D1011456

Nine Plays by
Eugene O'Neill

NINE PLAYS BY
EUGENE O'NEILL

THE EMPEROR JONES · "THE HAIRY APE"
ALL GOD'S CHILLUN GOT WINGS
DESIRE UNDER THE ELMS · "MARCO MILLIONS"
THE GREAT GOD BROWN · LAZARUS LAUGHED
STRANGE INTERLUDE
MOURNING BECOMES ELECTRA

SELECTED BY THE AUTHOR

THE MODERN LIBRARY
NEW YORK

Jacket portrait by Nickolas Muray

LIBRARY OF CONGRESS CATALOGING-IN-PUBLICATION DATA
O'Neill, Eugene, 1888–1953.
[Plays. Selections.]
Nine plays/by Eugene O'Neill.
p. cm.
Contents: The Emperor Jones—The Hairy ape—All God's chillun got wings—Desire
under the elms—Marco Millions—The Great god Brown—Lazarus laughed—Strange
interlude—Mourning becomes Electra.
ISBN 0-679-60045-0 (acid-free paper)
I. Title.
PS3529.N5A6 1992
812'.52—dc20   92-27149

Random House website address: http://www.randomhouse.com/

Printed in the United States of America on acid-free paper

2 4 6 8 9 7 5 3

EUGENE O'NEILL

Eugene O'Neill was born on October 16, 1888, in a hotel near Times Square in New York City. Both of O'Neill's parents were the children of Irish immigrants. His father became one of the best known actors of his day, although in his later years he was associated almost exclusively with a single role: Edmond Dantès in the melo-dramatic stage version of *The Count of Monte Cristo,* in which he toured the country year after year. Young Eugene spent his sum-mers in a cottage in New London, Connecticut, but was often on the road with his father.

As an adolescent, O'Neill rejected his parents' Catholicism and threw himself into the radical bohemianism of the day; the authors who influenced him most markedly were Ibsen, Strindberg, and Nietzsche. He also embarked on a pattern of heavy drinking typical of his family. He attended Princeton briefly but failed after two semesters. Before too long he was living off a meager allowance from his father and continuing his immersion in the saloons, brothels, and bohemian enclaves of the city.

In order to break up a love affair between Eugene and Kathleen Jenkins, a middle-class girl from an Episcopalian family, James O'Neill arranged for his son to embark on a gold-mining expedition to Honduras. The father was not aware that Eugene and Kathleen (who was already pregnant) had been secretly married before he left on the voyage. The expedition proved disastrous for O'Neill, who contracted malaria and had to be shipped back to New York in March 1910. Two months later a son, Eugene O'Neill, Jr., was born, but O'Neill had kept his distance from Kathleen and did not even see the baby. Instead he left for Buenos Aires, where he worked at a series of industrial and shipping jobs. Returning to New York a year later, he paid one visit to his wife and son (Kathleen filed for divorce not long after) but otherwise spent his time as a resident of Jimmy Condon's barroom and flophouse on Fulton Street.

In January 1912, in his room at Jimmy's, O'Neill made a failed suicide attempt. A brief stint as an actor accompanying his father's *Monte Cristo* tour and his first steps toward a writing career were interrupted by illness. Diagnosed with tuberculosis, O'Neill spent six months in a sanatorium in Connecticut, an experience that provided the basis for his play *The Straw*. By now O'Neill was actively writing plays, turning out a succession of one-acters which went unproduced; however, with the financial assistance of his father he did publish *Thirst and Other One Act Plays* in 1914. He also enrolled in Professor George Pierce Baker's renowned course in playwriting at Harvard.

A summer visit to Provincetown in 1916 introduced O'Neill to a community of artists and radicals in whose midst he would be able to realize the first productions of his work. O'Neill was one of the founders of the Provincetown Players, which expanded into a Greenwich Village theater, the Provincetown Playhouse, that autumn; their opening production was O'Neill's *Bound East for Cardiff.* Other productions, publications, and prizes followed. Many of O'Neill's early plays were based on his experiences as a merchant seaman.

In April 1918 O'Neill married a writer of magazine fiction named Agnes Boulton, and a year later their son Shane was born. With *Beyond the Horizon* he had his first Broadway production (1920), which enjoyed critical acclaim and a degree of commercial success. He was now writing plays at an extraordinary pace, and creating some of his best known works, including *Anna Christie, The Emperor Jones,* and *The Hairy Ape;* in 1922 he won the Pulitzer Prize for *Anna*

Christie and in 1923 received a gold medal from the National Institute of Arts and Letters. Just as he was achieving a certain measure of celebrity, O'Neill was hit by a series of family tragedies. His father, with whom he had only recently been reconciled, died in 1920. In 1922 his mother died, and the following year his older brother Jamie died of alcoholism in a New Jersey sanatorium.

O'Neill's plays attracted attention not only for their texts but for their frequently experimental productions. In collaboration with producer Kenneth Macgowan and stage designer Robert Edmond Jones, the playwright pioneered new techniques and innovative strategies, from the episodic expressionism of *The Hairy Ape* to the stylized masks of *The Great God Brown*. The interracial marriage depicted in *All God's Chillun Got Wings* aroused such animosity that the 1924 premiere, starring Paul Robeson and Mary Blair, took place amid death threats and political pressure from the city of New York. Likewise *Desire Under the Elms*—which enjoyed a great success in 1924, in a production starring Walter Huston—had to contend with threats of prosecution for indecency.

The novelistic *Strange Interlude,* a nine-act play incorporating interior monologues, was produced by the Theatre Guild in 1928 and (despite its enormous length, which necessitated a dinner break) ran for 426 performances, earning O'Neill a second Pulitzer Prize. After several less successful plays there followed the equally ambitious *Mourning Becomes Electra,* based on Aeschylus' Oresteian trilogy, which opened on Broadway in 1931 and confirmed O'Neill's unique stature in the American theater. At the same time, his plays were reaching a wider public through film adaptations; the movie of *Anna Christie*—advertised with the famous slogan "Garbo Talks!"—proved particularly popular. In 1936 O'Neill was awarded the Nobel Prize for literature.

O'Neill's second marriage had collapsed some years earlier, and in 1929 he married the actress Carlotta Monterey, with whom he had been having a sometimes turbulent affair for several years. O'Neill stopped drinking after 1926, aside from a few relapses, and following his marriage to Carlotta he also sought out increasingly remote habitations, so as to concentrate entirely on his writing. In 1931 he and Carlotta settled finally in Sea Island, Georgia. His health, however, was worsening.

After the popular *Ah, Wilderness!* (1933)—an uncharacteristic foray into nostalgic comedy—O'Neill embarked on an immense cycle of plays, never completed, which was to have traced the history of an Irish-American family from the early nineteenth century. For the remainder of his life O'Neill worked on aspects of this project, endlessly revising the plays *A Touch of the Poet* and *More Stately Mansions,* which were to have been part of it. The last of his works to be successfully produced in his lifetime was *The Iceman Cometh* (1939), an evocation of his days in Jimmy Condon's saloon. *A Moon for the Misbegotten* was tried out unsuccessfully in 1947 but didn't open on Broadway. The major accomplishment of O'Neill's final years was the autobiographical masterpiece *Long Day's Journey into Night,* completed in 1941 but not produced until 1956, three years after the playwright's death.

O'Neill's final years were dogged by tragedy and domestic difficulties: he broke off with his daughter Oona, angered by her marriage to Charlie Chaplin; Carlotta suffered severe psychiatric problems; his oldest son, Eugene, Jr., committed suicide, and his other son, Shane, was arrested for possession of heroin. O'Neill himself suffered from a rare degenerative disease resembling parkinsonism, which eventually make it impossible for him to continue writing. He died on November 27, 1953.

NINE PLAYS BY
EUGENE O'NEILL

In choosing the nine plays of full length or over which would best represent my work I have been guided not only by my own preferences but by the consensus of critical opinion, foreign as well as American, on either the published plays or productions of them in the theatre.

The plays are given here in the chronological order in which they were written: "The Emperor Jones," 1920; "The Hairy Ape," 1921; "All God's Chillun Got Wings," 1923; "Desire Under the Elms," 1924; "Marco Millions," 1923, 1924, 1925; "The Great God Brown," 1925; "Lazarus Laughed," 1925, 1926; "Strange Interlude," 1926, 1927; "Mourning Becomes Electra," 1929, 1931.

EUGENE O'NEILL

Contents

The Emperor Jones

CHARACTERS

BRUTUS JONES, *Emperor*

HENRY SMITHERS, *A Cockney Trader*

AN OLD NATIVE WOMAN

LEM, *A Native Chief*

SOLDIERS, *Adherents of Lem*

The Little Formless Fears; Jeff; The Negro Convicts; The Prison Guard; The Planters; The Auctioneer; The Slaves; The Congo Witch-Doctor; The Crocodile God.

The action of the play takes place on an island in the West Indies as yet not self-determined by White Marines. The form of native government is, for the time being, an Empire.

SCENES

Scene I: In the palace of the Emperor Jones. Afternoon.

Scene II: The edge of the Great Forest. Dusk.

Scene III: In the Forest. Night.

Scene IV: In the Forest. Night.

Scene V: In the Forest. Night.

Scene VI: In the Forest. Night.

Scene VII: In the Forest. Night.

Scene VIII: Same as Scene Two—the edge of the Great Forest. Dawn.

The Emperor Jones

Scene One

*T*HE *audience chamber in the palace of the Emperor—a spacious, high-ceilinged room with bare, white-washed walls. The floor is of white tiles. In the rear, to the left of center, a wide archway giving out on a portico with white pillars. The palace is evidently situated on high ground for beyond the portico nothing can be seen but a vista of distant hills, their summits crowned with thick groves of palm trees. In the right wall, center, a smaller arched doorway leading to the living quarters of the palace. The room is bare of furniture with the exception of one huge chair made of uncut wood which stands at center, its back to rear. This is very apparently the Emperor's throne. It is painted a dazzling, eye-smiting scarlet. There is a brilliant orange cushion on the seat and another smaller one is placed on the floor to serve as a footstool. Strips of matting, dyed scarlet, lead from the foot of the throne to the two entrances.*

It is late afternoon but the sunlight still blazes yellowly beyond the portico and there is an oppressive burden of exhausting heat in the air.

As the curtain rises, a native negro woman sneaks in cautiously from the entrance on the right. She is very old, dressed in cheap calico, bare-footed, a red bandana handkerchief covering all but a few stray wisps of white hair. A bundle bound in colored cloth is carried over her shoulder on the end of a stick. She hesitates beside the doorway, peering back as if in extreme dread of being discovered. Then she begins to glide noiselessly, a step at a time, toward the doorway in the rear. At this moment, SMITHERS *appears beneath the portico.*

SMITHERS *is a tall, stoop-shouldered man about forty. His bald head, perched on a long neck with an enormous Adam's apple, looks like an egg. The tropics have tanned his naturally pasty face with its small, sharp features to a sickly yellow, and native rum has painted his pointed nose to a startling red. His little, washy-blue eyes are red-rimmed and dart about him like a ferret's. His expression is one of unscrupulous meanness, cowardly and dangerous. He is dressed in a worn riding suit of dirty white drill, puttees, spurs, and wears a white cork helmet. A cartridge belt with an automatic revolver is around his waist. He carries a riding whip in his hand. He sees the woman and stops to watch her suspiciously. Then, making up his mind, he steps quickly on tiptoe into the room. The woman, looking back over her shoulder continually, does not see him until it is too late. When she does* SMITHERS *springs forward and grabs her firmly by the shoulder. She struggles to get away, fiercely but silently.*

SMITHERS: (*tightening his grasp—roughly*) Easy! None o' that, me birdie. You can't wiggle out, now I got me 'ooks on yer.

WOMAN: (*seeing the uselessness of struggling, gives way to frantic terror, and sinks to the ground, embracing his knees supplicatingly*) No tell him! No tell him, Mister!

SMITHERS: (*with great curiosity*) Tell 'im? (*Then scornfully*) Oh, you mean 'is bloomin' Majesty. What's the gaime, any'ow? What are you sneakin' away for? Been stealin' a bit, I s'pose. (*He taps her bundle with his riding whip significantly*).

WOMAN: (*shaking her head vehemently*) No, me no steal.

SMITHERS: Bloody liar! But tell me what's up. There's somethin' funny goin' on. I smelled it in the air first thing I got up this mornin'. You blacks are up to some devilment. This palace of 'is is like a bleedin' tomb. Where's all the 'ands? (*The woman keeps sullenly silent.* SMITHERS *raises his whip threateningly*) Ow, yer won't, won't yer? I'll show yer what's what.

WOMAN: (*coweringly*) I tell, Mister. You no hit. They go—all go. (*She makes a sweeping gesture toward the hills in the distance*).

SMITHERS: Run away—to the 'ills?

WOMAN: Yes, Mister. Him Emperor—Great Father (*She touches her forehead to the floor with a quick mechanical jerk*) Him sleep after eat. Then they go—all go. Me old woman. Me left only. Now me go too.

SMITHERS: (*his astonishment giving way to an immense, mean satisfaction*) Ow! So that's the ticket! Well, I know bloody well wot's in the air— when they runs orf to the 'ills. The tom-tom 'll be thumping out there bloomin' soon. (*With extreme vindictiveness*) And I'm bloody glad of it, for one! Serve 'im right! Puttin' on airs, the stinkin' nigger! 'Is Majesty! Gawd blimey! I only 'opes I'm there when they takes 'im out to shoot 'im. (*Suddenly*) 'E's still 'ere all right, ain't 'e?

WOMAN: Him sleep.

SMITHERS: 'E's bound to find out soon as 'e wakes up. 'E's cunnin' enough to know when 'is time's come. (*He goes to the doorway on right and whistles shrilly with his fingers in his mouth. The old woman springs to her feet and runs out of the doorway, rear.* SMITHERS *goes after her, reaching for his revolver*) Stop or I'll shoot! (*Then stopping—indifferently*) Pop orf then, if yer like, yer black cow. (*He stands in the doorway, looking after her*).

(JONES *enters from the right. He is a tall, powerfully-built, full-blooded negro of middle age. His features are typically negroid, yet there is something decidedly distinctive about his face—an underlying strength of will, a hardy, self-reliant confidence in himself that inspires respect. His eyes are alive with a keen, cunning intelligence. In manner he is shrewd, suspicious, evasive. He wears a light blue uniform coat, sprayed with brass buttons, heavy gold chevrons on his shoulders, gold braid on the collar, cuffs, etc. His pants are bright red with a light blue stripe down the side. Patent leather laced boots with brass spurs, and a belt with a long-barreled, pearl-handled revolver in a holster complete his make up. Yet there is something not altogether ridiculous about his grandeur. He has a way of carrying it off*).

JONES: (*not seeing anyone—greatly irritated and blinking sleepily—shouts*) Who dare whistle dat way in my palace? Who dare wake up de Emperor? I'll git de hide frayled off some o' you niggers sho'!

SMITHERS: (*showing himself—in a manner half-afraid and half-defiant*) It was me whistled to yer. (*As* JONES *frowns angrily*) I got news for yer.

JONES: (*putting on his suavest manner, which fails to cover up his contempt for the white man*) Oh, it's you, Mister Smithers. (*He sits down on his throne with easy dignity*) What news you got to tell me?

SMITHERS: (*coming close to enjoy his discomfiture*) Don't yer notice nothin' funny today?

JONES: (*coldly*) Funny? No. I ain't perceived nothin' of de kind!

SMITHERS: Then yer ain't so foxy as I thought yer was. Where's all your court? (*sarcastically*) the Generals and the Cabinet Ministers and all?

JONES: (*imperturbably*) Where dey mostly runs to minute I closes my eyes—drinkin' rum and talkin' big down in de town. (*Sarcastically*) How come you don't know dat? Ain't you sousin' with 'em most every day?

SMITHERS: (*stung but pretending indifference—with a wink*) That's part of the day's work. I got ter—ain't I—in my business?

JONES: (*contemptuously*) Yo' business!

SMITHERS: (*imprudently enraged*) Gawd blimey, you was glad enough for me ter take yer in on it when you landed here first. You didn' 'ave no 'igh and mighty airs in them days!

JONES: (*his hand going to his revolver like a flash—menacingly*) Talk polite, white man! Talk polite, you heah me! I'm boss heah now, is you fergettin'? (*The Cockney seems about to challenge this last statement with the facts but something in the other's eyes holds and cows him*).

SMITHERS: (*in a cowardly whine*) No 'arm meant, old top.

JONES: (*condescendingly*) I accepts yo' apology. (*Lets his hand fall from his revolver*) No use'n you rakin' up ole times. What I was den is one thing. What I is now 's another. You didn't let me in on yo' crooked work out o' no kind feelin's dat time. I done de dirty work fo' you— and most o' de brain work, too, fo' dat matter —and I was wu'th money to you, dat's de reason.

SMITHERS: Well, blimey, I give yer a start, didn't I?—when no one else would. I wasn't afraid to 'ire you like the rest was—'count of the story about your breakin' jail back in the States.

JONES: No, you didn't have no s'cuse to look down on me fo' dat. You been in jail you'self more'n once.

SMITHERS: (*furiously*) It's a lie! (*Then trying to pass it off by an attempt at scorn*) Garn! Who told yer that fairy tale?

JONES: Dey's some tings I ain't got to be tole. I kin see 'em in folk's eyes. (*Then after a pause—meditatively*) Yes, you sho' give me a start. And it didn't take long from dat time to git dese fool, woods' niggers right where I wanted dem. (*With pride*) From stowaway to Emperor in two years! Dat's goin' some!

SMITHERS: (*with curiosity*) And I bet you got yer pile o' money 'id safe some place.

JONES: (*with satisfaction*) I sho' has! And it's in a foreign bank where no pusson don't ever git it out but me no matter what come. You didn't s'pose I was holdin' down dis Emperor job for de glory in it, did you? Sho'! De fuss and glory part of it, dat's only to turn de heads o' de low-flung, bush niggers dat's here. Dey wants de big circus show for deir money. I gives it to 'em an' I gits de money. (*With a grin*) De long green, dat's me every time! (*Then rebukingly*) But you ain't got no kick agin me, Smithers. I'se paid you back all you done for me many times. Ain't I pertected you and winked at all de crooked tradin' you been doin' right out in de broad day? Sho' I has—and me makin' laws to stop it at de same time! (*He chuckles*).

SMITHERS: (*grinning*) But, meanin' no 'arm, you been grabbin' right and left yourself, ain't yer? Look at the taxes you've put on 'em! Blimey! You've squeezed 'em dry!

JONES: (*chuckling*) No, dey ain't *all* dry yet. I'se still heah, ain't I?

SMITHERS: (*smiling at his secret thought*) They're dry right now, you'll find out. (*Changing the subject abruptly*) And as for me breakin' laws, you've broke 'em all yerself just as fast as yer made 'em.

JONES: Ain't I de Emperor? De laws don't go for him. (*Judicially*) You heah what I tells you, Smithers. Dere's little stealin' like you does, and dere's big stealin' like I does. For de little stealin' dey gits you in jail soon or late. For de big stealin' dey makes you Emperor and puts you in de Hall o' Fame when you croaks. (*Reminiscently*) If dey's one thing I learns in ten years on de Pullman ca's listenin' to de

white quality talk, it's dat same fact. And when I gits a chance to use
it I winds up Emperor in two years.

SMITHERS: (*unable to repress the genuine admiration of the small fry for the
large*) Yes, yer turned the bleedin' trick, all right. Blimey, I never
seen a bloke 'as 'ad the bloomin' luck you 'as.

JONES: (*severely*) Luck? What you mean—luck?

SMITHERS: I suppose you'll say as that swank about the silver bullet ain't
luck—and that was what first got the fool blacks on yer side the time
of the revolution, wasn't it?

JONES: (*with a laugh*) Oh, dat silver bullet! Sho' was luck. But I makes
dat luck, you heah? I loads de dice! Yessuh! When dat murderin'
nigger ole Lem hired to kill me takes aim ten feet away and his gun
misses fire and I shoots him dead, what you heah me say?

SMITHERS: You said yer'd got a charm so's no lead bullet'd kill yer. You
was so strong only a silver bullet could kill yer, you told 'em. Blimey,
wasn't that swank for yer—and plain, fat-'eaded luck?

JONES: (*proudly*) I got brains and I uses 'em quick. Dat ain't luck.

SMITHERS: Yer know they wasn't 'ardly liable to get no silver bullets.
And it was luck 'e didn't 'it you that time.

JONES: (*laughing*) And dere all dem fool bush niggers was kneelin' down
and bumpin' deir heads on de ground like I was a miracle out o' de
Bible. Oh, Lawd, from dat time on I has dem all eatin' out of my
hand. I cracks de whip and dey jumps through.

SMITHERS: (*with a sniff*) Yankee bluff done it.

JONES: Ain't a man's talkin' big what makes him big—long as he makes
folks believe it? Sho', I talks large when I ain't got nothin' to back it
up, but I ain't talkin' wild just de same. I knows I kin fool 'em—I
knows it—and dat's backin' enough fo' my game. And ain't I got to
learn deir lingo and teach some of dem English befo' I kin talk to
'em? Ain't dat wuk? You ain't never learned ary word er it, Smithers,
in de ten years you been heah, dough you knows it's money in yo'
pocket tradin' wid 'em if you does. But you'se too shiftless to take
de trouble.

SMITHERS: (*flushing*) Never mind about me. What's this I've 'eard about yer really 'avin' a silver bullet moulded for yourself?

JONES: It's playin' out my bluff. I has de silver bullet moulded and I tells 'em when de time comes I kills myself wid it. I tells 'em dat's 'cause I'm de on'y man in de world big enuff to git me. No use'n deir tryin'. And dey falls down and bumps deir heads. (*He laughs*) I does dat so's I kin take a walk in peace widout no jealous nigger gunnin' at me from behind de trees.

SMITHERS: (*astonished*) Then you 'ad it made—'onest?

JONES: Sho' did. Heah she be. (*He takes out his revolver, breaks it, and takes the silver bullet out of one chamber*) Five lead an' dis silver baby at de last. Don't she shine pretty? (*He holds it in his hand, looking at it admiringly, as if strangely fascinated*).

SMITHERS: Let me see. (*Reaches out his hand for it*).

JONES: (*harshly*) Keep yo' hands whar dey b'long, white man.

(*He replaces it in the chamber and puts the revolver back on his hip*).

SMITHERS: (*snarling*) Gawd blimey! Think I'm a bleedin' thief, you would.

JONES: No, 'tain't dat. I knows you'se scared to steal from me. On'y I ain't 'lowin' nary body to touch dis baby. She's my rabbit's foot.

SMITHERS: (*sneering*) A bloomin' charm, wot? (*Venomously*) Well, you'll need all the bloody charms you 'as before long, s' 'elp me!

JONES: (*judicially*) Oh, I'se good for six months yit 'fore dey gits sick o' my game. Den, when I sees trouble comin', I makes my getaway.

SMITHERS: Ho! You got it all planned, ain't yer?

JONES: I ain't no fool. I knows dis Emperor's time is sho't. Dat why I make hay when de sun shine. Was you thinkin' I'se aimin' to hold down dis job for life? No, suh! What good is gittin' money if you stays back in dis raggedy country? I wants action when I spends. And when I sees dese niggers gittin' up deir nerve to tu'n me out, and I'se got all de money in sight, I resigns on de spot and beats it quick.

SMITHERS: Where to?

JONES: None o' yo' business.

SMITHERS: Not back to the bloody States, I'll lay my oath.

JONES: (*suspiciously*) Why don't I? (Then with an easy laugh) You mean 'count of dat story 'bout me breakin' from jail back dere? Dat's all talk.

SMITHERS: (*skeptically*) Ho, yes!

JONES: (*sharply*) You ain't 'sinuatin' I'se a liar, is you?

SMITHERS: (*hastily*) No, Gawd strike me! I was only thinkin' o' the bloody lies you told the blacks 'ere about killin' white men in the States.

JONES: (*angered*) How come dey're lies?

SMITHERS: You'd 'ave been in jail if you 'ad, wouldn't yer then? (*With venom*) And from what I've 'eard, it ain't 'ealthy for a black to kill a white man in the States. They burns 'em in oil, don't they?

JONES: (*with cool deadliness*) You mean lynchin' 'd scare me? Well, I tells you, Smithers, maybe I does kill one white man back dere. Maybe I does. And maybe I kills another right heah 'fore long if he don't look out.

SMITHERS: (*trying to force a laugh*) I was on'y spoofin' yer. Can't yer take a joke? And you was just sayin' you'd never been in jail.

JONES: (*in the same tone—slightly boastful*) Maybe I goes to jail dere for gettin' in an argument wid razors ovah a crap game. Maybe I gits twenty years when dat colored man die. Maybe I gits in 'nother argument wid de prison guard was overseer ovah us when we're wukin' de road. Maybe he hits me wid a whip and I splits his head wid a shovel and runs away and files de chain off my leg and gits away safe. Maybe I does all dat an' maybe I don't. It's a story I tells you so's you knows I'se de kind of man dat if you evah repeats one word of it, I ends yo' stealin' on dis yearth mighty damn quick!

SMITHERS: (*terrified*) Think I'd peach on yer? Not me! Ain't I always been yer friend?

JONES: (*suddenly relaxing*) Sho' you has—and you better be.

SMITHERS: (*recovering his composure—and with it his malice*) And just to show yer I'm yer friend, I'll tell yer that bit o' news I was goin' to.

JONES: Go ahead! Shoot de piece. Must be bad news from de happy way you look.

SMITHERS: (*warningly*) Maybe it's gettin' time for you to resign— with that bloomin' silver bullet, wot? (*He finishes with a mocking grin*).

JONES: (*puzzled*) What's dat you say? Talk plain.

SMITHERS: Ain't noticed any of the guards or servants about the place today, I 'aven't.

JONES: (*carelessly*) Dey're all out in de garden sleepin' under de trees. When I sleeps, dey sneaks a sleep, too, and I pretends I never suspicions it. All I got to do is to ring de bell and dey come flyin', makin' a bluff dey was wukin' all de time.

SMITHERS: (in *the same mocking tone*) Ring the bell now an' you'll bloody well see what I means.

JONES: (*startled to alertness, but preserving the same careless tone*) Sho' I rings. (*He reaches below the throne and pulls out a big, common dinner bell which is painted the same vivid scarlet as the throne. He rings this vigorously—then stops to listen. Then he goes to both doors, rings again, and looks out*).

SMITHERS: (*watching him with malicious satisfaction, after a pause —mockingly*) The bloody ship is sinkin' an' the bleedin' rats 'as slung their 'ooks.

JONES: (*in a sudden fit of anger flings the bell clattering into a corner*) Low-flung, woods' niggers! (*Then catching* SMITHERS' *eye on him, he controls himself and suddenly bursts into a low chuckling laugh*) Reckon I overplays my hand dis once! A man can't take de pot on a bob-tailed flush all de time. Was I sayin' I'd sit in six months mo'? Well, I'se changed my mind den. I cashes in and resigns de job of Emperor right dis minute.

SMITHERS: (*with real admiration*) Blimey, but you're a cool bird, and no mistake.

JONES: No use'n fussin'. When I knows de game's up I kisses it good-by widout no long waits. Dey've all run off to de hills, ain't dey?

SMITHERS: Yes—every bleedin' man jack of 'em.

JONES: Den de revolution is at de post. And de Emperor better git his feet smokin' up de trail. (*He starts for the door in rear*).

SMITHERS: Goin' out to look for your 'orse? Yer won't find any. They steals the 'orses first thing. Mine was gone when I went for 'im this mornin'. That's wot first give me a suspicion of wot was up.

JONES: (*alarmed for a second, scratches his head, then philosophically*) Well, den I hoofs it. Feet, do yo' duty! (*He pulls out a gold watch and looks at it*) Three-thuty. Sundown's at six-thuty or dereabouts. (*Puts his watch back—with cool confidence*) I got plenty o' time to make it easy.

SMITHERS: Don't be so bloomin' sure of it. They'll be after you 'ot and 'eavy. Ole Lem is at the bottom o' this business an' 'e 'ates you like 'ell. 'E'd rather do for you than eat 'is dinner, 'e would!

JONES: (*scornfully*) Dat fool no-count nigger! Does you think I'se scared o' him? I stands him on his thick head more'n once befo' dis, and I does it again if he comes in my way—(*Fiercely*) And dis time I leave him a dead nigger fo' sho'!

SMITHERS: You'll 'ave to cut through the big forest—an' these blacks 'ere can sniff and follow a trail in the dark like 'ounds. You'd 'ave to 'ustle to get through that forest in twelve hours even if you knew all the bloomin' trails like a native.

JONES: (*with indignant scorn*) Look-a-heah, white man! Does you think I'se a natural bo'n fool? Give me credit fo' havin' some sense, fo' Lawd's sake! Don't you s'pose I'se looked ahead and made sho' of all de chances? I'se gone out in dat big forest, pretendin' to hunt, so many times dat I knows it high an' low like a book. I could go through on dem trails wid my eyes shut. (*With great contempt*) Think dese ign'rent bush niggers dat ain't got brains enuff to know deir own names even can catch Brutus Jones? Huh, I s'pects not! Not on yo' life! Why, man, de white men went after me wid bloodhounds where I come from an' I jes' laughs at 'em. It's a shame to fool dese black trash around heah, dey're so easy. You watch me, man. I'll make dem look sick, I will. I'll be 'cross de plain to de edge of de forest by time dark comes. Once in de woods in de night, dey got a swell chance o' findin' dis baby! Dawn tomorrow I'll be out at de oder side and on de coast whar dat French gunboat is stayin'. She picks me up, takes me to Martinique when she go dar, and dere I is safe wid a mighty big bankroll in my jeans. It's easy as rollin' off a log.

SMITHERS: (*maliciously*) But s'posin' somethin' 'appens wrong an' they do nab yer?

JONES: (*decisively*) Dey don't—dat's de answer.

SMITHERS: But, just for argyment's sake—what'd you do?

JONES: (*frowning*) I'se got five lead bullets in dis gun good enuff fo' common bush niggers—and after dat I got de silver bullet left to cheat 'em out o' gittin' me.

SMITHERS: (*jeeringly*) Ho, I was fergettin' that silver bullet. You'll bump yourself orf in style, won't yer? Blimey!

JONES: (*gloomily*) You kin bet yo' whole roll on one thing, white man. Dis baby plays out his string to de end and when he quits, he quits wid a bang de way he ought. Silver bullet ain't none too good for him when he go, dat's a fac'! (*Then shaking off his nervousness—with a confident laugh*) Sho'! What is I talkin' about? Ain't come to dat yit and I never will—not wid trash niggers like dese yere. (*Boastfully*) Silver bullet bring me luck anyway. I kin outguess, outrun, outfight, an' outplay de whole lot o' dem all ovah de board any time o' de day er night! You watch me! (*From the distant hills comes the faint, steady thump of a tom-tom, low and vibrating. It starts at a rate exactly corresponding to normal pulse beat—72 to the minute—and continues at a gradually accelerating rate from this point uninterruptedly to the very end of the play*).

(JONES *starts at the sound. A strange look of apprehension creeps into his face for a moment as he listens. Then he asks, with an attempt to regain his most casual manner*) What's dat drum beatin' fo'?

SMITHERS: (*with a mean grin*) For you. That means the bleedin' ceremony 'as started. I've 'eard it before and I knows.

JONES: Cer'mony? What cer'mony?

SMITHERS: The blacks is 'oldin' a bloody meetin', 'avin' a war dance, gettin' their courage worked up b'fore they starts after you.

JONES: Let dem! Dey'll sho' need it!

SMITHERS: And they're there 'oldin' their 'eathen religious service— makin' no end of devil spells and charms to 'elp 'em against your silver bullet. (*He guffaws loudly*) Blimey, but they're balmy as 'ell!

JONES: (*a tiny bit awed and shaken in spite of himself*) Huh! Takes more'n dat to scare dis chicken!

SMITHERS: (*scenting the other's feeling—maliciously*) Ternight when it's pitch black in the forest, they'll 'ave their pet devils and ghosts 'oundin' after you. You'll find yer bloody 'air 'll be standin' on end before termorrow mornin'. (*Seriously*) It's a bleedin' queer place, that stinkin' forest, even in daylight. Yer don't know what might 'appen in there, it's that rotten still. Always sends the cold shivers down my back minute I gets in it.

JONES: (*with a contemptuous sniff*) I ain't no chicken-liver like you is. Trees an' me, we'se friends, and dar's a full moon comin' bring me light. And let dem po' niggers make all de fool spells dey'se a min' to. Does yo' s'pect I'se silly enuff to b'lieve in ghosts an' ha'nts an' all dat ole woman's talk? G'long, white man! You ain't talkin' to me. (*With a chuckle*) Doesn't you know dey's got to do wid a man was member in good standin' o' de Baptist Church? Sho' I was dat when I was porter on de Pullmans, befo' I gits into my little trouble. Let dem try deir heathen tricks. De Baptist Church done pertect me and land dem all in hell. (*Then with more confident satisfaction*) And I'se got little silver bullet o' my own, don't forgit!

SMITHERS: Ho! You 'aven't give much 'eed to your Baptist Church since you been down 'ere. I've 'eard myself you 'ad turned yer coat an' was takin' up with their blarsted witch-doctors, or whatever the 'ell yer calls the swine.

JONES: (*vehemently*) I pretends to! Sho' I pretends! Dat's part o' my game from de fust. If I finds out dem niggers believes dat black is white, den I yells it out louder 'n deir loudest. It don't git me nothin' to do missionary work for de Baptist Church. I'se after de coin, an' I lays my Jesus on de shelf for de time bein'. (*Stops abruptly to look at his watch—alertly*) But I ain't got de time to waste on no more fool talk wid you. I'se gwine away from heah dis secon'. (*He reaches in under the throne and pulls out an expensive Panama hat with a bright multi-colored band and sets it jauntily on his head*) So long, white man! (*With a grin*) See you in jail sometime, maybe!

SMITHERS: Not me, you won't. Well, I wouldn't be in yer bloody boots for no bloomin' money, but 'ere's wishin' yer luck just the same.

JONES: (*contemptuously*) You're de frightenedest man evah I see! I tells you I'se safe's 'f I was in New York City. It takes dem niggers from now to dark to git up de nerve to start somethin'. By dat time, I'se got a head start dey never kotch up wid.

SMITHERS: (*maliciously*) Give my regards to any ghosts yer meets up with.

JONES: (*grinning*) If dat ghost got money, I'll tell him never ha'nt you less'n he wants to lose it.

SMITHERS: (*flattered*) Garn! (*Then curiously*) Ain't yer takin' no luggage with yer?

JONES: I travels light when I wants to move fast. And I got tinned grub buried on de edge o' de forest. (*Boastfully*) Now say dat I don't look ahead an' use my brains! (*With a wide, liberal gesture*) I will all dat's left in de palace to you—and you better grab all you kin sneak away wid befo' dey gits here.

SMITHERS: (*gratefully*) Righto—and thanks ter yer. (*As JONES walks toward the door in rear—cautioningly*) Say! Look 'ere, you ain't goin' out that way, are yer?

JONES: Does you think I'd slink out de back door like a common nigger? I'se Emperor yit, ain't I? And de Emperor Jones leaves de way he comes, and dat black trash don't dare stop him—not yit, leastways. (*He stops for a moment in the doorway, listening to the far-off but insistent beat of the tom-tom*) Listen to dat roll-call, will you? Must be mighty big drum carry dat far. (*Then with a laugh*) Well, if dey ain't no whole brass band to see me off, I sho' got de drum part of it. So long, white man. (*He puts his hands in his pockets and with studied carelessness, whistling a tune, he saunters out of the doorway and off to the left*).

SMITHERS: (*looks after him with a puzzled admiration*) 'E's got 'is bloomin' nerve with 'im, s'elp me! (*Then angrily*) Ho—the bleedin' nigger—puttin' on 'is bloody airs! I 'opes they nabs 'im an' gives 'im what's what!

CURTAIN

SCENE TWO

*T*HE end of the plain where the Great Forest begins. The foreground is sandy, level ground dotted by a few stones and clumps of stunted bushes cowering close against the earth to escape the buffeting of the trade wind. In the rear the forest is a wall of darkness dividing the world. Only when the eye becomes accustomed to the gloom can the outlines of separate trunks of the nearest trees be made out, enormous pillars of deeper blackness. A somber monotone of wind lost in the leaves moans in the air. Yet this sound serves but to intensify the impression of the forest's relentless immobility, to form a background throwing into relief its brooding, implacable silence.*

(*JONES enters from the left, walking rapidly. He stops as he nears the edge of the forest, looks around him quickly, peering into the dark as if searching for some familiar landmark. Then, apparently satisfied that he is where he ought to be, he throws himself on the ground, dog-tired*).

Well, heah I is. In de nick o' time, too! Little mo' an' it'd be blacker'n de ace of spades heahabouts. (*He pulls a bandana handkerchief from his hip pocket and mops off his perspiring face*) Sho'! Gimme air! I'se tuckered out sho' 'nuff. Dat soft Emperor job ain't no trainin' fo' a long hike ovah dat plain in de brilin' sun. (*Then with a chuckle*) Cheer up, nigger, de worst is yet to come. (*He lifts his head and stares at the forest. His chuckle peters out abruptly. In a tone of awe*) My goodness, look at dem woods, will you? Dat no-count Smithers said dey'd be black an' he sho' called de turn. (*Turning away from them quickly and looking down at his feet, he snatches at a chance to change the subject—solicitously*) Feet, you is holdin' up yo' end fine an' I sutinly hopes you ain't blisterin' none. It's time you git a rest. (*He takes off his shoes, his eyes studiously avoiding the forest. He feels of the soles of his feet gingerly*) You is still in de pink—on'y a little mite feverish. Cool yo'selfs. Remember you done got a long journey yit befo' you. (*He sits in a weary attitude, listening to the rhythmic beating of the tom-tom. He grumbles in a loud tone to cover up a growing uneasiness*) Bush niggers! Wonder dey wouldn't git sick o' beatin' dat drum. Sound louder, seem like. I wonder if dey's startin' after me? (*He scrambles to his feet, looking back across the plain*) Couldn't see dem now, nohow, if dey was hundred feet away. (*Then shaking himself like a wet dog to get rid of these depressing thoughts*) Sho', dey's miles an' miles behind. What you gittin' fidgety about? (*But he sits down and begins to lace up his shoes in great haste, all the time muttering reassuringly*) You know what? Yo' belly is empty, dat's what's de matter wid you. Come time to eat! Wid nothin' but wind on yo' stumach, o' course you feels jiggedy. Well, we eats right heah an' now soon's I gits dese pesky shoes laced up. (*He finishes lacing up his shoes*) Dere! Now le's see! (*Gets on his hands and knees and searches the ground around him with his eyes*) White stone, white stone, where is you? (*He sees the first white stone and crawls to it—with satisfaction*) Heah you is! I knowed dis was de right place. Box of grub, come to me. (*He turns over the stone and feels in under it— in a tone of dismay*) Ain't heah! Gorry, is I in de right place or isn't I? Dere's 'nother stone. Guess dat's it. (*He scrambles to the next stone and turns it over*) Ain't heah, neither! Grub, whar is you? Ain't heah. Gorry, has I got to go hungry into dem woods—all de night? (*While he is talking he scrambles from one stone to another, turning them over in frantic haste. Finally, he jumps to his feet excitedly*) Is I lost de place? Must have!

But how dat happen when I was followin' de trail across de plain in broad daylight? (*Almost plaintively*) I'se hungry, I is! I gotta git my feed. Whar's my strength gonna come from if I doesn't? Gorry, I gotta find dat grub high an' low somehow! Why it come dark so quick like dat? Can't see nothin'. (*He scratches a match on his trousers and peers about him. The rate of the beat of the far-off tom-tom increases perceptibly as he does so. He mutters in a bewildered voice*) How come all dese white stones come heah when I only remembers one? (*Suddenly, with a frightened gasp, he flings the match on the ground and stamps on it*) Nigger, is you gone crazy mad? Is you lightin' matches to show dem whar you is? Fo' Lawd's sake, use yo' haid. Gorry, I'se got to be careful! (*He stares at the plain behind him apprehensively, his hand on his revolver*) But how come all dese white stones? And whar's dat tin box o' grub I hid all wrapped up in oilcloth?

(*While his back is turned, the* LITTLE FORMLESS FEARS *creep out from the deeper blackness of the forest. They are black, shapeless, only their glittering little eyes can be seen. If they have any describable form at all it is that of a grubworm about the size of a creeping child. They move noiselessly, but with deliberate, painful effort, striving to raise themselves on end, failing and sinking prone again.* JONES *turns about to face the forest. He stares up at the tops of the trees, seeking vainly to discover his whereabouts by their conformation*).

Can't tell nothin' from dem trees! Gorry, nothin' 'round heah looks like I evah seed it befo'. I'se done lost de place sho' 'nuff! (*With mournful foreboding*) It's mighty queer! It's mighty queer! (*With sudden forced defiance—in an angry tone*) Woods, is you tryin' to put somethin' ovah on me?

(*From the formless creatures on the ground in front of him comes a tiny gale of low mocking laughter like a rustling of leaves. They squirm upward toward him in twisted attitudes.* JONES *looks down, leaps backwards with a yell of terror, yanking out his revolver as he does so—in a quavering voice*) What's dat? Who's dar? What is you? Git away from me befo' I shoots you up! You don't?—

(*He fires. There is a flash, a loud report, then silence broken only by the far-off, quickened throb of the tom-tom. The formless creatures have scurried back into the forest.* JONES *remains fixed in his position, listening intently. The sound of the shot, the reassuring feel of the revolver in his hand, have somewhat restored his shaken nerve. He addresses himself with renewed confidence).*

Dey're gone. Dat shot fix 'em. Dey was only little animals—little wild pigs, I reckon. Dey've maybe rooted out yo' grub an' eat it. Sho', you fool nigger, what you think dey is—ha'nts? (*Excitedly*) Gorry, you give de game away when you fire dat shot. Dem niggers heah dat fo' su'tin! Time you beat it in de woods widout no long waits. (*He starts for the forest—hesitates before the plunge—then urging himself in with manful resolution*) Git in, nigger! What you skeered at? Ain't nothin' dere but de trees! Git in! (*He plunges boldly into the forest*).

SCENE THREE

*I*N *the forest. The moon has just risen. Its beams, drifting through the canopy of leaves, make a barely perceptible, suffused, eerie glow. A dense low wall of underbrush and creepers is in the nearer foreground, fencing in a small tri- angular clearing. Beyond this is the massed blackness of the forest like an encompassing barrier. A path is dimly discerned leading down to the clearing from left, rear, and winding away from it again toward the right. As the scene opens nothing can be distinctly made out. Except for the beating of the tom- tom, which is a trifle louder and quicker than at the close of the previous scene, there is silence, broken every few seconds by a queer, clicking sound. Then gradually the figure of the negro,* JEFF *can be discerned crouching on his haunches at the rear of the triangle. He is middle-aged, thin, brown in color, is dressed in a Pullman porter's uniform and cap. He is throwing a pair of dice on the ground before him, picking them up, shaking them, casting them out with the regular, rigid, mechanical movements of an automaton. The heavy, plodding footsteps of someone approaching along the trail from the left* *are heard and* JONES' *voice, pitched on a slightly higher key and strained in a cheery effort to overcome its own tremors.*

De moon's rizen. Does you heah dat, nigger? You gits more light from dis out. No mo' buttin' yo' fool head agin' de trunks an' scratchin' de hide off yo' legs in de bushes. Now you sees whar yo'se gwine. So cheer up! From now on you has a snap. (*He steps just to the rear of the triangular clearing and mops off his face on his sleeve. He has lost his Panama hat. His face is scratched, his brilliant uniform shows several large rents*) What time's it gittin' to be, I wonder? I dassent light no match to find out. Phoo'. It's wa'm an' dat's a fac'! (*Wearily*) How long I been makin' tracks in dese woods? Must be hours an' hours. Seems like fo'evah! Yit can't be, when de moon's jes' riz. Dis am a long night fo' yo', yo' Majesty! (*With a mournful chuckle*) Majesty! Der ain't much majesty 'bout dis baby now. (*With attempted cheerfulness*) Never min'. It's all part o' de game. Dis night come to an end like everything else. And when you gits dar safe and has dat bankroll in yo' hands you laughs at all dis. (*He starts to whistle but checks himself abruptly*) What yo' whistlin' for, you po' dope! Want all de worl' to heah you? (*He stops talking to listen*) Heah dat ole drum! Sho' gits nearer from de sound. Dey's packin' it along wid 'em. Time fo' me to move. (*He takes a step forward, then stops—worriedly*) What's dat odder queer clickety sound I heah? Dere it is! Sound close! Sound like—sound like—Fo' God sake, sound like some nigger was shootin' crap! (*Frightenedly*) I better beat it quick when I gits dem notions. (*He walks quickly into the clear space—then stands transfixed as he sees* JEFF—*in a terrified gasp*) Who dar? Who dat? Is dat you, Jeff? (*Starting toward the other, forgetful for a moment of his surroundings and really believing it is a living man that he sees—in a tone of happy relief*) Jeff! I'se sho' mighty glad to see you! Dey tol' me you done died from dat razor cut I gives you. (*Stopping suddenly, bewilderedly*) But how you come to be heah, nigger? (*He stares fascinatedly at the other who continues his mechanical play with the dice.* JONES' *eyes begin to roll wildly. He stutters*) Ain't you gwine—look up—can't you speak to me? Is you —is you—a ha'nt? (*He jerks out his revolver in a frenzy of terrified rage*) Nigger, I kills you dead once. Has I got to kill you ag'in? You take it den. (*He fires. When the smoke clears away* JEFF *has disappeared.* JONES *stands trembling— then with a certain reassurance*) He's gone, anyway. Ha'nt or not ha'nt, dat shot fix him. (*The beat of the far-off tom-tom is perceptibly louder and more rapid.* JONES *becomes conscious of it—with a start, looking back over his shoulder*) Dey's gittin' near! Dey's comin' fast! And heah I is shootin' shots to let 'em know jes' whar I is! Oh, Gorry, I'se got to run. (*Forgetting the path he plunges wildly into the underbrush in the rear and disappears in the shadow*).

Scene Four

*I*N *the forest. A wide dirt road runs diagonally from right, front, to left, rear. Rising sheer on both sides the forest walls it in. The moon is now up. Under its light the road glimmers ghastly and unreal. It is as if the forest had stood aside momentarily to let the road pass through and accomplish its veiled purpose. This done, the forest will fold in upon itself again and the road will be no more.* JONES *stumbles in from the forest on the right. His uniform is ragged and torn. He looks about him with numbed surprise when he sees the road, his eyes blinking in the bright moonlight. He flops down exhaustedly and pants heavily for a while. Then with sudden anger.*

I'm meltin' wid heat! Runnin' an' runnin' an' runnin'! Damn dis heah coat! Like a straitjacket! (*He tears off his coat and flings it away from him, revealing himself stripped to the waist*) Dere! Dat's better! Now I kin breathe! (*Looking down at his feet, the spurs catch his eye*) And to hell wid dese high-fangled spurs. Dey're what's been a-trippin' me up an' breakin' my neck. (*He unstraps them and flings them away disgustedly*) Dere! I gits rid o' dem frippety Emperor trappin's an' I travels lighter.

Lawd! I'se tired! (*After a pause, listening to the insistent beat of the tom-tom in the distance*) I must 'a' put some distance between myself an' dem— runnin' like dat—and yit—dat damn drum sounds jes' de same— nearer, even. Well, I guess I a'most holds my lead anyhow. De' won't never catch up. (*With a sigh*) If on'y my fool legs stands up. Oh, I'se sorry I evah went in for dis. Dat Emperor job is sho' hard to shake. (*He looks around him suspiciously*) How'd dis road evah git heah? Good level road, too. I never remembers seein' it befo'. (*Shaking his head apprehensively*) Dese woods is sho' full o' de queerest things at night. (*With a sudden terror*) Lawd God, don't let me see no more o' dem ha'nts! Dey gits my goat! (*Then trying to talk himself into confidence*) Ha'nts! You fool nigger, dey ain't no such things! Don't de Baptist parson tell you dat many time? Is you civilized, or is you like dese ign'rent black niggers heah? Sho'! Dat was all in yo' own head. Wasn't nothin' dere. Wasn't no Jeff! Know what? You jus' get seein' dem things 'cause yo' belly's empty and you's sick wid hunger inside. Hunger 'fects yo' head and yo' eyes. Any fool know dat. (*Then pleading fervently*) But bless God, I don't come across no more o' dem, whatever dey is! (*Then cautiously*) Rest! Don't talk! Rest! You needs it. Den you gits on yo' way again. (*Looking at the moon*) Night's half gone a'most. You hits de coast in de mawning! Den you's all safe.

(*From the right forward a small gang of negroes enter. They are dressed in striped convict suits, their heads are shaven, one leg drags limpingly, shackled to a heavy ball and chain. Some carry picks, the others shovels. They are followed by a white man dressed in the uniform of a prison guard. A Winchester rifle is slung across his shoulders and he carries a heavy whip. At a signal from the* GUARD *they stop on the road opposite where* JONES *is sitting.* JONES, *who has been staring up at the sky, unmindful of their noiseless approach, suddenly looks down and sees them. His eyes pop out, he tries to get to his feet and fly, but sinks back, too numbed by fright to move. His voice catches in a choking prayer*).

Lawd Jesus!

(*The* PRISON GUARD *cracks his whip—noiselessly—and at that signal all the convicts start to work on the road. They swing their picks, they shovel, but not a sound comes from their labor. Their movements, like those of* JEFF *in the preceding scene, are those of automatons,—rigid, slow, and mechanical. The* PRISON GUARD *points sternly at* JONES *with his whip, motions him to take his place among the other shovelers.* JONES *gets to his feet in a hypnotized stupor He mumbles subserviently).*

Yes, suh! Yes, suh! I'se comin'.

(As he shuffles, dragging one foot, over to his place, he curses under his breath with rage and hatred).

God damn yo' soul, I gits even wid you yit, sometime.

(As if there were a shovel in his hands he goes through weary, mechanical gestures of digging up dirt, and throwing it to the roadside. Suddenly the GUARD *approaches him angrily, threateningly. He raises his whip and lashes* JONES *viciously across the shoulders with it.* JONES *winces with pain and cowers abjectly. The* GUARD *turns his back on him and walks away contemptuously. Instantly* JONES *straightens up. With arms upraised as if his shovel were a club in his hands he springs murderously at the unsuspecting* GUARD: *In the act of crashing down his shovel on the white man's skull,* JONES *suddenly becomes aware that his hands are empty. He cries despairingly).*

Whar's my shovel? Gimme my shovel 'til I splits his damn head! *(Appealing to his fellow convicts)* Gimme a shovel, one o' you, fo' God's sake!

(They stand fixed in motionless attitudes, their eyes on the ground. The GUARD *seems to wait expectantly, his back turned to the attacker.* JONES *bellows with baffled, terrified rage, tugging frantically at his revolver).*

I kills you, you white debil, if it's de last thing I evah does! Ghost or debil, I kill you agin!

(He frees the revolver and fires point blank at the GUARD's *back. Instantly the walls of the forest close in from both sides, the road and the figures of the convict gang are blotted out in an enshrouding darkness. The only sounds are a crashing in the underbrush as* JONES *leaps away in mad flight and the throbbing of the tom-tom, still far distant, but increased in volume of sound and rapidity of beat).*

Scene Five

A LARGE *circular clearing, enclosed by the serried ranks of gigantic trunks of tall trees whose tops are lost to view. In the center is a big dead stump worn by time into a curious resemblance to an auction block. The moon floods the clearing with a clear light.* JONES *forces his way in through the forest on the left. He looks wildly about the clearing with hunted, fearful glances. His pants are in tatters, his shoes cut and misshapen, flapping about his feet. He slinks cautiously to the stump in the center and sits down in a tense position, ready for instant flight. Then he holds his head in his hands and rocks back and forth, moaning to himself miserably.*

Oh, Lawd, Lawd! Oh, Lawd, Lawd! (*Suddenly he throws himself on his knees and raises his clasped hands to the sky—in a voice of agonized pleading*) Lawd Jesus, heah my prayer! I'se a po' sinner, a po' sinner! I knows I done wrong, I knows it! When I cotches Jeff cheatin' wid loaded dice my anger overcomes me and I kills him dead! Lawd, I done wrong! When dat guard hits me wid de whip, my anger overcomes me, and I kills him dead. Lawd, I done wrong! And down heah whar dese fool bush niggers raises me up to the seat o' de mighty, I steals all I could grab. Lawd, I done wrong! I knows it! I'se sorry! Forgive me, Lawd! Forgive dis po' sinner! (*Then beseeching terrifiedly*) And keep dem away, Lawd! Keep dem away from me! And stop dat drum soundin' in my ears! Dat begin to sound ha'nted, too. (*He gets to his feet, evidently slightly reassured by his prayer—with attempted confidence*) De Lawd'll preserve me from dem ha'nts after dis. (*Sits down on the stump again*) I ain't skeered o' real men. Let dem come. But dem odders—(*He shudders— then looks down at his feet, working his toes inside the shoes—with a groan*) Oh, my po' feet! Dem shoes ain't no use no more 'ceptin' to hurt. I'se better off widout dem. (*He unlaces them and pulls them off—holds the wrecks of the shoes in his hands and regards them mournfully*) You was real,

A-one patin' leather, too. Look at you now. Emperor, you'se gittin'
mighty low!

(*He sighs dejectedly and remains with bowed shoulders, staring down at the
shoes in his hands as if reluctant to throw them away. While his attention is
thus occupied, a crowd of figures silently enter the clearing from all sides. All
are dressed in Southern costumes of the period of the fifties of the last century.
There are middle-aged men who are evidently well-to-do planters. There is
one spruce, authoritative individual—the* AUCTIONEER. *There is a crowd of
curious spectators, chiefly young belles and dandies who have come to the slave-
market for diversion. All exchange courtly greetings in dumb show and chat
silently together. There is something stiff, rigid, unreal, marionettish about
their movements. They group themselves about the stump. Finally a batch of
slaves is led in from the left by an attendant—three men of different ages, two
women, one with a baby in her arms, nursing. They are placed to the left of
the stump, beside* JONES.

*The white planters look them over appraisingly as if they were cattle, and
exchange judgments on each. The dandies point with their fingers and make
witty remarks. The belles titter bewitchingly. All this in silence save for the
ominous throb of the tom-tom. The* AUCTIONEER *holds up his hand, taking his
place at the stump. The groups strain forward attentively. He touches* JONES
*on the shoulder peremptorily, motioning for him to stand on the stump—the
auction block.*

JONES *looks up, sees the figures on all sides, looks wildly for some opening
to escape, sees none, screams and leaps madly to the top of the stump to get as
far away from them as possible. He stands there, cowering, paralyzed with
horror. The* AUCTIONEER *begins his silent spiel. He points to* JONES, *appeals to
the planters to see for themselves. Here is a good field hand, sound in wind
and limb as they can see. Very strong still in spite of his being middle-aged.
Look at that back. Look at those shoulders. Look at the muscles in his arms
and his sturdy legs. Capable of any amount of hard labor. Moreover, of a good
disposition, intelligent and tractable. Will any gentleman start the bidding?
The* PLANTERS *raise their fingers, make their bids. They are apparently all
eager to possess* JONES. *The bidding is lively, the crowd interested. While this*

has been going on, JONES *has been seized by the courage of desperation. He dares to look down and around him. Over his face abject terror gives way to mystification, to gradual realization—stutteringly*).

What you all doin', white folks? What's all dis? What you all lookin' at me fo'? What you doin' wid me, anyhow? (*Suddenly convulsed with raging hatred and fear*) Is dis a auction? Is you sellin' me like dey uster befo' de war? (*Jerking out his revolver just as the* AUCTIONEER *knocks him down to one of the planters—glaring from him to the purchaser*) And *you* sells me? And *you* buys me? I shows you I'se a free nigger, damn yo' souls! (*He fires at the* AUCTIONEER *and at the* PLANTER *with such rapidity that the two shots are almost simultaneous. As if this were a signal the walls of the forest fold in. Only blackness remains and silence broken by* JONES *as he rushes off, crying with fear—and by the quickened, ever louder beat of the tom-tom*).

Scene Six

A CLEARED *space in the forest. The limbs of the trees meet over it forming a low ceiling about five feet from the ground. The interlocked ropes of creepers reaching upward to entwine the tree trunks give an arched appearance to the sides. The space thus enclosed is like the dark, noisome hold of some ancient vessel. The moonlight is almost completely shut out and only a vague wan light filters through. There is the noise of someone approaching from the left, stumbling and crawling through the undergrowth.* JONES' *voice is heard between chattering moans.*

Oh, Lawd, what I gwine do now? Ain't got no bullet left on'y de silver one. If mo' o' dem ha'nts come after me, how I gwine skeer dem away? Oh, Lawd, on'y de silver one left—an' I gotta save dat fo' luck. If I shoots dat one I'm a goner sho'! Lawd, it's black heah! Whar's de moon? Oh, Lawd, don't dis night evah come to an end? (*By the sounds, he is feeling his way cautiously forward*) Dere! Dis feels like a clear space.

I gotta lie down an' rest. I don't care if dem niggers does cotch me. I gotta rest.

(*He is well forward now where his figure can be dimly made out. His pants have been so torn away that what is left of them is no better than a breech cloth. He flings himself full length, face downward on the ground, panting with exhaustion. Gradually it seems to grow lighter in the enclosed space and two rows of seated figures can be seen behind* JONES. *They are sitting in crumpled, despairing attitudes, hunched, facing one another with their backs touching the forest walls as if they were shackled to them. All are negroes, naked save for loin cloths. At first they are silent and motionless. Then they begin to sway slowly forward toward each and back again in unison, as if they were laxly letting themselves follow the long roll of a ship at sea. At the same time, a low, melancholy murmur rises among them, increasing gradually by rhythmic degrees which seem to be directed and controlled by the throb of the tom-tom in the distance, to a long, tremulous wail of despair that reaches a certain pitch, unbearably acute, then falls by slow gradations of tone into silence and is taken up again.* JONES *starts, looks up, sees the figures, and throws himself down again to shut out the sight. A shudder of terror shakes his whole body as the wail rises up about him again. But the next time, his voice, as if under some uncanny compulsion, starts with the others. As their chorus lifts he rises to a sitting posture similar to the others, swaying back and forth. His voice reaches the highest pitch of sorrow, of desolation. The light fades out, the other voices cease, and only darkness is left.* JONES *can be heard scrambling to his feet and running off, his voice sinking down the scale and receding as he moves farther and farther away in the forest. The tom-tom beats louder, quicker, with a more insistent, triumphant pulsation*).

SCENE SEVEN

*T*HE *foot of a gigantic tree by the edge of a great river. A rough structure of boulders, like an altar, is by the tree. The raised river bank is in the nearer background. Beyond this the surface of the river spreads out, brilliant and* *unruffled in the moonlight, blotted out and merged into a veil of bluish mist in the distance.* JONES' *voice is heard from the left rising and falling in the long, despairing wail of the chained slaves, to the rhythmic beat of the tom-tom. As his voice sinks into silence, he enters the open space. The expression of his face is fixed and stony, his eyes have an obsessed glare, he moves with a strange deliberation like a sleep-walker or one in a trance. He looks around at the tree, the rough stone altar, the moonlit surface of the river beyond, and passes his hand over his head with a vague gesture of puzzled bewilderment. Then, as if in obedience to some obscure impulse, he sinks into a kneeling, devotional posture before the altar. Then he seems to come to himself partly, to have an uncertain realization of what he is doing, for he straightens up and stares about him horrifiedly—in an incoherent mumble.*

What—what is I doin'? What is—dis place? Seems like I know dat tree—an' dem stones—an' de river. I remember—seems like I been heah befo'. (*Tremblingly*) Oh, Gorry, I'se skeered in dis place! I'se skeered. Oh, Lawd, pertect dis sinner!

(*Crawling away from the altar, he cowers close to the ground, his face hidden, his shoulders heaving with sobs of hysterical fright. From behind the trunk of the tree, as if he had sprung out of it, the figure of the* CONGO WITCH-DOCTOR *appears. He is wizened and old, naked except for the fur of some small animal tied about his waist, its bushy tail hanging down in front. His body is stained all over a bright red. Antelope horns are on each side of his head, branching upward. In one hand he carries a bone rattle, in the other a charm stick with a bunch of white cockatoo feathers tied to the end. A great number of glass beads and bone ornaments are about his neck, ears, wrists, and ankles. He struts noiselessly with a queer prancing step to a position in the clear ground between* JONES *and the altar. Then with a preliminary, summoning stamp of his foot on the earth, he begins to dance and to chant. As if in response to his summons the beating of the tom-tom grows to a fierce, exultant boom whose throbs seem to fill the air with vibrating rhythm.* JONES *looks up, starts to spring to his feet, reaches a half-kneeling, half-squatting position and remains rigidly fixed there, paralyzed with awed fascination by this new apparition. The* WITCH-DOCTOR *sways, stamping with his foot, his bone rattle clicking the time. His voice rises and falls in a weird, monotonous croon, without articulate word divisions. Gradually his dance becomes clearly one of a narrative in pantomime, his croon is an incantation, a charm to allay the fierceness of some implacable deity demanding sacrifice. He flees, he is pursued by devils, he hides, he flees again. Ever wilder and wilder becomes his flight, nearer and nearer draws the pursuing evil, more and more the spirit of terror gains possession of him. His croon, rising to intensity, is punctuated by shrill cries.* JONES *has become completely hypnotized. His voice joins in the incantation, in the cries, he beats time with his hands and sways his body to and fro from the waist. The whole spirit and meaning of the dance has entered into him, has become his spirit. Finally the theme of the pantomime halts on a howl of despair, and is taken up again in a note of savage hope. There is a salvation. The forces of evil demand sacrifice. They must be appeased. The* WITCH-DOCTOR *points with his wand to the sacred tree, to the river beyond, to the altar, and finally to* JONES *with a ferocious command.* JONES *seems to sense the meaning of this. It is he who must offer himself for sacrifice. He beats his forehead abjectly to the ground, moaning hysterically).*

Mercy, Oh, Lawd! Mercy! Mercy on dis po' sinner.

(*The* WITCH-DOCTOR *springs to the river bank. He stretches out his arms and calls to some God within its depths. Then he starts backward slowly, his arms remaining out. A huge head of a crocodile appears over the bank and its eyes, glittering greenly, fasten upon* JONES: *He stares into them fascinatedly. The* WITCH-DOCTOR *prances up to him, touches him with his wand, motions with hideous command toward the waiting monster.* JONES *squirms on his belly nearer and nearer, moaning continually).*

Mercy, Lawd! Mercy!

(*The crocodile heaves more of his enormous bulk onto the land.* JONES *squirms toward him. The* WITCH-DOCTOR'S *voice shrills out in furious exultation, the tom-tom beats madly.* JONES *cries out in a fierce, exhausted spasm of anguished pleading).*

Lawd, save me! Lawd Jesus, heah my prayer!

(*Immediately, in answer to his prayer, comes the thought of the one bullet left him. He snatches at his hip, shouting defiantly*).

De silver bullet! You don't git me yit!

(*He fires at the green eyes in front of him. The head of the crocodile sinks back behind the river bank, the* WITCH-DOCTOR *springs behind the sacred tree and disappears.* JONES *lies with his face to the ground, his arms outstretched, whimpering with fear as the throb of the tom-tom fills the silence about him with a somber pulsation, a baffled but revengeful power*).

SCENE EIGHT

*D*AWN. *Same as Scene Two, the dividing line of forest and plain. The nearest tree trunks are dimly revealed but the forest behind them is still a mass of glooming shadow. The tom-tom seems on the very spot, so loud and continuously vibrating are its beats.* LEM *enters from the left, followed by a small squad of his soldiers, and by the Cockney trader,* SMITHERS. LEM *is a heavy-set, ape-faced old savage of the extreme African type, dressed only in a loin cloth. A revolver and cartridge belt are about his waist. His soldiers are in different degrees of rag-concealed nakedness. All wear broad palmleaf hats. Each one carries a rifle.* SMITHERS *is the same as in Scene One. One of the soldiers, evidently a tracker, is peering about keenly on the ground. He points to the spot where* JONES *entered the forest.* LEM *and* SMITHERS *come to look.*

SMITHERS: (*after a glance, turns away in disgust*) That's where 'e went in right enough. Much good it'll do yer. 'E's miles orf by this an' safe to the Coast, damn 's 'ide! I tole yer yer'd lose im, didn't I?— wastin' the 'ole bloomin' night beatin' yer bloody drum and castin' yer silly spells! Gawd blimey, wot a pack!

LEM: (*gutturally*) We cotch him. (*He makes a motion to his soldiers who squat down on their haunches in a semi-circle*).

SMITHERS: (*exasperatedly*) Well, ain't yer goin' in an' 'unt 'im in the woods? What the 'ell's the good of waitin'?

LEM: (*imperturbably—squatting down himself*) We cotch him.

SMITHERS: (*turning away from him contemptuously*) Aw! Garn! 'E's a better man than the lot o' you put together. I 'ates the sight o' 'im but I'll say that for 'im. (*A sound comes from the forest. The soldiers jump to their feet, cocking their rifles alertly. LEM remains sitting with an imperturbable expression, but listening intently. He makes a quick signal with his hand. His followers creep quickly into the forest, scattering so that each enters at a different spot*).

SMITHERS: You ain't thinkin' that would be 'im, I 'ope?

LEM: (*calmly*) We cotch him.

SMITHERS: Blarsted fat 'eads! (*Then after a second's thought—wonderingly*) Still an' all, it might 'appen. If 'e lost 'is bloody way in these stinkin' woods 'e'd likely turn in a circle without 'is knowin' it.

LEM: (*peremptorily*) Sssh! (*The reports of several rifles sound from the forest, followed a second later by savage, exultant yells. The beating of the tom-tom abruptly ceases. LEM looks up at the white man with a grin of satisfaction*) We cotch him. Him dead.

SMITHERS: (*with a snarl*) 'Ow d'yer know it's 'im an' 'ow d'yer know 'e's dead?

LEM: My mens dey got um silver bullets. Lead bullet no kill him. He got um strong charm. I cook um money, make um silver bullet, make um strong charm, too.

SMITHERS: (*astonished*) So that's wot you was up to all night, wot? You was scared to put after 'im till you'd moulded silver bullets, eh?

LEM: (*simply stating a fact*) Yes. Him got strong charm. Lead no good.

SMITHERS: (*slapping his thigh and guffawing*) Haw-haw! If yer don't beat all 'ell! (*Then recovering himself—scornfully*) I'll bet yer it ain't 'im they shot at all, yer bleedin' looney!

LEM: (*calmly*) Dey come bring him now. (*The soldiers come out of the forest, carrying* JONES' *limp body. He is dead. They carry him to* LEM, *who examines his body with great satisfaction.* SMITHERS *leans over his shoulder—in a tone of frightened awe*) Well, they did for yer right enough, Jonesey, me lad! Dead as a 'erring! (*Mockingly*) Where's yer 'igh an' mighty airs now, yer bloomin' Majesty? (*Then with a grin*) Silver bullets! Gawd blimey, but yer died in the 'eighth o' style, any'ow!

CURTAIN

"The Hairy Ape"

A Comedy of Ancient and Modern Life in Eight Scenes

CHARACTERS

ROBERT SMITH, "YANK"

PADDY

LONG

MILDRED DOUGLAS

HER AUNT

SECOND ENGINEER

A GUARD

A SECRETARY OF AN ORGANIZATION

Stokers, Ladies, Gentlemen, etc.

SCENES

Scene I: The firemen's forecastle of an ocean liner
—an hour after sailing from New York.

Scene II: Section of promenade deck, two days out—
morning.

Scene III: The stokehole. A few minutes later.

Scene IV: Same as Scene I. Half an hour later.

Scene V: Fifth Avenue, New York. Three weeks later.

Scene VI: An island near the city. The next night.

Scene VII: In the city. About a month later.

Scene VIII: In the city. Twilight of the next day.

34

"The Hairy Ape"

Scene One

*T*HE *firemen's forecastle of a transatlantic liner an hour after sailing from New York for the voyage across. Tiers of narrow, steel bunks, three deep, on all sides. An entrance in rear. Benches on the floor before the bunks. The room is crowded with men, shouting, cursing, laughing, singing—a confused, inchoate uproar swelling into a sort of unity, a meaning—the bewildered, furious, baffled defiance of a beast in a cage. Nearly all the men are drunk. Many bottles are passed from hand to hand. All are dressed in dungaree pants, heavy ugly shoes. Some wear singlets, but the majority are stripped to the waist.*

The treatment of this scene, or of any other scene in the play, should by no means be naturalistic. The effect sought after is a cramped space in the bowels of a ship, imprisoned by white steel. The lines of bunks, the uprights supporting them, cross each other like the steel framework of a cage. The ceiling crushes down upon the men's heads. They cannot stand upright. This accentuates the natural stooping posture which shoveling coal and the resultant over-development of back and shoulder muscles have given them. The men themselves should resemble those pictures in which the appearance of Neanderthal Man is guessed at. All are hairy-chested, with long arms of tremendous power, and low, receding brows above their small, fierce, resentful eyes. All the civilized white races are represented, but except for the slight differentiation in color of hair, skin, eyes, all these men are alike.

The curtain rises on a tumult of sound. YANK *is seated in the foreground. He seems broader, fiercer, more truculent, more powerful, more sure of himself than the rest. They respect his superior strength—the grudging respect of fear. Then, too, he represents to them a self-expression, the very last word in what they are, their most highly developed individual.*

VOICES: Gif me trink dere, you!
'Ave a wet!
Salute!
Gesundheit!
Skoal!
Drunk as a lord, God stiffen you!
Here's how!
Luck!
Pass back that bottle, damn you!
Pourin' it down his neck!
Ho, Froggy! Where the devil have you been?
La Touraine.
I hit him smash in yaw, py Gott!
Jenkins—the First—he's a rotten swine—
And the coppers nabbed him—and I run—
I like peer better. It don't pig head gif you.
A slut, I'm sayin'! She robbed me aslape—
To hell with 'em all!
You're a bloody liar!
Say dot again! (*Commotion. Two men about to fight are pulled apart*).
No scrappin' now!
Tonight—
See who's the best man!
Bloody Dutchman!
Tonight on the for'ard square.
I'll bet on Dutchy.
He packa da wallop, I tella you!
Shut up, Wop!
No fightin', maties. We're all chums, ain't we?
(*A voice starts bawling a song*).

"Beer, beer, glorious beer!

Fill yourselves right up to here."

YANK: (*for the first time seeming to take notice of the uproar about him, turns around threateningly—in a tone of contemptuous authority*) Choke off dat noise! Where d'yuh get dat beer stuff? Beer, hell! Beer's for goils—and Dutchmen. Me for somep'n wit a kick to it! Gimme a drink, one of youse guys. (*Several bottles are eagerly offered. He takes a tremendous gulp at one of them; then, keeping the bottle in his hand, glares belligerently at the owner, who hastens to acquiesce in this robbery by saying*) All righto, Yank. Keep it and have another. (YANK *contemptuously turns his back on the crowd again. For a second there is an embarrassed silence. Then—*)

VOICES: We must be passing the Hook.

She's beginning to roll to it.

Six days in hell—and then Southampton.

Py Yesus, I vish somepody take my first vatch for me!

Gittin' seasick, Square-head?

Drink up and forget it!

What's in your bottle?

Gin.

Dot's nigger trink.

Absinthe? It's doped. You'll go off your chump, Froggy!

Cochon!

Whisky, that's the ticket!

Where's Paddy?

Going asleep.

Sing us that whisky song, Paddy. (*They all turn to an old, wizened Irishman who is dozing, very drunk, on the benches forward. His face is extremely monkey-like with all the sad, patient pathos of that animal in his small eyes*).

Singa da song, Caruso Pat!

He's gettin' old. The drink is too much for him.

He's too drunk.

PADDY: (*blinking about him, starts to his feet resentfully, swaying, holding on to the edge of a bunk*) I'm never too drunk to sing. 'Tis only when I'm dead to the world I'd be wishful to sing at all. (*With a sort of sad contempt*) "Whisky Johnny," ye want? A chanty, ye want? Now that's a queer wish from the ugly like of you, God help you. But no matther. (*He starts to sing in a thin, nasal, doleful tone*):

> Oh, whisky is the life of man!
> Whisky! O Johnny! (*They all join in on this*).
> Oh, whisky is the life of man!
> Whisky for my Johnny! (*Again chorus*).
>
> Oh, whisky drove my old man mad!
> Whisky! O Johnny!
> Oh, whisky drove my old man mad!
> Whisky for my Johnny!

YANK: (*again turning around scornfully*) Aw hell! Nix on dat old sailing ship stuff! All dat bull's dead, see? And you're dead, too, yuh damned old Harp, on'y yuh don't know it. Take it easy, see. Give us a rest. Nix on de loud noise. (*With a cynical grin*) Can't youse see I'm tryin' to t'ink?

ALL: (*repeating the word after him as one with the same cynical amused mockery*) Think! (*The chorused word has a brazen metallic quality as if their throats were phonograph horns. It is followed by a general uproar of hard, barking laughter*).

VOICES: Don't be cracking your head wit ut, Yank.

> You gat headache, py yingo!
> One thing about it—it rhymes with drink!
> Ha, ha, ha!
> Drink, don't think!
> Drink, don't think!
> Drink, don't think! (*A whole chorus of voices has taken up this refrain, stamping on the floor, pounding on the benches with fists*).

YANK: (*taking a gulp from his bottle—good-naturedly*) Aw right. Can de noise. I got yuh de foist time. (*The uproar subsides. A very drunken sentimental tenor begins to sing*):

"Far away in Canada,
   Far across the sea,
There's a lass who fondly waits
   Making a home for me—"

YANK: (*fiercely contemptuous*) Shut up, yuh lousy boob! Where d'yuh get dat tripe? Home? Home, hell! I'll make a home for yuh! I'll knock yuh dead. Home! T'hell wit home! Where d'yuh get dat tripe? Dis is home, see? What d'yuh want wit home? (*Proudly*) I runned away from mine when I was a kid. On'y too glad to beat it, dat was me. Home was lickings for me, dat's all. But yuh can bet your shoit no one ain't never licked me since! Wanter try it, any of youse? Huh! I guess not. (*In a more placated but still contemptuous tone*) Goils waitin' for yuh, huh? Aw, hell! Dat's all tripe. Dey don't wait for no one. Dey'd double-cross yuh for a nickel. Dey're all tarts, get me? Treat 'em rough, dat's me. To hell wit 'em. Tarts, dat's what, de whole bunch of 'em.

LONG: (*very drunk, jumps on a bench excitedly, gesticulating with a bottle in his hand*) Listen 'ere, Comrades! Yank 'ere is right. 'E says this 'ere stinkin' ship is our 'ome. And 'e says as 'ome is 'ell. And 'e's right! This is 'ell. We lives in 'ell, Comrades—and right enough we'll die in it. (*Raging*) And who's ter blame, I arsks yer? We ain't. We wasn't born this rotten way. All men is born free and ekal. That's in the bleedin' Bible, maties. But what d'they care for the Bible—them lazy, bloated swine what travels first cabin? Them's the ones. They dragged us down 'til we're on'y wage slaves in the bowels of a bloody ship, sweatin', burnin' up, eatin' coal dust! Hit's them's ter blame—the damned Capitalist clarss! (*There had been a gradual murmur of contemptuous resentment rising among the men until now he is interrupted by a storm of catcalls, hisses, boos, hard laughter*).

VOICES: Turn it off!
    Shut up!
    Sit down!
    Closa da face!
    Tamn fool! (*Etc.*).

YANK: (*standing up and glaring at* LONG) Sit down before I knock yuh down! (LONG *makes haste to efface himself.* YANK *goes on contemptuously*) De Bible, huh? De Cap'tlist class, huh? Aw nix on dat Salvation Army-Socialist bull. Git a soapbox! Hire a hall! Come and be saved, huh? Jerk us to Jesus, huh? Aw g'wan! I've listened to lots of guys like you, see. Yuh're all wrong. Wanter know what I t'ink? Yuh ain't no good for no one. Yuh're de bunk. Yuh ain't got no noive, get me? Yuh're yellow, dat's what. Yellow, dat's you. Say! What's dem slobs in de foist cabin got to do wit us? We're better men dan dey are, ain't we? Sure! One of us guys could clean up de whole mob wit one mit. Put one of 'em down here for one watch in de stokehole, what'd happen? Dey'd carry him off on a stretcher. Dem boids don't amount to nothin'. Dey're just baggage. Who makes dis old tub run? Ain't it us guys? Well den, we belong, don't we? We belong and dey don't. Dat's all. (*A loud chorus of approval.* YANK *goes on*) As for dis bein' hell—aw, nuts! Yuh lost your noive, dat's what. Dis is a man's job, get me? It belongs. It runs dis tub. No stiffs need apply. But yuh're a stiff, see? Yuh're yellow, dat's you.

VOICES: (*with a great hard pride in them*)
    Righto!
    A man's job!
    Talk is cheap, Long.
    He never could hold up his end.
    Divil take him!
    Yank's right. We make it go.
    Py Gott, Yank say right ting!
    We don't need no one cryin' over us.
    Makin' speeches.

Throw him out!

Yellow!

Chuck him overboard!

I'll break his jaw for him!

(*They crowd around* LONG *threateningly*).

YANK: (*half good-natured again—contemptuously*) Aw, take it easy. Leave him alone. He ain't woith a punch. Drink up. Here's how, whoever owns dis. (*He takes a long swallow from his bottle. All drink with him. In a flash all is hilarious amiability again, backslapping, loud talk, etc.*).

PADDY: (*who has been sitting in a blinking, melancholy daze—suddenly cries out in a voice full of old sorrow*) We belong to this, you're saying? We make the ship to go, you're saying? Yerra then, that Almighty God have pity on us! (*His voice runs into the wail of a keen, he rocks back and forth on his bench. The men stare at him, startled and impressed in spite of themselves*) Oh, to be back in the fine days of my youth, ochone! Oh, there was fine beautiful ships them days—clippers wid tall masts touching the sky—fine strong men in them—men that was sons of the sea as if 'twas the mother that bore them. Oh, the clean skins of them, and the clear eyes, the straight backs and full chests of them! Brave men they was, and bold men surely! We'd be sailing out, bound down round the Horn maybe. We'd be making sail in the dawn, with a fair breeze, singing a chanty song wid no care to it. And astern the land would be sinking low and dying out, but we'd give it no heed but a laugh, and never a look behind. For the day that was, was enough, for we was free men—and I'm thinking 'tis only slaves do be giving heed to the day that's gone or the day to come—until they're old like me. (*With a sort of religious exaltation*) Oh, to be scudding south again wid the power of the Trade Wind driving her on steady through the nights and the days! Full sail on her! Nights and days! Nights when the foam of the wake would be flaming wid fire, when the sky'd be blazing and winking wid stars. Or the full of the moon maybe. Then you'd see her driving through the gray night, her sails stretching aloft all silver and white, not a sound on the deck, the lot of us dreaming dreams, till you'd believe 'twas no real ship at all you was on but a ghost ship like the *Flying Dutchman* they say does be roaming the seas forevermore widout touching a port. And there was the days, too. A warm sun on the clean decks. Sun warming the blood of you, and wind over the miles of shiny green ocean like strong drink to your lungs. Work—aye, hard work—but who'd mind that at all? Sure, you worked under the sky and 'twas work wid skill and daring to it. And wid the day done, in the dog watch, smoking me pipe at ease, the lookout would be raising land maybe, and we'd see the mountains of South Americy wid the red fire of the setting sun painting their white tops and the clouds floating by them! (*His tone of exaltation ceases. He goes on mournfully*) Yerra, what's the use of talking? 'Tis a dead man's whisper. (*To* YANK *resentfully*) 'Twas them days men belonged to ships, not now. 'Twas them days a ship was part of the sea, and a man was part of a ship, and the sea joined all together and made it one. (*Scornfully*) Is it one wid this you'd be, Yank—black smoke from the funnels smudging the sea, smudging the decks—the bloody engines pounding and throbbing and shaking—wid divil a sight of sun or a breath of clean air—choking our lungs wid coal dust—breaking our backs and hearts in the hell of the stokehole—feeding the bloody furnace—feeding our lives along wid the coal, I'm thinking—caged in by steel from a sight of the sky like bloody apes in the Zoo! (*With a harsh laugh*) Ho-ho, divil mend you! Is it to belong to that you're wishing? Is it a flesh and blood wheel of the engines you'd be?

YANK: (*who has been listening with a contemptuous sneer, barks out the answer*) Sure ting! Dat's me. What about it?

PADDY: (*as if to himself—with great sorrow*) Me time is past due. That a great wave wid sun in the heart of it may sweep me over the side sometime I'd be dreaming of the days that's gone!

YANK: Aw, yuh crazy Mick! (*He springs to his feet and advances on* PADDY *threateningly—then stops, fighting some queer struggle within himself— lets his hands fall to his sides—contemptuously*) Aw, take it easy. Yuh're

aw right, at dat. Yuh're bugs, dat's all—nutty as a cuckoo. All dat
tripe yuh been pullin'— Aw, dat's all right. On'y it's dead, get me?
Yuh don't belong no more, see. Yuh don't get de stuff. Yuh're too
old. (*Disgustedly*) But aw say, come up for air onct in a while, can't
yuh? See what's happened since yuh croaked. (*He suddenly bursts forth
vehemently, growing more and more excited*) Say! Sure! Sure I meant it!
What de hell—Say, lemme talk! Hey! Hey, you old Harp! Hey, youse
guys! Say, listen to me—wait a moment—I gotter talk, see. I belong
and he don't. He's dead but I'm livin'. Listen to me! Sure I'm part
of de engines! Why de hell not! Dey move, don't dey? Dey're speed,
ain't dey? Dey smash trou, don't dey? Twenty five knots a hour!
Dat's goin' some! Dat's new stuff! Dat belongs! But him, he's too
old. He gets dizzy. Say, listen. All dat crazy tripe about nights and
days; all dat crazy tripe about stars and moons; all dat crazy tripe
about suns and winds, fresh air and de rest of it—Aw hell, dat's all a
dope dream! Hittin' de pipe of de past, dat's what he's doin'. He's
old and don't belong no more. But me, I'm young! I'm in de pink! I
move wit it! It, get me! I mean de ting dat's de guts of all dis. It
ploughs trou all de tripe he's been sayin'. It blows dat up! It knocks
dat dead! It slams dat offen de face of de oith! It, get me! De engines
and de coal and de smoke and all de rest of it! He can't breathe and
swallow coal dust, but I kin, see? Dat's fresh air for me! Dat's food
for me! I'm new, get me? Hell in de stokehole? Sure! It takes a man
to work in hell. Hell, sure, dat's my fav'rite climate. I eat it up! I git
fat on it! It's me makes it hot! It's me makes it roar! It's me makes it
move! Sure, on'y for me everyting stops. It all goes dead, get me?
De noise and smoke and all de engines movin' de woild, dey stop.
Dere ain't nothin' no more! Dat's what I'm sayin'. Everyting else dat
makes de woild move, somep'n makes it move. It can't move witout
somep'n else, see? Den yuh get down to me. I'm at de bottom, get
me! Dere ain't nothin' foither. I'm de end! I'm de start! I start
somep'n and de woild moves! It—dat's me!—de new dat's moiderin'
de old! I'm de ting in coal dat makes it boin; I'm steam and oil for

de engines; I'm de ting in noise dat makes yuh hear it; I'm smoke and express trains and steamers and factory whistles; I'm de ting in gold dat makes it money! And I'm what makes iron into steel! Steel, dat stands for de whole ting! And I'm steel—steel—steel! I'm de muscles in steel, de punch behind it! (*As he says this he pounds with his fist against the steel bunks. All the men, roused to a pitch of frenzied self-glorification by his speech, do likewise. There is a deafening metallic roar, through which* YANK's *voice can be heard bellowing*) Slaves, hell! We run de whole woiks. All de rich guys dat tink dey're somep'n, dey ain't nothin'! Dey don't belong. But us guys, we're in de move, we're at de bottom, de whole ting is us! (PADDY *from the start of* YANK's *speech has been taking one gulp after another from his bottle, at first frightenedly, as if he were afraid to listen, then desperately, as if to drown his senses, but finally has achieved complete indifferent, even amused, drunkenness.* YANK *sees his lips moving. He quells the uproar with a shout*) Hey, youse guys, take it easy! Wait a moment! De nutty Harp is sayin' somep'n.

PADDY: (*is heard now—throws his head back with a mocking burst of laughter*) Ho-ho-ho-ho-ho—

YANK: (*drawing back his fist, with a snarl*) Aw! Look out who yuh're givin' the bark!

PADDY: (*begins to sing the "Miller of Dee" with enormous good nature*)

> "I care for nobody, no, not I,
> And nobody cares for me."

YANK: (*good-natured himself in a flash, interrupts* PADDY *with a slap on the bare back like a report*) Dat's de stuff! Now yuh're gettin' wise to somep'n. Care for nobody, dat's de dope! To hell wit 'em all! And nix on nobody else carin'. I kin care for myself, get me! (*Eight bells sound, muffled, vibrating through the steel walls as if some enormous brazen gong were imbedded in the heart of the ship. All the men jump up mechanically, file through the door silently close upon each other's heels in what is very like a prisoners' lockstep.* YANK *slaps* PADDY *on the back*) Our watch, yuh old Harp! (*Mockingly*) Come on down in hell. Eat up de coal dust. Drink in de heat. It's it, see! Act like yuh liked it, yuh better—or croak yuhself.

PADDY: (*with jovial defiance*) To the divil wid it! I'll not report this watch. Let thim log me and be damned. I'm no slave the like of you. I'll be sittin' here at me ease, and drinking, and thinking, and dreaming dreams.

YANK: (*contemptuously*) Tinkin' and dreamin', what'll that get yuh? What's tinkin' got to do wit it? We move, don't we? Speed, ain't it? Fog, dat's all you stand for. But we drive trou dat, don't we? We split dat up and smash trou—twenty-five knots a hour! (*Turns his back on* PADDY *scornfully*) Aw, yuh make me sick! Yuh don't belong! (*He strides out the door in rear.* PADDY *hums to himself, blinking drowsily*).

CURTAIN

Scene Two

*T*wo *days out. A section of the promenade deck.* MILDRED DOUGLAS *and her aunt are discovered reclining in deck chairs. The former is a girl of twenty, slender, delicate, with a pale, pretty face marred by a self-conscious expression of disdainful superiority. She looks fretful, nervous and discontented, bored by her own anemia. Her aunt is a pompous and proud—and fat—old lady. She is a type even to the point of a double chin and lorgnettes. She is dressed pretentiously, as if afraid her face alone would never indicate her position in life.* MILDRED *is dressed all in white.*

The impression to be conveyed by this scene is one of the beautiful, vivid life of the sea all about—sunshine on the deck in a great flood, the fresh sea wind blowing across it. In the midst of this, these two incongruous, artificial figures, inert and disharmonious, the elder like a gray lump of dough touched up with rouge, the younger looking as if the vitality of her stock had been sapped before she was conceived, so that she is the expression not of its life energy but merely of the artificialities that energy had won for itself in the spending.

MILDRED: (*looking up with affected dreaminess*) How the black smoke swirls back against the sky! Is it not beautiful?

AUNT: (*without looking up*) I dislike smoke of any kind.

MILDRED: My great-grandmother smoked a pipe—a clay pipe.

AUNT: (*ruffling*) Vulgar!

MILDRED: She was too distant a relative to be vulgar. Time mellows pipes.

AUNT: (*pretending boredom but irritated*) Did the sociology you took up at college teach you that—to play the ghoul on every possible occasion, excavating old bones? Why not let your great-grandmother rest in her grave?

MILDRED: (*dreamily*) With her pipe beside her—puffing in Paradise.

AUNT: (*with spite*) Yes, you are a natural born ghoul. You are even getting to look like one, my dear.

MILDRED: (*in a passionless tone*) I detest you, Aunt. (*Looking at her critically*) Do you know what you remind me of? Of a cold pork pudding against a background of linoleum tablecloth in the kitchen of a—but the possibilities are wearisome. (*She closes her eyes*).

AUNT: (*with a bitter laugh*) Merci for your candor. But since I am and must be your chaperon—in appearance, at least—let us patch up some sort of armed truce. For my part you are quite free to indulge any pose of eccentricity that beguiles you—as long as you observe the amenities—

MILDRED: (*drawling*) The inanities?

AUNT: (*going on as if she hadn't heard*) After exhausting the morbid thrills of social service work on New York's East Side—how they must have hated you, by the way, the poor that you made so much poorer in their own eyes!—you are now bent on making your slumming international. Well, I hope Whitechapel will provide the needed nerve tonic. Do not ask me to chaperon you there, however. I told your father I would not. I loathe deformity. We will hire an army of detectives and you may investigate everything—they allow you to see.

MILDRED: (*protesting with a trace of genuine earnestness*) Please do not mock at my attempts to discover how the other half lives. Give me credit for some sort of groping sincerity in that at least. I would like to help them. I would like to be some use in the world. Is it my fault I don't know how? I would like to be sincere, to touch life somewhere. (*With weary bitterness*) But I'm afraid I have neither the vitality nor integrity. All that was burnt out in our stock before I was born. Grandfather's blast furnaces, flaming to the sky, melting steel, making millions—then father keeping those home fires burning, making more millions—and little me at the tail-end of it all. I'm a waste product in the Bessemer process—like the millions. Or rather, I inherit the acquired trait of the by-product, wealth, but none of the energy, none of the strength of the steel that made it. I am sired by gold and damned by it, as they say at the race track—damned in more ways than one. (*She laughs mirthlessly*).

AUNT: (*unimpressed—superciliously*) You seem to be going in for sincerity today. It isn't becoming to you, really—except as an obvious pose. Be as artificial as you are, I advise. There's a sort of sincerity in that, you know. And, after all, you must confess you like that better.

MILDRED: (*again affected and bored*) Yes, I suppose I do. Pardon me for my outburst. When a leopard complains of its spots, it must sound rather grotesque. (*In a mocking tone*) Purr, little leopard. Purr, scratch, tear, kill, gorge yourself and be happy—only stay in the jungle where your spots are camouflage. In a cage they make you conspicuous.

AUNT: I don't know what you are talking about.

MILDRED: It would be rude to talk about anything to you. Let's just talk. (*She looks at her wrist watch*) Well, thank goodness, it's about time for them to come for me. That ought to give me a new thrill, Aunt.

AUNT: (*affectedly troubled*) You don't mean to say you're really going? The dirt—the heat must be frightful—

MILDRED: Grandfather started as a puddler. I should have inherited an immunity to heat that would make a salamander shiver. It will be fun to put it to the test.

AUNT: But don't you have to have the captain's—or someone's— permission to visit the stokehole?

MILDRED: (*with a triumphant smile*) I have it—both his and the chief engineer's. Oh, they didn't want to at first, in spite of my social service credentials. They didn't seem a bit anxious that I should investigate how the other half lives and works on a ship. So I had to tell them that my father, the president of Nazareth Steel, chairman of the board of directors of this line, had told me it would be all right.

AUNT: He didn't.

MILDRED: How naïve age makes one! But I said he did, Aunt. I even said he had given me a letter to them—which I had lost. And they were afraid to take the chance that I might be lying. (*Excitedly*) So it's ho! for the stokehole. The second engineer is to escort me. (*Looking at her watch again*) It's time. And here he comes, I think. (*The* SECOND ENGINEER *enters. He is a husky, fine looking man of thirty-five or so. He stops before the two and tips his cap, visibly embarrassed and ill-at-ease*).

SECOND ENGINEER: Miss Douglas?

MILDRED: Yes. (*Throwing off her rugs and getting to her feet*) Are we all ready to start?

SECOND ENGINEER: In just a second, ma'am. I'm waiting for the Fourth. He's coming along.

MILDRED: (*with a scornful smile*) You don't care to shoulder this responsibility alone, is that it?

SECOND ENGINEER: (*forcing a smile*) Two are better than one. (*Disturbed by her eyes, glances out to sea—blurts out*) A fine day we're having.

MILDRED: Is it?

SECOND ENGINEER: A nice warm breeze—

MILDRED: It feels cold to me.

SECOND ENGINEER: But it's hot enough in the sun—

MILDRED: Not hot enough for me. I don't like Nature. I was never athletic.

SECOND ENGINEER: (*forcing a smile*) Well, you'll find it hot enough where you're going.

MILDRED: Do you mean hell?

SECOND ENGINEER: (*flabbergasted, decides to laugh*) Ho-ho! No, I mean the stokehole.

MILDRED: My grandfather was a puddler. He played with boiling steel.

SECOND ENGINEER: (*all at sea—uneasily*) Is that so? Hum, you'll excuse me, ma'am, but are you intending to wear that dress?

MILDRED: Why not?

SECOND ENGINEER: You'll likely rub against oil and dirt. It can't be helped.

MILDRED: It doesn't matter. I have lots of white dresses.

SECOND ENGINEER: I have an old coat you might throw over—

MILDRED: I have fifty dresses like this. I will throw this one into the sea when I come back. That ought to wash it clean, don't you think?

SECOND ENGINEER: (*doggedly*) There's ladders to climb down that are none too clean—and dark alleyways—

MILDRED: I will wear this very dress and none other.

SECOND ENGINEER: No offense meant. It's none of my business. I was only warning you—

MILDRED: Warning? That sounds thrilling.

SECOND ENGINEER: (*looking down the deck—with a sigh of relief*) There's the Fourth now. He's waiting for us. If you'll come—

MILDRED: Go on. I'll follow you. (*He goes.* MILDRED *turns a mocking smile on her aunt*) An oaf—but a handsome, virile oaf.

AUNT: (*scornfully*) Poser!

MILDRED: Take care. He said there were dark alleyways—

AUNT: (*in the same tone*) Poser!

MILDRED: (*biting her lips angrily*) You are right. But would that my millions were not so anemically chaste!

AUNT: Yes, for a fresh pose I have no doubt you would drag the name of Douglas in the gutter!

MILDRED: From which it sprang. Good-by, Aunt. Don't pray too hard that I may fall into the fiery furnace.

AUNT: Poser!

MILDRED: (*viciously*) Old hag! (*She slaps her aunt insultingly across the face and walks off, laughing gaily*).

AUNT: (*screams after her*) I said poser!

CURTAIN

SCENE THREE

*T*HE *stokehole. In the rear, the dimly-outlined bulks of the furnaces and boilers. High overhead one hanging electric bulb sheds just enough light through the murky air laden with coal dust to pile up masses of shadows everywhere. A line of men, stripped to the waist, is before the furnace doors. They bend over, looking neither to right nor left, handling their shovels as if they were part of their bodies, with a strange, awkward, swinging rhythm. They use the shovels to throw open the furnace doors. Then from these fiery round holes in the black a flood of terrific light and heat pours full upon the men who are outlined in silhouette in the crouching, inhuman attitudes of chained gorillas. The men shovel with a rhythmic motion, swinging as on a pivot from the coal which lies in heaps on the floor behind to hurl it into the flaming mouths before them. There is a tumult of noise—the brazen clang of the furnace doors as they are flung open or slammed shut, the grating, teeth-gritting grind of steel against steel, of crunching coal. This clash of sounds stuns one's ears with its rending dissonance. But there is order in it, rhythm, a mechanical regulated* *recurrence, a tempo. And rising above all, making the air hum with the quiver of liberated energy, the roar of leaping flames in the furnaces, the monotonous throbbing beat of the engines.*

As the curtain rises, the furnace doors are shut. The men are taking a breathing spell. One or two are arranging the coal behind them, pulling it into more accessible heaps. The others can be dimly made out leaning on their shovels in relaxed attitudes of exhaustion.

PADDY: (*from somewhere in the line—plaintively*) Yerra, will this divil's own watch nivir end? Me back is broke. I'm destroyed entirely.

YANK: (*from the center of the line—with exuberant scorn*) Aw, yuh make me sick! Lie down and croak, why don't yuh? Always beefin', dat's you! Say, dis is a cinch! Dis was made for me! It's my meat, get me! (*A whistle is blown—a thin, shrill note from somewhere overhead in the darkness.* YANK *curses without resentment*) Dere's de damn engineer crackin' de whip. He tinks we're loafin'.

PADDY: (*vindictively*) God stiffen him!

YANK: (*in an exultant tone of command*) Come on, youse guys! Git into de game! She's gittin' hungry! Pile some grub in her. Trow it into her belly! Come on now, all of youse! Open her up! (*At this last all the men, who have followed his movements of getting into position, throw open their furnace doors with a deafening clang. The fiery light floods over their shoulders as they bend round for the coal. Rivulets of sooty sweat have traced maps on their backs. The enlarged muscles form bunches of high light and shadow*).

YANK: (*chanting a count as he shovels without seeming effort*) One—two—tree— (*His voice rising exultantly in the joy of battle*) Dat's de stuff! Let her have it! All togedder now! Sling it into her! Let her ride! Shoot de piece now! Call de toin on her! Drive her into it! Feel her move! Watch her smoke! Speed, dat's her middle name! Give her coal, youse guys! Coal, dat's her booze! Drink it up, baby! Let's see yuh sprint! Dig in and gain a lap! Dere she go-o-es. (*This last in the chanting formula of the gallery gods at the six-day bike race. He slams his furnace door shut. The others do likewise with as much unison as their wearied bodies will permit. The effect is of one fiery eye after another being blotted out with a series of accompanying bangs).*

PADDY: (*groaning*) Me back is broke. I'm bate out—bate— (*There is a pause. Then the inexorable whistle sounds again from the dim regions above the electric light. There is a growl of cursing rage from all sides*).

YANK: (*shaking his fist upward—contemptuously*) Take it easy dere, you! Who d'yuh tink's runnin' dis game, me or you? When I git ready, we move. Not before! When I git ready, get me!

VOICES: (*approvingly*) That's the stuff!

Yank tal him, py golly!

Yank ain't affeerd.

Goot poy, Yank!

Give him hell!

Tell 'im 'e's a bloody swine!

Bloody slave-driver!

YANK: (*contemptuously*) He ain't got no noive. He's yellow, get me? All de engineers is yellow. Dey got streaks a mile wide. Aw, to hell wit him! Let's move, youse guys. We had a rest. Come on, she needs it! Give her pep! It ain't for him. Him and his whistle, dey don't belong. But we belong, see! We gotter feed de baby! Come on! (*He turns and flings his furnace door open. They all follow his lead. At this instant the* SECOND *and* FOURTH ENGINEERS *enter from the darkness on the left with* MILDRED *between them. She starts, turns paler, her pose is crumbling, she shivers with fright in spite of the blazing heat, but forces herself to leave the* ENGINEERS *and take a few steps nearer the men. She is right behind* YANK. *All this happens quickly while the men have their backs turned*).

YANK: Come on, youse guys! (*He is turning to get coal when the whistle sounds again in a peremptory, irritating note. This drives* YANK *into a sudden fury. While the other men have turned full around and stopped dumfounded by the spectacle of* MILDRED *standing there in her white dress,* YANK *does not turn far enough to see her. Besides, his head is thrown back, he blinks upward through the murk trying to find the owner of the whistle, he brandishes his shovel murderously over his head in one hand, pounding on his chest, gorilla-like, with the other, shouting*) Toin off dat whistle! Come down outa dere, yuh yellow, brass-buttoned, Belfast bum, yuh! Come down and I'll knock yer brains out! Yuh lousy, stinkin', yellow mut of a Catholic-moiderin' bastard! Come down and I'll moider yuh! Pullin' dat whistle on me, huh? I'll show yuh! I'll crash yer skull in! I'll drive yer teet' down yer troat! I'll slam yer nose trou de back of yer head! I'll cut yer guts out for a nickel, yuh lousy boob, yuh dirty, crummy, muck-eatin' son of a— (*Suddenly he becomes conscious of all the other men staring at something directly behind his back. He whirls defensively with a snarling, murderous growl, crouching to spring, his lips drawn back over his teeth, his small eyes gleaming ferociously. He sees* MILDRED, *like a white apparition in the full light from the open furnace doors. He glares into her eyes, turned to stone. As for her, during his speech she has listened, paralyzed with horror, terror, her whole personality crushed, beaten in, collapsed, by the terrific impact of this unknown, abysmal brutality, naked and shameless. As she looks at his gorilla face, as his eyes bore into hers, she utters a low, choking cry and shrinks away from him, putting both hands up before her eyes to shut out the sight of his face, to protect her own. This startles* YANK *to a reaction. His mouth falls open, his eyes grow bewildered*).

MILDRED: (*about to faint—to the* ENGINEERS, *who now have her one by each arm—whimperingly*) Take me away! Oh, the filthy beast! (*She faints. They carry her quickly back, disappearing in the darkness at the left, rear. An iron door clangs shut. Rage and bewildered fury rush back on* YANK. *He feels himself insulted in some unknown fashion in the very heart of his pride. He roars*) God damn yuh! (*And hurls his shovel after them at the door which has just closed. It hits the steel bulkhead with a clang and falls clattering on the steel floor. From overhead the whistle sounds again in a long, angry, insistent command*).

CURTAIN

Scene Four

*T*HE *firemen's forecastle.* YANK'S *watch has just come off duty and had din-*
ner. Their faces and bodies shine from a soap and water scrubbing but around
their eyes, where a hasty dousing does not touch, the coal dust sticks like black
make-up, giving them a queer, sinister expression. YANK *has not washed either*
face or body. He stands out in contrast to them, a blackened, brooding figure.
He is seated forward on a bench in the exact attitude of Rodin's "The Thinker."
The others, most of them smoking pipes, are staring at YANK *half-apprehen-*
sively, as if fearing an outburst; half-amusedly, as if they saw a joke somewhere
that tickled them.

VOICES: He ain't ate nothin'.
        Py golly, a fallar gat to gat grub in him.
        Divil a lie.
        Yank feeda da fire, no feeda da face.
        Ha-ha.
        He ain't even washed hisself.
        He's forgot.
        Hey, Yank, you forgot to wash.

YANK: (*sullenly*) Forgot nothin'! To hell wit washin'.

VOICES: It'll stick to you.
        It'll get under your skin.
        Give yer the bleedin' itch, that's wot.
        It makes spots on you—like a leopard.
        Like a piebald nigger, you mean.
        Better wash up, Yank.
        You sleep better.
        Wash up, Yank.
        Wash up! Wash up!

YANK: (*resentfully*) Aw say, youse guys. Lemme alone. Can't youse see I'm tryin' to tink?

ALL: (*repeating the word after him as one with cynical mockery*) Think! (*The word has a brazen, metallic quality as if their throats were phonograph horns. It is followed by a chorus of hard, barking laughter*).

YANK: (*springing to his feet and glaring at them belligerently*) Yes, tink! Tink, dat's what I said! What about it? (*They are silent, puzzled by his sudden resentment at what used to be one of his jokes.* YANK *sits down again in the same attitude of "The Thinker"*).

VOICES: Leave him alone.

He's got a grouch on.

Why wouldn't he?

PADDY: (*with a wink at the others*) Sure I know what's the matther. 'Tis aisy to see. He's fallen in love, I'm telling you.

ALL: (*repeating the word after him as one with cynical mockery*) Love! (*The word has a brazen, metallic quality as if their throats were phonograph horns. It is followed by a chorus of hard, barking laughter*).

YANK: (*with a contemptuous snort*) Love, hell! Hate, dat's what. I've fallen in hate, get me?

PADDY: (*philosophically*) 'Twould take a wise man to tell one from the other. (*With a bitter, ironical scorn, increasing as he goes on*) But I'm telling you it's love that's in it. Sure what else but love for us poor bastes in the stokehole would be bringing a fine lady, dressed like a white quane, down a mile of ladders and steps to be havin' a look at us? (*A growl of anger goes up from all sides*).

LONG: (*jumping on a bench—hecticly*) Hinsultin' us! Hinsultin' us, the bloody cow! And them bloody engineers! What right 'as they got to be exhibitin' us 's if we was bleedin' monkeys in a menagerie? Did we sign for hinsults to our dignity as 'onest workers? Is that in the ship's articles? You kin bloody well bet it ain't! But I knows why they done it. I arsked a deck steward 'o she was and 'e told me. 'Er old man's a bleedin' millionaire, a bloody Capitalist! 'E's got enuf bloody gold to sink this bleedin' ship! 'E makes arf the bloody steel in the

world! 'E owns this bloody boat! And you and me, Comrades, we're
'is slaves! And the skipper and mates and engineers, they're 'is slaves!
And she's 'is bloody daughter and we're all 'er slaves, too! And she
gives 'er orders as 'ow she wants to see the bloody animals below
decks and down they takes 'er! (*There is a roar of rage from all sides*).

YANK: (*blinking at him bewilderedly*) Say! Wait a moment! Is all dat
straight goods?

LONG: Straight as string! The bleedin' steward as waits on 'em, 'e told
me about 'er. And what're we goin' ter do, I arsks yer? 'Ave we got
ter swaller 'er hinsults like dogs? It ain't in the ship's articles. I tell
yer we got a case. We kin go to law—

YANK: (*with abysmal contempt*) Hell! Law!

ALL: (*repeating the word after him as one with cynical mockery*) Law! (*The
word has a brazen metallic quality as if their throats were phonograph
horns. It is followed by a chorus of hard, barking laughter*).

LONG: (*feeling the ground slipping from under his feet—desperately*) As vot-
ers and citizens we kin force the bloody governments—

YANK: (*with abysmal contempt*) Hell! Governments!

ALL: (*repeating the word after him as one with cynical mockery*) Governments! (*The word has a brazen metallic quality as if their throats were
phonograph horns. It is followed by a chorus of hard, barking laughter*).

LONG: (*hysterically*) We're free and equal in the sight of God—

YANK: (*with abysmal contempt*) Hell! God!

ALL: (*repeating the word after him as one with cynical mockery*) God! (*The
word has a brazen metallic quality as if their throats were phonograph
horns. It is followed by a chorus of hard, barking laughter*).

YANK: (*witheringly*) Aw, join de Salvation Army!

ALL: Sit down! Shut up! Damn fool! Sea-lawyer! (*LONG slinks back out of
sight*).

PADDY: (*continuing the trend of his thoughts as if he had never been interrupted—bitterly*) And there she was standing behind us, and the Second pointing at us like a man you'd hear in a circus would be saying:
In this cage is a queerer kind of baboon than ever you'd find in

darkest Africy. We roast them in their own sweat—and be damned if you won't heart some of thim saying they like it! (*He glances scornfully at* YANK).

YANK: (*with a bewildered uncertain growl*) Aw!

PADDY: And there was Yank roarin' curses and turning round wid his shovel to brain her—and she looked at him, and him at her—

YANK: (*slowly*) She was all white. I tought she was a ghost. Sure.

PADDY: (*with heavy, biting sarcasm*) 'Twas love at first sight, divil a doubt of it! If you'd seen the endearin' look on her pale mug when she shriveled away with her hands over her eyes to shut out the sight of him! Sure, 'twas as if she'd seen a great hairy ape escaped from the Zoo!

YANK: (*stung—with a growl of rage*) Aw!

PADDY: And the loving way Yank heaved his shovel at the skull of her, only she was out the door! (*A* grin breaking over his face) 'Twas touching, I'm telling you! It put the touch of home, swate home in the stokehole. (*There is a roar of laughter from all*).

YANK: (*glaring at* PADDY *menacingly*) Aw, choke dat off, see!

PADDY: (*not heeding him—to the others*) And her grabbin' at the Second's arm for protection. (*With a grotesque imitation of a woman's voice*) Kiss me, Engineer dear, for it's dark down here and me old man's in Wall Street making money! Hug me tight, darlin', for I'm afeerd in the dark and me mother's on deck makin' eyes at the skipper! (*Another roar of laughter*).

YANK: (*threateningly*) Say! What yuh tryin' to do, kid me, yuh old Harp?

PADDY: Divil a bit! Ain't I wishin' myself you'd brained her?

YANK: (*fiercely*) I'll brain her! I'll brain her yet, wait 'n' see! (*Coming over to* PADDY—*slowly*) Say, is dat what she called me—a hairy ape?

PADDY: She looked it at you if she didn't say the word itself.

YANK: (*grinning horribly*) Hairy ape, huh? Sure! Dat's de way she looked at me, aw right. Hairy ape! So dat's me, huh? (*Bursting into rage—as if she were still in front of him*) Yuh skinny tart! Yuh white-faced bum, yuh! I'll show yuh who's a ape! (*Turning to the others, bewilderment seizing him again*) Say, youse guys. I was bawlin' him out for pullin' de whistle on us. You heard me. And den I seen youse lookin' at somep'n and I tought he'd sneaked down to come up in back of me, and I hopped round to knock him dead wit de shovel. And dere she was wit de light on her! Christ, yuh coulda pushed me over with a finger! I was scared, get me? Sure! I tought she was a ghost, see? She was all in white like dey wrap around stiffs. You seen her. Kin yuh blame me? She didn't belong, dat's what. And den when I come to and seen it was a real skoit and seen de way she was lookin' at me—like Paddy said—Christ, I was sore, get me? I don't stand for dat stuff from nobody. And I flung de shovel—on'y she'd beat it. (*Furiously*) I wished it'd banged her! I wished it'd knocked her block off!

LONG: And be 'anged for murder or 'lectrocuted? She ain't bleedin' well worth it.

YANK: I don't give a damn what! I'd be square wit her, wouldn't I? Tink I wanter let her put somep'n over on me? Tink I'm goin' to let her git away wit dat stuff? Yuh don't know me! No one ain't never put nothin' over on me and got away wit it, see!—not dat kind of stuff—no guy and no skoit neither! I'll fix her! Maybe she'll come down again—

VOICE: No chance, Yank. You scared her out of a year's growth.

YANK: I scared her? Why de hell should I scare her? Who de hell is she? Ain't she de same as me? Hairy ape, huh? (*With his old confident bravado*) I'll show her I'm better'n her, if she on'y knew it. I belong and she don't, see! I move and she's dead! Twenty-five knots a hour, dat's me! Dat carries her but I make dat. She's on'y baggage. Sure! (*Again bewilderedly*) But, Christ, she was funny lookin'! Did yuh pipe her hands? White and skinny. Yuh could see de bones through 'em. And her mush, dat was dead white, too. And her eyes, dey was like dey'd seen a ghost. Me, dat was! Sure! Hairy ape! Ghost, huh? Look at dat arm! (*He extends his right arm, swelling out the great muscles*) I coulda took her wit dat, wit just my little finger even, and broke her in two. (*Again bewilderedly*) Say, who is dat skoit, huh? What is she? What's she come from? Who made her? Who give her de noive to look at me like dat? Dis ting's got my goat right. I don't get her. She's new to me. What does a skoit like her mean, huh? She don't belong, get me! I can't see her. (*With growing anger*) But one ting I'm wise to, aw right, aw right! Youse all kin bet your shoits I'll git even wit her. I'll show her if she tinks she— She grinds de organ and I'm on de string, huh? I'll fix her! Let her come down again and I'll fling her in de furnace! She'll move den! She won't shiver at nothin', den! Speed, dat'll be her! She'll belong den! (*He grins horribly*).

PADDY: She'll never come. She's had her belly-full, I'm telling you. She'll be in bed now, I'm thinking, wid ten doctors and nurses feedin' her salts to clean the fear out of her.

YANK: (*enraged*) Yuh tink I made her sick, too, do yuh? Just lookin' at me, huh? Hairy ape, huh? (*In a frenzy of rage*) I'll fix her! I'll tell her where to git off! She'll git down on her knees and take it back or I'll bust de face offen her! (*Shaking one fist upward and beating on his chest with the other*) I'll find yuh! I'm comin', d'yuh hear? I'll fix yuh, God damn yuh! (*He makes a rush for the door*).

VOICES: Stop him!
    He'll get shot!
    He'll murder her!
    Trip him up!
    Hold him!
    He's gone crazy!
    Gott, he's strong!
    Hold him down!
    Look out for a kick!
    Pin his arms!

(*They have all piled on him and, after a fierce struggle, by sheer weight of numbers have borne him to the floor just inside the door*).

PADDY: (*who has remained detached*) Kape him down till he's cooled off.

(*Scornfully*) Yerra, Yank, you're a great fool. Is it payin' attention at all you are to the like of that skinny sow widout one drop of rale blood in her?

YANK: (*frenziedly, from the bottom of the heap*) She done me doit! She done me doit, didn't she? I'll git square wit her! I'll get her some way! Git offen me, youse guys! Lemme up! I'll show her who's a ape!

CURTAIN

Scene Five

*T*HREE *weeks later. A corner of Fifth Avenue in the Fifties on a fine Sunday morning. A general atmosphere of clean, well-tidied, wide street; a flood of mellow, tempered sunshine; gentle, genteel breezes. In the rear, the show windows of two shops, a jewelry establishment on the corner, a furrier's next to it. Here the adornments of extreme wealth are tantalizingly displayed. The jeweler's window is gaudy with glittering diamonds, emeralds, rubies, pearls, etc., fashioned in ornate tiaras, crowns, necklaces, collars, etc. From each piece hangs an enormous tag from which a dollar sign and numerals in intermittent electric lights wink out the incredible prices. The same in the furrier's. Rich furs of all varieties hang there bathed in a downpour of artificial light. The general effect is of a background of magnificence cheapened and made grotesque by commercialism, a background in tawdry disharmony with the clear light and sunshine on the street itself.*

Up the side street YANK *and* LONG *come swaggering.* LONG *is dressed in shore clothes, wears a black Windsor tie, cloth cap.* YANK *is in his dirty dungarees. A fireman's cap with black peak is cocked defiantly on the side of his head. He has not shaved for days and around his fierce, resentful eyes—as around those of* LONG *to a lesser degree—the black smudge of coal dust still sticks like make-up. They hesitate and stand together at the corner, swaggering, looking about them with a forced, defiant contempt.*

LONG: (*indicating it all with an oratorical gesture*) Well, 'ere we are. Fif' Avenoo. This 'ere's their bleedin' private lane, as yer might say. (*Bitterly*) We're trespassers 'ere. Proletarians keep orf the grass!

YANK: (*dully*) I don't see no grass, yuh boob. (*Staring at the sidewalk*) Clean, ain't it? Yuh could eat a fried egg offen it. The white wings got some job sweepin' dis up. (*Looking up and down the avenue—surlily*) Where's all de white-collar stiffs yuh said was here—and de skoits—*her* kind?

LONG: In church, blarst 'em! Arskin' Jesus to give 'em more money.

YANK: Choich, huh? I useter go to choich onct—sure—when I was a kid. Me old man and woman, dey made me. Dey never went demselves, dough. Always got too big a head on Sunday mornin', dat was dem. (*With a grin*) Dey was scrappers for fair, bot' of dem. On Satiday nights when dey bot' got a skinful dey could put up a bout oughter been staged at de Garden. When dey got trough dere wasn't a chair or table wit a leg under it. Or else dey bot' jumped on me for somep'n. Dat was where I loined to take punishment. (*With a grin and a swagger*) I'm a chip offen de old block, get me?

LONG: Did yer old man follow the sea?

YANK: Naw. Worked along shore. I runned away when me old lady croaked wit de tremens. I helped at truckin' and in de market. Den I shipped in de stokehole. Sure. Dat belongs. De rest was nothin'. (*Looking around him*) I ain't never seen dis before. De Brooklyn waterfront, dat was where I was dragged up. (*Taking a deep breath*) Dis ain't so bad at dat, huh?

LONG: Not bad? Well, we pays for it wiv our bloody sweat, if yer wants to know!

YANK: (*with sudden angry disgust*) Aw, hell! I don't see no one, see—like her. All dis gives me a pain. It don't belong. Say, ain't dere a back room around dis dump? Let's go shoot a ball. All dis is too clean and quiet and dolled-up, get me! It gives me a pain.

LONG: Wait and yer'll bloody well see—

YANK: I don't wait for no one. I keep on de move. Say, what yuh drag me up here for, anyway? Tryin' to kid me, yuh simp, yuh?

LONG: Yer wants to get back at 'er, don't yer? That's what yer been sayin' every bloomin' hour since she hinsulted yer.

YANK: (*vehemently*) Sure ting I do! Didn't I try to get even wit her in Southampton? Didn't I sneak on de dock and wait for her by de gangplank? I was goin' to spit in her pale mug, see! Sure, right in her pop-eyes! Dat woulda made me even, see? But no chanct. Dere was a whole army of plainclothes bulls around. Dey spotted me and gimme de bum's rush. I never seen her. But I'll git square wit her yet, you watch! (*Furiously*) De lousy tart! She tinks she kin get away wit moider—but not wit me! I'll fix her! I'll tink of a way!

LONG: (*as disgusted as he dares to be*) Ain't that why I brought yer up 'ere—to show yer? Yer been lookin' at this 'ere 'ole affair wrong. Yer been actin' an' talkin' 's if it was all a bleedin' personal matter between yer and that bloody cow. I wants to convince yer she was on'y a representative of 'er clarss. I wants to awaken yer bloody clarss consciousness. Then yer'll see it's 'er clarss yer've got to fight, not 'er alone. There's a 'ole mob of 'em like 'er, Gawd blind 'em!

YANK: (*spitting on his hands—belligerently*) De more de merrier when I gits started. Bring on de gang!

LONG: Yer'll see 'em in arf a mo', when that church lets out. (*He turns and sees the window display in the two stores for the first time*) Blimey! Look at that, will yer? (*They both walk back and stand looking in the jeweler's.* LONG *flies into a fury*) Just look at this 'ere bloomin' mess! Just look at it! Look at the bleedin' prices on 'em—more'n our 'ole bloody stokehole makes in ten voyages sweatin' in 'ell! And they— 'er and 'er bloody clarss—buys 'em for toys to dangle on 'em! One of these 'ere would buy scoff for a starvin' family for a year!

YANK: Aw, cut de sob stuff! T' hell wit de starvin' family! Yuh'll be passin' de hat to me next. (*With naïve admiration*) Say, dem tings is pretty, huh? Bet yuh dey'd hock for a piece of change aw right. (*Then turning away, bored*) But, aw hell, what good are dey? Let her have 'em. Dey don't belong no more'n she does. (*With a gesture of sweeping the jewelers into oblivion*) All dat don't count, get me?

LONG: (*who has moved to the furrier's—indignantly*) And I s'pose this 'ere don't count neither—skins of poor, 'armless animals slaughtered so as 'er and 'ers can keep their bleedin' noses warm!

YANK: (*who has been staring at something inside—with queer excitement*) Take a slant at dat! Give it de once-over! Monkey fur—two t'ousand bucks! (*Bewilderedly*) Is dat straight goods—monkey fur? What de hell—?

LONG: (*bitterly*) It's straight enuf. (*With grim humor*) They wouldn't bloody well pay that for a 'airy ape's skin—no, nor for the 'ole livin' ape with all 'is 'ead, and body, and soul thrown in!

YANK: (*clenching his fists, his face growing pale with rage as if the skin in the window were a personal insult*) Trowin' it up in my face! Christ! I'll fix her!

LONG: (*excitedly*) Church is out. 'Ere they come, the bleedin' swine. (*After a glance at* YANK's *lowering face—uneasily*) Easy goes, Comrade. Keep yer bloomin' temper. Remember force defeats itself. It ain't our weapon. We must impress our demands through peaceful means—the votes of the on-marching proletarians of the bloody world!

YANK: (*with abysmal contempt*) Votes, hell! Votes is a joke, see. Votes for women! Let dem do it!

LONG: (*still more uneasily*) Calm, now. Treat 'em wiv the proper contempt. Observe the bleedin' parasites but 'old yer 'orses.

YANK: (*angrily*) Git away from me! Yuh're yellow, dat's what. Force, dat's me! De punch, dat's me every time, see! (*The crowd from church enter from the right, sauntering slowly and affectedly, their heads held stiffly up, looking neither to right nor left, talking in toneless, simpering voices. The women are rouged, calcimined, dyed, overdressed to the nth degree. The men are in Prince Alberts, high hats, spats, canes, etc. A procession of gaudy marionettes, yet with something of the relentless horror of Frankensteins in their detached, mechanical unawareness*).

VOICES: Dear Doctor Caiaphas! He is so sincere!

What was the sermon? I dozed off.

About the radicals, my dear—and the false doctrines that are being preached.

We must organize a hundred per cent American bazaar.

And let everyone contribute one one-hundredth per cent of their income tax.

What an original idea!

We can devote the proceeds to rehabilitating the veil of the temple.

But that has been done so many times.

YANK: (*glaring from one to the other of them—with an insulting snort of scorn*) Huh! Huh! (*Without seeming to see him, they make wide detours to avoid the spot where he stands in the middle of the sidewalk*).

LONG: (*frightenedly*) Keep yer bloomin' mouth shut, I tells yer.

YANK: (*viciously*) G'wan! Tell it to Sweeney! (*He swaggers away and deliberately lurches into a top-hatted gentleman, then glares at him pugnaciously*) Say, who d'yuh tink yuh're bumpin'? Tink yuh own de oith?

GENTLEMAN: (*coldly and affectedly*) I beg your pardon. (*He has not looked at* YANK *and passes on without a glance, leaving him bewildered*).

LONG: (*rushing up and grabbing* YANK's *arm*) 'Ere! Come away! This wasn't what I meant. Yer'll 'ave the bloody coppers down on us.

YANK: (*savagely—giving him a push that sends him sprawling*) G'wan!

LONG: (*picks himself up—hysterically*) I'll pop orf then. This ain't what I meant. And whatever 'appens, yer can't blame me. (*He slinks off left*).

YANK: T' hell wit youse! (*He approaches a lady—with a vicious grin and a smirking wink*) Hello, Kiddo. How's every little ting? Got anyting on for tonight? I know an old boiler down to de docks we kin crawl into. (*The lady stalks by without a look, without a change of pace.* YANK *turns to others—insultingly*) Holy smokes, what a mug! Go hide yuhself before de horses shy at yuh. Gee, pipe de heine on dat one! Say, youse, yuh look like de stoin of a ferryboat. Paint and powder! All dolled up to kill! Yuh look like stiffs laid out for de boneyard! Aw, g'wan, de lot of youse! Yuh give me de eye-ache. Yuh don't belong, get me! Look at me, why don't youse dare? I belong, dat's me! (*Pointing to a skyscraper across the street which is in process of construction—with bravado*) See dat building goin' up dere? See de steel work? Steel, dat's me! Youse guys live on it and tink yuh're somep'n. But I'm *in* it, see! I'm de hoistin' engine dat makes it go up! I'm it—de inside and bottom of it! Sure! I'm steel and steam and smoke and de rest of it! It moves—speed—twenty-five stories up—and me at de top and bottom—movin'! Youse simps don't move. Yuh're on'y dolls I winds up to see 'm spin. Yuh're de garbage, get me—de leavins— de ashes we dump over de side! Now, what 'a' yuh gotta say? (*But as they seem neither to see nor hear him, he flies into a fury*) Bums! Pigs! Tarts! Bitches! (*He turns in a rage on the men, bumping viciously into them but not jarring them the least bit. Rather it is he who recoils after each collision. He keeps growling*) Git off de oith! G'wan, yuh bum! Look where yuh're goin', can't yuh? Git outa here! Fight, why don't yuh? Put up yer mits! Don't be a dog! Fight or I'll knock yuh dead! (*But, without seeming to see him, they all answer with mechanical affected politeness*): I beg your pardon. (*Then at a cry from one of the women, they all scurry to the furrier's window*).

THE WOMAN: (*ecstatically, with a gasp of delight*) Monkey fur! (*The whole crowd of men and women chorus after her in the same tone of affected delight*) Monkey fur! ·

YANK: (*with a jerk of his head back on his shoulders, as if he had received a punch full in the face—raging*) I see yuh, all in white! I see yuh, yuh white-faced tart, yuh! Hairy ape, huh? I'll hairy ape yuh! (*He bends down and grips at the street curbing as if to pluck it out and hurl it. Foiled in this, snarling with passion, he leaps to the lamp-post on the corner and tries to pull it up for a club. Just at that moment a bus is heard rumbling up. A fat, highhatted, spatted gentleman runs out from the side street. He calls out plaintively*): Bus! Bus! Stop there! (*and runs full tilt into the bending, straining* YANK, *who is bowled off his balance*).

YANK: (*seeing a fight—with a roar of joy as he springs to his feet*) At last!

Bus, huh? I'll bust yuh! (*He lets drive a terrific swing, his fist landing full on the fat gentleman's face. But the gentleman stands unmoved as if nothing had happened*).

GENTLEMAN: I beg your pardon. (*Then irritably*) You have made me lose my bus. (*He claps his hands and begins to scream*): Officer! Officer! (*Many police whistles shrill out on the instant and a whole platoon of policemen rush in on* YANK *from all sides. He tries to fight but is clubbed to the pavement and fallen upon. The crowd at the window have not moved or noticed this disturbance. The clanging gong of the patrol wagon approaches with a clamoring din*).

CURTAIN

SCENE SIX

NIGHT *of the following day. A row of cells in the prison on Blackwells Island. The cells extend back diagonally from right front to left rear. They do not stop, but disappear in the dark background as if they ran on, numberless, into infinity. One electric bulb from the low ceiling of the narrow corridor sheds its light through the heavy steel bars of the cell at the extreme front and reveals part of the interior.* YANK *can be seen within, crouched on the edge of his cot in the attitude of Rodin's "The Thinker." His face is spotted with black and blue bruises. A blood-stained bandage is wrapped around his head.*

YANK: (*suddenly starting as if awakening from a dream, reaches out and shakes the bars—aloud to himself, wonderingly*) Steel. Dis is de Zoo, huh? (*A burst of hard, barking laughter comes from the unseen occupants of the cells, runs back down the tier, and abruptly ceases*).

VOICES: (*mockingly*) The Zoo? That's a new name for this coop—a damn good name!

Steel, eh? You said a mouthful. This is the old iron house.

Who is that boob talkin'?

He's the bloke they brung in out of his head. The bulls had beat him up fierce.

YANK: (*dully*) I musta been dreamin'. I tought I was in a cage at de Zoo—but de apes don't talk, do dey?

VOICES: (*with mocking laughter*) You're in a cage aw right.

A coop!

A pen!

A sty!

A kennel! (*Hard laughter—a pause*).

Say, guy! Who are you? No, never mind lying. What are you?

Yes, tell us your sad story. What's your game?

What did they jug yuh for?

YANK: (*dully*) I was a fireman—stokin' on de liners. (*Then with sudden rage, rattling his cell bars*) I'm a hairy ape, get me? And I'll bust youse all in de jaw if yuh don't lay off kiddin' me.

VOICES: Huh! You're a hard boiled duck, ain't you!

When you spit, it bounces! (*Laughter*).

Aw, can it. He's a regular guy. Ain't you?

What did he say he was—a ape?

YANK: (*defiantly*) Sure ting! Ain't dat what youse all are—apes?

(*A silence. Then a furious rattling of bars from down the corridor*).

A VOICE: (*thick with rage*) I'll show yuh who's a ape, yuh bum!

VOICES: Ssshh! Nix!

Can de noise!

Piano!

You'll have the guard down on us!

YANK: (*scornfully*) De guard? Yuh mean de keeper, don't yuh?

(*Angry exclamations from all the cells*).

VOICE: (*placatingly*) Aw, don't pay no attention to him. He's off his nut from the beatin'-up he got. Say, you guy! We're waitin' to hear what they landed you for—or ain't yuh tellin'?

YANK: Sure, I'll tell youse. Sure! Why de hell not? On'y—youse won't get me. Nobody gets me but me, see? I started to tell de Judge and all he says was: "Toity days to tink it over." Tink it over! Christ, dat's all I been doin' for weeks! (*After a pause*) I was tryin' to git even wit someone, see?—someone dat done me doit.

VOICES: (*cynically*) De old stuff, I bet. Your goil, huh?
Give yuh the double-cross, huh?
That's them every time!
Did yuh beat up de odder guy?

YANK: (*disgustedly*) Aw, yuh're all wrong! Sure dere was a skoit in it—but not what youse mean, not dat old tripe. Dis was a new kind of skoit. She was dolled up all in white—in de stokehole. I tought she was a ghost. Sure. (*A pause*).

VOICES: (*whispering*) Gee, he's still nutty.
Let him rave. It's fun listenin'.

YANK: (*unheeding—groping in his thoughts*) Her hands—dey was skinny and white like dey wasn't real but painted on somep'n. Dere was a million miles from me to her—twenty-five knots a hour. She was like some dead ting de cat brung in. Sure, dat's what. She didn't belong. She belonged in de window of a toy store, or on de top of a garbage can, see! Sure! (*He breaks out angrily*) But would yuh believe it, she had de noive to do me doit. She lamped me like she was seein' somep'n broke loose from de menagerie. Christ, yuh'd oughter seen her eyes! (*He rattles the bars of his cell furiously*) But I'll get back at her yet, you watch! And if I can't find her I'll take it out on de gang she runs wit. I'm wise to where dey hangs out now. I'll show her who belongs! I'll show her who's in de move and who ain't. You watch my smoke!

VOICES: (*serious and joking*) Dat's de talkin'!
Take her for all she's got!
What was this dame, anyway? Who was she, eh?

YANK: I dunno. First cabin stiff. Her old man's a millionaire, dey says—name of Douglas.

VOICES: Douglas? That's the president of the Steel Trust, I bet.

Sure. I seen his mug in de papers.

He's filthy with dough.

VOICE: Hey, feller, take a tip from me. If you want to get back at that dame, you better join the Wobblies. You'll get some action then.

YANK: Wobblies? What de hell's dat?

VOICE: Ain't you ever heard of the I. W. W.?

YANK: Naw. What is it?

VOICE: A gang of blokes—a tough gang. I been readin' about 'em today in the paper. The guard give me the *Sunday Times*. There's a long spiel about 'em. It's from a speech made in the Senate by a guy named Senator Queen. (*He is in the cell next to* YANK'S. *There is a rustling of paper*) Wait'll I see if I got light enough and I'll read you. Listen. (*He reads*): "There is a menace existing in this country today which threatens the vitals of our fair Republic—as foul a menace against the very life-blood of the American Eagle as was the foul conspiracy of Catiline against the eagles of ancient Rome!"

VOICE: (*disgustedly*) Aw, hell! Tell him to salt de tail of dat eagle!

VOICE: (*reading*): "I refer to that devil's brew of rascals, jailbirds, murderers and cutthroats who libel all honest working men by calling themselves the Industrial Workers of the World; but in the light of their nefarious plots, I call them the Industrious *Wreckers* of the World!"

YANK: (*with vengeful satisfaction*) Wreckers, dat's de right dope! Dat belongs! Me for dem!

VOICE: Ssshh! (*reading*): "This fiendish organization is a foul ulcer on the fair body of our Democracy—"

VOICE: Democracy, hell! Give him the boid, fellers—the raspberry! (*They do*).

VOICE: Ssshh! (*reading*): "Like Cato I say to this Senate, the I. W. W. must be destroyed! For they represent an ever-present dagger pointed at the heart of the greatest nation the world has ever known, where all men are born free and equal, with equal opportunities to all, where the Founding Fathers have guaranteed to each one happiness, where Truth, Honor, Liberty, Justice, and the Brotherhood of Man are a religion absorbed with one's mother's milk, taught at our father's knee, sealed, signed, and stamped upon in the glorious Constitution of these United States!" (*A perfect storm of hisses, catcalls, boos, and hard laughter*).

VOICES: (*scornfully*) Hurrah for de Fort' of July!

    Pass de hat!

    Liberty!

    Justice!

    Honor!

    Opportunity!

    Brotherhood!

ALL: (*with abysmal scorn*) Aw, hell!

VOICE: Give that Queen Senator guy the bark! All togedder now— one—two—tree— (*A terrific chorus of barking and yapping*).

GUARD: (*from a distance*) Quiet there, youse—or I'll git the hose. (*The noise subsides*).

YANK: (*with growling rage*) I'd like to catch dat senator guy alone for a second. I'd loin him some trute!

VOICE: Ssshh! Here's where he gits down to cases on the Wobblies. (*Reads*): "They plot with fire in one hand and dynamite in the other. They stop not before murder to gain their ends, nor at the outraging of defenseless womanhood. They would tear down society, put the lowest scum in the seats of the mighty, turn Almighty God's revealed plan for the world topsy-turvy, and make of our sweet and lovely civilization a shambles, a desolation where man, God's masterpiece, would soon degenerate back to the ape!"

VOICE: (*to* YANK) Hey, you guy. There's your ape stuff again.

YANK: (*with a growl of fury*) I got him. So dey blow up tings, do dey? Dey turn tings round, do dey? Hey, lend me dat paper, will yuh?

VOICE: Sure. Give it to him. On'y keep it to yourself, see. We don't wanter listen to no more of that slop.

VOICE: Here you are. Hide it under your mattress.

YANK: (*reaching out*) Tanks. I can't read much but I kin manage. (*He sits, the paper in the hand at his side, in the attitude of Rodin's "The Thinker." A pause. Several snores from down the corridor. Suddenly* YANK *jumps to his feet with a furious groan as if some appalling thought had crashed on him—bewilderedly*) Sure—her old man—president of de Steel Trust—makes half de steel in de world—steel—where I tought I belonged—drivin' trou—movin'—in dat—to make *her*—and cage me in for her to spit on! Christ! (*He shakes the bars of his cell door till the whole tier trembles. Irritated, protesting exclamations from those awakened or trying to get to sleep*) He made dis—dis cage! Steel! *It* don't belong, dat's what! Cages, cells, locks, bolts, bars—dat's what it means!—holdin' me down wit him at de top! But I'll drive trou! Fire, dat melts it! I'll be fire—under de heap—fire dat never goes out—hot as hell— breakin' out in de night—(*While he has been saying this last he has shaken his cell door to a clanging accompaniment. As he comes to the "breakin' out" he seizes one bar with both hands and, putting his two feet up against the others so that his position is parallel to the floor like a monkey's, he gives a great wrench backwards. The bar bends like a licorice stick under his tremendous strength. Just at this moment the* PRISON GUARD *rushes in, dragging a hose behind him*).

GUARD: (*angrily*) I'll loin youse bums to wake me up! (*Sees* YANK) Hello, it's you, huh? Got the D. Ts., hey? Well, I'll cure 'em. I'll drown your snakes for yuh! (*Noticing the bar*) Hell, look at dat bar bended! On'y a bug is strong enough for dat!

YANK: (*glaring at him*) Or a hairy ape, yuh big yellow bum! Look out! Here I come! (*He grabs another bar*).

GUARD: (*scared now—yelling off left*) Toin de hose on, Ben!—full pressure! And call de others—and a straitjacket! (*The curtain is falling. As it hides* YANK *from view, there is a splattering smash as the stream of water hits the steel of* YANK's *cell*).

CURTAIN

Scene Seven

NEARLY *a month later. An I. W. W. local near the waterfront, showing the interior of a front room on the ground floor, and the street outside. Moonlight on the narrow street, buildings massed in black shadow. The interior of the room, which is general assembly room, office, and reading room, resembles some dingy settlement boys' club. A desk and high stool are in one corner. A table with papers, stacks of pamphlets, chairs about it, is at center. The whole is decidedly cheap, banal, commonplace and unmysterious as a room could well be. The secretary is perched on the stool making entries in a large ledger. An eye shade casts his face into shadows. Eight or ten men, longshoremen, iron workers, and the like, are grouped about the table. Two are playing checkers. One is writing a letter. Most of them are smoking pipes. A big signboard is on the wall at the rear, "Industrial Workers of the World— Local No. 57."*

YANK: (*comes down the street outside. He is dressed as in Scene Five. He moves cautiously, mysteriously. He comes to a point opposite the door; tiptoes softly up to it, listens, is impressed by the silence within, knocks carefully, as if he were guessing at the password to some secret rite. Listens. No answer. Knocks again a bit louder. No answer. Knocks impatiently, much louder*).

SECRETARY: (*turning around on his stool*) What the hell is that— someone knocking? (*Shouts*): Come in, why don't you? (*All the men in the room look up.* YANK *opens the door slowly, gingerly, as if afraid of an ambush. He looks around for secret doors, mystery, is taken aback by the commonplaceness of the room and the men in it, thinks he may have gotten in the wrong place, then sees the signboard on the wall and is reassured*).

YANK: (*blurts out*) Hello.

MEN: (*reservedly*) Hello.

YANK: (*more easily*) I tought I'd bumped into de wrong dump.

SECRETARY: (*scrutinizing him carefully*) Maybe you have. Are you a member?

YANK: Naw, not yet. Dat's what I come for—to join.

SECRETARY: That's easy. What's your job—longshore?

YANK: Naw. Fireman—stoker on de liners.

SECRETARY: (*with satisfaction*) Welcome to our city. Glad to know you people are waking up at last. We haven't got many members in your line.

YANK: Naw. Dey're all dead to de woild.

SECRETARY: Well, you can help to wake 'em. What's your name? I'll make out your card.

YANK: (*confused*) Name? Lemme tink.

SECRETARY: (*sharply*) Don't you know your own name?

YANK: Sure; but I been just Yank for so long—Bob, dat's it— Bob Smith.

SECRETARY: (*writing*) Robert Smith. (*Fills out the rest of card*) Here you are. Cost you half a dollar.

YANK: Is dat all—four bits? Dat's easy. (*Gives the Secretary the money*).

SECRETARY: (*throwing it in drawer*) Thanks. Well, make yourself at home. No introductions needed. There's literature on the table. Take some of those pamphlets with you to distribute aboard ship. They may bring results. Sow the seed, only go about it right. Don't get caught and fired. We got plenty out of work. What we need is men who can hold their jobs—and work for us at the same time.

YANK: Sure. (*But he still stands, embarrassed and uneasy*).

SECRETARY: (*looking at him—curiously*) What did you knock for? Think we had a coon in uniform to open doors?

YANK: Naw. I tought it was locked—and dat yuh'd wanter give me the once-over trou a peep-hole or somep'n to see if I was right.

SECRETARY: (*alert and suspicious but with an easy laugh*) Think we were running a crap game? That door is never locked. What put that in your nut?

YANK: (*with a knowing grin, convinced that this is all camouflage, a part of the secrecy*) Dis burg is full of bulls, ain't it?

SECRETARY: (*sharply*) What have the cops got to do with us? We're breaking no laws.

YANK: (*with a knowing wink*) Sure. Youse wouldn't for woilds. Sure. I'm wise to dat.

SECRETARY: You seem to be wise to a lot of stuff none of us knows about.

YANK: (*with another wink*) Aw, dat's aw right, see. (*Then made a bit resentful by the suspicious glances from all sides*) Aw, can it! Youse needn't put me trou de toid degree. Can't youse see I belong? Sure! I'm reg'lar. I'll stick, get me? I'll shoot de woiks for youse. Dat's why I wanted to join in.

SECRETARY: (*breezily, feeling him out*) That's the right spirit. Only are you sure you understand what you've joined? It's all plain and above board; still, some guys get a wrong slant on us. (*Sharply*) What's your notion of the purpose of the I. W. W.?

YANK: Aw, I know all about it.

SECRETARY: (*sarcastically*) Well, give us some of your valuable information.

YANK: (*cunningly*) I know enough not to speak outa my toin. (*Then resentfully again*) Aw, say! I'm reg'lar. I'm wise to de game. I know yuh got to watch your step wit a stranger. For all youse know, I might be a plainclothes dick, or somep'n, dat's what yuh're tinkin', huh? Aw, forget it! I belong, see? Ask any guy down to de docks if I don't.

SECRETARY: Who said you didn't?

YANK: After I'm 'nitiated, I'll show yuh.

SECRETARY: (*astounded*) Initiated? There's no initiation.

YANK: (*disappointed*) Ain't there no password—no grip nor nothin'?

SECRETARY: What'd you think this is—the Elks—or the Black Hand?

YANK: De Elks, hell! De Black Hand, dey're a lot of yellow backstickin' Ginees. Naw. Dis is a man's gang, ain't it?

SECRETARY: You said it! That's why we stand on our two feet in the open. We got no secrets.

YANK: (*surprised but admiringly*) Yuh mean to say yuh always run wide open—like dis?

SECRETARY: Exactly.

YANK: Den yuh sure got your noive wit youse!

SECRETARY: (*sharply*) Just what was it made you want to join us? Come out with that straight.

YANK: Yuh call me? Well, I got noive, too! Here's my hand. Yuh wanter blow tings up, don't yuh? Well, dat's me! I belong!

SECRETARY: (*with pretended carelessness*) You mean change the unequal conditions of society by legitimate direct action—or with dynamite?

YANK: Dynamite! Blow it offen de oith—steel—all de cages—all de factories, steamers, buildings, jails—de Steel Trust and all dat makes it go.

SECRETARY: So—that's your idea, eh? And did you have any special job in that line you wanted to propose to us? (*He makes a sign to the men, who get up cautiously one by one and group behind* YANK).

YANK: (*boldly*) Sure, I'll come out wit it. I'll show youse I'm one of de gang. Dere's dat millionaire guy, Douglas—

SECRETARY: President of the Steel Trust, you mean? Do you want to assassinate him?

YANK: Naw, dat don't get yuh nothin'. I mean blow up de factory, de woiks, where he makes de steel. Dat's what I'm after—to blow up de steel, knock all de steel in de woild up to de moon. Dat'll fix tings! (*Eagerly, with a touch of bravado*) I'll do it by me lonesome! I'll show yuh! Tell me where his woiks is, how to git there, all de dope. Gimme de stuff, de old butter—and watch me do de rest! Watch de smoke and see it move! I don't give a damn if dey nab me—long as it's done! I'll soive life for it—and give 'em de laugh! (*Half to himself*) And I'll write her a letter and tell her de hairy ape done it. Dat'll square tings.

SECRETARY: (*stepping away from* YANK) Very interesting. (*He gives a signal. The men, huskies all, throw themselves on* YANK *and before he knows it they have his legs and arms pinioned. But he is too flabbergasted to make a struggle, anyway. They feel him over for weapons*).

MAN: No gat, no knife. Shall we give him what's what and put the boots to him?

SECRETARY: No. He isn't worth the trouble we'd get into. He's too stupid. (*He comes closer and laughs mockingly in* YANK's *face*) Ho-ho! By God, this is the biggest joke they've put up on us yet. Hey, you Joke! Who sent you—Burns or Pinkerton? No, by God, you're such a bonehead I'll bet you're in the Secret Service! Well, you dirty spy, you rotten agent provocator, you can go back and tell whatever skunk is paying you blood-money for betraying your brothers that he's wasting his coin. You couldn't catch a cold. And tell him that all he'll ever get on us, or ever has got, is just his own sneaking plots that he's framed up to put us in jail. We are what our manifesto says we are, neither more nor less—and we'll give him a copy of that any time he calls. And as for you— (*He glares scornfully at* YANK, *who is sunk in an oblivious stupor*) Oh, hell, what's the use of talking? You're a brainless ape.

YANK: (*aroused by the word to fierce but futile struggles*) What's dat, yuh Sheeny bum, yuh!

SECRETARY: Throw him out, boys. (*In spite of his struggles, this is done with gusto and éclat. Propelled by several parting kicks,* YANK *lands sprawling in the middle of the narrow cobbled street. With a growl he starts to get up and storm the closed door, but stops bewildered by the confusion in his brain, pathetically impotent. He sits there, brooding, in as near to the attitude of Rodin's "Thinker" as he can get in his position*).

YANK: (*bitterly*) So dem boids don't tink I belong, neider. Aw, to hell wit 'em! Dey're in de wrong pew—de same old bull—soapboxes and Salvation Army—no guts! Cut out an hour offen de job a day and make me happy! Gimme a dollar more a day and make me happy! Tree square a day, and cauliflowers in de front yard—ekal rights—a woman and kids—a lousy vote—and I'm all fixed for Jesus, huh? Aw, hell! What does dat get yuh? Dis ting's in your inside, but it ain't your belly. Feedin' your face—sinkers and coffee—dat don't touch it. It's way down—at de bottom. Yuh can't grab it, and yuh can't stop it. It moves, and everything moves. It stops and de whole woild stops. Dat's me now—I don't tick, see?—I'm a busted Ingersoll, dat's what. Steel was me, and I owned de woild. Now I ain't steel, and de woild owns me. Aw, hell! I can't see—it's all dark, get me? It's all wrong! (*He turns a bitter mocking face up like an ape gibbering at the moon*) Say, youse up dere, Man in de Moon, yuh look so wise, gimme de answer, huh? Slip me de inside dope, de information right from de stable—where do I get off at, huh?

A POLICEMAN: (*who has come up the street in time to hear this last—with grim humor*). You'll get off at the station, you boob, if you don't get up out of that and keep movin'.

YANK: (*looking up at him—with a hard, bitter laugh*) Sure! Lock me up! Put me in a cage! Dat's de on'y answer yuh know. G'wan, lock me up!

POLICEMAN: What you been doin'?

YANK: Enuf to gimme life for! I was born, see? Sure, dat's de charge. Write it in de blotter. I was born, get me!

POLICEMAN: (*jocosely*) God pity your old woman! (*Then matter-of-fact*) But I've no time for kidding. You're soused. I'd run you in but it's too long a walk to the station. Come on now, get up, or I'll fan your ears with this club. Beat it now! (*He hauls* YANK *to his feet*).

YANK: (*in a vague mocking tone*) Say, where do I go from here?

POLICEMAN: (*giving him a push—with a grin, indifferently*) Go to hell.

CURTAIN

Scene Eight

*T*WILIGHT *of the next day. The monkey house at the Zoo. One spot of clear gray light falls on the front of one cage so that the interior can be seen. The other cages are vague, shrouded in shadow from which chatterings pitched in a conversational tone can be heard. On the one cage a sign from which the word "gorilla" stands out. The gigantic animal himself is seen squatting on his haunches on a bench in much the same attitude as Rodin's "Thinker." YANK enters from the left. Immediately a chorus of angry chattering and screeching breaks out. The gorilla turns his eyes but makes no sound or move.*

YANK: (*with a hard, bitter laugh*) Welcome to your city, huh? Hail, hail, de gang's all here! (*At the sound of his voice the chattering dies away into an attentive silence.* YANK *walks up to the gorilla's cage and, leaning over the railing, stares in at its occupant, who stares back at him, silent and motionless. There is a pause of dead stillness. Then* YANK *begins to talk in a friendly confidential tone, half-mockingly, but with a deep undercurrent of sympathy*) Say, yuh're some hard-lookin' guy, ain't yuh? I seen lots of tough nuts dat de gang called gorillas, but yuh're de foist real one I ever seen. Some chest yuh got, and shoulders, and dem arms and mits! I bet yuh got a punch in eider fist dat'd knock 'em all silly! (*This with genuine admiration. The gorilla, as if he understood, stands upright, swelling out his chest and pounding on it with his fist.* YANK *grins sympathetically*) Sure, I get yuh. Yuh challenge de whole woild, huh? Yuh got what I was sayin' even if yuh muffed de woids. (*Then bitterness creeping in*) And why wouldn't yuh get me? Ain't we both members of de same club—de Hairy Apes? (*They stare at each other—a pause—then* YANK *goes on slowly and bitterly*) So yuh're what she seen when she looked at me, de white-faced tart! I was you to her, get me? On'y outa de cage—broke out—free to moider her, see? Sure! Dat's what she tought. She wasn't wise dat I was in a cage, too—worser'n yours—sure—a damn sight—'cause you got some chanct to bust loose—but me— (*He grows confused*) Aw, hell! It's all wrong, ain't it? (*A pause*) I s'pose yuh wanter know what I'm doin' here, huh? I been warmin' a bench down to de Battery—ever since last night. Sure. I seen de sun come up. Dat was pretty, too—all red and pink and green. I was lookin' at de skyscrapers—steel—and all de ships comin' in, sailin' out, all over de oith—and dey was steel, too. De sun was warm, dey wasn't no clouds, and dere was a breeze blowin'. Sure, it was great stuff. I got it aw right—what Paddy said about dat bein' de right dope—on'y I couldn't get *in* it, see? I couldn't belong in dat. It was over my head. And I kept tinkin'—and den I beat it up here to see what youse was like. And I waited till dey was all gone to git yuh alone. Say, how d'yuh feel sittin' in dat pen all de time, havin' to stand for 'em comin' and starin' at yuh—de white-faced, skinny tarts and de boobs what marry 'em—makin' fun of yuh, laughin' at yuh, gittin' scared of yuh—damn 'em! (*He pounds on the rail with his fist. The gorilla rattles the bars of his cage and snarls. All the other monkeys set up an angry chattering in the darkness.* YANK *goes on excitedly*) Sure! Dat's de way it hits me, too. On'y yuh're lucky, see? Yuh don't belong wit 'em and yuh know it. But me, I belong wit 'em—but I don't, see? Dey don't belong wit me, dat's what. Get me? Tinkin' is hard— (*He passes one hand across his forehead with a painful gesture. The gorilla growls impatiently.* YANK *goes on gropingly*) It's dis way, what I'm drivin' at. Youse can sit and dope dream in de past, green woods, de jungle and de rest of it. Den yuh belong and dey don't. Den yuh kin laugh at 'em, see? Yuh're de champ of de woild. But me—I ain't got no past to tink in, nor nothin' dat's comin', on'y what's now—and dat don't belong. Sure, you're de best off! Yuh can't tink, can yuh? Yuh can't talk neider. But I kin make a bluff at talkin' and tinkin'—a'most git away wit it—a'most!—and dat's where de joker comes in. (*He laughs*) I ain't on oith and I ain't in heaven, get me? I'm in de middle tryin' to separate 'em, takin' all de woist punches from bot' of 'em. Maybe dat's what dey call hell, huh? But you, yuh're at de bottom. You belong! Sure! Yuh're de on'y one in de woild dat does, yuh lucky stiff! (*The gorilla growls proudly*) And dat's why dey gotter put yuh in a cage, see? (*The gorilla roars angrily*) Sure! Yuh get me. It beats it when you try to tink it or talk it—it's way down—deep—behind—you 'n' me we feel it. Sure! Bot' members of dis club! (*He laughs—then in a savage tone*) What de hell! T' hell wit it! A little action, dat's our meat! Dat belongs! Knock 'em down and keep bustin' 'em till dey croaks yuh wit a gat—wit steel! Sure! Are yuh game? Dey've looked at youse, ain't dey—in a cage? Wanter git even? Wanter wind up like a sport 'stead of croakin' slow in dere? (*The gorilla roars an emphatic affirmative.* YANK *goes on with a sort of furious exaltation*) Sure! Yuh're reg'lar! Yuh'll stick to de finish! Me 'n' you, huh?—bot' members of this club! We'll put up one last star bout dat'll knock 'em offen deir seats! Dey'll have to make de cages stronger after we're trou! (*The gorilla is straining at his bars, growling, hopping from one foot to the other.* YANK *takes a jimmy from under his coat and forces the lock on the cage door. He throws this open*) Pardon from de governor! Step out and shake hands. I'll take yuh for a walk down Fif' Avenoo. We'll knock 'em offen de oith and croak wit de band playin'. Come on, Brother. (*The gorilla scrambles gingerly out of his cage. Goes to* YANK *and stands looking at him.* YANK *keeps his mocking tone—holds out his hand*) Shake—de secret grip of our order. (*Something, the tone of mockery, perhaps, suddenly enrages the animal. With a spring he wraps his huge arms around* YANK *in a murderous hug. There is a crackling snap of crushed ribs—a gasping cry, still mocking, from* YANK). Hey, I didn't say kiss me! (*The gorilla lets the crushed body slip to the floor; stands over it uncertainly, considering; then picks it up, throws it in the cage, shuts the door, and shuffles off menacingly into the darkness at left. A great uproar of frightened chattering and whimpering comes from the other cages. Then* YANK *moves, groaning, opening his eyes, and there is silence. He mutters painfully*) Say—dey oughter match him—wit Zybszko. He got me, aw right. I'm trou. Even him didn't tink I belonged. (*Then, with sudden passionate despair*). Christ, where do I get off at? Where do I fit in? (*Checking himself as suddenly*) Aw, what de hell! No squawkin', see! No quittin', get me! Croak wit your boots on! (*He grabs hold of the bars of the cage and hauls himself painfully to his feet—looks around him bewilderedly—forces a mocking laugh*) In de cage, huh? (*In the strident tones of a circus barker*) Ladies and gents, step forward and take a slant at de one and only— (*His voice weakening*)—one and original—Hairy Ape from de wilds of— (*He slips in a heap on the floor and dies. The monkeys set up a chattering, whimpering wail. And, perhaps, the Hairy Ape at last belongs*).

CURTAIN

All God's Chillun Got Wings

CHARACTERS

JIM HARRIS   SHORTY

MRS. HARRIS, *his mother*   JOE

HATTIE, *his sister*   MICKEY

ELLA DOWNEY   *Whites and Negroes.*

ACT ONE

ACT TWO

84

All God's Chillun Got Wings

Act One—Scene One

A corner *in lower New York, at the edge of a colored district. Three narrow streets converge. A triangular building in the rear, red brick, four-storied, its ground floor a grocery. Four-story tenements stretch away down the skyline of the two streets. The fire escapes are crowded with people. In the street leading left, the faces are all white; in the street leading right, all black. It is hot Spring. On the sidewalk are eight children, four boys and four girls. Two of each sex are white, two black. They are playing marbles. One of the black boys is* JIM HARRIS. *The little blonde girl, her complexion rose and white, who sits behind his elbow and holds his marbles is* ELLA DOWNEY. *She is eight. They play the game with concentrated attention for a while. People pass, black and white, the Negroes frankly participants in the spirit of Spring, the whites laughing constrainedly, awkward in natural emotion. Their words are lost. One hears only their laughter. It expresses the difference in race. There are street noises—the clattering roar of the Elevated, the puff of its locomotives, the ruminative lazy sound of a horse-car, the hooves of its team clacking on the cobbles. From the street of the whites a high-pitched, nasal tenor sings the chorus of "Only a Bird in a Gilded Cage." On the street of the blacks a Negro strikes up the chorus of: "I Guess I'll Have to Telegraph My Baby." As this singing ends, there is laughter, distinctive in quality, from both streets. Then silence. The light in the street begins to grow brilliant with the glow of the setting sun. The game of marbles goes on.*

WHITE GIRL: (*tugging at the elbow of her brother*) Come on, Mickey!

HER BROTHER: (*roughly*) Aw, gwan, youse!

85

WHITE GIRL: Aw right den. You kin git a lickin' if you wanter. (*Gets up to move off*).

HER BROTHER: Aw, git off de eart'!

WHITE GIRL: De old woman'll be madder'n hell!

HER BROTHER: (*worried now*) I'm comin', ain't I? Hold your horses.

BLACK GIRL: (*to a black boy*) Come on, you Joe. We gwine git frailed too, you don't hurry.

JOE: Go long!

MICKEY: Bust up de game, huh? I gotta run! (*Jumps to his feet*).

OTHER WHITE BOY: Me, too! (*Jumps up*).

OTHER BLACK GIRL: Lawdy, it's late!

JOE: Me for grub!

MICKEY: (*to* JIM HARRIS) You's de winner, Jim Crow. Yeh gotta play tomorrer.

JIM: (*readily*) Sure t'ing, Mick. Come one, come all! (*He laughs*).

OTHER WHITE BOY: Me, too! I gotta git back at yuh.

JIM: Aw right, Shorty.

LITTLE GIRLS: Hurry! Come on, come on! (*The six start off together. Then they notice that* JIM *and* ELLA *are hesitating, standing awkwardly and shyly together. They turn to mock*).

JOE: Look at dat Jim Crow! Land sakes, he got a gal! (*He laughs. They all laugh*).

JIM: (*ashamed*) Ne'er mind, you Chocolate!

MICKEY: Look at de two softies, will yeh! Mush! Mush! (*He and the two other boys take this up*).

LITTLE GIRLS: (*pointing their fingers at* ELLA) Shame! Shame! Everybody knows your name! Painty Face! Painty Face!

ELLA: (*hanging her head*) Shut up!

LITTLE WHITE GIRL: He's been carrying her books!

COLORED GIRL: Can't you find nuffin' better'n him, Ella? Look at de big feet he got! (*She laughs. They all laugh.* JIM *puts one foot on top of the other, looking at* ELLA).

ELLA: Mind yer own business, see! (*She strides toward them angrily. They jump up and dance in an ecstasy, screaming and laughing*).

ALL: Found yeh out! Found yeh out!

MICKEY: Mush-head! Jim Crow de Sissy! Stuck on Painty Face!

JOE: Will Painty Face let you hold her doll, boy?

SHORTY: Sissy! Softy! (ELLA *suddenly begins to cry. At this they all howl*).

ALL: Cry-baby! Cry-baby! Look at her! Painty Face!

JIM: (*suddenly rushing at them, with clenched fists, furiously*) Shut yo' moufs! I kin lick de hull of you! (*They all run away, laughing, shouting, and jeering, quite triumphant now that they have made him, too, lose his temper. He comes back to* ELLA, *and stands beside her sheepishly, stepping on one foot after the other. Suddenly he blurts out*): Don't bawl no more. I done chased 'em.

ELLA: (*comforted, politely*) T'anks.

JIM: (*swelling out*) It was a cinch. I kin wipe up de street wid any one of dem. (*He stretches out his arms, trying to bulge out his biceps*). Feel dat muscle!

ELLA: (*does so gingerly—then with admiration*) My!

JIM: (*protectingly*) You mustn't never be scared when I'm hanging round, Painty Face.

ELLA: Don't call me that, Jim—please!

JIM: (*contritely*) I didn't mean nuffin'. I didn't know you'd mind.

ELLA: I do—more'n anything.

JIM: You oughtn't to mind. Dey's jealous, dat's what.

ELLA: Jealous? Of what?

JIM: (*pointing to her face*) Of dat. Red 'n' white. It's purty.

ELLA: I hate it!

JIM: It's purty. Yes, it's—it's purty. It's—outa sight!

ELLA: I hate it. I wish I was black like you.

JIM: (*sort of shrinking*) No you don't. Dey'd call you Crow, den—or Chocolate—or Smoke.

ELLA: I wouldn't mind.

JIM: (*somberly*) Dey'd call you nigger sometimes, too.

ELLA: I wouldn't mind.

JIM: (*humbly*) You wouldn't mind?

ELLA: No, I wouldn't mind. (*An awkward pause*).

JIM: (*suddenly*) You know what, Ella? Since I been tuckin' yo' books to
school and back, I been drinkin' lots o' chalk 'n' water tree times a
day. Dat Tom, de barber, he tole me dat make me white, if I drink
enough. (*Pleadingly*) Does I look whiter?

ELLA: (*comfortingly*) Yes—maybe—a little bit—

JIM: (*trying a careless tone*) Reckon dat Tom's a liar, an' de joke's on me!
Dat chalk only makes me feel kinder sick inside.

ELLA: (*wonderingly*) Why do you want to be white?

JIM: Because—just because—I lak dat better.

ELLA: I wouldn't. I like black. Let's you and me swap. I'd like to be
black. (*Clapping her hands*) Gee, that'd be fun, if we only could!

JIM: (*hesitatingly*) Yes—maybe—

ELLA: Then they'd call me Crow, and you'd be Painty Face!

JIM: They wouldn't never dast call you nigger, you bet! I'd kill 'em! (*A
long pause. Finally she takes his hand shyly. They both keep looking as far
away from each other as possible*).

ELLA: I like you.

JIM: I like you.

ELLA: Do you want to be my feller?

JIM: Yes.

ELLA: Then I'm your girl.

JIM: Yes. (*Then grandly*) You kin bet none o' de gang gwine call you
Painty Face from dis out! I lam' 'em good! (*The sun has set. Twilight
has fallen on the street. An organ grinder comes up to the corner and plays
"Annie Rooney." They stand hand-in-hand and listen. He goes away. It is
growing dark*).

ELLA: (*suddenly*) Golly, it's late! I'll git a lickin'!

JIM: Me, too.

ELLA: I won't mind it much.

JIM: Me nuther.

ELLA: See you going to school tomorrow?

JIM: Sure.

ELLA: I gotta skip now.

JIM: Me, too.

ELLA: I like you, Jim.

JIM: I like you.

ELLA: Don't forget.

JIM: Don't you.

ELLA: Good-by.

JIM: So long. (*They run away from each other—then stop abruptly, and turn as at a signal*).

ELLA: Don't forget.

JIM: I won't, you bet!

ELLA: Here! (*She kisses her hand at him, then runs off in frantic embarrassment*).

JIM: (*overcome*) Gee! (*Then he turns and darts away as*

THE CURTAIN FALLS)

SCENE TWO

*T*HE *same corner. Nine years have passed. It is again late Spring at a time in the evening which immediately follows the hour of* SCENE ONE. *Nothing has changed much. One street is still all white, the other all black. The fire escapes are laden with drooping human beings. The grocery store is still at the corner. The street noises are now more rhythmically mechanical, electricity having taken the place of horse and steam. People pass, white and black. They laugh as in* SCENE ONE. *From the street of the whites the high-pitched nasal tenor sings: "Gee, I Wish That I Had a Girl," and the Negro replies with*

"All I Got Was Sympathy." The singing is followed again by laughter from both streets. Then silence. The dusk grows darker. With a spluttering flare the arc-lamp at the corner is lit and sheds a pale glare over the street. Two young roughs slouch up to the corner, as tough in manner as they can make themselves. One is the SHORTY *of* SCENE ONE; *the other the Negro,* JOE. *They stand loafing. A boy of seventeen or so passes by, escorting a girl of about the same age. Both are dressed in their best, the boy in black with stiff collar, the girl in white.*

SHORTY: (*scornfully*) Hully cripes! Pipe who's here. (*To the girl, sneeringly*) Wha's matter, Liz? Don't yer recernize yer old fr'ens?

GIRL: (*frightenedly*) Hello, Shorty.

SHORTY: Why de glad rags? Goin' to graduation? (*He tries to obstruct their way, but, edging away from him, they turn and run*)

JOE: Har-har! Look at dem scoot, will you! (SHORTY *grins with satisfaction*).

SHORTY: (looking *down other street*) Here comes Mickey.

JOE: He won de semi-final last night easy?

SHORTY: Knocked de bloke out in de thoid.

JOE: Dat boy's suah a-comin'! He'll be de champeen yit.

SHORTY: (*judicially*) Got a good chanct—if he leaves de broads alone. Dat's where he's wide open. (MICKEY *comes in from the left. He is dressed loudly, a straw hat with a gaudy band cocked over one cauliflower ear. He has acquired a typical "pug's" face, with the added viciousness of a natural bully. One of his eyes is puffed, almost closed, as a result of his battle the night before. He swaggers up*).

BOTH: Hello, Mickey.

MICKEY: Hello.

JOE: Hear you knocked him col'.

MICKEY: Sure. I knocked his block off. (*Changing the subject*). Say. Seen 'em goin' past to de graduation racket?

SHORTY: (*with a wink*) Why? You int'rested?

JOE: (*chuckling*) Mickey's gwine roun' git a good conduct medal.

MICKEY: Sure. Dey kin pin it on de seat o' me pants. (*They laugh*) Listen. Seen Ella Downey goin'?

SHORTY: Painty Face? No, she ain't been along.

MICKEY: (*with authority*) Can dat name, see! Want a bunch o' fives in yer kisser? Den nix! She's me goil, understan'?

JOE: (*venturing to joke*) Which one? Yo' number ten?

MICKEY: (*flattered*) Sure. De real K. O. one.

SHORTY: (*pointing right—sneeringly*) Gee! Pipe Jim Crow all dolled up for de racket.

JOE: (*with disgusted resentment*) You mean tell me dat nigger's graduatin'?

SHORTY: Ask him. (JIM HARRIS *comes in. He is dressed in black, stiff white collar, etc.—a quiet-mannered Negro boy with a queerly baffled, sensitive face*).

JIM: (*pleasantly*) Hello, fellows. (*They grunt in reply, looking over him scornfully*).

JOE: (*staring resentfully*) Is you graduatin' tonight?

JIM: Yes.

JOE: (*spitting disgustedly*) Fo' Gawd's sake! You *is* gittin' high-falutin'!

JIM: (*smiling deprecatingly*) This is my second try. I didn't pass last year.

JOE: What de hell does it git you, huh? Whatever is you gwine do wid it now you gits it? Live lazy on yo' ol' woman?

JIM: (*assertively*) I'm going to study and become a lawyer.

JOE: (*with a snort*) Fo' Chris' sake, nigger!

JIM: (*fiercely*) Don't you call me that—not before them!

JOE: (*pugnaciously*) Does you deny you's a nigger? I shows you—

MICKEY: (*gives them both a push—truculently*) Cut it out, see! I'm runnin' dis corner. (*Turning to* JIM *insultingly*) Say you! Painty Face's gittin' her ticket tonight, ain't she?

JIM: You mean Ella—

MICKEY: Painty Face Downey, dat's who I mean! I don't have to be perlite wit' her. She's me goil!

JIM: (*glumly*) Yes, she's graduating.

SHORTY: (*winks at* MICKEY) Smart, huh?

MICKEY: (*winks back—meaningly*) Willin' to loin, take it from me! (JIM *stands tensely as if a struggle were going on in him*).

JIM: (*finally blurts out*) I want to speak to you, Mickey—alone.

MICKEY: (*surprised—insultingly*) Aw, what de hell—!

JIM: (*excitedly*) It's important, I tell you!

MICKEY: Huh? (*Stares at him inquisitively—then motions the others back carelessly and follows* JIM *down front*).

SHORTY: Some noive!

JOE: (*vengefully*) I gits dat Jim alone, you wait!

MICKEY: Well, spill de big news. I ain't got all night. I got a date.

JIM: With—Ella?

MICKEY: What's dat to you?

JIM: (*the words tumbling out*) What—I wanted to say! I know—I've heard—all the stories—what you've been doing around the ward—with other girls—it's none of my business, with them—but she—Ella—it's different—she's not that kind—

MICKEY: (*insultingly*) Who told yuh so, huh?

JIM: (*draws back his fist threateningly*) Don't you dare—! (MICKEY *is so paralyzed by this effrontery that he actually steps back*).

MICKEY: Say, cut de comedy! (*Beginning to feel insulted*) Listen, you Jim Crow! Ain't you wise I could give yuh one poke dat'd knock yuh into next week?

JIM: I'm only asking you to act square, Mickey.

MICKEY: What's it to yuh? Why, yuh lousy goat, she wouldn't spit on yuh even! She hates de sight of a coon.

JIM: (*in agony*) I—I know—but once she didn't mind—we were kids together—

MICKEY: Aw, ferget dat! Dis is *now!*

JIM: And I'm still her friend always—even if she don't like colored people—

MICKEY: *Coons*, why don't yuh say it right! De trouble wit' you is yuh're gittin' stuck up, dat's what! Stay where yeh belong, see! Yer old man made coin at de truckin' game and yuh're tryin' to buy yerself white—graduatin' and law, for Christ sake! Yuh're gittin' yerself in Dutch wit' everyone in de ward—and it ain't cause yer a coon neider. Don't de gang all train wit' Joe dere and lots of others? But yuh're tryin' to buy white and it won't git yuh no place, see!

JIM: (*trembling*) Some day—I'll show you—

MICKEY: (*turning away*) Aw, gwan!

JIM: D'you think I'd change—be you—your dirty white—!

MICKEY: (*whirling about*) What's dat?

JIM: (*with hysterical vehemence*) You act square with her—or I'll show you up—I'll report you—I'll write to the papers—the sporting writers—I'll let them know how white you are!

MICKEY: (*infuriated*) Yuh damn nigger, I'll bust yer jaw in! (*Assuming his ring pose he weaves toward* JIM, *his face set in a cruel scowl.* JIM *waits helplessly but with a certain dignity*).

SHORTY: Cheese it! A couple bulls! And here's de Downey skoit comin', too.

MICKEY: I'll get yuh de next time! (ELLA DOWNEY *enters from the right. She is seventeen, still has the same rose and white complexion, is pretty but with a rather repelling bold air about her*).

ELLA: (*smiles with pleasure when she sees* MICKEY) Hello, Mick. Am I late? Say, I'm so glad you won last night. (*She glances from one to the other as she feels something in the air*) Hello! What's up?

MICKEY: Dis boob. (*He indicates* JIM *scornfully*).

JIM: (*diffidently*) Hello, Ella.

ELLA: (*shortly, turning away*) Hello. (*Then to* MICKEY) Come on, Mick. Walk down with me. I got to hurry.

JIM: (*blurts out*) Wait—just a second. (*Painfully*) Ella, do you hate—colored people?

MICKEY: Aw, shut up!

JIM: Please answer.

ELLA: (*forcing a laugh*) Say! What is this—another exam?

JIM: (*doggedly*) Please answer.

ELLA: (*irritably*) Of course I don't! Haven't I been brought up along-side— Why, some of my oldest—the girls I've been to public school the longest with—

JIM: Do you hate me, Ella?

ELLA: (*confusedly and more irritably*) Say, is he drunk? Why should I? I don't hate anyone.

JIM: Then why haven't you ever hardly spoken to me—for years?

ELLA: (*resentfully*) What would I speak about? You and me've got noth-ing in common any more.

JIM: (*desperately*) Maybe not any more—but—right on this corner—do you remember once—?

ELLA: I don't remember nothing! (*Angrily*) Say! What's got into you to be butting into my business all of a sudden like this? Because you finally managed to graduate, has it gone to your head?

JIM: No, I—only want to help you, Ella.

ELLA: Of all the nerve! You're certainly forgetting your place! Who's asking you for help, I'd like to know? Shut up and stop bothering me!

JIM: (*insistently*) If you ever need a friend—a true friend—

ELLA: I've got lots of friends among my own—kind, I can tell you. (*Exasperatedly*) You make me sick! Go to the devil! (*She flounces off. The three men laugh.* MICKEY *follows her.* JIM *is stricken. He goes and sinks down limply on a box in front of the grocery store*).

SHORTY: I'm going to shoot a drink. Come on, Joe, and I'll blow yuh.

JOE: (*who has never ceased to follow every move of* JIM'S *with angry, resentful eyes*) Go long. I'se gwine stay here a secon'. I got a lil' argyment. (*He points to* JIM).

SHORTY: Suit yerself. Do a good job. See yuh later. (*He goes, whistling*).

JOE: (*stands for a while glaring at* JIM, *his fierce little eyes peering out of his black face. Then he spits on his hands aggressively and strides up to the oblivious* JIM. *He stands in front of him, gradually working himself into a fury at the other's seeming indifference to his words*) Listen to me, nig-ger: I got a heap to whisper in yo' ear! Who is you, anyhow? Who does you think you is? Don't yo' old man and mine work on de docks togidder befo' yo' old man gits his own truckin' business? Yo' ol' man swallers his nickels, my ol' man buys him beer wid dem and swallers dat—dat's the on'y diff'rence. Don't you 'n' me drag up togidder?

JIM: (*dully*) I'm your friend, Joe.

JOE: No, you isn't! I ain't no fren o' yourn! I don't even know who you is! What's all dis schoolin' you doin'? What's all dis dressin' up and graduatin' an' sayin' you gwine study be a lawyer? What's all dis fakin' an' pretendin' and swellin' out grand an' talkin' soft and perlite? What's all dis denyin' you's a nigger—an' wid de white boys listenin' to you say it! Is you aimin' to buy white wid yo' ol' man's dough like Mickey say? What is you? (*In a rage at the other's silence*) You don't talk? Den I takes it out o' yo' hide! (*He grabs* JIM *by the throat with one hand and draws the other fist back*) Tell me befo' I wrecks yo' face in! Is you a nigger or isn't you? (*Shaking him*) Is you a nigger, Nigger? Nigger, is you a nigger?

JIM: (*looking into his eyes—quietly*) Yes. I'm a nigger. We're both niggers. (*They look at each other for a moment.* JOE'S *rage vanishes. He slumps onto a box beside* JIM'S. *He offers him a cigarette.* JIM *takes it.* JOE *scratches a match and lights both their cigarettes*).

JOE: (*after a puff, with full satisfaction*) Man, why didn't you 'splain dat in de fust place?

JIM: We're both niggers. (*The same hand-organ man of* SCENE ONE *comes to the corner. He plays the chorus of "Bon-bon Buddie The Chocolate Drop." They both stare straight ahead listening. Then the organ man goes away. A silence.* JOE *gets to his feet*).

JOE: I'll go get me a cold beer. (*He starts to move off—then turns*) Time you was graduatin', ain't it? (*He goes.* JIM *remains sitting on his box staring straight before him as*

THE CURTAIN FALLS)

SCENE THREE

*T*HE *same corner five years later. Nothing has changed much. It is a night in Spring. The arc-lamp discovers faces with a favorless cruelty. The street noises are the same but more intermittent and dulled with a quality of fatigue. Two people pass, one black and one white. They are tired. They both yawn, but neither laughs. There is no laughter from the two streets. From the street of the whites the tenor, more nasal than ever and a bit drunken, wails in high barber-shop falsetto the last half of the chorus of "When I Lost You." The Negro voice, a bit maudlin in turn, replies with the last half of "Waitin' for the Robert E. Lee." Silence.* SHORTY *enters. He looks tougher than ever, the typical gangster. He stands waiting, singing a bit drunkenly, peering down the street.*

SHORTY: (*indignantly*) Yuh bum! Ain't yuh ever comin'? (*He begins to sing:* "And sewed up in her yeller kimona, She had a blue-barreled forty-five gun, For to get her man Who'd done her wrong." *Then he comments scornfully*) Not her, dough! No gat for her. She ain't got de noive. A little sugar. Dat'll fix her. (ELLA *enters. She is dressed poorly, her face is pale and hollow-eyed, her voice cold and tired*).

SHORTY: Yuh got de message?

ELLA: Here I am.

SHORTY: How yuh been?

ELLA: All right. (*A pause. He looks at her puzzledly*).

SHORTY: (*a bit embarrassedly*) Well, I s'pose yuh'd like me to give yuh some dope on Mickey, huh?

ELLA: No.

SHORTY: Mean to say yuh don't wanter know where he is or what he's doin'?

ELLA: No.

SHORTY: Since when?

ELLA: A long time.

SHORTY: (*after a pause—with a rat-like viciousness*) Between you'n me, kid, you'll get even soon—you'n all de odder dames he's tossed. I'm on de inside. I've watched him trainin'. His next scrap, watch it! He'll go! It won't be de odder guy. It'll be all youse dames he's kidded— and de ones what's kidded him. Youse'll all be in de odder guy's corner. He won't need no odder seconds. Youse'll trow water on him, and sponge his face, and take de kinks out of his socker—and Mickey'll catch it on de button—and he won't be able to take it no more—'cause all your weight—you and de odders—'ll be behind dat punch. Ha ha! (*He laughs an evil laugh*) And Mickey'll go—down to his knees first—(*He sinks to his knees in the attitude of a groggy boxer*).

ELLA: I'd like to see him on his knees!

SHORTY: And den—flat on his pan—dead to de world—de boidies singin' in de trees—ten—out! (*He suits his action to the words, sinking flat on the pavement, then rises and laughs the same evil laugh*).

ELLA: He's been out—for me—a long time. (*A pause*) Why did you send for me?

SHORTY: He sent me.

ELLA: Why?

SHORTY: To slip you dis wad o' dough! (*He reluctantly takes a roll of bills from his pocket and holds it out to her*).

ELLA: (*looks at the money indifferently*) What for?

SHORTY: For you.

ELLA: No.

SHORTY: For de kid den.

ELLA: The kid's dead. He took diphtheria.

SHORTY: Hell yuh say! When?

ELLA: A long time.

SHORTY: Why didn't you write Mickey—?

ELLA: Why should I? He'd only be glad.

SHORTY: (*after a pause*) Well—it's better.

ELLA: Yes.

SHORTY: You made up wit yer family?

ELLA: No chance.

SHORTY: Livin' alone?

ELLA: In Brooklyn.

SHORTY: Workin'?

ELLA: In a factory.

SHORTY: You're a sucker. There's lots of softer snaps fer you, kid—

ELLA: I know what you mean. No.

SHORTY: Don't yuh wanter step out no more—have fun—live?

ELLA: I'm through.

SHORTY: (*mockingly*) Jump in de river, huh? T'ink it over, baby. I kin start yuh right in my stable. No one'll bodder yuh den. I got influence.

ELLA: (*without emphasis*) You're a dirty dog. Why doesn't someone kill you?

SHORTY: Is dat so! What're you? They say you been travelin' round with Jim Crow.

ELLA: He's been my only friend.

SHORTY: A nigger!

ELLA: The only white man in the world! Kind and white. You're all black—black to the heart.

SHORTY: Nigger-lover! (*He throws the money in her face. It falls to the street*) Listen, you! Mickey says he's off of yuh for keeps. Dis is de finish! Dat's what he sent me to tell you. (*Glances at her searchingly— a pause*) Yuh won't make no trouble?

ELLA: Why should I? He's free. The kid's dead. I'm free. No hard feelings—only—I'll be there in spirit at his next fight, tell him! I'll take your tip—the other corner—second the punch—nine—ten— out! He's free! That's all. (*She grins horribly at* SHORTY) Go away, Shorty.

SHORTY: (*looking at her and shaking his head—maudlinly*) Groggy! Groggy! We're all groggy! Gluttons for punishment! Me for a drink. So long. (*He goes. A Salvation Army band comes toward the corner. They are playing and singing "Till We Meet at Jesus' Feet." They reach the end as they enter and stop before* ELLA. THE CAPTAIN *steps forward*).

CAPTAIN: Sister—

ELLA: (*picks up the money and drops it in his hat—mockingly*) Here. Go save yourself. Leave me alone.

A WOMAN SALVATIONIST: Sister—

ELLA: Never mind that. I'm not in your line—yet. (*As they hesitate, wonderingly*) I want to be alone. (*To the thud of the big drum they march off.* ELLA *sits down on a box, her hands hanging at her sides. Presently* JIM HARRIS *comes in. He has grown into a quietly-dressed, studious-looking Negro with an intelligent yet queerly-baffled face*).

JIM: (*with a joyous but bewildered cry*) Ella! I just saw Shorty—

ELLA: (*smiling at him with frank affection*) He had a message from Mickey.

JIM: (*sadly*) Ah!

ELLA: (*pointing to the box behind her*) Sit down. (*He does so. A pause—then she says indifferently*) It's finished. I'm free, Jim.

JIM: (*wearily*) We're never free—except to do what we have to do.

ELLA: What are you getting gloomy about all of a sudden?

JIM: I've got the report from the school. I've flunked again.

ELLA: Poor Jim.

JIM: Don't pity me. I'd like to kick myself all over the block. Five years— and I'm still plugging away where I ought to have been at the end of two.

ELLA: Why don't you give it up?

JIM: No!

ELLA: After all, what's being a lawyer?

JIM: A lot—to me—what it means. (*Intensely*) Why, if I was a Member of the Bar right now, Ella, I believe I'd almost have the courage to—

ELLA: What?

JIM: Nothing. (*After a pause—gropingly*) I can't explain—just—but it hurts like fire. It brands me in my pride. I swear I know more'n any member of my class. I ought to, I study harder. I work like the devil. It's all in my head—all fine and correct to a T. Then when I'm called on—I stand up—all the white faces looking at me—and I can feel their eyes—I hear my own voice sounding funny, trembling—and all of a sudden it's all gone in my head—there's nothing remembered— and I hear myself stuttering—and give up—sit down— They don't laugh, hardly ever. They're kind. They're good people. (*In a frenzy*) They're considerate, damn them! But I feel branded!

ELLA: Poor Jim.

JIM: (*going on painfully*) And it's the same thing in the written exams. For weeks before I study all night. I can't sleep anyway. I learn it all, I see it, I understand it. Then they give me the paper in the exam room. I look it over, I know each answer—perfectly. I take up my pen. On all sides are white men starting to write. They're so sure— even the ones that I know know nothing. But I know it all—but I can't remember any more—it fades—it goes—it's gone. There's a blank in my head—stupidity—I sit like a fool fighting to remember a little bit here, a little bit there—not enough to pass—not enough for anything—when I know it all!

ELLA: (*compassionately*) Jim. It isn't worth it. You don't need to—

JIM: I need it more than anyone ever needed anything. I need it to live.

ELLA: What'll it prove?

JIM: Nothing at all much—but everything to me.

ELLA: You're so much better than they are in every other way.

JIM: (*looking up at her*) Then—you understand?

ELLA: Of course. (*Affectionately*) Don't I know how fine you've been to me! You've been the only one in the world who's stood by me—the only understanding person—and all after the rotten way I used to treat you.

JIM: But before that—way back so high—you treated me good. (*He smiles*).

ELLA: You've been white to me, Jim. (*She takes his hand*).

JIM: White—to you!

ELLA: Yes.

JIM: All love is white. I've always loved you. (*This with the deepest humility*).

ELLA: Even now—after all that's happened!

JIM: Always.

ELLA: I like you, Jim—better than anyone else in the world.

JIM: That's more than enough, more than I ever hoped for. (*The organ grinder comes to the corner. He plays the chorus of "Annie Laurie." They sit listening, hand in hand*) Would you ever want to marry me, Ella?

ELLA: Yes, Jim.

JIM: (*as if this quick consent alarmed him*) No, no, don't answer now. Wait! Turn it over in your mind! Think what it means to you! Consider it—over and over again! I'm in no hurry, Ella. I can wait months—years—

ELLA: I'm alone. I've got to be helped. I've got to help someone—or it's the end—one end or another.

JIM: (*eagerly*) Oh, I'll help—I know I can help—I'll give my life to help you—that's what I've been living for—

ELLA: But can I help you? Can I help you?

JIM: Yes! Yes! We'll go abroad where a man is a man—where it don't make that difference—where people are kind and wise to see the soul under skins. I don't ask you to love me—I don't dare to hope nothing like that! I don't want nothing—only to wait—to know you like me—to be near you—to keep harm away—to make up for the past—to never let you suffer any more—to serve you—to lie at your feet like a dog that loves you—to kneel by your bed like a nurse that watches over you sleeping—to preserve and protect and shield you from evil and sorrow—to give my life and my blood and all the strength that's in me to give you peace and joy—to become your slave!—yes, be your slave—your black slave that adores you as sacred! (*He has sunk to his knees. In a frenzy of self-abnegation, as he says the last words he beats his head on the flagstones*).

ELLA: (*overcome and alarmed*) Jim! Jim! You're crazy! I want to help you,
 Jim—I want to help—

CURTAIN

SCENE FOUR

*S*OME *weeks or so later. A street in the same ward in front of an old brick
church. The church sets back from the sidewalk in a yard enclosed by a rusty
iron railing with a gate at center. On each side of this yard are tenements.
The buildings have a stern, forbidding look. All the shades on the windows are
drawn down, giving an effect of staring, brutal eyes that pry callously at human
beings without acknowledging them. Even the two tall, narrow church windows
on either side of the arched door are blanked with dull green shades. It is a
bright sunny morning. The district is unusually still, as if it were waiting,
holding its breath.*

*From the street of the blacks to the right a Negro tenor sings in a voice of
shadowy richness—the first stanza with a contented, childlike melancholy—*

> Sometimes I feel like a mourning dove,
> Sometimes I feel like a mourning dove,
> Sometimes I feel like a mourning dove,
>   I feel like a mourning dove.
>   Feel like a mourning dove.

The second with a dreamy, boyish exultance—

> Sometimes I feel like an eagle in the air,
> Sometimes I feel like an eagle in the air,
> Sometimes I feel like an eagle in the air,
>   I feel like an eagle in the air.
>   Feel like an eagle in the air.

The third with a brooding, earthbound sorrow—

> Sometimes I wish that I'd never been born,
> Sometimes I wish that I'd never been born,
> Sometimes I wish that I'd never been born,
>   I wish that I'd never been born.
>   Wish that I'd never been born.

As the music dies down there is a pause of waiting stillness. This is broken by one startling, metallic clang of the church-bell. As if it were a signal, people—men, women, children—pour from the two tenements, whites from the tenement to the left, blacks from the one to the right. They hurry to form into two racial lines on each side of the gate, rigid and unyielding, staring across at each other with bitter hostile eyes. The halves of the big church door swing open and JIM *and* ELLA *step out from the darkness within into the sunlight. The doors slam behind them like wooden lips of an idol that has spat them out.* JIM *is dressed in black.* ELLA *in white, both with extreme plainness. They stand in the sunlight, shrinking and confused. All the hostile eyes are now concentrated on them. They become aware of the two lines through which they must pass; they hesitate and tremble; then stand there staring back at the people as fixed and immovable as they are. The organ grinder comes in from the right. He plays the chorus of "Old Black Joe." As he finishes the bell of the church clangs one more single stroke, insistently dismissing.*

JIM: (*as if the sound had awakened him from a trance, reaches out and takes her hand*) Come. Time we got to the steamer. Time we sailed away over the sea. Come, Honey! (*She tries to answer but her lips tremble; she cannot take her eyes off the eyes of the people; she is unable to move. He sees this and, keeping the same tone of profound, affectionate kindness, he points upward in the sky, and gradually persuades her eyes to look up*) Look up, Honey! See the sun! Feel his warm eye lookin' down! Feel how kind he looks! Feel his blessing deep in your heart, your bones! Look up, Honey! (*Her eyes are fixed on the sky now. Her face is calm.*

She tries to smile bravely back at the sun. Now he pulls her by the hand, urging her gently to walk with him down through the yard and gate, through the lines of people. He is maintaining an attitude to support them through the ordeal only by a terrible effort, which manifests itself in the hysteric quality of ecstasy which breaks into his voice) And look at the sky! Ain't it kind and blue! Blue for hope. Don't they say blue's for hope? Hope! That's for us, Honey. All those blessings in the sky! What's it the Bible says? Falls on just and unjust alike? No, that's the sweet rain. Pshaw, what am I saying? All mixed up. There's no unjust about it. We're all the same—equally just—under the sky—under the sun—under God—sailing over the sea—to the other side of the world—the side where Christ was born—the kind side that takes count of the soul—over the sea—the sea's blue, too—. Let's not be late—let's get that steamer! *(They have reached the curb now, passed the lines of people. She is looking up to the sky with an expression of trancelike calm and peace. He is on the verge of collapse, his face twitching, his eyes staring. He calls horsely)*: Taxi! Where is he? Taxi!

CURTAIN

Act Two—Scene One

Two years later. A flat of the better sort in the Negro district near the corner of Act One. This is the parlor. Its furniture is a queer clash. The old pieces are cheaply ornate, naïvely, childishly gaudy—the new pieces give evidence of a taste that is diametrically opposed, severe to the point of somberness. On one wall, in a heavy gold frame, is a colored photograph—the portrait of an elderly Negro with an able, shrewd face but dressed in outlandish lodge regalia, a get-up adorned with medals, sashes, a cocked hat with frills—the whole effect as absurd to contemplate as one of Napoleon's Marshals in full uniform. In the left corner, where a window lights it effectively, is a Negro primitive mask from the Congo—a grotesque face, inspiring obscure, dim connotations in one's mind, but beautifully done, conceived in a true religious spirit. In this room, however, the mask acquires an arbitrary accentuation. It dominates by a diabolical quality that contrast imposes upon it.

There are two windows on the left looking out in the street. In the rear, a door to the hall of the building. In the right, a doorway with red and gold portières leading into the bedroom and the rest of the flat. Everything is cleaned and polished. The dark brown wall paper is new, the brilliantly figured carpet also. There is a round mahogany table at center. In a rocking chair by the table MRS. HARRIS *is sitting. She is a mild-looking, gray-haired Negress of sixty-five, dressed in an old-fashioned Sunday-best dress. Walking about the room nervously is* HATTIE, *her daughter,* JIM's *sister, a woman of about thirty with a high-strung, defiant face—an intelligent head showing both power and courage. She is dressed severely, mannishly.*

It is a fine morning in Spring. Sunshine comes through the windows at the left.

MRS. HARRIS: Time dey was here, ain't it?

HATTIE: (*impatiently*) Yes.

105

MRS. H: (*worriedly*) You ain't gwine ter kick up a fuss, is you—like you done wid Jim befo' de weddin'?

HATTIE: No. What's done is done.

MRS. H: We mustn't let her see we hold it agin' her—de bad dat happened to her wid dat no-count fighter.

HATTIE: I certainly never give that a thought. It's what she's done to Jim—making him run away and give up his fight—!

MRS. H: Jim loves her a powerful lot, must be.

HATTIE: (*after a pause—bitterly*) I wonder if she loves Jim!

MRS. H: She must, too. Yes, she must, too. Don't you forget dat it was hard for her—mighty, mighty hard—harder for de white dan for de black!

HATTIE: (*indignantly*) Why should it be?

MRS. H: (*shaking her head*) I ain't talkin' of shoulds. It's too late for shoulds. Dey's o'ny one should. (*Solemnly*) De white and de black shouldn't mix dat close. Dere's one road where de white goes on alone; dere's anudder road where de black goes on alone—

HATTIE: Yes, if they'd only leave us alone!

MRS. H: Dey leaves your Pa alone. He comes to de top till he's got his own business, lots o' money in de bank, he owns a building even befo' he die. (*She looks up proudly at the picture.* HATTIE *sighs impatiently then her mother goes on*) Dey leaves me alone. I bears four children into dis worl', two dies, two lives, I helps you two grow up fine an' healthy and eddicated wid schoolin' and money fo' yo' comfort—

HATTIE: (*impatiently*) Ma!

MRS. H: I does de duty God set for me in dis worl'. Dey leaves me alone. (HATTIE *goes to the window to hide her exasperation. The mother broods for a minute—then goes on*) The worl' done change. Dey ain't no satisfaction wid nuffin' no more.

HATTIE: Oh! (*Then after a pause*) They'll be here any minute now.

MRS. H: Why didn't you go meet 'em at de dock like I axed you?

HATTIE: I couldn't. My face and Jim's among those hundreds of white faces— (*With a harsh laugh*) It would give her too much advantage!

MRS. H: (*impatiently*) Don't talk dat way! What makes you so proud? (*Then after a pause—sadly*) Hattie.

HATTIE: (*turning*) Yes, Ma.

MRS. H: I want to see Jim again—my only boy—but—all de same I'd ruther he stayed away. He say in his letter he's happy, she's happy, dey likes it dere, de folks don't think nuffin' but what's natural at seeing 'em married. Why don't dey stay?

HATTIE: (*vehemently*) No! They were cowards to run away. If they believe in what they've done, then let them face it out, live it out here, be strong enough to conquer all prejudice!

MRS. H: Strong? Dey ain't many strong. Dey ain't many happy neider. Dey was happy ovah yondah.

HATTIE: We don't deserve happiness till we've fought the fight of our race and won it! (*In the pause that follows there is a ring from back in the flat*) It's the door bell! You go, Ma. I—I—I'd rather not. (*Her mother looks at her rebukingly and goes out agitatedly through the portières. HATTIE waits, nervously walking about, trying to compose herself. There is a long pause. Finally the portières are parted and JIM enters. He looks much older, graver, worried*).

JIM: Hattie!

HATTIE: Jim! (*They embrace with great affection*).

JIM: It's great to see you again! You're looking fine.

HATTIE: (*looking at him searchingly*) You look well, too—thinner maybe—and tired. (*Then as she sees him frowning*) But where's Ella?

JIM: With Ma. (*Apologetically*) She sort of—broke down—when we came in. The trip wore her out.

HATTIE: (*coldly*) I see.

JIM: Oh, it's nothing serious. Nerves. She needs a rest.

HATTIE: Wasn't living in France restful?

JIM: Yes, but—too lonely—especially for her.

HATTIE: (*resentfully*) Why? Didn't the people there want to associate—?

JIM: (*quickly*) Oh, no indeed, they didn't think anything of that. (*After a pause*) But—she did. For the first year it was all right. Ella liked everything a lot. She went out with French folks and got so she could talk it a little—and I learned it—a little. We were having a right nice time. I never thought then we'd ever want to come back here.

HATTIE: (*frowning*) But—what happened to change you?

JIM: (*after a pause—haltingly*) Well—you see—the first year— she and I were living around—like friends—like a brother and sister—like you and I might.

HATTIE: (*her face becoming more and more drawn and tense*) You mean— then—? (*She shudders—then after a pause*) She loves you, Jim?

JIM: If I didn't know that I'd have to jump in the river.

HATTIE: Are you sure she loves you?

JIM: Isn't that why she's suffering?

HATTIE: (*letting her breath escape through her clenched teeth*) Ah!

JIM: (*suddenly springs up and shouts almost hysterically*) Why d'you ask me all those damn questions? Are you trying to make trouble between us?

HATTIE: (*controlling herself—quietly*) No, Jim.

JIM: (*after a pause—contritely*) I'm sorry, Hattie. I'm kind of on edge today. (*He sinks down on his chair—then goes on as if something forced him to speak*) After that we got to living housed in. Ella didn't want to see nobody, she said just the two of us was enough. I was happy then—and I really guess she was happy, too— in a way—for a while. (*Again a pause*) But she never did get to wanting to go out any place again. She got to saying she felt she'd be sure to run into someone she knew—from over here. So I moved us out to the country where no tourist ever comes—but it didn't make any difference to her. She got to avoiding the French folks the same as if they were Americans and I couldn't get it out of her mind. She lived in the house and got paler and paler, and more and more nervous and scary, always imagining things—until I got to imagining things, too. I got to feeling blue. Got to sneering at myself that I wasn't any better than a quitter because I sneaked away right after getting married, didn't face nothing, gave up trying to become a Member of the Bar—and I got to suspecting Ella must feel that way about me, too—that I wasn't a *real man!*

HATTIE: (*indignantly*) She couldn't!

JIM: (*with hostility*) You don't need to tell me! All this was only in my own mind. We never quarreled a single bit. We never said a harsh word. We were as close to each other as could be. We were all there was in the world to each other. We were alone together! (*A pause*) Well, one day I got so I couldn't stand it. I could see she couldn't stand it. So I just up and said: Ella, we've got to have a plain talk, look everything straight in the face, hide nothing, come out with the exact truth of the way we feel.

HATTIE: And you decided to come back!

JIM: Yes. We decided the reason we felt sort of ashamed was we'd acted like cowards. We'd run away from the thing—and taken it with us. We decided to come back and face it and live it down in ourselves, and prove to ourselves we were strong in our love—and then, and that way only, by being brave we'd free ourselves, and gain confidence, and be really free inside and able then to go anywhere and live in peace and equality with ourselves and the world without any guilty uncomfortable feeling coming up to rile us. (*He has talked himself now into a state of happy confidence*).

HATTIE: (*bending over and kissing him*) Good for you! I admire you so much, Jim! I admire both of you! And are you going to begin studying right away and get admitted to the Bar?

JIM: You bet I am!

HATTIE: You must, Jim! Our race needs men like you to come to the front and help— (*As voices are heard approaching she stops, stiffens, and her face grows cold*).

JIM: (*noticing this—warningly*) Remember Ella's been sick! (*Losing control—threateningly*) You be nice to her, you hear! (MRS. HARRIS *enters, showing* ELLA *the way. The colored woman is plainly worried and perplexed.* ELLA *is pale, with a strange, haunted expression in her eyes. She runs to*

JIM *as to a refuge, clutching his hands in both of hers, looking from* MRS. HARRIS *to* HATTIE *with a frightened defiance*).

MRS. H: Dere he is, child, big's life! She was afraid we'd done kidnapped you away, Jim.

JIM: (*patting her hand*) This place ought to be familiar, Ella. Don't you remember playing here with us sometimes as a kid?

ELLA: (*queerly—with a frown of effort*) I remember playing marbles one night—but that was on the street.

JIM: Don't you remember Hattie?

HATTIE: (*coming forward with a forced smile*) It was a long time ago—but I remember Ella. (*She holds out her hand*).

ELLA: (*taking it—looking at* HATTIE *with the same queer defiance*) I remember. But you've changed so much.

HATTIE: (*stirred to hostility by* ELLA's *manner—condescendingly*) Yes, I've grown older, naturally. (*Then in a tone which, as if in spite of herself, becomes bragging*) I've worked so hard. First I went away to college, you know—then I took up post-graduate study—when suddenly I decided I'd accomplish more good if I gave up learning and took up teaching. (*She suddenly checks herself, ashamed, and stung by* ELLA's *indifference*) But this sounds like stupid boasting. I don't mean that. I was only explaining—

ELLA: (*indifferently*) I didn't know you'd been to school so long. (*A pause*) Where are you teaching? In a colored school, I suppose. (*There is an indifferent superiority in her words that is maddening to* HATTIE).

HATTIE: (*controlling herself*) Yes. A private school endowed by some wealthy members of our race.

ELLA: (*suddenly—even eagerly*) Then you must have taken lots of examinations and managed to pass them, didn't you?

HATTIE: (*biting her lips*) I always passed with honors!

ELLA: Yes, we both graduated from the same High School, didn't we? That was dead easy for me. Why I hardly even looked at a book. But Jim says it was awfully hard for him. He failed one year, remember?

(*She turns and smiles at* JIM—*a tolerant, superior smile but one full of genuine love.* HATTIE *is outraged, but* JIM *smiles*).

JIM: Yes, it was hard for me, Honey.

ELLA: And the law school examinations Jim hardly ever could pass at all. Could you? (*She laughs lovingly*).

HATTIE: (*harshly*) Yes, he could! He can! He'll pass them now— if you'll give him a chance!

JIM: (*angrily*) Hattie!

MRS. HARRIS:. Hold yo' fool tongue!

HATTIE: (*sullenly*) I'm sorry. (ELLA *has shrunk back against* JIM. *She regards* HATTIE *with a sort of wondering hatred. Then she looks away about the room. Suddenly her eyes fasten on the primitive mask and she gives a stifled scream*).

JIM: What's the matter, Honey?

ELLA: (*pointing*) That! For God's sake, what is it?

HATTIE: (*scornfully*) It's a Congo mask. (*She goes and picks it up*) I'll take it away if you wish. I thought you'd like it. It was my wedding present to Jim.

ELLA: What is it?

HATTIE: It's a mask which used to be worn in religious ceremonies by my people in Africa. But, aside from that, it's beautifully made, a work of Art by a real artist—as real in his way as your Michael Angelo. (*Forces* ELLA *to take it*) Here. Just notice the workmanship.

ELLA: (*defiantly*) I'm not scared of it if you're not. (*Looking at it with disgust*) Beautiful? Well, some people certainly have queer notions! It looks ugly to me and stupid—like a kid's game—making faces! (*She slaps it contemptuously*) Pooh! You needn't look hard at me. I'll give you the laugh. (*She goes to put it back on the stand*).

JIM: Maybe, if it disturbs you, we better put it in some other room.

ELLA: (*defiantly aggressive*) No. I want it here where I can give it the laugh! (*She sets it there again—then turns suddenly on* HATTIE *with aggressive determination*) Jim's not going to take any more examinations! I won't let him!

HATTIE: (*bursting forth*) Jim! Do you hear that? There's white justice!—
their fear for their superiority!—

ELLA: (*with a terrified pleading*) Make her go away, Jim!

JIM: (*losing control—furiously to his sister*) Either you leave here—or we
will!

MRS. H: (*weeping—throws her arms around* HATTIE) Let's go, chile! Let's
go!

HATTIE: (*calmly now*) Yes, Ma. All right. (*They go through the portières.
As soon as they are gone,* JIM *suddenly collapses into a chair and hides his
head in his hands.* ELLA *stands beside him for a moment. She stares distractedly about her, at the portrait, at the mask, at the furniture, at* JIM.
*She seems fighting to escape from some weight on her mind. She throws
this off and, completely her old self for the moment, kneels by* JIM *and pats
his shoulder*).

ELLA: (*with kindness and love*) Don't, Jim! Don't cry, please! You don't
suppose I really meant that about the examinations, do you? Why,
of course, I didn't mean a word! I couldn't mean it! I want you to
take the examinations! I want you to pass! I want you to be a lawyer!
I want you to be the best lawyer in the country! I want you to show
'em—all the dirty sneaking, gossiping liars that talk behind our
backs—what a man I married. I want the whole world to know you're
the whitest of the white! I want you to climb and climb—and step
on 'em, stamp right on their mean faces! I love you, Jim. You know
that!

JIM: (*calm again—happily*) I hope so, Honey—and I'll make myself worthy.

HATTIE: (*appears in the doorway—quietly*) We're going now, Jim.

ELLA: No. Don't go.

HATTIE: We were going to, anyway. This is your house—Mother's gift
to you, Jim.

JIM: (*astonished*) But I can't accept— Where are you going?

HATTIE: We've got a nice flat in the Bronx—(*with bitter pride*) in the
heart of the Black Belt—the Congo—among our own people!

JIM: (*angrily*) You're crazy—I'll see Ma— (*He goes out.* HATTIE *and* ELLA *stare at each other with scorn and hatred for a moment, then* HATTIE *goes.* ELLA *remains kneeling for a moment by the chair, her eyes dazed and strange as she looks about her. Then she gets to her feet and stands before the portrait of* JIM's *father—with a sneer*).

ELLA: It's his Old Man—all dolled up like a circus horse! Well, they can't help it. It's in the blood, I suppose. They're ignorant, that's all there is to it. (*She moves to the mask—forcing a mocking tone*) Hello, sport! Who d'you think you're scaring? Not me! I'll give you the laugh. He won't pass, you wait and see. Not in a thousand years! (*She goes to the window and looks down at the street and mutters*) All black! Every one of them! (*Then with sudden excitement*) No, there's one. Why, it's Shorty! (*She throws the window open and calls*) Shorty! Shorty! Hello, Shorty! (*She leans out and waves—then stops, remains there for a moment looking down, then shrinks back on the floor suddenly as if she wanted to hide—her whole face in an anguish*) Say! Say! I wonder?—No, he didn't hear you. Yes, he did, too! He must have! I yelled so loud you could hear me in Jersey! No, what are you talking about? How would he hear with all the kids yelling down there? He never heard a word, I tell you! He did, too! He didn't want to hear you! He didn't want to let anyone know he knew you! Why don't you acknowledge it? What are you lying about? I'm not! Why shouldn't he? Where does he come in to—for God's sake, who is Shorty, anyway? A pimp! Yes, and a dope-peddler, too! D'you mean to say he'd have the nerve to hear me call him and then deliberately—? Yes, I mean to say it! I do say it! And it's true, and you know it, and you might as well be honest for a change and admit it! He heard you but he didn't want to hear you! He doesn't want to know you any more. No, not even him! He's afraid it'd get him in wrong with the old gang. Why? You know well enough! Because you married a—a—a—well, I won't say it, but you know without my mentioning names! (ELLA *springs to her feet in horror and shakes off her obsession with a frantic effort*) Stop! (*Then whimpering like a frightened child*) Jim! Jim! Jim! Where are you? I want you, Jim! (*She runs out of the room as*

THE CURTAIN FALLS)

SCENE TWO

*T*HE *same. Six months later. It is evening. The walls of the room appear shrunken in, the ceiling lowered, so that the furniture, the portrait, the mask look unnaturally large and domineering.* JIM *is seated at the table studying, law books piled by his elbows. He is keeping his attention concentrated only by a driving physical effort which gives his face the expression of a runner's near the tape. His forehead shines with prespiration. He mutters one sentence from Blackstone over and over again, tapping his forehead with his fist in time to the rhythm he gives the stale words. But, in spite of himself, his attention wanders, his eyes have an uneasy, hunted look, he starts at every sound in the house or from the street. Finally, he remains rigid, Blackstone forgotten, his eyes fixed on the portières with tense grief. Then he groans, slams the book shut, goes to the window and throws it open and sinks down beside it, his arms on the sill, his head resting wearily on his arms, staring out into the night, the pale glare from the arc-lamp on the corner throwing his face into relief. The portières on the right are parted and* HATTIE *comes in.*

HATTIE: (*not seeing him at the table*) Jim! (*Discovering him*) Oh, there you are. What're you doing?

JIM: (*turning to her*) Resting. Cooling my head. (*Forcing a smile*) These law books certainly are a sweating proposition! (*Then, anxiously*) How is she?

HATTIE: She's asleep now. I felt it was safe to leave her for a minute. (*After a pause*) What did the doctor tell you, Jim?

JIM: The same old thing. She must have rest, he says, her mind needs rest— (*Bitterly*) But he can't tell me any prescription for that rest—leastways not any that'd work.

HATTIE: (*after a pause*) I think you ought to leave her, Jim—or let her leave you—for a while, anyway.

JIM: (*angrily*) You're like the doctor. Everything's so simple and easy. Do this and that happens. Only it don't. Life isn't simple like that—not in this case, anyway—no, it isn't simple a bit. (*After a pause*) I can't leave her. She can't leave me. And there's a million little reasons combining to make one big reason why we can't. (*A pause*) For her sake—if it'd do her good—I'd go—I'd leave—I'd do anything—because I love her. I'd kill myself even—jump out of this window this second—I've thought it over, too—but that'd only make matters worse for her. I'm all she's got in the world! Yes, that isn't bragging or fooling myself. I know that for a fact! Don't you know that's true? (*There is a pleading for the certainty he claims*).

HATTIE: Yes, I know she loves you, Jim. I know that now.

JIM: (*simply*) Then we've got to stick together to the end, haven't we, whatever comes—and hope and pray for the best? (*A pause—then hopefully*) I think maybe this is the crisis in her mind. Once she settles this in herself, she's won to the other side. And me—once I become a Member of the Bar—then I win, too! We're both free—by our own fighting down our own weakness! We're both really, truly free! Then we can be happy with ourselves here or anywhere. She'll be proud then! Yes, she's told me again and again, she says she'll be actually proud!

HATTIE: (*turning away to conceal her emotion*) Yes, I'm sure—but you mustn't study too hard, Jim! You mustn't study too awfully hard!

JIM: (*gets up and goes to the table and sits down wearily*) Yes, I know. Oh, I'll pass easily. I haven't got any scary feeling about that any more. And I'm doing two years' work in one here alone. That's better than schools, eh?

HATTIE: (*doubtfully*) It's wonderful, Jim.

JIM: (*his spirit evaporating*) If I can only hold out! It's hard! I'm worn out. I don't sleep. I get to thinking and thinking. My head aches and burns like fire with thinking. Round and round my thoughts go chasing like crazy chickens hopping and flapping before the wind. It gets me crazy mad—'cause I can't stop!

HATTIE: (*watching him for a while and seeming to force herself to speak*) The doctor didn't tell you all, Jim.

JIM: (*dully*) What's that?

HATTIE: He told me you're liable to break down too, if you don't take care of yourself.

JIM: (*abjectly weary*) Let 'er come! I don't care what happens to me. Maybe if I get sick she'll get well. There's only so much bad luck allowed to one family, maybe. (*He forces a wan smile*).

HATTIE: (*hastily*) Don't give in to that idea, for the Lord's sake!

JIM: I'm tired—and blue—that's all.

HATTIE: (*after another long pause*) I've got to tell you something else, Jim.

JIM: (*dully*) What?

HATTIE: The doctor said Ella's liable to be sick like this a very long time.

JIM: He told me that too—that it'd be a long time before she got back her normal strength. Well, I suppose that's got to be expected.

HATTIE: (*slowly*) He didn't mean convalescing—what he told me. (*A long pause*).

JIM: (*evasively*) I'm going to get other doctors in to see Ella— specialists. This one's a damn fool.

HATTIE: Be sensible, Jim. You'll have to face the truth—sooner or later.

JIM: (*irritably*) I know the truth about Ella better'n any doctor.

HATTIE: (*persuasively*) She'd get better so much sooner if you'd send her away to some nice sanitarium—

JIM: No! She'd die of shame there!

HATTIE: At least until after you've taken your examinations—

JIM: To hell with me!

HATTIE: Six months. That wouldn't be long to be parted.

JIM: What are you trying to do—separate us? (*He gets to his feet—furiously*) Go on out! Go on out!

HATTIE: (*calmly*) No, I won't. (*Sharply*) There's something that's got to be said to you and I'm the only one with the courage— (*Intensly*) Tell me, Jim, have you heard her raving when she's out of her mind?

JIM: (*with a shudder*) No!

HATTIE: You're lying, Jim. You must have—if you don't stop your ears—and the doctor says she may develop a violent mania, dangerous for you—get worse and worse until—Jim, you'll go crazy too—living this way. Today she raved on about "Black! Black!" and cried because she said her skin was turning black—that you had poisoned her—

JIM: (*in anguish*) That's only when she's out of her mind.

HATTIE: And then she suddenly called me a dirty nigger.

JIM: No! She never said that ever! She never would!

HATTIE: She did—and kept on and on! (*A tense pause*) She'll be saying that to you soon.

JIM: (*torturedly*) She don't mean it! She isn't responsible for what she's saying!

HATTIE: I know she isn't—yet she is just the same. It's deep down in her or it wouldn't come out.

JIM: Deep down in her people—not deep in her.

HATTIE: I can't make such distinctions. The race in me, deep in me, can't stand it. I can't play nurse to her any more, Jim,—not even for your sake. I'm afraid—afraid of myself—afraid sometime I'll kill her dead to set you free! (*She loses control and begins to cry*).

JIM: (*after a long pause—somberly*) Yes, I guess you'd better stay away from here. Good-by.

HATTIE: Who'll you get to nurse her, Jim,—a white woman?

JIM: Ella'd die of shame. No, I'll nurse her myself.

HATTIE: And give up your studies?

JIM: I can do both.

HATTIE: You can't! You'll get sick yourself! Why, you look terrible even as it is—and it's only beginning!

JIM: I can do anything for her! I'm all she's got in the world! I've got to prove I can be all to her! I've got to prove worthy! I've got to prove she can be proud of me! I've got to prove I'm the whitest of the white!

HATTIE: (*stung by this last—with rebellious bitterness*) Is that the ambition she's given you? Oh, you soft, weak-minded fool, you traitor to your race! And the thanks you'll get—to be called a dirty nigger—to hear her cursing you because she can never have a child because it'll be born black—!

JIM: (*in a frenzy*) Stop!

HATTIE: I'll say what must be said even though you kill me, Jim. Send her to an asylum before you both have to be sent to one together.

JIM: (*with a sudden wild laugh*) Do you think you're threatening me with something dreadful now? Why, I'd like that. Sure, I'd like that! Maybe she'd like it better, too. Maybe we'd both find it all simple then—like you think it is now. Yes. (*He laughs again*).

HATTIE: (*frightenedly*) Jim!

JIM: Together! You can't scare me even with hell fire if you say she and I go together. It's heaven then for me! (*With sudden savagery*) You go out of here! All you've ever been aiming to do is to separate us so we can't be together!

HATTIE: I've done what I did for your own good.

JIM: I have no own good. I only got a good together with her. I'm all she's got in the world! Let her call me nigger! Let her call me the whitest of the white! I'm all she's got in the world, ain't I? She's all I've got! You with your fool talk of the black race and the white race! Where does the human race get a chance to come in? I suppose that's simple for you. You lock it up in asylums and throw away the key! (*With fresh violence*) Go along! There isn't going to be no more people coming in here to separate—excepting the doctor. I'm going to lock the door and it's going to stay locked, you hear? Go along, now!

HATTIE: (*confusedly*) Jim!

JIM: (*pushes her out gently and slams the door after her—vaguely*) Go along! I got to study. I got to nurse Ella, too. Oh, I can do it! I can do anything for her! (*He sits down at the table and, opening the book, begins again to recite the line from Blackstone in a meaningless rhythm, tapping his forehead with his fist. ELLA enters noiselessly through the portières. She wears a red dressing-gown over her night-dress but is in her bare feet. She has a carving-knife in her right hand. Her eyes fasten on JIM with a murderous mania. She creeps up behind him. Suddenly he senses something and turns. As he sees her he gives a cry, jumping up and catching her wrist. She stands fixed, her eyes growing bewildered and frightened*).

JIM: (*aghast*) Ella! For God's sake! Do you want to murder me? (*She does not answer. He shakes her*).

ELLA: (*whimperingly*) They kept calling me names as I was walking along—I can't tell you what, Jim—and then I grabbed a knife—

JIM: Yes! See! This! (*She looks at it frightenedly*).

ELLA: Where did I—? I was having a nightmare— Where did they go— I mean, how did I get here? (*With sudden terrified pleading—like a little girl*) Oh, Jim—don't ever leave me alone! I have such terrible dreams, Jim—promise you'll never go away!

JIM: I promise, Honey.

ELLA: (*her manner becoming more and more childishly silly*) I'll be a little girl—and you'll be old Uncle Jim who's been with us for years and years— Will you play that?

JIM: Yes, Honey. Now you better go back to bed.

ELLA: (*like a child*) Yes, Uncle Jim. (*She turns to go. He pretends to be occupied by his book. She looks at him for a second— then suddenly asks in her natural woman's voice*) Are you studying hard, Jim?

JIM: Yes, Honey. Go to bed now. You need to rest, you know.

ELLA: (*stands looking at him, fighting with herself. A startling transformation comes over her face. It grows mean, vicious, full of jealous hatred. She cannot contain herself but breaks out harshly with a cruel, venomous grin*) You dirty nigger!

JIM: (*starting as if he'd been shot*) Ella! For the good Lord's sake!

ELLA: (*coming out of her insane mood for a moment, aware of something terrible, frightened*) Jim! Jim! Why are you looking at me like that?

JIM: What did you say to me just then?

ELLA: (*gropingly*) Why, I—I said—I remember saying, are you studying hard, Jim? Why? You're not mad at that, are you?

JIM: No, Honey. What made you think I was mad? Go to bed now.

ELLA: (*obediently*) Yes, Jim. (*She passes behind the portières.* JIM *stares before him. Suddenly her head is thrust out at the side of the portières. Her face is again that of a vindictive maniac*). Nigger! (*The face disappears—she can be heard running away, laughing with cruel satisfaction.* JIM *bows his head on his outstretched arms but he is too stricken for tears*).

CURTAIN

SCENE THREE

*T*HE *same, six months later. The sun has just gone down. The Spring twilight sheds a vague, gray light about the room, picking out the Congo mask on the stand by the window. The walls appear shrunken in still more, the ceiling now seems barely to clear the people's heads, the furniture and the characters appear enormously magnified. Law books are stacked in two great piles on each side of the table.* ELLA *comes in from the right, the carving-knife in her hand. She is pitifully thin, her face is wasted, but her eyes glow with a mad energy, her movements are abrupt and springlike. She looks stealthily about the room, then advances and stands before the mask, her arms akimbo, her attitude one of* *crazy mockery, fear and bravado. She is dressed in the red dressing-gown, grown dirty and ragged now, and is in her bare feet.*

ELLA: I'll give you the laugh, wait and see! (*Then in a confidential tone*) He thought I was asleep! He called, Ella, Ella—but I kept my eyes shut, I pretended to snore. I fooled him good. (*She gives a little hoarse laugh*) This is the first time he's dared to leave me alone for months and months. I've been wanting to talk to you every day but this is the only chance— (*With sudden violence—flourishing her knife*) What're you grinning about, you dirty nigger, you? How dare you grin at me? I guess you forget what you are! That's always the way. Be kind to you, treat you decent, and in a second you've got a swelled head, you think you're somebody, you're all over the place putting on airs; why, it's got so I can't even walk down the street without seeing niggers, niggers everywhere. Hanging around, grinning, grinning—going to school—pretending they're white—taking examinations— (*She stops, arrested by the word, then suddenly*) That's where he's gone—down to the mail-box—to see if there's a letter from the Board—telling him— But why is he so long? (*She calls pitifully*) Jim! (*Then in a terrified whimper*) Maybe he's passed! Maybe he's passed! (*In a frenzy*) No! No! He can't! I'd kill him! I'd kill myself! (*Threatening the Congo mask*) It's you who're to blame for this! Yes, you! Oh, I'm on to you! (*Then appealingly*) But why d'you want to do this to us? What have I ever done wrong to you? What have you got against me? I married you, didn't I? Why don't you let Jim alone? Why don't you let him be happy as he is—with me? Why don't you let me be happy? He's white, isn't he—the whitest man that ever lived? Where do you come in to interfere? Black! Black! Black as dirt! You've poisoned me! I can't wash myself clean! Oh, I hate you! I hate you! Why don't you let Jim and I be happy? (*She sinks down in his chair, her arms outstretched on the table. The door from the hall is slowly opened and* JIM *appears. His bloodshot, sleepless eyes stare from deep hollows. His expression is one of crushed numbness. He holds an open letter in his hand*).

JIM: (*seeing* ELLA—*in an absolutely dead voice*) Honey— I thought you were asleep.

ELLA: (*starts and wheels about in her chair*) What's that? You got—you got a letter—?

JIM: (*turning to close the door after him*) From the Board of Examiners for admission to the Bar, State of New York—God's country! (*He finishes up with a chuckle of ironic self-pity so spent as to be barely audible*).

ELLA: (*writhing out of her chair like some fierce animal, the knife held behind her—with fear and hatred*) You didn't—you didn't—you didn't pass, did you?

JIM: (*looking at her wildly*) Pass? Pass? (*He begins to chuckle and laugh between sentences and phrases, rich, Negro laughter, but heart-breaking in its mocking grief*) Good Lord, child, how come you can ever imagine such a crazy idea? Pass? Me? Jim Crow Harris? Nigger Jim Harris— become a full-fledged Member of the Bar! Why the mere notion of it is enough to kill you with laughing! It'd be against all natural laws, all human right and justice. It'd be miraculous, there'd be earthquakes and catastrophes, the seven Plagues'd come again and locusts'd devour all the money in the banks, the second Flood'd come roaring and Noah'd fall overboard, the sun'd drop out of the sky like a ripe fig, and the Devil'd perform miracles, and God'd be tipped head first right out of the Judgment seat! (*He laughs, maudlinly uproarious*).

ELLA: (*her face beginning to relax, to light up*) Then you—you didn't pass?

JIM: (*spent—giggling and gasping idiotically*) Well, I should say not! I should certainly say not!

ELLA: (*with a cry of joy, pushes all the law books crashing to the floor—then with childish happiness she grabs* JIM *by both hands and dances up and down*) Oh, Jim, I knew it! I knew you couldn't! Oh, I'm so glad, Jim! I'm so happy! You're still my old Jim—and I'm so glad! (*He looks at her dazedly, a fierce rage slowly gathering on his face. She dances away from him. His eyes follow her. His hands clench. She stands in front of the mask—triumphantly*) There! What did I tell you? I told you I'd give you the laugh! (*She begins to laugh with wild unrestraint, grabs the mask from its place, sets it in the middle of the table and plunging the knife down through it pins it to the table*) There! Who's got the laugh now?

JIM: (*his eyes bulging—hoarsely*) You devil! You white devil woman! (*In a terrible roar, raising his fists above her head*) You devil!

ELLA: (*looking up at him with a bewildered cry of terror*) Jim! (*Her appeal recalls him to himself. He lets his arms slowly drop to his sides, bowing his head.* ELLA *points tremblingly to the mask*) It's all right, Jim! It's dead. The devil's dead. See! It couldn't live—unless you passed. If you'd passed it would have lived in you. Then I'd have had to kill you, Jim, don't you see?—or it would have killed me. But now I've killed it. (*She pats his hand*) So you needn't ever be afraid any more, Jim.

JIM: (*dully*) I've got to sit down, Honey. I'm tired. I haven't had much chance for sleep in so long— (*He slumps down in the chair by the table*).

ELLA: (*sits down on the floor beside him and holds his hand. Her face is gradually regaining an expression that is happy, childlike and pretty*) I know, Jim! That was my fault. I wouldn't let you sleep. I couldn't let you. I kept thinking if he sleeps good then he'll be sure to study good and then he'll pass—and the devil'll win!

JIM: (*with a groan*) Don't, Honey!

ELLA: (*with a childish grin*) That was why I carried that knife around— (*she frowns—puzzled*)—one reason—to keep you from studying and sleeping by scaring you.

JIM: I wasn't scared of being killed. I was scared of what they'd do to you after.

ELLA: (*after a pause—like a child*) Will God forgive me, Jim?

JIM: Maybe He can forgive what you've done to me; and maybe He can forgive what I've done to you; but I don't see how He's going to forgive—Himself.

ELLA: I prayed and prayed. When you were away taking the examinations and I was alone with the nurse, I closed my eyes and pretended to be asleep but I was praying with all my might: O God, don't let Jim pass!

JIM: (*with a sob*) Don't, Honey, don't! For the good Lord's sake! You're hurting me!

ELLA: (*frightenedly*) How, Jim? Where? (*Then after a pause—suddenly*) I'm sick, Jim. I don't think I'll live long.

JIM: (*simply*) Then I won't either. Somewhere yonder maybe—together—our luck'll change. But I wanted—here and now—before you—we—I wanted to prove to you—to myself—to become a full-fledged Member—so you could be proud— (*He stops. Words fail and he is beyond tears*).

ELLA: (*brightly*) Well, it's all over, Jim. Everything'll be all right now. (*Chattering along*) I'll be just your little girl, Jim—and you'll be my little boy—just as we used to be, remember, when we were beaux; and I'll put shoe blacking on my face and pretend I'm black and you can put chalk on your face and pretend you're white just as we used to do—and we can play marbles—only you mustn't all the time be a boy. Sometimes you must be my old kind Uncle Jim who's been with us for years and years. Will you, Jim?

JIM: (*with utter resignation*) Yes, Honey.

ELLA: And you'll never, never, never, never leave me, Jim?

JIM: Never, Honey.

ELLA: 'Cause you're all I've got in the world—and I love you, Jim. (*She kisses his hand as a child might, tenderly and gratefully*).

JIM: (*suddenly throws himself on his knees and raises his shining eyes, his transfigured face*) Forgive me, God—and make me worthy! Now I see Your Light again! Now I hear Your Voice! (*He begins to weep in an ecstasy of religious humility*) Forgive me, God, for blaspheming You! Let this fire of burning suffering purify me of selfishness and make me worthy of the child You send me for the woman You take away!

ELLA: (*jumping to her feet—excitedly*) Don't cry, Jim! You mustn't cry! I've got only a little time left and I want to play. Don't be old Uncle Jim now. Be my little boy, Jim. Pretend you're Painty Face and I'm Jim Crow. Come and play!

JIM: (*still deeply exalted*) Honey, Honey, I'll play right up to the gates of Heaven with you! (*She tugs at one of his hands, laughingly trying to pull him up from his knees as*

THE CURTAIN FALLS)

Desire Under the Elms

CHARACTERS

EPHRAIM CABOT

SIMEON

PETER   } *His sons*

EBEN

ABBIE PUTNAM

Young Girl, Two Farmers, The Fiddler, A Sheriff, and other folk from the neighboring farms.

The action of the entire play takes place in, and immediately outside of, the Cabot farmhouse in New England, in the year 1850. The south end of the house faces front to a stone wall with a wooden gate at center opening on a country road. The house is in good condition but in need of paint. Its walls are a sickly grayish, the green of the shutters faded. Two enormous elms are on each side of the house. They bend their trailing branches down over the roof. They appear to protect and at the same time subdue. There is a sinister maternity in their aspect, a crushing, jealous absorption. They have developed from their intimate contact with the life of man in the house an appalling humaneness. They brood oppressively over the house. They are like exhausted women resting their sagging breasts and hands and hair on its roof, and when it rains their tears trickle down monotonously and rot on the shingles.

There is a path running from the gate around the right corner of the house to the front door. A narrow porch is on this side. The end wall facing us has two windows in its upper story, two larger ones on the floor below. The two upper are those of the father's bedroom and that of the brothers. On the left, ground floor, is the kitchen—on the right, the parlor, the shades of which are always drawn down.

128

Desire Under the Elms

Part One—Scene One

*E*XTERIOR *of the Farmhouse. It is sunset of a day at the beginning of summer in the year 1850. There is no wind and everything is still. The sky above the roof is suffused with deep colors, the green of the elms glows, but the house is in shadow, seeming pale and washed out by contrast.*

A door opens and EBEN CABOT *comes to the end of the porch and stands looking down the road to the right. He has a large bell in his hand and this he swings mechanically, awakening a deafening clangor. Then he puts his hands on his hips and stares up at the sky. He sighs with a puzzled awe and blurts out with halting appreciation.*

EBEN: God! Purty! (*His eyes fall and he stares about him frowningly. He is twenty-five, tall and sinewy. His face is well-formed, good-looking, but its expression is resentful and defensive. His defiant, dark eyes remind one of a wild animal's in captivity. Each day is a cage in which he finds himself trapped but inwardly unsubdued. There is a fierce repressed vitality about him. He has black hair, mustache, a thin curly trace of beard. He is dressed in rough farm clothes.*

He spits on the ground with intense disgust, turns and goes back into the house.

SIMEON *and* PETER *come in from their work in the fields. They are tall men, much older than their half-brother [*SIMEON *is thirty-nine and* PETER *thirty-seven], built on a squarer, simpler model, fleshier in body, more bovine and homelier in face, shrewder and more practical. Their shoulders* *stoop a bit from years of farm work. They clump heavily along in their clumsy thick-soled boots caked with earth. Their clothes, their faces, hands, bare arms and throats are earth-stained. They smell of earth. They stand together for a moment in front of the house and, as if with the one impulse, stare dumbly up at the sky, leaning on their hoes. Their faces have a compressed, unresigned expression. As they look upward, this softens).*

SIMEON: (*grudgingly*) Purty.

PETER: Ay-eh.

SIMEON: (*suddenly*) Eighteen year ago.

PETER: What?

SIMEON: Jenn. My woman. She died.

PETER: I'd fergot.

SIMEON: I rec'lect—now an' agin. Makes it lonesome. She'd hair long's a hoss' tail—an' yaller like gold!

PETER: Waal—she's gone. (*This with indifferent finality—then after a pause*) They's gold in the West, Sim.

SIMEON: (*still under the influence of sunset—vaguely*) In the sky?

PETER: Waal—in a manner o' speakin'—thar's the promise. (*Growing excited*) Gold in the sky—in the West—Golden Gate—Californi-a! —Goldest West!—fields o' gold!

SIMEON: (*excited in his turn*) Fortunes layin' just atop o' the ground waitin' t' be picked! Solomon's mines, they says! (*For a moment they continue looking up at the sky—then their eyes drop*).

PETER: (*with sardonic bitterness*) Here—it's stones atop o' the ground— stones atop o' stones—makin' stone walls—year atop o' year —him 'n' yew 'n' me 'n' then Eben—makin' stone walls fur him to fence us in!

SIMEON: We've wuked. Give our strength. Give our years. Plowed 'em under in the ground,—(*he stamps rebelliously*)—rottin'—makin' soil for his crops! (*A pause*) Waal—the farm pays good for hereabouts.

PETER: If we plowed in Californi-a, they'd be lumps o' gold in the furrow!

SIMEON: Californi-a's t'other side o' earth, a'most. We got t' calc'late—

PETER: (*after a pause*) 'Twould be hard fur me, too, to give up what we've 'arned here by our sweat. (*A pause.* EBEN *sticks his head out of the dining-room window, listening*).

SIMEON: Ay-eh. (*A pause*) Mebbe—he'll die soon.

PETER: (*doubtfully*) Mebbe.

SIMEON: Mebbe—fur all we knows—he's dead now.

PETER: Ye'd need proof.

SIMEON: He's been gone two months—with no word.

PETER: Left us in the fields an evenin' like this. Hitched up an' druv off into the West. That's plum onnateral. He hain't never been off this farm 'ceptin' t' the village in thirty year or more, not since he married Eben's maw. (*A pause. Shrewdly*) I calc'late we might git him declared crazy by the court.

SIMEON: He skinned 'em too slick. He got the best o' all on 'em. They'd never b'lieve him crazy. (*A pause*) We got t' wait—till he's under ground.

EBEN: (*with a sardonic chuckle*) Honor thy father! (*They turn, startled, and stare at him. He grins, then scowls*) I pray he's died. (*They stare at him. He continues matter-of-factly*) Supper's ready.

SIMEON *and* PETER: (*together*) Ay-eh.

EBEN: (*gazing up at the sky*) Sun's downin' purty.

SIMEON *and* PETER: (*together*) Ay-eh. They's gold in the West.

EBEN: Ay-eh. (*Pointing*) Yonder atop o' the hill pasture, ye mean?

SIMEON *and* PETER: (*together*) In Californi-a!

EBEN: Hunh? (*Stares at them indifferently for a second, then drawls*) Waal—supper's gittin' cold. (*He turns back into kitchen*).

SIMEON: (*startled—smacks his lips*) I air hungry!

PETER: (*sniffing*) I smells bacon!

SIMEON: (*with hungry appreciation*) Bacon's good!

PETER: (*in same tone*) Bacon's bacon! (*They turn, shouldering each other, their bodies bumping and rubbing together as they hurry clumsily to their food, like two friendly oxen toward their evening meal. They disappear around the right corner of house and can be heard entering the door).*

CURTAIN

Scene Two

*T*HE *color fades from the sky. Twilight begins. The interior of the kitchen is now visible. A pine table is at center, a cookstove in the right rear corner, four rough wooden chairs, a tallow candle on the table. In the middle of the rear wall is fastened a big advertising poster with a ship in full sail and the word "California" in big letters. Kitchen utensils hang from nails. Everything is neat and in order but the atmosphere is of a men's camp kitchen rather than that of a home.*

Places for three are laid. EBEN *takes boiled potatoes and bacon from the stove and puts them on the table, also a loaf of bread and a crock of water.* SIMEON *and* PETER *shoulder in, slump down in their chairs without a word.* EBEN *joins them. The three eat in silence for a moment, the two elder as naturally unrestrained as beasts of the field,* EBEN *picking at his food without appetite, glancing at them with a tolerant dislike.*

SIMEON: (*suddenly turns to* EBEN) Looky here! Ye'd oughtn't t' said that, Eben.

PETER: 'Twa'n't righteous.

EBEN: What?

SIMEON: Ye prayed he'd died.

EBEN: Waal—don't yew pray it? (*A pause*).

PETER: He's our Paw.

EBEN: (*violently*) Not mine!

SIMEON: (*dryly*) Ye'd not let no one else say that about yer Maw! Ha!
   (*He gives one abrupt sardonic guffaw.* PETER *grins*).

EBEN: (*very pale*) I meant—I hain't his'n—I hain't like him—he hain't me!

PETER: (*dryly*) Wait till ye've growed his age!

EBEN: (*intensely*) I'm Maw—every drop o' blood! (*A pause. They stare at him with indifferent curiosity*).

PETER: (*reminiscently*) She was good t' Sim 'n' me. A good Stepmaw's scurse.

SIMEON: She was good t' everyone.

EBEN: (*greatly moved, gets to his feet and makes an awkward bow to each of them—stammering*) I be thankful t' ye. I'm her—her heir. (*He sits down in confusion*).

PETER: (*after a pause—judicially*) She was good even t' him.

EBEN: (*fiercely*) An' fur thanks he killed her!

SIMEON: (*after a pause*) No one never kills nobody. It's allus somethin'. That's the murderer.

EBEN: Didn't he slave Maw t' death?

PETER: He's slaved himself t' death. He's slaved Sim 'n' me 'n' yew t' death—on'y none o' us hain't died—yit.

SIMEON: It's somethin'—drivin' him—t' drive us!

EBEN: (*vengefully*) Waal—I hold him t' jedgment! (*Then scornfully*) Somethin'? What's somethin'?

SIMEON: Dunno.

EBEN: (*sardonically*) What's drivin' yew to Californi-a, mebbe? (*They look at him in surprise*) Oh, I've heerd ye! (*Then, after a pause*) But ye'll never go t' the gold fields!

PETER: (*assertively*) Mebbe!

EBEN: Whar'll ye git the money?

PETER: We kin walk. It's an a'mighty ways—Californi-a—but if yew was t' put all the steps we've walked on this farm end t' end we'd be in the moon!

EBEN: The Injuns'll skulp ye on the plains.

SIMEON: (*with grim humor*) We'll mebbe make 'em pay a hair fur a hair!

EBEN: (*decisively*) But t'aint that. Ye won't never go because ye'll wait here fur yer share o' the farm, thinkin' allus he'll die soon.

SIMEON: (*after a pause*) We've a right.

PETER: Two-thirds belongs t'us.

EBEN: (*jumping to his feet*) Ye've no right! She wa'n't yewr Maw! It was her farm! Didn't he steal it from her? She's dead. It's my farm.

SIMEON: (*sardonically*) Tell that t' Paw—when he comes! I'll bet ye a dollar he'll laugh—fur once in his life. Ha! (*He laughs himself in one single mirthless bark*).

PETER: (*amused in turn, echoes his brother*) Ha!

SIMEON: (*after a pause*) What've ye got held agin us, Eben? Year arter year it's skulked in yer eye—somethin'.

PETER: Ay-eh.

EBEN: Ay-eh. They's somethin'. (*Suddenly exploding*) Why didn't ye never stand between him 'n' my Maw when he was slavin' her to her grave—t' pay her back fur the kindness she done t' yew? (*There is a long pause. They stare at him in surprise*).

SIMEON: Waal—the stock'd got t' be watered.

PETER: 'R they was woodin' t' do.

SIMEON: 'R plowin'.

PETER: 'R hayin'.

SIMEON: 'R spreadin' manure.

PETER: 'R weedin'.

SIMEON: 'R prunin'.

PETER: 'R milkin'.

EBEN: (*breaking in harshly*) An' makin' walls—stone atop o' stone—makin' walls till yer heart's a stone ye heft up out o' the way o' growth onto a stone wall t' wall in yer heart!

SIMEON: (*matter-of-factly*) We never had no time t' meddle.

PETER: (*to EBEN*) Yew was fifteen afore yer Maw died—an' big fur yer age. Why didn't ye never do nothin'?

EBEN: (*harshly*) They was chores t' do, wa'n't they? (*A pause—then slowly*) It was on'y arter she died I come to think o' it. Me cookin'—

doin' her work—that made me know her, suffer her sufferin'—she'd come back t' help—come back t' bile potatoes—come back t' fry bacon—come back t' bake biscuits—come back all cramped up t' shake the fire, an' carry ashes, her eyes weepin' an' bloody with smoke an' cinders same's they used t' be. She still comes back—stands by the stove thar in the evenin'—she can't find it nateral sleepin' an' restin' in peace. She can't git used t' bein' free—even in her grave.

SIMEON: She never complained none.

EBEN: She'd got too tired. She'd got too used t' bein' too tired. That was what he done. (*With vengeful passion*) An' sooner'r later, I'll meddle. I'll say the thin's I didn't say then t' him! I'll yell 'em at the top o' my lungs. I'll see t' it my Maw gits some rest an' sleep in her grave! (*He sits down again, relapsing into a brooding silence. They look at him with a queer indifferent curiosity*).

PETER: (*after a pause*) Whar in tarnation d'ye s'pose he went, Sim?

SIMEON: Dunno. He druv off in the buggy, all spick an' span, with the mare all breshed an' shiny, druv off clackin' his tongue an' wavin' his whip. I remember it right well. I was finishin' plowin', it was spring an' May an' sunset, an' gold in the West, an' he druv off into it. I yells "Whar ye goin', Paw?" an' he hauls up by the stone wall a jiffy. His old snake's eyes was glitterin' in the sun like he'd been drinkin' a jugful an' he says with a mule's grin: "Don't ye run away till I come back!"

PETER: Wonder if he knowed we was wantin' fur Californi-a?

SIMEON: Mebbe. I didn't say nothin' and he says, lookin' kinder queer an' sick: "I been hearin' the hens cluckin' an' the roosters crowin' all the durn day. I been listenin' to the cows lowin' an' everythin' else kickin' up till I can't stand it no more. It's spring an' I'm feelin' damned," he says. "Damned like an old bare hickory tree fit on'y fur burnin'," he says. An' then I calc'late I must've looked a mite hopeful, fur he adds real spry and vicious: "But don't git no fool idee I'm dead. I've sworn t' live a hundred an' I'll do it, if on'y t' spite yer sinful greed! An' now I'm ridin' out t' learn God's message t' me in the spring, like the prophets done. An' yew git back t' yer plowin'," he says. An' he druv off singin' a hymn. I thought he was drunk—'r I'd stopped him goin'.

EBEN: (*scornfully*) No, ye wouldn't! Ye're scared o' him. He's stronger—inside—than both o' ye put together!

PETER: (*sardonically*) An' yew—be yew Samson?

EBEN: I'm gittin' stronger. I kin feel it growin' in me—growin' an' growin'—till it'll bust out—! (*He gets up and puts on his coat and a hat. They watch him, gradually breaking into grins. EBEN avoids their eyes sheepishly*) I'm goin' out fur a spell—up the road.

PETER: T' the village?

SIMEON: T' see Minnie?

EBEN: (*defiantly*) Ay-eh!

PETER: (*jeeringly*) The Scarlet Woman!

SIMEON: Lust—that's what's growin' in ye!

EBEN: Waal—she's purty!

PETER: She's been purty fur twenty year!

SIMEON: A new coat o' paint'll make a heifer out of forty.

EBEN: She hain't forty!

PETER: If she hain't, she's teeterin' on the edge.

EBEN: (*desperately*) What d'yew know—

PETER: All they is . . . Sim knew her—an' then me arter—

SIMEON: An' Paw kin tell yew somethin' too! He was fust!

EBEN: D'ye mean t' say he . . . ?

SIMEON: (*with a grin*) Ay-eh! We air his heirs in everythin'!

EBEN: (*intensely*) That's more to it! That grows on it! It'll bust soon! (*Then violently*) I'll go smash my fist in her face! (*He pulls open the door in rear violently*).

SIMEON: (*with a wink at* PETER—*drawlingly*) Mebbe—but the night's wa'm—purty—by the time ye git thar mebbe ye'll kiss her instead!

PETER: Sart'n he will! (*They both roar with coarse laughter.* EBEN *rushes out and slams the door—then the outside front door—comes around the corner of the house and stands still by the gate, staring up at the sky*).

SIMEON: (*looking after him*) Like his Paw.

PETER: Dead spit an' image!

SIMEON: Dog'll eat dog!

PETER: Ay-eh. (*Pause. With yearning*) Mebbe a year from now we'll be in Californi-a.

SIMEON: Ay-eh. (*A pause. Both yawn*) Let's git t'bed. (*He blows out the candle. They go out door in rear.* EBEN *stretches his arms up to the sky— rebelliously*).

EBEN: Waal—thar's a star, an' somewhar's they's him, an' here's me, an' thar's Min up the road—in the same night. What if I does kiss her? She's like t'night, she's soft 'n' wa'm, her eyes kin wink like a star, her mouth's wa'm, her arms're wa'm, she smells like a wa'm plowed field, she's purty . . . Ay-eh! By God A'mighty she's purty, an' I don't give a damn how many sins she's sinned afore mine or who she's sinned 'em with, my sin's as purty as any one on 'em! (*He strides off down the road to the left*).

Scene Three

*I*T *is the pitch darkness just before dawn.* EBEN *comes in from the left and goes around to the porch, feeling his way, chuckling bitterly and cursing half-aloud to himself.*

EBEN: The cussed old miser! (*He can be heard going in the front door. There is a pause as he goes upstairs, then a loud knock on the bedroom door of the brothers*) Wake up!

SIMEON: (*startedly*) Who's thar?

EBEN: (*pushing open the door and coming in, a lighted candle in his hand. The bedroom of the brothers is revealed. Its ceiling is the sloping roof. They can stand upright only close to the center dividing wall of the upstairs.* SIMEON *and* PETER *are in a double bed, front.* EBEN'S *cot is to the rear.* EBEN *has a mixture of silly grin and vicious scowl on his face*) I be!

PETER: (*angrily*) What in hell's-fire . . . ?

EBEN: I got news fur ye! Ha! (*He gives one abrupt sardonic guffaw*).

SIMEON: (*angrily*) Couldn't ye hold it 'til we'd got our sleep?

EBEN: It's nigh sunup. (*Then explosively*) He's gone an' married agen!

SIMEON *and* PETER: (*explosively*) Paw?

EBEN: Got himself hitched to a female 'bout thirty-five—an' purty, they says . . .

SIMEON: (*aghast*) It's a durn lie!

PETER: Who says?

SIMEON: They been stringin' ye!

EBEN: Think I'm a dunce, do ye? The hull village says. The preacher from New Dover, he brung the news—told it t'our preacher —New Dover, that's whar the old loon got himself hitched—that's whar the woman lived—

PETER: (*no longer doubting—stunned*) Waal . . . !

SIMEON: (*the same*) Waal . . . !

EBEN: (*sitting down on a bed—with vicious hatred*) Ain't he a devil out o' hell? It's jest t' spite us—the damned old mule!

PETER: (*after a pause*) Everythin'll go t' her now.

SIMEON: Ay-eh. (*A pause—dully*) Waal—if it's done—

PETER: It's done us. (Pause—then persuasively) They's gold in the fields o' Californi-a, Sim. No good a-stayin' here now.

SIMEON: Jest what I was a-thinkin'. (*Then with decision*) S'well fust's last! Let's light out and git this mornin'.

PETER: Suits me.

EBEN: Ye must like walkin'.

SIMEON: (*sardonically*) If ye'd grow wings on us we'd fly thar!

EBEN: Ye'd like ridin' better—on a boat, wouldn't ye? (*Fumbles in his pocket and takes out a crumpled sheet of foolscap*) Waal, if ye sign this ye kin ride on a boat. I've had it writ out an' ready in case ye'd ever go. It says fur three hundred dollars t' each ye agree yewr shares o' the farm is sold t' me. (*They look suspiciously at the paper. A pause*).

SIMEON: (*wonderingly*) But if he's hitched agen—

PETER: An' whar'd yew git that sum o' money, anyways?

EBEN: (*cunningly*) I know whar it's hid. I been waitin'—Maw told me. She knew whar it lay fur years, but she was waitin' . . . It's her'n—the money he hoarded from her farm an' hid from Maw. It's my money by rights now.

PETER: Whar's it hid?

EBEN: (*cunningly*) Whar yew won't never find it without me. Maw spied on him—'r she'd never knowed. (*A pause. They look at him suspiciously, and he at them*) Waal, is it fa'r trade?

SIMEON: Dunno.

PETER: Dunno.

SIMEON: (*looking at window*) Sky's grayin'.

PETER: Ye better start the fire, Eben.

SIMEON: An' fix some vittles.

EBEN: Ay-eh. (*Then with a forced jocular heartiness*) I'll git ye a good one. If ye're startin' t' hoof it t' Californi-a ye'll need somethin' that'll stick t' yer ribs. (*He turns to the door, adding meaningly*) But ye kin ride on a boat if ye'll swap. (*He stops at the door and pauses. They stare at him*).

SIMEON: (*suspiciously*) Whar was ye all night?

EBEN: (*defiantly*) Up t' Min's. (*Then slowly*) Walkin' thar, fust I felt 's if I'd kiss her; then I got a-thinkin' o' what ye'd said o' him an' her an' I says, I'll bust her nose fur that! Then I got t' the village an' heerd the news an' I got madder'n hell an' run all the way t' Min's not knowin' what I'd do— (*He pauses—then sheepishly but more defiantly*) Waal—when I seen her, I didn't hit her—nor I didn't kiss her nuther—I begun t' beller like a calf an' cuss at the same time, I was so durn mad—an' she got scared—an' I jest grabbed holt an' tuk her! (*Proudly*) Yes, sirree! I tuk her. She may've been his'n—an' your'n, too—but she's mine now!

SIMEON: (*dryly*) In love, air yew?

EBEN: (*with lofty scorn*) Love! I don't take no stock in sech slop!

PETER: (*winking at* SIMEON) Mebbe Eben's aimin' t' marry, too.

SIMEON: Min'd make a true faithful he'pmeet! (*They snicker*).

EBEN: What do I care fur her—'ceptin' she's round an' wa'm? The p'int is she was his'n—an' now she b'longs t' me! (*He goes to the door— then turns—rebelliously*) An' Min hain't sech a bad un. They's worse'n Min in the world, I'll bet ye! Wait'll we see this cow the Old Man's hitched t'! She'll beat Min, I got a notion! (*He starts to go out*).

SIMEON: (*suddenly*) Mebbe ye'll try t' make her your'n, too?

PETER: Ha! (*He gives a sardonic laugh of relish at this idea*).

EBEN: (*spitting with disgust*) Her—here—sleepin' with him— stealin' my Maw's farm! I'd as soon pet a skunk 'r kiss a snake! (*He goes out. The two stare after him suspiciously. A pause. They listen to his steps receding*).

PETER: He's startin' the fire.

SIMEON: I'd like t' ride t' Californi-a—but—

PETER: Min might o' put some scheme in his head.

SIMEON: Mebbe it's all a lie 'bout Paw marryin'. We'd best wait an' see the bride.

PETER: An' don't sign nothin' till we does!

SIMEON: Nor till we've tested it's good money! (*Then with a grin*) But if Paw's hitched we'd be sellin' Eben somethin' we'd never git nohow!

PETER: We'll wait an' see. (*Then with sudden vindictive anger*) An' till he comes, let's yew 'n' me not wuk a lick, let Eben tend to thin's if he's a mind t', let's us jest sleep an' eat an' drink likker, an' let the hull damned farm go t' blazes!

SIMEON: (*excitedly*) By God, we've 'arned a rest! We'll play rich fur a change. I hain't a-going to stir outa bed till breakfast's ready.

PETER: An' on the table!

SIMEON: (*after a pause—thoughtfully*) What d'ye calc'late she'll be like— our new Maw? Like Eben thinks?

PETER: More 'n' likely.

SIMEON: (*vindictively*) Waal—I hope she's a she-devil that'll make him wish he was dead an' livin' in the pit o' hell fur comfort!

PETER: (*fervently*) Amen!

SIMEON: (*imitating his father's voice*) "I'm ridin' out t' learn God's message t' me in the spring like the prophets done," he says. I'll bet right then an' thar he knew plumb well he was goin' whorin', the stinkin' old hypocrite!

Scene Four

*S*AME *as Scene Two—shows the interior of the kitchen with a lighted candle on table. It is gray dawn outside.* SIMEON *and* PETER *are just finishing their breakfast.* EBEN *sits before his plate of untouched food, brooding frowningly.*

PETER: (*glancing at him rather irritably*) Lookin' glum don't help none.

SIMEON: (*sarcastically*) Sorrowin' over his lust o' the flesh!

PETER: (*with a grin*) Was she yer fust?

EBEN: (*angrily*) None o' yer business. (*A pause*) I was thinkin' o' him. I got a notion he's gittin' near—I kin feel him comin' on like yew kin feel malaria chill afore it takes ye.

PETER: It's too early yet.

SIMEON: Dunno. He'd like t' catch us nappin'—jest t' have somethin' t' hoss us 'round over.

PETER: (*mechanically gets to his feet.* SIMEON *does the same*) Waal—let's git t' wuk. (*They both plod mechanically toward the door before they realize. Then they stop short*).

SIMEON: (*grinning*) Ye're a cussed fool, Pete—and I be wuss! Let him see we hain't wukin'! We don't give a durn!

PETER: (*as they go back to the table*) Not a damned durn! It'll serve t' show him we're done with him. (*They sit down again.* EBEN *stares from one to the other with surprise*).

SIMEON: (*grins at him*) We're aimin' t' start bein' lilies o' the field.

PETER: Nary a toil 'r spin 'r lick o' wuk do we put in!

SIMEON: Ye're sole owner—till he comes—that's what ye wanted. Waal, ye got t' be sole hand, too.

PETER: The cows air bellerin'. Ye better hustle at the milkin'.

EBEN: (*with excited joy*) Ye mean ye'll sign the paper?

SIMEON: (*dryly*) Mebbe.

PETER: Mebbe.

SIMEON: We're considerin'. (*Peremptorily*) Ye better git t' wuk.

EBEN: (*with queer excitement*) It's Maw's farm agen! It's my farm! Them's my cows! I'll milk my durn fingers off fur cows o' mine! (*He goes out door in rear, they stare after him indifferently*).

SIMEON: Like his Paw.

PETER: Dead spit 'n' image!

SIMEON: Waal—let dog eat dog! (EBEN *comes out of front door and around the corner of the house. The sky is beginning to grow flushed with sunrise.* EBEN *stops by the gate and stares around him with glowing, possessive eyes. He takes in the whole farm with his embracing glance of desire*).

EBEN: It's purty! It's damned purty! It's mine! (*He suddenly throws his head back boldly and glares with hard, defiant eyes at the sky*) Mine, d'ye hear? Mine! (*He turns and walks quickly off left, rear, toward the barn. The two brothers light their pipes*).

SIMEON: (*putting his muddy boots up on the table, tilting back his chair, and puffing defiantly*) Waal—this air solid comfort—fur once.

PETER: Ay-eh. (*He follows suit. A pause. Unconsciously they both sigh*).

SIMEON: (*suddenly*) He never was much o' a hand at milkin', Eben wa'n't.

PETER: (*with a snort*) His hands air like hoofs! (*A pause*).

SIMEON: Reach down the jug thar! Let's take a swaller. I'm feelin' kind o' low.

PETER: Good idee! (*He does so—gets two glasses—they pour out drinks of whisky*) Here's t' the gold in Californi-a!

SIMEON: An' luck t' find it! (*They drink—puff resolutely—sigh—take their feet down from the table*).

PETER: Likker don't 'pear t' sot right.

SIMEON: We hain't used t' it this early. (*A pause. They become very restless*).

PETER: Gittin' close in this kitchen.

SIMEON: (*with immense relief*) Let's git a breath o' air. (*They arise briskly and go out rear—appear around house and stop by the gate. They stare up at the sky with a numbed appreciation*).

PETER: Purty!

SIMEON: Ay-eh. Gold's t' the East now.

PETER: Sun's startin' with us fur the Golden West.

SIMEON: (*staring around the farm, his compressed face tightened, unable to conceal his emotion*) Waal—it's our last mornin'—mebbe.

PETER: (*the same*) Ay-eh.

SIMEON: (*stamps his foot on the earth and addresses it desperately*) Waal—ye've thirty year o' me buried in ye—spread out over ye—blood an' bone an' sweat—rotted away—fertilizin' ye—richin' yer soul—prime manure, by God, that's what I been t' ye!

PETER: Ay-eh! An' me!

SIMEON: An' yew, Peter. (*He sighs—then spits*) Waal—no use'n cryin' over spilt milk.

PETER: They's gold in the West—an' freedom, mebbe. We been slaves t' stone walls here.

SIMEON: (*defiantly*) We hain't nobody's slaves from this out—nor no thin's slaves nuther. (*A pause—restlessly*) Speakin' o' milk, wonder how Eben's managin'?

PETER: I s'pose he's managin'.

SIMEON: Mebbe we'd ought t' help—this once.

PETER: Mebbe. The cows knows us.

SIMEON: An' likes us. They don't know him much.

PETER: An' the hosses, an' pigs, an' chickens. They don't know him much.

SIMEON: They knows us like brothers—an' likes us! (*Proudly*). Hain't we raised 'em t' be fust-rate, number one prize stock?

PETER: We hain't—not no more.

SIMEON: (*dully*) I was fergittin'. (*Then resignedly*) Waal, let's go help Eben a spell an' git waked up.

PETER: Suits me. (*They are starting off down left, rear, for the barn when* EBEN *appears from there hurrying toward them, his face excited*).

EBEN: (*breathlessly*) Waal—har they be! The old mule an' the bride! I seen 'em from the barn down below at the turnin'.

PETER: How could ye tell that far?

EBEN: Hain't I as far-sight as he's near-sight? Don't I know the mare 'n' buggy, an' two people settin' in it? Who else . . . ? An' I tell ye I kin feel 'em a-comin', too! (*He squirms as if he had the itch*).

PETER: (*beginning to be angry*) Waal—let him do his own unhitchin'!

SIMEON: (*angry in his turn*) Let's hustle in an' git our bundles an' be a-goin' as he's a-comin'. I don't want never t' step inside the door agen arter he's back. (*They both start back around the corner of the house.* EBEN *follows them*).

EBEN: (*anxiously*) Will ye sign it afore ye go?

PETER: Let's see the color o' the old skinflint's money an' we'll sign. (*They disappear left. The two brothers clump upstairs to get their bundles. EBEN appears in the kitchen, runs to window, peers out, comes back and pulls up a strip of flooring in under stove, takes out a canvas bag and puts it on table, then sets the floorboard back in place. The two brothers appear a moment after. They carry old carpet bags*).

EBEN: (*puts his hand on bag guardingly*) Have ye signed?

SIMEON: (*shows paper in his hand*) Ay-eh. (*Greedily*) Be that the money?

EBEN: (*opens bag and pours out pile of twenty-dollar gold pieces*) Twenty-dollar pieces—thirty on 'em. Count 'em. (*Peter does so, arranging them in stacks of five, biting one or two to test them*).

PETER: Six hundred. (*He puts them in bag and puts it inside his shirt carefully*).

SIMEON: (*handing paper to EBEN*) Har ye be.

EBEN: (*after a glance, folds it carefully and hides it under his shirt—gratefully*) Thank yew.

PETER: Thank yew fur the ride.

SIMEON: We'll send ye a lump o' gold fur Christmas. (*A pause. EBEN stares at them and they at him*).

PETER: (*awkwardly*) Waal—we're a-goin'.

SIMEON: Comin' out t' the yard?

EBEN: No. I'm waitin' in here a spell. (*Another silence. The brothers edge awkwardly to door in rear—then turn and stand*).

SIMEON: Waal—good-by.

PETER: Good-by.

EBEN: Good-by. (*They go out. He sits down at the table, faces the stove and pulls out the paper. He looks from it to the stove. His face, lighted up by the shaft of sunlight from the window, has an expression of trance. His lips move. The two brothers come out to the gate*).

PETER: (*looking off toward barn*) Thar he be—unhitchin'.

SIMEON: (*with a chuckle*) I'll bet ye he's riled!

PETER: An' thar she be.

SIMEON: Let's wait 'n' see what our new Maw looks like.

PETER: (*with a grin*) An' give him our partin' cuss!

SIMEON: (*grinning*) I feel like raisin' fun. I feel light in my head an' feet.

PETER: Me, too. I feel like laffin' till I'd split up the middle.

SIMEON: Reckon it's the likker?

PETER: No. My feet feel itchin' t' walk an' walk—an' jump high over thin's—an' . . . .

SIMEON: Dance? (*A pause*).

PETER: (*puzzled*) It's plumb onnateral.

SIMEON: (*a light coming over his face*) I calc'late it's 'cause school's out. It's holiday. Fur once we're free!

PETER: (*dazedly*) Free?

SIMEON: The halter's broke—the harness is busted—the fence bars is down—the stone walls air crumblin' an' tumblin'! We'll be kickin' up an' tearin' away down the road!

PETER: (*drawing a deep breath—oratorically*) Anybody that wants this stinkin' old rock-pile of a farm kin hev it. T'ain't our'n, no sirree!

SIMEON: (*takes the gate off its hinges and puts it under his arm*) We harby 'bolishes shet gates, an' open gates, an' all gates, by thunder!

PETER: We'll take it with us fur luck an' let 'er sail free down some river.

SIMEON: (*as a sound of voices comes from left, rear*) Har they comes! (*The two brothers congeal into two stiff, grim-visaged statues. EPHRAIM CABOT and ABBIE PUTNAM come in. CABOT is seventy-five, tall and gaunt, with great, wiry, concentrated power, but stoop-shouldered from toil. His face is as hard as if it were hewn out of a boulder, yet there is a weakness in it, a petty pride in its own narrow strength. His eyes are small, close together, and extremely near-sighted, blinking continually in the effort to focus on objects, their stare having a straining, ingrowing quality. He is dressed in his dismal black Sunday suit. ABBIE is thirty-five, buxom, full of vitality. Her round face is pretty but marred by its rather gross sensuality. There is strength and obstinacy in her jaw, a hard determination in her eyes, and about her whole personality the same unsettled, untamed, desperate quality which is so apparent in EBEN*).

CABOT: (*as they enter—a queer strangled emotion in his dry cracking voice*) Har we be t' hum, Abbie.

ABBIE: (*with lust for the word*) Hum! (*Her eyes gloating on the house without seeming to see the two stiff figures at the gate*) It's purty—purty! I can't b'lieve it's r'ally mine.

CABOT: (*sharply*) Yewr'n? Mine! (*He stares at her penetratingly. She stares back. He adds relentingly*) Our'n—mebbe! It was lonesome too long. I was growin' old in the spring. A hum's got t' hev a woman.

ABBIE: (*her voice taking possession*) A woman's got t' hev a hum!

CABOT: (*nodding uncertainly*) Ay-eh. (*Then irritably*) Whar be they? Ain't thar nobody about—'r wukin'—r' nothin'?

ABBIE: (*sees the brothers. She returns their stare of cold appraising contempt with interest—slowly*) Thar's two men loafin' at the gate an' starin' at me like a couple o' strayed hogs.

CABOT: (*straining his eyes*) I kin see 'em—but I can't make out . . . .

SIMEON: It's Simeon.

PETER: It's Peter.

CABOT: (*exploding*) Why hain't ye wukin'?

SIMEON: (*dryly*) We're waitin' t' welcome ye hum—yew an' the bride!

CABOT: (*confusedly*) Huh? Waal—this be yer new Maw, boys. (*She stares at them and they at her*).

SIMEON: (*turns away and spits contemptuously*) I see her!

PETER: (*spits also*) An' I see her!

ABBIE: (*with the conqueror's conscious superiority*) I'll go in an' look at *my* house. (*She goes slowly around to porch*).

SIMEON: (*with a snort*) Her house!

PETER: (*calls after her*) Ye'll find Eben inside. Ye better not tell him it's *yewr* house.

ABBIE: (*mouthing the name*) Eben. (*Then quietly*) I'll tell Eben.

CABOT: (*with a contemptuous sneer*) Ye needn't heed Eben. Eben's a dumb fool—like his Maw—soft an' simple!

SIMEON: (*with his sardonic burst of laughter*) Ha! Eben's a chip o' yew—

spit 'n' image—hard 'n' bitter's a hickory tree! Dog'll eat dog. He'll eat ye yet, old man!

CABOT: (*commandingly*) Ye git t' wuk!

SIMEON: (*as* ABBIE *disappears in house—winks at* PETER *and says tauntingly*) So that thar's our new Maw, be it? Whar in hell did ye dig her up? (*He and* PETER *laugh*).

PETER: Ha! Ye'd better turn her in the pen with the other sows. (*They laugh uproariously, slapping their thighs*).

CABOT: (*so amazed at their effrontery that he stutters in confusion*) Simeon! Peter! What's come over ye? Air ye drunk?

SIMEON: We're free, old man—free o' yew an' the hull damned farm! (*They grow more and more hilarious and excited*).

PETER: An' we're startin' out fur the gold fields o' Californi-a!

SIMEON: Ye kin take this place an' burn it!

PETER: An' bury it—fur all we cares!

SIMEON: We're free, old man! (*He cuts a caper*).

PETER: Free! (*He gives a kick in the air*).

SIMEON: (*in a frenzy*) Whoop!

PETER: Whoop! (*They do an absurd Indian war dance about the old man who is petrified between rage and the fear that they are insane*).

SIMEON: We're free as Injuns! Lucky we don't skulp ye!

PETER: An' burn yer barn an' kill the stock!

SIMEON: An' rape yer new woman! Whoop! (*He and* PETER *stop their dance, holding their sides, rocking with wild laughter*).

CABOT: (*edging away*) Lust fur gold—fur the sinful, easy gold o' Californi-a! It's made ye mad!

SIMEON: (*tauntingly*) Wouldn't ye like us to send ye back some sinful gold, ye old sinner?

PETER: They's gold besides what's in Californi-a! (*He retreats back beyond the vision of the old man and takes the bag of money and flaunts it in the air above his head, laughing*).

SIMEON: And sinfuller, too!

PETER: We'll be voyagin' on the sea! Whoop! (*He leaps up and down*).

SIMEON: Livin' free! Whoop! (*He leaps in turn*).

CABOT: (*suddenly roaring with rage*) My cuss on ye!

SIMEON: Take our'n in trade fur it! Whoop!

CABOT: I'll hev ye both chained up in the asylum!

PETER: Ye old skinflint! Good-by!

SIMEON: Ye old blood sucker! Good-by!

CABOT: Go afore I . . . !

PETER: Whoop! (*He picks a stone from the road.* SIMEON *does the same*).

SIMEON: Maw'll be in the parlor.

PETER: Ay-eh! One! Two!

CABOT: (*frightened*) What air ye . . . ?

PETER: Three! (*They both throw, the stones hitting the parlor window with a crash of glass, tearing the shade*).

SIMEON: Whoop!

PETER: Whoop!

CABOT: (*in a fury now, rushing toward them*) If I kin lay hands on ye— I'll break yer bones fur ye! (*But they beat a capering retreat before him,* SIMEON *with the gate still under his arm.* CABOT *comes back, panting with impotent rage. Their voices as they go off take up the song of the gold-seekers to the old tune of "Oh, Susannah!"*)

> "I jumped aboard the Liza ship,
> And traveled on the sea,
> And every time I thought of home
> I wished it wasn't me!
> Oh! Californi-a,
> That's the land fur me!
> I'm off to Californi-a!
> With my wash bowl on my knee."

(*In the meantime, the window of the upper bedroom on right is raised and* ABBIE *sticks her head out. She looks down at* CABOT— *with a sigh of relief*).

ABBIE: Waal—that's the last o' them two, hain't it? (*He doesn't answer. Then in possessive tones*) This here's a nice bedroom, Ephraim. It's a r'al nice bed. Is it my room, Ephraim?

CABOT: (*grimly—without looking up*) Our'n! (*She cannot control a grimace of aversion and pulls back her head slowly and shuts the window. A sudden horrible thought seems to enter* CABOT's *head*) They been up to some-thin'! Mebbe—mebbe they've pizened the stock—'r somethin'! (*He almost runs off down toward the barn. A moment later the kitchen door is slowly pushed open and* ABBIE *enters. For a moment she stands looking at* EBEN. *He does not notice her at first. Her eyes take him in penetratingly with a calculating appraisal of his strength as against hers. But under this her desire is dimly awakened by his youth and good looks. Suddenly he becomes conscious of her presence and looks up. Their eyes meet. He leaps to his feet, glowering at her speechlessly*).

ABBIE: (*in her most seductive tones which she uses all through this scene*) Be you—Eben? I'm Abbie— (*She laughs*) I mean, I'm yer new Maw.

EBEN: (*viciously*) No, damn ye!

ABBIE: (*as if she hadn't heard—with a queer smile*) Yer Paw's spoke a lot o' yew . . . .

EBEN: Ha!

ABBIE: Ye mustn't mind him. He's an old man. (*A long pause. They stare at each other*) I don't want t' pretend playin' Maw t' ye, Eben. (*Ad-miringly*) Ye're too big an' too strong fur that. I want t' be frens with ye. Mebbe with me fur a fren ye'd find ye'd like livin' here better. I kin make it easy fur ye with him, mebbe. (*With a scornful sense of power*) I calc'late I kin git him t' do most anythin' fur me.

EBEN: (*with bitter scorn*) Ha! (*They stare again,* EBEN *obscurely moved, physically attracted to her—in forced stilted tones*) Yew kin go t' the devil!

ABBIE: (*calmly*) If cussin' me does ye good, cuss all ye've a mind t'. I'm all prepared t' have ye agin me—at fust. I don't blame ye nuther. I'd feel the same at any stranger comin' t' take my Maw's place. (*He shudders. She is watching him carefully*) Yew must've cared a lot fur yewr Maw, didn't ye? My Maw died afore I'd growed. I don't re-member her none. (*A pause*) But yew won't hate me long, Eben. I'm not the wust in the world—an' yew an' me've got a lot in common. I kin tell that by lookin' at ye. Waal—I've had a hard life, too—

oceans o' trouble an' nuthin' but wuk fur reward. I was a orphan early an' had t' wuk fur others in other folks' hums. Then I married an' he turned out a drunken spreer an' so he had to wuk fur others an' me too agen in other folks' hums, an' the baby died, an' my husband got sick an' died too, an' I was glad sayin' now I'm free fur once, on'y I diskivered right away all I was free fur was t' wuk agen in other folks' hums, doin' other folks' wuk till I'd most give up hope o' ever doin' my own wuk in my own hum, an' then your Paw come. . . . (*Cabot appears returning from the barn. He comes to the gate and looks down the road the brothers have gone. A faint strain of their retreating voices is heard: "Oh, Californi-a! That's the place for me." He stands glowering, his fist clenched, his face grim with rage*).

EBEN: (*fighting against his growing attraction and sympathy— harshly*) An' bought yew—like a harlot! (*She is stung and flushes angrily. She has been sincerely moved by the recital of her troubles. He adds furiously*) An' the price he's payin' ye—this farm—was my Maw's, damn ye!—an' mine now!

ABBIE: (*with a cool laugh of confidence*) Yewr'n? We'll see 'bout that! (*Then strongly*) Waal—what if I did need a hum? What else'd I marry an old man like him fur?

EBEN: (*maliciously*) I'll tell him ye said that!

ABBIE: (*smiling*) I'll say ye're lyin' a-purpose—an' he'll drive ye off the place!

EBEN: Ye devil!

ABBIE: (*defying him*) This be my farm—this be my hum—this be my kitchen—!

EBEN: (*furiously, as if he were going to attack her*) Shut up, damn ye!

ABBIE: (*walks up to him—a queer coarse expression of desire in her face and body—slowly*) An' upstairs—that be my bedroom—an' my bed! (*He stares into her eyes, terribly confused and torn. She adds softly*) I hain't bad nor mean—'ceptin' fur an enemy—but I got t' fight fur what's due me out o' life, if I ever 'spect t' git it. (*Then putting her hand on his arm—seductively*) Let's yew 'n' me be frens, Eben.

EBEN: (*stupidly—as if hypnotized*) Ay-eh. (*Then furiously flinging off her arm*) No, ye durned old witch! I hate ye! (*He rushes out the door*).

ABBIE: (*looks after him smiling satisfiedly—then half to herself, mouthing the word*) Eben's nice. (*She looks at the table, proudly*) I'll wash up *my* dishes now. (EBEN *appears outside, slamming the door behind him. He comes around corner, stops on seeing his father, and stands staring at him with hate*).

CABOT: (*raising his arms to heaven in the fury he can no longer control*) Lord God o' Hosts, smite the undutiful sons with Thy wust cuss!

EBEN: (*breaking in violently*) Yew 'n' yewr God! Allus cussin' folks—allus naggin' 'em!

CABOT: (*oblivious to him—summoningly*) God o' the old! God o' the lonesome!

EBEN: (*mockingly*) Naggin' His sheep t' sin! T' hell with yewr God! (CABOT *turns. He and* EBEN *glower at each other*).

CABOT: (*harshly*) So it's yew. I might've knowed it. (*Shaking his finger threateningly at him*) Blasphemin' fool! (*Then quickly*) Why hain't ye t' wuk?

EBEN: Why hain't yew? They've went. I can't wuk it all alone.

CABOT: (*contemptuously*) Nor noways! I'm wuth ten o' ye yit, old's I be! Ye'll never be more'n half a man! (*Then, matter-of-factly*) Waal—let's git t' the barn. (*They go. A last faint note of the "Californi-a" song is heard from the distance.* ABBIE *is washing her dishes*).

CURTAIN

*T*HE *exterior of the farmhouse, as in Part One—a hot Sunday afternoon two months later.* ABBIE, *dressed in her best, is discovered sitting in a rocker at the end of the porch. She rocks listlessly, enervated by the heat, staring in front of her with bored, half-closed eyes.*

EBEN *sticks his head out of his bedroom window. He looks around furtively and tries to see—or hear—if anyone is on the porch, but although he has been careful to make no noise,* ABBIE *has sensed his movement. She stops rocking, her face grows animated and eager, she waits attentively.* EBEN *seems to feel her presence, he scowls back his thoughts of her and spits with exaggerated disdain—then withdraws back into the room.* ABBIE *waits, holding her breath as she listens with passionate eagerness for every sound within the house.*

EBEN *comes out. Their eyes meet. His falter, he is confused, he turns away and slams the door resentfully. At this gesture,* ABBIE *laughs tantalizingly, amused but at the same time piqued and irritated. He scowls, strides off the porch to the path and starts to walk past her to the road with a grand swagger of ignoring her existence. He is dressed in his store suit, spruced up, his face shines from soap and water.* ABBIE *leans forward on her chair, her eyes hard and angry now, and, as he passes her, gives a sneering, taunting chuckle.*

EBEN: (*stung—turns on her furiously*) What air yew cacklin' 'bout?

ABBIE: (*triumphant*) Yew!

EBEN: What about me?

ABBIE: Ye look all slicked up like a prize bull.

EBEN: (*with a sneer*) Waal—ye hain't so durned purty yerself, be ye? (*They stare into each other's eyes, his held by hers in spite of himself, hers glowingly possessive. Their physical attraction becomes a palpable force quivering in the hot air*).

ABBIE: (*softly*) Ye don't mean that, Eben. Ye may think ye mean it, mebbe, but ye don't. Ye can't. It's agin nature, Eben. Ye been fightin' yer nature ever since the day I come—tryin' t' tell yerself I hain't

153

purty t'ye. (*She laughs a low humid laugh without taking her eyes from his. A pause—her body squirms desirously—she murmurs languorously*) Hain't the sun strong an' hot? Ye kin feel it burnin' into the earth—Nature—makin' thin's grow—bigger 'n' bigger—burnin' inside ye—makin' ye want t' grow—into somethin' else—till ye're jined with it—an' it's your'n—but it owns ye, too— an' makes ye grow bigger—like a tree—like them elums— (*She laughs again softly, holding his eyes. He takes a step toward her, compelled against his will*) Nature'll beat ye, Eben. Ye might's well own up t' it fust 's last.

EBEN: (*trying to break from her spell—confusedly*) If Paw'd hear ye goin' on. . . . (*Resentfully*) But ye've made such a damned idjit out o' the old devil . . . ! (ABBIE *laughs*).

ABBIE: Waal—hain't it easier fur yew with him changed softer?

EBEN: (*defiantly*) No. I'm fightin' him—fightin' yew—fightin' fur Maw's rights t' her hum! (*This breaks her spell for him. He glowers at her*) An' I'm onto ye. Ye hain't foolin' me a mite. Ye're aimin' t' swaller up everythin' an' make it your'n. Waal, you'll find I'm a heap sight bigger hunk nor yew kin chew! (*He turns from her with a sneer*).

ABBIE: (*trying to regain her ascendancy—seductively*) Eben!

EBEN: Leave me be! (*He starts to walk away*).

ABBIE: (*more commandingly*) Eben!

EBEN: (*stops—resentfully*) What d'ye want?

ABBIE: (*trying to conceal a growing excitement*) Whar air ye goin'?

EBEN: (*with malicious nonchalance*) Oh—up the road a spell.

ABBIE: T' the village?

EBEN: (*airily*) Mebbe.

ABBIE: (*excitedly*) T' see that Min, I s'pose?

EBEN: Mebbe.

ABBIE: (*weakly*) What d'ye want t' waste time on her fur?

EBEN: (*revenging himself now—grinning at her*) Ye can't beat Nature, didn't ye say? (*He laughs and again starts to walk away*).

ABBIE: (*bursting out*) An ugly old hake!

EBEN: (*with a tantalizing sneer*) She's purtier'n yew be!

ABBIE: That every wuthless drunk in the country has. . . .

EBEN: (*tauntingly*) Mebbe—but she's better'n yew. She owns up fa'r 'n' squar' t' her doin's.

ABBIE: (*furiously*) Don't ye dare compare. . . .

EBEN: She don't go sneakin' an' stealin'—what's mine.

ABBIE: (*savagely seizing on his weak point*) Your'n? Yew mean—my farm?

EBEN: I mean the farm yew sold yerself fur like any other old whore— my farm!

ABBIE: (*stung—fiercely*) Ye'll never live t' see the day when even a stinkin' weed on it 'll belong t' ye! (*Then in a scream*) Git out o' my sight! Go on t' yer slut—disgracin' yer Paw 'n' me! I'll git yer Paw t' horsewhip ye off the place if I want t'! Ye're only livin' here 'cause I tolerate ye! Git along! I hate the sight o' ye! (*She stops, panting and glaring at him*).

EBEN: (*returning her glance in kind*) An' I hate the sight o' yew! (*He turns and strides off up the road. She follows his retreating figure with concentrated hate. Old CABOT appears coming up from the barn. The hard, grim expression of his face has changed. He seems in some queer way softened, mellowed. His eyes have taken on a strange, incongruous dreamy quality. Yet there is no hint of physical weakness about him—rather he looks more robust and younger. ABBIE sees him and turns away quickly with unconcealed aversion. He comes slowly up to her*).

CABOT: (*mildly*) War yew an' Eben quarrelin' agen?

ABBIE: (*shortly*) No.

CABOT: Ye was talkin' a'mighty loud. (*He sits down on the edge of porch*).

ABBIE: (*snappishly*) If ye heerd us they hain't no need askin' questions.

CABOT: I didn't hear what ye said.

ABBIE: (*relieved*) Waal—it wa'n't nothin' t' speak on.

CABOT: (*after a pause*) Eben's queer.

ABBIE: (*bitterly*) He's the dead spit 'n' image o' yew!

CABOT: (*queerly interested*) D'ye think so, Abbie? (*After a pause, ruminatingly*) Me 'n' Eben's allus fit 'n' fit. I never could b'ar him noways. He's so thunderin' soft—like his Maw.

ABBIE: (*scornfully*) Ay-eh! 'Bout as soft as yew be!

CABOT: (*as if he hadn't heard*) Mebbe I been too hard on him.

ABBIE: (*jeeringly*) Waal—ye're gittin' soft now—soft as slop! That's what Eben was sayin'.

CABOT: (*his face instantly grim and ominous*) Eben was sayin'? Waal, he'd best not do nothin' t' try me 'r he'll soon diskiver . . . . (*A pause. She keeps her face turned away. His gradually softens. He stares up at the sky*) Purty, hain't it?

ABBIE: (*crossly*) I don't see nothin' purty.

CABOT: The sky. Feels like a wa'm field up thar.

ABBIE: (*sarcastically*) Air yew aimin' t' buy up over the farm too? (*She snickers contemptuously*).

CABOT: (*strangely*) I'd like t' own my place up thar. (*A pause*) I'm gittin' old, Abbie. I'm gittin' ripe on the bough. (*A pause. She stares at him mystified. He goes on*) It's allus lonesome cold in the house—even when it's bilin' hot outside. Hain't yew noticed?

ABBIE: No.

CABOT: It's wa'm down t' the barn—nice smellin' an' warm—with the cows. (*A pause*) Cows is queer.

ABBIE: Like yew?

CABOT: Like Eben. (*A pause*) I'm gittin' t' feel resigned t' Eben— jest as I got t' feel 'bout his Maw. I'm gittin' t' learn to b'ar his softness—jest like her'n. I calc'late I c'd a'most take t' him—if he wa'n't sech a dumb fool! (*A pause*) I s'pose it's old age a-creepin' in my bones.

ABBIE: (*indifferently*) Waal—ye hain't dead yet.

CABOT: (*roused*) No, I hain't, yew bet—not by a hell of a sight—I'm sound 'n' tough as hickory! (*Then moodily*) But arter three score and ten the Lord warns ye t' prepare. (*A pause*) That's why Eben's come in my head. Now that his cussed sinful brothers is gone their path t' hell, they's no one left but Eben.

ABBIE: (*resentfully*) They's me, hain't they? (*Agitatedly*) What's all this sudden likin' ye've tuk to Eben? Why don't ye say nothin' 'bout me? Hain't I yer lawful wife?

CABOT: (*simply*) Ay-eh. Ye be. (*A pause—he stares at her desirously—his eyes grow avid—then with a sudden movement he seizes her hands and squeezes them, declaiming in a queer camp meeting preacher's tempo*) Yew air my Rose o' Sharon! Behold, yew air fair; yer eyes air doves; yer lips air like scarlet; yer two breasts air like two fawns; yer navel be like a round goblet; yer belly be like a heap o' wheat .... (*He covers her hand with kisses. She does not seem to notice. She stares before her with hard angry eyes*).

ABBIE: (*jerking her hands away—harshly*) So ye're plannin' t' leave the farm t' Eben, air ye?

CABOT: (*dazedly*) Leave ...? (*Then with resentful obstinacy*) I hain't a-givin' it t' no one!

ABBIE: (*remorselessly*) Ye can't take it with ye.

CABOT: (*thinks a moment—then reluctantly*) No, I calc'late not. (*After a pause—with a strange passion*) But if I could, I would, by the Etarnal! 'R if I could, in my dyin' hour, I'd set it afire an' watch it burn—this house an' every ear o' corn an' every tree down t' the last blade o' hay! I'd sit an' know it was all a-dying with me an' no one else'd ever own what was mine, what I'd made out o' nothin' with my own sweat 'n' blood! (*A pause—then he adds with a queer affection*) 'Ceptin' the cows. Them I'd turn free.

ABBIE: (*harshly*) An me?

CABOT: (*with a queer smile*) Ye'd be turned free, too.

ABBIE: (*furiously*) So that's the thanks I git fur marryin' ye—t' have ye change kind to Eben who hates ye, an' talk o' turnin' me out in the road.

CABOT: (*hastily*) Abbie! Ye know I wa'n't ....

ABBIE: (*vengefully*) Just let me tell ye a thing or two 'bout Eben! Whar's he gone? T' see that harlot, Min! I tried fur t' stop him. Disgracin' yew an' me—on the Sabbath, too!

CABOT: (*rather guiltily*) He's a sinner—nateral-born. It's lust eatin' his heart.

ABBIE: (*enraged beyond endurance—wildly vindictive*) An' his lust fur me! Kin ye find excuses fur that?

CABOT: (*stares at her—after a dead pause*) Lust—fur yew?

ABBIE: (*defiantly*) He was tryin' t' make love t' me—when ye heerd us quarrelin'.

CABOT: (*stares at her—then a terrible expression of rage comes over his face—he springs to his feet shaking all over*) By the A'mighty God—I'll end him!

ABBIE: (*frightened now for* EBEN) No! Don't ye!

CABOT: (*violently*) I'll git the shotgun an' blow his soft brains t' the top o' them elums!

ABBIE: (*throwing her arms around him*) No, Ephraim!

CABOT: (*pushing her away violently*) I will, by God!

ABBIE: (*in a quieting tone*) Listen, Ephraim. 'Twa'n't nothin' bad—on'y a boy's foolin'—'twa'n't meant serious—jest jokin' an' teasin' . . . .

CABOT: Then why did ye say—lust?

ABBIE: It must hev sounded wusser'n I meant. An' I was mad at thinkin'—ye'd leave him the farm.

CABOT: (*quieter but still grim and cruel*) Waal then, I'll horsewhip him off the place if that much'll content ye.

ABBIE: (*reaching out and taking his hand*) No. Don't think o' me! Ye mustn't drive him off. 'Tain't sensible. Who'll ye get to help ye on the farm? They's no one hereabouts.

CABOT: (*considers this—then nodding his appreciation*) Ye got a head on ye. (*Then irritably*) Waal, let him stay. (*He sits down on the edge of the porch. She sits beside him. He murmurs contemptuously*) I oughtn't t' git riled so—at that 'ere fool calf. (*A pause*) But har's the p'int. What son o' mine'll keep on here t' the farm—when the Lord does call me? Simeon an' Peter air gone t' hell—an' Eben's follerin' 'em.

ABBIE: They's me.

CABOT: Ye're on'y a woman.

ABBIE: I'm yewr wife.

CABOT: That hain't me. A son is me—my blood—mine. Mine ought t' git mine. An' then it's still mine—even though I be six foot under. D'ye see?

ABBIE: (*giving him a look of hatred*) Ay-eh. I see. (*She becomes very thoughtful, her face growing shrewd, her eyes studying* CABOT *craftily*).

CABOT: I'm gittin' old—ripe on the bough. (*Then with a sudden forced reassurance*) Not but what I hain't a hard nut t' crack even yet—an' fur many a year t' come! By the Etarnal, I kin break most o' the young fellers' backs at any kind o' work any day o' the year!

ABBIE: (*suddenly*) Mebbe the Lord'll give *us* a son.

CABOT: (*turns and stares at her eagerly*) Ye mean—a son—t' me 'n' yew?

ABBIE: (*with a cajoling smile*) Ye're a strong man yet, hain't ye? 'Tain't noways impossible, be it? We know that. Why d'ye stare so? Hain't ye never thought o' that afore? I been thinkin' o' it all along. Ay-eh—an' I been prayin' it'd happen, too.

CABOT: (*his face growing full of joyous pride and a sort of religious ecstasy*) Ye been prayin', Abbie?—fur a son?—t' us?

ABBIE: Ay-eh. (*With a grim resolution*) I want a son now.

CABOT: (*excitedly clutching both of her hands in his*) It'd be the blessin' o' God, Abbie—the blessin' o' God A'mighty on me—in my old age— in my lonesomeness! They hain't nothin' I wouldn't do fur ye then, Abbie. Ye'd hev on'y t' ask it—anythin' ye'd a mind t'!

ABBIE: (*interrupting*) Would ye will the farm t' me then—t' me an' it . . . ?

CABOT: (*vehemently*) I'd do anythin' ye axed, I tell ye! I swar it! May I be everlastin' damned t' hell if I wouldn't! (*He sinks to his knees pulling her down with him. He trembles all over with the fervor of his hopes*) Pray t' the Lord agen, Abbie. It's the Sabbath! I'll jine ye! Two prayers air better nor one. "An' God hearkened unto Rachel"! An' God hearkened unto Abbie! Pray, Abbie! Pray fur him to hearken! (*He bows his head, mumbling. She pretends to do likewise but gives him a side glance of scorn and triumph*).

Scene Two

*A*BOUT *eight in the evening. The interior of the two bedrooms on the top floor is shown.* EBEN *is sitting on the side of his bed in the room on the left. On account of the heat he has taken off everything but his undershirt and pants. His feet are bare. He faces front, brooding moodily, his chin propped on his hands, a desperate expression on his face.*

In the other room CABOT *and* ABBIE *are sitting side by side on the edge of their bed, an old four-poster with feather mattress. He is in his night shirt, she in her nightdress. He is still in the queer, excited mood into which the notion of a son has thrown him. Both rooms are lighted dimly and flickeringly by tallow candles.*

CABOT: The farm needs a son.

ABBIE: I need a son.

CABOT: Ay-eh. Sometimes ye air the farm an' sometimes the farm be yew. That's why I clove t' ye in my lonesomeness. (*A pause. He pounds his knee with his fist*) Me an' the farm has got t' beget a son!

ABBIE: Ye'd best go t' sleep. Ye're gittin' thin's all mixed.

CABOT: (*with an impatient gesture*) No, I hain't. My mind's clear's a well. Ye don't know me, that's it. (*He stares hopelessly at the floor*).

ABBIE: (*indifferently*) Mebbe. (*In the next room* EBEN *gets up and paces up and down distractedly.* ABBIE *hears him. Her eyes fasten on the intervening wall with concentrated attention.* EBEN *stops and stares. Their hot glances seem to meet through the wall. Unconsciously he stretches out his arms for her and she half rises. Then aware, he mutters a curse at himself and flings himself face downward on the bed, his clenched fists above his head, his face buried in the pillow.* ABBIE *relaxes with a faint sigh but her eyes remain fixed on the wall; she listens with all her attention for some movement from* EBEN).

CABOT: (*suddenly raises his head and looks at her—scornfully*) Will ye ever know me—'r will any man 'r woman? (*Shaking his head*) No. I calc'late 't wa'n't t' be. (*He turns away.* ABBIE *looks at the wall. Then, evidently unable to keep silent about his thoughts, without looking at his wife, he puts out his hand and clutches her knee. She starts violently, looks at him, sees he is not watching her, concentrates again on the wall and pays no attention to what he says*) Listen, Abbie. When I come here fifty odd year ago—I was jest twenty an' the strongest an' hardest ye ever seen—ten times as strong an' fifty times as hard as Eben. Waal—this place was nothin' but fields o' stones. Folks laughed when I tuk it. They couldn't know what I knowed. When ye kin make corn sprout out o' stones, God's livin' in yew! They wa'n't strong enuff fur that! They reckoned God was easy. They laughed. They don't laugh no more. Some died hereabouts. Some went West an' died. They're all under ground—fur follerin' arter an easy God. God hain't easy. (*He shakes his head slowly*) An' I growed hard. Folks kept allus sayin' he's a hard man like 'twas sinful t' be hard, so's at last I said back at 'em: Waal then, by thunder, ye'll git me hard an' see how ye like it! (*Then suddenly*) But I give in t' weakness once. 'Twas arter I'd been here two year. I got weak—despairful—they was so many stones. They was a party leavin', givin' up, goin' West. I jined 'em. We tracked on 'n' on. We come t' broad medders, plains, whar the soil was black an' rich as gold. Nary a stone. Easy. Ye'd on'y to plow an' sow an' then set an' smoke yer pipe an' watch thin's grow. I could o' been a rich man—but somethin' in me fit me an' fit me—the voice o' God sayin': "This hain't wuth nothin' t' Me. Git ye back t' hum!" I got afeerd o' that voice an' I lit out back t' hum here, leavin' my claim an' crops t' whoever'd a mind t' take 'em. Ay-eh. I actoolly give up what was rightful mine! God's hard, not easy! God's in the stones! Build my church on a rock—out o' stones an' I'll be in them! That's what He meant t' Peter! (*He sighs heavily—a pause*) Stones. I picked 'em up an' piled 'em into walls. Ye kin read the years o' my life in them walls, every day a hefted stone, climbin' over the hills up and down, fencin' in the fields that was mine, whar I'd made thin's grow out o' nothin'—like the will o' God, like the servant o' His hand. It wa'n't easy. It was hard an' He made me hard fur it. (*He pauses*) All the time I kept gittin' lonesomer. I tuk a wife. She bore Simeon an' Peter. She was a good woman. She wuked hard. We was married twenty year. She never knowed me. She helped but she never knowed what she was helpin'. I was allus lonesome. She died. After that it wa'n't so lonesome fur a spell. (*A pause*) I lost count o' the years. I had no time t' fool away countin' 'em. Sim an' Peter helped. The farm growed. It was all mine! When I thought o' that I didn't feel lonesome. (*A pause*) But ye can't hitch yer mind t' one thin' day an' night. I tuk another wife—Eben's Maw. Her folks was contestin' me at law over my deeds t' the farm—my farm! That's why Eben keeps a-talkin' his fool talk o' this bein' his Maw's farm. She bore Eben. She was purty—but soft. She tried t' be hard. She couldn't. She never knowed me nor nothin'. It was lonesomer 'n hell with her. After a matter o' sixteen odd years, she died. (*A pause*) I lived with the boys. They hated me 'cause I was hard. I hated them 'cause they was soft. They coveted the farm without knowin' what it meant. It made me bitter 'n wormwood. It aged me—them coveting what I'd made fur mine. Then this spring the call come—the voice o' God cryin' in my wilderness, in my lonesomeness—t' go out an' seek an' find! (*Turning to her with strange passion*) I sought ye an' I found ye! Yew air my Rose o' Sharon! Yer eyes air like.... (*She has turned a blank face, resentful eyes to his. He stares at her for a moment—then harshly*) Air ye any the wiser fur all I've told ye?

ABBIE: (*confusedly*) Mebbe.

CABOT: (*pushing her away from him—angrily*) Ye don't know nothin'— nor never will. If ye don't hev a son t' redeem ye.... (*This in a tone of cold threat*).

ABBIE: (*resentfully*) I've prayed, hain't I?

CABOT: (*bitterly*) Pray agen—fur understandin'!

ABBIE: (*a veiled threat in her tone*) Ye'll have a son out o' me, I promise ye.

CABOT: How kin ye promise?

ABBIE: I got second-sight mebbe. I kin foretell. (*She gives a queer smile*).

CABOT: I believe ye have. Ye give me the chills sometimes. (*He shivers*) It's cold in this house. It's oneasy. They's thin's pokin' about in the dark—in the corners. (*He pulls on his trousers, tucking in his night shirt, and pulls on his boots*).

ABBIE: (*surprised*) Whar air ye goin'?

CABOT: (*queerly*) Down whar it's restful—whar it's warm—down t' the barn. (*Bitterly*) I kin talk t' the cows. They know. They know the farm an' me. They'll give me peace. (*He turns to go out the door*).

ABBIE: (*a bit frightenedly*) Air ye ailin' tonight, Ephraim?

CABOT: Growin'. Growin' ripe on the bough. (*He turns and goes, his boots clumping down the stairs.* EBEN *sits up with a start, listening.* ABBIE *is conscious of his movement and stares at the wall.* CABOT *comes out of the house around the corner and stands by the gate, blinking at the sky. He stretches up his hands in a tortured gesture*) God A'mighty, call from the dark! (*He listens as if expecting an answer. Then his arms drop, he shakes his head and plods off toward the barn.* EBEN *and* ABBIE *stare at each other through the wall.* EBEN *sighs heavily and* ABBIE *echoes it. Both become terribly nervous, uneasy. Finally* ABBIE *gets up and listens, her ear to the wall. He acts as if he saw every move she was making, he becomes resolutely still. She seems driven into a decision—goes out the door in rear determinedly. His eyes follow her. Then as the door of his room is opened softly, he turns away, waits in an attitude of strained fixity.* ABBIE *stands for a second staring at him, her eyes burning with desire. Then with a little cry she runs over and throws her arms about his neck, she pulls his head back and covers his mouth with kisses. At first, he submits dumbly; then he puts his arms about her neck and returns her kisses, but finally, suddenly aware of his hatred, he hurls her away from him, springing to his feet. They stand speechless and breathless, panting like two animals*).

ABBIE: (at *last—painfully*) Ye shouldn't, Eben—ye shouldn't—I'd make ye happy!

EBEN: (*harshly*) I don't want t' be happy—from yew!

ABBIE: (*helplessly*) Ye do, Eben! Ye do! Why d'ye lie?

EBEN: (*viciously*) I don't take t'ye, I tell ye! I hate the sight o' ye!

ABBIE: (*with an uncertain troubled laugh*) Waal, I kissed ye anyways—an' ye kissed back—yer lips was burnin'—ye can't lie 'bout that! (*Intensely*) If ye don't care, why did ye kiss me back—why was yer lips burnin'?

EBEN: (*wiping his mouth*) It was like pizen on 'em. (*Then tauntingly*) When I kissed ye back, mebbe I thought 'twas someone else.

ABBIE: (*wildly*) Min?

EBEN: Mebbe.

ABBIE: (*torturedly*) Did ye go t' see her? Did ye r'ally go? I thought ye mightn't. Is that why ye throwed me off jest now?

EBEN: (*sneeringly*) What if it be?

ABBIE: (*raging*) Then ye're a dog, Eben Cabot!

EBEN: (*threateningly*) Ye can't talk that way t' me!

ABBIE: (*with a shrill laugh*) Can't I? Did ye think I was in love with ye— a weak thin' like yew? Not much! I on'y wanted ye fur a purpose o' my own—an' I'll hev ye fur it yet 'cause I'm stronger'n yew be!

EBEN: (*resentfully*) I knowed well it was on'y part o' yer plan t' swaller everythin'!

ABBIE: (*tauntingly*) Mebbe!

EBEN: (*furious*) Git out o' my room!

ABBIE: This air my room an' ye're on'y hired help!

EBEN: (*threateningly*) Git out afore I murder ye!

ABBIE: (*quite confident now*) I hain't a mite afeerd. Ye want me, don't ye? Yes, ye do! An' yer Paw's son'll never kill what he wants! Look at yer eyes! They's lust fur me in 'em, burnin' 'em up! Look at yer lips now! They're tremblin' an' longin' t' kiss me, an' yer teeth t' bite! (*He is watching her now with a horrible fascination. She laughs a crazy triumphant laugh*) I'm a-goin' t' make all o' this hum my hum! They's one room hain't mine yet, but it's a-goin' t' be tonight. I'm a-goin' down now an' light up! (*She makes him a mocking bow*) Won't ye come courtin' me in the best parlor, Mister Cabot?

EBEN: (*staring at her—horribly confused—dully*) Don't ye dare! It hain't been opened since Maw died an' was laid out thar! Don't ye . . . ! (*But her eyes are fixed on his so burningly that his will seems to wither before hers. He stands swaying toward her helplessly*).

ABBIE: (*holding his eyes and putting all her will into her words as she backs out the door*) I'll expect ye afore long, Eben.

EBEN: (*stares after her for a while, walking toward the door. A light appears in the parlor window. He murmurs*) In the parlor? (*This seems to arouse connotations for he comes back and puts on his white shirt, collar, half ties the tie mechanically, puts on coat, takes his hat, stands barefooted looking about him in bewilderment, mutters wonderingly*) Maw! Whar air yew? (*Then goes slowly toward the door in rear*).

Scene Three

A FEW *minutes later. The interior of the parlor is shown. A grim, repressed room like a tomb in which the family has been interred alive.* ABBIE *sits on the edge of the horsehair sofa. She has lighted all the candles and the room is revealed in all its preserved ugliness. A change has come over the woman. She looks awed and frightened now, ready to run away.*

The door is opened and EBEN *appears. His face wears an expression of obsessed confusion. He stands staring at her, his arms hanging disjointedly from his shoulders, his feet bare, his hat in his hand.*

ABBIE: (*after a pause—with a nervous, formal politeness*) Won't ye set?

EBEN: (*dully*) Ay-eh. (*Mechanically he places his hat carefully on the floor near the door and sits stiffly beside her on the edge of the sofa. A pause. They both remain rigid, looking straight ahead with eyes full of fear*).

ABBIE: When I fust come in—in the dark—they seemed somethin' here.

EBEN: (*simply*) Maw.

ABBIE: I kin still feel somethin'. . . .

EBEN: It s Maw.

ABBIE: At fust I was feered o' it. I wanted t' yell an' run. Now—since yew come—seems like it's growin' soft an' kind t' me. (*Addressing the air—queerly*) Thank yew.

EBEN: Maw allus loved me.

ABBIE: Mebbe it knows I love yew, too. Mebbe that makes it kind t' me.

EBEN: (*dully*) I dunno. I should think she'd hate ye.

ABBIE: (*with certainty*) No. I kin feel it don't—not no more.

EBEN: Hate ye fur stealin' her place—here in her hum—settin' in her parlor whar she was laid— (*He suddenly stops, staring stupidly before him*).

ABBIE: What is it, Eben?

EBEN: (*in a whisper*) Seems like Maw didn't want me t' remind ye.

ABBIE: (*excitedly*) I knowed, Eben! It's kind t' me! It don't b'ar me no grudges fur what I never knowed an' couldn't help!

EBEN: Maw b'ars him a grudge.

ABBIE: Waal, so does all o' us.

EBEN: Ay-eh. (*With passion*) I does, by God!

ABBIE: (*taking one of his hands in hers and patting it*) Thar! Don't git riled thinkin' o' him. Think o' yer Maw who's kind t' us. Tell me about yer Maw, Eben.

EBEN: They hain't nothin' much. She was kind. She was good.

ABBIE: (*putting one arm over his shoulder. He does not seem to notice— passionately*) I'll be kind an' good t' ye!

EBEN: Sometimes she used t' sing fur me.

ABBIE: I'll sing fur ye!

EBEN: This was her hum. This was her farm.

ABBIE: This is my hum! This is my farm!

EBEN: He married her t' steal 'em. She was soft an' easy. He couldn't 'preciate her.

ABBIE: He can't 'preciate me!

EBEN: He murdered her with his hardness.

ABBIE: He's murderin' me!

EBEN: She died. (*A pause*) Sometimes she used to sing fur me. (*He bursts
into a fit of sobbing*).

ABBIE: (*both her arms around him—with wild passion*) I'll sing fur ye! I'll
die fur ye! (*In spite of her overwhelming desire for him, there is a sincere
maternal love in her manner and voice—a horribly frank mixture of lust
and mother love*) Don't cry, Eben! I'll take yer Maw's place! I'll be
everythin' she was t' ye! Let me kiss ye, Eben! (*She pulls his head
around. He makes a bewildered pretense of resistance. She is tender*) Don't
be afeered! I'll kiss ye pure, Eben—same 's if I was a Maw t' ye—an'
ye kin kiss me back 's if yew was my son—my boy—sayin' good-
night t' me! Kiss me, Eben. (*They kiss in restrained fashion. Then
suddenly wild passion overcomes her. She kisses him lustfully again and
again and he flings his arms about her and returns her kisses. Suddenly,
as in the bedroom, he frees himself from her violently and springs to his
feet. He is trembling all over, in a strange state of terror.* ABBIE *strains her
arms toward him with fierce pleading*) Don't ye leave me, Eben! Can't
ye see it hain't enuf—lovin' ye like a Maw—can't ye see it's got t' be
that an' more—much more—a hundred times more—fur me t' be
happy—fur yew t' be happy?

EBEN: (*to the presence he feels in the room*) Maw! Maw! What d'ye want?
What air ye tellin' me?

ABBIE: She's tellin' ye t' love me. She knows I love ye an' I'll be good
t' ye. Can't ye feel it? Don't ye know? She's tellin' ye t' love me,
Eben!

EBEN: Ay-eh. I feel—mebbe she—but—I can't figger out—why— when
ye've stole her place—here in her hum—in the parlor whar she was—

ABBIE: (*fiercely*) She knows I love ye!

EBEN: (*his face suddenly lighting up with a fierce, triumphant grin*) I see it!
I sees why. It's her vengeance on him—so's she kin rest quiet in her
grave!

ABBIE: (*wildly*) Vengeance o' God on the hull o' us! What d'we give a
durn? I love ye, Eben! God knows I love ye! (*She stretches out her
arms for him*).

EBEN: (*throws himself on his knees beside the sofa and grabs her in his arms—releasing all his pent-up passion*) An' I love yew, Abbie!—now I kin say it! I been dyin' fur want o' ye—every hour since ye come! I love ye! (*Their lips meet in a fierce, bruising kiss*).

Scene Four

Exterior of the farmhouse. It is just dawn. The front door at right is opened and EBEN *comes out and walks around to the gate. He is dressed in his working clothes. He seems changed. His face wears a bold and confident expression, he is grinning to himself with evident satisfaction. As he gets near the gate, the window of the parlor is heard opening and the shutters are flung back and* ABBIE *sticks her head out. Her hair tumbles over her shoulders in disarray, her face is flushed, she looks at* EBEN *with tender, languorous eyes and calls softly*).

ABBIE: Eben. (*As he turns—playfully*) Jest one more kiss afore ye go. I'm goin' to miss ye fearful all day.

EBEN: An' me yew, ye kin bet! (*He goes to her. They kiss several times. He draws away, laughingly*) Thar. That's enuff, hain't it? Ye won't hev none left fur next time.

ABBIE: I got a million o' 'em left fur yew! (*Then a bit anxiously*) D'ye r'ally love me, Eben?

EBEN: (*emphatically*) I like ye better'n any gal I ever knowed! That's gospel!

ABBIE: Likin' hain't lovin'.

EBEN: Waal then—I love ye. Now air yew satisfied?

ABBIE: Ay-eh, I be. (*She smiles at him adoringly*).

EBEN: I better git t' the barn. The old critter's liable t' suspicion an' come sneakin' up.

ABBIE: (*with a confident laugh*) Let him! I kin allus pull the wool over his eyes. I'm goin' t' leave the shutters open and let in the sun 'n' air. This room's been dead long enuff. Now it's goin' t' be my room!

EBEN: (*frowning*) Ay-eh.

ABBIE: (*hastily*) I meant—our room.

EBEN: Ay-eh.

ABBIE: We made it our'n last night, didn't we? We give it life—our lovin' did. (*A pause*).

EBEN: (*with a strange look*) Maw's gone back t' her grave. She kin sleep now.

ABBIE: May she rest in peace! (*Then tenderly rebuking*) Ye oughtn't t' talk o' sad thin's—this mornin'.

EBEN: It jest come up in my mind o' itself.

ABBIE: Don't let it. (*He doesn't answer. She yawns*) Waal, I'm a-goin' t' steal a wink o' sleep. I'll tell the Old Man I hain't feelin' pert. Let him git his own vittles.

EBEN: I see him comin' from the barn. Ye better look smart an' git upstairs.

ABBIE: Ay-eh. Good-by. Don't ferget me. (*She throws him a kiss. He grins—then squares his shoulders and awaits his father confidently.* CABOT *walks slowly up from the left, staring up at the sky with a vague face*).

EBEN: (*jovially*) Mornin', Paw. Star-gazin' in daylight?

CABOT: Purty, hain t it?

EBEN: (*looking around him possessively*) It's a durned purty farm.

CABOT: I mean the sky.

EBEN: (*grinning*) How d'ye know? Them eyes o' your'n can't see that fur. (*This tickles his humor and he slaps his thigh and laughs*) Ho-ho! That's a good un!

CABOT: (*grimly sarcastic*) Ye're feelin' right chipper, hain't ye? Whar'd ye steal the likker?

EBEN: (*good-naturedly*) 'Tain't likker. Jest life. (*Suddenly holding out his hand—soberly*) Yew 'n' me is quits. Let's shake hands.

CABOT: (*suspiciously*) What's come over ye?

EBEN: Then don't. Mebbe it's jest as well. (*A moment's pause*) What's come over me? (*Queerly*) Didn't ye feel her passin'—goin' back t' her grave?

CABOT: (*dully*) Who?

EBEN: Maw. She kin rest now an' sleep content. She's quits with ye.

CABOT: (*confusedly*) I rested. I slept good—down with the cows. They know how t' sleep. They're teachin' me.

EBEN: (*suddenly jovial again*) Good fur the cows! Waal—ye better git t' work.

CABOT: (*grimly amused*) Air yew bossin' me, ye calf?

EBEN: (*beginning to laugh*) Ay-eh! I'm bossin' yew! Ha-ha-ha! See how ye like it! Ha-ha-ha! I'm the prize rooster o' this roost. Ha-ha-ha! (*He goes off toward the barn laughing*).

CABOT: (*looks after him with scornful pity*) Soft-headed. Like his Maw. Dead spit 'n' image. No hope in him! (*He spits with contemptuous disgust*) A born fool! (*Then matter-of-factly*) Waal—I'm gittin' peckish. (*He goes toward door*).

CURTAIN

PART THREE—SCENE ONE

A NIGHT *in late spring the following year. The kitchen and the two bedrooms upstairs are shown. The two bedrooms are dimly lighted by a tallow candle in each.* EBEN *is sitting on the side of the bed in his room, his chin propped on his fists, his face a study of the struggle he is making to understand his conflicting emotions. The noisy laughter and music from below where a kitchen dance is in progress annoy and distract him. He scowls at the floor.*

In the next room a cradle stands beside the double bed.

In the kitchen all is festivity. The stove has been taken down to give more room to the dancers. The chairs, with wooden benches added, have been pushed back against the walls. On these are seated, squeezed in tight against one another, farmers and their wives and their young folks of both sexes from the neighboring farms. They are all chattering and laughing loudly. They evidently have some secret joke in common. There is no end of winking, of nudging, of meaning nods of the head toward CABOT *who, in a state of extreme hilarious excitement increased by the amount he has drunk, is standing near the rear door where there is a small keg of whisky and serving drinks to all the men. In the left corner, front, dividing the attention with her husband,* ABBIE *is sitting in a rocking chair, a shawl wrapped about her shoulders. She is very pale, her face is thin and drawn, her eyes are fixed anxiously on the open door in rear as if waiting for someone.*

The musician is tuning up his fiddle, seated in the far right corner. He is a lanky young fellow with a long, weak face. His pale eyes blink incessantly and he grins about him slyly with a greedy malice.

ABBIE: (*suddenly turning to a young girl on her right*) Whar's Eben?

YOUNG GIRL: (*eying her scornfully*) I dunno, Mrs. Cabot. I hain't seen Eben in ages. (*Meaningly*) Seems like he's spent most o' his time t' hum since yew come.

ABBIE: (*vaguely*) I tuk his Maw's place.

YOUNG GIRL: Ay-eh. So I've heerd. (*She turns away to retail this bit of*

171

gossip to her mother sitting next to her. ABBIE *turns to her left to a big stoutish middle-aged man whose flushed face and starting eyes show the amount of "likker" he has consumed*).

ABBIE: Ye hain't seen Eben, hev ye?

MAN: No, I hain't. (*Then he adds with a wink*) If yew hain't, who would?

ABBIE: He's the best dancer in the county. He'd ought t' come an' dance.

MAN: (*with a wink*) Mebbe he's doin' the dutiful an' walkin' the kid t' sleep. It's a boy, hain't it?

ABBIE: (*nodding vaguely*) Ay-eh—born two weeks back—purty's a picter.

MAN: They all is—t' their Maws. (*Then in a whisper, with a nudge and a leer*) Listen, Abbie—if ye ever git tired o' Eben, remember me! Don't fergit now! (*He looks at her uncomprehending face for a second—then grunts disgustedly*) Waal—guess I'll likker agin. (*He goes over and joins* CABOT *who is arguing noisily with an old farmer over cows. They all drink*).

ABBIE: (*this time appealing to nobody in particular*) Wonder what Eben's a-doin'? (*Her remark is repeated down the line with many a guffaw and titter until it reaches the fiddler. He fastens his blinking eyes on* ABBIE).

FIDDLER: (*raising his voice*) Bet I kin tell ye, Abbie, what Eben's doin'! He's down t' the church offerin' up prayers o' thanksgivin'. (*They all titter expectantly*).

A MAN: What fur? (*Another titter*).

FIDDLER: 'Cause unto him a—(*He hesitates just long enough*) brother is born! (*A roar of laughter. They all look from* ABBIE *to* CABOT. *She is oblivious, staring at the door.* CABOT, *although he hasn't heard the words, is irritated by the laughter and steps forward, glaring about him. There is an immediate silence*).

CABOT: What're ye all bleatin' about like—flock o' goats? Why don't ye dance, damn ye? I axed ye here t' dance—t' eat, drink an' be merry—an' thar ye set cacklin' like a lot o' wet hens with the pip! Ye've swilled my likker an' guzzled my vittles like hogs, hain't ye? Then dance fur me, can't ye? That's fa'r an' squar', hain't it? (*A grumble of resentment goes around but they are all evidently in too much awe of him to express it openly*).

FIDDLER: (*slyly*) We're waitin' fur Eben. (*A suppressed laugh*).

CABOT: (*with a fierce exultation*) T'hell with Eben! Eben's done fur now! I got a new son! (*His mood switching with drunken suddenness*) But ye needn't t' laugh at Eben, none o' ye! He's my blood, if he be a dumb fool. He's better nor any o' yew! He kin do a day's work a'most up t' what I kin—an' that'd put any o' yew pore critters t' shame!

FIDDLER: An' he kin do a good night's work, too! (*A roar of laughter*).

CABOT: Laugh, ye damn fools! Ye're right jist the same, Fiddler. He kin work day an' night too, like I kin, if need be!

OLD FARMER: (*from behind the keg where he is weaving drunkenly back and forth—with great simplicity*) They hain't many t' touch ye, Ephraim— a son at seventy-six. That's a hard man fur ye! I be on'y sixty-eight an' I couldn't do it. (*A roar of laughter in which* CABOT *joins uproariously*).

CABOT: (*slapping him on the back*) I'm sorry fur ye, Hi. I'd never suspicion sech weakness from a boy like yew!

OLD FARMER: An' I never reckoned yew had it in ye nuther, Ephraim. (*There is another laugh*).

CABOT: (*suddenly grim*) I got a lot in me—a hell of a lot—folks don't know on. (*Turning to the* FIDDLER) Fiddle 'er up, durn ye! Give 'em somethin' t' dance t'! What air ye, an ornament? Hain't this a celebration? Then grease yer elbow an' go it!

FIDDLER: (*seizes a drink which the* OLD FARMER *holds out to him and downs it*) Here goes! (*He starts to fiddle "Lady of the Lake." Four young fellows and four girls form in two lines and dance a square dance. The* FIDDLER *shouts directions for the different movements, keeping his words in the rhythm of the music and interspersing them with jocular personal remarks to the dancers themselves. The people seated along the walls stamp their feet and clap their hands in unison.* CABOT *is especially active in this respect. Only* ABBIE *remains apathetic, staring at the door as if she were alone in a silent room*).

FIDDLER: Swing your partner t' the right! That's it, Jim! Give her a b'ar hug! Her Maw hain't lookin'. (*Laughter*) Change partners! That suits ye, don't it, Essie, now ye got Reub afore ye? Look at her redden up, will ye? Waal, life is short an' so's love, as the feller says. (*Laughter*).

CABOT: (*excitedly, stamping his foot*) Go it, boys! Go it, gals!

FIDDLER: (*with a wink at the others*) Ye're the spryest seventy-six ever I sees, Ephraim! Now if ye'd on'y good eye-sight...! (*Suppressed laughter. He gives* CABOT *no chance to retort but roars*) Promenade! Ye're walkin' like a bride down the aisle, Sarah! Waal, while they's life they's allus hope, I've heerd tell. Swing your partner to the left! Gosh A'mighty, look at Johnny Cook high-steppin'! They hain't goin' t'be much strength left fur howin' in the corn lot t'morrow. (*Laughter*).

CABOT: Go it! Go it! (*Then suddenly, unable to restrain himself any longer, he prances into the midst of the dancers, scattering them, waving his arms about wildly*) Ye're all hoofs! Git out o' my road! Give me room! I'll show ye dancin'. Ye're all too soft! (*He pushes them roughly away. They crowd back toward the walls, muttering, looking at him resentfully*).

FIDDLER: (*jeeringly*) Go it, Ephraim! Go it! (*He starts "Pop, Goes the Weasel," increasing the tempo with every verse until at the end he is fiddling crazily as fast as he can go*).

CABOT: (*starts to dance, which he does very well and with tremendous vigor. Then he begins to improvise, cuts incredibly grotesque capers, leaping up and cracking his heels together, prancing around in a circle with body bent in an Indian war dance, then suddenly straightening up and kicking as high as he can with both legs. He is like a monkey on a string. and all the while he intersperses his antics with shouts and derisive comments*) Whoop! Here's dancin' fur ye! Whoop! See that! Seventy-six, if I'm a day! Hard as iron yet! Beatin' the young 'uns like I allus done! Look at me! I'd invite ye t' dance on my hundredth birthday on'y ye'll all be dead by then. Ye're a sickly generation! Yer hearts air pink, not red! Yer veins is full o' mud an' water! I be the on'y man in the county! Whoop! See that! I'm a Injun! I've killed Injuns in the West afore ye was born—an' skulped 'em too! They's a arrer wound on my

backside I c'd show ye! The hull tribe chased me. I outrun 'em all—
with the arrer stuck in me! An' I tuk vengeance on 'em. Ten eyes fur
an eye, that was my motter! Whoop! Look at me! I kin kick the
ceilin' off the room! Whoop!

FIDDLER: (*stops playing—exhaustedly*) God A' mighty, I got enuf. Ye got
the devil's strength in ye.

CABOT: (*delightedly*) Did I beat yew, too? Wa'al, ye played smart. Hev
a swig. (*He pours whisky for himself and* FIDDLER. *They drink. The others
watch* CABOT *silently with cold, hostile eyes. There is a dead pause. The*
FIDDLER *rests.* CABOT *leans against the keg, panting, glaring around him
confusedly. In the room above,* EBEN *gets to his feet and tiptoes out the door
in rear, appearing a moment later in the other bedroom. He moves silently,
even frightenedly, toward the cradle and stands there looking down at the
baby. His face is as vague as his reactions are confused, but there is a trace
of tenderness, of interested discovery. At the same moment that he reaches
the cradle,* ABBIE *seems to sense something. She gets up weakly and goes to*
CABOT).

ABBIE: I m goin up t' the baby.

CABOT: (*with real solicitation*) Air ye able fur the stairs? D'ye want me t'
help ye, Abbie?

ABBIE: No. I'm able. I'll be down agen soon.

CABOT: Don't ye git wore out! He needs ye, remember—our son does!
(*He grins affectionately, patting her on the back. She shrinks from his
touch*).

ABBIE: (*dully*) Don't—tech me. I'm goin'—up. (*She goes.* CABOT *looks
after her. A whisper goes around the room.* CABOT *turns. It ceases. He
wipes his forehead streaming with sweat. He is breathing pantingly*).

CABOT: I'm a-goin' out t' git fresh air. I'm feelin' a mite dizzy. Fiddle
up thar! Dance, all o' ye! Here's likker fur them as wants it. Enjoy
yerselves. I'll be back. (*He goes, closing the door behind him*).

FIDDLER: (*sarcastically*) Don't hurry none on our account! (*A suppressed
laugh. He imitates* ABBIE) Whar's Eben? (*More laughter*).

A WOMAN: (*loudly*) What's happened in this house is plain as the nose on yer face! (ABBIE *appears in the doorway upstairs and stands looking in surprise and adoration at* EBEN *who does not see her*).

A MAN: Ssshh! He's li'ble t' be listenin' at the door. That'd be like him. (*Their voices die to an intensive whispering. Their faces are concentrated on this gossip. A noise as of dead leaves in the wind comes from the room.* CABOT *has come out from the porch and stands by the gate, leaning on it, staring at the sky blinkingly.* ABBIE *comes across the room silently.* EBEN *does not notice her until quite near*).

EBEN: (*starting*) Abbie!

ABBIE: Ssshh! (*She throws her arms around him. They kiss—then bend over the cradle together*) Ain't he purty?—dead spit 'n' image o' yew!

EBEN: (*pleased*) Air he? I can't tell none.

ABBIE: E-zactly like!

EBEN: (*frowningly*) I don't like this. I don't like lettin' on what's mine's his'n. I been doin' that all my life. I'm gittin' t' the end o' b'arin' it!

ABBIE: (*putting her finger on his lips*) We're doin' the best we kin. We got t' wait. Somethin's bound t' happen. (*She puts her arms around him*) I got t' go back.

EBEN: I'm goin' out. I can't b'ar it with the fiddle playin' an' the laughin'.

ABBIE: Don't git feelin' low. I love ye, Eben. Kiss me. (*He kisses her. They remain in each other's arms*).

CABOT: (*at the gate, confusedly*) Even the music can't drive it out—somethin'. Ye kin feel it droppin' off the elums, climbin' up the roof, sneakin' down the chimney, pokin' in the corners! They's no peace in houses, they's no rest livin' with folks. Somethin's always livin' with ye. (*With a deep sigh*) I'll go t' the barn an' rest a spell. (*He goes wearily toward the barn*).

FIDDLER: (*tuning up*) Let's celebrate the old skunk gittin' fooled! We kin have some fun now he's went. (*He starts to fiddle "Turkey in the Straw." There is real merriment now. The young folks get up to dance*).

Scene Two

A HALF *hour later—Exterior—*EBEN *is standing by the gate looking up at the sky, an expression of dumb pain bewildered by itself on his face.* CABOT *appears, returning from the barn, walking wearily, his eyes on the ground. He sees* EBEN *and his whole mood immediately changes. He becomes excited, a cruel, triumphant grin comes to his lips, he strides up and slaps* EBEN *on the back. From within comes the whining of the fiddle and the noise of stamping feet and laughing voices.*

CABOT: So har ye be!

EBEN: (*startled, stares at him with hatred for a moment—then dully*) Ay-eh.

CABOT: (*surveying him jeeringly*) Why hain't ye been in t' dance? They was all axin' fur ye.

EBEN: Let 'em ax!

CABOT: They's a hull passel o' purty gals.

EBEN: T' hell with 'em!

CABOT: Ye'd ought t' be marryin' one o' 'em soon.

EBEN: I hain't marryin' no one.

CABOT: Ye might 'arn a share o' a farm that way.

EBEN: (*with a sneer*) Like yew did, ye mean? I hain't that kind.

CABOT: (*stung*) Ye lie! 'Twas yer Maw's folks aimed t' steal my farm from me.

EBEN: Other folks don't say so. (*After a pause—defiantly*) An' I got a farm, anyways!

CABOT: (*derisively*) Whar?

EBEN: (*stamps a foot on the ground*) Har!

CABOT: (*throws his head back and laughs coarsely*) Ho-ho! Ye hev, hev ye? Waal, that's a good un!

EBEN: (*controlling himself—grimly*) Ye'll see!

CABOT: (*stares at him suspiciously, trying to make him out—a pause—then with scornful confidence*) Ay-eh. I'll see. So'll ye. It's ye that's blind— blind as a mole underground. (EBEN *suddenly laughs, one short sardonic bark: "Ha." A pause.* CABOT *peers at him with renewed suspicion*) Whar air ye hawin' 'bout? (EBEN *turns away without answering.* CABOT *grows angry*) God A'mighty, yew air a dumb dunce! They's nothin' in that thick skull o' your'n but noise—like a empty keg it be! (EBEN *doesn't seem to hear.* CABOT's *rage grows*) Yewr farm! God A'mighty! If ye wa'n't a born donkey ye'd know ye'll never own stick nor stone on it, specially now arter him bein' born. It's his'n, I tell ye—his'n arter I die—but I'll live a hundred jest t' fool ye all—an' he'll be growed then—yewr age a'most! (EBEN *laughs again his sardonic "Ha." This drives* CABOT *into a fury*) Ha? Ye think ye kin git 'round that some- ways, do ye? Waal, it'll be her'n, too—Abbie's—ye won't git 'round her—she knows yer tricks—she'll be too much fur ye—she wants the farm her'n—she was afeerd o' ye—she told me ye was sneakin' 'round tryin' t' make love t' her t' git her on yer side . . . ye . . . ye mad fool, ye! (*He raises his clenched fists threateningly*).

EBEN: (*is confronting him, choking with rage*) Ye lie, ye old skunk! Abbie never said no sech thing!

CABOT: (*suddenly triumphant when he sees how shaken* EBEN *is*) She did. An' I says, I'll blow his brains t' the top o' them elums—an' she says no, that hain't sense, who'll ye git t'help ye on the farm in his place— an' then she says yew'n me ought t' have a son—I know we kin, she says—an' I says, if we do, ye kin have anythin' I've got ye've a mind t'. An' she says, I wants Eben cut off so's this farm'll be mine when ye die! (*With terrible gloating*) An' that's what's happened, hain't it? An' the farm's her'n! An' the dust o' the road—that's you'rn! Ha! Now who's hawin'?

EBEN: (*has been listening, petrified with grief and rage—suddenly laughs wildly and brokenly*) Ha-ha-ha! So that's her sneakin' game—all along!—like I suspicioned at fust—t' swaller it all—an' me, too . . . !

(*Madly*) I'll murder her! (*He springs toward the porch but* CABOT *is quicker and gets in between*).

CABOT: No, ye don't!

EBEN: Git out o' my road! (*He tries to throw* CABOT *aside. They grapple in what becomes immediately a murderous struggle. The old man's concentrated strength is too much for* EBEN. CABOT *gets one hand on his throat and presses him back across the stone wall. At the same moment,* ABBIE *comes out on the porch. With a stifled cry she runs toward them*).

ABBIE: Eben! Ephraim! (*She tugs at the hand on* EBEN'S *throat*) Let go, Ephraim! Ye're chokin' him!

CABOT: (*removes his hand and flings* EBEN *sideways full length on the grass, gasping and choking. With a cry,* ABBIE *kneels beside him, trying to take his head on her lap, but he pushes her away.* CABOT *stands looking down with fierce triumph*) Ye needn't t've fret, Abbie, I wa'n't aimin' t' kill him. He hain't wuth hangin' fur—not by a hell of a sight! (*More and more triumphantly*) Seventy-six an' him not thirty yit—an' look whar he be fur thinkin' his Paw was easy! No, by God, I hain't easy! An' him upstairs, I'll raise him t' be like me! (*He turns to leave them*) I'm goin' in an' dance!—sing an' celebrate! (*He walks to the porch—then turns with a great grin*) I don't calc'late it's left in him, but if he gits pesky, Abbie, ye jest sing out. I'll come a-runnin' an' by the Etarnal, I'll put him across my knee an' birch him! Ha-ha-ha! (*He goes into the house laughing. A moment later his loud "whoop" is heard*).

ABBIE: (*tenderly*) Eben. Air ye hurt? (*She tries to kiss him but he pushes her violently away and struggles to a sitting position*).

EBEN: (*gaspingly*) T'hell—with ye!

ABBIE: (*not believing her ears*) It's me, Eben—Abbie—don't ye know me?

EBEN: (*glowering at her with hatred*) Ay-eh—I know ye—now! (*He suddenly breaks down, sobbing weakly*).

ABBIE: (*fearfully*) Eben—what's happened t' ye—why did ye look at me 's if ye hated me?

EBEN: (*violently, between sobs and gasps*) I do hate ye! Ye're a whore—a damn trickin' whore!

ABBIE: (*shrinking back horrified*) Eben! Ye don't know what ye're sayin'!

EBEN: (*scrambling to his feet and following her—accusingly*) Ye're nothin' but a stinkin' passel o' lies! Ye've been lyin' t' me every word ye spoke, day an' night, since we fust—done it. Ye've kept sayin' ye loved me. . . .

ABBIE: (*frantically*) I do love ye! (*She takes his hand but he flings hers away*).

EBEN: (*unheeding*) Ye've made a fool o' me—a sick, dumb fool—a-purpose! Ye've been on'y playin' yer sneakin', stealin' game all along—gittin' me t' lie with ye so's ye'd hev a son he'd think was his'n, an' makin' him promise he'd give ye the farm and let me eat dust, if ye did git him a son! (*Staring at her with anguished, bewildered eyes*) They must be a devil livin' in ye! T'ain't human t' be as bad as that be!

ABBIE: (*stunned—dully*) He told yew . . . ?

EBEN: Hain't it true? It hain't no good in yew lyin'.

ABBIE: (*pleadingly*) Eben, listen—ye must listen—it was long ago—afore we done nothin'—yew was scornin' me—goin' t' see Min—when I was lovin' ye—an' I said it t' him t' git vengeance on ye!

EBEN: (*unheedingly. With tortured passion*) I wish ye was dead! I wish I was dead along with ye afore this come! (*Ragingly*) But I'll git my vengeance too! I'll pray Maw t' come back t' help me—t' put her cuss on yew an' him!

ABBIE: (*brokenly*) Don't ye, Eben! Don't ye! (*She throws herself on her knees before him, weeping*) I didn't mean t' do bad t'ye! Fergive me, won't ye?

EBEN: (*not seeming to hear her—fiercely*) I'll git squar' with the old skunk—an' yew! I'll tell him the truth 'bout the son he's so proud o'! Then I'll leave ye here t' pizen each other—with Maw comin' out o' her grave at nights—an' I'll go t' the gold fields o' Californi-a whar Sim an' Peter be!

ABBIE: (*terrified*) Ye won't—leave me? Ye can't!

EBEN: (*with fierce determination*) I'm a-goin', I tell ye! I'll git rich thar an' come back an' fight him fur the farm he stole—an' I'll kick ye both out in the road—t' beg an' sleep in the woods—an' yer son along with ye—t' starve an' die! (*He is hysterical at the end*).

ABBIE: (*with a shudder—humbly*) He's yewr son, too, Eben.

EBEN: (*torturedly*) I wish he never was born! I wish he'd die this minit! I wish I'd never sot eyes on him! It's him—yew havin' him—a-purpose t' steal—that's changed everythin'!

ABBIE: (*gently*) Did ye believe I loved ye—afore he come?

EBEN: Ay-eh—like a dumb ox!

ABBIE: An' ye don't believe no more?

EBEN: B'lieve a lyin' thief! Ha!

ABBIE: (*shudders—then humbly*) An' did ye r'ally love me afore?

EBEN: (*brokenly*) Ay-eh—an' ye was trickin' me!

ABBIE: An' ye don't love me now!

EBEN: (*violently*) I hate ye, I tell ye!

ABBIE: An' ye're truly goin' West—goin' t' leave me—all account o' him being born?

EBEN: I'm a-goin' in the mornin'—or may God strike me t' hell!

ABBIE: (*after a pause—with a dreadful cold intensity—slowly*) If that's what his comin's done t' me—killin' yewr love—takin' yew away—my on'y joy—the on'y joy I ever knowed—like heaven t' me—purtier'n heaven—then I hate him, too, even if I be his Maw!

EBEN: (*bitterly*) Lies! Ye love him! He'll steal the farm fur ye! (*Brokenly*) But t'ain't the farm so much—not no more—it's yew foolin' me—gittin' me t' love ye—lyin' yew loved me—jest t' git a son t' steal!

ABBIE: (*distractedly*) He won't steal! I'd kill him fust! I do love ye! I'll prove t' ye . . . !

EBEN: (*harshly*) T'ain't no use lyin' no more. I'm deaf t' ye! (*He turns away*) I hain't seein' ye agen. Good-by!

ABBIE: (*pale with anguish*) Hain't ye even goin' t' kiss me—not once—arter all we loved?

EBEN: (*in a hard voice*) I hain't wantin' t' kiss ye never agen! I'm wantin' t' forgit I ever sot eyes on ye!

ABBIE: Eben!—ye mustn't—wait a spell—I want t' tell ye. . . .

EBEN: I'm a-goin' in t' git drunk. I'm a-goin' t' dance.

ABBIE: (*clinging to his arm—with passionate earnestness*) If I could make it—'s if he'd never come up between us—if I could prove t' ye I wa'n't schemin' t' steal from ye—so's everythin' could be jest the same with us, lovin' each other jest the same, kissin' an' happy the same's we've been happy afore he come—if I could do it—ye'd love me agen, wouldn't ye? Ye'd kiss me agen? Ye wouldn't never leave me, would ye?

EBEN: (*moved*) I calc'late not. (*Then shaking her hand off his arm—with a bitter smile*) But ye hain't God, be ye?

ABBIE: (*exultantly*) Remember ye've promised! (*Then with strange intensity*) Mebbe I kin take back one thin' God does!

EBEN: (*peering at her*) Ye're gittin' cracked, hain't ye? (*Then going towards door*) I'm a-goin' t' dance.

ABBIE: (*calls after him intensely*) I'll prove t' ye! I'll prove I love ye better'n. . . . (*He goes in the door, not seeming to hear. She remains standing where she is, looking after him—then she finishes desperately*) Better'n everythin' else in the world!

SCENE THREE

*J*UST *before dawn in the morning—shows the kitchen and* CABOT'S *bedroom. In the kitchen, by the light of a tallow candle on the table,* EBEN *is sitting, his chin propped on his hands, his drawn face blank and expressionless. His carpetbag is on the floor beside him. In the bedroom, dimly lighted by a small whale-oil lamp,* CABOT *lies asleep.* ABBIE *is bending over the cradle, listening, her face full of terror yet with an undercurrent of desperate triumph. Suddenly,* *she breaks down and sobs, appears about to throw herself on her knees beside the cradle; but the old man turns restlessly, groaning in his sleep, and she controls herself, and, shrinking away from the cradle with a gesture of horror, backs swiftly toward the door in rear and goes out. A moment later she comes into the kitchen and, running to* EBEN, *flings her arms about his neck and kisses him wildly. He hardens himself, he remains unmoved and cold, he keeps his eyes straight ahead.*

ABBIE: (*hysterically*) I done it, Eben! I told ye I'd do it! I've proved I love ye—better'n everythin'—so's ye can't never doubt me no more!

EBEN: (*dully*) Whatever ye done, it hain't no good now.

ABBIE: (*wildly*) Don't ye say that! Kiss me, Eben, won't ye? I need ye t' kiss me arter what I done! I need ye t' say ye love me!

EBEN: (*kisses her without emotion—dully*) That's fur good-by. I'm a-goin' soon.

ABBIE: No! No! Ye won't go—not now!

EBEN: (*going on with his own thoughts*) I been a-thinkin'—an' I hain't goin' t' tell Paw nothin'. I'll leave Maw t' take vengeance on ye. If I told him, the old skunk'd jest be stinkin' mean enuff to take it out on that baby. (*His voice showing emotion in spite of him*) An' I don't want nothin' bad t' happen t' him. He hain't t' blame fur yew. (*He adds with a certain queer pride*) An' he looks like me! An' by God, he's mine! An' some day I'll be a-comin' back an' . . . !

ABBIE: (*too absorbed in her own thoughts to listen to him—pleadingly*) They's no cause fur ye t' go now—they's no sense—it's all the same's it was—they's nothin' come b'tween us now—arter what I done!

EBEN: (*something in her voice arouses him. He stares at her a bit frightenedly*) Ye look mad, Abbie. What did ye do?

ABBIE: I—I killed him, Eben.

EBEN: (*amazed*) Ye killed him?

ABBIE: (*dully*) Ay-eh.

EBEN: (*recovering from his astonishment—savagely*) An' serves him right!

But we got t' do somethin' quick t' make it look s'if the old skunk'd killed himself when he was drunk. We kin prove by 'em all how drunk he got.

ABBIE: (*wildly*) No! No! Not him! (*Laughing distractedly*) But that's what I ought t' done, hain't it? I oughter killed him instead! Why didn't ye tell me?

EBEN: (*appalled*) Instead? What d'ye mean?

ABBIE: Not him.

EBEN: (*his face grown ghastly*) Not—not that baby!

ABBIE: (*dully*) Ay-eh!

EBEN: (*falls to his knees as if he'd been struck—his voice trembling with horror*) Oh, God A'mighty! A'mighty God! Maw, whar was ye, why didn't ye stop her?

ABBIE: (*simply*) She went back t' her grave that night we fust done it, remember? I hain't felt her about since. (*A pause.* EBEN *hides his head in his hands, trembling all over as if he had the ague. She goes on dully*) I left the piller over his little face. Then he killed himself. He stopped breathin'. (*She begins to weep softly*).

EBEN: (*rage beginning to mingle with grief*) He looked like me. He was mine, damn ye!

ABBIE: (*slowly and brokenly*) I didn't want t' do it. I hated myself fur doin' it. I loved him. He was so purty—dead spit 'n' image o' yew. But I loved yew more—an' yew was goin' away—far off whar I'd never see ye agen, never kiss ye, never feel ye pressed agin me agen— an' ye said ye hated me fur havin' him—ye said ye hated him an' wished he was dead—ye said if it hadn't been fur him comin' it'd be the same's afore between us.

EBEN: (*unable to endure this, springs to his feet in a fury, threatening her, his twitching fingers seeming to reach out for her throat*) Ye lie! I never said—I never dreamed ye'd— I'd cut off my head afore I'd hurt his finger!

ABBIE: (*piteously, sinking on her knees*) Eben, don't ye look at me like that—hatin' me—not after what I done fur ye—fur us—so's we could be happy agen—

EBEN: (*furiously now*) Shut up, or I'll kill ye! I see yer game now—the same old sneakin' trick—ye're aimin' t' blame me fur the murder ye done!

ABBIE: (*moaning—putting her hands over her ears*) Don't ye, Eben! Don't ye! (*She grasps his legs*).

EBEN: (*his mood suddenly changing to horror, shrinks away from her*) Don't ye tech me! Ye're pizen! How could ye—t' murder a pore little critter— Ye must've swapped yer soul t' hell! (*Suddenly raging*) Ha! I kin see why ye done it! Not the lies ye jest told—but 'cause ye wanted t' steal agen—steal the last thin' ye'd left me—my part o' him—no, the hull o' him—ye saw he looked like me—ye knowed he was all mine—an' ye couldn't b'ar it—I know ye! Ye killed him fur bein' mine! (*All this has driven him almost insane. He makes a rush past her for the door—then turns—shaking both fists at her, violently*) But I'll take vengeance now! I'll git the Sheriff! I'll tell him everythin'! Then I'll sing "I'm off to Californi-a!" an' go—gold—Golden Gate—gold sun—fields o' gold in the West! (*This last he half shouts, half croons incoherently, suddenly breaking off passionately*) I'm a-goin' fur the Sheriff t' come an' git ye! I want ye tuk away, locked up from me! I can't stand t' luk at ye! Murderer an' thief 'r not, ye still tempt me! I'll give ye up t' the Sheriff! (*He turns and runs out, around the corner of house, panting and sobbing, and breaks into a swerving sprint down the road*).

ABBIE: (*struggling to her feet, runs to the door, calling after him*) I love ye, Eben! I love ye! (*She stops at the door weakly, swaying, about to fall*) I don't care what ye do—if ye'll on'y love me agen—(*She falls limply to the floor in a faint*).

Scene Four

*A*BOUT *an hour later. Same as Scene Three. Shows the kitchen and* CABOT'S *bedroom. It is after dawn. The sky is brilliant with the sunrise. In the kitchen,* ABBIE *sits at the table, her body limp and exhausted, her head bowed down over her arms, her face hidden. Upstairs,* CABOT *is still asleep but awakens with a start. He looks toward the window and gives a snort of surprise and irritation—throws back the covers and begins hurriedly pulling on his clothes. Without looking behind him, he begins talking to* ABBIE *whom he supposes beside him.*

CABOT: Thunder 'n' lightin', Abbie! I hain't slept this late in fifty year! Looks 's if the sun was full riz a'most. Must've been the dancin' an' likker. Must be gittin' old. I hope Eben's t' wuk. Ye might've tuk the trouble t' rouse me, Abbie. (*He turns—sees no one there—surprised*) Waal—whar air she? Gittin' vittles, I calc'late. (*He tiptoes to the cradle and peers down—proudly*) Mornin', sonny. Purty's a picter! Sleepin' sound. He don't beller all night like most o' 'em. (*He goes quietly out the door in rear—a few moments later enters kitchen—sees* ABBIE—*with satisfaction*) So thar ye be. Ye got any vittles cooked?

ABBIE: (*without moving*) No.

CABOT: (*coming to her, almost sympathetically*) Ye feelin' sick?

ABBIE: No.

CABOT: (*pats her on shoulder. She shudders*) Ye'd best lie down a spell. (*Half jocularly*) Yer son'll be needin' ye soon. He'd ought t' wake up with a gnashin' appetite, the sound way he's sleepin'.

ABBIE: (*shudders—then in a dead voice*) He hain't never goin' t' wake up.

CABOT: (*jokingly*) Takes after me this mornin'. I hain't slept so late in . . .

ABBIE: He's dead.

CABOT: (*stares at her—bewilderedly*) What . . . .

ABBIE: I killed him.

CABOT: (*stepping back from her—aghast*) Air ye drunk—'r crazy—'r . . . !

ABBIE: (*suddenly lifts her head and turns on him—wildly*) I killed him, I tell ye! I smothered him. Go up an' see if ye don't b'lieve me! (CABOT *stares at her a second, then bolts out the rear door, can be heard bounding up the stairs, and rushes into the bedroom and over to the cradle.* ABBIE *has sunk back lifelessly into her former position.* CABOT *puts his hand down on the body in the crib. An expression of fear and horror comes over his face*).

CABOT: (*shrinking away—tremblingly*) God A'mighty! God A'mighty. (*He stumbles out the door—in a short while returns to the kitchen—comes to* ABBIE, *the stunned expression still on his face—hoarsely*) Why did ye do it? Why? (*as she doesn't answer, he grabs her violently by the shoulder and shakes her*) I ax ye why ye done it! Ye'd better tell me 'r . . . !

ABBIE: (*gives him a furious push which sends him staggering back and springs to her feet—with wild rage and hatred*) Don't ye dare tech me! What right hev ye t' question me 'bout him? He wa'n't yewr son! Think I'd have a son by yew? I'd die fust! I hate the sight o' ye an' allus did! It's yew I should've murdered, if I'd had good sense! I hate ye! I love Eben. I did from the fust. An' he was Eben's son—mine an' Eben's—not your'n!

CABOT: (*stands looking at her dazedly—a pause—finding his words with an effort—dully*) That was it—what I felt—pokin' round the corners—while ye lied—holdin' yerself from me—sayin' ye'd a'ready conceived— (*He lapses into crushed silence—then with a strange emotion*) He's dead, sart'n. I felt his heart. Pore little critter! (*He blinks back one tear, wiping his sleeve across his nose*).

ABBIE: (*hysterically*) Don't ye! Don't ye! (*She sobs unrestrainedly*).

CABOT: (*with a concentrated effort that stiffens his body into a rigid line and hardens his face into a stony mask—through his teeth to himself*) I got t' be—like a stone—a rock o' jedgment! (*A pause. He gets complete control over himself—harshly*) If he was Eben's, I be glad he air gone! An' mebbe I suspicioned it all along. I felt they was somethin' onnateral—somewhars—the house got so lonesome—an' cold—drivin' me down t' the barn—t' the beasts o' the field. . . . Ay-eh. I must've suspi-

cioned—somethin'. Ye didn't fool me—not altogether, leastways—
I'm too old a bird—growin' ripe on the bough. . . . (*He becomes aware
he is wandering, straightens again, looks at* ABBIE *with a cruel grin*) So
ye'd liked t' hev murdered me 'stead o' him, would ye? Waal, I'll live
to a hundred! I'll live t' see ye hung! I'll deliver ye up t' the jedgment
o' God an' the law! I'll git the Sheriff now. (*Starts for the door*).

ABBIE: (*dully*) Ye needn't. Eben's gone fur him.

CABOT: (*amazed*) Eben—gone fur the Sheriff?

ABBIE: Ay-eh.

CABOT: T' inform agen ye?

ABBIE: Ay-eh.

CABOT: (*considers this—a pause—then in a hard voice*) Waal, I'm thankful
fur him savin' me the trouble. I'll git t' wuk. (*He goes to the door—
then turns—in a voice full of strange emotion*) He'd ought t' been my
son, Abbie. Ye'd ought t' loved me. I'm a man. If ye'd loved me, I'd
never told no Sheriff on ye no matter what ye did, if they was t' brile
me alive!

ABBIE: (*defensively*) They's more to it nor yew know, makes him tell.

CABOT: (*dryly*) Fur yewr sake, I hope they be. (*He goes out—comes around
to the gate—stares up at the sky. His control relaxes. For a moment he is
old and weary. He murmurs despairingly*) God A'mighty, I be lonesomer'n ever! (*He hears running footsteps from the left, immediately is
himself again.* EBEN *runs in, panting exhaustedly, wild-eyed and mad
looking. He lurches through the gate.* CABOT *grabs him by the shoulder.*
EBEN *stares at him dumbly*) Did ye tell the Sheriff?

EBEN: (*nodding stupidly*) Ay-eh.

CABOT: (*gives him a push away that sends him sprawling—laughing with
withering contempt*) Good fur ye! A prime chip o' yer Maw ye be! (*He
goes toward the barn, laughing harshly.* EBEN *scrambles to his feet. Suddenly
CABOT turns—grimly threatening*) Git off this farm when the Sheriff
takes her—or, by God, he'll have t' come back an' git me fur murder,
too! (*He stalks off.* EBEN *does not appear to have heard him. He runs to
the door and comes into the kitchen.* ABBIE *looks up with a cry of anguished*

joy. EBEN *stumbles over and throws himself on his knees beside her—sobbing* brokenly).

EBEN: Fergive me!

ABBIE: (*happily*) Eben! (*She kisses him and pulls his head over against her breast*).

EBEN: I love ye! Fergive me!

ABBIE: (*ecstatically*) I'd fergive ye all the sins in hell fur sayin' that! (*She kisses his head, pressing it to her with a fierce passion of possession*).

EBEN: (*brokenly*) But I told the Sheriff. He's comin' fur ye!

ABBIE: I kin b'ar what happens t' me—now!

EBEN: I woke him up. I told him. He says, wait 'til I git dressed. I was waiting. I got to thinkin' o' yew. I got to thinkin' how I'd loved ye. It hurt like somethin' was bustin' in my chest an' head. I got t' cryin'. I knowed sudden I loved ye yet, an' allus would love ye!

ABBIE: (*caressing his hair—tenderly*) My boy, hain't ye?

EBEN: I begun t' run back. I cut across the fields an' through the woods. I thought ye might have time t' run away—with me— an' . . .

ABBIE: (*shaking her head*) I got t' take my punishment—t' pay fur my sin.

EBEN: Then I want t' share it with ye.

ABBIE: Ye didn't do nothin'.

EBEN: I put it in yer head. I wisht he was dead! I as much as urged ye t' do it!

ABBIE: No. It was me alone!

EBEN: I'm as guilty as yew be! He was the child o' our sin.

ABBIE: (*lifting her head as if defying God*) I don't repent that sin! I hain't askin' God t' fergive that!

EBEN: Nor me—but it led up t' the other—an' the murder ye did, ye did 'count o' me—an' it's my murder, too, I'll tell the Sheriff—an' if ye deny it, I'll say we planned it t'gether—an' they'll all b'lieve me, fur they suspicion everythin' we've done, an' it'll seem likely an' true to 'em. An' it is true—way down. I did help ye—somehow.

ABBIE: (*laying her head on his—sobbing*) No! I don't want yew t' suffer!

EBEN: I got t' pay fur my part o' the sin! An' I'd suffer wuss leavin' ye, goin' West, thinkin' o' ye day an' night, bein' out when yew was in—(*Lowering his voice*) 'r bein' alive when yew was dead. (*A pause*) I want t' share with ye, Abbie—prison 'r death 'r hell 'r anythin'! (*He looks into her eyes and forces a trembling smile*) If I'm sharin' with ye, I won't feel lonesome, leastways.

ABBIE: (*weakly*) Eben! I won't let ye! I can't let ye!

EBEN: (*kissing her—tenderly*) Ye can't he'p yerself. I got ye beat fur once!

ABBIE: (*forcing a smile—adoringly*) I hain't beat—s'long's I got ye!

EBEN: (*hears the sound of feet outside*) Ssshh! Listen! They've come t' take us!

ABBIE: No, it's him. Don't give him no chance to fight ye, Eben. Don't say nothin'—no matter what he says. An' I won't neither. (*It is* CABOT. *He comes up from the barn in a great state of excitement and strides into the house and then into the kitchen.* EBEN *is kneeling beside* ABBIE, *his arm around her, hers around him. They stare straight ahead*).

CABOT: (*stares at them, his face hard. A long pause—vindictively*) Ye make a slick pair o' murderin' turtle doves! Ye'd ought t' be both hung on the same limb an' left thar t' swing in the breeze an' rot—a warnin' t' old fools like me t' b'ar their lonesomeness alone—an' fur young fools like ye t' hobble their lust. (*A pause. The excitement returns to his face, his eyes snap, he looks a bit crazy*) I couldn't work today. I couldn't take no interest. T' hell with the farm! I'm leavin' it! I've turned the cows an' other stock loose! I've druv 'em into the woods whar they kin be free! By freein' 'em, I'm freein' myself! I'm quittin' here today! I'll set fire t' house an' barn an' watch 'em burn, an' I'll leave yer Maw t' haunt the ashes, an' I'll will the fields back t' God, so that nothin' human kin never touch 'em! I'll be a-goin' to California—t' jine Simeon an' Peter—true sons o' mine if they be dumb fools—an' the Cabots'll find Solomon's Mines t'gether! (*He suddenly cuts a mad caper*) Whoop! What was the song they sung? "Oh, Californi-a! That's the land fur me." (*He sings this—then gets on his knees by the floor-board under which the money was hid*) An' I'll sail thar

on one o' the finest clippers I kin find! I've got the money! Pity ye
didn't know whar this was hidden so's ye could steal.... (*He has
pulled up the board. He stares—feels—stares again. A pause of dead silence.
He slowly turns, slumping into a sitting position on the floor, his eyes like
those of a dead fish, his face the sickly green of an attack of nausea. He
swallows painfully several times—forces a weak smile at last*) So—ye did
steal it!

EBEN: (*emotionlessly*) I swapped it t' Sim an' Peter fur their share o' the
farm—t' pay their passage t' Californi-a.

CABOT: (*with one sardonic*) Ha! (*He begins to recover. Gets slowly to his
feet—strangely*) I calc'late God give it to 'em—not yew! God's hard,
not easy! Mebbe they's easy gold in the West but it hain't God's
gold. It hain't fur me. I kin hear His voice warnin' me agen t' be
hard an' stay on my farm. I kin see his hand usin' Eben t' steal t'
keep me from weakness. I kin feel I be in the palm o' His hand, His
fingers guidin' me. (*A pause—then he mutters sadly*) It's a-goin' t' be
lonesomer now than ever it war afore—an' I'm gittin' old, Lord—
ripe on the bough.... (*Then stiffening*) Waal—what d'ye want?
God's lonesome, hain't He? God's hard an' lonesome! (*A pause. The
Sheriff with two men comes up the road from the left. They move cautiously
to the door. The Sheriff knocks on it with the butt of his pistol*).

SHERIFF: Open in the name o' the law! (*They start*).

CABOT: They've come fur ye. (*He goes to the rear door*) Come in, Jim!
(*The three men enter.* CABOT *meets them in doorway*) Jest a minit, Jim.
I got 'em safe here. (*The Sheriff nods. He and his companions remain in
the doorway*).

EBEN: (*suddenly calls*) I lied this mornin', Jim. I helped her to do it. Ye
kin take me, too.

ABBIE: (*brokenly*) No!

CABOT: Take 'em both. (*He comes forward—stares at* EBEN *with a trace of
grudging admiration*) Purty good—fur yew! Waal, I got t' round up
the stock. Good-by.

EBEN: Good by.

ABBIE: Good-by. (CABOT *turns and strides past the men—comes out and around the corner of the house, his shoulders squared, his face stony, and stalks grimly toward the barn. In the meantime the Sheriff and men have come into the room*).

SHERIFF: (*embarrassedly*) Wall—we'd best start.

ABBIE: Wait. (*Turns to* EBEN) I love ye, Eben.

EBEN: I love ye, Abbie. (*They kiss. The three men grin and shuffle embarrassedly.* EBEN *takes* ABBIE'S *hand. They go out the door in rear, the men following, and come from the house, walking hand in hand to the gate.* EBEN *stops there and points to the sunrise sky*) Sun's a-rizin'. Purty, hain't it?

ABBIE: Ay-eh. (*They both stand for a moment looking up raptly in attitudes strangely aloof and devout*).

SHERIFF: (*looking around at the farm enviously—to his companion*) It's a jim-dandy farm, no denyin'. Wished I owned it!

CURTAIN

"Marco Millions"

CHARACTERS

CHRISTIANS (*in the order in which they appear*):

A TRAVELER

MARCO POLO

DONATA

NICOLO POLO, *Marco's father*

MAFFEO POLO, *Marco's uncle*

TEDALDO, *Legate of Syria* (*afterward Pope Gregory X*)

A DOMINICAN MONK

A KNIGHT-CRUSADER

A PAPAL COURIER

PAULO LOREDANO, *Donata's father, a gentleman from Venice*

Ladies and gentlemen of Venice, soldiers, people of Acre, musicians, servants, etc.

HEATHEN (*in the order in which they appear*):

A MAGIAN TRAVELER

A BUDDHIST TRAVELER

A MAHOMETAN CAPTAIN OF
   GHAZAN'S ARMY

THE ALI BROTHERS,
   Mahometan merchants

A PROSTITUTE

A DERVISH

TWO BUDDHIST MERCHANTS

TWO TARTAR MERCHANTS

A MONGOL PRIEST

194

EMISSARY FROM KUBLAI	GHAZAN, KHAN OF PERSIA
KUBLAI, THE GREAT KAAN	A BUDDHIST PRIEST
PRINCESS KUKACHIN, *his granddaughter*	A TAOIST PRIEST
	A CONFUCIAN PRIEST
CHU-YIN, *a Cathayan sage*	
	A MOSLEM PRIEST
GENERAL BAYAN	
	A TARTAR CHRONICLER
A MESSENGER FROM PERSIA	

People of Persia, India, Mongolia, Cathay, courtiers, nobles, ladies, wives, warriors of Kublai's court, musicians, dancers, Chorus of Mourners.

SCENES

Prologue: A sacred tree in Persia near the confines of India toward the close of the thirteenth century.

ACT ONE

Scene I: Exterior of DONATA's house, Venice—twenty-three years earlier.

Scene II: Palace of the Papal Legate of Syria at Acre—six months later.

Scene III: Persia—four months later.

Scene IV: India—eight months later.

Scene v: Mongolia—eleven months later.

Scene vi: Cathay—The Grand Throne Room in KUBLAI's palace at
             Cambaluc—one month later.

Act Two

Scene i: The Little Throne Room in KUBLAI's summer palace at Xan-
             adu, "the city of Peace," fifteen years later.

Scene ii: The royal wharf at the seaport of Zayton, several weeks later.

Scene iii: Deck of the royal junk of the Princess Kukachin at anchor in
             the harbor of Hormuz, Persia—two years later.

Act Three

Scene i: The Grand Throne Room in the Imperial Palace at Cam-
             baluc, one year later—and later the Dining Room of the Polo
             Home in Venice at the same time.

Scene ii: The Grand Throne Room at Cambaluc—one year later.

Epilogue: The theatre.

"Marco Millions"

Prologue

*S*cene: *A sacred tree on a vast plain in Persia near the confines of India. Votive offerings, pieces of cloth torn from clothing, bangles, armlets, ornaments, tapers, have been nailed on the trunk or tied to the branches. The heavy limbs spread out to a great distance from the trunk. Beneath them is deep cool shade, contrasting with the blinding glare of the noon sun on the sandy plain in the background. A merchant carrying in each hand a strapped box that resembles a modern sample case, plods wearily to the foot of the tree. He puts the boxes down and takes out a handkerchief to mop his forehead. He is a white Christian, middle-aged, average-looking, with a moustache and beard beginning to show gray. His clothes in the style of the Italian merchant class of the thirteenth century are travel-worn. He sighs, tired and hot.*

Phoo!

(*From the left a* MAGIAN, *a Persian, dressed in the fashion of a trader, comes in. He carries a small, square bag. He also is hot, weary, and dust-covered. In age and appearance, making allowance for the difference in race, he closely resembles the* CHRISTIAN. *He and the latter stare at each other, then bow perfunctorily. The* MAGIAN *sets down his bag and wipes his brow*).

CHRISTIAN: (*sympathetically*) Hot as hell!
MAGIAN: (*grimly*) Hotter! (*They both chuckle. A* BUDDHIST, *a Kashmiri traveling merchant comes in, puffing and sweating, from the right. He has a pack strapped on his back. He resembles the other two in the essential character of his body and face. He stops on seeing them. After eyeing him for an appraising second, the two bow and the* BUDDHIST *comes forward to set his pack beside the bags of the others*).

BUDDHIST: (*with relief*) Phoo! (*Then breaking the ice*) The sun would cook you!

MAGIAN: It is hot certainly.

CHRISTIAN: (*as they all sit down to rest, looks from one to the other—jovially*) Funny! you'd think we three had an appointment here. Your faces look familiar. Haven't I see you somewheres before?

MAGIAN: In the house of the courtezans at Shiraz. You were drunk.

BUDDHIST: I happened to be there that night, too. You danced and sang lewd songs.

CHRISTIAN: (*a bit embarrassed, but grinning*) Humn—oh, yes—I remember. It was my birthday and I'd taken a drop too much—a very unusual thing for me. (*Then abruptly changing the subject*) How are conditions down your way?

BUDDHIST: (*pursing his lips*) Slow. I come from Delhi. There is a new import tax and trade is very unsettled. We make prayer beads.

MAGIAN: (*gloomily*) And I, for my sins, am hawking a novelty, a block-printed book, for an Arab house. It contains one thousand Arabian lies, with one over for good measure, all full of lechery— at least so they instructed me to tell people to get them to buy.

CHRISTIAN: Did your trip take you down around Ispahan way?

MAGIAN: I just came from there. It is a sad city now. All the bazaars have been closed by an imperial edict in mourning for Queen Kukachin.

CHRISTIAN: (*bounding to his feet as if a wasp had stung him*) Is Queen Kukachin dead? (*Stunned*) Why, I've got a letter of introduction to her from the head of my firm—Marco Polo of Polo Brothers and Son, Venice. He acted as her official escort, and took her from Cathay to Persia to be married! Why, I was counting on selling her and her husband a whole fleet load of goods!

MAGIAN: (*suddenly, pointing off left*) What makes that cloud of dust? (*They all stare and begin to grow worried*).

CHRISTIAN: It doesn't look like camels.

BUDDHIST: (*fearfully*) It has a strange look!

CHRISTIAN: It's coming directly this way.

MAGIAN: These plains are haunted by evil spirits.

CHRISTIAN: (*very frightened, but striving to put up a brave front*) I've heard those rumors. And I know for a fact that people are sometimes possessed by devils, but I don't believe—

BUDDHIST: (*suddenly, pointing to the tree*) I am going to offer a prayer for protection to this tree sacred to Buddha.

CHRISTIAN:⎫
⎬ (*in chorus—irritably*) Sacred to Buddha?
MAGIAN: ⎭

BUDDHIST: Certainly! Do you not know the legend of how the Holy Sakya picked a twig to cleanse his teeth, and then throwing it away, it took root, and sprang up into this mighty tree to testify forever to his miraculous power?

CHRISTIAN: (*resentfully*) You're absolutely all wrong! This tree was the staff of our first father, Adam. It was handed down to Moses who used it to tap water out of stones and finally planted it. The cross our Lord was crucified on was made of this wood. And ever since this tree has been sacred to Him!

MAGIAN: (*cuttingly*) You have both of you been duped by childish lies! This tree is sacred to the founder of the one true religion, Zoroaster, who brought a shoot of the Tree of Life down from Paradise and planted it here!

BUDDHIST: (*scornfully*) You are a pair of superstitious sheep!

CHRISTIAN: You are a couple of idolatrous dogs!

MAGIAN: The two of you are blasphemous hogs! (*They glare at each other insultingly, their hands on their daggers. Suddenly they hear a noise from the left. Their eyes at once are turned in that direction and, forgetting personal animosities, they give a startled exclamation at what they see*).

BUDDHIST: They are pulling a chariot!

CHRISTIAN: They must be slaves. See how the driver lashes them!

BUDDHIST: But what can that be on the wagon—like a coffin!

CHRISTIAN: It must be treasure!

MAGIAN: No. It is a coffin. (*Trembling*) Ssst! I have a foreboding of evil.

(*They prostrate themselves, their faces to the ground. A moment later, preceded by shouts, a cracking of whips, and the dull stamping of feet, a double file of thirty men of different ages, stripped to the waist, harnessed to each other waist-to-waist and to the long pole of a two-wheeled wagon, stagger in, straining forward under the lashes of two soldiers who run beside them and the long whips of the* CAPTAIN *and a* CORPORAL *who are riding on the wagon, the* CAPTAIN *driving. As they reach the middle of the shade they stop. Lashed on the wagon is a coffin covered with a white pall*).

CAPTAIN: (*a brutal, determined-looking man of forty, bellows*). Halt! (*The files of bleeding and sweating men collapse in panting, groaning heaps. The* SOLDIERS *sprawl down beside them. The* CAPTAIN *springs off the wagon*) Phoo! This shade is grateful. (*He looks at the tree—then in an awed tone*) This must be the Holy Tree which was once the staff of Mahomet and, passing down through generations, was buried in the grave of Abu Abdallah where it struck root and grew by the will of Allah into this tree. (*He makes obeisance and prays to the tree as do the* SOLDIERS. *He gets up and takes a gulp of water—then, looking around, notices the three merchants—with startled surprise, drawing his sword*) Ho! What are you? Get up! (*They do so frightenedly. He stares at them and laughs coarsely with relief*) By all the demons, you startled me! But you traders are like fleas, one finds you everywhere! (*Then with a scowl*) Three dogs of unbelievers, too! (*Sharply*) Give an account of yourselves!

BUDDHIST: I was proceeding westward on a business venture, good sir.

MAGIAN: And I to the northward.

CHRISTIAN: And I to the court of Ghazan Khan to present this letter to Queen Kukachin. But I hear she's dead. (*He hands him the letter but the* CAPTAIN *backs away superstitiously*).

CAPTAIN: Allah forbid I touch what belongs to a corpse. (*Then with forced laughter*) You need not journey farther. She is in there! (*His voice has dropped, he points toward the coffin. The others stare at it, dumbfounded and awed. The* CAPTAIN *goes on dryly*) You cannot cheat her now, Christian! (*Then lowering his voice as if afraid he will be overheard*) And yet, to look at her face you would think her only sleeping.

CHRISTIAN: (*astonished*) What? Can you look at her?

CAPTAIN: Her coffin is glass. Her body was anointed by Egyptians so that she preserves the appearance of life. This was done by command of her grandfather Kublai, the Great Kaan. She is being taken home to Cathay for burial—and under penalty of torture I must transport her over the first stage by dark tonight! (*Suddenly lamenting*) But Allah afflicted me! When I reached the last village with my camels foundering, I found the accursed villagers had driven off their beasts to escape requisition. But the dogs could not balk me. I hitched them to the pole instead. (*He looks at the moaning figures with a cruel appraising eye*) But will they last till night? Hi, there! Water to revive them! (*The soldiers carry around jugs of water which the panting men reach out for avidly, then sink back. But three of the more elderly men are too spent to move*).

CHRISTIAN: (*timorously—anxious to change the subject*) Was the Queen very beautiful?

CAPTAIN: (*with bravado*) Would you care to see? You had a letter to her. It can do no harm—and it is a very great wonder!

CHRISTIAN: (*reassuringly, because he is now extremely curious*) Dead Queens in the West usually lie in state.

CAPTAIN: You pull back the cloth then, since that is your custom. (*The* CHRISTIAN *goes to the wagon and gingerly pulls back the pall from the head of the coffin—then retreats with an exclamation as* KUKACHIN'S *face, that of a beautiful Tartar princess of twenty-three, is revealed inside the glass. Her calm expression seems to glow with the intense peace of a life beyond death, the eyes are shut as if she were asleep. The men stare fascinatedly*).

CHRISTIAN: (*after a pause—crossing himself awedly*) Are you certain she's dead?

CAPTAIN: (*in an awed whisper*) In the palace I commanded the company who guarded her coffin at night. I could not take my eyes from her face. It seemed that any moment she must awake and speak! (*While they have been speaking, unnoticed by them, it has grown dark. An unearthly glow, like a halo, lights up the face of* KUKACHIN. *From the branches of the tree comes a sound of sweet sad music as if the leaves were tiny harps strummed by the wind. The face of* KUKACHIN *becomes more and more living. Finally her lips part and her eyes open to look up at the tree*).

CAPTAIN: (*kneeling down to pray*) Allah, be pitiful!

BUDDHIST: Buddha, protect Thy servant!

MAGIAN: Mithra, All-Powerful One!

CHRISTIAN: Jesus, have mercy! (*A voice which is* KUKACHIN's *and yet more musical than a human voice, comes from the coffin as her lips are seen to move*).

KUKACHIN: Say this, I loved and died. Now I am love, and live. And living, have forgotten. And loving, can forgive. (*Here her lips part in a smile of beautiful pity*) Say this for me in Venice! (*A sound of tender laughter, of an intoxicating, supernatural gaiety, comes from her lips and is taken up in chorus in the branches of the tree as if every harp-leaf were laughing in music with her. The laughter recedes heavenward and dies as the halo of light about her face fades and noonday rushes back in a blaze of baking plain. Everyone is prostrate, the harnessed wretches in the exhausted attitudes of sleep, the others visibly trembling with superstitious horror*).

CHRISTIAN: (*the first to recover—bewilderedly*) Venice! It must have been a message she wished me to take back to Marco Polo!

CAPTAIN: (*his terror going and rage taking its place, leaps to his feet*) It was the voice of some Christian devil you summoned! It bewitched even me until Allah drove it back to hell! (*He draws his sword*) Cover her face, accursed sorcerer!

CHRISTIAN: (*pulls the covering over the head of the coffin with indecent haste*) I pledge you my word, good Captain—!

CAPTAIN: (*to his* SOLDIERS) Attention! Kick them up! We must get away from here! (*With blows and kicks the* SOLDIERS *get their human beasts to their feet. There are groans and curses and cries of pain. But three cannot be roused. The* CAPTAIN *growls savagely at the* CHRISTIAN *to keep up his courage*) Pig of an infidel! (*Then glaring at the* BUDDHIST *and* MAGIAN) You too! You were in league with him! (*He grips his sword*).

ALL THREE: (*kneeling—pitiably*) Mercy! Spare us!

A CORPORAL: (*comes up and salutes*) We cannot get three of them up, sir.

CAPTAIN: (*raging*) Lash them!

CORPORAL: They are dead, sir.

CAPTAIN: (*glumly*) Oh. (*Then an idea comes—with cruel satisfaction*) Three, did you say? That is fortunate. Allah has provided! Cut them out and put these in their places! (*At a sign, the* SOLDIERS *fall upon the three merchants, strip off their upper clothes, untie the dead men, and hitch them in their places. All the time the three set up miserable screams of protest, punctuated by the blows and kicks they receive. The others look on with exhausted indifference*).

CHRISTIAN: (*making himself heard above the tumult*) My letter! It was to the Queen! When Polo Brothers hear of this outrage they'll get the Kaan to flay you alive!

CAPTAIN: (*taken aback a moment—then craftily*) Show me your letter again!

CHRISTIAN: (*holding it out with frantic eagerness*) Here! Now set me free!

CAPTAIN: (*takes it and calmly tears it up*) I cannot read but I think you are lying. At any rate, now you have no letter! (*The* CHRISTIAN *sets up a wailing cry and receives a blow. The* CAPTAIN *and* CORPORALS *spring up on the wagon*) And now forward march! (*With a great cracking of whips and shouts of pain the wagon is pulled swiftly away. On the ground under the sacred tree three bodies lie in crumpled heaps. The same sweet sad music comes from the tree again as if its spirit were playing on the leaves a last lamenting farewell to the dead* PRINCESS. *It rises softly and as softly dies away until it is nothing but a faint sound of wind rustling the leaves.*

CURTAIN

*S*CENE: *Twenty-three years earlier. A fresh boy's voice is heard singing a love song in a subdued tone. The light slowly reveals the exterior of* DONATA'S *home on a canal, Venice.* MARCO POLO, *a boy of fifteen, youthfully handsome and well made, is standing in a gondola beneath a barred window of the house, a guitar over his shoulder. The song finished, he waits anxiously. A hand is thrust out to him through the bars. He kisses it passionately. It is hurriedly withdrawn.* DONATA'S *face appears pressed against the bars. She is a girl of twelve, her face pale and pretty in the moonlight.*

DONATA: (*coyly and tenderly*) You mustn't, Mark.

MARCO: There's no harm in that—just kissing your hand!

DONATA: (*demurely*) It's a sin, I'm sure of it.

MARCO: (*with a quick movement of his own hand, captures hers through the bars*) Then I'll have to steal it, and that's a worse sin. (*He pulls her willing hand down toward his lips*).

DONATA: You're hurting my fingers.

MARCO: (*boldly now*) Then I know how to cure them. (*He kisses them one by one*) There!

DONATA: (*tenderly*) You silly boy! Why do you do that?

MARCO: (*very seriously*) You know, Donata.

DONATA: Know what? (*Softly*) Go on and tell me, Mark.

MARCO: (*blurts out gruffly*) I love you, that's what. I've loved you ever since I can remember. And you've known it right along, too, so there's no good pretending.

DONATA: (*softly*) I wasn't sure.

MARCO: (*recklessly*) And how about you? Do you love me? You've got to answer me that!

DONATA: You know—without my saying it.

MARCO: Please say it!

DONATA: (*in a whisper*) I love you. There, silly!

MARCO: And you'll promise to marry me when I come back?

DONATA: Yes, but you'll have to ask my parents.

MARCO: (*easily*) Don't worry about them. They'll be glad, and my folks, too. It'll bring the two firms into closer contact.

DONATA: (*practically*) Yes, I think so, too. (*A pause. Songs and music come from near and far-off in the night about them.* MARCO *has gained possession of her two hands now and his face is closer to the bars of her window*).

MARCO: (*with a sigh*) It's beautiful tonight. I wish I didn't have to go away.

DONATA: I wish, too! Do you really have to?

MARCO: Yes. And I want to, too—all but leaving you. I want to travel and see the world and all the different people, and get to know their habits and needs from first-hand knowledge. You've got to do that if you want to become really big and important. That's what Father says—and Uncle.

DONATA: But won't this trip so very far away be full of danger?

MARCO: (*boastfully*) I can take care of myself. Uncle says taking chances—*necessary* chances, of course—is the best schooling for a real merchant and Father has a saying that where there's nothing risked, there's nothing gained. And they ought to know, oughtn't they, after spending nine years at the court of the Great Kaan and traveling there and back?

DONATA: Is that where you're going?

MARCO: Yes. He's the richest king in the world and Uncle and Father are personal friends of his. They did a lot of work for him. I'll be on the right side of him from the start, and Father and Uncle both say there's millions to be made in his service if you're not afraid of work and keep awake to opportunity.

DONATA: I'm sure you'll succeed. But I wish you weren't going for so long.

MARCO: I'll miss you as much as you miss me. (*Huskily*) I hate to leave you, Donata—but I've got to make my own way—so we can marry—

DONATA: (*hurriedly*) Yes—of course—only come back as soon as you can.

MARCO: But you'll wait, won't you, no matter how long?

DONATA: (*solemnly*) Yes, I swear to, Mark.

MARCO: And I swear by God I'll come back and marry you, and I'll always be true and never forget or do anything—

DONATA: (*startled by a noise from within*) Ssshh! There's someone moving inside. You'll have to go. Here. (*She hands him a locket*) It's a medallion of me painted by an artist who owed Father for spices and couldn't pay with money. Will you keep looking at this all the time you're away and never forget me?

MARCO: (*kissing it passionately*) Every day!

DONATA: And you'll write me?

MARCO: I promise. Every chance I get.

DONATA: (*hesitatingly*) Will you write me—a poem? I won't care how short it is if it's only a poem.

MARCO: I'll try, Donata. I'll do my best.

DONATA: I'll just love it to death, Mark! (*Startledly*) Ssshh! I hear it again. It must be Father. I've got to sneak back.

MARCO: (*desperately*) Won't you kiss me—let me really kiss you—just once—for good-bye?

DONATA: I mustn't.

MARCO: Just once—when I'm going so far away? (*Desperately*) I—I—I'll die if you don't!

DONATA: Well—just once. (*The moonlight fades into darkness as their lips meet. Then from the darkness are their voices heard in hushed tones*) Good-bye, Mark.

MARCO: Good-bye, Donata. (*The sentimental singing voices and guitars are heard from all corners of the night in celebration of love. The sound gradually grows fainter and fainter, receding into the distance, as if* MARCO *were already leaving Venice behind him*).

DARKNESS

Scene Two

Scene: Six months later. The tolling of a church bell is first heard. Then the interior of the Papal Legate's palace at Acre is revealed—a combination of church and government building.

The Legate, TEDALDO, *a man of sixty with a strong, intelligent face, is seated on a sort of throne placed against the rear wall. On his right, stands a warrior noble, a* KNIGHT-CRUSADER, *in full armor, leaning on his sword. On his left, a* DOMINICAN MONK, *his adviser. On the left of the room is an altar with candles burning. On the right, an open portal with a sentry pacing up and down, spear in hand.*

The two elder Polos, NICOLO *and* MAFFEO, *stand in attitudes of patient servility before the throne.* MARCO'S *father,* NICOLO, *is a small thin middle-aged man, with a dry, shrewd face.* MAFFEO, *MARCO'S uncle, is around the same age, but he is tall and stout with a round, jovial face and small, cunning eyes. There is a strong general resemblance between both of them and* MARCO. MARCO *is sitting on a stool in the foreground, his body all screwed up into an awkward intensity, striving with all his might to compose a poem to* DONATA, *but constantly distracted in spite of himself.*

TEDALDO: (*bored but tolerantly*) What can I do except advise you to be patient? I'm sure the Conclave of Cardinals must soon select a Pope.

NICOLO: Two years in session! (*Then suddenly—consoled*) Well, it's a new world's record, anyway.

MAFFEO: (*shaking his head*) This uncertainty is bad for trade.

TEDALDO: (*with a bored yawn*) No doubt. (*Then rather impatiently*) Then, when your business so evidently calls you to the East, why delay longer? Why not simply explain to the Great Kaan, Kublai, that there was no Pope to whom you could deliver his message?

NICOLO: He mightn't understand. His instructions to us were pretty emphatic.

MAFFEO: To request the Pope to send him a hundred wise men of the West—

TEDALDO: (*dryly*) This Kublai is an optimist!

MAFFEO: —to argue with his Buddhists and Taoists and Confucians which religion in the world is best.

MONK: (*outraged*) Impudent ignoramus! Does he imagine the Church would stoop to such bickering?

TEDALDO: (*with a weary smile*) I begin to think Kublai is a humorist, too.

MAFFEO: (*craftily*) It'd pay to convert him. He's the richest king in the world. He rules over millions of subjects, his empire covers millions of square miles of great undeveloped natural resources, his personal wealth in cash and jewels and goods alone easily runs into millions of millions!

MARCO: (*stares at his uncle—then mutters fascinatedly*) Millions! (*Then, shaking away this interruption, bends to his writing again*).

TEDALDO: (*wearily*) I am bored with your millions, Messrs. Polo. Even if they are true, it is too much effort to conceive them. (*They bow humbly and retire backward. His eyes following them listlessly* TEDALDO *sees* MARCO, *who at this moment is scratching himself, twisting and turning his legs and feet, tearing his hair in a perfect frenzy of balked inspiration.* TEDALDO *smiles and addresses him in an affectionate, humorous tone*) God's mercy on you, Master Marco! Are you suddenly possessed by a devil—or is it only these infernal Mahometan fleas the Almighty sends us for our sins?

MARCO: (*coming out of his fit—sheepishly*) I'm only writing something.

MAFFEO: Mark is surprisingly quick at figures.

NICOLO: But still heedless. A dreamer! (*To* MARCO, *with a condescending paternal air*) What are you writing, son? (*He and* MAFFEO *draw near* MARCO).

MARCO: (*more confused*) Nothing, sir—just—something. (*He tries to hide it*).

MAFFEO: Why are you so mysterious? Come, let's see.

MARCO: No—please, Uncle.

MAFFEO: (*with a sudden cunning motion, he snatches it from* MARCO's *hand, glances at it and bursts into laughter*) Look, Nicolo, look!

MARCO: (*rebelliously*) Give that back!

NICOLO: (*sternly*) Behave yourself, Mark! (*To* MAFFEO) What is it?

MAFFEO: See for yourself. (*He hands it to him*) Did you know you'd hatched a nightingale? (*He laughs coarsely*) (NICOLO *reads, a scornful grin coming to his lips*).

TEDALDO: Surely it cannot be a song he has written?

NICOLO: (*going to him—laughing*) A rhyme! A love poem, no less!

TEDALDO: (*severely, as he takes the poem*) Do not mock at him! Rather be grateful if a thistle can bring forth figs. (MARCO *remains sullenly apart, shamefaced and angry, his fists clenched.* TEDALDO *reads—frowns— laughs—then smilingly to* NICOLO) Your fear that this is a poem is— humn—exaggerated! (*He reads amusedly as* MARCO *squirms*):

"You are lovely as the gold in the sun
Your skin is like silver in the moon
Your eyes are black pearls I have won.
I kiss your ruby lips and you swoon,
Smiling your thanks as I promise you
A large fortune if you will be true,
While I am away earning gold
And silver so when we are old
I will have a million to my credit
And in the meantime can easily afford
A big wedding that will do us credit
And start having children, bless the Lord!"

(*There is a roar of laughter in which* TEDALDO *joins.* MARCO *looks about for a hole into which to crawl.* TEDALDO *addresses him amusedly but with kindness*) Come, Marco. Here is your poem. Your lady is a bit too mineral, your heaven of love a trifle monetary—but, never mind, you will be happier as a Polo than as a poet. Here. (*He gives it to* MARCO.

The latter fiercely crumples it up and throws it on the floor and stamps on it).

NICOLO: (*approvingly*) Sensibly done, my boy.

TEDALDO: (*looking searchingly at* MARCO's *face—gently*) Perhaps I was too critical. Your poem had merits of its own. I am sure it would touch your lady's heart.

MARCO: (*with a great bluster of manliness*) Oh, I don't mind your making fun. I can take a joke. It *was* silly. Poetry's all stupid, anyway. I was only trying it for fun, to see if I could. You won't catch me ever being such a fool again!

MONK: (*as a noise of shouting comes toward them*) Ssstt! What's that? (*The* KNIGHT *hurries to the portal*).

KNIGHT: Someone is running here, and a crowd behind. I hear them shouting "Pope."

MONK: Then the Conclave has chosen!

POLOS: (*joyfully*) At last! (*The cries of many voices. The* SENTINEL *and* KNIGHT *admit the* MESSENGER *but push back the others*).

MESSENGER: (*exhausted—falls on his knees before* TEDALDO, *holding out a sealed paper*) I come from the Conclave. You were chosen. Your Holiness—(*He falls fainting. The crowds cheer and sweep in*).

TEDALDO: (*rising—pale and trembling*) What does he say?

MONK: (*has picked up the document—joyfully*) See! The official seal! You are the Pope! (*He kneels humbly*) Your Holiness, let me be the first—(*He kisses* TEDALDO's *hand. All are kneeling now, their heads bowed. The bells of the churches begin to ring*).

TEDALDO: (*raising his hands to heaven—dazedly*) Lord, I am not worthy! (*Then to those about him—tremblingly*) Leave me. I must pray to God for strength—for guidance!

CROWD: (*in a clamor*) Your blessing! (TEDALDO *with a simple dignity and power, blesses them. They back out slowly, the* MONK *and* KNIGHT *last. The* POLOS *group together in the foreground, holding a whispered conference.* TEDALDO *kneels before the altar*).

MAFFEO: Now that he's the Pope, if we could get an answer from him, we could start right away.

NICOLO: We couldn't hope for better weather.

MAFFEO: He seems to have taken a fancy to Mark. You speak to him, Mark.

MARCO: (*unwillingly*) He's praying.

MAFFEO: He'll have time enough for that, but with us time is money. (*Giving the unwilling* MARCO *a push*) This will test your nerve, Mark! Don't shirk!

MARCO: (*gritting his teeth*) All right. I'll show you I'm not scared! (*He advances boldly toward the altar, stands there for a moment awkwardly as* TEDALDO *remains oblivious—then he falls on his knees—humbly but insistently*) Your Holiness. Forgive me, Your Holiness—

TEDALDO: (*turns to him and springs to his feet—imperiously*) I wish to be alone! (*Then as* MARCO *is shrinking back—more kindly*) Well, what is it? I owe you a recompense, perhaps—for an injury.

MARCO: (*stammeringly*) Your Holiness—if you could give us some answer to deliver to the Great Kaan—we could start now—with such favorable weather—

TEDALDO: (*amused in spite of himself*) On the last day one of your seed will interrupt Gabriel to sell him another trumpet! (*Then sardonically to the elder* POLOS) I have no hundred wise men—nor one! Tell the Great Kaan he must have been imposed upon by your patriotic lies, or he could never make such a request.

POLOS: (*terrified*) But, Your Holiness, we dare not repeat— He'd have us killed!

TEDALDO: I will send him a monk or two. That is quite sufficient to convert a Tartar barbarian!

MAFFEO: But, Your Holiness, he's not a barbarian! Why, every plate on his table is solid gold!

TEDALDO: (*smiling*) And has he millions of plates, too? (*Then with a sudden whimsicality*) But if the monks fail, Master Marco can be my missionary. Let him set an example of virtuous Western manhood amid all the levities of paganism, shun the frailty of poetry, have a million to his credit, as he so beautifully phrased it, and I will wager a million of something or other myself that the Kaan will soon be driven to seek spiritual salvation somewhere! Mark my words, Marco will be worth a million wise men—in the cause of wisdom! (*He laughs gaily, raising his hand over* MARCO's *head*) Go with my blessing! But what need have you for a blessing? You were born with success in your pocket! (*With a last gesture he turns, going quickly out the door in rear*).

MAFFEO: (*as he goes—approvingly*) Mark is making a good impression already!

NICOLO: Well, he's got a head on him!

MARCO: (*beginning to swell out a bit matter-of-factly*) Never mind about me. When do we start?

POLOS: (*hurriedly*) At once. Let's go and pack. (*They go out left*) Come, Mark! Hurry!

MARCO: I'm coming. (*He waits, looks after them, picks up the crumpled poem, starts to hide it in his jacket, stops, mutters with brave self-contempt*) Aw! You damn fool! (*He throws the poem down again, starts to go, hesitates, suddenly turns back, picks it up, crams it into his doublet and runs wildly out the door. The scene fades into darkness. For a time the church bells, which have never ceased ringing, are heard acclaiming the new Pope; but the* POLOS *proceed speedily on their journey and the sound is soon left behind them*).

DARKNESS

Scene Three

*S*CENE: *Light comes, gradually revealing the scene. In the rear is the front of a Mahometan mosque. Before the mosque, is a throne on which sits a Mahometan ruler. On the right, the inevitable warrior—on his left, the inevitable priest—the two defenders of the State. At the ruler's feet his wives crouch like slaves. Everything is jeweled, high-colored, gorgeous in this background. Squatted against the side walls, forming a sort of semi-circle with the throne at center, counting from left to right consecutively, are a mother nursing a baby, two children playing a game, a young girl and a young man in a loving embrace, a middle-aged couple, an aged couple, a coffin. All these Mahometan figures remain motionless. Only their eyes move, staring fixedly but indifferently at the* POLOS, *who are standing at center.* MARCO *is carrying in each hand bags which curiously resemble modern sample cases. He sets these down and gazes around with a bewildered awe.*

NICOLO: (*turning on him—genially*) Well, son, here we are in Islam.

MARCO: (*round-eyed*) A man told me that Noah's Ark is still somewhere around here on top of a mountain. (*Eagerly*) And he proved it to me, too. Look! (*He shows them a piece of wood*) He broke this off of the Ark. See, it's got Noah's initials on it!

MAFFEO: (*grimly*) How much did you pay him for it?

MARCO: Ten soldi in silver.

NICOLO: (*dashing it out of* MARCO's *hand—bitterly*) Muttonhead! Do you suppose Almighty God would allow infidels to cut up Noah's Ark into souvenirs to sell to Christians?

MAFFEO: (*teasingly*) Your son and your money are soon parted, Brother. (*Then placatingly*) But he's only a boy. He'll learn. And before we go farther, Nicolo, we better read him from the notes we made on our last trip all there is to remember about this corner of the world.

NICOLO: (*they take out note-books closely resembling a modern business man's date-book and read*) We're now passing through Kingdoms where they worship Mahomet.

MAFFEO: There's one kingdom called Musul and in it a district of Baku where there's a great fountain of oil. There's a growing demand for it. (*Then speaking*) Make a mental note of that.

MARCO: Yes, sir.

NICOLO: Merchants make great profits. The people are simple creatures. It's very cold in winter. The women wear cotton drawers. This they do to look large in the hips, for the men think that a great beauty. (*The two* MAHOMETAN MERCHANTS *enter from the left.* MAFFEO *recognizes them immediately—in a swift aside to his brother*).

MAFFEO: There's those damned Ali brothers. They'll cut under our prices with their cheap junk as usual. (*The* ALI *brothers have seen the* POLOS *and a whispered aside, evidently of the same nature, passes between them. Then simultaneously the two firms advance to meet each other putting on expressions of the utmost cordiality*) Well, well. You folks are a welcome sight!

ONE ALI: My dear, dear friends! Praise be to Allah! (*They embrace*).

MAFFEO: (*with a cunning smirk*) Selling a big bill of goods hereabouts, I'll wager, you old rascals?

THE OLDER ALI: (*airily*) My dear friend, don't speak of business. But you, you are on a venture to the court of the Great Kaan, we hear?

MAFFEO: What lies get around! Nothing in it—absolutely nothing!

NICOLO: For heaven's sake, let's not talk business! Let's have a nice friendly chat. (*The four squat together in a circle*).

MAFFEO: (*with a wink*) I'll tell you a good one an Armenian doily-dealer told me down in Bagdad. (*They all bend their heads toward him with expectant grins. He looks around—then begins in a cautious lowered tone*) Well, there was an old Jew named Ikey and he married a young girl named Rebecca— (*He goes on telling the rest of the story with much exaggerated Jewish pantomime but in a voice too low to be heard. In the meantime,* MARCO *has slipped off, full of curiosity and wonder, to look at this strange life. He goes first to the left, stops before the mother and baby, smiles down at it uncertainly, then bends down to take hold of its hand).*

MARCO: Hello! (*Then to the mother*) He's fat as butter! (*Both remain silent and motionless, staring at him from a great distance with indifferent calm.* MARCO *is rebuffed, grows embarrassed, turns away to the children, who, frozen in the midst of their game of jackstraws, are looking at him.* MARCO *adopts a lofty condescending air*) Humh! Do you still play that game here? I remember it—when I was a kid. (*They stare silently. He mutters disgustedly*) Thickheads! (*And turns to the lovers who with their arms about each other, cheek to cheek, stare at him. He looks at them, fascinated and stirred, and murmurs enviously*) She's pretty. I suppose they're engaged—like Donata and me. (*He fumbles and pulls out the locket which is hung around his neck on a ribbon*) Donata's prettier. (*Then embarrassedly, he holds it out for them to see*) Don't you think she's pretty? She and I are going to be married some day. (*They do not look except into his eyes. He turns away, hurt and angry*) Go to the devil, you infidels! (*He stuffs the locket back—stops before the throne—tries to stare insolently at the king but, awed in spite of himself, makes a grudging bow and passes on, stops before the family group, sneers and passes on, stops before the old couple and cannot restrain his curiosity*) Would you tell me how old you are? (*He passes on, rebuffed again, stops fascinatedly before the coffin, leans out and touches it with defiant daring, shudders superstitiously and shrinks away, going to the merchant group who are roaring with laughter as* MAFFEO *ends his story*).

THE OLDER ALI: (*to* NICOLO) Your son?

NICOLO: Yes, and a chip of the old block.

THE OLDER ALI: Will he follow in your footsteps?

NICOLO: (*jocosely*) Yes, and you better look out then! He's as keen as a hawk already.

THE OLDER ALI: (*with a trace of a biting smile*) He greatly resembles a youth I saw back on the road buying a piece of Noah's Ark from a wayside sharper.

MAFFEO: (*hastily coming to the rescue as* NICOLO *cannot hide his chagrin—boastfully*) It wasn't Mark. Mark would have sold him the lions of St. Mark's for good mousers! (*The* PROSTITUTE *enters from the right. She is painted, half-naked, alluring in a brazen, sensual way. She smiles at* MARCO *enticingly*).

MARCO: (*with a gasp*) Look! Who's that? (*They all turn, and, recognizing her, laugh with coarse familiarity*).

MAFFEO: (*jokingly*) So here you are again. You're like a bad coin—always turning up.

PROSTITUTE: (*smiling*) Shut up. You can bet it isn't old fools like you that turn me.

NICOLO: (*with a lecherous grin at her*) No? But it's the old who have the money.

PROSTITUTE: Money isn't everything, not always. Now I wouldn't ask money from him. (*She points to* MARCO).

NICOLO: (*crossly and jealously*) Leave him alone, you filth!

MAFFEO: (*broad-mindedly*) Come, come, Nicolo. Let the boy have his fling.

PROSTITUTE: (*her eyes on* MARCO) Hello, Handsome.

MARCO: (*bewilderedly*) You've learned our language?

PROSTITUTE: I sell to all nations.

MARCO: What do you sell?

PROSTITUTE: (*mockingly*) A precious jewel. Myself. (*Then desirously*) But for you I'm a gift. (*Putting her hands on his shoulder and lifting her lips*) Why don't you kiss me?

MARCO: (*terribly confused—strugglingly*) I—I don't know—I mean, I'm sorry but—you see I promised someone I'd never—(*Suddenly freeing himself—frightenedly*) Leave go! I don't want your kisses. (*A roar of coarse taunting laughter from the men.* MARCO *runs away, off left*).

NICOLO: (*between his teeth*). What a dolt!

MAFFEO: (*slapping the* PROSTITUTE *on the bare shoulder*) Better luck next time. He'll learn!

PROSTITUTE: (*trying to hide her pique—forcing a cynical smile*) Oh, yes, but I won't be a gift then. I'll make him pay, just to show him! (*She laughs harshly and goes out left. A pause. All four squat again in silence*).

THE OLDER ALI: (*suddenly*) Many wonders have come to pass in these regions. They relate that in old times three kings from this country went to worship a Prophet that was born and they carried with them three manner of offerings—Gold and Frankincense and Myrrh—and when they had come to the place where the Child was born, they marveled and knelt before him.

MAFFEO: That's written in the Bible. The child was Jesus Christ, our Lord. (*He blesses himself,* NICOLO *does likewise*).

THE OLDER ALI: Your Jesus was a great prophet.

NICOLO: (*defiantly*) He was the Son of God!

BOTH ALIS: (*stubbornly*) There is no God but Allah! (*A strained pause. A dervish of the desert runs in shrieking and begins to whirl. No one is surprised except the two* POLOS *who get up to gape at him with the thrilled appreciation inspired by a freak in a sideshow.* MARCO *comes back and joins them*).

MAFFEO: (*with appreciation*) If we had him in Venice we could make a mint of money exhibiting him. (NICOLO *nods*).

MARCO: I'll have to write Donata all about this. (*Wonderingly*) Is he crazy?

MAFFEO: (*in a low aside to him*) My boy, all Mahometans are crazy. That's the only charitable way to look at it. (*Suddenly the call to prayer sounds from Muezzins in the minarets of the mosque. The* DERVISH *falls on his face. Everyone sinks into the attitude of prayer except the* POLOS *who stand embarrassedly, not knowing what to do*).

MARCO: Are they praying?

NICOLO: Yes, they call it that. Much good it does them!

MAFFEO: Ssshh! Come! This is a good time to move on again. Marco! Wake up! (*They go quickly out right,* MARCO *following with the sample cases. The scene fades quickly into darkness as the call of the Muezzins is heard again).*

DARKNESS

Scene Four

S CENE: *The slowly-rising light reveals an Indian snake-charmer squatted on his haunches at center. A snake is starting to crawl from the basket in front of him, swaying its head to the thin, shrill whine of a gourd. Otherwise, the scene, in the placing of its people and the characters and types represented, is the exact duplicate of the last except that here the locale is Indian. The background for the ruler's throne is now a Buddhist temple instead of a mosque. The motionless staring figures are all Indians. Looming directly above and in back of the ruler's throne is an immense Buddha. The* POLOS *stand at center as before,* MARCO *still lugging the sample cases. He is seventeen now. Some of the freshness of youth has worn off.*

They stare at the snake-charmer, the two older men cynically. MARCO *gasps with enthralled horror.*

MARCO: Look at that deadly snake!

MAFFEO: (*cynically*) He's a fake, like everything else here. His fangs have been pulled out.

MARCO: (*disillusioned*) Oh! (*He turns away. The snake-charmer glares at them, stops playing, pushes his snake back into the box and carries it off, after spitting on the ground at their feet with angry disgust.* MARCO *sits on one of the cases and glances about with a forced scorn; looks finally at the Buddha—in a smart-Aleck tone*) So that is Buddha!

NICOLO: (*begins to read from his note-book*) These people are idolaters. The climate is so hot if you put an egg in their rivers it will be boiled.

MAFFEO: (*taking up the reading from his book in the same tone*) The merchants make great profits. Ginger, pepper, and indigo. Largest sheep in the world. Diamonds of great size. The Kings have five hundred wives apiece.

MARCO: (*disgustedly*) It's too darn hot here!

MAFFEO: (*warningly*) Sshhh! Don't let the natives hear you. Remember any climate is healthy where trade is brisk.

MARCO: (*walks sullenly off to left. At the same moment two merchants, this time Buddhists, come in. The same interplay goes on with them as with the* ALI BROTHERS *in the previous scene, only this time it is all done in pantomime until the loud laughter at the end of* MAFFEO'S *story. As* MAFFEO *tells the story,* MARCO *is looking at the people but this time he assumes the casual, indifferent attitude of the worldly-wise. He makes a silly gesture to attract the baby's attention, passes by the two children with only a contemptuous glance, but stops and stares impudently at the lovers—finally spits with exaggerated scorn*) Where do you think you are—home with the light out? Why don't you charge admission? (*He stalks on—pauses before the middle-aged couple who have a bowl of rice between them—in astonishment as though this evidence of a humanity common with his struck him as strange*) Real rice! (*He ignores the throne, passes quickly by the old people with a glance of aversion and very obviously averts his head from the coffin. As he returns to the group at center,* MAFFEO *has just finished his story. There is a roar of laughter*).

MARCO: (*grinning eagerly*) What was it, Uncle?

MAFFEO: (*grinning teasingly*) You're too young.

MARCO: (*boastfully*) Is that so?

NICOLO: (*severely*) Mark! (*The* PROSTITUTE, *the same but now in Indian garb, has entered from left and comes up behind* MARCO).

PROSTITUTE: A chip of the old block, Nicolo!

NICOLO: (*angrily*) You again!

MARCO: (*pleased to see her—embarrassedly*) Why, hello.

PROSTITUTE: (*cynically*) I knew you'd want to see me. (*She raises her lips*) Will you kiss me now? (*as he hesitates*) Forget your promise. You know you want to.

MAFFEO: (*grinning*) There's no spirit in the youngsters nowadays. I'll bet he won't.

PROSTITUTE: (*her eyes on* MARCO's) How much will you bet?

MAFFEO: Ten— (MARCO *suddenly kisses her*).

PROSTITUTE: (*turning to* MAFFEO) I win, Uncle.

MARCO: (*with a grin*) No. I kissed you before he said ten what.

MAFFEO: That's right! Good boy, Mark!

PROSTITUTE: (*turning to* MARCO—*cynically*) You're learning, aren't you? You're becoming shrewd even about kisses. You need only me now to make you into a real man—for ten pieces of gold.

MARCO: (*genuinely overcome by a sudden shame*) No, please.—I—I didn't mean it. It was only in fun.

PROSTITUTE: (*with a sure smile*) Later, then—when we meet again. (*She walks off left*).

MARCO: (*looks after her. As she evidently turns to look back at him, he waves his hand and grins—then abashed*) She's pretty. It's to bad she's—what she is.

MAFFEO: Don't waste pity. Her kind are necessary evils. All of us are human. (*A long pause*).

THE OLDER BUDDHIST MERCHANT: (*suddenly*) The Buddha taught that one's loving-kindness should embrace all forms of life, that one's compassion should suffer with the suffering, that one's sympathy should understand all things, and last that one's judgment should regard all persons and things as of equal importance.

NICOLO: (*harshly*) Who was this Buddha?

THE OLDER BUDDISH MERCHANT: The Incarnation of God.

NICOLO: You mean Jesus?

THE OLDER BUDDHIST MERCHANT: (*unheedingly*) He was immaculately conceived. The Light passed into the womb of Maya, and she bore a son who, when he came to manhood, renounced wife and child, riches and power, and went out as a beggar on the roads to seek the supreme enlightenment which would conquer birth and death; and at last he attained the wisdom where all desire has ended and experienced the heaven of peace, Nirvana. And when he died he became a God again. (*The temple bells begin to ring in chorus. All except the* POLOS *prostrate themselves before the Buddha*).

MARCO: (*to his uncle—in a whispered chuckle*) Died and became a God? So that's what they believe about that stone statue, is it?

MAFFEO: They're all crazy, like the Mahometans. They're not responsible.

MARCO: (*suddenly*) I saw two of them with a bowl of rice—

MAFFEO: Oh, yes. They eat the same as we do. (*Then abruptly*) Come on! This is our chance to make a start. Don't forget our cases, Mark. (*They go out left followed by* MARCO *with the sample cases. The scene fades into darkness. The clamor of the temple bells slowly dies out in the distance*).

DARKNESS

Scene Five

Scene: *From the darkness comes the sound of a small Tartar kettledrum, its beats marking the rhythm for a crooning, nasal voice, rising and falling in a wordless chant.*

The darkness gradually lifts. In the rear is a section of the Great Wall of China with an enormous shut gate. It is late afternoon, just before sunset. Immediately before the gate is a rude throne on which sits a Mongol ruler with warrior and sorcerer to right and left of him. At the sides are Mongol circular huts. The motionless figures sit before these. The MINSTREL, *squatting at center, is the only one whose body moves. In the back of the throne and above it is a small idol made of felt and cloth. The clothes of the ruler and his court are of rich silk stuffs, lined with costly furs. The squatting figures of the people are clothed in rough robes.*

The POLOS *stand at center,* MARCO *still lugging the battered sample cases. He is now nearly eighteen, a brash, self-confident young man, assertive and talky. All the* POLOS *are weary and their clothes shabby and travel-worn.*

MARCO: (*setting down the bags with a thump and staring about with an appraising contempt*) Welcome to that dear old Motherland, Mongolia!

MAFFEO: (*wearily takes out his guide-book and begins to read in the monotone of a boring formula*) Flocks—goats—horses—cattle. The women do all the buying and selling. Business is all in cattle and crops. In short, the people live like beasts.

NICOLO: (*reading from his book*) They have two Gods—a God of Heaven to whom they pray for health of mind, and a God of Earth, who watches over their earthly goods. They pray to him also and do many other stupid things.

MARCO: (*boredly*) Well—let them! (*He walks away and makes the circuit of the figures, but now he hardly glances at them. The* TWO TARTAR MERCHANTS *enter and there is the same pantomime of greeting between them and the* POLOS *as with the* BUDDHIST MERCHANTS *in the previous scene.* MARCO *joins them. It is apparent the whole company is extremely weary. They yawn and prepare to lie down*).

MAFFEO: We'll have time to steal a nap before they open the Gate.

MARCO: (*with an assertive importance*) Just a moment! I've got a good one an idol-polisher told me in Tibet. This is the funniest story you ever heard! It seems an Irishman got drunk in Tangut and wandered into a temple where he mistook one of the female statues for a real woman and— (*He goes on, laughing and chuckling to himself, with endless comic pantomime. The two* TARTAR MERCHANTS *fall asleep.* NICOLO *stares at his son bitterly,* MAFFEO *with contemptuous pity. Finally* MARCO *finishes to his own uproarious amusement*).

NICOLO: (*bitterly*) Dolt!

MAFFEO: (*mockingly. With a yawn*) Youth will have its laugh! (MARCO *stops open-mouthed and stares from one to the other*).

MARCO: (*faintly*) What's the matter?

NICOLO: (*pettishly*) Unless your jokes improve you'll never sell anything.

MAFFEO: I'll have to give Marco some lessons in how to tell a short story. (*Warningly*) And until I pronounce you graduated, mum's the word, understand! The people on the other side of that wall may look simple but they're not. (*The* PROSTITUTE *enters dressed now as a Tartar. She comes and puts her hand on* MARCO's *head*).

PROSTITUTE: What has this bad boy been doing now?

MAFFEO: He's getting too witty! (*He rests his head on his arms and goes to sleep*).

PROSTITUTE: Shall I expect you again tonight?

MARCO: No. You've got all my money. (*Suddenly gets to his feet and faces her—disgustedly*) And I'm through with you, anyway.

PROSTITUTE: (*with a scornful smile*) And I with you—now that you're a man. (*She turns away*).

MARCO: (*angrily*) Listen here! Give me back what you stole! I know I had it on a ribbon around my neck last night and this morning it was gone. (*Threateningly*) Give it to me, you, or I'll make trouble!

PROSTITUTE: (*takes a crumpled paper from her bosom*) Do you mean this?

MARCO: (*tries to snatch it*) No!

PROSTITUTE: (*she unfolds it and reads*)

> "I'll have a million to my credit
> And in the meantime can easily afford
> A big wedding that will do us credit
> And start having children, Bless the Lord!"

(*She laughs*) Are you a poet, too?

MARCO: (*abashed and furious*) I didn't write that.

PROSTITUTE: You're lying. You must have. Why deny it? Don't sell your soul for nothing. That's bad business. (*She laughs, waving the poem in her upraised hand, staring mockingly*) Going! Going! Gone! (*She lets it fall and grinds it under her feet into the earth—laughing*) Your soul! Dead and buried! You strong man! (*She laughs*).

MARCO: (*threateningly*) Give me what was wrapped up in that, d'you hear!

PROSTITUTE: (*scornfully. Takes the miniature from her bosom*) You mean this? I was bringing it back to you. D'you think I want her ugly face around? Here! (*She throws it at his feet. He leans down and picks it up, polishing it on his sleeve remorsefully. The* PROSTITUTE *walking away, calls back over her shoulder*) I kissed it so you'd remember my kiss whenever you kiss her! (*She laughs.* MARCO *starts as if to run after her angrily. Suddenly a shout rises from the lips of all the Tartars, the* MINSTREL *and his drum become silent, and with one accord they raise their arms and eyes to the sky. Then the* MINSTREL *chants*).

MINSTREL: God of the Heaven, be in our souls! (*Then they all prostrate themselves on the ground as he chants*) God of the Earth, be in our bodies! (*The Tartars sit up. The* MINSTREL *begins again his drum beat, crooning in a low monotone. The* POLOS *rise and stretch sleepily*).

MARCO: (*inquisitively*) Two Gods? Are they in one Person like our Holy Trinity?

MAFFEO: (*shocked*) Don't be impious! These are degraded pagans—or crazy, that's a more charitable way to— (*From behind the wall comes the sound of martial Chinese music. The gate opens. The blinding glare of the setting sun floods in from beyond. A file of soldiers, accompanying a richly-dressed* COURT MESSENGER, *come through. He walks directly up to the* POLOS *and bows deeply*).

MESSENGER: The Great Kaan, Lord of the World, sent me— (*He looks around*) But where are the hundred wise men of the West?

NICOLO: (*confusedly*) We had two monks to start with—but they left us and went back.

MAFFEO: (*warningly*) Ssst!

MESSENGER: (*indifferently*) You will explain to the Kaan. I was ordered to arrange a welcome for them.

MAFFEO: (*claps him on the back*) Well, here we are—and hungry as hunters! So your welcome will be welcome, Brother. (*The* MESSENGER *bows, starts back, the* POLOS *following him,* MAFFEO *calling*) Get on the job, Mark! (*They pass through the gate*).

MARCO: (*wearily picks up the cases—then goading himself on*) Giddap! Cathay or bust! (*He struggles through the gate. For a second he is framed in it, outlined against the brilliant sky, tugging a sample case in each hand. Then the gate shuts, the light fades out. The drum beat and the chanting recede into the distance*).

DARKNESS

SCENE SIX

SCENE: *Music from full Chinese and Tartar bands crashes up to a tremendous blaring crescendo of drums, gongs, and the piercing shrilling of flutes. The light slowly comes to a pitch of blinding brightness. Then, as light and sound attain their highest point, there is a sudden dead silence. The scene is revealed as the Grand Throne Room in the palace of Kublai, the Great Kaan, in the city of Cambaluc, Cathay—an immense octagonal room, the lofty walls adorned in gold and silver. In the far rear wall, within a deep recess like the shrine of an idol, is the throne of the Great Kaan. It rises in three tiers, three steps to a tier. On golden cushions at the top* KUBLAI *sits dressed in his heavy gold robes of state. He is a man of sixty but still in the full prime of his powers, his face proud and noble, his expression tinged with an ironic humor and bitterness yet full of a sympathetic humanity. In his person are combined the conquering indomitable force of a descendant of Chinghiz with the humanizing culture of the conquered Chinese who have already begun to absorb their conquerors.*

On the level of the throne below Kublai are: on his right a Mongol warrior in full armor with shield and spear, his face grim, cruel and fierce. On his left CHU-YIN, *the Cathayan sage and adviser to the Kaan, a venerable old man with white hair, dressed in a simple black robe. On the main floor, grouped close to the throne, are: on the right, the sons of the Kaan. Farther away, the nobles and warriors of all degrees with their wives behind them. On the left, the wives and concubines of the Kaan, then the courtiers, officers, poets, scholars, etc.—all the non-military officials and hangers-on of government, with their women beside them.* MARCO *stands, a sample case in each hand, bewildered and dazzled, gawking about him on every side. His father and uncle, bowing, walk to the foot of the throne and kneel before the Kaan. They make frantic signals to* MARCO *to do likewise but he is too dazed to notice. All the people in the room are staring at him. The Kaan is looking at the two brothers with a stern air. An usher of the palace comes quietly to* MARCO *and makes violent gestures to him to kneel down.*

MARCO: (*misunderstanding him—gratefully*) Thank you, Brother. (*He sits down on one of the sample cases to the gasping horror of all the Court. The Kaan is still looking frowningly at the two* POLOS *as he listens to the report of their Messenger escort. He does not notice. An outraged Chamberlain rushes over to* MARCO *and motions him to kneel down*).

MARCO: (*bewilderedly*) What's the trouble now?

KUBLAI: (*dismissing the* MESSENGER, *having heard his report—addresses the* POLOS *coldly*) I bid you welcome, Messrs. Polo. But where are the hundred wise men of the West who were to dispute with my wise men of the sacred teachings of Lao-Tseu and Confucius and the Buddha and Christ?

MAFFEO: (*hurriedly*) There was no Pope elected until just before—

NICOLO: And he had no wise men, anyway. (*The Kaan now sees* MARCO *and a puzzled expression of interest comes over his face*).

KUBLAI: Is he with you?

NICOLO: (*hesitantly*) My son, Marco, your Majesty—still young and graceless.

KUBLAI: Come here, Marco Polo. (MARCO *comes forward, trying feebly to assume a bold, confident air*).

MAFFEO: (*in a loud, furious aside*) Kneel, you ass! (MARCO *flounders to his knees*).

KUBLAI: (*with a smile*) I bid you welcome, Master Marco.

MARCO: Thank you, sir—I mean, your Lordship—your—(*then suddenly*) Before I forget—the Pope gave me a message for you, sir.

KUBLAI: (*smiling*) Are you his hundred wise men?

MARCO: (*contentedly*) Well—almost. He sent me in their place. He said I'd be worth a million wise men to you.

NICOLO: (*hastily*) His Holiness meant that Marco, by leading an upright life—not neglecting the practical side, of course—might set an example that would illustrate, better than wise words, the flesh and blood product of our Christian civilization.

KUBLAI: (*with a quiet smile*) I shall study this apotheosis with unwearied interest, I foresee it.

MARCO: (*suddenly—with a confidential air*) Wasn't that just a joke, your asking for the wise men? His Holiness thought you must have a sense of humor. Or that you must be an optimist.

KUBLAI: (*with a smile of appreciation*) I am afraid your Holy Pope is a most unholy cynic. (*Trying to solve a riddle in his own mind—musingly*) Could he believe this youth possesses that thing called soul which the West dreams lives after death—and might reveal it to me? (*Suddenly to* MARCO) Have you an immortal soul?

MARCO: (*in surprise*) Of course! Any fool knows that.

KUBLAI: (*humbly*) But I am not a fool. Can you prove it to me?

MARCO: Why, if you didn't have a soul, what would happen when you die?

KUBLAI: What, indeed?

MARCO: Why, nothing. You'd be dead—just like an animal.

KUBLAI: Your logic is irrefutable.

MARCO: Well, I'm not an animal, am I? That's certainly plain enough. (*Then proudly*) No, sir! I'm a man made by Almighty God in His Own Image for His greater glory!

KUBLAI: (*staring at him for a long moment with appalled appreciation—ecstatically*) So you are the Image of God! There is certainly something about you, something complete and unanswerable—but wait—a test! (*He claps his hands, pointing to* MARCO. *Soldiers with drawn swords leap forward and seize him, trussing him up his hands behind his back*).

MAFFEO: (*groveling*) Mercy! He is only a boy!

NICOLO: (*groveling*) Mercy! He is only a fool!

KUBLAI: (*sternly*) Silence! (*To* MARCO, *with inhuman calm*) Since you possess eternal life, it can do you no harm to cut off your head. (*He makes a sign to a soldier who flourishes his sword*).

MARCO: (*trying to conceal his fear under a quavering, joking tone*) I might—catch—cold!

KUBLAI: You jest, but your voice trembles. What! Are you afraid to die, immortal youth? Well, then, if you will confess that your soul is a stupid invention of your fear and that when you die you will be dead as a dead dog is dead—

MARCO: (*with sudden fury*) You're a heathen liar! (*He glares defiantly. His father and uncle moan with horror*).

KUBLAI: (*laughs and claps his hands.* MARCO *is freed. The Kaan studies his sullen but relieved face with amusement*) Your pardon, Marco! I suspected a flaw but you are perfect. You cannot imagine your death. You are a born hero. I must keep you near me. You shall tell me about your soul and I will listen as to a hundred wise men from the West! Is it agreed?

MARCO: (*hesitatingly*) I know it's a great honor, sir—but forgetting the soul side of it, I've got to eat.

KUBLAI: (*astonished*) To eat?

MARCO: I mean, I'm ambitious. I've got to succeed, and— (*Suddenly blurts out*) What can you pay me?

KUBLAI: Ha! Well, you will find me a practical man, too. I can start you upon any career you wish. What is your choice?

MAFFEO: (*interposing eagerly*) If I might speak to the boy in private a minute—give him my humble advice—he is so young— (MAFFEO *and* NICOLO *hurriedly lead* MARCO *down to the foreground*).

MAFFEO: You've made a favorable impression—God knows why—but strike while the iron is hot, you ninny! Ask to be appointed a Second Class government commission-agent.

MARCO: (*offendedly*) No! I'll be first-class or nothing!

MAFFEO: Don't be a fool! A First Class agent is all brass buttons and no opportunities. A Second Class travels around, is allowed his expenses, gets friendly with all the dealers, scares them into letting him in on everything—and gets what's rightfully coming to him! (*Then with a crafty look and a nudge in the ribs*) And, being always in the secret, you'll be able to whisper to us in time to take advantage—

MARCO: (*a bit flustered—with bluff assertion*) I don't know. The Kaan's been square with me. After all, honesty's the best policy, isn't it?

MAFFEO: (*looking him over scathingly*) You'd think I was advising you to steal—I, Maffeo Polo, whose conservatism is unquestioned!

MARCO: (*awed*) I didn't mean—

MAFFEO: (*solemnly*) Do you imagine the Kaan is such a Nero as to expect you to live on your salary?

MARCO: (*uncertainly*) No, I suppose not. (*He suddenly looks at* MAFFEO *with a crafty wink*) When I do give you a tip, what do I get from Polo Brothers?

MAFFEO: (*between appreciation and dismay*) Ha! You learn quickly, don't you? (*Then hastily*) Why, we—we've already thought of that—trust us to look after your best interests—and decided to—to make you a junior partner in the firm—eh, Nick?—Polo Brothers and Son—doesn't that sound solid, eh?

MARCO: (*with a sly grin*) It's a great honor—a very great honor. (*Then meaningly*) But as neither of you are Neros, naturally you'll also offer me—

MAFFEO: (*grinning in spite of himself*) Hmm! Hmm! You Judas!

MARCO: A fair commission—

NICOLO: (*blustering—but his eyes beaming with paternal pride*) You young scamp!

MAFFEO: (*laughing*) Ha-ha! Good boy, Mark! Polos will be Polos! (*They all embrace laughingly.* KUBLAI, *who has been observing them intently, turns to* CHU-YIN *and they both smile*).

KUBLAI: Did their Pope mean that a fool is a wiser study for a ruler of fools than a hundred wise men could be? This Marco touches me, as a child might, but at the same time there is something warped, deformed—Tell me, what shall I do with him?

CHU-YIN: Let him develop according to his own inclination and give him also every opportunity for true growth if he so desires. And let us observe him. At least, if he cannot learn, we shall.

KUBLAI: (*smilingly*) Yes. And be amused. (*He calls commandingly*) Marco Polo! (MARCO *turns rather frightenedly and comes to the throne and kneels*) Have you decided?

MARCO: (*promptly*) I'd like to be appointed a commission-agent of the Second Class.

KUBLAI: (*somewhat taken aback, puzzledly*) You are modest enough!

MARCO: (*manfully*) I want to start at the bottom!

KUBLAI: (*with mocking grandeur*) Arise then, Second Class Marco! You will receive your agent's commission at once. (*Then with a twinkle in his eye*) But each time you return from a journey you must relate to me all the observations and comments of your soul on the East. Be warned and never fail me in this!

MARCO: (*confused but cocksuredly*) I won't. I'll take copious notes. (*Then meaningly*) And I can memorize any little humorous incidents—

MAFFEO: (*apprehensively*) Blessed Savior! (*He gives a violent fit of coughing*).

MARCO: (*looks around at him questioningly*) Hum? (*Misinterpreting his signal*) And may I announce to your Majesty that a signal honor has just been conferred on me? My father and uncle have taken me into the firm. It will be Polo Brothers and Son from now on, and any way we can serve your Majesty—

KUBLAI: (*a light coming over his face*) Aha! I begin to smell all the rats in Cathay! (*The two elder* POLOS *are bowed to the ground, trembling with apprehension.* KUBLAI *laughs quietly*) Well, I am sure you wish to celebrate this family triumph together, so you may go. And accept my congratulations, Marco!

MARCO: Thank you, your Majesty. You will never regret it. I will always serve your best interests, so help me God! (*He goes grandly, preceded hurriedly by the trembling* NICOLO *and* MAFFEO. KUBLAI *laughs and turns to* CHU-YIN *who is smiling*).

CURTAIN

SCENE: *The Little Throne Room in the bamboo summer palace of the Kaan at Xanadu, the City of Peace—smaller, more intimate than the one at Cambaluc, but possessing an atmosphere of aloof dignity and simplicity fitting to the philosopher ruler who retreats here to contemplate in peace the vanity of his authority.*

About fifteen years have elapsed. It is a beautiful sunlit morning in late June. The Kaan reclines comfortably on his cushioned bamboo throne. His face has aged greatly. The expression has grown mask-like, full of philosophic calm. He has the detached air of an idol. KUKACHIN, *a beautiful young girl of twenty, pale and delicate, is sitting at his feet. Her air is grief-stricken. A flute player in the garden is playing a melancholy air.* KUKACHIN *recites in a low tone:*

KUKACHIN:

> My thoughts in this autumn are lonely and sad,
> A chill wind from the mountain blows in the garden.
> The sky is gray, a snowflake falls, the last chrysanthemum
> Withers beside the deserted summer-house.
> I walk along the path in which weeds have grown.
> My heart is bitter and tears blur my eyes.
> I grieve for the days when we lingered together
> In this same garden, along these paths between flowers.
> In the spring we sang of love and laughed with youth
> But now we are parted by many leagues and years,
> And I weep that never again shall I see your face.

(*She finishes and relapses into her attitude of broken resignation. The flute player ceases his playing.* KUBLAI *looks down at her tenderly*).

KUBLAI: (*musingly*) Sing while you can. When the voice fails, listen to song. When the heart fails, be sung asleep. (*Chidingly*) That is a sad

232

poem, Little Flower. Are you sad because you must soon become
Queen of Persia? But Arghun is a great hero, a Khan of the blood
of Chinghiz. You will be blessed with strong sons able to dare the
proud destiny of our blood.

KUKACHIN: (*dully*) Your will is my law.

KUBLAI: Not my will. The will of life to continue the strong. (*Forcing a
consoling tone*) Come, Little Flower. You have been fading here. See
how pale you have grown! Your eyes are listless! Your lips droop
even in smiling! But life at the Court of Persia is gay. There will be
feasts, celebrations, diverting pleasures. You will be their Queen of
Beauty.

KUKACHIN: (*with a sigh*) A Queen may be only a woman who is unhappy.

KUBLAI: (*teasingly*) What despair! You talk like the ladies in poems who
have lost their lovers! (KUKACHIN *gives a violent start which he does not
notice and a spasm of pain comes over her face*) But, never mind, Arghun
of Persia is a hero no woman could fail to love.

KUKACHIN: (*starting to her feet—desperately*) No! I can bear his children,
but you cannot force me to— (*She breaks down, weeping*).

KUBLAI: (*astonished—gazing at her searchingly*) Have I ever forced you to
anything? (*Then resuming his tone of tender teasing*) I would say, rather,
that ever since you were old enough to talk, the Ruler of Earth, as
they innocently call your grandfather, has been little better than your
slave.

KUKACHIN: (*taking his hand and kissing it*) Forgive me. (*Then smiling at
him*) Have I been so bad as that? Has my love for you who have been
both father and mother to me, brought you no happiness?

KUBLAI: (*with deep emotion*) You have been a golden bird singing beside
a black river. You took your mother's place in my heart when she
died. I was younger then. The river was not so black—the river of
man's life so deep and silent—flowing with an insane obsession—
whither?—and why? (*Then suddenly forcing a smile*) Your poem has
made me melancholy. And I am too old, if not too wise, to afford
anything but optimism! (*Then sadly*) But now you in your turn must

leave me, the river seems black indeed! (*Then after a pause—tenderly*) If it will make you unhappy, you need not marry Arghun Khan.

KUKACHIN: (*recovering herself—resolutely*) No. Your refusal would insult him. It might mean war. (*Resignedly*) And Arghun is as acceptable as any other. Forgive my weakness. You once told me a Princess must never weep. (*She forces a smile*) It makes no difference whether I stay or go, except that I shall be homesick for you. (*She kisses his hand again*).

KUBLAI: (*gratefully*) My little one. (*He strokes her hair. After a pause during which he looks at her thoughtfully—tenderly*) We have never had secrets from each other, you and I. Tell me, can you have fallen in love?

KUKACHIN: (*after a pause—tremblingly*) You must not ask that—if you respect my pride! (*With a pitiful smile*) You see—he does not even know— (*She is blushing and hanging her head with confusion.* CHU-YIN *enters hurriedly from the right. He is very old but still upright. He is a bit breathless from haste but his face is wreathed in smile*).

CHU-YIN: (*making an obeisance*) Your Majesty, do you hear that martial music? His Honor, Marco Polo, Mayor of Yang-Chau, seems about to visit you in state! (*The strains of a distant band can be heard*).

KUBLAI: (*still looking at* KUKACHIN *who has started violently at the mention of* MARCO's *name—worriedly*) Impossible! In love? . . . (*Then to* CHU-YIN—*preoccupiedly*) Eh? Marco? I have given no orders for him to return.

CHU-YIN: (*ironically*) No doubt he comes to refresh your humor with new copious notes on his exploits. Our Marco has made an active mayor. Yang-Chau, according to the petition for mercy you have received from its inhabitants, is the most governed of all your cities. I talked recently with a poet who had fled from there in horror. Yang-Chau used to have a soul, he said. Now it has a brand new Court House. And another, a man of wide culture, told me, our Christian mayor is exterminating our pleasures and our rats as if they were twin breeds of vermin!

KUBLAI: (*irritably*) He is beginning to weary me with his grotesque antics. A jester inspires mirth only so long as his deformity does not revolt one. Marco's spiritual hump begins to disgust me. He has not even a mortal soul, he has only an acquisitive instinct. We have given him every opportunity to learn. He has memorized everything and learned nothing. He has looked at everything and seen nothing. He has lusted for everything and loved nothing. He is only a shrewd and crafty greed. I shall send him home to his native wallow.

CHU-YIN: (*in mock alarm*) What? Must we lose our clown?

KUKACHIN: (*who has been listening with growing indignation*) How dare you call him a clown? Just because he is not a dull philosopher you think—

KUBLAI: (*astounded—admonishingly*) Princess!

KUKACHIN: (*turns to him—on the verge of tears—rebelliously*) Why are you both so unjust? Has he not done well everything he was ever appointed to do? Has he not always succeeded where others failed? Has he not by his will-power and determination risen to the highest rank in your service? (*Then her anger dying—more falteringly*) He is strange, perhaps, to people who do not understand him, but that is because he is so different from other men, so much stronger! And he has a soul! I know he has!

KUBLAI: (*whose eyes have been searching her face—aghast*) Kukachin! (*She sees he has guessed her secret and at first she quails and shrinks away, then stiffens regally and returns his gaze unflinchingly.* CHU-YIN *looks from one to the other comprehendingly. Finally* KUBLAI *addresses her sternly*) So, because I have allowed this fool a jester's latitude, because I permitted him to amuse you when you were a little girl, and since then, on his returns, to speak with you—a Princess!— (*Then brusquely*) I shall inform the ambassadors you will be ready to sail for Persia within ten days. You may retire. (*She bows with a proud humility and walks off left.* KUBLAI *sits in a somber study, frowning and biting his lips. The blaring of* MARCO'*s band grows steadily nearer*).

CHU-YIN: (*gently*) Is intolerance wisdom? (*A pause. Then he goes on*) I
have suspected her love for him for a long time.

KUBLAI: Why didn't you warn me?

CHU-YIN: Love is to wisdom what wisdom seems to love—a folly. I
reasoned, love comes like the breath of wind on water and is gone
leaving calm and reflection. I reasoned, but this is an enchanted
moment for her and it will remain a poignant memory to recompense
her when she is no longer a girl but merely a Queen. And I reasoned,
who knows but some day this Marco may see into her eyes and his
soul may be born and that will make a very interesting study—for
Kukachin, and her grandfather, the Son of Heaven and Ruler of the
World! (*He bows mockingly*) And for the old fool who is I!

KUBLAI: (*bewilderedly*) I cannot believe it! Why, since she was a little
girl, she has only talked to him once or twice every two years or so!

CHU-YIN: That was unwise, for thus he has remained a strange, mysterious dream-knight from the exotic West, an enigma with something
about him of a likable boy who brought her home each time a
humble, foolish, touching little gift! And also remember that on each
occasion he returned in triumph, having accomplished a task—a vic-
tor, more or less, acting the hero. (*The band has crashed and dinned its
way into the courtyard*) As now! Listen! (*He goes to the window and looks
down—with ironical but intense amusement*) Ah! He wears over his
Mayor's uniform, the regalia of Cock of Paradise in his secret fra-
ternal order of the Mystic Knights of Confucius! The band of the
Xanadu lodge is with him as well as his own! He is riding on a very
fat white horse. He dismounts, aided by the steps of your Imperial
Palace! He slaps a policeman on the back and asks his name! He
chucks a baby under the chin and asks the mother its name. She lies
and says "Marco" although the baby is a girl. He smiles. He is talking
loudly so everyone can overhear. He gives the baby one yen to start
a savings account and encourage its thrift. The mother looks savagely
disappointed. The crowd cheers. He keeps his smile frozen as he
notices an artist sketching him. He shakes hands with a one-legged

veteran of the Manzi campaign and asks his name. The veteran is touched. Tears come to his eyes. He tells him—but the Polo forgets his name even as he turns to address the crowd. He waves one hand for silence. The band stops. It is the hand on which he wears five large jade rings. The other hand rests upon—and pats—the head of a bronze dragon, our ancient symbol of Yang, the celestial, male principle of the Cosmos. He clears his throat, the crowd stands petrified, he is about to draw a deep breath and open his mouth carefully in position one of the five phonetic exercises— (*Here* CHU-YIN *chuckles*) But I am an old man full of malice and venom and it embitters me to see others unreasonably happy so— (*Here just as* MARCO *is heard starting to speak, he throws open the window and calls in a loud, commanding tone*) Messer Polo, His Imperial Majesty commands that you stop talking, dismiss your followers, and repair to his presence at once!

MARCO'S VOICE: (*very faint and crestfallen*) Oh—all right—I'll be right there.

KUBLAI: (*cannot control a laugh in spite of himself—helplessly*) How can one deal seriously with such a child-actor?

CHU-YIN: (*coming back from the window—ironically*) Most women, including Kukachin, love children—and all women must take acting seriously in order to love at all. (*Just as he finishes speaking,* KUKACHIN *enters from the left. She is terribly alarmed. She throws herself at* KUBLAI'S *feet*).

KUKACHIN: Why did you summon him? I told you he does not know. It is all my fault! Punish me, if you will! But promise me you will not harm him!

KUBLAI: (*looking down at her—sadly*). Is it my custom to take vengeance? (*Then as people are heard approaching—quickly*) Compose yourself! Remember again, Princesses may not weep! (*She springs to her feet, turns away for a moment, then turns back, her face rigidly calm and emotionless.* KUBLAI *nods with appreciation of her control*) Good. You will make a Queen. (*She bows and retires backward to the left side of the*

throne. At the same moment, NICOLO *and* MAFFEO POLO *enter ceremoniously from the right. They wear the regalia of officers in the Mystic Knights
of Confucius over their rich merchants' robes. (This costume is a queer
jumble of stunning effects that recall the parade uniforms of our modern
Knights Templar, of Columbus, of Pythias, Mystic Shriners, the Klan, etc.)
They are absurdly conscious and proud of this get-up—like two old men in
a children's play.* KUBLAI *and* CHU-YIN *regard them with amused astonishment. Even* KUKACHIN *cannot restrain a smile. They prostrate themselves
at the foot of the throne. Then just at the right moment, preceded by a
conscious cough,* MARCO POLO *makes his entrance. Over his gorgeous uniform of Mayor, he wears his childishly fantastic regalia as chief of the Mystic
Knights of Confucius. As he steps on, he takes off his gilded, laced hat with
its Bird of Paradise plumes and bows with a mechanical dignity on all sides.
He has the manner and appearance of a successful movie star at a mas-
querade ball, disguised so that no one can fail to recognize him. His regular,
good-looking, well-groomed face is carefully arranged into the grave responsible expression of a Senator from the South of the United States of
America about to propose an amendment to the Constitution restricting the
migration of non-Nordic birds into Texas, or prohibiting the practice of the
laws of biology within the twelve-mile limit. He moves in stately fashion to
the throne and prostrates himself before the* KAAN. KUKACHIN *stares at him
with boundless admiration, hoping to catch his eye. The* KAAN *looks from
her to him and his face grows stern.* CHU-YIN *is enjoying himself).*

KUBLAI: Rise. (MARCO *does so.* KUBLAI *continues dryly*) To what do I owe
the honor of this unexpected visit?

MARCO: (*hastily, but with full confidence*) Well, I was sending in to your
treasury the taxes of Yang-Chau for the fiscal year, and I knew you'd
be so astonished at the unprecedented amount I had sweated out of
them that you'd want to know how I did it—so here I am. (*An
awkward pause.* MARCO *is disconcerted at the* KAAN's *steady impersonal
stare. He glances about—sees the* PRINCESS—*welcomes this opportunity for
diverting attention. Bowing with humble respect*) Pardon me, Princess.

I didn't recognize you before, you've gotten so grown up. (*Flatteringly*) You look like a Queen.

KUKACHIN: (*falteringly*) I bid you welcome, Your Honor.

KUBLAI: (*as a warning to* KUKACHIN *to control her emotion*) The Princess will soon be Queen of Persia.

MARCO: (*flustered and awed, bowing to her again—flatteringly*) Then— Your Majesty—if I may be humbly permitted (*Bowing to* KUBLAI)— to offer my congratulations—and before I settle down to discussing business—if her Highness—Majesty—will accept a small token of my esteem— (*Here he stamps his foot. An* AFRICAN SLAVE, *dressed in a pink livery with green hat and shoes and stockings and carrying a golden wicker basket, enters. He kneels, presents the basket to* MARCO, *who lifts the cover and pulls out a small chow puppy with a pink ribbon tied around its neck. He steps forward and offers this to the* PRINCESS, *with a boyish grin*) A contribution to your ZOO—from your most humble servant!

KUKACHIN: (*taking it—flushing with pleasure*) Oh, what a little darling! (*She cuddles the puppy in her arms*).

MARCO: (*Boastfully*) He's a genuine, pedigreed pup. I procured him at great cost—I mean he's extra well-bred.

KUKACHIN: Oh, thank you so much, Marco Polo! (*Stammering*) I mean, Your Honor.

KUBLAI: (*warningly*) His Honor wishes to talk business, Princess.

KUKACHIN: (*controlling herself*) I ask pardon. (*She bows and retires to left, rear, where she stands fondling the puppy and watching* MARCO).

MARCO: (*plunging in confidently on what he thinks is a sure point of attack*) My tax scheme, Your Majesty, that got such wonderful results is simplicity itself. I simply reversed the old system. For one thing I found they had a high tax on excess profits. Imagine a profit being excess! Why, it isn't humanly possible! I repealed it. And I repealed the tax on luxuries. I found out the great majority in Yang-Chau couldn't afford luxuries. The tax wasn't democratic enough to make it pay! I crossed it off and I wrote on the statute books a law that taxes every necessity in life, a law that hits every man's pocket equally, be he beggar or banker! And I got results!

CHU-YIN: (*gravely*) In beggars?

KUBLAI: (*with a chilling air*) I have received a petition from the inhabitants of Yang-Chau enumerating over three thousand cases of your gross abuse of power!

MARCO: (*abashed only for a moment*). Oh, so they've sent that vile slander to you, have they? That's the work of a mere handful of radicals—

KUBLAI: (*dryly*) Five hundred thousand names are signed to it. (*Still more dryly*) Half a million citizens accuse you of endeavoring to stamp out their ancient culture!

MARCO: What! Why, I even had a law passed that anyone caught interfering with culture would be subject to a fine! It was Section One of a blanket statute that every citizen must be happy or go to jail. I found it was the unhappy ones who were always making trouble and getting discontented. You see, here's the way I figure it; if a man's good, he's happy—and if he isn't happy, it's a sure sign he's no good to himself or anyone else and he better be put where he can't do harm.

KUBLAI: (*a bit helplessly now*) They complain that you have entirely prohibited all free expression of opinion.

MARCO: (*feelingly*) Well, when they go to the extreme of circulating such treasonable opinions against me, isn't it time to protect your sovereignty by strong measures? (KUBLAI *stares at this effrontery with amazement.* MARCO *watches this impression and hurries on with an injured dignity*) I can't believe, Your Majesty, that this minority of malcontents can have alienated your long-standing high regard for me!

KUBLAI: (*conquered—suddenly overpowered by a great smile*) Not so! You are the marvel of mankind! And I would be lost without you!

MARCO: (*flattered but at the same time nonplussed*) I thank you! (*Hesitatingly*) But, to tell the truth, I want to resign anyhow. I've done all I could. I've appointed five hundred committees to carry on my work and I retire confident that with the system I've instituted everything will go on automatically and brains are no longer needed. (*He adds as a bitter afterthought*) And it's lucky they're not or Yang-Chau would soon be a ruin!

KUBLAI: (*with mock seriousness*) In behalf of the population of Yang-Chau I accept your resignation, with deep regret for the loss of your unique and extraordinary services. (*Then suddenly in a strange voice*) Do you still possess your immortal soul, Marco Polo?

MARCO: (*flustered*) Ha-ha! Yes, of course—at least I hope so. But I see the joke. You mean that Yang-Chau used to be a good place to lose one. Well, you wouldn't know the old town now. Sin is practically unseen. (*Hurrying on to another subject—boisterously*). But however much I may have accomplished there, it's nothing to the big surprise I've got in reserve far you. May I demonstrate? (*Without waiting for permission, takes a piece of printed paper like a dollar bill from his pocket*) What is it? Paper. Correct! What is it worth? Nothing. That's where you're mistaken. It's worth ten yen. No, I'm not a liar! See ten yen written on it, don't you? Well, I'll tell you the secret. This is money, legally valued at ten yens' worth of anything you wish to buy, by order of His Imperial Majesty, the Great Kaan! Do you see my point? Its advantages over gold and silver coin are obvious. It's light, easy to carry,— (*Here he gives a prodigious wink*) wears out quickly, can be made at very slight expense and yields enormous profit. Think of getting ten yen for this piece of paper. Yet it can be done. If you make the people believe it's worth it, it is! After all, when you stop to think, who was it first told them gold was money? I'll bet anything it was some quick-thinker who'd just discovered a gold mine! (KUBLAI *and* CHU-YIN *stare at him in petrified incredulity. He mistakes it for admiration and is flattered. Bows and lays his paper money on the* KAAN's *knee*) You're stunned, I can see that. It's so simple—and yet, who ever thought of it before me? I was amazed myself. Think it over, Your Majesty, and let the endless possibilities dawn on you! And now I want to show another little aid to government that I thought out. (*He makes a sign to his uncle and father. The former takes a mechanical contrivance out of a box and sets it up on the floor. It is a working model of a clumsy cannon.* NICOLO, *meanwhile, takes children's blocks out of his box and builds them into a fortress wall.* MARCO *is talking. His manner and voice have become grave and portentous*) It all came to me, like an inspiration, last Easter Sunday when Father and Uncle and I were holding a little service. Uncle read a prayer which spoke of Our Lord as the Prince of Peace. Somehow, that took hold of me. I thought to myself, well, it's funny, there always have been wars and there always will be, I suppose, because I've never read much in any history about heroes who waged peace. Still, that's wrong. War is a waste of money which eats into the profits of life like thunder! Then why war, I asked myself? But how are you going to end it? Then the flash came! There's only one workable way and that's to conquer everybody else in the world so they'll never dare fight you again! An impossible task, you object? Not any more! This invention you see before you makes conquering easy. Let me demonstrate with these models. On our right, you see the fortress wall of a hostile capital. Under your present system with battering rams, to make an effective breach in this wall would cost you the lives of ten thousand men. Valuing each life conservatively at ten yen, this amounts to one hundred thousand yen! This makes the cost of breaching prohibitive. But all of this waste can be saved. How? Just keep your eyes on your right and permit my exclusive invention to solve this problem. (*He addresses the fortress in a matter-of-fact tone*) So you won't surrender, eh? (*Then in a mock-heroic falsetto, answering himself like a ventriloquist*) We die but we never surrender! (*Then matter-of-factly*) Well, Brother, those heroic sentiments do you a lot of credit, but this is war and not a tragedy. You're up against new methods this time, and you better give in and avoid wasteful bloodshed. (*Answering himself*) No! Victory or Death! (*Then again*) All right, Brother, don't blame me. Fire! (*His uncle fires the gun. There is a bang, and a leaden ball is shot out which knocks a big breach in the wall of blocks.* MARCO *beams.* KUKACHIN *gives a scream of fright, then a gasp of delight, and claps her hands.* MARCO *bows to her the more gratefully as* KUBLAI *and* CHU-YIN *are staring at him with a queer appalled wonder that puzzles him although he cannot imagine it is not admiration*) I see you are stunned again. What made it do that, you're wondering? This! (*He takes a little package out of his pocket and pours some black powder out of it on his palm*) It's the same powder they've been using here in children's fire works. They've had it under their noses for years without a single soul ever having creative imagination enough to visualize the enormous possibilities. But you can bet I did! It was a lad crying with a finger half blown off where he held a firecracker too long that first opened my eyes. I learned the formula, improved on it, experimented in secret, and here's the gratifying result! (*He takes the cannon ball from his father who has retrieved it*) You see? Now just picture this little ball magnified into one weighing twenty pounds or so and then you'll really grasp my idea. The destruction of property and loss of life would be tremendous! No one could resist you!

KUBLAI: (*after a pause—musingly*) I am interested in the hero of that city who preferred death to defeat. Did you conquer his immortal soul?

MARCO: (*with frankness*) Well, you can't consider souls when you're dealing with soldiers, can you? (*He takes his model and places it on the* KAAN's *knee with the paper money*) When you have time, I wish you'd look this over. In fact—and this is the big idea I've been saving for the last—consider these two inventions of mine in combination. You conquer the world with this—(*He pats the cannon-model*) and you pay for it with this. (*He pats the paper money—rhetorically*) You become the bringer of peace on earth and good-will to men, and it doesn't cost you a yen hardly. Your initial expense—my price—is as low as I can possibly make it out of my deep affection for your Majesty—only a million yen.

KUBLAI: (*quickly*) In paper?

MARCO: (*with a grin and a wink*) No. I'd prefer gold, if you don't mind.

(*Silence.* MARCO *goes on meaningly*) Of course, I don't want to force them on you. I'm confident there's a ready market for them elsewhere.

KUBLAI: (*grimly smiling*) Oh, I quite realize that in self-protection I've got to buy them—or kill you!

MARCO: (*briskly*) Then it's a bargain? But I've still got one proviso—that you give us permission to go home. (KUKACHIN *gives a little gasp.* MARCO *goes on feelingly*) We're homesick, Your Majesty. We've served you faithfully, and frankly now that we've made our fortune we want to go home and enjoy it. There's no place like home, Your Majesty! I'm sure even a King in his palace appreciates that.

KUBLAI: (*with smiling mockery*) But—who can play your part? And your mission—your example? What will your Pope say when you tell him I'm still unconverted?

MARCO: (*confidently*) Oh, you will be—on your death-bed, if not before—a man of your common sense.

KUBLAI: (*ironically*) Courtier! (*Then solemnly*) But my last objection is insurmountable. You haven't yet proved you have an immortal soul!

MARCO: It doesn't need proving.

KUBLAI: If you could only bring forward one reliable witness.

MARCO: My Father and Uncle can swear—

KUBLAI: They think it is a family trait. Their evidence is prejudiced.

MARCO: (*worried now—looks at* CHU-YIN *hopefully*) Mr. Chu-Yin ought to be wise enough to acknowledge—

CHU-YIN: (*smiling*) But I believe that what can be proven cannot be true. (MARCO *stands puzzled, irritated, looking stubborn, frightened and foolish. His eyes wander about the room, finally resting appealingly on* KUKACHIN).

KUKACHIN: (*suddenly steps forward—flushed but proudly*) I will bear witness he has a soul. (KUBLAI *looks at her with a sad wonderment,* CHU-YIN *smilingly,* MARCO *with gratitude,* NICOLO *and* MAFFEO *exchange a glance of congratulation*).

KUBLAI: How can you know, Princess?

KUKACHIN: Because I have seen it—once, when he bound up my dog's leg, once when he played with a slave's baby, once when he listened to music over water and I heard him sigh, once when he looked at sunrise, another time at sunset, another at the stars, another at the moon, and each time he said that Nature was wonderful. And all the while, whenever he has been with me I have always felt—something strange and different—and that something must be His Honor's soul, must it not?

KUBLAI: (*with wondering bitterness*) The eye sees only its own sight.

CHU-YIN: But a woman may feel life in the unborn.

KUBLAI: (*mockingly but sadly*) I cannot contest the profound intuitions of virgins and mystics. Go home, Your Honor, Immortal Marco, and live forever! (*With forced gaiety*) And tell your Pope your example has done much to convert me to wisdom—if I could find the true one!

KUKACHIN: (*boldly now*) And may I humbly request, since His Honor, and his father and uncle, are experienced masters of navigation, that they be appointed, for my greater safety, to attend me and command the fleet on my voyage to Persia?

KUBLAI: (*astonished at her boldness—rebukingly*) Princess!

KUKACHIN: (*returning his look—simply*) It is the last favor I shall ever ask. I wish to be converted to wisdom, too—one or another—before I become a name.

KUBLAI: (*bitterly*) I cannot deny your last request, even though you wish your own unhappiness. (*To the* POLOS) You will accompany the Princess.

MARCO: (*jubilantly*) I'll be only too glad! (*Turning to the* PRINCESS) It'll be a great pleasure! (*Then briskly*) And have we your permission to trade in the ports along the way?

KUKACHIN: (*to* MARCO *embarrassedly*) As you please, Your Honor.

MARCO: (*bowing low*) I'll promise it won't disturb you. It's really a scheme to while away the hours, for I warn you in advance this is liable to be a mighty long trip.

KUKACHIN: (*impulsively*) I do not care how long— (*She stops in confusion*).

MARCO: Now if I had the kind of ships we build in Venice to work with I could promise you a record passage, but with your tubby junks it's just as well to expect the worst and you'll never be disappointed. (*Familiarly*) And the trouble with any ship, for a man of action, is that there's so little you can do. I hate idleness where there's nothing to occupy your mind but thinking. I've been so used to being out, overcoming obstacles, getting things done, creating results where there weren't any before, going after the impossible—well— (*Here he gives a little deprecating laugh*) all play and no work makes Jack a dull boy. I'm sure I'd make a pretty dull person to have around if there wasn't plenty to do. You might not believe it, but when I'm idle I actually get gloomy sometimes!

KUKACHIN: (*eagerly*) But we shall have dancers on the ship and actors who will entertain us with plays—

MARCO: (*heartily*) That'll be grand. There's nothing better than to sit down in a good seat at a good play after a good day's work in which you know you've accomplished something, and after you've had a good dinner, and just take it easy and enjoy a good wholesome thrill or a good laugh and get your mind off serious things until it's time to go to bed.

KUKACHIN: (*vaguely*) Yes. (*Then eager to have him pleased*) And there will be poets to recite their poems—

MARCO: (*not exactly overjoyed*) That'll be nice. (*Then very confidentially— in a humorous whisper*) I'll tell you a good joke on me, Your Highness. I once wrote a poem myself; would you ever believe it to look at me?

KUKACHIN: (*smiling at him as at a boy—teasingly*) No?

MARCO: (*smiling back like a boy*) Yes, I did too, when I was young and foolish. It wasn't bad stuff either, considering I'd had no practice. (*Frowning with concentration*) Wait! Let me see if I can remember any—oh, yes—"You are lovely as the gold in the sun." (*He hesitates*).

KUKACHIN: (*thrilled*) That is beautiful!

MARCO: That's only the first line. (*Then jokingly*) You can consider yourself lucky. I don't remember the rest.

KUKACHIN: (*dropping her eyes—softly*) Perhaps on the voyage you may be inspired to write another.

KUBLAI: (*who has been staring at them with weary amazement*) Life is so stupid, it is mysterious!

DARKNESS

SCENE TWO

*S*CENE: *The wharves of the Imperial Fleet at the seaport of Zayton —several weeks later. At the left, stern to, is an enormous junk, the flagship. The wharf extends out, rear, to the right of her. At the right is a warehouse, from a door in which a line of half-naked slaves, their necks, waists, and right ankles linked up by chains, form an endless chain which revolves mechanically, as it were, on sprocket wheels in the interiors of the shed and the junk. As each individual link passes out of the shed it carries a bale on its head, moves with mechanical precision across the wharf, disappears into the junk, and reappears a moment later having dumped its load and moves back into the shed. The whole process is a man-power original of the modern devices with bucket scoops that dredge, load coal, sand, etc. By the side of the shed, a foreman sits with a drum and gong with which he marks a perfect time for the slaves, a four beat rhythm, three beats of the drum, the fourth a bang on the gong as one slave at each end loads and unloads. The effect is like the noise of a machine. A bamboo stair leads up to the high poop of the junk from front, left. It is just getting dawn. A forest of masts, spars, sails of woven bamboo laths, shuts out all view of the harbor at the end of the wharf. At the foot of the stairs, CHU-YIN stands like a sentinel. Above on top of the poop, the figures of KUBLAI and KUKACHIN are outlined against the lightening sky.*

KUBLAI: (*brokenly*) I must go. (*He takes her in his arms*) We have said all we can say. Little Daughter, all rare things are secrets which cannot be revealed to anyone. That is why life must be so lonely. But I love you more dearly than anything on earth. And I know you love me. So perhaps we do not need to understand. (*Rebelliously*) Yet I wish some Power could give me assurance that in granting your desire I am acting for your happiness, and for your eventual deliverance from sorrow to acceptance and peace. (*He notices she is weeping—in self-reproach*) Old fool! I have made you weep again! I am death advising life how to live! Be deaf to me! Strive after what your heart desires! Who can ever know which are the mistakes we make? One should be either sad or joyful. Contentment is a warm sty for the eaters and sleepers! (*Impulsively*) Do not weep! Even now I can refuse your hand to Arghun. Let it mean war!

KUKACHIN: (*looking up and controlling herself—with a sad finality*) You do not understand. I wish to take this voyage.

KUBLAI: (*desperately*) But I could keep Polo here. (*With impotent anger*) He shall pray for his soul on his knees before you!

KUKACHIN: (*with calm sadness*) Do I want a slave? (*Dreamily*) I desire a captain of my ship on a long voyage in dangerous, enchanted seas.

KUBLAI: (*with a fierce defiance of fate*) I am the Great Kaan! I shall have him killed! (a *pause*).

CHU-YIN: (*from below, recites in a calm, soothing tone*) The noble man ignores self. The wise man ignores action. His truth acts without deeds. His knowledge venerates the unknowable. To him birth is not the beginning, nor is death the end. (KUBLAI's *head bends in submission.* CHU-YIN *continues tenderly*) I feel there are tears in your eyes. The Great Kaan, Ruler of the World, may not weep.

KUBLAI: (*brokenly*) Ruler? I am my slave! (*Then controlling himself—forcing an amused teasing tone*) Marco will soon be here, wearing the self-assurance of an immortal soul and his new admiral's uniform! I must fly in retreat from what I can neither laugh away nor kill. Write when you reach Persia. Tell me—all you can tell—particularly what his immortal soul is like! (*Then tenderly*) Farewell, Little Flower! Live. There is no other advice possible from one human being to another.

KUKACHIN: Live—and love!

KUBLAI: (*trying to renew his joking tone*) One's ancestors, particularly one's grandfather. Do not forget me!

KUKACHIN: Never! (*They embrace*).

KUBLAI: (*chokingly*) Farewell. (*He hurries down the ladder—to* CHU-YIN) You remain—see him—bring me word— (*He turns his head up to* KUKACHIN) For the last time, farewell, Little Flower of my life! May you know happiness! (*He turns quickly and goes*).

KUKACHIN: Farewell! (*She bows her head on the rail and weeps*).

CHU-YIN: (*after a pause*) You are tired, Princess. Your eyes are red from weeping and your nose is red. You look old—a little homely, even. The Admiral Polo will not recognize you. (KUKACHIN *dries her eyes hastily*).

KUKACHIN: (*half-smiling and half-weeping at his teasing*) I think you are a very horrid old man!

CHU-YIN: A little sleep, Princess, and you will be beautiful. The old dream passes. Sleep and awake in the new. Life is perhaps most wisely regarded as a bad dream between two awakenings, and every day is a life in miniature.

KUKACHIN: (*wearily and drowsily*) Your wisdom makes me sleep. (*Her head sinks back on her arms and she is soon asleep*).

CHU-YIN: (*after a pause—softly*) Kukachin! (*He sees she is asleep—chuckles*) I have won a convert. (*Then speculatively*) Youth needs so much sleep and old age so little. Is that not a proof that from birth to death one grows steadily closer to complete life? Hum. (*He ponders on this. From the distance comes the sound of* POLOS's *band playing the same martial air as in the previous scene.* CHU-YIN *starts—then smiles. The music quickly grows louder. The* PRINCESS *awakes with a start*).

KUKACHIN: (*startledly*) Chu-Yin! Is that the Admiral coming?

CHU-YIN: (*dryly*) I suspect so. It is like him not to neglect a person in the city when saying good-bye.

KUKACHIN: (*flurriedly*) I must go to my cabin for a moment. (*She hurries back*).

CHU-YIN: (*listens with a pleased, ironical smile as the band gets rapidly nearer. Finally it seems to turn a corner nearby, and a moment later, to a deafening clangor, MARCO enters, dressed in a gorgeous Admiral's uniform. Two paces behind, side by side, walk MAFFEO and NICOLO, dressed only a trifle less gorgeously as Commodores. Behind them comes the band. MARCO halts as he sees CHU-YIN, salutes condescendingly, and signals the band to be silent. CHU-YIN bows gravely and remarks as if answering an argument in his own mind*) Still, even though they cannot be house-broken, I prefer monkeys because they are so much less noisy.

MARCO: (*with a condescending grin*) What's that—more philosophy? (*Clapping him on the back*) Well, I like your determination. (*He wipes his brow with a handkerchief*) Phew! I'll certainly be glad to get back home where I can hear some music that I can keep step to. My feet just won't give in to your tunes. (*With a grin*) And look at the Old Man and Uncle. They're knock-kneed for life. (*Confidentially*) Still, I thought the band was a good idea—to sort of cheer up the Princess, and let people know she's leaving at the same time. (*As people begin to come in and stare at the poop of the ship*) See the crowd gather? I got them out of bed, too!

CHU-YIN: (*ironically*) You also woke up the Princess. You sail at sunrise?

MARCO: (*briskly—taking operations in hand*) Thank you for reminding me. I've got to hurry. (*To his FATHER and UNCLE*) You two better get aboard your ships and be ready to cast off when I signal. (*They go off. He suddenly bawls to someone in the ship*) Much more cargo to load?

A VOICE: Less than a hundred bales, sir.

MARCO: Good. Call all hands on deck and stand by to put sail on her.

A VOICE: Aye-aye, sir.

MARCO: And look lively, damn your lazy souls! (*To* CHU-YIN—*complacently*) You've got to impose rigid discipline on shipboard.

CHU-YIN: (*inquisitively*) I suppose you feel your heavy responsibility as escort to the future Queen of Persia?

MARCO: (*soberly*) Yes, I do. I'll confess I do. If she were a million yen's worth of silk or spices, I wouldn't worry an instant, but a Queen, that's a different matter. However, when you give my last word to His Majesty, you can tell him that I've always done my duty by him and I won't fail him this time. As long as I've a breath in me, I'll take care of her!

CHU-YIN: (*with genuine appreciation*) That is bravely spoken.

MARCO: I don't know anything about brave speaking. I'm by nature a silent man, and I let my actions do the talking. But, as I've proved to you people in Cathay time and again, when I say I'll do a thing, I do it!

CHU-YIN: (*suddenly with a sly smile to himself*) I was forgetting. His Majesty gave me some secret last instructions for you. You are, at some time every day of the voyage, to look carefully and deeply into the Princess's eyes and note what you see there.

MARCO: What for? (*Then brightly*) Oh, he's afraid she'll get fever in the tropics. Well, you tell him I'll see to it she keeps in good condition. I'll do what's right by her without considering fear or favor. (*Then practically*) Then, of course, if her husband thinks at the end of the voyage that my work deserves a bonus—why, that's up to him. (*Inquisitively*) She's never seen him, has she?

CHU-YIN: No.

MARCO: (*with an air of an independent thinker*) Well, I believe in love matches myself, even for Kings and Queens. (*With a grin*) Come to think of it, I'll be getting married to Donata myself when I get home.

CHU-YIN: Donata?

MARCO: (*proudly*) The best little girl in the world! She's there waiting for me.

CHU-YIN: You have heard from her?

MARCO: I don't need to hear. I can trust her. And I've been true to her, too. I haven't ever thought of loving anyone else. Of course, I don't mean I've been any he-virgin. I've played with concubines at odd moments when my mind needed relaxation—but that's only human nature. (*His eyes glistening reminiscently*) Some of them were beauties, too! (*With a sigh*) Well, I've had my fun and I suppose it's about time I settled down.

CHU-YIN: Poor Princess!

MARCO: What's that? Oh, I see, yes, I sympathize with her, too—going into a harem. If there's one thing more than another that proves you in the East aren't responsible, it's that harem notion. (*With a grin*) Now in the West we've learned by experience that one at a time is trouble enough.

CHU-YIN: (*dryly*) Be sure and converse on love and marriage often with the Princess. I am certain you will cure her.

MARCO: (*mystified*) Cure her?

CHU-YIN: Cure her mind of any unreasonable imaginings.

MARCO: (*easily*) Oh, I'll guarantee she'll be contented, if that's what you mean. (*The human chain in back finishes its labors and disappears into the shed. The crowd of people has been steadily augmented by new arrivals, until a small multitude is gathered standing in silence staring up at the poop.* MARCO *says with satisfaction*) Well, cargo's all aboard, before schedule, too. We killed six slaves but, by God, we did it! And look at the crowd we've drawn, thanks to my band!

CHU-YIN: (*disgustedly*) They would have come without noise. They love their Princess.

MARCO: (*cynically*) Maybe, but they love their sleep, too. I know 'em! (*A cry of adoration goes up from the crowd. With one movement they prostrate themselves as the* PRINCESS *comes from the cabin dressed in a robe of silver and stands at the rail looking down*).

THE CROWD: (*in a long, ululating whisper*) Farewell—farewell—farewell—farewell!

KUKACHIN: (*silences them with a motion of her hand*)

I shall know the long sorrow of an exile
As I sail over the green water and the blue water

Alone under a strange sky amid alien flowers and faces.
My eyes shall be ever red with weeping, my heart bleeding,
While I long for the land of my birth and my childhood
Remembering with love the love of my people.

(*A sound of low weeping comes from the crowd*) Farewell!

THE CROWD: Farewell—farewell—farewell—farewell!

MARCO: (*feeling foolish because he is moved*) Damn it! Reciting always makes me want to cry about something. Poetry acts worse on me than wine that way. (*He calls up—very respectfully*) Princess! We'll be sailing at once. Would you mind retiring to your cabin? I'm afraid you're going to catch cold standing bareheaded in the night air.

KUKACHIN: (*tremulously—grateful for his solicitude*) I am in your charge, Admiral. I am grateful that you should think of my health, and I obey. (*She turns and goes back into her cabin. The crowd silently filters away, leaving only the band*).

MARCO: (*proudly and fussily*) You can't have women around when you're trying to get something done. I can see where I'll have to be telling her what to do every second. Well, I hope she'll take it in good part and not forget I'm acting in her husband's interests, not my own. (*Very confidentially*) You know, apart from her being a Princess, I've always respected her a lot. She's not haughty and she's—well, human, that's what I mean. I'd do anything I could for her, Princess or not! Yes, sir!

CHU-YIN: (*wonderingly*) There may be hope—after all.

MARCO: What's that?

CHU-YIN: Nothing. Enigma!

MARCO: There's always hope! Don't be a damned pessimist! (*Clapping him on the back*) Enigma, eh? Well, if that isn't like a philosopher—to start in on riddles just at the last moment! (*He ascends half-way up the ladder to the poop, then turns back to* CHU-YIN *with a chuckle*) Take a fool's advice and don't think so much or you'll get old before your time! (*More oratorically*) If you look before you leap, you'll decide to sit down. Keep on going ahead and you can't help being right! You're bound to get somewhere! (*He suddenly breaks into a grin again*) There! Don't ever say I never gave you good advice! (*He springs swiftly to the top deck and bellows*) Cast off there amidships! Where the hell are you—asleep? Set that foresail! Hop, you kidney-footed gang of thumb-fingered infidels! (*He turns with a sudden fierceness on the band who are standing stolidly, awaiting orders*) Hey you! Didn't I tell you to strike up when I set foot on the deck? What do you think I paid you in advance for—to wave me good-by? (*The band plunges madly into it. A frenzied cataract of sound results.* CHU-YIN *covers his ears and moves away, shaking his head, as* MARCO *leans over the rail and bawls after him*) And tell the Kaan—anything he wants—write me—just Ven-ice—they all know me there—and if they don't, by God, they're going to!

DARKNESS

Scene Three

Scene: *Poop deck of the royal junk of the* PRINCESS KUKACHIN *at anchor in the harbor of Hormuz, Persia—a moonlight night some two years later. On a silver throne at center* KUKACHIN *is sitting dressed in a gorgeous golden robe of ceremony. Her beauty has grown more intense, her face has undergone a change, it is the face of a woman who has known real sorrow and suffering. In the shadow of the highest deck in rear her women-in-waiting are in a group, sitting on cushions. On the highest deck in rear* SAILORS *lower and furl the sail of the mizzenmast, every movement being carried out in unison with a machine-like rhythm. The bulwarks of the junk are battered and splintered, the sail is frayed and full of jagged holes and patches. In the foreground (the port side of deck) the two elder* POLOS *are squatting. Each has a bag of money before him from which they are carefully counting gold coins and packing stacks of these into a chest that stands between them.*

MARCO: (*his voice, hoarse and domineering, comes from the left just before the curtain rises*) Let go that anchor! (*A meek "Aye-Aye, sir," is heard replying and then a great splash and a long rattling of chains. The curtain then rises discovering the scene as above.* MARCO'S *voice is again heard, "Lower that mizzensail! Look lively now!"*)

BOATSWAIN: (*with the sailors*) Aye-aye, sir! (*They lower the sail, and begin to tie it up trimly*).

MAFFEO: (*looking up and straightening his cramped back—with a relieved sigh*) Here's Persia! I'll be glad to get on dry land again. Two years on this foreign tub are too much.

NICOLO: (*with a grunt, intent on the money*) Keep counting if you want to finish before we go ashore. It's nine hundred thousand now in our money, isn't it?

MAFFEO: (*nods—counting again*) This lot will bring it to a million. (*He begins stacking and packing again*).

BOATSWAIN: (*chanting as his men work*)

    Great were the waves
    Volcanoes of foam
    Ridge after ridge
    To the rim of the world!
    Great were the waves!

CHORUS OF SAILORS: Great were the waves!

BOATSWAIN:

    Fierce were the winds!
    Demons screamed!
    Their claws rended
    Sails into rags,
    Fierce were the winds!

CHORUS: Fierce were the winds!

BOATSWAIN: Fire was the sun!
                     Boiled the blood black,
                     Our veins hummed
                     Like bronze kettles.
                     Fire was the sun!

CHORUS: Fire was the sun!

BOATSWAIN: Long was the voyage!
                     Life drifted becalmed,
                     A dead whale awash
                     In the toil of tides.
                     Long was the voyage!

CHORUS: Long was the voyage!

BOATSWAIN: Many have died!
                     Sleep in green water.
                     Wan faces at home
                     Pray to the sea.
                     Many have died!

CHORUS: Many have died!

KUKACHIN: (*chants the last line after them—sadly*)

                     Many have died!

(*After a brooding pause she rises and chants in a low voice*)

If I were asleep in green water,
No pang could be added to my sorrow,
Old grief would be forgotten,
I would know peace.

SAILORS: There is peace deep in the sea
But the surface is sorrow.

WOMEN: Kukachin will be a Queen!
A Queen may not sorrow
Save for her King!

KUKACHIN: When love is not loved it loves death.
When I sank drowning, I loved Death.
When the pirate's knife gleamed, I loved Death.
When fever burned me I loved Death.
But the man I love saved me.

SAILORS: Death lives in a silent sea,
Gray and cold under cold gray sky,
Where there is neither sun nor wind
Nor joy nor sorrow!

WOMEN: Kukachin will be a wife.
A wife must not sorrow
Save for her man.

KUKACHIN: A hero is merciful to women.
Why could not this man see or feel or know?
Then he would have let me die.

SAILORS: There are harbors at every voyage-end
             Where we rest from the sorrows of the sea.

WOMEN: Kukachin will be a mother
             A mother may not sorrow
             Save for her son.

KUKACHIN: (*bows her head in resignation. A pause of silence*) (MARCO POLO *enters briskly from below on the left. He is dressed in full uniform, looking spick and span and self-conscious. His face wears an expression of humorous scorn. He bows ceremoniously to the* PRINCESS, *his attitude a queer mixture of familiarity and an uncertain awe*).

MARCO: Your Highness— (*Then ingratiatingly*)—or I suppose I'd better say Majesty now that we've reached Persia—I've got queer news for you. A boat just came from the shore with an official notification that your intended husband, Arghun Khan, is dead and I'm to hand you over to his son, Ghazan, to marry. (*He hands her a sealed paper*) See!

KUKACHIN: (*letting the paper slip from her hand without a glance—dully*) What does it matter?

MARCO: (*admiringly—as he picks it up*) I must say you take it coolly. Of course, come to think of it, never having seen either, one's as good as another. (*He winds up philosophically*) And you'll be Queen just the same, that's the main thing.

KUKACHIN: (*with bitter irony*) So you think that is happiness? (*Then as* MARCO *stares at her uncertainly, she turns away and looks out over the sea with a sigh—after a pause*) There, where I see the lights, is that Hormuz?

MARCO: Yes. And I was forgetting, the messenger said Ghazan Khan would come to take you ashore tonight.

KUKACHIN: (*with sudden fear*) So soon? Tonight? (*Then rebelliously*) Is the granddaughter of the Great Kublai no better than a slave? I will not go until it pleases me!

MARCO: Good for you! That's the spirit! (*Then alarmed at his own te-*

merity—hastily) But don't be rash! The Khan probably meant whenever you were willing. And don't mind what I just said.

KUKACHIN: (*looks at him with a sudden dawning of hope—gently*) Why should you be afraid of what you said?

MARCO: (*offended*) I'm not afraid of anything—when it comes to the point!

KUKACHIN: What point?

MARCO: (*nonplussed*) Why—well—when I feel someone's trying to steal what's rightfully mine, for instance.

KUKACHIN: And now—here—you do not feel that?

MARCO: (*with a forced laugh, thinking she is joking*) Ha! Well— (*Uncertainly*) That is—I don't catch your meaning— (*Then changing the subject abruptly*) But here's something I want to ask you. Your grandfather entrusted you to my care. He relied on me to prove equal to the task of bringing you safe and sound to your husband. Now I want to ask you frankly if you yourself won't be the first to acknowledge that in spite of typhoons, shipwrecks, pirates and every other known form of bad luck, I've brought you through in good shape?

KUKACHIN: (*with an irony almost hysterical*) More than anyone in the world, I can appreciate your devotion to duty! You have been a prodigy of heroic accomplishment! In the typhoon when a wave swept me from the deck, was it not you who swam to me as I was drowning?

MARCO: (*modestly*) It was easy. Venetians make the best swimmers in the world.

KUKACHIN: (*even more ironically*) When the pirates attacked us, was it not your brave sword that warded off their curved knives from my breast and struck them dead at my feet?

MARCO: I was out of practice, too. I used to be one of the crack swordsmen of Venice—and they're the world's foremost, as everyone knows.

KUKACHIN: (*with a sudden change—softly*) And when the frightful fever wasted me, was it not you who tended me night and day, watching by my bedside like a gentle nurse, even brewing yourself the medicines that brought me back to life?

MARCO: (*with sentimental solemnity*) My mother's recipes. Simple home remedies—from the best friend I ever had!

KUKACHIN: (*a trifle wildly*) Oh, yes, you have been a model guardian, Admiral Polo!

MARCO: (*quickly*) Thank you, Princess. If I have satisfied you—then if I might ask you a favor, that you put in writing all you've just said in your first letter to the Great Kaan, and also tell your husband?

KUKACHIN: (*suddenly wildly bitter*) I will assuredly! I will tell them both of your heroic cruelty in saving me from death! (*Intensely*) Why could you not let me die?

MARCO: (*confusedly*) You're joking. You certainly didn't want to die, did you?

KUKACHIN: (*slowly and intensely*) Yes!

MARCO: (*puzzled and severe*) Hum! You shouldn't talk that way.

KUKACHIN: (*longingly*) I would be asleep in green water!

MARCO: (*worriedly, suddenly reaches out and takes her hand*) Here now, young lady! Don't start getting morbid!

KUKACHIN: (*with a thrill of love*) Marco!

MARCO: I believe you're feverish. Let me feel your pulse!

KUKACHIN: (*violently*) No! (*She draws her hand from his as if she had been stung*).

MARCO: (*worriedly*) Please don't be unreasonable. There'd be the devil to pay if you should suffer a relapse of that fever after I sweated blood to pull you through once already! Do you feel hot?

KUKACHIN: (*wildly*) No! Yes! On fire!

MARCO: Are your feet cold?

KUKACHIN: No! Yes! I don't know! (*Gravely* MARCO *kneels, removes a slipper, and feels the sole of her foot—then pats her foot playfully*).

MARCO: No. They're all right. (*He gets up—professionally*) Any cramps?

KUKACHIN: You fool! No! Yes! My heart feels as if it were bursting!

MARCO: It burns?

KUKACHIN: Like a red ember flaring up for the last time before it chills into gray ash forever!

MARCO: Then something must have disagreed with you. Will you let me see your tongue?

KUKACHIN: (*in a queer hysterical state where she delights in self-humiliation*) Yes! Yes! Anything! I am a Princess of the Imperial blood of Chinghiz and you are a dog! Anything! (*She sticks out her tongue, the tears streaming down her face as he looks at it*).

MARCO: (*shakes his head*) No sign of biliousness. There's nothing seriously wrong. If you would only try to sleep a while—

KUKACHIN: O Celestial God of the Heavens! What have I done that Thou shouldst torture me? (*Then wildly to* MARCO) I wished to sleep in the depths of the sea. Why did you awaken me?

MARCO: (*worried again*) Perhaps it's brain fever. Does your head ache?

KUKACHIN: No! Does your immortal soul?

MARCO: Don't blaspheme! You're talking as if you were delirious! (*Then pleadingly*) For Heaven's sake, try and be calm, Princess! What if your husband, Ghazan Khan, should find you in such a state?

KUKACHIN: (*calming herself with difficulty—after a pause, bitterly*) I suppose you are relieved to get me here alive and deliver me—like a cow!

MARCO: (*injuredly*) I've only carried out your own grandfather's orders!

KUKACHIN: (*forcing a smile*) Won't you miss being my guardian? (*Striving pitifullly to arouse his jealousy*) When you think of Ghazan protecting me and nursing me when I am sick—and—and loving me? Yes! I will compel him to love me, even though I never love him! He shall look into my eyes and see that I am a woman and beautiful!

MARCO: That's a husband's privilege.

KUKACHIN: Or a man's—a man who has a soul! (*Mockingly but intensely*) And that reminds me, Admiral Polo! You are taking advantage of this being the last day to shirk your duty!

MARCO: Shirk! No one can ever say—!

KUKACHIN: It was my grandfather's special command, given to you by Chu-Yin, you told me, that every day you should look into my eyes.

MARCO: (*resignedly*) Well, it isn't too late yet, is it? (*He moves toward her with a sigh of half-impatience with her whims*).

KUKACHIN: Wait. This is the one part of your duty in which I shall have to report you incompetent.

MARCO: (*hurt*) I've done my best. I never could discover anything out of the way.

KUKACHIN: There must be something he wished you to find. I myself feel there is something, something I cannot understand, something you must interpret for me! And remember this is your last chance! There is nothing in life I would not give—nothing I would not do— even now it is not too late! See my eyes as those of a woman and not a Princess! Look deeply! I will die if you do not see what is there! (*She finishes hysterically and beseechingly*).

MARCO: (*worried—soothingly*) There! There! Certainly, Princess! Of course, I'll look. And will you promise me that afterwards you'll lie down?

KUKACHIN: Look! See! (*She throws her head back, her arms outstretched. He bends over and looks into her eyes. She raises her hands slowly above his head as if she were going to pull it down to hers. Her lips part, her whole being strains out to him. He looks for a moment critically, then he grows tense, his face moves hypnotically toward hers, their lips seem about to meet in a kiss. She murmurs*) Marco!

MARCO: (*his voice thrilling for this second with oblivious passion*) Kukachin!

MAFFEO: (*suddenly slapping a stack of coins into the chest with a resounding clank*) One million!

MARCO: (*with a start, comes to himself and backs away from the* PRINCESS *in terror*) What, Uncle? Did you call?

MAFFEO: One million in God's money! (*He and* NICOLO *lock and fasten the box jubilantly*).

KUKACHIN: (*in despair*) Marco!

MARCO: (*flusteredly*) Yes, Princess. I saw something queer! It made me feel feverish too! (*Recovering a bit—with a sickly smile*) Oh, there's trouble there, all right! You must be delirious! I advise you to go to sleep.

KUKACHIN: (*with wild despair pulls out a small dagger from the bosom of her dress*) I obey! I shall sleep forever! (*But* MARCO, *the man of action, springs forward and wresting the dagger from her hand, flings it over the side. She confronts him defiantly, her eyes wild with grief and rage. He stares at her, dumbfounded and bewildered*).

MARCO: (*bewilderedly*) I never believed people—sane people—ever seriously tried—

KUKACHIN: (*intensely*) I implored an ox to see my soul! I no longer can endure the shame of living!

MARCO: (*sheepishly*) You mean it was a terrible insult when I called you—by your name?

KUKACHIN: (*bursting into hysterical laughter*) Yes! How dared you!

MARCO: (*hastily*) I ask pardon, Princess! Please forgive me! My only excuse is, I forgot myself. I guess I'll have to stop overworking or I'll suffer a nervous breakdown. I felt like one of those figures in a puppet show with someone jerking the wires. It wasn't me, you understand. My lips spoke without me saying a word. And here's the funniest part of it all, and what'll explain matters in full, if you can believe it. It wasn't you I was seeing and talking to, not a Princess at all, you'd changed into someone else, someone I've got a good right to—just a girl—

KUKACHIN: (*again clutching at hope*) A girl—a woman—you saw in me?

MARCO: (*enthusiastically, groping in his shirt front*) Yes. Here she is! (*He jerks the locket out of an under pocket and presents it to her proudly*) The future Mrs. Marco Polo! (*The* PRINCESS *takes it mechanically and stares at it in a stupor as* MARCO *rambles on*).

MARCO: You may believe it or not but like a flash she was standing there in your place and I was talking to her, not you at all!

KUKACHIN: (*dully*) But it was my name you spoke.

MARCO: (*confused*) I meant to say Donata. That's her name. We're going to be married as soon as I get home. (*Then as she stares at the miniature—proudly*) Pretty, isn't she?

KUKACHIN: (*dully*) She may have married another.

MARCO: (*confidently*) No. Her family needs an alliance with our house.

KUKACHIN: She may have had lovers.

MARCO: (*simply*) Oh, no. She's not that kind.

KUKACHIN: (*staring at the picture*) She will be middle-aged—fat—and stupid!

MARCO: (*with a grin*) Well, I don't mind a wife being a bit plump—and who wants a great thinker around the house? Sound common sense and a home where everything runs smooth, that's what I'm after.

KUKACHIN: (*looks from him to the miniature*).There is no soul even in your love, which is no better than a mating of swine! And I—! (*A spasm of pain covers her face—then with hatred and disdain*) Pig of a Christian! Will you return to this sow and boast that a Princess and a Queen—? (*With rage*) Shall I ask as my first wedding present from Ghazan Khan that he have you flayed and thrown into the street to be devoured by dogs?

MAFFEO AND NICOLO: (*who have pricked up their ears at this last, rush to the* PRINCESS, *dragging their box between them and prostrate themselves at her feet*) Mercy! Mercy! (*She seems not to hear or to see them but stares ahead stonily.* MARCO *beckons* MAFFEO *to one side*).

MARCO: (*in a whisper*) Don't be afraid. She doesn't mean a word of it. She's hysterical. Listen, I just noticed the royal barge coming. I'll go and meet the Khan. You keep her from doing anything rash until he gets here.

MAFFEO: Yes. (*He goes back and crouches again before the* PRINCESS, *keeping a wary eye on her, but she seems turned to stone.* MARCO *comes down and goes off left. There is the blare of a trumpet, the reflections of lanterns and torches, the sound of running about on deck and* MARCO's *voice giving commands. The* WOMEN *come out to attend the* PRINCESS. *She remains rigid, giving no sign*).

WOMEN: (*in chorus*)

> The lover comes,
> Who becomes a husband,
> Who becomes a son,
> Who becomes a father—
> In this contemplation lives the woman.

KUKACHIN: (*her face now a fatalistic mask of acceptance*)

> I am not.
> Life is.
> A cloud hides the sun.
> A life is lived.
> The sun shines again.
> Nothing has changed.
> Centuries wither into tired dust.
> A new dew freshens the grass.
> Somewhere this dream is being dreamed.

(*From the left* MARCO *comes escorting* GHAZAN KHAN, *attended by a train of nobles and slaves with lights. He can be heard saying: "She is a little feverish—the excitement—" All are magnificently dressed, glittering with jewels.* GHAZAN *is a young man, not handsome but noble and manly looking. He comes forward and bows low before her, his attendants likewise. Then he looks into her face and stands fascinated by her beauty. She looks back at him with a calm indifference*).

GHAZAN: (*after a pause—his voice thrilling with admiration*) If it were possible for a son who loved a noble father to rejoice at that father's death, then I should be that guilty son! (*As she makes no reply*) You have heard? Arghun Khan is dead. You must bear the humiliation of accepting his son for husband, a crow to replace an eagle! Forgive me. But with your eyes to watch I may become at least a shadow of his greatness.

KUKACHIN: (*calmly*) What am I? I shall obey the eternal will which governs your destiny and mine.

GHAZAN: (*impetuously*) You are more beautiful than I had dared to dream! It shall not be I who rules, but you! I shall be your slave! Persia shall be your conquest and everywhere where songs are sung they shall be in praise of your beauty! You shall be Queen of Love—!

KUKACHIN: (*sharply with pain*) No! (*She drops the locket on the floor and grinds it into pieces under her foot*).

MARCO: (*excitedly*) Princess! Look out! You're stepping on— (*She kicks it away from her.* MARCO *stoops on his knees and begins picking up the wreckage in his handkerchief.* KUKACHIN *turns to* GHAZAN *and points to* MARCO) My first request of you, my Lord, is that you reward this Christian who has brought me here in safety. I ask, as a fitting tribute to his character, that you give an immense feast in his honor. Let there be food in tremendous amounts! He is an exquisite judge of quantity. Let him be urged to eat and drink until he can hold no more, until he becomes his own ideal figure, an idol of stuffed self-satisfaction! Will you do this? (*She is a trifle hectic now and her manner has grown wilder*).

CHAZAN: Your wish is my will!

KUKACHIN: (*pointing to a magnificent lion in diamonds on his breast*) What is that wonderful glittering beast?

GHAZAN: It is the emblem of the Order of the Lion which only great heroes and kings of men may wear.

KUKACHIN: (*gives a laugh of wild irony*) Great heroes—kings of men? (*Then eagerly*) Will you give it to me? I implore you! (GHAZAN, *fascinated, yet with a wondering glance, unpins it and hands it to her without a word. She prods* MARCO, *who is still collecting the pieces of the locket with her foot*) Arise! Let me give you the noble Order of the

Lion! (*She pins the blazing diamond figure on the breast of the stunned* MARCO, *laughing with bitter mockery*) How well it is set off on the bosom of a sheep! (*She laughs more wildly*) Kneel again! Bring me a chest of gold! (GHAZAN *makes a sign. Two slaves bring a chest of gold coins to her. She takes handfuls and throws them over the kneeling forms of the* POLOS, *laughing*) Here! Guzzle! Grunt! Wallow for our amusement! (*The two elder are surreptitiously snatching at the coins but* MARCO *jumps to his feet, his face flushing*).

MARCO: (*in a hurt tone*) I don't see why you're trying to insult me—just at the last moment. What have I done? (*Then suddenly forcing a smile*) But I realize you're not yourself.

GHAZAN: (*sensing something*) Has this man offended you? Shall he be killed?

KUKACHIN: (*wearily*) No. He has amused me. Let him be fed. Stuff him with food and gold and send him home. And you, My Lord, may I ask that this first night I be allowed to remain on board alone with my women? I am weary!

GHAZAN: Again your wish is my will, even though I will not live until I see you again!

KUKACHIN: (*exhaustedly*) I am humbly grateful. Good night, My Lord. (*She bows.* GHAZAN *and the Court bow before her. They retire toward the left,* MARCO *talking earnestly to the oblivious* GHAZAN *whose eyes are riveted on the* PRINCESS, *who has turned away from them. The two elder* POLOS, *carrying their chest, their pockets stuffed, trudge along last*).

MARCO: The close confinement of a long voyage. I think probably her spleen is out of order. (*They are gone from sight.* KUKACHIN's *shoulders quiver as, her head bowed in her hands, she sobs quietly. The ship can be heard making off*).

WOMEN: Weep, Princess of the Wounded Heart,
           Weeping heals the wounds of sorrow
           Till only the scars remain
           And the heart forgets.

KUKACHIN: (*suddenly runs up to the upper deck and stands outlined against the sky, her arms outstretched—in a voice which is a final, complete renunciation, calls*) Farewell, Marco Polo!

MARCO: (*his voice comes from over the water cheery and relived*) Good-bye, Your Majesty—and all best wishes for long life and happiness! (*The* PRINCESS *sinks to her knees, her face hidden in her arms on the bulwark*).

CURTAIN

*S*CENE: *One year later.*

The Grand Throne Room in the Imperial palace at Cambaluc. KUBLAI *squats on his throne, aged and sad, listening with an impassive face to* GENERAL BAYAN *who, dressed in the full military uniform and armor of the Commander-in-Chief is explaining earnestly with several maps in his hand. On* KUBLAI'S *left stands* CHU-YIN, *who is reading. Behind* BAYAN *are grouped at attention all the generals of his army with a multitude of young staff officers, all gorgeously uniformed and armored. From the room on the right, the ballroom, a sound of dance music and laughter comes through the closed doors.*

BAYAN: (*impressively—pointing to the map*) Here, Your Majesty, is the line of the river Danube which marks the Western boundary of your Empire. Beyond it, lies the West. Our spies report their many petty states are always quarreling. So great is their envy of each other that we could crush each singly and the rest would rejoice. We can mobilize one million horsemen on the Danube within a month. (*Proudly*) We would ride their armies down into the sea! Your Empire would extend from ocean to ocean!

KUBLAI: (*wearily*) It is much too large already. Why do you want to conquer the West? It must be a pitiful land, poor in spirit and material wealth. We have everything to lose by contact with its greedy hypocrisy. The conqueror acquires first of all the vices of the conquered. Let the West devour itself.

BAYAN: (*helplessly*) But—everywhere in the East there is peace!

KUBLAI: (*with hopeless irony*) Ah! And you are becoming restless?

BAYAN: (*proudly*) I am a Mongol—a man of action!

KUBLAI: (*looking at him with musing irony*) Hum! You have already conquered the West, I think.

BAYAN: (*puzzled*) What, Your Majesty? (*Then persuasively*) The West may not be strong but it is crafty. Remember how that Christian, Polo, invented the engine to batter down walls? It would be better to wipe out their cunning now before they make too many engines to weaken the power of men. (*Then with a sudden inspiration*) And it would be a righteous war! We would tear down their Christian Idols and set up the image of the Buddha!

KUBLAI: Buddha, the Prince of Peace?

BAYAN: (*bowing his head as do all his retinue*) The Gentle One, The Good, The Kind, The Pitiful, The Merciful, The Wise, The Eternal Contemplative One!

KUBLAI: In His Name?

BAYAN: (*fiercely*) Death to those who deny Him!

ALL: (*with a great fierce shout and a clanking of swords*) Death!

KUBLAI: (*looks up at the ceiling quizzically*) A thunderbolt? (*Waits*) No? Then there is no God! (*Then to* BAYAN *with a cynical bitter smile*) August Commander, if you must have war, let it be one without fine phrases—a practical war of few words, as that Polo you admire would say. Leave the West alone. Our interests do not conflict—yet. But there is a group of islands whose silk industry is beginning to threaten the supremacy of our own. Lead your gallant million there—and see to it your war leaves me in peace!

BAYAN: I hear and I obey! (*He turns to his staff exultantly*) His Majesty has declared war!

ALL: (*with a fierce cheer*) Down with the West!

BAYAN: (*hastily*) No. Not yet. Down with Japan! (*They cheer with equal enthusiasm—then he harangues them with the air of a patriotic exhorter*) His Majesty's benevolence and patience have been exhausted by the continued outrages against our silk nationals perpetrated by unscrupulous Japanese trade-pirates who, in spite of his protests, are breeding and maintaining silkworms for purposes of aggression! We fight in the cause of moral justice, that our silk-makers may preserve their share of the eternal sunlight! (*A long cheer*).

KUBLAI: (*smiling—distractedly*) War without rhetoric, please! Polo has infected you with cant! The West already invades us! Throw open the doors! Music! (*The doors are thrown open. The dance music sounds loudly*) Go in and dance, everyone! You, too, General! I revoke my declaration of war—unless you learn to dance and be silent! (*They all go into the ballroom,* BAYAN *stalking majestically with an injured mien*) But dancing makes me remember Kukachin whose little dancing feet—! Shut the doors! Music brings back her voice singing! (*Turning to* CHU-YIN—*harshly*) Wisdom! No, do not read! What good are wise writings to fight stupidity? One must have stupid writings that men can understand. In order to live even wisdom must be stupid!

A CHAMBERLAIN: (*enters hurriedly and prostrates himself*) A courier from Persia!

KUBLAI: (*excitedly*) From Kukachin! Bring him here! (*The* CHAMBERLAIN *dashes to the door and a moment later the* COURIER *enters, travel-stained and weary. He sinks into a heap before the throne.* KUBLAI *shouts at him impatiently*).

KUBLAI: Have you a letter?

COURIER: (*with a great effort holds out a letter*) Here! (*He collapses.* CHU-YIN *hands the letter up to* KUBLAI *who takes it eagerly from him. He begins to read at once. The* CHAMBERLAIN *comes back with a cup of wine. The* COURIER *is revived and gets to his knees, waiting humbly*).

CHU-YIN: (*goes back to* KUBLAI *who has finished reading the short note and is staring somberly before him*) And did the Little Flower save his Immortal Soul? (*KUBLAI does not look at him but mutely hands him the letter.* CHU-YIN *becomes grave. He reads aloud*) "Arghun had died. I am the wife of his son, Ghazan. It does not matter. He is kind but I miss my home and you. I doubt if I shall be blessed with a son. I do not care. I have lost my love of life. My heart beats more and more wearily. Death wooes me. You must not grieve. You wish me to be happy, do you not? And my body may resist Death for a long time yet. Too long. My soul he has already possessed. I wish to commend the unremitting attention to his duty of Admiral Polo. He saved my life three times at the risk of his own. He delivered me to Ghazan. Send him another million. You were right about his soul. What I had mistaken for one I discovered to be a fat woman with a patient virtue. By the time you receive this they will be married in Venice. I do not blame him. But I cannot forgive myself—nor forget—nor believe again in any beauty in the world. I love you the best in life. And tell Chu-Yin I love him too." (*He lets the letter in his hand drop to his side, his eyes filling, his voice grown husky.* KUBLAI *stares bleakly ahead of him*).

KUBLAI: (*at last rouses himself—harshly to the* COURIER) Did the Queen give you this in person?

COURIER: Yes, Your Majesty—with a generous gift.

KUBLAI: I can be generous too. Did she appear—ill?

COURIER: Yes. I could scarcely hear her voice.

KUBLAI: You brought no other word?

COURIER: Not from the Queen. I came privately from her. But Admiral Polo suspected my departure and gave me a verbal message which he caused me to memorize.

KUBLAI: (*harshly—his eyes beginning to gleam with anger*) Ha! Go on! Repeat!

COURIER: (*stopping for a moment to freshen his memory*) He said, tell the Great Kaan that "in spite of perils too numerous to relate, I have delivered my charge safely to Ghazan Khan. In general, she gave but little trouble on the voyage, for although flighty in temper and of a passionate disposition, she never refused to heed my advice for her welfare and as I informed His Majesty, King Ghazan, the responsibilities of marriage and the duties of motherhood will sober her spirit and she will settle down as a sensible wife should. This much I further add, that in humble obedience to your final instructions given me by Mr. Chu-Yin, I looked daily into her eyes."

KUBLAI: (*bewilderedly to* CHU-YIN) What? Did you—?

CHU-YIN: (*miserably*) Forgive an old fool! I meant it partly in jest as a last chance—to cure her—or to awaken him.

COURIER: (*continuing*) "But I have never noted any unnatural change in them except toward the termination of our trip, particularly on the last day, when I noticed a rather strained expression but this I took to be fever due to her Highness's spleen being sluggish after the long confinement on shipboard."

KUBLAI: (*choking with wrath*) O God of the Somber Heavens!

COURIER: And he gave me no money for delivering the message but he promised that you would reward me nobly.

KUBLAI: (*with wild laughter*) Ha-ha-ha! Stop! Do you dare to madden me? (*Then suddenly raging*) Out of my sight, dog, before I have you impaled! (*The terror-stricken* COURIER *scrambles out like a flash.* KUBLAI *stands up with flashing eyes—revengefully*). I have reconsidered! I shall conquer the West! I shall lead my armies in person! I shall not leave one temple standing nor one Christian alive who is not enslaved! Their cities shall vanish in flame, their fields shall be wasted! Famine shall finish what I leave undone! And of the city of Venice not one vestige shall remain! And of the body of Marco Polo there shall not be a fragment of bone nor an atom of flesh which will not have shrieked through ten days' torture before it died!

CHU-YIN: Master! (*He throws himself on his face at* KUBLAI's *feet*) Do not torture yourself! Is this Wisdom? Is this the peace of the soul?

KUBLAI: (*distractedly*) To revenge oneself—that brings a kind of peace!

CHU-YIN: To revenge equally the wrong of an equal perhaps, but this—? Can you confess yourself weaker than his stupidity?

KUBLAI: He has murdered her!

CHU-YIN: She does not accuse him. What would be her wish?

KUBLAI: (*his anger passing—wearily and bitterly, after a pause*) Rise, my old friend, it is I who should be at your feet, not you at mine! (*He sinks dejectedly on his throne again. After a pause, sadly*) She will die. Why is this? What purpose can it serve? My hideous suspicion is that God is only an infinite, insane energy which creates and destroys without other purpose than to pass eternity in avoiding thought. Then the stupid man becomes the Perfect Incarnation of Omnipotence and the Polos are the true children of God! (*He laughs bitterly*) Ha! How long before we shall be permitted to die, my friend? I begin to resent life as the insult of an ignoble inferior with whom it is a degradation to fight! (*Broodingly—after a pause*) I have had a foreboding she would die. Lately, to while away time, I experimented with the crystal. I do not believe the magic nonsense about it but I do consider that, given a focus, the will can perhaps overcome the limits of the senses. Whatever the explanation be, I looked into the crystal and willed to see Kukachin in Persia and she appeared, sitting alone in a garden, beautiful and sad, apart from life, waiting— (*Brokenly*) My eyes filled with tears. I cried out to her—and she was gone! (*Then suddenly— to the* CHAMBERLAIN) Bring me the crystal! (*To* CHU-YIN *as the* CHAMBERLAIN *goes*) Marco, the true ruler of the world, will have come to Venice by this time. My loathing grows so intense I feel he must jump into the crystal at my bidding. And—in the cause of wisdom, say—we must see what he is doing now. (*The* CHAMBERLAIN *returns with the crystal.* KUBLAI *takes it eagerly from his hand and stares fixedly into it*).

CHU-YIN: (*protestingly*) Why do you wish to hurt yourself further?

KUBLAI: (*staring fixedly*) I shall observe dispassionately. It is a test of myself I want to make as a penalty for my weakness a moment ago. (*He sees something*) Ah—it begins. (*A pause. The light grows dimmer and dimmer on the stage proper as it begins to come up on the extreme foreground*) I see—a city whose streets are canals—it is evening—a house. I begin to see through the walls— Ah! (*The lights come up again on the back stage as the forestage is fully revealed. The* KAAN *on his throne and* CHU-YIN *are seen dimly, behind and above, like beings on another plane. At the center of the forestage is a great banquet table garishly set with an ornate gold service. A tall majordomo in a gorgeous uniform enters and stands at attention as the procession begins. First come the Guests, male and female, a crowd of good substantial bourgeois, who stare about with awe and envy and are greatly impressed by the gold plate*).

A MAN: They've laid out a pile of money here!

A WOMAN: Is that gold service really gold?

ANOTHER: Absolutely. I can tell without biting it.

A MAN: They must have cash, whoever they are.

A WOMAN: Do you think they're really the Polos?

ANOTHER: They looked like greasy Tartars to me.

ANOTHER: That was their queer clothes.

A MAN: And remember they've been gone twenty-odd years.

ANOTHER: In spite of that, I thought I could recognize MAFFEO

A WOMAN: Will Donata know Marco, I wonder?

A MAN: What's more to her point, will he recognize her?

A WOMAN: Imagine her waiting all this time!

ANOTHER: How romantic! He must be terribly rich—if it's really him.

A MAN: We'll soon know. That's why we were invited.

A WOMAN: Ssshh! Here comes Donata now. How old she's getting to look!

ANOTHER: And how fat in the hips!

A MAN: (*jokingly*) That's the way I like 'em, and perhaps Marco— (DON-ATA *enters on the arm of her father, a crafty, wizened old man. She has grown into a stout middle-age but her face is unlined and still pretty in a bovine, good-natured way. All bow and they return this salutation*).

ALL: Congratulations, Donata! (*She blushes and turns aside in an incongruous girlish confusion*).

FATHER: (*proud but pretending querulousness*) Don't tease her now! The girl's nervous enough already. And it may not be Marco after all but only a joke someone's put up on us.

A WOMAN: No one could be so cruel!

ALL: (*suddenly with a great gasp*) Oh, listen! (*An orchestra vigorously begins a flowery, sentimental Italian tune. This grows into quite a blare as the musicians enter from the right, six in number, in brilliant uniforms*) Oh, look! (*The musicians form a line, three on each side by the stairs on right*) Oh, see! (*A procession of servants begins to file one by one through the ranks of musicians, each carrying on his head or upraised hand an enormous platter on which are whole pigs, fowl of all varieties, roasts, vegetables, salads, fruits, nuts, dozens of bottles of wine. The servants arrange these on the table, in symmetrical groups, with the trained eye for display of window-dressers, until the table, with the bright light flooding down on it, closely resembles the front of a pretentious delicatessen store. Meanwhile*) See! What a turkey! Such a goose! The fattest pig I ever saw! What ducks! What vegetables! Look at the wine! A feast for the Gods! And all those servants! An army! And the orchestra! What expense! Lavish! They must be worth millions! (*The three* POLOS *make their grand entrance from the stairs on right, walking with bursting self-importance between the files of musicians who now blare out a triumphant march. The two elder precede* MARCO *All three are dressed in long robes of embroidered crimson satin reaching almost to the ground. The guests give a new united gasp of astonishment*) Is it they? Is that old Nicolo? That's Maffeo's nose! No! It isn't them at all! Well, if it's a joke, I don't see the point. But such robes! Such hand embroidery! Such material! They must be worth millions.

DONATA: (*falteringly*) Is that him, father? I can't tell. (*She calls faintly*) Marco! (*But he pretends not to hear. He gives a sign at which the three take off their robes and hand them to the servants. They have even more gorgeous blue ones underneath.* MARCO *addresses the servants in a false voice*).

MARCO: My good men, you may sell these rich robes and divide the proceeds among yourselves! And here is a little something extra. (*He tosses a handful of gold to the servants and another to the musicians. A mad scramble results. The guests gasp. They seem inclined to join in the scramble*).

GUESTS: How generous! What prodigality! What indifference to money! They throw it away like dirt. They must be worth millions!

MARCO: (*in the same false voice*) Our guests look thirsty. Pass around the wine. (*The servants do so. The guests gaze, smell, taste*).

ALL: What a vintage! What flavor! What bouquet! How aged! It must have cost twenty lire a bottle! (*At another signal the three* POLOS *take off their blue robes*).

MARCO: (*regally*) Give those to the musicians! (*They are revealed now in their old dirty, loose Tartar traveling dress and look quite shabby. The guests gape uncertainly. Then* MARCO *declares grandly*) You look astonished, good people, but this is a moral lesson to teach you not to put too much faith in appearances, for behold! (*He slits up the wide sleeves of his own robe, as do his father and uncle, and now the three, standing beside a big empty space which has been purposely left at the very center of the table at the front, lower their opened sleeves, and, as the musicians, obeying this signal, start up a great blare, let pour from them a perfect stream of precious stones which forms a glittering multicolored heap. This is the final blow. The guests stare pop-eyed, open-mouthed, speechless for a second. Then their pent-up admiration breaks forth*).

ALL: Extraordinary! Jewels! Gems! Rubies! Emeralds! Diamonds! Pearls! A king's ransom! Millions!

MARCO: (*suddenly with his hail-fellow-well-met joviality*) Well folks, are you all tongue-tied? Isn't one of you going to say welcome home? And Miss Donata, don't I get a kiss? I'm still a bachelor! (*Immediately with mad shouts of "Bravo!" "Welcome home!" "Hurrah for the Polos!" etc., etc., the guests bear down on them in a flood. There is a confused whirl of embraces, kisses, backslaps, handshakes and loud greetings of all sorts.* MARCO *manages to get separated and pulls* DONATA *down front to the foreground*).

DONATA: (*half swooning*). Marco!

MARCO: (*moved*) My old girl! (*They kiss, then he pushes her away*) Here! Let me get a good look at you! Why, you're still as pretty as a picture and you don't look a day older!

DONATA: (*exaltedly*) My beloved prince!

MARCO: (*jokingly*) No, if I was a prince I'd never have remained single all these years in the East! I'm a hero, that's what! And all the twenty-odd years I kept thinking of you, and I was always intending to write— (*He pulls the pieces of the miniature wrapped in the handkerchief out of his pocket*) Here's proof for you! Look at yourself! You're a bit smashed but that was done in a hand-to-hand fight with pirates. Now don't I deserve another kiss?

DONATA: (*giving it*) My hero! (*Then jealously*) But I know all the heathen women must have fallen in love with you.

MARCO: Oh, maybe one or two or so—but I didn't have time to waste on females. I kept my nose to the grindstone every minute. (*Proudly*) And I got results. I don't mind telling you, Donata, I'm worth over two millions! How's that for keeping my promise? Worth while your waiting, eh? (*He slaps her on the back*).

DONATA: Yes, my wonder boy! (*Then worriedly*) You said there were one or two women? But you were true in spite of them, weren't you?

MARCO: I tell you I wouldn't have married the prettiest girl in Cathay! (*This with emphasis. Then abruptly*) But never mind any other girl. (*He chucks her under the chin*) What I want to know is when this girl is going to marry me?

DONATA: (*softly*) Any time! (*They hug. The guests group about them kittenishly, pointing and murmuring, "What a romance! What a romance!"*).

DONATA'S FATHER: (*seizing the opportunity*) Friends, I take this opportunity to publicly announce the betrothal of my daughter, Donata, to Marco Polo of this City! (*Another wild round of congratulations, kisses, etc.*).

MARCO: (*his voice sounding above the hubbub*) Let's eat, friends! (*They swirl to their places behind the long table. When they stand their faces can be seen above the piles of food but when they sit they are out of sight*) No ceremony among friends. Just pick your chair. All ready? Let's sit down then! (*with one motion they disappear*).

VOICE OF DONATA'S FATHER: But, first, before we regale ourselves with your cheer, won't you address a few words to your old friends and neighbors who have gathered here on this happy occasion? (*Applause. MARCO is heard expostulating but finally he gives in*).

MARCO: All right, if you'll promise to go ahead and eat and not wait for me. (*His head appears, his expression full of importance. Servants flit about noisily. He coughs and begins with dramatic feeling*) My friends and neighbors of old, your generous and wholehearted welcome touches me profoundly. I would I had the gift of oratory to thank you fittingly, but I am a simple man, an ordinary man, I might almost say,—a man of affairs used to dealing in the hard facts of life, a silent man given to deeds not words— (*Here he falters fittingly*) And so now—forgive my emotion—words fail me— (*Here he clears his throat with an important cough and bursts forth into a memorized speech in the grand Chamber of Commerce style*) But I'll be glad to let you have a few instructive facts about the silk industry as we observed it in the Far East, laying especial emphasis upon the keystone of the whole silk business—I refer to the breeding of worms! (*A few hungry guests start to eat. Knives and forks and spoons rattle against plates. Soup is heard.* MARCO *strikes a good listening attitude so he will be sure not to miss a word his voice utters and warms to his work*) Now, to begin with, there are millions upon millions of capital invested in this industry, millions of contented slaves labor unremittingly millions of hours per annum to obtain the best results in the weaving and dyeing of the finished product, but I don't hesitate to state that all this activity is relatively unimportant beside the astounding fact that in the production of the raw material there are constantly employed millions upon millions upon millions of millions of worms!

ONE VOICE: (*rather muffled by roast pig*) Hear! (*But the rest are all absorbed in eating and a perfect clamor of knives and forks resounds.* MARCO *begins again but this time the clamor is too great, his words are lost, only the one he lays such emphasis upon can be distinguished*).

MARCO: Millions! . . . millions! . . . millions! . . . millions!

KUBLAI: (*who from the height of his golden throne, crystal in hand, has watched all this with fascinated disgust while* CHU-YIN *has sat down to read again, now turns away with a shudder of loathing—and, in spite of himself, a shadow of a smile—and lets the crystal fall from his hand and shatter into bits with a loud report. Instantly there is darkness and from high up in the darkness* KUBLAI's *voice speaking with a pitying scorn*). The Word became their flesh, they say. Now all is flesh! And can their flesh become the Word again?

DARKNESS

SCENE TWO

SCENE: *Grand Throne Room in the Imperial Palace at Cambaluc, about two years later. The walls tower majestically in shadow, their elaborate detail blurred into a background of half-darkness.*

KUBLAI *sits at the top of his throne, cross-legged in the posture of an idol, motionless, wrapped in contemplation. He wears a simple white robe without adornment of any sort. A brilliant light floods down upon him in one concentrated ray. His eyes are fixed on a catafalque, draped in heavy white silk, which stands in the center of the room, emphasized by another downpouring shaft of light.*

CHU-YIN *stands on the level below, on* KUBLAI's *left. On the main floor are the nobles and people of the court, grouped as in Act One, Scene Six.*

There is a long pause clamorous with the pealing of the thousands of bells in the city, big and little, near and far. Every figure in the room is as motionless as the KAAN *himself. Their eyes are kept on him with the ardent humility and respect of worship. Behind their impassive faces, one senses a tense expectancy of some sign from the throne. At last,* KUBLAI *makes a slight but imperious motion of command with his right hand. Immediately the women all turn with arms outstretched toward the catafalque. Their voices rise together in a long, rhythmic wail of mourning; their arms with one motion move slowly up; their voices attain a prolonged note of unbearable poignancy; their heads are thrown* back, their arms appeal to Heaven in one agonized gesture of despair. Here the KAAN makes the same barely perceptible sign of command again. The voices are instantly silenced. With one motion, the women throw themselves prostrate on the floor. The bells, except for one slow deep-toned one in the palace itself, are almost instantly hushed. At the same instant, from outside, at first faint, but growing momentarily in volume, comes the sound of funeral music. A moment later the funeral procession enters. The men sink to the cross-legged position of prayer, their heads bowed.

First come the musicians, nine in number, men in robes of bright red. They are followed by the chorus of nine singers, five men and four women, all of them aged, with bent bodies, their thin, cracked voices accompanying the music in queer, breaking waves of lamentation. These are masked, the men with a male mask of grief, the women with a female. All are dressed in deep black with white edging to their robes. After them comes a troupe of young girls and boys, dressed in white with black edging, moving slowly backward in a gliding, interweaving dance pattern. Their faces are not masked but are fixed in a disciplined, traditional expression of bewildered, uncomprehending grief that is like a mask. They carry silver censers which they swing in unison toward the corpse of the PRINCESS KUKACHIN, carried on a bier directly behind them on the shoulders of eight princes of the blood in black armor.

Accompanying the bier, one at each corner, are four priests—the foremost two, a Confucian and a Taoist, the latter two, a Buddhist and a Moslem. Each walks with bent head reading aloud to himself from his Holy Book.

The princes lift the bier of KUKACHIN to the top of the catafalque. Her body is wrapped in a winding sheet of deep blue, a jeweled golden head-dress is on her black hair, her face is white and clear as a statue's. The young boys and girls place their smoking censers about the catafalque, the incense ascending in clouds about the Princess as if it were bearing her soul with it. The music and the singing cease as the dancers, singers, and musicians form on each side, and to the rear, of the catafalque and sink into attitudes of prayer.

KUBLAI speaks to the priests in a voice of command in which is weariness and disbelief.

KUBLAI: Peace! She does not need your prayers. She was a prayer! (*With one motion they shut their books, raise their heads and stare before them in silence.* KUBLAI *continues—sadly*) Can words recall life to her beauty? (*To the* PRIEST OF TAO) Priest of Tao, will you conquer death by your mystic Way?

PRIEST OF TAO: (*bowing his head in submission—fatalistically*) Which is the greater evil, to possess or to be without? Death is.

CHORUS: (*in an echo of vast sadness*) Death is.

KUBLAI: (*to the* CONFUCIAN) Follower of Confucius, the Wise, have you this wisdom?

PRIEST OF CONFUCIUS: (*slowly*) Before we know life, how can we know death? (*Then as the* TAOIST, *submissively*) Death is.

CHORUS: (*as before*) Death is.

KUBLAI: (*to the* BUDDHIST PRIEST) Worshiper of Buddha, can your self-overcoming overcome that greatest overcomer of self?

BUDDHIST PRIEST: This is a thing which no god can bring about: that what is subject to death should not die. (*Then as the others, submissively*) Death is.

CHORUS: (*as before*) Death is.

KUBLAI: (*wearily*) And your answer, priest of Islam?

PRIEST OF ISLAM: It is the will of Allah! (*Submissively*) Death is.

CHORUS: Death is. Death is. Death is. (*Their voices die away*).

KUBLAI: (*after a pause*) What is death? (*A long pause. His eyes rest in loving contemplation on the body of* KUKACHIN: *Finally he speaks tenderly to her with a sad smile*) Girl whom we call dead, whose beauty is even in death more living than we, smile with infinite silence upon our speech, smile with infinite forbearance upon our wisdom, smile with infinite remoteness upon our sorrow, smile as a star smiles! (*His voice appears about to break. A muffled sound of sobbing comes from the prostrate women.* KUBLAI *regains control over his weakness and rises to his feet—with angry self-contempt*) No more! That is for poets! (*With over-stressed arrogance—assertively*) I am the Great Kaan! (*Everyone in the room rises with one motion of assertion*).

CHORUS: (*accompanied by a clangor of brass from the musicians—recite with discordant vigor*)

Greatest of the Great!
Son of Heaven!
Lord of Earth!
Sovereign of the World!
Ruler over Life and Death!

KUBLAI: (*silences them by an imperious gesture—and now even the great palace bell is stilled—half-mockingly but assertively*) The Son of Heaven? Then I should know a prayer. Sovereign of the World? Then I command the World to pray! (*With one motion all sink to the position of prayer*) In silence! Prayer is beyond words! Contemplate the eternal life of Life! Pray thus! (*He himself sinks to the position of prayer—a pause—then slowly*) In silence—for one concentrated moment—be proud of life! Know in your heart that the living of life can be noble! Know that the dying of death can be noble! Be exalted by life! Be inspired by death! Be humbly proud! Be proudly grateful! Be immortal because life is immortal. Contain the harmony of womb and grave within you! Possess life as a lover —then sleep requited in the arms of death! If you awake, love again! If you sleep on, rest in peace! Who knows which? What does it matter? It is nobler not to know! (*A pause of silence. He rises to his feet. With one motion all do likewise.* KUBLAI *sits back on his cushions again, withdrawing into contemplation. The Mongol* CHRONICLER *comes forward to fulfill his function of chanting the official lament for the dead. He declaims in a high wailing voice accompanied by the musicians and by the* CHORUS *who sway rhythmically and hum a rising and falling mourning accompaniment*).

CHRONICLER: We lament the shortness of life. Life at its longest is brief enough.

Too brief for the wisdom of joy, too long for the knowledge of sorrow.

Sorrow becomes despair when death comes to the young, untimely.

Oh, that her beauty could live again, that her youth could be born anew.

Our Princess was young as Spring, she was beautiful as a bird or flower.

Cruel when Spring is smitten by Winter, when birds are struck dead in full song, when the budding blossom is blighted!

Alas that our Princess is dead, she was the song of songs, the perfume of perfumes, the perfect one!

Our sobs stifle us, our tears wet the ground, our lamentations sadden the wind from the West.

(*Bows submissively—speaks*)

Yet we must bow humbly before the Omnipotent.

CHORUS: We must be humble.

CHRONICLER: Against Death all Gods are powerless.

CHORUS: All Gods are powerless. (*Their voices die into silence*).

KUBLAI: (*after a pause—wearily*) Leave her in peace. Go. (*The Court leaves silently at his command in a formal, expressionless order. The four priests go first, beginning to pray silently again. They are followed by the nobles and officials with their women coming after. Finally the young boys and girls take up their censers and dance their pattern out backward, preceded by the musicians. Only the* CHORUS *remain, grouped in a semi-circle behind the catafalque, motionless, and* CHU-YIN *who stays at the left hand of* KUBLAI. *The music fades away.* KUBLAI *takes his eyes from the dead girl with a sigh of bitter irony*).

KUBLAI: Oh, Chu-Yin, my Wise Friend, was the prayer I taught them wisdom?

CHU-YIN: It was the wisdom of pride. It was thy wisdom.

CHORUS: (*echoing sadly*) Thy wisdom.

KUBLAI: Was it not truth?

CHU-YIN: It was the truth of power. It was thy truth.

CHORUS: (*as before*) Thy truth.

KUBLAI: My pride, my power? My wisdom, my truth? For me there remains only—her truth! (*Then after staring at* KUKACHIN *for a second, bitterly*) Her truth! She died for love of a fool!

CHU-YIN: No. She loved love. She died for beauty.

KUBLAI: Your words are hollow echoes of the brain. Do not wound me with wisdom. Speak to my heart! (*Sadly—his eyes again on* KUKA-CHIN) Her little feet danced away the stamp of armies. Her smile made me forget the servile grin on the face of the World. In her eyes' mirror I watched myself live protected from life by her affection—a simple old man dying contentedly a little, day after pleasant day.

CHU-YIN: (*bowing—compassionately*) Then weep, old man. Be humble and weep for your child. The old should cherish sorrow. (*He bows again and goes out silently*).

KUBLAI: (*after a pause, gets up and descending from his throne, slowly approaches the catafalque, speaking to the dead girl softly as he does so—with a trembling smile*) I think you are hiding your eyes, Kukachin. You are a little girl again. You are playing hide and seek. You are pretending. Did we not once play such games together, you and I? You have made your face still, you have made your face cold, you have set your lips in a smile so remote—you are pretending even that you are dead! (*He is very near her now. His voice breaks—more and more intensely*) Let us stop playing! It is late. It is time you were asleep. Open your eyes and laugh! Laugh now that the game is over. Take the blindfold from my dim eyes. Whisper your secret in my ear. I— I am dead and you are living! Weep for me, Kukachin! Weep for the dead! (*He stretches his arms out to her beseechingly—pauses, standing beside the body, staring down at her; then, after a moment, he passes his hand over her face—tremblingly—with a beautiful tenderness of grief*) So, little Kukachin—so, Little Flower—you have come back—they could not keep you—you were too homesick—you wanted to return—to gladden my last days— (*He no longer tries to control his grief. He sobs like a simple old man, bending and kissing his granddaughter on the forehead—with heart-breaking playfulness*) I bid you welcome home, Little Flower! I bid you welcome home! (*He weeps, his tears falling on her calm white face*).

CURTAIN

Epilogue

*T*HE *play is over. The lights come up brilliantly in the theatre. In an aisle seat in the first row a* MAN *rises, conceals a yawn in his palm, stretches his legs as if they had become cramped by too long an evening, takes his hat from under the seat and starts to go out slowly with the others in the audience. But although there is nothing out of the ordinary in his actions, his appearance excites general comment and surprise for he is dressed as a Venetian merchant of the later Thirteenth Century. In fact, it is none other than* MARCO POLO *himself, looking a bit sleepy, a trifle puzzled, and not a little irritated as his thoughts, in spite of himself, cling for a passing moment to the play just ended. He appears quite unaware of being unusual and walks in the crowd without self-consciousness, very much as one of them. Arrived in the lobby his face begins to clear of all disturbing memories of what had happened on the stage. The noise, the lights of the streets, recall him at once to himself. Impatiently he waits for his car, casting a glance here and there at faces in the groups around him, his eyes impersonally speculative, his bearing stolid with the dignity of one who is sure of his place in the world. His car, a luxurious limousine, draws up at the curb. He gets in briskly, the door is slammed, the car edges away into the traffc and* MARCO POLO, *with a satisfied sigh at the sheer comfort of it all, resumes his life.*

THE END

The Great God Brown

CHARACTERS

WILLIAM A. BROWN

HIS FATHER, *a contractor*

HIS MOTHER

DION ANTHONY

HIS FATHER, *a builder*

HIS MOTHER

MARGARET

HER THREE SONS

CYBEL

TWO DRAFTSMEN ⎱ *in Brown's*
A STENOGRAPHER ⎰ *Office*

SCENES

Prologue: The Pier of the Casino. Moonlight in middle June.

ACT ONE

Scene I: Sitting room, Margaret Anthony's apartment. Afternoon, seven years later.

Scene II: Billy Brown's office. The same afternoon.

Scene III: Cybel's parlor. That night.

ACT TWO

Scene I: Cybel's parlor. Seven years later. Dusk.

Scene II: Drafting room, William A. Brown's office. That evening.

Scene III: Library, William A. Brown's home. That night.

ACT THREE

Scene I: Brown's office, a month later. Morning.

Scene II: Library, Brown's home. That evening.

Scene III: Sitting room, Margaret's home. That night.

ACT FOUR

Scene I: Brown's office, weeks later. Late afternoon.

Scene II: Library, Brown's house, hours later. The same night.

Epilogue: The Pier of the Casino. Four years later.

290

The Great God Brown

Prologue

SCENE: *A cross section of the pier of the Casino. In the rear, built out beyond the edge, is a rectangular space with benches on the three sides. A rail encloses the entire wharf at the back.*

It is a moonlight night in mid-June. From the Casino comes the sound of the school quartet rendering "Sweet Adeline" with many ultra-sentimental barber-shop quavers. There is a faint echo of the ensuing hand-clapping—then nothing but the lapping of ripples against the piles and their swishing on the beach—then footsteps on the boards and BILLY BROWN *walks along from right with his* MOTHER *and* FATHER. *The* MOTHER *is a dumpy woman of forty-five, overdressed in black lace and spangles. The* FATHER *is fifty or more, the type of bustling, genial, successful, provincial business man, stout and hearty in his evening dress.*

BILLY BROWN *is a handsome, tall and athletic boy of nearly eighteen. He is blond and blue-eyed, with a likeable smile and a frank good-humored face, its expression already indicating a disciplined restraint. His manner has the easy self-assurance of a normal intelligence. He is in evening dress.*

They walk arm in arm, the MOTHER *between.*

MOTHER: (*always addressing the* FATHER) This Commencement dance is badly managed. Such singing! Such poor voices! Why doesn't Billy sing?

BILLY: (to *her*) Mine is a regular fog horn! (*He laughs*).

MOTHER: (*to the air*) I had a pretty voice, when I was a girl. (*Then, to the* FATHER, *caustically*) Did you see young Anthony strutting around the ballroom in dirty flannel pants?

FATHER: He's just showing off.

MOTHER: Such impudence! He's as ignorant as his father.

FATHER: The old man's all right. My only kick against him is he's been too damned conservative to let me branch out.

MOTHER: (*bitterly*) He has kept you down to his level—out of pure jealousy.

FATHER: But he took me into partnership, don't forget—

MOTHER: (*sharply*) Because you were the brains! Because he was afraid of losing you! (*A pause*).

BILLY: (*admiringly*) Dion came in his old clothes on a bet with me. He's a real sport. He wouldn't have been afraid to appear in his pajamas! (*He grins with appreciation*).

MOTHER: Isn't the moonlight clear! (*She goes and sits on the center bench. BILLY stands at the left corner, forward, his hand on the rail, like a prisoner at the bar, facing the judge. His FATHER stands in front of the bench on right. The MOTHER announces, with finality*) After he's through college, Billy must study for a profession of some sort, I'm determined on that! (*She turns to her husband, defiantly, as if expecting opposition*).

FATHER: (*eagerly and placatingly*) Just what I've been thinking, my dear. Architecture! How's that? Billy a first-rate, number-one architect! That's my proposition! What I've always wished I could have been myself! Only I never had the opportunity. But Billy—we'll make him a partner in the firm after. Anthony, Brown *and Son*, *architects* and builders—instead of *contractors* and builders!

MOTHER: (*yearning for the realization of a dream*) And we won't lay sidewalks or—dig sewers—ever again?

FATHER: (*a bit ruffled*) I and Anthony can build anything your pet can draw—even if it's a church! (*Then, selling his idea*) It's a great chance for him! He'll design—expand us—make the firm famous.

MOTHER: (*to the air—musingly*) When you proposed, I thought your future promised success—my future—(*with a sigh*)—Well, I suppose we've been comfortable. Now, it's his future. How would Billy like to be an architect? (*She does not look at him*).

BILLY: (*to her*) All right, Mother. (*Then sheepishly*) I guess I've never bothered much about what I'd like to do after college—but architecture sounds all right to me, I guess.

MOTHER: (*to the air—proudly*) Billy used to draw houses when he was little.

FATHER: (*jubilantly*) Billy's got the stuff in him to win, if he'll only work hard enough.

BILLY: (*dutifully*) I'll work hard, Dad.

MOTHER: Billy can do anything!

BILLY: (*embarrassed*) I'll try, Mother. (*There is a pause*).

MOTHER: (*with a sudden shiver*) The nights are so much colder than they used to be! Think of it, I once went moonlight bathing in June when I was a girl—but the moonlight was so warm and beautiful in those days, do you remember, Father?

FATHER: (*puts his arm around her affectionately*) You bet I do, Mother. (*He kisses her. The orchestra at the Casino strikes up a waltz*) There's the music. Let's go back and watch the young folks dance. (*They start off, leaving* BILLY *standing there*).

MOTHER: (*suddenly calls back over her shoulder*) I want to watch Billy dance.

BILLY: (*dutifully*) Yes, Mother! (*He follows them. For a moment the faint sound of the music and the lapping of waves is heard. Then footsteps again and the three* ANTHONYS *come in. First come the* FATHER *and* MOTHER, *who are not masked. The* FATHER *is a tall lean man of fifty-five or sixty with a grim, defensive face, obstinate to the point of stupid weakness. The* MOTHER *is a thin frail faded woman, her manner perpetually nervous and distraught, but with a sweet and gentle face that had once been beautiful. The* FATHER *wears an ill-fitting black suit, like a mourner. The* MOTHER *wears a cheap, plain, black dress. Following them, as if he were a stranger, walking alone, is their son,* DION. *He is about the same height as young* BROWN *but lean and wiry, without repose, continually in restless nervous movement. His face is masked. The mask is a fixed forcing of his own face— dark, spiritual, poetic, passionately supersensitive, helplessly unprotected in*) *its childlike, religious faith in life—into the expression of a mocking, reckless, defiant, gayly scoffing and sensual young Pan. He is dressed in a gray flannel shirt, open at the neck, sneakers over bare feet, and soiled white flannel trousers. The* FATHER *strides to the center bench and sits down. The* MOTHER, *who has been holding to his arm, lets go and stands by the bench at the right. They both stare at* DION, *who, with a studied carelessness, takes his place at the rail, where young* BROWN *had stood. They watch him, with queer, puzzled eyes.*

MOTHER: (*suddenly—pleading*) You simply must send him to college!

FATHER: I won't. I don't believe in it. Colleges turn out lazy loafers to sponge on their poor old fathers! Let him slave like I had to! That'll teach him the value of a dollar! College'll only make him a bigger fool than he is already! I never got above grammar school but I've made money and established a sound business. Let him make a man out of himself like I made of myself!

DION: (*mockingly—to the air*) This Mr. Anthony is my father, but he only imagines he is God the Father. (*They both stare at him*).

FATHER: (*with angry bewilderment*) What—what—what's that?

MOTHER: (*gently remonstrating to her son*) Dion, dear! (*Then to her husband—tauntingly*) Brown takes all the credit! He tells everyone the success is all due to his energy—that you're only an old stick-in-the-mud!

FATHER: (*stung, harshly*) The damn fool! He knows better'n anyone if I hadn't held him down to common sense, with his crazy wild-cat notions, he'd have had us ruined long ago!

MOTHER: He's sending Billy to college—Mrs. Brown just told me—going to have him study architecture afterwards, too, so's he can help expand your firm!

FATHER: (*angrily*) What's that? (*Suddenly turns on* DION *furiously*) Then you can make up your mind to go, too! And you'll learn to be a better architect than Brown's boy or I'll turn you out in the gutter without a penny! You hear?

DION: (*mockingly—to the air*) It's difficult to choose—but architecture sounds less laborious.

MOTHER: (*fondly*) You ought to make a wonderful architect, Dion. You've always painted pictures so well—

DION: (*with a start—resentfully*) Why must she lie? Is it my fault? She knows I only try to paint. (*Passionately*) But I will, some day! (*Then quickly, mocking again*) On to college! Well, it won't be home, anyway, will it? (*He laughs queerly and approaches them. His* FATHER *gets up defensively.* DION *bows to him*) I thank Mr. Anthony for this splendid opportunity to create myself— (*He kisses his mother, who bows with a strange humility as if she were a servant being saluted by the young master—then adds lightly*)—in my mother's image, so she may feel her life comfortably concluded. (*He sits in his* FATHER'S *place at center and his mask stares with a frozen mockery before him. They stand on each side, looking dumbly at him*).

MOTHER: (*at last, with a shiver*) It's cold. June didn't use to be cold. I remember the June when I was carrying you, Dion—three months before you were born. (*She stares up at the sky*) The moonlight was warm, then. I could feel the night wrapped around me like a gray velvet gown lined with warm sky and trimmed with silver leaves!

FATHER: (*gruffly—but with a certain awe*) My mother used to believe the full of the moon was the time to sow. She was terrible old-fashioned. (*With a grunt*) I can feel it's bringing on my rheumatism. Let's go back indoors.

DION: (*with intense bitterness*) Hide! Be ashamed! (*They both start and stare at him*).

FATHER: (*with bitter hopelessness. To his wife—indicating their son*) Who is he? You bore him!

MOTHER: (*proudly*) He's my boy! He's Dion!

DION: (*bitterly resentful*) What else, indeed! The identical son! (*Then mockingly*) Are Mr. Anthony and his wife going in to dance? The nights grow cold! The days are dimmer than they used to be! Let's play hide-and-seek! Seek the monkey in the moon! (*He suddenly cuts a grotesque caper, like a harlequin and darts off, laughing with forced abandon. They stare after him—then slowly follow. Again there is silence except for the sound of the lapping waves. Then* MARGARET *comes in, followed by the humbly worshiping* BILLY BROWN. *She is almost seventeen, pretty and vivacious, blonde, with big romantic eyes, her figure lithe and strong, her facial expression intelligent but youthfully dreamy, especially now in the moonlight. She is in a simple white dress. On her entrance, her face is masked with an exact, almost transparent reproduction of her own features, but giving her the abstract quality of a Girl instead of the individual,* MARGARET).

MARGARET: (*looking upward at the moon and singing in low tone as they enter*) "Ah, moon of my delight that knowest no wane!"

BILLY: (*eagerly*) I've got that record—John McCormack. It's a peach! Sing some more. (*She looks upward in silence. He keeps standing respectfully in back of her, glancing embarrassedly toward her averted face. He tries to make conversation*) I think the *Rubáiyát's* great stuff, don't you? I never could memorize poetry worth a darn. Dion can recite lots of Shelley's poems by heart.

MARGARET: (*slowly takes off her mask—to the moon*) Dion! (*A pause*).

BILLY: (*fidgeting*) Margaret!

MARGARET: (*to the moon*) Dion is so wonderful!

BILLY: (*blunderingly*) I asked you to come out here because I wanted to tell you something.

MARGARET: (*to the moon*) Why did Dion look at me like that? It made me feel so crazy!

BILLY: I wanted to ask you something, too.

MARGARET: That one time he kissed me—I can't forget it! He was only joking—but I felt—and he saw and just laughed!

BILLY: Because that's the uncertain part. My end of it is a sure thing, and has been for a long time, and I guess everybody in town knows it—they're always kidding me—so it's a cinch you must know—how I feel about you.

MARGARET: Dion's so different from all the others. He can paint beautifully and write poetry and he plays and sings and dances so marvelously. But he's sad and shy, too, just like a baby sometimes, and he understands what I'm really like inside—and—and I'd love to run my fingers through his hair—and I love him! Yes, I love him! (*She stretches out her arms to the moon*) Oh, Dion, I love you!

BILLY: I love you, Margaret.

MARGARET: I wonder if Dion— I saw him looking at me again tonight— Oh, I wonder . . . !

BILLY: (*takes her hand and blurts out*) Can't you love me? Won't you marry me—after college—

MARGARET: Where is Dion now, I wonder?

BILLY: (*shaking her hand in an agony of uncertainty*) Margaret! Please answer me!

MARGARET: (*her dream broken, puts on her mask and turns to him—matter-of-factly*) It's getting chilly. Let's go back and dance, Billy.

BILLY: (*desperately*) I love you! (*He tries clumsily to kiss her*).

MARGARET: (*with an amused laugh*) Like a brother! You can kiss me if you like. (*She kisses him*) A big-brother kiss. It doesn't count. (*He steps back crushed, with head bowed. She turns away and takes off her mask—to the moon*) I wish Dion would kiss me again!

BILLY: (*painfully*) I'm a poor boob. I ought to know better. I'll bet I know. You're in love with Dion. I've seen you look at him. Isn't that it?

MARGARET: Dion! I love the sound of it!

BILLY: (*huskily*) Well—he's always been my best friend—I'm glad it's him—and I guess I know how to lose— (*He takes her hand and shakes it*)—so here's wishing you all the success and happiness in the world, Margaret—and remember I'll always be your best friend! (*He gives her hand a final shake—swallows hard—then manfully*) Let's go back in!

MARGARET: (*to the moon—faintly annoyed*) What is Billy Brown doing here? I'll go down to the end of the dock and wait. Dion is the moon and I'm the sea. I want to feel the moon kissing the sea. I want Dion to leave the sky to me. I want the tides of my blood to leave my heart and follow him! (*She whispers like a little girl*) Dion! Margaret! Peggy! Peggy is Dion's girl—Peggy is Dion's little girl— (*She sings laughingly, elfishly*) Dion is my Daddy-O! (*She is walking toward the end of the dock, off left*).

BILLY: (*who has turned away*, I'm going. I'll tell Dion you're here.

MARGARET: (*more and more strongly and assertively, until at the end she is a wife and a mother*) And I'll be Mrs. Dion—Dion's wife—and he'll be my Dion—my own Dion—my little boy—my baby! The moon is drowned in the tides of my heart, and peace sinks deep through the sea! (*She disappears off left, her upturned unmasked face like that of a rapturous visionary. There is silence again, in which the dance music is heard. Then this stops and* DION *comes in. He walks quickly to the bench at center and throws himself on it, hiding his masked face in his hands. After a moment, he lifts his head, peers about, listens huntedly, then slowly takes off his mask. His real face is revealed in the bright moonlight, shrinking, shy and gentle, full of a deep sadness*).

DION: (*with a suffering bewilderment*) Why am I afraid to dance, I who love music and rhythm and grace and song and laughter? Why am I afraid to live, I who love life and the beauty of flesh and the living colors of earth and sky and sea? Why am I afraid of love, I who love love? Why am I afraid, I who am not afraid? Why must I pretend to scorn in order to pity? Why must I hide myself in self-contempt in order to understand? Why must I be so ashamed of my strength, so proud of my weakness? Why must I live in a cage like a criminal, defying and hating, I who love peace and friendship? (*Clasping his hands above in supplication*) Why was I born without a skin, O God, that I must wear armor in order to touch or to be touched? (*A second's pause of waiting silence—then he suddenly claps his mask over his face again, with a gesture of despair and his voice becomes bitter and sardonic*) Or rather, Old Graybeard, why the devil was I ever born at all? (*Steps are heard from the right.* DION *stiffenes and his mask stares straight ahead.*

BILLY *comes in from the right. He is shuffling along disconsolately. When he sees* DION, *he stops abruptly and glowers resentfully—but at once the "good loser" in him conquers this*).

BILLY: (*embarrassedly*) Hello, Dion. I've been looking all over for you. (*He sits down on the bench at right, forcing a joking tone*) What are you sitting here for, you nut—trying to get more moonstruck? (*A pause—awkwardly*) I just left Margaret—

DION: (*gives a start—immediately defensively mocking*) Bless you, my children!

BILLY: (*gruffly and slangily*) I'm out of it—she gave me the gate. You're the original white-haired boy. Go on in and win! We've been chums ever since we were kids, haven't we?—and—I'm glad it's you, Dion. (*This huskily—he fumbles for* DION's *hand and gives it a shake*).

DION: (*letting his hand fall back—bitterly*) Chums? Oh, no, Billy Brown would despise me!

BILLY: She's waiting for you now, down at the end of the dock.

DION: For me? Which? Who? Oh, no, girls only allow themselves to look at what is seen!

BILLY: She's in love with you.

DION: (*moved—a pause—stammers*) Miracle? I'm afraid! (*He chants flippantly*) I love, thou lovest, he loves, she loves! She loves, she loves—what?

BILLY: And I know damn well, underneath your nuttiness, you're gone on her.

DION: (*moved*) Underneath? I love love! I'd love to be loved! But I'm afraid! (*Then aggressively*) *Was* afraid! Not now! Now I can make love—to anyone! Yes, I love Peggy! Why not? Who is she? Who am I? We love, you love, they love, one loves! No one loves! All the world loves a lover, God loves us all and we love Him! Love is a word—a shameless ragged ghost of a word—begging at all doors for life at any price!

BILLY: (*always as if he hadn't listened to what the other said*) Say, let's you and me room together at college—

DION: Billy wants to remain by her side!

BILLY: It's a bet, then! (*Forcing a grin*) You can tell her I'll see that you behave! (*Turns away*) So long. Remember she's waiting. (*He goes*).

DION: (*dazedly, to himself*) Waiting—waiting for me! (*He slowly removes his mask. His face is torn and transfigured by joy. He stares at the sky raptly*) O God in the moon, did you hear? She loves me! I am not afraid! I am strong! I can love! She protects me! Her arms are softly around me! She is warmly around me! She is my skin! She is my armor! Now I am born—I—the I!—one and indivisible—I who love Margaret! (*He glances at his mask triumphantly—in tones of deliverance*) You are outgrown! I am beyond you! (*He stretches out his arms to the sky*) O God, now I believe! (*From the end of the wharf, her voice is heard*).

MARGARET: Dion!

DION: (*raptly*) Margaret!

MARGARET: (*nearer*) Dion!

DION: Margaret!

MARGARET: Dion! (*She comes running in, her mask in her hands. He springs toward her with outstretched arms but she shrinks away with a frightened shriek and hastily puts on her mask.* DION *starts back. She speaks coldly and angrily*) Who are you? Why are you calling me? I don't know you!

DION: (*heart-brokenly*) I love you!

MARGARET: (*freezingly*) Is this a joke—or are you drunk?

DION: (*with a final pleading whisper*) Margaret! (*But she only glares at him contemptuously. Then with a sudden gesture he claps his mask on and laughs wildly and bitterly*) Ha-ha-ha! That's one on you, Peg!

MARGARET: (*with delight, pulling off her mask*) Dion! How did you ever— Why, I never knew you!

DION: (*puts his arm around her boldly*) How? It's the moon—the crazy moon—the monkey in the moon—playing jokes on us! (*He kisses her with his masked face with a romantic actor's passion again and again*) You love me! You know you do! Say it! Tell me! I want to hear! I want to feel! I want to know! I want to want! To want you as you want me!

MARGARET: (*in ecstasy*) Oh, Dion, I do! I do love you!

DION: (*with ironic mastery—rhetorically*) And I love you! Oh, madly! Oh, forever and ever, amen! You are my evening star and all my Pleiades! Your eyes are blue pools in which gold dreams glide, your body is a young white birch leaning backward beneath the lips of spring. So! (*He has bent her back, his arms supporting her, his face above hers*) So! (*He kisses her*).

MARGARET: (*with overpowering passionate languor*) Oh, Dion! Dion! I love you!

DION: (*with more and more mastery in his tone*) I love, you love, we love! Come! Rest! Relax! Let go your clutch on the world! Dim and dimmer! Fading out in the past behind! Gone! Death! Now! Be born! Awake! Live! Dissolve into dew—into silence—into night—into earth—into space—into peace—into meaning—into joy—into God—into the Great God Pan! (*While he has been speaking, the moon has passed gradually behind a black cloud, its light fading out. There is a moment of intense blackness and silence. Then the light gradually comes on again. DION's voice, at first in a whisper, then increasing in volume with the light, is heard*) Wake up! Time to get up! Time to exist! Time for school! Time to learn! Learn to pretend! Cover your nakedness! Learn to lie! Learn to keep step! Join the procession! Great Pan is dead! Be ashamed!

MARGARET: (*with a sob*) Oh, Dion, I am ashamed!

DION: (*mockingly*) Sssshh! Watch the monkey in the moon! See him dance! His tail is a piece of string that was left when he broke loose from Jehovah and ran away to join Charley Darwin's circus!

MARGARET: I know you must hate me now! (*She throws her arms around him and hides her head on his shoulder*).

DION: (*deeply moved*) Don't cry! Don't—! (*He suddenly tears off his mask—in a passionate agony*) Hate you? I love you with all my soul! Love me! Why can't you love me, Margaret? (*He tries to kiss her but she jumps to her feet with a frightened cry holding up her mask before her face protectingly*).

MARGARET: Don't! Please! I don't know you! You frighten me!

DION: (*puts on his mask again—quietly and bitterly*) All's well. I'll never let you see again. (*He puts his arm around her—gently mocking*) By proxy, I love you. There! Don't cry! Don't be afraid! Dion Anthony will marry you some day. (*He kisses her*) "I take this woman—" (*Tenderly joking*) Hello, woman! Do you feel older by æons? Mrs. Dion Anthony, shall we go in and may I have the next dance?

MARGARET: (*tenderly*) You crazy child! (*Then, laughing with joy*) Mrs. Dion Anthony! It sounds wonderful doesn't it? (*They go out as*

THE CURTAIN FALLS*)

ACT ONE—SCENE ONE

*S*CENE: *Seven years later.*

   The sitting room of MRS. DION ANTHONY'S *half of a two-family house in the homes section of the town—one of those one-design districts that daze the eye with multiplied ugliness. The four pieces of furniture shown are in keeping—an armchair at left, a table with a chair in back of it at center, a sofa at right. The same court-room effect of the arrangement of benches in Act One is held to here. The background is a backdrop on which the rear wall is painted with the intolerable lifeless realistic detail of the stereotyped paintings which usually adorn the sitting rooms of such houses. It is late afternoon of a gray day in winter.*

   DION *is sitting behind the table, staring before him. The mask hangs on his breast below his neck, giving the effect of two faces. His real face has aged greatly, grown more strained and tortured, but at the same time, in some queer way, more selfless and ascetic, more fixed in its resolute withdrawal from life. The mask, too, has changed. It is older, more defiant and mocking, its sneer more forced and bitter, its Pan quality becoming Mephisthophelean. It has already begun to show the ravages of dissipation.*

DION: (*suddenly reaches out and takes up a copy of the* New Testament *which is on the table and, putting a finger in at random, opens and reads aloud the text at which it points*) "Come unto me all ye who are heavy laden and I will give you rest." (*He stares before him in a sort of trance, his face lighted up from within but painfully confused—in an uncertain whisper*) I will come—but where are you, Savior? (*The noise of the outer door shutting is heard.* DION *starts and claps the mocking mask on his face again. He tosses the Testament aside contemptuously*) Blah! Fixation on old Mama Christianity! You infant blubbering in the dark, you! (*He laughs, with a bitter self-contempt. Footsteps approach. He picks up a newspaper and hides behind it hurriedly.* MARGARET *enters. She is dressed in*

*stylish, expensive clothes and a fur coat, which look as if they had been
remodeled and seen service. She has grown mature and maternal, in spite
of her youth. Her pretty face is still fresh and healthy but there is the
beginning of a permanently worried, apprehensive expression about the nose
and mouth—an uncomprehending hurt in her eyes.* DION *pretends to be
engrossed in his paper. She bends down and kisses him*).

MARGARET: (*with a forced gayety*) Good morning—at four in the afternoon! You were snoring when I left!

DION: (*puts his arms around her with a negligent, accustomed gesture—
mockingly*) The Ideal Husband!

MARGARET: (*already preoccupied with another thought—comes and sits in
chair on left*) I was afraid the children would disturb you, so I took
them over to Mrs. Young's to play. (*A pause. He picks up the paper
again. She asks anxiously*) I suppose they'll be all right over there,
don't you? (*He doesn't answer. She is more hurt than offended*) I wish
you'd try to take more interest in the children, Dion.

DION: (*mockingly*) Become a father—before breakfast? I'm in too delicate a condition. (*She turns away, hurt. Penitently he pats her hand—
vaguely*) All right. I'll try.

MARGARET: (*squeezing his hand—with possessive tenderness*) Play with
them. You're a bigger kid than they are—underneath.

DION: (*self-mockingly—flipping the Bible*) Underneath—I'm becoming
downright infantile! "Suffer these little ones!"

MARGARET: (*keeping to her certainty*) You're my oldest.

DION: (*with mocking appreciation*) She puts the Kingdom of Heaven in
its place!

MARGARET: (*withdrawing her hand*) I was serious.

DION: So was I—about something or other. (*He laughs*) This domestic
diplomacy! We communicate in code—when neither has the other's
key!

MARGARET: (*frowns confusedly—then forcing a playful tone*) I want to have
a serious talk with you, young man! In spite of your promises, you've

kept up the hard drinking and gambling you started the last year abroad.

DION: From the time I realized it wasn't in me to be an artist— except in living—and not even in that! (*He laughs bitterly*).

MARGARET: (*with conviction*) But you *can* paint, Dion—beautifully!

DION: (*with deep pain*) No! (*He suddenly takes her hand and kisses it gratefully*) I love Margaret! Her blindness surpasseth all understanding! (*Then bitterly*)—or is it pity?

MARGARET: We've only got about one hundred dollars left in the bank.

DION: (*with dazed surprise*) What! Is all the money from the sale of the house gone?

MARGARET: (*wearily*) Every day or so you've been cashing checks. You've been drinking—you haven't counted—

DION: (*irritably*) I know! (*A pause—soberly*) No more estate to fall back on, eh? Well, for five years it kept us living abroad in peace. It bought us a little happiness—of a kind—didn't it?—living and loving and having children— (*A slight pause—bitterly*)—thinking one was creating before one discovered one couldn't!

MARGARET: (*this time with forced conviction*) But you *can* paint—beautifully!

DION: (*angrily*) Shut up! (*A pause—then jeeringly*) So my wife thinks it behooves me to settle down and support my family in the meager style to which they'll have to become accustomed?

MARGARET: (*shamefacedly*) I didn't say—still—something's got to be done.

DION: (*harshly*) Will Mrs. Anthony helpfully suggest what?

MARGARET: I met Billy Brown on the street. He said you'd have made a good architect, if you'd stuck to it.

DION: Flatterer! Instead of leaving college when my Old Man died? Instead of marrying Peggy and going abroad and being happy?

MARGARET: (*as if she hadn't heard*) He spoke of how well you used to draw.

DION: Billy was in love with Margaret at one time.

MARGARET: He wanted to know why you've never been in to see him.

DION: He's bound heaven-bent for success. It's the will of Mammon!
Anthony and Brown, contractors and builders—death subtracts Anthony and I sell out—Billy graduates—Brown and Son, architects
and builders—old man Brown perishes of paternal pride—and now
we have William A. Brown, architect! Why his career itself already
has an architectural design! One of God's mud pies!

MARGARET: He particularly told me to ask you to drop in.

DION: (*springs to his feet—assertively*) No! Pride! I have been alive!

MARGARET: Why don't you have a talk with him?

DION: Pride in my failure!

MARGARET: You were always such close friends.

DION: (*more and more desperately*) The pride which came after man's
fall—by which he laughs as a creator at his self-defeats!

MARGARET: Not for my sake—but for your own—and, above all, for the
children's!

DION: (*with terrible despair*) Pride! Pride without which the Gods are
worms!

MARGARET: (*after a pause, meekly and humbly*) You don't want to? It
would hurt you? All right, dear. Never mind. We'll manage somehow—you mustn't worry—you must start your beautiful painting
again—and I can get that position in the library—it would be such
fun for me working there! . . . (*She reaches out and takes his hand—
tenderly*) I love you, dear. I understand.

DION: (*slumps down into his chair, crushed, his face averted from hers, as
hers is from him, although their hands are still clasped—in a trembling,
expiring voice*) Pride is dying! (*As if he were suffocating, he pulls the
mask from his resigned, pale, suffering face. He prays like a Saint in the
desert, exorcizing a demon*) Pride is dead! Blessed are the meek! Blessed
are the poor in spirit!

MARGARET: (*without looking at him—in a comforting, motherly tone*) My
poor boy!

DION: (*resentfully—clapping on his mask again and springing to his feet—derisively*) Blessed are the meek for they shall inherit graves! Blessed are the poor in spirit for they are blind! (*Then with tortured bitterness*) All right! Then I ask my wife to go and ask Billy Brown—that's more deadly than if I went myself! (*With wild mockery*) Ask him if he can't find an opening for a talented young man who is only honest when he isn't sober—implore him, beg him in the name of old love, old friendship—to be a generous hero and save the woman and her children! (*He laughs with a sort of diabolical, ironical glee now, and starts to go out*).

MARGARET: (*meekly*) Are you going up street, Dion?

DION: Yes.

MARGARET: Will you stop at the butchers' and have them send two pounds of pork chops?

DION: Yes.

MARGARET: And stop at Mrs. Young's and ask the children to hurry right home?

DION: Yes.

MARGARET: Will you be back for dinner, Dion?

DION: No. (*He goes, the outer door slams.* MARGARET *sighs with a tired incomprehension and goes to the window and stares out*).

MARGARET: (*worriedly*) I hope they'll watch out, crossing the street.

CURTAIN

SCENE TWO

SCENE: BILLY BROWN'S *Office, at five in the afternoon. At center, a fine mahogany desk with a swivel chair in back of it. To the left of desk, an office armchair. To the right of desk, an office lounge. The background is a backdrop of an office wall, treated similarly to that of Scene One in its over-meticulous representation of detail.*

BILLY BROWN *is seated at the desk looking over a blue print by the light of a desk lamp. He has grown into a fine-looking, well-dressed, capable, college-bred American business man, boyish still and with the same engaging personality.*

The telephone rings.

BROWN: (*answering it*) Yes? Who? (*This in surprise—then with eager pleasure*) Let her come right in. (*He gets up and goes to the door, expectant and curious.* MARGARET *enters. Her face is concealed behind the mask of the pretty young matron, still hardly a woman, who cultivates a naïvely innocent and bravely hopeful attitude toward things and acknowledges no wound to the world. She is dressed as in Scene One but with an added touch of effective primping here and there*).

MARGARET: (*very gayly*) Hello, Billy Brown!

BROWN: (*awkward in her presence, shakes her hand*) Come in. Sit down. This is a pleasant surprise, Margaret. (*She sits down on the lounge. He sits in his chair behind the desk, as before*).

MARGARET: (*looking around*). What lovely offices! My, but Billy Brown is getting grand!

BROWN: (*pleased*) I've just moved in. The old place was too stuffy.

MARGARET: It looks so prosperous—but then, Billy is doing so wonderfully well, everyone says.

BROWN: (*modestly*) Well, to be frank, it's been mostly luck. Things have come my way without my doing much about it. (*Then, with an abashed pride*) Still—I have done a little something myself. (*He picks the plan from the desk*) See this? It's my design for the new Municipal Building. It's just been accepted— provisionally—by the Committee.

MARGARET: (*taking it—vaguely*) Oh? (*She looks at it abstractedly. There is a pause. Suddenly*) You mentioned the other day how well Dion used to draw—

BROWN: (*a bit stiffly*) Yes, he certainly did. (*He takes the drawing from*

her and at once becomes interested and squints at it frowningly) Did you
notice that anything seemed lacking in this?

MARGARET: (*indifferently*) Not at all.

BROWN: (*with a cheerful grin*) The Committee want it made a little more
American. It's too much of a conventional Greco-Roman tomb, they
say. (*Laughs*) They want an original touch of modern novelty stuck
in to liven it up and make it look different from other town halls.
(*Putting the drawing back on his desk*) And I've been figuring out how
to give it to them but my mind doesn't seem to run that way. Have
you any suggestion?

MARGARET: (*as if she hadn't heard*) Dion certainly draws well, Billy
Brown was saying?

BROWN: (*trying not to show his annoyance*) Why, yes—he did— and still
can, I expect. (*A pause. He masters what he feels to be an unworthy pique
and turns to her generously*) Dion would have made a cracking good
architect.

MARGARET: (*proudly*) I know. He could be anything he wanted to.

BROWN: (*a pause—embarrassedly*) Is he working at anything these
days?

MARGARET: (*defensively*) Oh, yes! He's painting wonderfully!
But he's just like a child, he's so impractical. He doesn't try to have an
exhibition anywhere, or anything.

BROWN: (*surprised*) The one time I ran into him, I thought he told me
he'd destroyed all his pictures—that he'd gotten sick of painting and
completely given it up.

MARGARET: (*quickly*) He always tells people that. He doesn't want anyone even to look at his things, imagine! He keeps saying they're
rotten—when they're really too beautiful! He's too modest for his
own good, don't you think? But it is true he hasn't done so much
lately since we've been back. You see the children take up such a lot
of his time. He just worships them! I'm afraid he's becoming a hopeless family man, just the opposite of what anyone would expect who
knew him in the old days.

BROWN: (*painfully embarrassed by her loyalty and his knowledge of the facts*) Yes, I know. (*He coughs self-consciously*).

MARGARET: (*aroused by something in his manner*) But I suppose the gossips are telling the same silly stories about him they always did. (*She forces a laugh*) Poor Dion! Give a dog a bad name! (*Her voice breaks a little in spite of herself*).

BROWN: (*hastily*) I haven't heard any stories—(*he stops uncertainly, then decides to plunge in*)—except about money matters.

MARGARET: (*forcing a laugh*) Oh, perhaps they're true enough. Dion is such a generous fool with his money, like all artists.

BROWN: (*with a certain doggedness*) There's a rumor that you've applied for a position at the Library.

MARGARET: (*forcing a gay tone*) Yes, indeed! Won't it be fun! Maybe it'll improve my mind! And one of us has got to be practical, so why not me? (*She forces a gay, girlish laugh*).

BROWN: (*impulsively reaches out and takes her hand—awkwardly*) Listen, Margaret. Let's be perfectly frank, will you? I'm such an old friend, and I want like the deuce to . . . . You know darn well I'd do anything in the world to help you—or Dion.

MARGARET: (*withdrawing her hand, coldly*) I'm afraid I—don't under-stand, Billy Brown.

BROWN: (*acutely embarrassed*) Well, I—I just meant—you know, if you needed— (*A pause. He looks questioningly at her averted face—then ventures on another tack, matter-of-factly*) I've got a proposition to make to Dion—if I could ever get hold of him. It's this way: business has been piling up on me—a run of luck—but I'm short-handed. I need a crack chief draftsman darn badly—or I'm liable to lose out. Do you think Dion would consider it—as a temporary stop-gap— until he felt in the painting mood again?

MARGARET: (*striving to conceal her eagerness and relief—judicially*) Yes—I really do. He's such a good sport and Billy and he were such pals once. I know he'd be only too tickled to help him out.

BROWN: (*diffidently*) I thought he might be sensitive about working for—I mean, with me—when, if he hadn't sold out to Dad he'd be my partner now—(*earnestly*)—and, by jingo! I wish he was! (*Then, abruptly*) Let's try to nail him down right away, Margaret. Is he home now? (*He reaches for the phone*).

MARGARET: (*hurriedly*) No, he—he went out for a long walk.

BROWN: Perhaps I can locate him later around town somewhere.

MARGARET: (*with a note of pleading*) Please don't trouble. It isn't necessary. I'm sure when I talk to him—he's coming home to dinner—(*Getting up*) Then it's all settled, isn't it? Dion will be so glad to be able to help an old friend—he's so terribly loyal, and he's always liked Billy Brown so much! (*Holding out her hand*) I really must go now!

BROWN: (*shakes her hand*) Good-by, Margaret. I hope you'll be dropping in on us a lot when Dion gets here.

MARGARET: Yes. (*She goes*).

BROWN: (*sits at his desk again, looking ahead in a not unsatisfying melancholy reverie. He mutters admiringly but pityingly*) Poor Margaret! She's a game sport, but it's pretty damn tough on her! (*Indignantly*) By God, I'm going to give Dion a good talking-to one of these days!

CURTAIN

Scene Three

SCENE: *Cybel's parlor. An automatic, nickel-in-the-slot player-piano is at center, rear. On its right is a dirty gilt second-hand sofa. At the left is a bald-spotted crimson plush chair. The backdrop for the rear wall is cheap wall-paper of a dull yellow-brown, resembling a blurred impression of a fallow field in early spring. There is a cheap alarm clock on top of the piano. Beside it her mask is lying.*

DION *is sprawled on his back, fast asleep on the sofa. His mask has fallen down on his chest. His pale face is singularly pure, spiritual and sad.*

The player-piano is groggily banging out a sentimental medley of "Mother—Mammy" tunes.

CYBEL *is seated on the stool in front of the piano. She is a strong, calm, sensual, blonde girl of twenty or so, her complexion fresh and healthy, her figure full-breasted and wide-hipped, her movements slow and solidly languorous like an animal's, her large eyes dreamy with the reflected stirring of profound instincts. She chews gum like a sacred cow forgetting time with an eternal end. Her eyes are fixed, incuriously, on* DION's *pale face.*

CYBEL: (*as the tune runs out, glances at the clock, which indicates midnight, then goes slowly over to* DION *and puts her hand gently on his forehead*) Wake up!

DION: (*stirs, sighs and murmurs dreamily*) "And He laid his hands on them and healed them." (*Then with a start he opens his eyes and, half sitting up, stares at her bewilderedly*) What—where—who are you? (*He reaches for his mask and claps it on defensively*).

CYBEL: (*placidly*) Only another female. You was camping on my steps, sound asleep. I didn't want to run any risk getting into more trouble with the cops pinching you there and blaming me, so I took you in to sleep it off.

DION: (*mockingly*) Blessed are the pitiful, Sister! I'm broke—but you will be rewarded in Heaven!

CYBEL: (*calmly*) I wasn't wasting my pity. Why should I? You were happy, weren't you?

DION: (*approvingly*) Excellent! You're not a moralist, I see.

CYBEL: (*going on*) And you look like a good boy, too—when you're asleep. Say, you better beat it home to bed or you'll be locked out.

DION: (*mockingly*) Now you're becoming maternal, Miss Earth. Is that the only answer—to pin my soul into every vacant diaper? (*She stares down at his mask, her face growing hard. He laughs*) But please don't stop stroking my aching brow. Your hand is a cool mud poultice on the sting of thought!

CYBEL: (*calmly*) Stop acting. I hate ham fats. (*She looks at him as if waiting for him to remove his mask—then turns her back indifferently and goes to the piano*) Well, if you simply got to be a regular devil like all the other visiting sports, I s'pose I got to play with you. (*She takes her mask and puts it on—then turns. The mask is the rouged and eye-blackened countenance of the hardened prostitute. In a coarse, harsh voice*) Kindly state your dishonorable intentions, if any! I can't sit up all night keeping company! Let's have some music! (*She puts a plug in the machine. The same sentimental medley begins to play. The two masks stare at each other. She laughs*) Shoot! I'm all set! It's your play, Kid Lucifer!

DION: (*slowly removes his mask. She stops the music with a jerk. His face is gentle and sad—humbly*) I'm sorry. It has always been such agony for me to be touched!

CYBEL: (*taking off her mask—sympathetically as she comes back and sits down on her stool*) Poor kid! I've never had one, but I can guess. They hug and kiss you and take you on their laps and pinch you and want to see you getting dressed and undressed—as if they owned you—I bet you I'd never let them treat one of mine that way!

DION: (*turning to her*) You're lost in blind alleys, too. (*Suddenly holding out his hand to her*) But you're strong. Let's be friends.

CYBEL: (*with a strange sternness, searches his face*) And never nothing more?

DION: (*with a strange smile*) Let's say, never anything less! (*She takes his hand. There is a ring at the outside door bell. They stare at each other. There is another ring*).

CYBEL: (*puts on her mask, DION does likewise. Mockingly*) When you got to love to live it's hard to love living. I better join the A. F. of L. and soap-box for the eight-hour night! Got a nickel, baby? Play a tune. (*She goes out. DION puts a nickel in. The same sentimental tune starts. CYBEL returns, followed by BILLY BROWN. His face is rigidly composed, but his superior disgust for DION can be seen. DION jerks off the music and he and BILLY look at each other for a moment, CYBEL watching them both— then, bored, she yawns*) He's hunting for you. Put out the lights when you go. I'm going to sleep. (*She starts to go—then, as if reminded of something—to* DION) Life's all right, if you let it alone. (*Then mechanically flashing a trade smile at* BILLY) Now you know the way, Handsome, call again! (*She goes*).

BROWN: (*after an awkward pause*) Hello, Dion! I've been looking all over town for you. This place was the very last chance. . . . (*Another pause—embarrassedly*) Let's take a walk.

DION: (*mockingly*) I've given up exercise. They claim it lengthens your life.

BROWN: (*persuasively*) Come on, Dion, be a good fellow. You're certainly not staying here—

DION: Billy would like to think me taken in *flagrante delicto*, eh?

BROWN: Don't be a damn fool! Listen to me! I've been looking you up for purely selfish reasons. I need your help.

DION: (*astonished*) What?

BROWN: I've a proposition to make that I hope you'll consider favorably out of old friendship. To be frank, Dion, I need you to lend me a hand down at the office.

DION: (*with a harsh laugh*) So it's the job, is it? Then my poor wife did a-begging go!

BROWN: (*repelled—sharply*) On the contrary, I had to beg her to beg you to take it! (*More angrily*) Look here, Dion! I won't listen to you talk that way about Margaret! And you wouldn't if you weren't drunk! (*Suddenly shaking him*) What in hell has come over you, anyway! You didn't use to be like this! What the devil are you going to do with yourself—sink into the gutter and drag Margaret with you? If you'd heard her defend you, lie about you, tell me how hard you were working, what beautiful things you were painting, how you stayed at home and idolized the children!—when everyone knows you've been out every night sousing and gambling away the last of your estate. . . . (*He stops, ashamed, controlling himself*).

DION: (*wearily*) She was lying about her husband, not me, you fool! But it's no use explaining. (*Then, in a sudden, excitable passion*) What do you want? I agree to anything—except the humiliation of yelling secrets at the deaf!

BROWN: (*trying a bullying tone—roughly*) Bunk! Don't try to crawl out! There's no excuse and you know it. (*Then as* DION *doesn't reply— penitently*) But I know I shouldn't talk this way, old man! It's only because we're such old pals—and I hate to see you wasting yourself— you who had more brains than any of us! But, damn it, I suppose you're too much of a rotten cynic to believe I mean what I've just said!

DION: (*touched*) I know Billy was always Dion Anthony's friend.

BROWN: You're damn right I am—and I'd have proved it long ago if you'd only given me half a chance! After all, I couldn't keep chasing after you and be snubbed every time. A man has some pride!

DION: (*bitterly mocking*) Dead wrong! Never more! None whatever! It's unmoral! Blessed are the poor in spirit, Brother! When shall I report?

BROWN: (*eagerly*) Then you'll take the—you'll help me?

DION: (*wearily bitter*) I'll take the job. One must do something to pass away the time, while one is waiting—for one's next incarnation.

BROWN: (*jokingly*) I'd say it was a bit early to be worrying about that. (*Trying to get* DION *started*) Come along, now. It's pretty late.

DION: (*shakes his hand off his shoulder and walks away from him—after a pause*) Is my father's chair still there?

BROWN: (*turns away—embarrassed*) I—I don't really remember, Dion— I'll look it up.

DION: (*taking off his mask—slowly*) I'd like to sit where he spun what I have spent. What aliens we were to each other! When he lay dead, his face looked so familiar that I wondered where I had met that man before. Only at the second of my conception. After that, we grew hostile with concealed shame. And my mother? I remember a sweet, strange girl, with affectionate, bewildered eyes as if God had locked her in a dark closet without any explanation. I was the sole doll our ogre, her husband, allowed her and she played mother and child with me for many years in that house until at last through two tears I watched her die with the shy pride of one who has lengthened her dress and put up her hair. And I felt like a forsaken toy and cried to be buried with her, because her hands alone had caressed without clawing. She lived long and aged greatly in the two days before they closed her coffin. The last time I looked, her purity had forgotten me, she was stainless and imperishable, and I knew my sobs were ugly and meaningless to her virginity; so I shrank away, back into life, with naked nerves jumping like fleas, and in due course of nature another girl called me her boy in the moon and married me and became three mothers in one person, while I got paint on my paws in an endeavor to see God! (*He laughs wildly—claps on his mask*) But that Ancient Humorist had given me weak eyes, so now I'll have to foreswear my quest for Him and go in for the Omnipresent Successful Serious One, the Great God Mr. Brown, instead! (*He makes him a sweeping, mocking bow*).

BROWN: (*repelled but cajolingly*) Shut up, you nut! You're still drunk. Come on! Let's start! (*He grabs* DION *by the arm and switches off the light*).

DION: (*from the darkness—mockingly*) I am thy shorn, bald, nude sheep! Lead on, Almighty Brown, thou Kindly Light!

CURTAIN

SCENE: Cybel's parlor—about sunset in spring seven years later. The arrangement of furniture is the same but the chair and sofa are new, brightcolored, costly pieces. The old automatic piano at center looks exactly the same. The cheap alarm clock is still on top of it. On either side of the clock, the masks of DION *and* CYBEL *are lying. The background backdrop is brilliant, stunning wallpaper, on which crimson and purple flowers and fruits tumble over one another in a riotously profane lack of any apparent design.*

DION sits in the chair on left, CYBEL *on the sofa. A cardtable is between them. Both are playing solitaire.* DION *is now prematurely gray. His face is that of an ascetic, a martyr, furrowed by pain and self-torture, yet lighted from within by a spiritual calm and human kindliness.*

CYBEL has grown stouter and more voluptuous, but her face is still unmarked and fresh, her calm more profound. She is like an unmoved idol of Mother Earth.

The piano is whining out its same old sentimental medley. They play their cards intently and contentedly. The music stops.

CYBEL: (*musingly*) I love those rotten old sob tunes. They make me wise to people. That's what's inside them—what makes them love and murder their neighbor—crying jags set to music!

DION: (*compassionately*) Every song is a hymn. They keep trying to find the Word in the Beginning.

CYBEL: They try to know too much. It makes them weak. I never puzzled them with myself. I gave them a Tart. They understood her and knew their parts and acted naturally. And on both sides we were able to keep our real virtue, if you get me (*She plays her last card—indifferently*) I've made it again.

DION: (*smiling*) Your luck is uncanny. It never comes out for me.

CYBEL: You keep getting closer, but it knows you still want to win—a

317

little bit—and it's wise all I care about is playing. (*She lays out another game*) Speaking of my canned music, our Mr. Brown hates that old box. (*At the mention of* BROWN, DION *trembles as if suddenly possessed, has a terrible struggle with himself, then while she continues to speak, gets up like an automaton and puts on his mask. The mask is now terribly ravaged. All of its Pan quality has changed into a diabolical Mephistophelean cruelty and irony*) He doesn't mind the music inside. That gets him somehow. But he thinks the case looks shabby and he wants it junked. But I told him that just because he's been keeping me so long, he needn't start bossing like a husband or I'll— (*She looks up and sees the masked* DION *standing by the piano—calmly*) Hello! Getting jealous again?

DION: (*jeeringly*) Are you falling in love with your keeper, old Sacred Cow?

CYBEL: (*without taking offense*) Cut it! You've been asking me that for years. Be yourself! He's healthy and handsome—but he's too guilty. What makes you pretend you think love is so important, anyway? It's just one of a lot of things you do to keep life living.

DION: (*in same tone*) Then you've lied when you've said you loved me, have you, Old Filth?

CYBEL: (*affectionately*) You'll never grow up! We've been friends, haven't we, for seven years? I've never let myself want you nor you me. Yes, I love you. It takes all kinds of love to make a world! Ours is the living cream, I say, living rich and high! (*A pause. Coaxingly*) Stop hiding. I know you.

DION: (*taking off his mask, wearily comes and sits down at her feet and lays his head in her lap—with a grateful smile*) You're strong. You always give. You've given my weakness strength to live.

CYBEL: (*tenderly, stroking his hair maternally*) You're not weak. You were born with ghosts in your eyes and you were brave enough to go looking into your own dark—and you got afraid (*After a pause*) I don't blame your being jealous of Mr. Brown sometimes. I'm jealous of your wife, even though I know you do love her.

DION: (*slowly*) I love Margaret. I don't know who my wife is.

CYBEL: (*after a pause—with a queer broken laugh*) Oh, God, sometimes the truth hits me such a sock between the eyes I can see the stars!— and then I'm so damn sorry for the lot of you, every damn mother's son-of-a-gun of you, that I'd like to run out naked into the street and love the whole mob to death like I was bringing you all a new brand of dope that'd make you forget everything that ever was for good! (*Then, with a twisted smile*) But they wouldn't see me, any more than they see each other. And they keep right on moving along and dying without my help anyway.

DION: (*sadly*) You've given me strength to die.

CYBEL: You may be important but your life's not. There's millions of it born every second. Life can cost too much even for a sucker to afford it—like everything else. And it's not sacred—only the you inside is. The rest is earth.

DION: (*gets to his knees and with clasped hands looks up raptly and prays with an ascetic fervor*) "Into thy hands, O Lord," . . . (*Then suddenly, with a look of horror*) Nothing! To feel one's life blown out like the flame of a cheap match . . . ! (*He claps on his mask and laughs harshly*) To fall asleep and know you'll never, never be called to get on the job of existence again! "Swift be thine approaching flight! Come soon— soon!" (*He quotes this last with a mocking longing*).

CYBEL: (*pats his head maternally*) There, don't be scared. It's born in the blood. When the time comes, you'll find it's easy.

DION: (*jumps to his feet and walks about excitedly*) It won't be long. My wife dragged in a doctor the day before yesterday. He says my heart is gone—booze— He warned me, never another drop or— (*Mockingly*) What say? Shall we have a drink?

CYBEL: (*like an idol*) Suit yourself. It's in the pantry. (*Then, as he hesitates*) What set you off on this bat? You were raving on about some cathedral plans . . . .

DION: (*wildly mocking*) They've been accepted—Mr. Brown's designs! My designs really! You don't need to be told that. He hands me one mathematically correct barn after another and I doctor them up with cute allurements so that fools will desire to buy, sell, breed, sleep, love, hate, curse and pray in them! I do this with devilish cleverness to their entire delight! Once I dreamed of painting wind on the sea and the skimming flight of cloud shadows over the tops of trees! Now . . . (*He laughs*) But pride is a sin—even in a memory of the long deceased! Blessed are the poor in spirit! (*He subsides weakly on his chair, his hand pressed to his heart*).

CYBEL: (*like an idol*) Go home and sleep. Your wife'll be worried.

DION: She knows—but she'll never admit to herself that her husband ever entered your door. (*Mocking*) Aren't women loyal—to their vanity and their other things!

CYBEL: Brown is coming soon, don't forget.

DION: He knows too and can't admit. Perhaps he needs me here—unknown. What first aroused his passion to possess you exclusively, do you think? Because he knew you loved me and he felt himself cheated. He wanted what he thought was my love of the flesh! He feels I have no right to love. He'd like to steal it as he steals my ideas—complacently—righteously. Oh, the good Brown!

CYBEL: But you like him, too! You're brothers, I guess, somehow. Well, remember he's paying, he'll pay—in some way or other.

DION: (*raises his head as if starting to remove the mask*) I know. Poor Billy! God forgive me the evil I've done him!

CYBEL: (*reaches out and takes his hand*) Poor boy!

DION: (*presses her convulsively—then with forced harshness*) Well, home-ward Christian Soldier! I'm off! By-bye, Mother Earth! (*He starts to go off right. She seems about to let him go*).

CYBEL: (*suddenly starts and calls with deep grief*) Dion! (*He looks at her. A pause. He comes slowly back. She speaks strangely in a deep, far-off voice—and yet like a mother talking to her little son*) You mustn't forget to kiss me before you go, Dion. (*She removes his mask*) Haven't I told you to take off your mask in the house? Look at me, Dion. I've—just—seen—something. I'm afraid you're going away a long, long ways.

I'm afraid I won't see you again for a long, long time. So it's good-by, dear. (*She kisses him gently. He begins to sob. She hands him back his mask*) Here you are. Don't get hurt. Remember, it's all a game, and after you're asleep I'll tuck you in.

DION: (*in a choking, heart-broken cry*) Mother! (*Then he claps on his mask with a terrible effort of will—mockingly*) Go to the devil, you senti-mental old pig! See you tomorrow! (*He goes, whistling, slamming the door*).

CYBEL: (*like an idol again*) What's the good of bearing children? What's the use of giving birth to death? (*She sighs wearily, turns, puts a plug in the piano, which starts up its old sentimental tune. At the same moment BROWN enters quietly from the left. He is the ideal of the still youthful, good-looking, well-groomed, successful provincial American of forty. Just now, he is plainly perturbed. He is not able to see either CYBEL's face or her mask*).

BROWN: Cybel! (*She starts, jams off the music and reaches for her mask but has no time to put it on*) Wasn't that Dion I just saw going out—after all your promises never to see him! (*She turns like an idol, holding the mask behind her. He stares, bewildered— stammers*) I—I beg your par-don—I thought—

CYBEL: (*in her strange voice*) Cybel's gone out to dig in the earth and pray.

BROWN: (*with more assurance*) But—aren't those her clothes?

CYBEL: Cybel doesn't want people to see me naked. I'm her sister. Dion came to see me.

BROWN: (*relieved*) So that's what he's up to, is it? (*Then with a pitying sigh*) Poor Margaret! (*Then with playful reproof*) You really shouldn't encourage him. He's married and got three big sons.

CYBEL: And you haven t.

BROWN: (*stung*) No, I'm not married.

CYBEL: He and I were friends.

BROWN: (*with a playful wink*) Yes, I can imagine how the platonic must appeal to Dion's pure, innocent type! It's no good your kidding me about Dion. We've been friends since we were kids. I know him in and out. I've always stood up for him whatever he's done—so you can be perfectly frank. I only spoke as I did on account of Margaret—his wife—it's pretty tough on her.

CYBEL: You love his wife.

BROWN: (*scandalized*) What? What are you talking about? (*Then uncertainly*) Don't be a fool! (*A pause—then as if impelled by an intense curiosity*) So Dion is your lover, eh? That's very interesting. (*He pulls his chair closer to hers*) Sit down. Let's talk. (*She continues to stand, the mask held behind her*) Tell me—I've always been curious—what is it that makes Dion so attractive to women— especially certain types of women, if you'll pardon me? He always has been and yet I never could see exactly what they saw in him. Is it his looks—or because he's such a violent sensualist—or because he poses as artistic and temperamental—or because he's so wild—or just what is it?

CYBEL: He's alive!

BROWN: (*suddenly takes one of her hands and kisses it—insinuatingly*) Well, don't you think I'm alive, too? (*Eagerly*) Listen. Would you consider giving up Dion—and letting me take care of you under a similar arrangement to the one I've made with Cybel? I like you, you can see that. I won't bother you much—I'm much too busy—you can do what you like—lead your own life—except for seeing him. (*He stops. A pause. She stares ahead unmoved as if she hadn't heard. He pleads*) Well—what do you say? Please do!

CYBEL: (*her voice very weary*) Cybel said to tell you she'd be back next week, Mr. Brown.

BROWN: (*with queer agony*) You mean you won't? Don't be so cruel! I love you! (*She walks away. He clutches at her pleadingly*) At least—I'll give you anything you ask!—please promise me you won't see Dion Anthony again!

CYBEL: (*with deep grief*) He will never see me again, I promise you. Good-by!

BROWN: (*jubilantly, kissing her hand—politely*) Thank you! Thank you!

I'm exceedingly grateful. (*Tactfully*) I won't disturb you any further. Please forgive my intrusion, and remember me to Cybel when you write. (*He bows, turns, and goes off left*).

CURTAIN

SCENE TWO

*S*CENE: *The drafting room in* BROWN'S *office.* DION'S *drafting table with a high stool in front is at center. Another stool is to the left of it. At the right is a bench. It is in the evening of the same day. The black wall drop has windows painted on it with a dim, street-lighted view of black houses across the way.*

   DION *is sitting on the stool in back of the table, reading aloud from the "Imitation of Christ" by Thomas à Kempis to his mask, which is on the table before him. His own face is gentler, more spiritual, more saintlike and ascetic than ever before.*

DION: (*like a priest, offering up prayers for the dying*) "Quickly must thou be gone from hence, see then how matters stand with thee. Ah, fool—learn now to die to the world that thou mayst begin to live with Christ! Do now, beloved, do now all thou canst because thou knowst not when thou shalt die; nor dost thou know what shall befall thee after death. Keep thyself as a pilgrim, and a stranger upon earth, to whom the affairs of this world do not—belong! Keep thy heart free and raised upwards to God because thou hast not here a lasting abode. 'Because at what hour you know not the Son of Man will come!' " Amen. (*He raises his hand over the mask as if he were blessing it, closes the book and puts it back in his pocket. He raises the mask in his hands and stares at it with a pitying tenderness*) Peace, poor tortured one, brave pitiful pride of man, the hour of our deliverance comes. Tomorrow we may be with Him in Paradise! (*He kisses it on the lips and sets it down again. There is the noise of footsteps climbing the stairs in the hallway. He grabs up the mask in a sudden panic and, as a knock comes on the door, he claps it on and calls mockingly*) Come in, Mrs. Anthony, come in! (MARGARET *enters. In one hand behind her, hidden from him, is the mask of the brave face she puts on before the world to hide her suffering and disillusionment, and which she has just taken off. Her own face is still sweet and pretty but lined, drawn and careworn for its years, sad, resigned, but a bit querulous*).

MARGARET: (*wearily reproving*) Thank goodness I've found you! Why haven't you been home the last two days? It's bad enough your drinking again without your staying away and worrying us to death!

DION: (*bitterly*) My ears knew her footsteps. One gets to recognize everything—and to see nothing!

MARGARET: I finally sent the boys out looking for you and came myself. (*With tired solicitude*) I suppose you haven't eaten a thing, as usual. Won't you come home and let me fry you a chop?

DION: (*wonderingly*) Can Margaret still love Dion Anthony? Is it possible she does?

MARGARET: (*forcing a tired smile*) I suppose so, Dion. I certainly oughtn't to, had I?

DION: (*in same tone*) And I love Margaret! What haunted, haunting ghosts we are! We dimly remember so much it will take us so many million years to forget! (*He comes forward, putting one arm around her bowed shoulders, and they kiss*).

MARGARET: (*patting his hand affectionately*) No, you certainly don't deserve it. When I stop to think of all you've made me go through in the years since we settled down here . . . ! I really don't believe I could ever have stood it if it weren't for the boys! (*Forcing a smile*) But perhaps I would, I've always been such a big fool about you.

DION: (*a bit mockingly*) The boys! Three strong sons! Margaret can afford to be magnanimous!

MARGARET: If they didn't find you, they were coming to meet me here.

DION: (*with sudden wildness—torturedly, sinking on his knees beside her*)

Margaret! Margaret! I'm lonely! I'm frightened! I'm going away! I've got to say good-by!

MARGARET: (*patting his hair*) Poor boy! Poor Dion! Come home and sleep.

DION: (*springs up frantically*) No! I'm a man! I'm a lonely man! I can't go back! I have conceived myself! (*Then with desperate mockery*) Look at me, Mrs. Anthony! It's the last chance! Tomorrow I'll have moved on to the next hell! Behold your man—the sniveling, cringing, life-denying Christian slave you have so nobly ignored in the father of your sons! Look! (*He tears the mask from his face, which is radiant with a great pure love for her and a great sympathy and tenderness*) O woman—my love—that I have sinned against in my sick pride and cruelty—forgive my sins—forgive my solitude—forgive my sickness—forgive me! (*He kneels and kisses the hem of her dress*).

MARGARET: (*who has been staring at him with terror, raising her mask to ward off his face*) Dion! Don't! I can't bear it! You're like a ghost! You're dead! Oh, my God! Help! Help! (*She falls back fainting on the bench. He looks at her—then takes her hand which holds her mask and looks at that face—gently*) And now I am permitted to understand and love you, too! (*He kisses the mask first— then kisses her face, murmuring*) And you, sweetheart! Blessed, thrice blessed are the meek! (*There is a sound of heavy, hurrying footsteps on the stairs. He puts on his mask in haste. The* THREE SONS *rush into the room. The Eldest is about fourteen, the two others thirteen and twelve. They look healthy, normal, likeable boys, with much the same quality as* BILLY BROWN's *in Act One, Scene One. They stop short and stiffen all in a row, staring from the woman on the bench to their father, accusingly*).

ELDEST: We heard someone yell. It sounded like Mother.

DION: (*defensively*) No. It was this lady—my wife.

ELDEST: But hasn't Mother come yet?

DION: (*going to* MARGARET) Yes. Your Mother is here. (*He stands between them and puts her mask over* MARGARET's *face—then steps back*) She has fainted. You'd better bring her to.

BOYS: Mother! (*They run to her side, kneel and rub her wrists. The* ELDEST *smooths back her hair*).

DION: (*watching them*) At least I am leaving her well provided for. (*He addresses them directly*) Tell your mother she'll get word from Mr. Brown's house. I must pay him a farewell call. I am going. Good-by. (*They stop, staring at him fixedly, with eyes a mixture of bewilderment, distrust and hurt*).

ELDEST: (*awkwardly and shamefacedly*) Honest, I think you ought to have . . .

SECOND: Yes, honest you ought . . .

YOUNGEST: Yes, honest . . .

DION: (*in a friendly tone*) I know. But I couldn't. That's for you who can. You must inherit the earth for her. Don't forget now, boys. Good-by.

BOYS: (*in the same awkward, self-conscious tone, one after another*) Good-by—good-by—good-by. (DION *goes*).

CURTAIN

Scene Three

*S*CENE: *The library of* WILLIAM BROWN'S *home—night of the same day. A backdrop of carefully painted, prosperous, bourgeois culture, bookcases filled with sets, etc. The heavy table at center is expensive. The leather armchair at left of it and the couch at right are opulently comfortable. The reading lamp on the table is the only light.*

BROWN *sits in the chair at left reading an architectural periodical. His expression is composed and gravely receptive. In outline, his face suggests a Roman consul on an old coin. There is an incongruous distinction about it, the quality of unquestioning faith in the finality of its achievement.*

There is a sudden loud thumping on the front door and the ringing of the bell. BROWN *frowns and listens as a servant answers.* DION'S *voice can be heard, raised mockingly.*

DION: Tell him it's the devil come to conclude a bargain.

BROWN: (*suppressing annoyance, calls out with forced good nature*) Come on in, Dion. (DION *enters. He is in a wild state. His clothes are disheveled, his masked face has a terrible deathlike intensity, its mocking irony becomes so cruelly malignant as to give him the appearance of a real demon, tortured into torturing others*) Sit down.

DION: (*stands and sings*) William Brown's soul lies moldering in the crib but his body goes marching on!

BROWN: (*maintaining the same indulgent, big-brotherly tone, which he tries to hold throughout the scene*) Not so loud, for Pete's sake! I don't mind—but I've got neighbors.

DION: Hate them! Fear thy neighbor as thyself! That's the leaden rule for the safe and sane. (*Then advancing to the table with a sort of deadly calm*) Listen! One day when I was four years old, a boy sneaked up behind when I was drawing a picture in the sand he couldn't draw and hit me on the head with a stick and kicked out my picture and laughed when I cried. It wasn't what he'd done that made me cry, but him! I had loved and trusted him and suddenly the good God was disproved in his person and the evil and injustice of Man was born! Everyone called me cry-baby, so I became silent for life and designed a mask of the Bad Boy Pan in which to live and rebel against that other boy's God and protect myself from His cruelty. And that other boy, secretly he felt ashamed but he couldn't acknowledge it; so from that day he instinctively developed into the good boy, the good friend, the good man, William Brown!

BROWN: (*shamefacedly*) I remember now. It was a dirty trick. (*Then with a trace of resentment*) Sit down. You know where the booze is. Have a drink, if you like. But I guess you've had enough already.

DION: (*looks at him fixedly for a moment—then strangely*) Thanks be to

Brown for reminding me. I must drink. (*He goes and gets a bottle of whisky and a glass*).

BROWN: (*with a good-humored shrug*) All right. It's your funeral.

DION: (*returning and pouring out a big drink in the tumbler*) And William Brown's! When I die, he goes to hell! Shöal! (*He drinks and stares malevolently. In spite of himself,* BROWN *is uneasy. A pause*).

BROWN: (*with forced casualness*) You've been on this toot for a week now.

DION: (*tauntingly*) I've been celebrating the acceptance of *my* design for the cathedral.

BROWN: (*humorously*) You certainly helped me a lot on it.

DION: (*with a harsh laugh*) O perfect Brown! Never mind! I'll make him look in my mirror yet—and drown in it! (*He pours out another big drink*).

BROWN: (*rather tauntingly*) Go easy. I don't want your corpse on my hands.

DION: But I do (*He drinks*) Brown will still need me—to reassure him he's alive! I've loved, lusted, won and lost, sang and wept! I've been life's lover! I've fulfilled her will and if she's through with me now it's only because I was too weak to dominate her in turn. It isn't enough to be her creature, you've got to create her or she requests you to destroy yourself.

BROWN: (*good-naturedly*) Nonsense. Go home and get some sleep.

DION: (*as if he hadn't heard—bitingly*) But to be neither creature nor creator! To exist only in her indifference! To be unloved by life! (BROWN *stirs uneasily*) To be merely a successful freak, the result of some snide neutralizing of life forces—a spineless cactus—a wild boar of the mountains altered into a packer's hog eating to become food— a Don Juan inspired to romance by a monkey's glands—and to have Life not even think you funny enough to see!

BROWN: (*stung—angrily*) Bosh!

DION: Consider Mr. Brown. His parents bore him on earth as if they were thereby entering him in a baby parade with prizes for the fattest—and he's still being wheeled along in the procession, too fat now to learn to walk, let alone to dance or run, and he'll never live until his liberated dust quickens into earth!

BROWN: (*gruffly*) Rave on! (*Then with forced good-nature*) Well, Dion, at any rate, I'm satisfied.

DION: (*quickly and malevolently*) No! Brown isn't satisfied! He's piled on layers of protective fat, but vaguely, deeply he feels at his heart the gnawing of a doubt! And I'm interested in that germ which wriggles like a question mark of insecurity in his blood, because it's part of the creative life Brown's stolen from me!

BROWN: (*forcing a sour grin*) Steal germs? I thought you caught them.

DION: (*as if he hadn't heard*) It's mine—and I'm interested in seeing it thrive and breed and become multitudes and eat until Brown is consumed!

BROWN: (*cannot restrain a shudder*) Sometimes when you're drunk, you're positively evil, do you know it?

DION: (*somberly*) When Pan was forbidden the light and warmth of the sun he grew sensitive and self-conscious and proud and revengeful—and became Prince of Darkness.

BROWN: (*jocularly*) You don't fit the role of Pan, Dion. It sounds to me like Bacchus, alias the Demon Rum, doing the talking. (DION *recovers from his spasm with a start and stares at* BROWN *with terrible hatred. There is a pause. In spite of himself,* BROWN *squirms and adopts a placating tone*) Go home. Be a good scout. It's all well enough celebrating our design being accepted but—

DION: (*in a steely voice*) I've been the brains! I've been the design! I've designed even his success—drunk and laughing at him—laughing at his career! Not proud! Sick! Sick of myself and him! Designing and getting drunk! Saving my woman and children! (*He laughs*) Ha! And this cathedral is my masterpiece! It will make Brown the most eminent architect in this state of God's Country. I put a lot into it—what was left of my life! It's one vivid blasphemy from sidewalk to the tips of its spires!—but so concealed that the fools will never know. They'll kneel and worship the ironic Silenus who tells them the best good is never to be born! (*He laughs triumphantly*) Well, blasphemy is faith, isn't it? In self-preservation the devil must believe! But Mr. Brown, the Great Brown, has no faith! He couldn't design a cathedral without it looking like the First Supernatural Bank! He only believes in the immortality of the moral belly! (*He laugh wildly—then sinks down in his chair, gasping, his hands pressed to his heart. Then suddenly becomes deadly calm and pronounces like a cruel malignant condemnation*) From now on, Brown will never design anything. He will devote his life to renovating the house of my Cybel into a home for my Margaret!

BROWN: (*springing to his feet, his face convulsed with strange agony*) I've stood enough! How dare you . . . !

DION: (*his voice like a probe*) Why has no woman ever loved him? Why has he always been the Big Brother, the Friend? Isn't their trust—a contempt?

BROWN: You lie!

DION: Why has he never been able to love—since my Margaret? Why has he never married? Why has he tried to steal Cybel, as he once tried to steal Margaret? Isn't it out of revenge—and envy?

BROWN: (*violently*) Rot! I wanted Cybel, and I bought her!

DION: Brown bought her for me! She has loved me more than he will ever know!

BROWN: You lie! (*Then furiously*) I'll throw her back on the street!

DION: To me! To her fellow creature! Why hasn't Brown had children—he who loves children—he who loves *my* children—he who envies me *my* children?

BROWN: (*brokenly*) I'm not ashamed to envy you them!

DION: They like Brown, too—as a friend—as an equal—as Margaret has always liked him—

BROWN: (*brokenly*) And as I've liked her!

DION: How many million times Brown has thought how much better for her it would have been if she'd chosen him instead!

BROWN: (*torturedly*) You lie! (*Then with sudden frenzied defiance*) All right. If you force me to say it, I do love Margaret! I always have loved her and you've always known I did!

DION: (*with a terrible composure*) No! That is merely the appearance, not the truth! Brown loves me! He loves me because I have always possessed the power he needed for love, because I am love!

BROWN: (*frenziedly*) You drunken bum! (*He leaps on* DION *and grabs him by the throat*)

DION: (*triumphantly, staring into his eyes*) Ah! Now he looks into the mirror! Now he sees his face! (BROWN *lets go of him and staggers back to his chair, pale and trembling*).

BROWN: (*humbly*) Stop, for God's sake! You're mad!

DION: (*sinking in his chair, more and more weakly*) I'm done. My heart, not Brown— (*Mockingly*) My last will and testament! I leave Dion Anthony to William Brown—for him to love and obey—for him to become me—then my Margaret will love me—my children will love me—Mr. and Mrs. Brown and sons, happily ever after! (*Staggering to his full height and looking upward defiantly*) Nothing more—but Man's last gesture—by which he conquers—to laugh! *Ha*— (*He begins, stops as if paralyzed, and drops on his knees by* BROWN'S *chair, his mask falling off, his Christian Martyr's face at the point of death*) Forgive me, Billy. Bury me, hide me, forget me for your own happiness! May Margaret love you! May you design the Temple of Man's Soul! Blessed are the meek and the poor in spirit! (*He kisses* BROWN'S *feet— then more and more weakly and childishly*) What was the prayer, Billy? I'm getting so sleepy . . . .

BROWN: (*in a trancelike tone*) "Our Father who art in Heaven."

DION: (*drowsily*) "Our Father.". . . (*He dies. A pause.* BROWN *remains in a stupor for a moment—then stirs himself, puts his hand on* DION'S *breast*).

BROWN: (*dully*) He's dead—at last. (*He says this mechanically but the last two words awaken him—wonderingly*) At last? (*Then with triumph*) At last! (*He stares at* DION'S *real face contemptuously*) So that's the poor weakling you really were! No wonder you hid! And I've always been afraid of you—yes, I'll confess it now, in awe of you! Paugh! (*He picks up the mask from the floor*) No, not of you! Of this! Say what you like, it's strong if it is bad! And this is what Margaret loved, not you! Not you! This man!—this man who willed himself to me! (*Struck by an idea, he jumps to his feet*) By God! (*He slowly starts to put the mask on. A knocking comes on the street door. He starts guiltily, laying the mask on the table. Then he picks it up again quickly, takes the dead body and carries it off left. He reappears immediately and goes to the front door as the knocking recommences—gruffly*) Hello! Who's there?

MARGARET: It's Margaret, Billy. I m looking for Dion.

BROWN: (*uncertainly*) Oh—all right—(*Unfastening door*) Come in. Hello, Margaret. Hello, Boys! He's here. He's asleep. I—I was just dozing off too. (MARGARET *enters. She is wearing her mask. The* THREE SONS *are with her*).

MARGARET: (*seeing the bottle, forcing a laugh*) Has he been celebrating?

BROWN: (*with strange glibness now*) No. I was. He wasn't. He said he'd sworn off tonight—forever—for your sake—and the kids!

MARGARET: (*with amazed joy*) Dion said that? (*Then hastily defensive*) But of course he never does drink much. Where is he?

BROWN: Upstairs. I'll wake him. He felt bad. He took off his clothes to take a bath before he lay down. You just wait here. (*She sits in the chair where* DION *had sat and stares straight before her. The* SONS *group around her, as if for a family photo.* BROWN *hurries out left*).

MARGARET: It's late to keep you boys up. Aren't you sleepy?

BOYS: No, Mother.

MARGARET: (*proudly*) I'm glad to have three such strong boys to protect me.

ELDEST: (*boastingly*) We'd kill anyone that touched you, wouldn't we?

NEXT: You bet! We'd make him wish he hadn't!

YOUNGEST: You bet!

MARGARET: You're Mother's brave boys! (*She laughs fondly— then curiously*) Do you like Mr. Brown?

ELDEST: Sure thing! He's a regular fellow.

NEXT: He's all right!

YOUNGEST: Sure thing!

MARGARET: (*half to herself*) Your father claims he steals his ideas.

ELDEST: (*with a sheepish grin*) I'll bet father said that when he was—just talking.

NEXT: Mr. Brown doesn't have to steal, does he?

YOUNGEST: I should say not! He's awful rich.

MARGARET: Do you love your father?

ELDEST: (*scuffling—embarrassed*) Why—of course—

NEXT: (*ditto*) Sure thing!

YOUNGEST: Sure I do.

MARGARET: (*with a sigh*) I think you'd better start on before—right now—before your father comes— He'll be very sick and nervous and he'll want to be quiet. So run along!

BOYS: All right. (*They file out and close the front door as* BROWN, *dressed in* DION'S *clothes and wearing his mask, appears at left*).

MARGARET: (*taking off her mask, gladly*) Dion! (*She stares wonderingly at him and he at her; goes to him and puts an arm around him*) Poor dear, do you feel sick? (*He nods*) But you look—(*squeezing his arms*)—why, you actually feel stronger and better already! Is it true what Billy told me—about your swearing off forever? (*He nods. She exclaims intensely*) Oh, if you'll only—and get well—we can still be so happy! Give Mother a kiss. (*They kiss. A shudder passes through both of them. She breaks away laughing with aroused desire*) Why, Dion? Aren't you ashamed? You haven't kissed me like that in ages!

BROWN: (*his voice imitating* DION'S *and muffled by the mask*) I've wanted to, Margaret!

MARGARET: (*gayly and coquettishly now*) Were you afraid I'd spurn you?

Why, Dion, something has happened. It's like a miracle! Even your voice is changed! It actually sounds younger, do you know it? (*Then, solicitously*) But you must be worn out. Let's go home. (*With an impulsive movement she flings her arms wide open, throwing her mask away from her as if suddenly no longer needing it*) Oh, I'm beginning to feel so happy, Dion—so happy!

BROWN: (*stifledly*) Let's go home. (*She puts her arm around him. They walk to the door*).

CURTAIN

*S*cene: *The drafting room and private office of* brown *are both shown. The former is at left, the latter at right of a dividing wall at center. The arrangement of furniture in each room is the same as in previous scenes. It is ten in the morning of a day about a month later. The backdrop for both rooms is of plain wall with a few tacked-up designs and blue prints painted on it.*

two draftsmen, *a middle-aged and a young man, both stoop shouldered, are sitting on stools behind what was formerly* dion's *table. They are tracing plans. They talk as they work.*

older draftsman: W. B. is late again.

younger draftsman: Wonder what's got into him the last month? (*A pause. They work silently*).

older draftsman: Yes, ever since he fired Dion . . . .

younger draftsman: Funny his firing him all of a sudden like that. (*A pause. They work*).

older draftsman: I haven't seen Dion around town since then. Have you?

younger draftsman: No, not since Brown told us he'd canned him. I suppose he's off drowning his sorrow!

older draftsman: I heard someone had seen him at home and he was sober and looking fine. (*A pause. They work*).

younger draftsman: What got into Brown? They say he fired all his old servants that same day and only uses his house to sleep in.

older draftsman: (*with a sneer*) Artistic temperament, maybe—the real name of which is swelled head! (*There is a noise of footsteps from the hall. Warningly*) Ssstt! (*They bend over their table.* margaret *enters. She does not need to wear a mask now. Her face has regained the self-confident spirit of its youth, her eyes shine with happiness*).

margaret: (*heartily*) Good morning! What a lovely day!

BOTH: (*perfunctorily*) Good morning, Mrs. Anthony.

MARGARET: (*looking around*) You've been changing around in here, haven't you? Where is Dion? (*They stare at her*) I forgot to tell him something important this morning and our phone's out of order. So if you'll tell him I'm here— (*They don't move. A pause.* MARGARET *says stiffly*) Oh, I realize Mr. Brown has given strict orders Dion is not to be disturbed, but surely . . . . (*Sharply*) Where is my husband, please?

OLDER DRAFTSMAN: We don't know.

MARGARET: You don't know?

YOUNGER DRAFTSMAN: We haven't seen him.

MARGARET: Why, he left home at eight-thirty!

OLDER DRAFTSMAN: To come here?

YOUNGER DRAFTSMAN: This morning?

MARGARET: (*provoked*) Why, of course, to come here—as he does every day! (*They stare at her. A pause*).

OLDER DRAFTSMAN: (*evasively*) We haven't seen him.

MARGARET: (*with asperity*) Where is Mr. Brown?

YOUNGER DRAFTSMAN: (*at a noise of footsteps from the hall—sulkily*) Coming now. (BROWN *enters. He is now wearing a mask which is an exact likeness of his face as it was in the last scene—the self-assured success. When he sees* MARGARET, *he starts back apprehensively*).

BROWN: (*immediately controlling himself—breezily*) Hello, Margaret! This is a pleasant surprise! (*He holds out his hand*).

MARGARET: (*hardly taking it—reservedly*) Good morning.

BROWN: (*turning quickly to the* DRAFTSMEN) I hope you explained to Mrs. Anthony how busy Dion . . .

MARGARET: (*interrupting him—stiffly*) I certainly can't understand—

BROWN: (*hastily*) I'll explain. Come in here and be comfortable. (*He throws open the door and ushers her into his private office*).

OLDER DRAFTSMAN: Dion must be putting over some bluff on her.

YOUNGER DRAFTSMAN: Pretending he's still here—and Brown's helping him . . . .

OLDER DRAFTSMAN: But why should Brown, after he . . . ?

YOUNGER DRAFTSMAN: Well, I suppose— Search me. (*They work*).

BROWN: Have a chair, Margaret. (*She sits on the chair stiffly. He
sits behind the desk*).

MARGARET: (*coldly*) I'd like some explanation . . . .

BROWN: (*coaxingly*) Now, don't get angry, Margaret! Dion is hard at
work on his design for the new State Capitol, and I don't want him
disturbed, not even by you! So be a good sport! It's for his own good,
remember! I asked him to explain to you.

MARGARET: (*relenting*) He told me you'd agreed to ask me and the boys
not to come here—but then, we hardly ever did.

BROWN: But you might! (*Then with confidential friendliness*) This is for
his sake, Margaret. I know Dion. He's got to be able to work without
distractions. He's not the ordinary man, you appreciate that. And
this design means his whole future! He's to get full credit for it, and
as soon as it's accepted, I take him into partnership. It's all agreed.
And after that I'm going to take a long vacation—go to Europe for
a couple of years—and leave everything here in Dion's hands! Hasn't
he told you all this?

MARGARET: (*jubilant now*) Yes—but I could hardly believe . . . (*Proudly*)
I'm sure he can do it. He's been like a new man lately, so full of
ambition and energy! It's made me so happy! (*She stops in confusion*).

BROWN: (*deeply moved, takes her hand impulsively*) And it has made me
happy, too!

MARGARET: (*confused—with an amused laugh*) Why, Billy Brown! For a
moment, I thought it was Dion, your voice sounded so much . . . !

BROWN: (*with sudden desperation*) Margaret, I've got to tell you! I can't
go on like this any longer! I've got to confess . . . ! There's something . . . !

MARGARET: (*alarmed*) Not—not about Dion?

BROWN: (*harshly*) To hell with Dion! To hell with Billy Brown! (*He
tears off his mask and reveals a suffering face that is ravaged and haggard,*

his own face tortured and distorted by the demon of Dion's mask) Think of me! I love you, Margaret! Leave him! I've always loved you! Come away with me! I'll sell out here! We'll go abroad and be happy!

MARGARET: (*amazed*) Billy Brown, do you realize what you're saying? (*With a shudder*) Are you crazy? Your face—is terrible. You're sick! Shall I phone for a doctor?

BROWN: (*turning away slowly and putting on his mask—dully*) No. I've been on the verge—of a breakdown—for some time. I get spells . . . . I'm better now. (*He turns back to her*) Forgive me! Forget what I said! But, for all our sakes, don't come here again.

MARGARET: (*coldly*) After this—I assure you . . . ! (*Then looking at him with pained incredulity*) Why, Billy—I simply won't believe—after all these years . . . !

BROWN: It will never happen again. Good-by.

MARGARET: Good-by. (*Then, wishing to leave on a pleasant change of subject—forcing a smile*) Don't work Dion to death! He's never home for dinner any more. (*She goes out past the* DRAFTSMEN *and off right, rear.* BROWN *sits down at his desk, taking off the mask again. He stares at it with bitter, cynical amusement*).

BROWN: You're dead, William Brown, dead beyond hope of resurrection! It's the Dion you buried in your garden who killed you, not you him! It's Margaret's husband who . . . (*He laughs harshly*) Paradise by proxy! Love by mistaken identity! God! (*This is almost a prayer—then fiercely defiant*) But it *is* paradise! I *do* love! (*As he is speaking, a well-dressed, important, stout man enters the drafting room. He is carrying a rolled-up plan in his hand. He nods condescendingly and goes directly to* BROWN'S *door, on which he raps sharply, and, without waiting for an answer, turns the knob.* BROWN *has just time to turn his head and get his mask on*).

MAN: (*briskly*) Ah, good morning! I came right in. Hope I didn't disturb . . . ?

BROWN: (*the successful architect now—urbanely*) Not at all, sir. How are you? (*They shake hands*) Sit down. Have a cigar. And now what can I do for you this morning?

MAN: (*unrolling his plan*) It's your plan. My wife and I have been going over it again. We like it—and we don't—and when a man plans to lay out half a million, why he wants everything exactly right, eh? (BROWN *nods*) It's too cold, too spare, too like a tomb, if you'll pardon me, for a liveable home. Can't you liven it up, put in some decorations, make it fancier and warmer—you know what I mean. (*Looks at him a bit doubtfully*) People tell me you had an assistant, Anthony, who was a real shark on these details but that you've fired him—

BROWN: (*suavely*) Gossip! He's still with me but, for reasons of his own, doesn't wish it known. Yes, I trained him and he's very ingenious. I'll turn this right over to him and instruct him to carry out your wishes . . . .

CURTAIN

Scene Two

*S*CENE: *The same as Act Two, Scene Three—the library of* BROWN'S *home about eight the same night. He can be heard feeling his way in through the dark. He switches on the reading lamp on the table. Directly under it on a sort of stand is the mask of* DION, *its empty eyes staring front.*

BROWN *takes off his own mask and lays it on the table before* DION'S. *He flings himself down in the chair and stares without moving into the eyes of* DION'S *mask. Finally, he begins to talk to it in a bitter, mocking tone.*

BROWN: Listen! Today was a narrow escape—for us! We can't avoid discovery much longer. We must get our plot to working! We've already made William Brown's will, leaving you his money and business. We must hustle off to Europe now—and murder him there! (*A bit tauntingly*) Then you—the I in you—*I* will live with Margaret happily ever after. (*More tauntingly*) She will have children by me! (*He seems to hear some mocking denial from the mask. He bends toward it*) What? (*Then with a sneer*) Anyway, that doesn't matter! Your children already love me more than they ever loved you! And Margaret loves me more! You think you've won, do you—that I've got to vanish into you in order to live? Not yet, my friend! Never! Wait! Gradually Margaret will love what is beneath—me! Little by little I'll teach her to know me, and then finally I'll reveal myself to her, and confess that I stole your place out of love for her, and she'll understand and forgive and love me! And you'll be forgotten! Ha! (*Again he bends down to the mask as if listening—torturedly*) What's that? She'll never believe? She'll never see? She'll never understand? You lie, devil! (*He reaches out his hands as if to take the mask by the throat, then shrinks back with a shudder of hopeless despair*) God have mercy! Let me believe! Blessed are the merciful! Let me obtain mercy! (*He waits, his face upturned—pleadingly*) Not yet? (*Despairingly*) Never? (*A pause. Then, in a sudden panic of dread, he reaches out for the mask of* DION *like a dope fiend after a drug. As soon as he holds it, he seems to gain strength and is able to force a sad laugh*) Now I am drinking your strength, Dion—strength to love in this world and die and sleep and become fertile earth, as you are becoming now in my garden—your weakness the strength of my flowers, your failure as an artist painting their petals with life! (*Then, with bravado*) Come with me while Margaret's bridegroom dresses in your clothes, Mr. Anthony! I need the devil when I'm in the dark! (*He goes off left, but can be heard talking*) Your clothes begin to fit me better than my own! Hurry, Brother! It's time we were home. Our wife is waiting! (*He reappears, having changed his coat and trousers*) Come with me and tell her again I love her! Come and hear her tell me how she loves you!

(*He suddenly cannot help kissing the mask*) I love you because she loves you! My kisses on your lips are for her! (*He puts the mask over his face and stands for a moment, seeming to grow tall and proud—then with a laugh of bold self-assurance*) Out by the back way! I mustn't forget I'm a desperate criminal, pursued by God, and by myself! (*He goes out right, laughing with amused satisfaction*).

CURTAIN

Scene Three

Scene: *Is the same as Scene One of Act One—the sitting-room of* MARGARET's *home. It is about half an hour after the last scene.* MARGARET *sits on the sofa, waiting with the anxious, impatient expectancy of one deeply in love. She is dressed with a careful, subtle extra touch to attract the eye. She looks young and happy. She is trying to read a book. The front door is heard opening and closing. She leaps up and runs back to throw her arms around* BROWN *as he enters from right, rear. She kisses him passionately.*

MARGARET: (*as he recoils with a sort of guilt—laughingly*) Why, you hateful old thing, you! I really believe you were trying to avoid kissing me! Well, just for that, I'll never . . .

BROWN: (*with fierce, defiant passion, kisses her again and again*) Margaret!

MARGARET: Call me Peggy again. You used to when you really loved me. (*Softly*) Remember the school commencement dance— you and I on the dock in the moonlight?

BROWN: (*with pain*) No. (*He takes his arms from around her*).

MARGARET: (*still holding him—with a laugh*) Well, I like that! You old bear, you! Why not?

BROWN: (*sadly*) It was so long ago.

MARGARET: (*a bit melancholy*) You mean you don't want to be reminded that we're getting old?

BROWN: Yes. (*He kisses her gently*) I'm tired. Let's sit down. (*They sit on the sofa, his arm about her, her head on his shoulder*).

MARGARET: (*with a happy sigh*) I don't mind remembering—now I'm happy. It's only when I'm unhappy that it hurts—and I've been so happy lately, dear—and so grateful to you! (*He stirs uneasily. She goes on joyfully*) Everything's changed! I'd gotten pretty resigned to—and sad and hopeless, too—and then all at once you turn right around and everything is the same as when we were first married—much better even, for I was never sure of you then. You were always so strange and aloof and alone, it seemed I was never really touching you. But now I feel you've become quite human—like me—and I'm so happy, dear! (*She kisses him*).

BROWN: (*his voice trembling*) Then I have made you happy—happier than ever before—no matter what happens? (*She nods*) Then—that justifies everything! (*He forces a laugh*).

MARGARET: Of course it does! I've always known that. But you—you wouldn't be—or you couldn't be—and I could never help you—and all the time I knew you were so lonely! I could always hear you calling to me that you were lost, but I couldn't find the path to you because I was lost, too! That's an awful way for a wife to feel! (*She laughs—joyfully*) But now you're here! You're mine! You're my long-lost lover, and my husband, and my big boy, too!

BROWN: (*with a trace of jealousy*) Where are your other big boys tonight?

MARGARET: Out to a dance. They've all acquired girls, I'll have you know.

BROWN: (*mockingly*) Aren't you jealous?

MARGARET: (*gayly*) Of course! Terribly! But I'm diplomatic. I don't let them see. (*Changing the subject*) Believe me, they've noticed the change in you! The eldest was saying to me today: "It's great not to have Father so nervous, any more. Why, he's a regular sport when

he gets started!" And the other two said very solemnly: "You bet!"
(*She laughs*).

BROWN: (*brokenly*) I—I'm glad.

MARGARET: Dion! You're crying!

BROWN: (*stung by the name, gets up—harshly*) Nonsense! Did you ever
know Dion to cry about anyone?

MARGARET: (*sadly*) You couldn't—then. You were too lonely. You had
no one to cry to.

BROWN: (*goes and takes a rolled-up plan from the table drawer— dully*) I've
got to do some work.

MARGARET: (*disappointedly*) What, has that old Billy Brown got you to
work at home again, too?

BROWN: (*ironically*) It's for Dion's good, you know—and yours.

MARGARET: (*making the best of it—cheerfully*) All right. I won't be selfish.
It really makes me proud to have you so ambitious. Let me help.
(*She brings his drawing-board, which he puts on the table and pins his plan
upon. She sits on sofa and picks up her book*).

BROWN: (*carefully casual*) I hear you were in to see me today?

MARGARET: Yes, and Billy wouldn't hear of it! I was quite furious until
he convinced me it was all for the best. When is he going to take
you into partnership?

BROWN: Very soon now.

MARGARET: And will he really give you full charge when he goes abroad?

BROWN: Yes.

MARGARET: (*practically*) I'd pin him down if I could. Promises are all
right, but—(*she hesitates*) I don't trust him.

BROWN: (*with a start, sharply*) What makes you say that?

MARGARET: Oh, something that happened today.

BROWN: What?

MARGARET: I don't mean I blame him, but—to be frank, I think the
Great God Brown, as you call him, is getting a bit queer and it's time
he took a vacation. Don't you?

BROWN: (*his voice a bit excited—but guardedly*) But why? What did he do?

MARGARET: (*hesitatingly*) Well—it's really too silly—he suddenly got awfully strange. His face scared me. It was like a corpse. Then he raved on some nonsense about he'd always loved me. He went on like a perfect fool! (*She looks at* BROWN *who is staring at her. She becomes uneasy*) Maybe I shouldn't tell you this. He simply wasn't responsible. Then he came to himself and was all right and begged my pardon and seemed dreadfully sorry, and I felt sorry for him. (*Then with a shudder*) But honestly, Dion, it was just too disgusting for words to hear him! (*With kind, devastating contempt*) Poor Billy!

BROWN: (*with a show of tortured derision*) Poor Billy! Poor Billy the Goat! (*With mocking frenzy*) I'll kill him for you! I'll serve you his heart for breakfast!

MARGARET: (*jumping up—frightenedly*) Dion!

BROWN: (*waving his pencil knife with grotesque flourishes*) I tell you I'll murder this God-damned disgusting Great God Brown who stands like a fatted calf in the way of our health and wealth and happiness!

MARGARET: (*bewilderedly, not knowing how much is pretending, puts an arm about him*) Don't, dear! You're being horrid and strange again. It makes me afraid you haven't really changed, after all.

BROWN: (*unheeding*) And then my wife can be happy! Ha! (*He laughs. She begins to cry. He controls himself—pats her head— gently*) All right, dear. Mr. Brown is now safely in hell. Forget him!

MARGARET: (*stops crying—but still worriedly*) I should never have told you—but I never imagined you'd take it seriously. I've never thought of Billy Brown except as a friend, and lately not even that! He's just a stupid old fool!

BROWN: Ha-ha! Didn't I say he was in hell? They're torturing him! (*Then controlling himself again—exhaustedly*) Please leave me alone now. I've got to work.

MARGARET: All right, dear. I'll go into the next room and anything you want, just call. (*She pats his face—cajolingly*) Is it all forgotten?

BROWN: Will you be happy?

MARGARET: Yes.

BROWN: Then it's dead, I promise! (*She kisses him and goes out. He stares ahead, then shakes off his thoughts and concentrates on his work—mockingly*) Our beautiful new Capitol calls you, Mr. Dion! To work! We'll adroitly hide old Silenus on the cupola! Let him dance over their law-making with his eternal leer! (*He bends over his work*)

CURTAIN

SCENE: *Same as Scene One of Act Three—the drafting room and* BROWN'S *office. It is dusk of a day about a month later. The* TWO DRAFTSMEN *are bent over their table, working.*

BROWN: (*at his desk, is working feverishly over a plan. He is wearing the mask of* DION. *The mask of* WILLIAM BROWN *rests on the desk beside him. As he works, he chuckles with malicious glee—finally flings down his pencil with a flourish*). Done! In the name of the Almighty Brown, amen, amen! Here's a wondrous fair capitol! The design would do just as well for a Home for Criminal Imbeciles! Yet to them, such is my art, it will appear to possess a pure common-sense, a fat-bellied finality, as dignified as the suspenders of an assemblyman! Only to me will that pompous façade reveal itself as the wearily ironic grin of Pan as, his ears drowsy with the crumbling hum of past and future civilizations, he half-listens to the laws passed by his fleas to enslave him! Ha-ha-ha! (*He leaps grotesquely from behind his desk and cuts a few goatish capers, laughing with lustful merriment*) Long live Chief of Police Brown! District Attorney Brown! Alderman Brown! Assemblyman Brown! Mayor Brown! Congressman Brown! Governor Brown! Senator Brown! President Brown! (*He chants*) Oh, how many persons in one God make up the good God Brown? Hahahaha! (*The* TWO DRAFTSMEN *in the next room have stopped work and are listening*).

YOUNGER DRAFTSMAN: Drunk as a fool!

OLDER DRAFTSMAN: At least Dion used to have the decency to stay away from the office—

YOUNGER DRAFTSMAN: Funny how it's got hold of Brown so quick!

OLDER DRAFTSMAN: He was probably hitting it up on the Q.T. all the time.

BROWN: (*has come back to his desk, laughing to himself and out of breath*)

346

Time to become respectable again! (*He takes off the* DION *mask and reaches out for the* WILLIAM BROWN *one—then stops, with a hand on each, staring down on the plan with fascinated loathing. His real face is now sick, ghastly, tortured, hollow-cheeked and feverish-eyed*) Ugly! Hideous! Despicable! Why must the demon in me pander to cheapness—then punish me with self-loathing and life-hatred? Why am I not strong enough to perish—or blind enough to be content? (*To heaven, bitterly but pleadingly*) Give me the strength to destroy this!—and myself!— and him!—and I will believe in Thee! (*While he has been speaking there has been a noise from the stairs. The* TWO DRAFTSMEN *have bent over their work.* MARGARET *enters, closing the door behind her. At this sound,* BROWN *starts. He immediately senses who it is—with alarm*) Margaret! (*He grabs up both masks and goes into room off right*).

MARGARET: (*she looks healthy and happy, but her face wears a worried, solicitous expression—pleasantly to the staring* DRAFTSMEN) Good morning. Oh, you needn't look worried, it's Mr. Brown I want to see, not my husband.

YOUNGER DRAFTSMAN: (*hesitatingly*) He's locked himself in—but maybe if you'll knock—

MARGARET: (*knocks—somewhat embarrassedly*) Mr. Brown! (BROWN *enters his office, wearing the* WILLIAM BROWN *mask. He comes quickly to the other door and unlocks it*).

BROWN: (*with a hectic cordiality*) Come on, Margaret! Enter! This is delightful! Sit down! What can I do for you?

MARGARET: (*taken aback—a bit stiffly*) Nothing much.

BROWN: Something about Dion, of course. Well, your darling pet is all right—never better!

MARGARET: (*coldly*) That's a matter of opinion. I think you're working him to death.

BROWN: Oh, no, not him. It's Brown who is to die. We've agreed on that.

MARGARET: (*giving him a queer look*) I'm serious.

BROWN: So am I. Deadly serious! Hahaha!

MARGARET: (*checking her indignation*) That's what I came to see you about. Really, Dion has acted so hectic and on edge lately I'm sure he's on the verge of a breakdown.

BROWN: Well, it certainly isn't drink. He hasn't had a drop. He doesn't need it! Haha! And I haven't either, although the gossips are beginning to say I'm soused all the time! It's because I've started to laugh! Hahaha! They can't believe in joy in this town except by the bottle! What funny little people! Hahaha! When you're the Great God Brown, eh, Margaret? Hahaha!

MARGARET: (*getting up—uneasily*) I'm afraid I—

BROWN: Don't be afraid, my dear! I won't make love to you again! Honor bright! I'm too near the grave for such folly! But it must have been funny for you when you came here the last time—watching a disgusting old fool like me, eh?—too funny for words! Hahaha! (*Then with a sudden movement he flourishes the design before her*) Look! We've finished it! Dion has finished it! His fame is made!

MARGARET: (*tartly*) Really, Billy, I believe you are drunk!

BROWN: Nobody kisses me—so you can all believe the worst! Hahaha!

MARGARET: (*chillingly*) Then if Dion is through, why can't I see him?

BROWN: (*crazily*) See Dion? See Dion? Well, why not? It's an age of miracles. The streets are full of Lazaruses. Pray! I mean—wait a moment, if you please.

(BROWN *disappears into the room off right. A moment later he reappears in the mask of* DION: *He holds out his arms and* MARGARET *rushes into them. They kiss passionately. Finally he sits with her on the lounge*).

MARGARET: So you've finished it.

BROWN: Yes. The Committee is coming to see it soon. I've made all the changes they'll like, the fools!

MARGARET: (*lovingly*) And can we go on that second honeymoon, right away now?

BROWN: In a week or so, I hope—as soon as I've gotten Brown off to Europe.

MARGARET: Tell me—isn't he drinking hard?

BROWN: (*laughing as* BROWN *did*) Haha! Soused to the ears all the time! Soused on life! He can't stand it! It's burning his insides out!

MARGARET: (*alarmed*) Dear! I'm worried about you. You sound as crazy as he did—when you laugh! You must rest!

BROWN: (*controlling himself*) I'll rest in peace—when he's gone!

MARGARET: (*with a queer look*) Why, Dion, that isn't your suit. It's just like—

BROWN: It's his! We're getting to be like twins. I'm inheriting his clothes already! (*Then calming himself as he sees how frightened she is*) Don't be worried, dear. I'm just a trifle elated, now the job's done. I guess I'm a bit soused on life, too! (*The* COMMITTEE, *three important-looking, average personages, come into the drafting-room*).

MARGARET: (*forcing a smile*) Well, don't let it burn *your* insides out!

BROWN: No danger! Mine were tempered in hell! Hahaha!

MARGARET: (*kissing him, coaxingly*) Come home, dear—please!

OLDER DRAFTSMAN: (*knocks on the door*) The Committee is here, Mr. Brown.

BROWN: (*hurriedly to* MARGARET) You receive them. Hand them the design. I'll get Brown. (*He raises his voice*) Come right in, gentlemen. (*He goes off right, as the* COMMITTEE *enter the office. When they see* MARGARET, *they stop in surprise*).

MARGARET: (*embarrassedly*) Good afternoon. Mr. Brown will be right with you. (*They bow.* MARGARET *holds out the design to them*) This is my husband's design. He finished it today.

COMMITTEE: Ah! (*They crowd around to look at it—with enthusiasm*) Perfect! Splendid! Couldn't be better! Exactly what we suggested!

MARGARET: (*joyfully*) Then you accept it? Mr. Anthony will be so pleased!

MEMBER: Mr. Anthony?

ANOTHER: Is he working here again?

THIRD: Did I understand you to say this was your husband's design?

MARGARET: (*excitedly*) Yes! Entirely his! He's worked like a dog— (*Appalled*) You don't mean to say—Mr. Brown never told you? (*They shake their heads in solemn surprise*) Oh, the contemptible cad! I hate him!

BROWN: (*appearing at right—mockingly*) Hate me, Margaret? Hate Brown? How superfluous! (*Oratorically*) Gentlemen, I have been keeping a secret from you in order that you might be the more impressed when I revealed it. That design is entirely the inspiration of Mr. Dion Anthony's genius. I had nothing to do with it.

MARGARET: (*contritely*) Oh, Billy! I m sorry! Forgive me!

BROWN: (*ignoring her, takes the plan from the* COMMITTEE *and begins unpinning it from the board—mockingly*) I can see by your faces you have approved this. You are delighted, aren't you? And why not, my dear sirs? Look at it, and look at you! Hahaha! It'll immortalize you, my good men! You'll be as death-defying a joke as any in Joe Miller! (*Then with a sudden complete change of tone—angrily*) You damn fools! Can't you see this is an insult—a terrible, blasphemous insult!—that this embittered failure Anthony is hurling in the teeth of our success—an insult to you, to me, to you, Margaret—and to Almighty God! (*In a frenzy of fury*) And if you are weak and cowardly enough to stand for it, I'm not! (*He tears the plan into four pieces. The* COMMITTEE *stands aghast.* MARGARET *runs forward*).

MARGARET: (*in a scream*) You coward! Dion! Dion! (*She picks up the plan and hugs it to her bosom*).

BROWN: (*with a sudden goatish caper*) I'll tell him you're here. (*He disappears, but reappears almost immediately in the mask of* DION. *He is imposing a terrible discipline on himself to avoid dancing and laughing. He speaks suavely*) Everything is all right—all for the best—you mustn't get excited! A little paste, Margaret! A little paste, gentlemen! And all will be well! Life is imperfect, Brothers! Men have their faults, Sister! But with a few drops of glue much may be done! A little dab of pasty resignation here and there—and even broken hearts may be repaired to do yeoman service! (*He has edged toward the door. They are all staring at him with petrified bewilderment. He puts his fingers to his lips*) Ssssh! This is Daddy's bedtime secret for today: Man is born broken. He lives by mending. The grace of God is glue! (*With a quick prancing movement, he has opened the door, gone through, and closed it after him silently, shaking with suppressed laughter. He springs lightly to the side of the petrified* DRAFTSMEN—*in a whisper*) They will find him in the little room. Mr. William Brown is dead! (*With light leaps he vanishes, his head thrown back, shaking with silent laughter. The sound of his feet leaping down the stairs, five at a time, can be heard. Then a pause of silence. The people in the two rooms stare. The* YOUNGER DRAFTSMEN *is the first to recover*).

YOUNGER DRAFTSMAN: (*rushing into the next room, shouts in terrified tones*) Mr. Brown is dead!

COMMITTEE: He murdered him! (*They all run into the little room off right.* MARGARET *remains, stunned with horror. They return in a moment, carrying the mask of* WILLIAM BROWN, *two on each side as if they were carrying a body by the legs and shoulders. They solemnly lay him down on the couch and stand looking down at him*).

FIRST COMMITTEEMAN: (*with a frightened awe*) I can't believe he's gone.

SECOND COMMITTEEMAN: (*in same tone*) I can almost hear him talking. (*As if impelled, he clears his throat and addresses the mask importantly*) Mr. Brown— (*Then stops short*).

THIRD COMMITTEEMAN: (*shrinking back*) No. Dead, all right! (*Then suddenly, hysterically angry and terrified*) We must take steps at once to run Anthony to earth!

MARGARET: (*with a heart-broken cry*) Dion's innocent!

YOUNGER DRAFTSMAN: I'll phone for the police, sir! (*He rushes to the phone*).

CURTAIN

Scene Two

*S*CENE: *The same as Scene Two of Act Three—the library of* WILLIAM BROWN'S *home. The mask of* DION *stands on the table beneath the light, facing front. On his knees beside the table, facing front, stripped naked except for a white cloth around his loins, is* BROWN. *The clothes he has torn off in his agony are scattered on the floor. His eyes, his arms, his whole body strain upward, his muscles writhe with his lips as they pray silently in their agonized supplication. Finally a voice seems torn out of him.*

BROWN: Mercy, Compassionate Savior of Man! Out of my depths I cry to you! Mercy on thy poor clod, thy clod of unhallowed earth, thy clay, the Great God Brown! Mercy, Savior! (*He seems to wait for an answer—then leaping to his feet he puts out one hand to touch the mask like a frightened child reaching out for its nurse's hand—then with immediate mocking despair*) Bah! I am sorry, little children, but your kingdom is empty. God has become disgusted and moved away to some far ecstatic star where life is a dancing flame! We must die without him. (*Then—addressing the mask—harshly*) Together, my friend! You, too! Let Margaret suffer! Let the whole world suffer as I am suffering! (*There is a sound of a door being pushed violently open, padding feet in slippers, and* CYBEL, *wearing her mask, runs into the room. She stops short on seeing* BROWN *and the mask, and stares from one to the other for a second in confusion. She is dressed in a black kimono robe and wears slippers over her bare feet. Her yellow hair hangs down in a great mane over her shoulders. She has grown stouter, has more of the deep objective calm of an idol*).

BROWN: (*staring at her—fascinated—with great peace as if her presence comforted him*) Cybel! I was coming to you! How did you know?

CYBEL: (*takes off her mask and looks from* BROWN *to the* DION *mask, now with a great understanding*) So that's why you never came to me again! You are Dion Brown!

BROWN: (*bitterly*) I am the remains of William Brown! (*He points to the mask of* DION) I am his murderer and his murdered!

CYBEL: (*with a laugh of exasperated pity*) Oh, why can't you ever learn to leave yourselves alone and leave me alone!

BROWN: (*boyishly and naïvely*) I am Billy.

CYBEL: (*immediately, with a motherly solicitude*) Then run, Billy, run! They are hunting for someone! They came to my place, hunting for a murderer, Dion! They must find a victim! They've got to quiet their fears, to cast out their devils, or they'll never sleep soundly again! They've got to absolve themselves by finding a guilty one! They've got to kill someone now, to live! You're naked! You must be Satan! Run, Billy, run! They'll come here! I ran here to warn— someone! So run away if you want to live!

BROWN: (*like a sulky child*) I'm too tired. I don't want to.

CYBEL: (*with motherly calm*) All right, you needn't, Billy. Don't sulk. (*As a noise comes from outside*) Anyway, it's too late. I hear them in the garden now.

BROWN: (*listening, puts out his hand and takes the mask of* DION—*as he gains strength, mockingly*) Thanks for this one last favor, Dion! Listen! Your avengers! Standing on your grave in the garden! Hahaha! (*He puts on the mask and springs to the left and makes a gesture as if flinging French windows open. Gayly moving*) Welcome, dumb worshippers! I am your Great God Brown! I have been advised to run from you but it is my almighty whim to dance into escape over your prostrate souls! (*Shouts from the garden and a volley of shots.* BROWN *staggers back and falls on the floor by the couch, mortally wounded*).

CYBEL: (*runs to his side, lifts him on to the couch and takes off the mask of* DION) You can't take this to bed with you. You've got to go to sleep alone. (*She places the mask of* DION *back on its stand under the light and puts on her own, just as, after a banging of doors, crashing of glass, trampling of feet, a Squad of Police with drawn revolvers, led by a grizzly, brutal-faced* CAPTAIN, *run into the room. They are followed by* MARGARET, *still distractedly clutching the pieces of the plan to her breast*).

CAPTAIN: (*pointing to the mask of* DION—*triumphantly*) Got him! He's dead!

MARGARET: (*throws herself on her knees, takes the mask and kisses it—heartbrokenly*) Dion! Dion! (*Her face hidden in her arms, the mask in her hands above her bowed head, she remains, sobbing with deep, silent grief*).

CAPTAIN: (*noticing* CYBEL *and* BROWN—*startled*) Hey! Look at this! What're you doin' here? Who's he?

CYBEL: You ought to know. You croaked him!

CAPTAIN: (*with a defensive snarl—hastily*) It was Anthony! I saw his mug! This feller's an accomplice, I bet yuh! Serves him right! Who is he? Friend o' yours! Crook! What's his name? Tell me or I'll fix yuh!

CYBEL: Billy.

CAPTAIN: Billy what?

CYBEL: I don't know. He's dying. (*Then suddenly*) Leave me alone with him and maybe I'll get him to squeal it.

CAPTAIN: Yuh better! I got to have a clean report. I'll give yuh a couple o' minutes. (*He motions to the Policemen, who follow him off left.* CYBEL *takes off her mask and sits down by* BROWN's *head. He makes an effort to raise himself toward her and she helps him, throwing her kimono over his bare body, drawing his head on to her shoulder*).

BROWN: (*snuggling against her—gratefully*) The earth is warm.

CYBEL: (*soothingly, looking before her like an idol*) Ssshh! Go to sleep, Billy.

BROWN: Yes, Mother. (*Then explainingly*) It was dark and I couldn't see where I was going and they all picked on me.

CYBEL: I know. You're tired.

BROWN: And when I wake up . . . ?

CYBEL: The sun will be rising again.

BROWN: To judge the living and the dead! (*Frightenedly*) I don't want justice. I want love.

CYBEL: There is only love.

BROWN: Thank you, Mother. (*Then feebly*) I'm getting sleepy. What's the prayer you taught me— Our Father—?

CYBEL: (*with calm exultance*) Our Father Who Art!

BROWN: (*taking her tone—exultantly*) Who art! Who art! (*Suddenly—with ecstasy*) I know! I have found Him! I hear Him speak! "Blessed are they that weep, for they shall laugh!" Only he that has wept can laugh! The laughter of Heaven sows earth with a rain of tears, and out of Earth's transfigured birth-pain the laughter of Man returns to bless and play again in innumerable dancing gales of flame upon the knees of God! (*He dies*).

CYBEL: (*gets up and fixes his body on the couch. She bends down and kisses him gently—she straightens up and looks into space—with a profound pain*) Always spring comes again bearing life! Always again! Always, always forever again!—Spring again!—life again!—summer and fall and death and peace again!—(*with agonized sorrow*)—but always, always, love and conception and birth and pain again—spring bearing the intolerable chalice of life again!—(*then with agonized exultance*)—bearing the glorious, blazing crown of life again! (*She stands like an idol of Earth, her eyes staring out over the world*).

MARGARET: (*lifting her head adoringly to the mask—triumphant tenderness mingled with her grief*) My lover! My husband! My boy! (*She kisses the mask*) Good-by. Thank you for happiness! And you're not dead, sweetheart! You can never die till my heart dies! You will live forever! You will sleep under my heart! I will feel you stirring in your sleep, forever under my heart! (*She kisses the mask again. There is a pause*).

CAPTAIN: (*comes just into sight at left and speaks front without looking at them—gruffly*) Well, what's his name?

CYBEL: Man!

CAPTAIN: (*taking a grimy notebook and an inch-long pencil from his pocket*) How d'yuh spell it?

CURTAIN

EPILOGUE

*S*CENE: *Four years later. The same spot on the same dock as in Prologue on another moonlight night in June. The sound of the waves and of distant dance music.*

MARGARET *and her* THREE SONS *appear from the right. The eldest is now eighteen. All are dressed in the height of correct Prep-school elegance. They are all tall, athletic, strong and handsome-looking. They loom up around the slight figure of their mother like protecting giants, giving her a strange aspect of lonely, detached, small femininity. She wears her mask of the proud, indulgent Mother. She has grown appreciably older. Her hair is now a beautiful gray. There is about her manner and voice the sad but contented feeling of one who knows her life-purpose well accomplished but is at the same time a bit empty and comfortless with the finality of it. She is wrapped in a gray cloak.*

ELDEST: Doesn't Bee look beautiful tonight, Mother?

NEXT: Don't you think Mabel's the best dancer in there, Mother?

YOUNGEST: Aw, Alice has them both beat, hasn't she, Mother?

MARGARET: (*with a sad little laugh*) Each of you is right. (*Then, with strange finality*) Good-by, boys.

BOYS: (*surprised*) Good-by.

MARGARET: It was here on a night just like this your father first—proposed to me. Did you ever know that?

BOYS: (*embarrassedly*) No.

MARGARET: (*yearningly*) But the nights now are so much colder than they used to be. Think of it, I went in moonlight bathing in June when I was a girl. It was so warm and beautiful in those days. I remember the Junes when I was carrying you boys— (*A pause. They fidget uneasily. She asks pleadingly*) Promise me faithfully never to forget your father!

BOYS: (*uncomfortably*) Yes, Mother.

356

MARGARET: (*forcing a joking tone*) But you mustn't waste June on an old woman like me! Go in and dance. (*As they hesitate dutifully*) Go on. I really want to be alone—with my Junes.

BOYS: (*unable to conceal their eagerness*) Yes, Mother. (*They go away*).

MARGARET: (*slowly removes her mask, laying it on the bench, and stares up at the moon with a wistful, resigned sweetness*) So long ago! And yet I'm still the same Margaret. It's only our lives that grow old. We *are* where centuries only count as seconds and after a thousand lives our eyes begin to open—(*She looks around her with a rapt smile*)—and the moon rests in the sea! I want to feel the moon at peace in the sea! I want Dion to leave the sky for me! I want him to sleep in the tides of my heart! (*She slowly takes from under her cloak, from her bosom, as if from her heart, the mask of* DION *as it was at the last and holds it before her face*) My lover! My husband! My boy! You can never die till my heart dies! You will live forever. You are sleeping under my heart! I feel you stirring in your sleep, forever under my heart. (*She kisses him on the lips with a timeless kiss*).

CURTAIN

Lazarus Laughed

❧

CHARACTERS

LAZARUS OF BETHANY

HIS FATHER

HIS MOTHER

MARTHA ⎫ *his sisters*

MARY ⎭

MIRIAM, *his wife*

SEVEN GUESTS, *neighbors of Lazarus*

CHORUS OF OLD MEN

AN ORTHODOX PRIEST

CHORUS OF LAZARUS' FOLLOWERS

A CENTURION

GAIUS CALIGULA

CRASSUS, *a Roman General*

CHORUS OF GREEKS

SEVEN CITIZENS OF ATHENS

CHORUS OF ROMAN SENATORS

SEVEN SENATORS

CHORUS OF LEGIONARIES

FLAVIUS, *a centurion*

MARCELLUS, *a patrician*

CHORUS OF THE GUARD

TIBERIUS CÆSAR

POMPEIA

CHORUS OF YOUTHS AND GIRLS

CHORUS OF THE ROMAN POPULACE

CROWDS

SCENES

ACT ONE

Scene I: Lazarus' home in Bethany—a short time after the miracle.

Scene II: Months later. Outside the House of Laughter in Bethany. Late evening.

ACT TWO

Scene I: A street in Athens. A night months later.

Scene II: A temple immediately inside the walls of Rome. Mid-night. Months later.

ACT THREE

Scene I: Garden of Tiberius' palace. A night a few days later.

Scene II: Inside the palace. Immediately after.

ACT FOUR

Scene I: The same. A while after.

Scene II: Interior of a Roman theatre. Dawn of the same night.

360

LAZARUS LAUGHED

ACT ONE—SCENE ONE

SCENE: *Exterior and interior of* LAZARUS' *home at Bethany. The main room at the front end of the house is shown—a long, low-ceilinged, sparely furnished chamber, with white walls gray in the fading daylight that enters from three small windows at the left. To the left of center several long tables placed lengthwise to the width of the room, around which many chairs for guests have been placed. In the rear wall, right, a door leading into the rest of the house. On the left, a doorway opening on a road where a crowd of men has gathered. On the right, another doorway leading to the yard where there is a crowd of women.*

Inside the house, on the men's side, seven male Guests are grouped by the door, watching LAZARUS *with frightened awe, talking hesitantly in low whispers. The Chorus of Old Men, seven in number, is drawn up in a crescent, in the far corner, right, facing* LAZARUS.

(All of these people are masked in accordance with the following scheme: There are seven periods of life shown: Boyhood (or Girlhood), Youth, Young Manhood (or Womanhood), Manhood (or Womanhood), Middle Age, Maturity and Old Age; and each of these periods is represented by seven different masks of general types of character as follows: The Simple, Ignorant; the Happy, Eager; the Self-Tortured, Introspective; the Proud, Self-Reliant; the Servile, Hypocritical; the Revengeful, Cruel; the Sorrowful, Resigned. Thus in each crowd (this includes among the men the Seven Guests who are composed of one male of each period-type as period one—type one, period two—type two, and so on up to period seven—type seven) there are forty-nine different combinations of period and type. Each type has a distinct predominant color for its costumes which varies in kind according to its period. The masks of the Chorus

of Old Men are double the size of the others. They are all seven in the Sorrowful, Resigned type of Old Age).

On a raised platform at the middle of the one table placed lengthwise at center sits LAZARUS, *his head haloed and his body illumined by a soft radiance as of tiny phosphorescent flames.*

LAZARUS, *freed now from the fear of death, wears no mask.*

In appearance LAZARUS *is tall and powerful, about fifty years of age, with a mass of gray-black hair and a heavy beard. His face recalls that of a statue of a divinity of Ancient Greece in its general structure and particularly in its quality of detached serenity. It is dark-complected, ruddy and brown, the color of rich earth upturned by the plow, calm but furrowed deep with the marks of former suffering endured with a grim fortitude that had never softened into resignation. His forehead is broad and noble, his eyes black and deep-set. Just now he is staring straight before him as if his vision were still fixed beyond life.*

Kneeling beside him with bowed heads are his wife, MIRIAM, *his sisters,* MARTHA *and* MARY, *and his* FATHER *and* MOTHER.

MIRIAM *is a slender, delicate woman of thirty-five, dressed in deep black, who holds one of his hands in both of hers, and keeps her lips pressed to it. The upper part of her face is covered by a mask which conceals her forehead, eyes and nose, but leaves her mouth revealed. The mask is the pure pallor of marble, the expression that of a statue of Woman, of her eternal acceptance of the compulsion of motherhood, the inevitable cycle of love into pain into joy and new love into separation and pain again and the loneliness of age. The eyes of the mask are almost closed. Their gaze turns within, oblivious to the life outside, as they dream down on the child forever in memory at her breast. The mouth of* MIRIAM *is sensitive and sad, tender with an eager, understanding smile of self-forgetful love, the lips still fresh and young. Her skin, in contrast to the mask, is sunburned and earth-colored like that of* LAZARUS. MARTHA, MARY *and the two parents all wear full masks which broadly reproduce their own characters.* MARTHA *is a buxom middle-aged housewife, plain and pleasant.* MARY *is young and pretty, nervous and high-strung. The* FATHER *is a small, thin, feeble old man of over eighty, meek and pious. The* MOTHER *is tall and stout, over sixty-five, a gentle, simple woman.*

All the masks of these Jews of the first two scenes of the play are pronouncedly Semitic.

A background of twilight sky. A dissolving touch of sunset still lingers on the horizon.

It is some time after the miracle and Jesus has gone away.

CHORUS OF OLD MEN: (*in a quavering rising and falling chant—their arms outstretched toward* LAZARUS)

> Jesus wept!
> Behold how he loved him!
> He that liveth,
> He that believeth,
> Shall never die!

CROWD: (*on either side of house, echo the chant*)

> He that believeth
> Shall never die!
> Lazarus, come forth!

FIRST GUEST: (*a Simple Boy—in a frightened whisper after a pause of dead silence*) That strange light seems to come from within him! (*With awe*) Think of it! For four days he lay in the tomb! (*Turns away with a shudder*).

SECOND GUEST: (*a Happy Youth—with reassuring conviction*) It is a holy light. It came from Jesus.

FIFTH GUEST: (*an Envious, Middle-Aged Man*) Maybe if the truth were known, our friend there never really died at all!

FOURTH GUEST: (*a Defiant Man, indignantly*) Do you doubt the miracle? I tell you I was here in this house when Lazarus died!

SEVENTH GUEST: (*an Aged, Sorrowful Man*) And I used to visit him every day. He knew himself his hour was near.

FOURTH GUEST: He wished for death! He said to me one day: "I have known my fill of life and the sorrow of living. Soon I shall know peace." And he smiled. It was the first time I had seen him smile in years.

THIRD GUEST: (*a Self-Tortured Man—gloomily*) Yes, of late years his life had been one long misfortune. One after another his children died—

SIXTH GUEST: (*a Mature Man with a cruel face—with a harsh laugh*) They were all girls. Lazarus had no luck.

SEVENTH GUEST: The last was a boy, the one that died at birth. You are forgetting him.

THIRD GUEST: Lazarus could never forget. Not only did his son die but Miriam could never bear him more children.

FIFTH GUEST: (*practically*) But he could not blame bad luck for everything. Take the loss of his father's wealth since he took over the management. That was his own doing. He was a bad farmer, a poor breeder of sheep, and a bargainer so easy to cheat it hurt one's conscience to trade with him!

SIXTH GUEST: (*with a sneer—maliciously*) You should know best about that! (*A suppressed laugh from those around him*).

FIRST GUEST: (*who has been gazing at* LAZARUS—*softly*) Ssssh! Look at his face! (*They all stare. A pause*).

SECOND GUEST: (*with wondering awe*) Do you remember him, neighbors, before he died? He used to be pale even when he worked in the fields. Now he seems as brown as one who has labored in the earth all day in a vineyard beneath the hot sun! (*A pause*).

FOURTH GUEST: The whole look of his face has changed. He is like a stranger from a far land. There is no longer any sorrow in his eyes. They must have forgotten sorrow in the grave.

FIFTH GUEST: (*grumblingly*) I thought we were invited here to eat—and all we do is stand and gape at him!

FOURTH GUEST: (*sternly*) Be silent! We are waiting for him to speak.

THIRD GUEST: (*impressively*) He did speak once. And he laughed!

ALL THE GUESTS: (*amazed and incredulous*) Laughed?

THIRD GUEST: (*importantly*) Laughed! I heard him! It was a moment after the miracle—

MIRIAM: (*her voice, rich with sorrow, exultant now*) Jesus cried, "Lazarus, come forth!" (*She kisses his hand. He makes a slight movement, a stirring in his vision. The* GUESTS *stare. A frightened pause*).

FIFTH GUEST: (*nudging the* SECOND—*uneasily*) Go on with your story!

THIRD GUEST: Just as he appeared in the opening of the tomb, wrapped in his shroud—

SECOND GUEST: (*excitedly—interrupting*) My heart stopped! I fell on my face! And all the women screamed! (*Sceptically*) You must have sharp ears to have heard him laugh in that uproar!

THIRD GUEST: I helped to pry away the stone so I was right beside him. I found myself kneeling, but between my fingers I watched Jesus and Lazarus. Jesus looked into his face for what seemed a long time and suddenly Lazarus said "Yes" as if he were answering a question in Jesus' eyes.

ALL THE GUEST: (*mystified*) Yes? What could he mean by yes?

THIRD GUEST: Then Jesus smiled sadly but with tenderness, as one who from a distance of years of sorrow remembers happiness. And then Lazarus knelt and kissed Jesus' feet and both of them smiled and Jesus blessed him and called him "My Brother" and went away; and Lazarus, looking after Him, began to laugh softly like a man in love with God! Such a laugh I never heard! It made my ears drunk! It was like wine! And though I was half-dead with fright I found myself laughing, too!

MIRIAM: (*with a beseeching summons*) Lazarus, come forth!

CHORUS: (*chanting*) Lazarus! Come forth!

CROWD: (*on either side of the house—echoing the chant*) Come forth! Come forth!

LAZARUS: (*suddenly in a deep voice—with a wonderful exultant acceptance in it*) Yes! (*The* GUESTS *in the room, the* CROWDS *outside all cry out in fear and joy and fall on their knees*).

CHORUS: (*chanting exultantly*)

The stone is taken away!
The spirit is loosed!
The soul let go!

LAZARUS: (*rising and looking around him at everyone and everything—with an all-embracing love—gently*) Yes! (*His family and the* GUESTS *in the room now throng about* LAZARUS *to embrace him. The* CROWDS *of men and women on each side push into the room to stare at him. He is in the arms of his* MOTHER *and* MIRIAM *while his* SISTERS *and* FATHER *kiss and press his hands. The five are half hysterical with relief and joy, sobbing and laughing*).

FATHER: My son is reborn to me!

CHORUS: Hosannah!

ALL: (*with a great shout*) Hosannah!

FATHER: Let us rejoice! Eat and drink! Draw up your chairs, friends! Music! Bring wine! (*Music begins in the room off right, rear—a festive dance tune. The company sit down in their places, the* FATHER *and* MOTHER *at* LAZARUS' *right and left,* MIRIAM *next to the* MOTHER, MARTHA *and* MARY *beside the* FATHER. *But* LAZARUS *remains standing. And the* CHORUS OF OLD MEN *remain in their formation at the rear. Wine is poured and all raise their goblets toward* LAZARUS—*then suddenly they stop, the music dies out, and an awed and frightened stillness prevails, for* LAZARUS *is a strange, majestic figure whose understanding smile seems terrible and enigmatic to them*).

FATHER: (*pathetically uneasy*) You frighten us, my son. You are strange—standing there— (*In the midst of a silence more awkward than before he rises to his feet, goblet in hand—forcing his voice, falteringly*) A toast, neighbors!

CHORUS: (*in a forced echo*) A toast!

ALL: (*echoing them*) A toast!

FATHER: To my son, Lazarus, whom a blessed miracle has brought back from death!

LAZARUS: (*suddenly laughing softly out of his vision, as if to himself, and*

*speaking with a strange unearthly calm in a voice that is like a loving
whisper of hope and confidence*) No! There is no death! (*A moment's
pause. The people remain with goblets uplifted, staring at him. Then all
repeat after him questioningly and frightenedly*).

ALL: There—is—no—death?

SIXTH GUEST: (*suddenly blurts out the question which is in the minds of all*)
What did you find beyond there, LAZARUS? (*A pause of silence*).

LAZARUS: (*smiles gently and speaks as if to a group of inquisitive children*) O
Curious Greedy Ones, is not one world in which you know not how
to live enough for you?

SIXTH GUEST: (*emboldened*) Why did you say yes, Lazarus?

FOURTH GUEST: Why did you laugh?

ALL THE GUESTS: (*with insistent curiosity but in low awed tones*) What is
beyond there, Lazarus?

CHORUS: (*in a low murmur*) What is beyond there? What is beyond?

CROWD: (*carrying the question falteringly back into silence*) What is beyond?

LAZARUS: (*suddenly again—now in a voice of loving exaltation*) There is
only life! I heard the heart of Jesus laughing in my heart; "There is
Eternal Life in No," it said, "and there is the same Eternal Life in
Yes! Death is the fear between!" And my heart reborn to love of life
cried "Yes!" and I laughed in the laughter of God! (*He begins to laugh,
softly at first—a laugh so full of a complete acceptance of life, a profound
assertion of joy in living, so devoid of all self-consciousness or fear, that it is
like a great bird song triumphant in depths of sky, proud and powerful,
infectious with love, casting on the listener an enthralling spell. The crowd
in the room are caught by it. Glancing sideways at one another, smiling
foolishly and self-consciously, at first they hesitate, plainly holding themselves
in for fear of what the next one will think*).

CHORUS: (*in a chanting murmur*)

Lazarus laughs!
Our hearts grow happy!

Laughter like music!
The wind laughs!
The sea laughs!
Spring laughs from the earth!
Summer laughs in the air!
Lazarus laughs!

LAZARUS: (*on a final note of compelling exultation*)

Laugh! Laugh with me! Death is dead! Fear is no more!
There is only life! There is only laughter!

CHORUS: (*chanting exultingly now*)

Laugh! Laugh!
Laugh with Lazarus!
Fear is no more!
There is no death!

(*They laugh in a rhythmic cadence dominated by the laughter of* LAZARUS).

CROWD: (*who, gradually, joining in by groups or one by one—including* LAZ-
ARUS' *family with the exception of* MIRIAM, *who does not laugh but watches
and listens to his laughter with a tender smile of being happy in his happiness—have now all begun to laugh in rhythm with the* CHORUS—*in a
great, full-throated pæan as the laughter of* LAZARUS *rises higher and
higher*)

Laugh! Laugh!
Fear is no more!
There is no death!

CHORUS:

Laugh! Laugh!
There is only life!
There is only laughter!
Fear is no more!
Death is dead!

CROWD: (*in a rhythmic echo*)

> Laugh! Laugh!
> Death is dead!
> There is only laughter!

(*The room rocks, the air outside throbs with the rhythmic beat of their liberated laughter—still a bit uncertain of its freedom, harsh, discordant, frenzied, desperate and drunken, but dominated and inspired by the high, free, aspiring, exulting laughter of* LAZARUS).

CURTAIN

SCENE TWO

SCENE: *Some months later. Exterior of* LAZARUS' *home in Bethany, now known as the House of Laughter. It is a clear, bright night, the sky sparkling with stars. At the extreme front is a road. Between this and the house is a small raised terrace. The house is low, of one story only, its walls white. Four windows are visible with a closed door in the middle of the wall. Steps lead up to this door, and to the left of door a flight of stairs goes up to the balustrated roof. The windows shine brilliantly with the flickering light of many candles which gives them a throbbing star-like effect. From within comes the sound of flutes and dance music. The dancers can be seen whirling swiftly by the windows. There is continually an overtone of singing laughter emphasizing the pulsing rhythm of the dance. On the road in the foreground, at left and right, two separate groups of Jews are gathered. They are not divided according to sex as in the previous scene. Each is composed about equally of men and women, forty-nine in each, masked and costumed as before. It is religious belief that now divides them. The adherents of Jesus, the Nazarenes, among whom may be noted* MARTHA *and* MARY, *are on the left; the Orthodox, among whom are*

LAZARUS' FATHER *and* MOTHER *and a* PRIEST, *are at right. Between the two hostile groups is the same* CHORUS OF OLD MEN, *in a formation like a spearhead, whose point is placed at the foot of the steps leading to the terrace. All these people are staring fascinatedly at the house, listening entranced, their feet moving, their bodies swaying to the music's beat, stiffly, constrainedly, compelled against their wills. Then the music suddenly stops and the chant of youthful voices is heard:*

FOLLOWERS OF LAZARUS: (*from within the house*)

> Laugh! Laugh!
> There is only life!
> There is only laughter.

CHORUS OF OLD MEN: (*as if they were subjects moved by hypnotic suggestion—miserably and discordantly*)

> Ha-ha-ha-ha!
> There is only laughter!
> Ha-ha—

CROWD: (*in the same manner*) Ha-ha—

MARY: Ha—(*Then frantically—half-weeping with indignant rage—to the* Nazarenes) Stop! Oh, how can we laugh! We are betraying Jesus! My brother Lazarus has become a devil!

THE ORTHODOX PRIEST: (*his mask is that of a religious fanatic. He is sixty or so*) Ha—ha— (*Tearing his beard and stamping with rage*). Stop it, you fools! It is a foul sin in the sight of Jehovah! Why do you come here every night to listen and watch their abominations? The Lord God will punish you!

MARY: (*echoing him—to her people*) Jesus will never forgive you!

THE PRIEST: (*angrily*) Jesus? (*He turns to look at the Nazarenes disdainfully and spits on the ground insultingly. The members of the two groups begin to glare at each other. The* CHORUS *falls back, three on each side, leaving one neutral figure before the steps. The* PRIEST *goes on tauntingly*) Did you hear her, friends? These renegade Nazarenes will soon deny they are Jews at all! They will begin to worship in filthy idolatry the sun and stars and man's body—as Lazarus in there, (*points to the house*) the disciple of their Jesus, has so well set them the example! (*This is followed by an outburst of insulting shouts of accusation and denial from both sides*).

A NAZARENE: (*the* FOURTH GUEST *of Scene One*) You lie! Lazarus is no disciple! He is a traitor to Jesus! We scorn him!

PRIEST: (*sneeringly*) But your pretended Messiah did not scorn him. According to your stupid lies, he raised him from the dead! And answer me, has your Jesus ever denied Lazarus, or denounced his laughter? No! No doubt he is laughing, too, at all you credulous fools—for if Lazarus is not his disciple, in the matter of the false miracle he was his accomplice! (*This provokes a furious protest from the Nazarenes and insulting hoots and jeers from the Orthodox, penetrated by a piercing scream from* LAZARUS' MOTHER, *who, crushed in the crowd, sinks fainting to the ground. The* FATHER *bends over her. The group of the Orthodox falls back from them. With frightened cries* MARTHA *and* MARY *run from the group of Nazarenes and kneel beside her*).

FATHER: (*pitifully*) Rachel! Darling! Speak to me!

MARTHA: (*practically*) She has only fainted.

MARY: She is opening her eyes! Mother, dear!

MOTHER: (*weakly*) Did I fall? (*Recognizing* MARTHA *and* MARY) Martha—and Mary—my dear ones! (*They embrace her, weeping*) I have not kissed you since you left home to follow that Jesus—Oh, if we were only at home again—and if, also, my poor boy, Lazarus— (*She sobs*).

FATHER: (*gruffly*) You must not speak of him!

MARTHA: Do not worry your head about Lazarus. He is not worth it!

MARY: (*with surprising vindictiveness*) He is accursed! He has betrayed our Lord!

PRIEST: (*to those around him—mockingly*) Do you hear? They already call the Nazarene "Lord!" A Lord who is in the common prison at Jerusalem, I heard today! A fine Lord whom our High Priests have had arrested like a thief!

MARY: (*with fanatic fervor*) He is a king! Whenever He chooses He will gather a great army and He will seize His kingdom and all who deny Him shall be crucified!

PRIEST: (*tauntingly*) Now their jail-bird is a king, no less! Soon they will make him a god, as the Romans do their Caesars!

MARY: (*her eyes flashing*) He is the Messiah!

PRIEST: (*furiously*) The Messiah! May Jehovah smite you in your lies! Step back among your kind! You defile us! (As *she stands defiantly he appeals to the* FATHER) Have you no authority? She called him the Messiah—that common beggar, that tramp! Curse her!

FATHER: (*confused, pitifully harried, collecting his forces*) Wait! Go back, Mary! You chose to follow that impostor—

MARY: (*defiantly*) The Messiah!

MARTHA: (*trying to calm her*) Ssssh! Remember he is our father!

MARY: (*fanatically*) I deny him! I deny all who deny Jesus!

MOTHER: (*tearfully*) And me, darling?

MARY: You must come to us, Mother! You must believe in Jesus and leave all to follow Him!

FATHER: (*enraged*) So! You want to steal your mother away, to leave me lonely in my old age! You are an unnatural daughter! I disown you! Go, before I curse—

MOTHER: (*beseechingly*) Father!

MARTHA: (*pulling* MARY *away*) Mary! Jesus teaches to be kind.

MARY: (*hysterically*) He teaches to give up all and follow Him! I want to give Him everything! I want my father to curse me!

FATHER: (*frenziedly*) Then I do curse you! No—not you—but the devil in you! And the devil in Martha! And the great mocking devil that dwells in Lazarus and laughs from his mouth! I curse these devils and that Prince of Devils, that false prophet, Jesus! It is he who has brought division to my home and many homes that were happy before. I curse him! I curse the day he called my good son, Lazarus, from the grave to walk again with a devil inside him! It was not my son who came back but a devil! My son is dead! And you, my daughters, are dead! I am the father only of devils! (*His voice has risen to a wailing lament*) My children are dead!

LAZARUS: (*his voice rings from within the house in exultant denial*) Death is dead! There is only laughter! (*He laughs. The voices of all his* FOLLOWERS *echo his laughter. They pour in a laughing rout from the doorway onto the terrace. At the same moment the* CHORUS OF FOLLOWERS *appears on the roof and forms along the balustrade, facing front. These* FOLLOWERS OF LAZARUS, *forty-nine in number, composed about equally of both sexes, wear a mask that, while recognizably Jewish, is a* LAZARUS *mask, resembling him in its expression of fearless faith in life, the mouth shaped by laughter. The* CHORUS OF FOLLOWERS, *seven in number, all men, have identical masks of double size, as before. The Period of all these masks is anywhere between Youth and Manhood (or Womanhood). The music continues to come from within. Laughing, the* FOLLOWERS *dance to it in weaving patterns on the terrace. They are dressed in bright-colored diaphanous robes. Their chorused laughter, now high and clear, now dying to a humming murmur, stresses the rhythmic flow of the dance*).

CHORUS OF FOLLOWERS:

> Laugh! Laugh!
> There is no death!
> There is only laughter!

FOLLOWERS:

> There is only laughter!
> Death is dead!
> Laugh! Laugh!

CROWD: (*the two groups of Nazarenes and Orthodox, on the appearance of the* FOLLOWERS, *immediately forget their differences and form into one mob, led by their* CHORUS OF OLD MEN, *whose jeering howls they echo as one voice*) Yaah! Yaah! Yaah! (*But they cannot keep it up. The music and laughter rise above their hooting. They fall into silence. Then they again begin to feel impelled by the rhythm and laughter, their feet move, their bodies sway. Their lips quiver, their mouths open as if to laugh. Their* CHORUS OF OLD MEN *are the first to be affected. It is as if this reaction were transmitted through the* CHORUS *to the* CROWD).

PRIEST: (*his mouth twitching—fighting against the compulsion in him—stammers*) Brothers—listen—we must unite—in one cause—to—stamp out—this abomination! (*It is as if he can no longer control his speech. He presses his hand over his mouth convulsively*).

AN AGED ORTHODOX JEW: (*the* SEVENTH GUEST *of Scene One—starts to harangue the crowd. He fights the spell but cannot control his jerking body nor his ghastly, spasmodic laughter*) Neighbors! Our young people are corrupted! They are leaving our farms—to dance and sing! To laugh! Ha—! Laugh at everything! Ha-ha—! (*He struggles desperately to control himself*).

CHORUS OF OLD MEN: (*A barking laugh forced from them*) Ha-ha—!

CROWD: (*echoing this*) Ha-ha—!

THE AGED JEW: They have no respect for life! When I said in kindness, "You must go back to work," they laughed at me! Ha—! "We desire joy. We go to Lazarus," they said—and left my fields! I begged them to stay—with tears in my eyes! I even offered them more money! They laughed! "What is money? Can the heart eat gold?" They laughed at money! Ha-ha—! (*He chokes with exasperated rage*).

CHORUS OF OLD MEN: (*echoing him*) Ha-ha—!

CROWD: (*echoing the* CHORUS) Ha-ha—!

AGED JEW: (*shaking his fist at* LAZARUS' FOLLOWERS) That loafer taught them that! They come to him and work for nothing! For nothing! And they are glad, these undutiful ones! While they sow, they dance! They sing to the earth when they are plowing! They tend his flocks and laugh toward the sun! Ha-ha-ha—! (*He struggles again*).

CHORUS OF OLD MEN: (*as before*) Ha-ha-ha—

CROWD: (*as before*) Ha-ha-ha—

AGED JEW: How can we compete with labor for laughter! We will have no harvest. There will be no food! Our children will starve! Our race will perish! And he will laugh! Ha-ha-ha-ha! (*He howls with furious, uncontained laughter*).

CHORUS OF OLD MEN: (*echoing his tone*)

> Our children will starve!
> Our race will perish!
> Lazarus laughs!
> Ha-ha-ha-ha! Ha-ha-ha-ha!

CROWD: (*as before*) Ha-ha-ha-ha! Ha-ha-ha-ha! (*Their former distinctions of Nazarenes and Orthodox are now entirely forgotten. The members of* LAZARUS' *family are grouped in the center as if nothing had ever happened to separate them. The* CHORUS OF OLD MEN *is again joined in its spearhead formation at the stairs. Apparent first in this* CHORUS, *a queer excitement begins to pervade this mob. They begin to weave in and out, clasping each other's hands now and then, moving mechanically in jerky steps to the music in a grotesque sort of marionettes' country dance. At first this is slow but it momentarily becomes more hectic and peculiar. They raise clenched fists or hands distended into threatening talons. Their voices sound thick and harsh and animal-like with anger as they mutter and growl, each one aloud to himself or herself*).

CHORUS OF OLD MEN: (*threateningly, gradually rising to hatred*)

> Hear them laugh!
> See them dance!
> Shameless! Wanton!
> Dirty! Evil!
> Infamous! Bestial!
> Madness! Blood!
> Adultery! Murder!
> We burn!
> We kill!

We crucify!
Death! Death!
Beware, Lazarus!

(*This last in a wild frenzy*).
CROWD: (*frenziedly*)

Beware, Lazarus!
We burn! We kill!
We crucify!
Death! Death!

(*They crowd toward the gateway, their arms stretched out as if demanding* LAZARUS *for a sacrificial victim. Meanwhile they never cease to hop up and down, to mill around, to twist their bodies toward and away from each other in bestial parody of the dance of the* FOLLOWERS. *The tall figure of* LAZARUS, *dressed in a white robe, suddenly appears on the roof of the house. He stands at the balustrade in the middle of the* CHORUS. *Beside him, a little behind,* MIRIAM *appears dressed in black, her face upturned, her lips praying. She appears to have grown older, to be forty now.* LAZARUS' *body is softly illumined by its inner light. The change in him is marked. He seems ten years younger, at the prime of forty. His body has become less angular and stiff. His movements are graceful and pliant. The change is even more noticeable in his face, which has filled out, become purer in outline, more distinctly Grecian. His complexion is the red-brown of rich earth, the gray in his black, curly beard has almost disappeared. He makes a sign and the music ceases. His* FOLLOWERS *remain fixed in their dancing attitudes like figures in a frieze. Each member of the mob remains frozen in a distorted posture. He stares down at the mob pityingly, his face calm*).
LAZARUS: (*speaks amid a profound silence. His voice releases his own dancers and the mob from their fixed attitudes. The music begins to play again within the house, very soft and barely audible, swelling up and down like the sound of an organ from a distant church*) You laugh, but your

laughter is guilty! It laughs a hyena laughter, spotted, howling its hungry fear of life! That day I returned did I not tell you your fear was no more, that there is no death? You believed then—for a moment! You laughed—discordantly, hoarsely, but with a groping toward joy. What! Have you so soon forgotten, that now your laughter curses life again as of old? (*He pauses—then sadly*) That is your tragedy! You forget! You forget the God in you! You wish to forget! Remembrance would imply the high duty to live as a son of God—generously!—with love!—with pride!—with laughter! This is too glorious a victory for you, too terrible a loneliness! Easier to forget, to become only a man, the son of a woman, to hide from life against her breast, to whimper your fear to her resigned heart and be comforted by her resignation! To live by denying life! (*Then exhortingly*) Why are your eyes always either fixed on the ground in weariness of thought, or watching one another with suspicion? Throw your gaze upward! To Eternal Life! To the fearless and deathless! The everlasting! To the stars! (*He stretches out his arms to the sky—then suddenly points*) See! A new star has appeared! It is the one that shone over Bethlehem! (*His voice becomes a little bitter and mocking*) The Master of Peace and Love has departed this earth. Let all stars be for you henceforth symbols of Saviors—Sons of God who appeared on worlds like ours to tell the saving truth to ears like yours, inexorably deaf! (*Then exaltedly*) But the greatness of Saviors is that they may not save! The greatness of Man is that no god can save him—until he becomes a god! (*He stares up at the stars, rapt in contemplation, oblivious to all around him now. Rapidly approaching from the left a man's voice jarring in high-pitched cruel laughter is heard. They all listen, huddled together like sheep*).

MESSENGER: (*the* THIRD GUEST *of Scene One rushes in breathlessly, shouting*) The Nazarene has been crucified!

PRIEST: (*with fierce triumph*) Jehovah is avenged! Hosannah!

ORTHODOX: Hosannah! The false prophet is dead! The pretended Mes-

siah is dead! (*They jump and dance, embracing one another. The* NAZA-
RENES *stand paralyzed and stunned. The two groups mechanically separate
to right and left again, the* CHORUS OF OLD MEN *dividing itself as before*).

MARY: (*in a frenzy of grief*) Do not believe him! Jesus could not die!
(*But at this moment a Nazarene youth, exhausted by grief and tears,
staggers in from the left*).

MESSENGER: (SECOND GUEST *of Scene One*) Jesus is dead! Our Lord is
murdered! (*He sinks on his knees sobbing. All the* NAZARENES *do likewise,
wailing, rending their garments, tearing their hair, some even beating
their heads on the ground in the agony of their despair*).

MARY: (*insane with rage now*) They have murdered Him! (*To her followers—savagely*) An eye for an eye! Avenge the Master! (*Their frenzy of
grief turned into rage, the* NAZARENES *leap to their feet threateningly.
Concealed swords and knives are brought out by both sides*).

MIRIAM: (*leaning over the balustrade—in a voice of entreaty*) Mary! Brothers! (*But none heed her or seem to see her.* LAZARUS *and his* FOLLOWERS
*remain oblivious to men, arms upstretched toward the stars, their heads
thrown back*).

MARY: (*wildly*) Vengeance! Death to His murderers!

PRIEST: (*fiercely to his followers*) Death to the Nazarenes! (*With cries of
rage the two groups rush on one another. There is a confused tumult of
yells, groans, curses, the shrieks of women, the sounds of blows as they meet
in a pushing, whirling, struggling mass in which individual figures are
indistinguishable. Knives and swords flash above the heads of the mass,
hands in every tense attitude of striking, clutching, tearing are seen
upraised. As the fight is at its height a* ROMAN CENTURION *and a squad of
eight* SOLDIERS *come tramping up at the double-quick. They all are masked.
These Roman masks now and henceforth in the play are carried out according to the same formula of Seven Periods, Seven Types, as those of the Jews
seen previously, except that the basis of each face is Roman—heavy, domineering, self-complacent, the face of a confident dominant race. The* CEN-
TURION *differs from his soldiers only in being more individualized. He is*

middle-aged, his soldiers belong to the Period of Manhood. All are of the Simple, Ignorant Type).

CENTURION: *(shouts commandingly)* Disperse! *(But no one hears him—with angry disgust to his* SOLDIERS*)* Charge! Cut them down! *(The* SOLDIERS *form a wedge and charge with a shout. They soon find it necessary to use their swords, and strike down everyone in their way).*

MIRIAM: Mercy, Romans! *(As they pay no attention to her, in desperation she embraces* LAZARUS *beseechingly, forcing his attention back to earth)* Lazarus! Mercy!

LAZARUS: *(looks down upon the struggling mass and cries in a ringing voice)* Hold! *(Each person stands transfixed, frozen in the last movement, even the Roman soldiers and the* CENTURION *himself. Ten dead and mortally wounded lie on the ground, trampled by the feet of friend and foe alike.* LAZARUS *looks at the* CROWD. *To each he seems to look at him or her alone. His eyes are accusing and stern. As one head, the heads of all are averted. Even the* CENTURION *stares at the ground humbly, in spite of himself. Finally* LAZARUS *speaks in a voice of infinite disdain)* Sometimes it is hard to laugh—even *at* men! *(He turns his eyes from them, staring straight before him. This seems to release them from their fixed positions. The* NAZARENES *and the* ORTHODOX *separate and slink guiltily apart. The* CHORUS OF OLD MEN *forms again, the apex at the center of the steps as before. A low wail of lamentation arises from them. The two crowds of Nazarenes and Orthodox echo this).*

CHORUS OF OLD MEN: *(in a wailing chant)*

> Woe unto Israel!
> Woe unto thee, Jerusalem!
> O divided house,
> Thou shalt crumble to dust,
> And swine shall root
> Where thy Temple stood!
> Woe unto us!

CROWD: (*in a great echoing cry*) Woe unto us!

CENTURION: (*gruffly to hide his embarrassment at being awed by* LAZARUS) Here, you! Drag your carcasses away! (*From each side men and women come forward to identify and mourn their dead. The wail of lamentation rises and falls. The* CENTURION *looks up at* LAZARUS—*harshly*) You, there! Are you he whom they call the Laugher?

LAZARUS: (*without looking at him—his voice seeming to come from some dream within him*) I am Lazarus.

CENTURION: Who was brought back from death by enchantment?

LAZARUS: (*looking down at him now—with a smile, simply*) No. There is no death!

CHORUS OF FOLLOWERS: (*chanting joyously*)

There is no death!

FOLLOWERS: (*echoing*)

There is no death!

AN ORTHODOX MAN: (*bending beside the body of* LAZARUS' FATHER) Here is your father, Lazarus. He is dead.

AN ORTHODOX WOMAN: This is your mother, Lazarus. She is dead.

A NAZARENE: Here is your sister, Martha, Lazarus. She is dead.

A NAZARENE WOMAN: And this is Mary, Lazarus. She is dead.

MIRIAM: (*suddenly—with deep grief*) And Jesus who was the Son of Man, who loved you and gave you life again has died, Lazarus—has died!

LAZARUS: (*in a great triumphant voice*) Yes! Yes!! Yes!!! Men die! Even a Son of Man must die to show men that Man may live! But there is no death!

CENTURION: (*at first in a tone of great awe—to his* SOLDIERS) Is he a god? (*Then gruffly, ashamed of his question*) Come down, Jew! I have orders to bring you to Rome to Cæsar!

LAZARUS: (*as if he were answering not the* CENTURION *but the command of his fate from the sky*) Yes! (*He walks down the narrow stairs and,* MIRIAM *following him, comes down the path to the road. He goes and kneels for a moment each beside the bodies of his* FATHER, MOTHER, *and* SISTERS *and kisses each in turn on the forehead. For a moment the struggle with his grief can be seen in his face. Then he looks up to the stars and, as if answering a question, again says simply and acceptingly*) Yes! (*Then exultantly*) Yes!! (*And begins to laugh from the depths of his exalted spirit. The laughter of his* CHORUS *and then of his* FOLLOWERS *echoes his. The music and dancing begin again. The* CENTURION *grins sheepishly. The* SOLDIERS *chuckle. The* CENTURION *laughs awkwardly. The* SOLDIERS *laugh. The music from the house and the laughter of the* FOLLOWERS *grow louder. The infection spreads to the* CHROUS OF OLD MEN *whose swaying grief falls into the rhythm of the laughter and music as does that of the mourners*).

LAZARUS' FOLLOWERS: (*led by their* CHORUS)

    Laugh! Laugh!

CHORUS OF OLD MEN: (*torn by the conflict—torturedly*)

    Ha-ha-ha—
    Woe to us, woe!

CROWD: (*beside the bodies*)

    Woe to us, woe!
    Ha-ha—!

CENTURION: (*laughingly*) You are brave, you Laugher! Remember Tiberius never laughs! And boast not to Cæsar there is no death, or he will invent a new one for you!

LAZARUS: (*with a smile*) But all death is men's invention! So laugh! (*He laughs and the* CENTURION *and* SOLDIERS *laugh with him, half dancing clumsily now to the beat of the music*).

CHORUS OF LAZARUS' FOLLOWERS:

    Laugh! Laugh!
    Fear is no more!
    There is no death!

There is only life!
There is only laughter!

FOLLOWERS: (*dancing*)

Laugh! Laugh!
Fear is no more!
Death is dead!

CHORUS OF OLD MEN: (*forgetting their grief—their eyes on* LAZARUS *now, their arms outstretched to him as are those of the crowd grouped around the bodies but forgetting them*)

Death is no more!
Death is dead!
Laugh!

CROWD:

Laugh! Laugh!
Death is no more!

CENTURION: (*laughing, to his laughing* SOLDIERS) Forward! (*They tramp, dancing, off.* LAZARUS *and* MIRIAM *start to follow*).

MIRIAM: (*suddenly pointing to his* FOLLOWERS *who are dancing and laughing obliviously—pityingly*) But your faithful ones who love you, Lazarus?

LAZARUS: (*simply, with a trace of a sad sternness*) This is their test. Their love must remember—or it must forget. Come! (*With a last gesture back like a blessing on all he is leaving, he goes. The laughter of the* SOLDIERS *recedes. That of the* CHORUS OF OLD MEN *and of the* CROWD *falters and breaks into lamenting grief again, guilt-stricken because of its laughter*).

CHORUS OF OLD MEN:

Laugh! Laugh!
Death is dead!

Laugh!—But woe!
There lie our dead!
Oh, shame and guilt!
We forget our dead!

CROWD: (*with fierce remorseful grief*)

Woe to us, woe!
There lie our dead!

CHORUS OF LAZARUS' FOLLOWERS: (*their voices and the music growing more
and more hesitating and faint*)

Laugh! Laugh!
There is only life!
There is only—
Laugh—

(*Their dance is faltering and slow now*)

Fear is no—
Death is—
Laugh—

(*The music and dancing and voices cease. The lights in the windows, which
have been growing dim, go out. There is a second of complete, death-like
silence. The mourning folk in the foreground are frozen figures of grief.
Then a sudden swelling chorus of forlorn bewilderment, a cry of lost children
comes from the* CHORUS OF FOLLOWERS *and the* FOLLOWERS *themselves.
They huddle into groups on the roof and on the terrace. They stretch their
arms out in every direction supplicatingly*).

CHORUS OF FOLLOWERS:

Oh, Lazarus, laugh!
Do not forsake us!
We forget!

Where is thy love fled?
Give back thy laughter,
Thy fearless laughter!
We forget!

FOLLOWERS:

Give back thy laughter!
We forget!

CHORUS OF FOLLOWERS: (*with dull, resigned terror now*)

Death slinks out
Of his grave in the heart!
Ghosts of fear
Creep back in the brain!
We remember fear!
We remember death!

FOLLOWERS:

Death in the heart!
Fear in the brain!
We remember fear!
We remember death!

CHORUS OF FOLLOWERS: (*wailing hopelessly now*)

Forgotten is laughter!
We remember
Only death!
Fear is God!
Forgotten is laughter!
Life is death!

FOLLOWERS:

> Forgotten is laughter!
> Life is death!

ALL: (*the* CHORUS OF OLD MEN *and the* CROWD *joining in*)

> Life is a fearing,
> A long dying,
> From birth to death!
> God is a slayer!
> Life is death!

CURTAIN

SCENE: *Some months later. A square in Athens about ten o'clock at night. In the rear, pure and beautiful in the light of a full moon, is the façade of a temple. An excited crowd of Greeks of both sexes is gathered in the square as if for some public festival. They are masked according to the scheme of Seven Periods in Seven Types of Character for each sex. Here, of course, the foundation of the mask is the Grecian type of face.*

On the left, the CHORUS OF GREEKS *is grouped, seven in number, facing front, in the spearhead formation. As before the* CHORUS *wears masks double the life size of the* CROWD *masks. They are all of the Proud Self-Reliant type, in the period of Young Manhood.*

These seven are clad in goat skins, their tanned bodies and masks daubed and stained with wine lees, in imitation of the old followers of Dionysus. Rumor has led them to hope and believe that LAZARUS *may be the reincarnation of this deity.*

The people in the crowd are holding themselves in restraint with difficulty, they stir and push about restlessly with an eager curiosity and impatience. All eyes are fixed off left. A buzz of voices hums in the air.

Acting as police, a number of Roman legionaires (masked like the soldiers of Scene Two) armed with staves, keep back the crowd from the line of the street that runs from left to right, front. They resent this duty, which has already kept them there a long time, and are surly and quick-tempered with the Greeks.

At front, pacing impatiently up and down, is a young Roman noble of twenty-one, clad richly, wearing beautifully wrought armor and helmet. This is GAIUS, *the heir of Tiberius Cæsar, nicknamed* CALIGULA *by the soldiers in whose encampments he was born and where he spent his childhood. His body is bony and angular, almost malformed, with wide, powerful shoulders and long arms and hands, and short, skinny, hairy legs like an ape's. He wears a half-mask of crimson, dark with a purplish tinge, that covers the upper part of his face to below the nose. This mask accentuates his bulging, prematurely wrinkled forehead, his hollow temples and his bulbous, sensual nose. His large troubled eyes, of a glazed greenish-blue, glare out with a shifty feverish suspicion at everyone. Below his mask his own skin is of an anæmic transparent pallor. Above it, his hair is the curly blond hair of a child of six or seven. His mouth also is childish, the red lips soft and feminine in outline. Their expression is spoiled, petulant and self-obsessed, weak but domineering. In combination with the rest of the face there is an appalling morbid significance to his mouth. One feels that its boyish cruelty, encouraged as a manly attribute in the coarse brutality of camps, has long ago become naïvely insensitive to any human suffering but its own.*

Walking with CALIGULA *is* CNEIUS CRASSUS, *a Roman general—a squat, muscular man of sixty, his mask that of a heavy battered face full of coarse humor.*

CHORUS OF GREEKS: (*intoning solemnly*)

> Soon the God comes!
> Redeemer and Savior!
> Dionysus, Son of Man and a God!

GREEK CROWD: (*echoing*)

> Soon the God comes
> Redeemer and Savior!
> Dionysus!

FIRST GREEK: They say an unearthly flame burns in this Lazarus!

SECOND GREEK: The sacred fire! He must be the Fire-born, the son of Zeus!

THIRD GREEK: Many who have seen him swear he is Dionysus, rearisen from Hades!

FOURTH GREEK: (*importantly*) I saw Lazarus at Antioch where the galley on which they were taking him to Rome had been thrice blown back by a storm. Fear of this warning omen is why they now march with him by land.

FIRST GREEK: Does he truly resemble a god?

FOURTH GREEK: (*impressively*) One look in his eyes while his laughter sings in your ears and you forget sorrow! You dance! You laugh! It is as if a heavy weight you had been carrying all your life without knowing it suddenly were lifted. You are like a cloud, you can fly, your mind reels with laughter, you are drunk with joy! (*Solemnly*) Take my word for it, he is indeed a god. Everywhere the people have acclaimed him. He heals the sick, he raises the dead, by laughter.

SEVENTH GREEK: But I have heard that when he has gone people cannot remember his laughter, that the dead are dead again and the sick die, and the sad grow more sorrowful.

FIFTH GREEK: Well, we shall soon see with our own eyes. But why should the God return in the body of a Jew?

SIXTH GREEK: What better disguise if he wishes to remain unknown? The fools of Romans will never suspect him!

THIRD GREEK: (*laughing*) Never! They are beginning to claim he is a Roman!

FIFTH GREEK: So much the better! He will be in their confidence!

FOURTH GREEK: He will lead us against Rome! He will laugh our tyrants into the sea! Ha! (*He turns toward the Romans and laughs sneeringly. This is taken up by the* CROWD—*unpleasant, resentful laughter. They push forward aggressively and almost sweep the soldiers from their feet*).

CRASSUS: (*angrily*) Drive them back!

CALIGULA: (*suddenly with a distorted warped smile*) Order them to use their swords, Cneius. Let the scum look at their dead and learn respect for us!

SOLDIERS: (*shoving and whacking*) Back! Step back! Back there! (*The crowd push back to their former line. There are muttered curses, groans, protests, which subside into the former hum of expectancy*).

CALIGULA: (*with the same smile*) The sword, my old hyena! Corpses are so educational!

CRASSUS: (*surlily*) I would like to, I promise you! When I see how they hate us—!

CALIGULA: (*carelessly*) Let them hate—so long as they fear us! We must keep death dangling (*He makes the gesture of doing so*) before their eyes! (*He gives a soft, cruel laugh*) Will you not sacrifice in my honor? What are a few Greeks? (*Queerly*) I like to watch men die.

CRASSUS: I dare not, Caligula. Cæsar has forbidden bloodshed.

CALIGULA: Tiberius is a miser. He wants to hoard all of death for his own pleasure! (*He laughs again*).

CRASSUS: (*with rough familiarity*) I wager no one will make that complaint against you when you are Cæsar! (*He chuckles*).

CALIGULA: (*with the sudden grandiose posturing of a bad actor unintentionally burlesquing grandeur*) When I, Gaius Caligula, am Cæsar, I— (Then superstitiously looking up at the sky with cringing foreboding) But it brings bad luck to anticipate fate. (*He takes off his helmet and spits in it—then with a grim smile*) The heirs of a Cæsar take sick so mysteriously! Even with you who used to ride me on your knee, I do not eat nor drink until you have tasted first.

CRASSUS: (*nodding approvingly*) You are sensible. I suppose I, too, have my price—if they were only clever enough to discover it! (*He laughs hoarsely*).

CALIGULA: (*steps back from him with an uneasy shudder*) You are honest, at least—too honest, Cneius! (*Grimly*) If my father Germanicus had had you for his counselor, he might have escaped their poison. (*Then gloomily*) I must fear everyone. The world is my enemy.

CRASSUS: Kill it then! (*He laughs again*).

CHORUS: (*stretching out their arms in the direction from which* LAZARUS *is expected—supplicatingly*)

> Son of the Lightning!
> Deadly thy vengeance!
> Swift thy deliverance!
> Beholding thy Mother,

Greece, our Mother,
Her beauty in bondage,
Her pride in chains!
Hasten, Redeemer!

CROWD: (*as before—echoing the chant*)

Hasten, Redeemer!
Son of the Lightning!
Deadly thy vengeance!
Swift thy deliverance!

CALIGULA: (*disdainfully*) What clods! Mob is the same everywhere, eager to worship any new charlatan! They have already convinced themselves this Lazarus is a reincarnation of Dionysus! A Jew become a god! By the breasts of Venus that *is* a miracle! (*He laughs*).

CRASSUS: (*seriously*) But he must be expert in magic. He was buried four days and came out unharmed. Maybe he is not a Jew. Some say his father was really a legionary of our garrison in Judea. And he teaches people to laugh at death. That smacks of Roman blood!

CALIGULA: (*ironically*) Better still! He tells them there is no death at all! Hence the multitude of fools who have acclaimed him everywhere since he left his own country—and why Tiberius has begun to fear his influence.

CRASSUS: (*sententiously*) Whom Cæsar fears—disappears!

CALIGULA: Yes, the dupes who follow Lazarus will be killed. But Tiberius believes this Lazarus may know a cure for death or for renewing youth, and the old lecher hopes he can worm the secret out of him—before he kills him. (*He laughs ironically, then disgustedly*) That is why I must escort this Jew to Rome—as a special honor! (*With fierce, haughty resentment*) I, the heir of Cæsar! (*Savagely*) Oh, if I were Cæsar—!

CRASSUS: (*with a coarse, meaning smirk*) Patience. Tiberius is old.

CALIGULA: (*suddenly becoming terribly uneasy at some thought*) Cneius!

What if this Lazarus has really discovered a cure for old age and should reveal it to Tiberius! (*His lips tremble, his eyes are terrified, he shrinks against* CRASSUS *for protection—with boyish pleading*) Oh, Cneius, what could I do then?

CRASSUS: (*matter-of-factly*) Kill him before Cæsar can talk to him.

CALIGULA: (*almost in tears*) But if he knows a charm against death how could he be slain, old fool?

CRASSUS: (*gruffly*) Bah! (*Then with grim humor*) Death in bed I suspect, but when men are killed I know they stay dead! (*Disgustedly*) A moment ago you were laughing at him! (*Scornfully*) Do you fear him now?

CALIGULA: (*rather shamefacedly pulls himself together—then broodingly*) I fear everyone who lives. Even you. As you advised me. (*He turns away*).

CRASSUS: (*contemptuously*) Well, maybe he can teach you to laugh at fear. You would welcome him then, eh, cry baby?

CALIGULA: (*with sudden passionate intensity but only half aloud as if to himself*) I would love him, Cneius! As a father! As a god! (*He stands staring before him strangely. There is a new stir from the crowd who again push forward*).

CRASSUS: (*pointing off right*) Look! I see a great crowd! Your Lazarus must be coming at last!

CHORUS: (*chanting in a deep, rhythmic monotone like the rising and falling cadences of waters on a beach*)

> He comes, the Redeemer and Savior!
> Laughing along the mountains!
> To give back our lost laughter
> To raise from the dead our freedom
> To free us from Rome!

CROWD: (*echoing this chant*)

> Fire-born! Redeemer! Savior!
> Raise from the dead our freedom!

Give back our lost laughter!
Free us from Rome!

(*They have been pushing forward, more and more fiercely and defiantly. The* ROMAN SOLDIERS *in spite of their efforts are pushed backward step by step*).

SOLDIERS: (*angrily*) Back! Back! (*The* SOLDIERS *work with a will, dealing out blows with their staves at everyone in reach. But now these blows seem only to infuriate the* CROWD *which steadily pushes them back into the street. At the same time the distant sound of exultant music, singing and laughter becomes steadily louder. Both* SOLDIERS *and* CROWD *are inspired to battle by these strains without their knowing it.* CALIGULA *is listening spell-bound, his mouth open, his body swaying and twitching. Even* CRASSUS *stares off at the oncomers, forgetful of the growing plight of his* SOLDIERS).

CROWD: (*led by their* CHORUS—*angrily*)

Cowards! Pigs!
Strike! Hit!
Stones! Knives!
Stab! Kill!
Death to the Romans!
Death!

A SOLDIER: (*alarmed, calls to* CRASSUS) General! Let us use our swords!
SOLDIERS: (*enraged—eagerly*) Yes! Swords!
CROWD: Death!
CRASSUS: (*turning—uneasy but afraid to give any drastic order*) Bah! Staves are enough. Crack their skulls!
CROWD: (*led by the* CHORUS—*defiantly*)

Death to Crassus!
Drunkard! Coward!
Death to him!

(*They continue to push forward, hooting and jeering*).

CRASSUS: (*exploding for a second*) By the gods—! (to the SOLDIERS) Draw
   your swords! (*The troops do so eagerly. The* CROWD *sag back momentarily
   with exclamations of fear*).
CALIGULA: (*listening as in a trance to the music and what is going on behind
   him—in a queer whisper*) Kill, Cneius! Let me dance! Let me sing!
   (*The music and crashing of cymbals and the ferment of passions around
   him cause him to lose all control over himself. He gives a crazy leap in the
   air and begins to dance grotesquely and chant in a thick voice*) He is
   coming! Death, the Deliverer! Kill, soldiers! I command you! I, Caligula! I will be Cæsar! Death!
CROWD: (*led by the* CHORUS—*savage now*)

   Beast! Cur!
   Death to Caligula!

(*They crowd forward*).
CALIGULA: (*drawing his sword and flourishing it drunkenly—his eyes glazed*)
   Death!
CRASSUS: (*drawing his own sword in a frenzy*) Strike! Death! (*His* SOLDIERS
   raise their swords. The CROWD *have raised whatever weapons they have
   found—knifes, clubs, daggers, stones, bare fists*).
CHORUS: (*chanting fiercely*)

   Death!

ALL: (ROMANS *and* GREEKS *alike as one great voice*)

   Death!

(*The chorused word beats down all sound into a stricken silence. The wild
joyous music ceases. The Romans and Greeks seem to lean back from one
another and collect strength to leap forward. At this moment the voice of
LAZARUS comes ringing through the air like a command from the sky*).
LAZARUS: There is no death! (*The* SOLDIERS *and* GREEKS *remain frozen in*

their attitudes of murderous hate. Following his words the laughter of
LAZARUS *is heard, exultant and gaily mocking, filling them with the sheep-*
ish shame of children caught in mischief. Their hands hang, their arms
sink to their sides. The music starts once more with a triumphant clash of
cymbals, LAZARUS' *laughter is echoed from the throats of the multitude of*
his FOLLOWERS *who now come dancing into the square, preceded by a band*
of masked musicians and by their CHORUS. *This* CHORUS *wears, in double*
size, the laughing mask of LAZARUS' FOLLOWERS *in the same Period and*
Type as in the preceding scene, except that here the mask of each member
of the CHORUS *has a different racial basis—Egyptian, Syrian, Cappadocian,*
Lydian, Phrygian, Cilician, Parthian. The FOLLOWERS *are costumed and*
masked as in the preceding scene, seven Types in seven Periods, except that,
as in the CHORUS, *racially there are many nations represented. All have*
wreaths of ivy in their hair and flowers in their hands which they scatter
about. They whirl in between the SOLDIERS *and* CROWD, *forcing them back*
from each other, teasing them, sifting into the CROWD, *their* CHORUS *in a*
half circle, confronting the CHORUS *of* GREEKS).

CHORUS OF FOLLOWERS:

> Laugh! Laugh!
> There is no death!
> There is only life!
> There is only laughter!

FOLLOWERS: (*echoing*)

> Laugh! Laugh!
> There is no death!

(CALIGULA *and* CRASSUS *are swept to one side, left. Then the cries and*
laughter of all become mingled into one exclamation:
ALL:

> Lazarus! Lazarus!

(*The squad of* ROMAN SOLDIERS *led by the* CENTURION, *who had taken* LAZARUS *prisoner, march in with dancers' steps, like a proud guard of honor now, laughing, pulling a chariot in which* LAZARUS *stands dressed in a tunic of white and gold, his bronzed face and limbs radiant in the halo of his own glowing light.* LAZARUS *now looks less than thirty-five. His countenance now might well be that of the positive masculine Dionysus, closest to the soil of the Grecian Gods, a Son of Man, born of a mortal. Not the coarse, drunken Dionysus, nor the effeminate God, but Dionysus in his middle period, more comprehensive in his symbolism, the soul of the recurring seasons, of living and dying as processes in eternal growth, of the wine of life stirring forever in the sap and blood and loam of things.* MIRIAM *is beside him, dressed in black, smiling the same sad tender smile, holding* LAZARUS' *arm as if for protection and in protection. She appears older, a woman over forty-five*).

CHORUS OF GREEKS: (*rushing to* LAZARUS' *car*)

> Hail, Dionysus!
> Iacchus!
> Lazarus!
> Hail!

(*They surround him, throw over his shoulders and head the finely dressed hide of a bull with great gilded horns, force into his right hand the mystic rod of Dionysus with a pine cone on top, then prostrate themselves*)

> Hail, Savior!
> Redeemer!
> Conqueror of Death!

ALL: (*in a repeated chorus which finally includes even the* ROMAN SOLIDERS, *raising their arms to him*)

> Hail, Lazarus!
> Redeemer!
> Hail!

(They are silent. LAZARUS *looks at them, seeming to see each and all at the same time, and his laughter, as if in answer to their greetings, is heard rising from his lips like a song).*

CRASSUS: *(awed)* Look! He is more than man!

CALIGULA: *(trembling, in a queer agitation)* I dare not look!

CRASSUS: Do you hear his laughter?

CALIGULA: *(chokingly—puts his hands over his ears)* I will not hear!

CRASSUS: But you must welcome him in Cæsar's name!

CALIGULA: *(his teeth chattering)* I must kill him!

LAZARUS: *(looking directly at him—gaily mocking)* Death is dead, Caligula! *(He begins to laugh again softly).*

CALIGULA: *(with an hysterical cry of defiant terror)* You lie! *(Sword in hand he whirls to confront* LAZARUS, *but at the first sight of his face he stops in his tracks, trembling, held fascinated by* LAZARUS' *eyes, mumbling with a last pitiful remainder of defiance)* But—you lie—whatever you are! I say there *must* be death! *(The sword has fallen to his side. He stares open-mouthed at* LAZARUS. *There is something of a shy, wondering child about his attitude now.* LAZARUS *looks at him, laughing with gentle understanding.* CALIGULA *suddenly drops his sword and covering his face with his hands weeps like a boy who has been hurt)* You have murdered my only friend, Lazarus! Death would have been my slave when I am Cæsar. He would have been my jester and made me laugh at fear! *(He weeps bitterly).*

LAZARUS: *(gaily)* Be your own jester instead, O Caligula! Laugh at yourself, O Cæsar-to-be! *(He laughs. The* CROWD *now all join in with him.* CALIGULA *suddenly uncovers his face, grins his warped grin, gives a harsh cackle which cracks through the other laughter with a splitting discord, cuts a hopping caper like some grotesque cripple which takes him to the side of* LAZARUS' *chariot where he squats on his hams and, stretching out his hand, fingers* LAZARUS' *robe inquisitively and stares up into his face in the attitude of a chained monkey).*

CALIGULA: *(with a childish, mischievous curiosity)* Then if there is no death, O Teacher, tell me why I love to kill?

LAZARUS: Because you fear to die! (*Then gaily mocking*) But what do you matter, O Deathly-Important One? Put yourself that question—as a jester! (*Exultantly*) Are you a speck of dust danced in the wind? Then laugh, dancing! Laugh yes to your insignificance! Thereby will be born your new greatness! As Man, Petty Tyrant of Earth, you are a bubble pricked by death into a void and a mocking silence! But as dust, you are eternal change, and everlasting growth, and a high note of laughter soaring through chaos from the deep heart of God! Be proud, O Dust! Then you may love the stars as equals! (*Then mockingly again*) And then perhaps you may be brave enough to love even your fellow men without fear of their vengeance!

CALIGULA: (*dully*) I cannot understand. I hate men. I am afraid of their poison and their swords and the cringing envy in their eyes that only yields to fear!

LAZARUS: (*gaily mocking*) Tragic is the plight of the tragedian whose only audience is himself! Life is for each man a solitary cell whose walls are mirrors. Terrified is Caligula by the faces he makes! But I tell you to laugh in the mirror, that seeing your life gay, you may begin to live as a guest, and not as a condemned one! (*Raising his hands for silence—with a playful smile*) Listen! In the dark peace of the grave the man called Lazarus rested. He was still weak, as one who recovers from a long illness—for, living, he had believed his life a sad one! (*He laughs softly, and softly they all echo his laughter*) He lay dreaming to the croon of silence, feeling as the flow of blood in his own veins the past reënter the heart of God to be renewed by faith into the future. He thought: "Men call this death"—for he had been dead only a little while and he still remembered. Then, of a sudden, a strange gay laughter trembled from his heart as though his life, so long repressed in him by fear, had found at last its voice and a song for singing. "Men call this death," it sang. "Men call life death and fear it. They hide from it in horror. Their lives are spent in hiding. Their fear becomes their living. They worship life as death!"

CHORUS OF FOLLOWERS: (*in a chanting echo*)

> Men call life death and fear it.
> They hide from it in horror.
> Their lives are spent in hiding.
> Their fear becomes their living.
> They worship life as death!

LAZARUS: And here the song of Lazarus' life grew pitiful. "Men must learn to live," it mourned. "Before their fear invented death they knew, but now they have forgotten. They must be taught to laugh again!" And Lazarus answered "Yes!" (*He now addresses the crowd—especially* CALIGULA, *directly, laughingly*) Thus sang his life to Lazarus while he lay dead! Man must learn to live by laughter! (*He laughs*).

CHORUS OF FOLLOWERS:

> Laugh! Laugh!
> There is only life!
> There is only laughter!
> Fear is no more!
> Death is dead!

CHORUS OF GREEKS:

> Laugh! Laugh!
> Hail, Dionysus!
> Fear is no more!
> Thou hast conquered death!

ALL: (*laughing—in a great laughing chorus*)

> Laugh! Laugh!
> Fear is no more!
> Death is dead!

LAZARUS: (*as to a crowd of children—laughingly*) Out with you! Out into the woods! Upon the hills! Cities are prisons wherein man locks himself from life. Out with you under the sky! Are the stars too pure for your sick passions? Is the warm earth smelling of night too desirous of love for your pale introspective lusts? Out! Let laughter be your new clean lust and sanity! So far man has only learned to snicker meanly at his neighbor! Let a laughing away of self be your new right to live forever! Cry in your pride, "I am Laughter, which is Life, which is the Child of God!" (*He laughs and again his voice leads and dominates the rhythmic chorus of theirs. The music and dancing begin again*).

THE TWO CHORUSES: (*chanting in unison*)

> Laugh! Laugh!
> There is only God!
> We are His Laughter!

ALL: (*echoing*)

> There is only God!
> We are His Laughter!
> Laugh! Laugh!

(*They take hold of his chariot traces, and as he had come in the midst of a happy multitude, now augmented by all the* GREEKS, *and the* ROMAN SOLDIERS *who had awaited him, dancing, playing, singing, laughing, he is escorted off. The noise of their passing recedes.* CALIGULA *and* CRASSUS *are left in the empty square, the former squatting on his hams, monkey-wise, and brooding somberly*).

CRASSUS: (*is swaying and staggering, like a man in a drunken stupor, in a bewildered, stubborn struggle to control himself. He stammers after the* SOLDIERS) Ha-ha-ha— Halt! Halt, I say! No use—they are gone— mutiny—Halt! (*He continues to stumble toward left*) Ha-ha—Stop it, curse you! Am I laughing? Where am I going? After Lazarus? Thirty years of discipline and I— Halt, traitor! Remember Cæsar! Remember Rome! Halt, traitor! (*He faints with the violence of his struggle and falls in a limp heap*).

CALIGULA: (*startled by his fall, terrified, hops to his feet and snatches up his sword defensively, glancing over his shoulder and whirling around as if he expected someone to stab him in the back. Then, forcing a twisted grin of self-contempt—harshly*). Coward! What do I fear—if there is no death? (*As if he had to cut something, he snatches up a handful of flowers—desperately*) You must laugh, Caligula! (*He starts to lop off the flowers from their stems with a savage intentness*) Laugh! Laugh! Laugh! (*Finally, impatiently, he cuts off all the remaining with one stroke*) Laugh! (*He grinds the petals under his feet and breaks out into a terrible hysterical giggle*) Ha-ha—

CURTAIN

Scene Two

SCENE: *A midnight, months later. Immediately inside the walls of Rome. In the foreground is the portico of a temple between whose massive columns one looks across a street on a lower level to the high wall of Rome at the extreme rear. In the center of the wall is a great metal gate. The night is thick and oppressive. In the sky overhead lightning flashes and thunder rumbles and crashes but there is no rain.*

Within the portico on rows of chairs placed on a series of wide steps which are on each side, members of the Senate are seated in their white robes. High hanging lamps cast a wan light over their faces. They are all masked in the Roman mask, refined in them by nobility of blood but at the same time with strength degenerated, corrupted by tyranny and debauchery to an exhausted cynicism. The three periods of Middle Age, Maturity and Old Age are represented in the types of the Self-Tortured, Introspective; Proud, Self-Reliant;

the Servile, Hypocritical; the Cruel, Revengeful; and the Resigned, Sorrowful. The SENATORS *are divided into two groups on each side, thirty in each. Seated in the middle of the lower of the three high broad stairs that lead to the level from which the columns rise is the* CHORUS OF SENATORS, *seven in number, facing front, in double-sized masks of the Servile, Hypocritical type of Old Age.*

LAZARUS, *in his robe of white and gold, the aura of light surrounding his body seeming to glow more brightly than ever, stands in the rear at the edge of the portico, center, gazing upward into the pall of sky beyond the wall. His figure appears in its immobility to be the statue of the god of the temple. Near him, but to the rear and to the left of him, facing right,* MIRIAM *is kneeling in her black robes, swaying backward and forward, praying silently with moving lips like a nun who asks mercy for the sins of the world. She has grown much older, her hair is gray, her shoulders are bowed.*

On the other side, placed similarly in relation to LAZARUS *and facing* MIRIAM, CALIGULA *is squatting on his hams on a sort of throne-chair of ivory and gold. He is dressed with foppish richness in extreme bright colors, a victory wreath around his head. He stares blinkingly and inquisitively at* LAZARUS, *then at* MIRIAM. *He is half-drunk. A large figured goblet of gold is in his hand. A slave with an amphora of wine crouches on the steps by his chair. The slave wears a black negroid mask.*

At the opening of the scene there is heard the steady tramp of departing troops, whose masks, helmets and armored shoulders can be seen as they pass through the street before LAZARUS *to the gate beyond. Finally with a metallic clash the gate is shut behind them and there is a heavy and oppressive silence in which only the murmured prayers of* MIRIAM *are heard.*

CHORUS OF THE SENATE: (*intones wearily, as if under a boring compulsion*)

> The Roman Senate
> Is the Roman Senate
> The Mighty Voice
> Of the Roman People
> As long as Rome is Rome.

CALIGULA: (*as if he hadn't heard—sings hoarsely an old camp song of the Punic Wars, pounding with his goblet*)

> A bold legionary am I!
> March, oh march on!
> A Roman eagle was my daddy,
> My mother was a drunken drabby
> Oh, march on to the wars!
>
> Since lived that lady Leda
> March, oh march on!
> Women have loved high-fliers
> And we are eagles of Rome!
> Oh, march on to the wars!
>
> Comrades, march to the wars!
> There's pretty girls in Carthage
> And wine to swill in Carthage,
> So we must capture Carthage
> And fight for Mother Rome!

(*Holds out his goblet to be refilled. There is silence again. He stares at* LAZARUS *with a somber intentness. He says thickly*) The legions have gone, Lazarus. (LAZARUS *gives no evidence of having heard him.* CALIGULA *gulps at his wine. The* SENATORS *begin to talk to each other in low voices*).

FIRST SENATOR: How does that Jew make that light come from him, I wonder? It is a well-contrived bit of magic.

SECOND SENATOR: What are we waiting for? A messenger came to me with Cæsar's command that the Senate meet here at midnight.

THIRD SENATOR: (*bored*) Some new whim of Tiberius, naturally— (*With a meaning titter*) —or rather I should say, unnaturally!

FOURTH SENATOR: Perhaps Cæsar has decided to abolish our august body by a massacre in mass!

THIRD SENATOR: (*yawning*) There was a feast at Cinna's last night that lasted until this evening. I could welcome my own murder as an excuse for sleeping!

FIFTH SENATOR: (*pompously*) Tiberius would not dare harm the Senate. He may mistreat individual Senators, but the Roman Senate is the Roman Senate!

CHORUS OF THE SENATE: (*as before—wearily as if under a boring compulsion—intones*)

> While Rome is Rome
> The Senate is the Senate
> The Mighty Voice of the Roman People.

FIRST SENATOR: (*with the ghost of a laugh—wearily*). The Senate is an empty name—a pack of degenerate cowards with no trace of their ancient nobility or courage remaining—that and no more!

THIRD SENATOR: (*flippantly*) You are too severe with yourself, Lucius! (*A titter of laughter*).

FIRST SENATOR: (*wearily*) A degenerate coward. I am, I confess it. So are you too, Sulpicius—a hundred fold!—whether you admit it or not. (SULPICIUS *laughs weakly without taking offense*).

SIXTH SENATOR: (*after a pause—sighing*) In truth, the Senate is not what it used to be. I can remember—

FIRST SENATOR: Let us forget, if we can! (*Then impatiently*) What are we doing here?

SECOND SENATOR: I imagine it has something to do with the followers of this Lazarus encamped outside the wall. Probably the legions are to butcher them in their sleep.

SEVENTH SENATOR: And what part do we play—official witnesses? But how can we witness at night and through a wall? (*With bored resignation*). Ah, well, the moods of Tiberius are strange, to say the least. But Cæsar is Cæsar.

CHORUS: (*again with bored weariness as before*)

> Hail!
> Cæsar is Cæsar

The August One
Prince of the Senate
Tribune over Tribunes
Consul of Consuls
Supreme Pontiff
Emperor of Rome
God among Gods
Hail!

FIRST SENATOR: (*after a pause of silence—dryly*) Cæsar is a beast—and a madman!

FIFTH SENATOR: (*pompously*) Respect, sir! More respect for Cæsar!

THIRD SENATOR: (*mockingly*) Or caution, Lucius. One of us might repeat your opinion to him.

FIRST SENATOR: You would if it would pay you. But all my money is squandered. My death is worthless to Tiberius. He would not reward you. Moreover, you would not be revenged on me, for I long for death.

THIRD SENATOR: (*dryly*) Your stomach must be out of order.

FIRST SENATOR: The times are out of order. But let us change the subject. Is it true Tiberius has fled to Capri?

FOURTH SENATOR: Yes. He was terrified by the multitude of laughing idiots who appeared today with that charlatan. (*He points to* LAZARUS).

SECOND SENATOR: There are thousands of them outside the wall. Cæsar refused to let them enter the city. The story is, this Lazarus was dead four days and then restored himself to life by magic.

FIRST SENATOR: I have a mind to question him. (*Calls as to a slave*) You, there! Jew, turn round! In the name of the Senate! (LAZARUS *seems not to hear him.* LUCIUS *remarks with a weary smile*) So much for our authority!

SIXTH SENATOR: (*with injured dignity*) What insolence! (*In a rage*) Ho, barbarian cur, turn round! The Senate commands you! (LAZARUS *does not seem to hear, but* CALIGULA *turns on them fiercely*).

CALIGULA: Silence! Leave him alone! (*With insulting scorn*) I, Caligula, command you! (*The* SENATORS *seem to shrink back from him in fear, all but* LUCIUS, *who answers with a mocking servility*).

FIRST SENATOR: At least, grant us the boon to see this corpse's face, O Gracious Gaius!

CALIGULA: (*fixing his cruel, burning eyes on him—softly*) I heard you wish for death, Lucius. When I am Cæsar you shall scream and pray for it!

FIRST SENATOR: (*dryly and haughtily*) You were bred in camp, Gaius. You should have learned more courage there along with your coarseness. But accept my gratitude for your warning. I shall take care to die before you become Cæsar—and life becomes too idiotic!

CALIGULA: (*his grin becoming ferocious with cruelty*) No. You are too weak to kill yourself. Look at me, Lucius! I am imagining what I shall have done to you! (*The* SENATORS *are now trembling. Even* LUCIUS *cannot repress a shudder of horror at the face glaring at him. Suddenly* CALIGULA *throws the cup from him and springs to his feet*) What good is wine if it cannot kill thought? Lazarus! It is time. I must give the signal! The legions are waiting. It is Cæsar's command that they spare none of your followers. (*He has walked toward* LAZARUS).

MIRIAM: (*stretches out her hands to* CALIGULA *imploringly*) Mercy! Spare them who are so full of life and joy!

CALIGULA: (*harshly*) For their joy I will revenge myself upon them! Mercy? If there is no death, then death is a mercy! Ask that man! (*He points accusingly to* LAZARUS) And why should you plead for them, Jewess? There are few Jews among them. They are mostly those whom your people call idolaters and would gladly see murdered.

MIRIAM: (*with deep grief*) I am a mother of dead children. I plead for the mothers of those about to die.

CALIGULA: (*contemptuously*) Pah! (*He turns from her and puts his hand on* LAZARUS' *shoulder*) Lazarus! Do you hear? I must signal to the legions!

LAZARUS: (*turns. He has grown more youthful. He seems no more than thirty. His face is exalted and calm and beautiful. His eyes shine with an unearthly glory. The* SENATORS *lean forward in their seats, fascinated by his face. A low murmur of admiration comes from them.* LAZARUS *speaks commandingly*) Wait! I will awaken my beloved ones that their passing may be a symbol to the world that there is no death! (*He turns, throwing back his head and stretching up his arms, and begins to laugh low and tenderly, like caressing music at first but gradually gaining in volume, becoming more and more intense and insistent, finally ending up on a triumphant, blood-stirring call to that ultimate attainment in which all prepossession with self is lost in an ecstatic affirmation of Life. The voices of his* FOLLOWERS *from beyond the wall, at first one by one, then several at a time, then multitudes, join in his laughter. Even the* SENATORS *are drawn into it. Now every one of these is standing up, stretching out his arms toward* LAZARUS, *laughing harshly and discordantly and awkwardly in his attempt to laugh. Terrific flashes of lightning and crashes of thunder seem a responsive accompaniment from the heavens to this laughter of thousands which throbs in beating waves of sound in the air. Mingled with the laughing from beyond the wall comes the sound of singing and the music of flutes and cymbals.* MIRIAM *has crawled on her knees to the edge of the portico where her black figure of grief is outlined below and to the left of* LAZARUS, *her arms raised outward like the arms of a cross*).

FOLLOWERS OF LAZARUS: (*in a great chanting singing chorus*)

> Laugh! Laugh!
> There is only God!
> Life is His Laughter!
> We are His Laughter!
> Fear is no more!
> Death is dead!

CHORUS OF SENATORS: (*taking it up in a tone between chanting and their old solemn intoning*)

Laugh! Laugh!
Fear is no more!
Death is dead!

ALL: (*the multitude beyond the wall, all the* SENATORS, *everyone except the never-laughing* MIRIAM *and* CALIGULA *and the* MEN OF THE LEGIONS)

Laugh! Laugh!
Death is dead!

CALIGULA: (*in a queer state of mingled exaltation and fear—hopping restlessly about from foot to foot—shouting*) The signal! Shall I give the signal to kill, Lazarus?

MEN OF THE LEGIONS: (*following a brazen trumpet call, are suddenly heard from beyond the wall beginning to laugh their hoarse, bass laughter, a deeper note than all the others*) Laugh! Laugh!

CALIGULA: (*listening—with dismay*) I hear the legions, Lazarus! They are laughing with them! (*He cries with a strange pitifulness and beseeching*) You are playing me false, Lazarus! You are trying to evade death! You are trying to spare your people! You are small and weak like other men when the test comes! You give way to pity! Your great laughter becomes pitiful! (*Working himself into a rage*) You are a traitor, Lazarus! You betray Cæsar! Have you forgotten I will be Cæsar? You betray me, Lazarus! (*He rushes to the edge and, making a megaphone of his hands, bellows*) You on the wall! Sentry! It is I, Caligula! Kill! (*The brazen trumpets of the* LEGIONS *sound from beyond the wall. He springs near* LAZARUS *again, in a fiendish ecstasy, dancing a hopping grotesque sword dance behind him, chanting as he does so*) Kill! Kill laughter! Kill those who deny Cæsar! I will be Cæsar! Kill those who deny Death! I will be Death! My face will be bright with blood! My laughing face, Lazarus! Laughing because men fear me! My face of victorious Fear! Look at me! I am laughing, Lazarus! *My* laughter! Laughter of Gods and Cæsars! Ha-ha-ha-ha! (*He laughs, his laughter fanatically cruel and savage, forced from his lips with a desperate, destroying abandon. For a moment, above all the chorus of other sounds, his voice fights to overcome that of* LAZARUS, *whose laughter seems now to have attained the most exultant heights of spiritual affirmation. Then* CALIGULA *breaks into a cry of fear and a sob, and, casting his sword aside, he hides his face in his hands and cries beseechingly*) Forgive me! I love you, Lazarus! Forgive me! (*At this second the blaring trumpets of the* LEGIONS *are heard approaching and their great bass chorus of marching tramping laughter*).

MEN OF THE LEGIONS: (*chanting*)

> Laugh! Laugh! Laugh!
> Fear, no more!
> Death, no more!
> Death is dead!

(*There is now no sound of the singing or the laughter or music of* LAZARUS' FOLLOWERS. MIRIAM *rocks to and fro and raises a low wail of lamentation. The* SENATORS *cheer and shout as at a triumph*).

CHORUS OF SENATORS: (*saluting* LAZARUS)

> Hail, Victor!
> Hail, Divine One!
> Thou hast slain fear!
> Thou hast slain death!
> Hail! Triumph!

SENATORS:

> Hail! Hail!
> Slayer of Fear!
> Slayer of Death!

(*The gate in the wall is clanged open. The returning* LEGIONS *burst through and gather in a dense mob in the street below* LAZARUS, *who looks down upon them, silent but smiling gently now. They stare at him with admiration. Only a sea of their masks can be seen, their eyes shining exultantly.* CRASSUS, *their general, ascends the steps until he stands a little below* LAZARUS. *Their* CHORUS OF LEGIONARIES *in double-sized masks climb to the step below* CRASSUS, *forming behind him. They are in the Period of Manhood, of the Simple, Ignorant Type. No weapons can be seen—only their masks and helmets and armor gleaming in the lightning flashes and in the flickering light of torches. Their laughter seems to shake the walls and make the pillars of the temple dance*).

CHORUS OF THE LEGIONS:

> Fear, no more!
> Death, no more!
> Death is dead!

LEGIONARIES: (*echoing*)

> Laugh! Laugh! Laugh!
> Death is dead!

CRASSUS: (*raising his hand*) Silence! (*They obey. He turns to* LAZARUS *and bows his head, falling on one knee, raising his right arm*) Hail!

LEGIONARIES: (*as one man—raising their arms*). Hail!

CALIGULA: (*suddenly pushes forward impudently and strikes a grandiose attitude*) I am here, my brave ones! (*There is a roar of mocking laughter from the* LEGIONARIES).

CRASSUS: (*not unkindly*) Not you, Little Killer! We hail the Great Laugher!

CALIGULA: (*harshly*) Have you killed all his followers?

CRASSUS: No. They died. They did not wait for our attack. They charged upon us, laughing! They tore our swords away from us, laughing, and we laughed with them! They stabbed themselves, dancing as though it were a festival! They died, laughing, in one another's arms! We laughed, too, with joy because it seemed it was not they who died but death itself they killed! (*He stops uncertainly, bowing to* LAZARUS, *awkwardly*) I do not understand this. I am a soldier. But there is a god in it somewhere! For I know they were drunk, and so were we, with a happiness no mortal ever felt on earth before! And death was dead! (*In a sudden outburst as if he were drunk with excitement, he takes off his helmet and waves it*) Hail, Deliverer! Death is dead! We left our swords with them! What virtue in killing when there is no death? Your foe laughs. The joke is on you. What a fool's game, eh? One can only laugh! Now we want peace to laugh in—to laugh at war! Let Cæsars fight—that is all they are good for—and not much good for that!

CALIGULA: (*frenziedly*) Silence, impious traitor!

CRASSUS: (*smiling drunkenly*) Shut up, yourself, camp-brat! Though you were Cæsar this minute I would laugh at you! Your death is dead! We will make Lazarus Cæsar! What say you? (*He appeals to the* SOLDIERS).

CALIGULA: No!

CHORUS OF THE LEGIONS: (*with laughing intoxication*) Hail, Lazarus Cæsar! Hail!

LEGIONARIES: Lazarus Cæsar, hail!

CRASSUS: (*appealing to* SENATE) And you, Senators!

CHORUS OF SENATORS: (*with the same joyous intoxication as the* SOLDIERS) Hail, Lazarus Cæsar! Hail!

SENATORS: Lazarus Cæsar, hail!

CALIGULA: (*piteously*) No, Lazarus! Say no for my sake!

LAZARUS: (*with gay mockery*) What is—Cæsar? (*He begins to laugh with mockery. All except* CALIGULA *and* MIRIAM *join in this laughter*).

CRASSUS: Ha-ha! What is Cæsar? You are right! You deserve better from us. A god? How is that? We will build you a temple, Lazarus, and make you a god!

LAZARUS: (*laughingly*) When men make gods, there is no God! (*He laughs. They all laugh*).

CRASSUS: (*with puzzled good-nature*) I do not understand. But there is a god in it somewhere—a god of peace—a god of happiness! Perhaps you are already he, eh? Are you? Well, never mind now, remember our offer. Give us your answer tomorrow. Good night to you!

LAZARUS: (*as the* SOLDIERS *start to march away behind* CRASSUS, *and the* SENATORS *turn to retire, he stops them all for a moment with a gesture— with a deep earnestness*) Wait! When you awake tomorrow, try to remember! Remember that death is dead! Remember to laugh!

ALL: (*as if taking an oath with one voice*) We will remember, Lazarus!

CRASSUS: (*making a sign to the regimental musicians jovially*) And we will laugh! Play there! (*The bands crash out. The* LEGIONS *tramp away*).

CHORUS OF THE LEGIONS: (*chanting to the music*)

> Laugh! Laugh! Laugh!
> Cæsar, no more!
> War, no more!
> Wounds, no more!
> Death is dead!
> Dead! Dead! Dead!

LEGIONARIES:

> Laugh! Laugh! Laugh!
> Death is dead!
> Dead! Dead! Dead!

CHORUS OF SENATORS: (*following them*)

> Cæsar, no more!
> Fear, no more!
> Death, no more!
> Laugh! Laugh! Laugh!

SENATE: (*elated, excited as a crowd of schoolboys going on a vacation. Marching after them*)

Laugh! Laugh! Laugh!
Death is dead!

(LAZARUS, MIRIAM and CALIGULA *remain*).

LAZARUS: (*with a great yearning*) If men would remember! If they could!
(*He stares after them compassionately*).

CALIGULA: (*crouching beside* LAZARUS. *Plucks at his robe humbly*) You will
not laugh at Cæsar, Lazarus, will you—when I am Cæsar? You will
not laugh at gods when they make me a god? (LAZARUS *does not answer.*
CALIGULA *forces a cruel vindictive smile*) I swear you shall not laugh at
death when I am Death! Ha-ha— (*He starts to laugh harshly—then
suddenly, terrified, slinks away and sidles off at right*).

MIRIAM: (*from where she kneels bowed grief grief—brokenly*) Those who
have just died were like your children, Lazarus. They believed in you
and loved you.

LAZARUS: And I loved them!

MIRIAM: Then how could you laugh when they were dying?

LAZARUS: (*exultingly*) Did they not laugh? That was their victory and
glory! (*With more and more of a passionate, proud exultation*) Eye to
eye with the Fear of Death, did they not laugh with scorn? "Death
to old Death," they laughed! "Once as squirming specks we crept
from the tides of the sea. Now we return to the sea! Once as quivering
flecks of rhythm we beat down from the sun. Now we reënter the
sun! Cast aside is our pitiable pretense, our immortal egohood, the
holy lantern behind which cringed our Fear of the Dark! Flung off
is that impudent insult to life's nobility which gibbers: 'I, this Jew,
this Roman, this noble or this slave, must survive in my pettiness
forever!' Away with such cowardice of spirit! We will to die! We
will to change! Laughing we lived with our gift, now with laughter
give we back that gift to become again the Essence of the Giver!
Dying we laugh with the Infinite. We are the Giver and the Gift!
Laughing, we will our own annihilation! Laughing, we give our lives
for Life's sake!" (*He laughs up to heaven ecstatically*) This must Man

will as his end and his new beginning! He must conceive and desire his own passing as a mood of eternal laughter and cry with pride, "Take back, O God, and accept in turn a gift from me, my grateful blessing for Your gift—and see, O God, now I am laughing with You! I am Your laughter—and You are mine!" (*He laughs again, his laughter dying lingeringly and tenderly on his lips like a strain af music receding into the silence over still waters*).

MIRIAM: (*with a sigh—meekly*) I cannot understand, Lazarus. (*Sadly*) They were like your children—and they have died. Must you not mourn for them?

LAZARUS: (*gently*) Mourn? When they laughed?

MIRIAM: (*sadly*) They are gone from us. And their mothers weep.

LAZARUS: (*puts his arm around her and raises her to her feet— tenderly*) But God, their Father, laughs! (*He kisses her on the forehead*).

CURTAIN

ACT THREE—SCENE ONE

SCENE: *Some days later—exterior of* TIBERIUS' *villa-palace at Capri. It is about two in the morning of a clear black night. In the rear, the walls of the villa, which is built entirely of marble on the brow of a cliff, loom up with a startling clarity against the sky. The rear foreground is a marble terrace at the middle of which is a triumphal arch. On each side, leading up to it, are massive marble columns standing like the mummies of legionaries at attention. In the exact centre of the arch itself a cross is set up on which a full grown male lion has been crucified. A lamp reflecting downward has been fixed at the top of the cross to light up an inscription placed over the lion's head. Below the steps to the terrace, in a line facing front, on each side of the cross, is the* CHORUS OF THE GUARD *in their double masks and gorgeous uniforms and armor. Their masks are the same as the* LEGIONARY CHORUS *of the previous scene.*

The windows of the palace glow crimson-purple with the reflection of many shaded lamps. The sound of music in a strained theme of that joyless abandon which is vice is heard above a confused drunken clamor of voices, punctuated by the high, staccato laughter of women and youths. A squad of the GUARD *in the same uniforms as the* CHORUS, *masked as all the* ROMAN SOLDIERS *previously, enter from the left, front, climbing up from the beach below. They are commanded by a Centurion,* FLAVIUS. *His mask is that of a typical young patrician officer. They are followed by* LAZARUS *and* MIRIAM. CALIGULA *walks behind, his drawn sword in his hand. He is in a state of queer conflicting emotion, seeming to be filled with a nervous dread and terror of everything about him, while at the same time perversely excited and elated by his own morbid tension.* LAZARUS, *looking no more than twenty-five, haloed in his own mystic light, walks in a deep, detached serenity.*

MIRIAM, *in black, her hair almost white now, her figure bowed and feeble, seems more than ever a figure of a sad, resigned mother of the dead. The soldiers form in line with the columns.*

414

FLAVIUS: (*saluting* CALIGULA—*with an awed glance at* LAZARUS) I will announce your coming— (*As if in spite of himself he bows awkwardly to* LAZARUS)—and that of this man. Cæsar was not expecting you so soon, I think.

CALIGULA: (*forcing a light tone*) Lazarus laughed and the galley slaves forgot their fetters and made their oars fly as if they were bound for the Blessed Isles of Liberty! (*Then with an ironic smile*) But you need not tell Tiberius that, good Flavius. Say it was due to my extreme zeal.

FLAVIUS: (*smiles with respectful understanding.* CALIGULA *nods in dismissal.* FLAVIUS *turns to go—apologetically*) You may have to wait. I dare not speak before he questions me. (FLAVIUS *salutes and hastens to the villa, walking under an arm of the cross unconcernedly without an upward glance. As they follow him with their eyes* CALIGULA *and* MIRIAM *see the lion for the first time. He steps back with a startled exclamation. She gives a cry of horror and covers her eyes with her hands to shut out the sight*).

LAZARUS: (*immediately puts his arms around her protectingly*) What is it, Beloved? (*She hides her face on his breast, pointing toward the lion with a trembling hand*).

CALIGULA: (*pointing—curiously now, but with entire callousness*) This lion they have crucified. Are you frightened, Jewess? (*With a cruel laugh*) My grandfather frequently plants whole orchards of such trees, but usually they bear human fruit!

MIRIAM: (*with a shudder*) Monster!

CALIGULA: (*with genuine surprise—turning to her*) Who? Why? (*He approaches the cross and stares at it moodily*) But why did he have it placed here where he knew you must pass? Tiberius does not go to such pains to frighten women. (*His eyes fasten on the inscription above the lion's head*) Aha! I see! (*He reads*) "From the East, land of false gods and superstition, this lion was brought to Rome to amuse Cæsar." (*A silence.* CALIGULA *shrugs his shoulders, turning away—lightly*) A lesson for you, Lazarus. An example for other lions—not to roar—or laugh—at Cæsar! (*He gives a harsh laugh*) Tiberius must be terribly afraid of you. (*Then somberly*) You should never have come here. I would have advised you not to—but what are you to me? My duty, if I wish to become Cæsar, is to Cæsar. Besides, you are no fool. Evidently you must desire your own death. Last night *you* might have been Cæsar. The legions were yours.

LAZARUS: (*smiling without bitterness—with a sad comprehension*) But this morning the legions had forgotten. They only remembered—to go out and pick up their swords! They also pillaged the bodies a little, as their right, believing now that they had slain them! (*This last a bit bitterly*).

CALIGULA: (*tauntingly*) The legions did slay them! It was only by some magician's trick you made them think your followers killed themselves.

LAZARUS: (*not answering him—ironically to himself*) It is too soon. Men still need their swords to slash at ghosts in the dark. Men, those haunted heroes! (*He laughs softly*).

CALIGULA: (*irritably*) What are you laughing at?

LAZARUS: At Lazarus when I find him feeling wronged because men are men! (*He laughs again, softly and musically*).

CALIGULA: (*again taunting brutally*) You may be in his place soon! (*He points to the lion*) Will you laugh then? (MIRIAM *gives a cry of terror*).

LAZARUS: (*calmly*) Yes. (*Then humbly, bowing his head*) I will laugh with the pride of a beggar set upon the throne of Man!

CALIGULA: (*sneeringly*) You boast. (*Then as* LAZARUS *does not answer, touching the lion with intentional provoking brutality*) This one from Africa seems almost gone. They do not last as long as men.

LAZARUS: (*walks up the steps to the cross and, stretching to his full height, gently pushes the lion's hair out of its eyes—tenderly*) Poor brother! Cæsar avenges himself on you because of me. Forgive me your suffering!

CALIGULA: (*with a start backward—with frightened awe*) Gods! He licks your hand! I could swear he smiles—with his last breath! (*Then with relief*) Now he is dead!

LAZARUS: (*gently*) There is no death.

CALIGULA: (*pointing to the lion*) What is that then?

LAZARUS: Your fear of life.

CALIGULA: (*impatiently*) Bah! (*Then somberly*) A little fear is useful even for lions—or teachers of laughter if they wish to laugh long! (*Then with a sudden exasperation*) Escape now, you fool, while there is still time!

LAZARUS: (*laughing softly*) Escape—what?

CALIGULA: (*in a frenzy*) You know, you ass, you lunatic! Escape death! Death! Death! (*To* MIRIAM) You, woman! Talk to him! Do you want him nailed up like that?

MIRIAM: (*with a pitiful cry*) Lazarus! Come! Caligula will help us!

CALIGULA: (*harshly*) You presume, Jewess! I have no wish to die! (*Then with his wry smile*) But I will turn my back—and shut my eyes— (*He walks away to left*).

MIRIAM: (*beseechingly*) Lazarus! I could not bear that aching hunger of my empty heart if you should die again!

LAZARUS: (*coming to her—tenderly*) I will not leave you! Believe in me! (*He kisses her forehead tenderly*).

MIRIAM: (*after a pause—slowly and lamentingly*) I wish we were home, Lazarus. This Roman world is full of evil. These skies threaten. These hearts are heavy with hatred. There is a taint of blood in the air that poisons the breath of the sea. These columns and arches and thick walls seem waiting to fall, to crush these rotten men and then to crumble over the bones that raised them until both are dust. It is a world deadly to your joy, Lazarus. Its pleasure is a gorging of dirt, its fulfilled desire a snoring in a sty in the mud among swine. Its will is so sick that it must kill in order to be aware of life at all. I wish we were home, Lazarus. I begin to feel horror gnawing at my breast. I begin to know the torture of the fear of death, Lazarus—not of my death but of yours—not of the passing of your man's body but of the going away from me of your laughter which is to me as my son, my little boy!

LAZARUS: (*soothing her*) Be comforted, Beloved. Your fear shall never be!

MIRIAM: On the hills near Bethany you might pray at noon and laugh your boy's laughter in the sun and there would be echoing laughter from the sky and up from the grass and distantly from the shining sea. We would adopt children whose parents the Romans had butchered, and their laughter would be around me in my home where I cooked and weaved and sang. And in the dawn at your going out, and in the evening on your return, I would hear in the hushed air the bleating of sheep and the tinkling of many little bells and your voice. And my heart would know peace.

LAZARUS: (*tenderly*) Only a little longer! There is God's laughter on the hills of space, and the happiness of children, and the soft healing of innumerable dawns and evenings, and the blessing of peace!

CALIGULA: (*looks around at* LAZARUS *impatiently. Then he makes a beckoning gesture to* MIRIAM) Ssstt! (*Wonderingly she leaves* LAZARUS' *side and follows him.* LAZARUS *remains, his eyes fixed on the cross, directly in front of it.* CALIGULA *speaks gruffly to* MIRIAM *with a sneer*) Jewess, your Lazarus is mad, I begin to think. (*Then confusedly but helplessly inquisitive and confiding—bursting out*) What is it troubles me about him? What makes me dream of him? Why should I—love him, Jewess? Tell me! You love him, too. I do not understand this. Why, wherever he goes, is there joy? You heard even the galley slaves laugh and clank time with their chains! (*Then with exasperation*) And yet why can I not laugh, Jewess?

MIRIAM: (*in a tone of hushed grief*) I may not laugh either. My heart remains a little dead with Lazarus in Bethany. The miracle could not revive all his old husband's life in my wife's heart.

CALIGULA: (*disgustedly*) What answer is that to me? (*Then brusquely*) But I called you to put you on your guard. (*He points*) There is death in there—Tiberius' death, a kind from which no miracles can recall one! (*He smiles his twisted smile*) Since Lazarus will not help himself, you must protect him. I will not, for once in there I am (*Mockingly*) the heir of Cæsar, and you are scum whom I will kill at his order as I would two beetles! So keep watch! Taste first of what he eats— even were I the one to give it to him!

LAZARUS: (*suddenly laughs softly*) Why do you delight in believing evil of yourself, Caligula?

CALIGULA: (*flying into a queer rage*) You lie! I am what I am! (*With grandiose pride*) What could you know of a Cæsar?

LAZARUS: (*still laughing with an affectionate understanding*) What—I know! (*As he finishes speaking all the sound of music and voices from the house ceases abruptly and there is a heavy silence*).

MIRIAM: (*shaking her head and turning away sadly*) That is too far, Lazarus. Let us go home.

CALIGULA: (*harshly*) Sst! Do you hear? Flavius has told Cæsar. (*Grimly forcing a harsh snicker*) Now we will soon know— (*There is the sudden blaring of a trumpet from within the palace. A wide door is flung open and a stream of reddish light comes out against which the black figures of several men are outlined. The door is shut again quickly. Several SLAVES bearing lamps on poles escort the patrician, MARCELLUS, forward to the arch. He passes under the crucified lion without a glance—then stands, cool and disdainful, to look about him. He is a man of about thirty-five, wearing the type mask of a Roman patrician to which are added the dissipated courtier's characteristics of one who leans to evil more through weakness than any instinctive urge. He is dressed richly. His smile is hypocritical and his eyes are hard and cold but when they come to rest on LAZARUS he gives a start of genuine astonishment*).

CALIGULA: (*who has moved to LAZARUS' side defensively—in a quick whisper*) Beware of this man, Lazarus! (*Then advancing—with a condescending hauteur*) Greeting, Marcellus!

MARCELLUS: (*in an ingratiating tone*) Greeting, Gaius. I have a message from Cæsar for the man called Lazarus.

LAZARUS: (*calmly*) I am Lazarus.

MARCELLUS: (*makes a deep bow—flatteringly*) I had surmised it, sir. Although I cannot pretend to virtue in myself at least I may claim the merit of recognizing it in others. (*He advances toward* LAZARUS, *smiling, with one hand kept hidden beneath his cloak*).

CALIGULA: (*stepping between them—sharply*) What is your message?

MARCELLUS: (*surprised—placatingly*) I am sorry, Gaius, but it was Cæsar's command I speak to Lazarus alone.

CALIGULA: (*fiercely*) And then, Marcellus? (MARCELLUS *shrugs his shoulders and smiles deprecatingly*).

LAZARUS: (*with a compelling dignity*) Let him speak. (*Inclining his head to* MARCELLUS—*strangely*) Over here where it is dark you will not be seen—nor see yourself. (*He walks to the darkness at right*).

CALIGULA: (*turning his back on them, with angry boyish resentfulness that is close to tears*) Idiot! Go and die, then!

MIRIAM: (*with a terrified cry*) Lazarus! (*She starts to go to him*).

LAZARUS: (*motioning her to remain where she is—gently*) Believe, Beloved! (*He turns his back on them all and stands waiting*).

MARCELLUS: (*stares at* LAZARUS—*then over his shoulder at* CALIGULA—*uncertainly*) What does he mean, Gaius? (*Then suddenly putting on a brave front, he strides up behind* LAZARUS) Cæsar wished me to bid you welcome, to tell you how much regard he has for you, but he desired me to ask whether you propose to laugh here—in Cæsar's palace? He has heard that you laugh at death—that you have caused others to laugh—even his legionaries. (*A pause,* MARCELLUS *remains behind* LAZARUS' *back, the latter standing like a victim*) Briefly, Cæsar requires your pledge that you will not laugh. Will you give it? (*He frees his dagger from under his robe. A pause. Arrogantly*) I am waiting! Answer when Cæsar commands! (*Then angrily, baffled*) I will give you while I count three—or take your silence as a refusal! One! Two! Three! (*He raises his hand to stab* LAZARUS *in the back.* MIRIAM *stifles a scream. At the same instant,* LAZARUS *begins to laugh, softly and affectionately.* MARCELLUS *stops, frozen in mid-action, the dagger upraised.* CALIGULA *has*

whirled around and stands staring, a smile gradually coming to his face.
LAZARUS *turns, his laughter grown a trifle louder, and faces* MARCELLUS.
*The latter steps back from him, staring openmouthed, fascinated. His arm
sinks to his side. The dagger falls from his fingers. He smiles back at*
LAZARUS—*the curious, sheepish, bashful smile of one who has fallen in love
and been discovered*).

LAZARUS: (*going to him, puts both hands on his shoulders and looks in his
eyes, laughing affectionately—then quizzically*) Here is another one who
believes in death! But soon you will laugh with life! I see it in your
eyes. Farewell, Marcellus! (*He turns away from him and walk's, laughing, toward the arch in rear. With bowed head the black-robed figure of*
MIRIAM *follows him.* MARCELLUS *hides his face in his hands, half-sobbing,
and half-laughing hysterically.* LAZARUS *pauses before the cross for a moment—raises his hand as if blessing the dead lion, then passes below it,
moving slowly on toward the palace in the rear. His laughter rises with
more and more summoning power. The files of the* GUARD, *as he passes
them, two by two join in his laughter, saluting him as if in spite of them
selves*).

CALIGULA: (*sidling up to* MARCELLUS, *cruel and mocking*) Are you weeping,
Marcellus? Laugh at that blundering fool, yourself! What will Cæsar
say? Will he laugh when he has your body broken one bone at a time
with hammers? Why did you not kill? For shame! A patrician exposed
to laughter by a Jew! Poor craven! Why could you not strike? There
must be death! Coward! Why did you not stab? (*Then in a queer awed
whisper*) I know! Was it not because of a sudden you loved him and
could not?

MARCELLUS: (*suddenly—eagerly*) Yes! That was it! I loved him!

CALIGULA: (*craftily and cruelly*) You were about to murder him!

MARCELLUS: (*tortured with remorse*) No! No! How could I? What in-
famy! (*Cries tearfully*) Forgive me, Lazarus!

CALIGULA: (*with vindictive insistence*) Judge yourself! (*He takes up the
dagger*) Here is your dagger! Avenge him on yourself!

MARCELLUS: (*trying to laugh*) Ha-ha— Yes! (*He stabs himself and falls. Suddenly his laughter is released*) I laugh! You are a fool, Caligula! There is no death! (*He dies, laughing up at the sky*).

CALIGULA: (*kicks his body with savage cruelty*) You lie! (*Then suddenly kneels and bends over it imploringly*) Tell me you lie, Marcellus! Do me that mercy!—and when I am Cæsar, I— (*He begins to weep like a frightened boy, his head in his hands. Meanwhile* LAZARUS *has arrived with* MIRIAM *at the steps before the door of the palace. As he starts to ascend these, the crimson-purple lights of the many windows of the palace go out one by one as if fleeing in terror from the laughter which now beats at the walls*).

CHORUS OF THE GUARD:

> Fear, no more!
> Death, no more!
> Laugh! Laugh! Laugh!
> Death is dead!

ALL THE GUARDS: (*now all in a great chorus, raising their spears aloft and saluting* LAZARUS *as if they were his own triumphal body guard*).

> Laugh! Laugh! Laugh!
> Death is dead!

(LAZARUS *has ascended the steps. He walks into the black archway of the darkened palace, his figure radiant and unearthly in his own light.* MIRIAM *follows him. They disappear in the darkness. There is a pause of dead silence*).

CALIGULA: (*raises his head uneasily, looks back toward the palace, jumps to his feet in a panic of terror, and runs toward the palace door, calling*) Lazarus! Wait! I will defend you! There is death inside there—death! Beware, Lazarus!

CHORUS OF THE GUARD: (*as the laughter of* LAZARUS *is heard again from the dark palace*).

> Laugh! Laugh! Laugh!
> Death is dead!

ALL THE GUARDS:

> Dead! Dead! Dead!
> Death is dead!

CURTAIN

Scene Two

S<small>CENE</small>: *The banquet hall in the palace of* TIBERIUS—*an immense high-ceilinged room. In the rear, center, is a great arched doorway. Smaller arches in the middle of the side walls lead into other rooms. Long couches are placed along the walls at right and left, and along the rear wall on either side of the arch. Before these couches, a series of narrow tables is set. In the center of the room on a high dais is the ivory and gold chair of* CÆSAR, *a table in front of it; couches for him to recline on at either side. On this table, and on all the tables for his guests, gold lamps with shades of crimson purple are placed.*

Reclining on the couches on the right are young women and girls, on the left, youths of an equal number.

(*The masks are based on the Roman masks of the periods of Boyhood (or Girlhood), Youth, and Young Manhood (or Womanhood) and there are seven individuals of each period and sex in each of the three types of the Introspective, Self-Tortured; the Servile, Hypocritical; and the Cruel, Revengeful—a crowd of forty-two in all. There is a distinctive character to the masks of each sex, the stamp of an effeminate corruption on all the male, while the female have a bold, masculine expression. The male masks are a blotched heliotrope in shade. These youths wear female wigs of curled wire like frizzed hair of a yellow gold. They are dressed in women's robes of pale heliotrope, they wear anklets and bracelets and necklaces. The women are dressed as males in crimson or deep purple. They also wear wire wigs but of straight hair cut in short boyish mode, dyed either deep purple or crimson. Those with crimson hair are dressed in purple, and vice versa. The female voices are harsh, strident, mannish—those of the youths affected, lisping, effeminate. The whole effect of these two groups is of sex corrupted and warped, of invented lusts and artificial vices.*

The CHORUS *in this scene and the next is composed of three males and four females—the males in the period of Youth, one in each of the types represented, and three of the females in similar type-period masks. The fourth female is masked in the period of Womanhood in the Proud, Self-Reliant type. They sit, facing front in their double-sized masks, on the side steps of the dais, four on right, three on left).*

POMPEIA, *a Roman noblewoman, the favorite mistress of* CÆSAR, *sits at front, right.*

She wears a half-mask on the upper part of her face, olive-colored with the red of blood smoldering through, with great, dark, cruel eyes—a dissipated mask of intense evil beauty, of lust and perverted passion. Beneath the mask, her own complexion is pale, her gentle, girlish mouth is set in an expression of agonized self-loathing and weariness of spirit. Her body is strong and beautiful. Her wig and dress are purple.

TIBERIUS CÆSAR *stands on the dais, dressed in deep purple, fringed and ornamented with crimson and gold. An old man of seventy-six, tall, broad and corpulent but of great muscular strength still despite his age, his shiny white cranium rises like a polished shell above his half-masked face. This mask is a pallid purple blotched with darker color, as if the imperial blood in his veins had been sickened by age and debauchery. The eyes are protuberant, leering, cynical slits, the long nose, once finely modeled, now gross and thickened, the forehead lowering and grim. Beneath the mask, his own mouth looks as incongruous as* CALIGULA'S. *The lips are thin and stern and self-contained—the lips of an able soldier-statesman of rigid probity. His chin is forceful and severe. The complexion of his own skin is that of a healthy old campaigner.*

As the curtain rises, slaves are hurriedly putting out the many lamps. From outside, the laughter of LAZARUS *rises on the deep ground swell of the* GUARD'S *laughter. The walls and massive columns seem to reverberate with the sound. In the banquet room all are listening fascinatedly. Every reaction, from the extreme of panic fear or hypnotized ecstasy to a feigned cynical amusement or a pretended supercilious indifference, is represented in their frozen attitudes.*

TIBERIUS *stands, shrinking back, staring at the doorway in the rear with superstitious dread. A squad of the* GUARD *surround the dais, commanded by* FLAVIUS.

TIBERIUS: (*in a strained voice shaken by apprehension and awe*) Marcellus! Strike him down! Stab him!

SOLDERS OF THE GUARD: (*from without*).

Laugh! Laugh! Laugh!
Death is dead!

TIBERIUS: (*as he suddenly sees the shining figure of* LAZARUS *appear at the end of the dark hall beyond the archway*) Gods! Flavius, look! (*He points with a shaking finger.* FLAVIUS *has leaped up to his side*).

FLAVIUS: (*not without dread himself*) That is the man, Cæsar.

TIBERIUS: Man? Say a dæmon! (*To the slaves who are turning out the few remaining lamps*) Quick! Darkness! (*He puts out the lamp on his table himself. Then as nothing is seen but the light from the approaching* LAZARUS) Flavius! Stand here in my place! It will think you are Cæsar! (*He clumps heavily down the steps of the dais*) Guards! Here! Cover me with your shields! (*He goes to the extreme right corner, front, and crouches there. His* GUARDS *follow him. They hold their shields so that they form a wall around him and half over him. Then* CALIGULA's *voice is heard screaming above the chorus of laughter as he enters the hall behind* LAZARUS).

CALIGULA: Beware of death! I will defend you, Lazarus! (*He is seen to rush past* LAZARUS, *flourishing his sword and comes running into the room, shouting*) Cæsar! Dare not to murder Lazarus! (*He leaps to the dais and up its steps in a frenzy*) Dare not, I say! (*He stabs* FLAVIUS *with a savage cry*) Ah! (*Then, as the body of* FLAVIUS *falls heavily and rolls down the steps at right, he begins to laugh, at first a clear laughter of selfless joy, sounding startlingly incongruous from him*) I have saved you, Lazarus— at the risk of my own life—and now, hear me, I can laugh! (LAZARUS *appears in the archway,* MIRIAM *behind him. He stops laughing and im-*

mediately there is silence, except for CALIGULA. LAZARUS *casts a luminous glow over the whole room in which the masked faces appear distorted and livid.* CALIGULA *stands with upraised sword by the chair of* CÆSAR. *Suddenly his laughter cracks, changes, becomes full of his old fear and blood-lust*).

CALIGULA: Ha-ha-ha! See, Lazarus! (*He points to the body of* FLAVIUS *with his sword*) Welcome in the name of Cæsar, now Cæsar is slain and I am Cæsar! (*He assumes the absurd grandiose posture of his imperial posing. No one looks at him or hears him. Their eyes are on* LAZARUS *as he moves directly to where* TIBERIUS *crouches behind the shields of the* GUARDS. MIRIAM *follows him.* CALIGULA *turns and stares toward him, and then down at the body of* FLAVIUS *and back, in a petrified, bewildered stupor.* LAZARUS *steps up beside* TIBERIUS. *The* GUARDS *make way for him fearfully*).

TIBERIUS: (*feeling his nearness—straightening himself with a certain dignity*) Strike! I have been a soldier. Thou canst not make me fear death, Dæmon! (*He draws his toga over his face*).

LAZARUS: (*smiling gently*) Then fear not fear, Tiberius! (*He reaches out and pulls back the toga from his face.* TIBERIUS *looks into his eyes, at first shrinkingly, then with growing reassurance, his own masked face clearly revealed now in the light from* LAZARUS).

TIBERIUS: (*at first falteringly*) So—thou art not evil? Thou art not come to contrive my murder? (*As* LAZARUS *smilingly shakes his head,* TIBERIUS *frowns*) Then why dost thou laugh against Cæsar? (*Then bitterly— with a twisted attempt at a smile*) Yet I like thy laughter. It is young. Once I laughed somewhat like that—so I pardon thee. I will even laugh at thee in return. Ha ha! (*His laughter is cold, cruel and merciless as the grin of a skeleton*).

CALIGULA: (*who has been staring in a bewildered stupor from* TIBERIUS, *whom he thought he had killed, to the body of* FLAVIUS—*quaking with terror now as if this laugh was meant for him, drops to his knees, his sword clattering down the steps to the floor*). Mercy, Tiberius! I implore you forgive your Caligula!

TIBERIUS: (*not understanding. Fixing his eyes on* CALIGULA *with a malevolent irony*) Come down from my throne, Caligula. (CALIGULA *slinks down warily*) You are too impatient. But I must pardon you, too—for where could I find another heir so perfect for serving my spite upon mankind? (*He has walked toward the throne while he is speaking,* CALIGULA *backing away from him.* LAZARUS *remains where he is,* MIRIAM *beside and to the rear of him.* TIBERIUS, *his eyes fixed on* CALIGULA, *stumbles against the body of* FLAVIUS. *He gives a startled gasp and shrinks back, calling*) Lights! A light here! (*A crowd of masked slaves obey his orders. One runs to him with a lantern. He looks down at* FLAVIUS' *corpse—half to himself*) I did wisely to stand him in my place. (*To* CALIGULA—*with sinister emphasis*) Too impatient, my loving grandchild! Take care lest I become impatient also—with your impatience! (CALIGULA *shudders and backs away to the extreme left corner, front, where he crouches on his haunches as inconspicuously as possible.* TIBERIUS *suddenly whirls around as if he felt a dagger at his back*).

TIBERIUS: Where—? (*Seeing* LAZARUS *where he had been—with relief—staring at his face now that the room is flooded with the purplish-crimson glow from all the lamps*) Ah, you are there. More lights! Darkness leads men into error. My heir mistakes a man for Cæsar and Cæsar, it appears, has mistaken a man for a dæmon! (*Scrutinizing him—with sinister finality*) I can deal with men. I know them well. Too well! (*He laughs grimly*) Therefore I hate them. (*He mounts the steps of the dais and sits on the couch at left of table—staring at* LAZARUS, *wonderingly*) But you seem—something other than man! That light! (*Then he forces a harsh laugh*) A trick! I had forgotten you are a magician. (*Arrogantly*) Stand there, Jew. I would question you about your magic. (*Smilingly* LAZARUS *ascends to where* TIBERIUS *points at the top of the dais.* MIRIAM *remains standing at the foot.* TIBERIUS *stares for a while with somber intensity at* LAZARUS) They say you died and have returned from death?

LAZARUS: (*smiling—as if he were correcting a child*) There is no death, Cæsar.

TIBERIUS: (*with a sneer of scepticism but with an underlying eagerness*) I have heard you teach that folly. (*Then threateningly*) You shall be given full opportunity to prove it! (*A pause—then in a low voice, bending down toward* LAZARUS) Do you foretell the future? (*Trembling but with a pretense of carelessness*) Must I die soon?

LAZARUS: (*simply*) Yes, Cæsar.

TIBERIUS: (*jumping up with a shuddering start*) Soon? Soon? (*Then his fear turning to rage*) What do you say? Vile Jew, do you dare threaten me with death! (LAZARUS, *looking into his eyes, begins to laugh softly.* TIBERIUS *sinks back on his couch, fighting to control himself—confusedly*) Laugh not, I ask you. I am old. It is not seemly. (LAZARUS *ceases his low laughter. A pause.* TIBERIUS *broods—then suddenly*) And you were really dead? (*He shudders*) Come nearer. I need to watch your face. I have learned to read the lies in faces. A Cæsar gets much practice—from childhood on—too much! (*With awe*) Your eyes are dark with death. While I watch them, answer me, what cured thee of death?

LAZARUS: (*gently*) There is only life, Cæsar. (*Then gaily mocking but compellingly*) And laughter! Look! Look well into my eyes, old Reader of Lies, and see if you can find aught in them that is not life—and laughter! (*He laughs softly. A ripple of soft laughter from the motionless figures about the room echoes his.* TIBERIUS *stares into his eyes. In the silence that ensues* POMPEIA *gets up and walks over to the dais. She stops to stare for a moment with cruel contempt at* MIRIAM, *then stands and looks up at* LAZARUS, *trying in vain to attract his or* CÆSAR'S *attention. Failing in this, she passes over and sits beside* CALIGULA, *whose attention is concentrated on* LAZARUS).

POMPEIA: I admire your strange magician, Caligula.

CALIGULA: (*without looking at her*) He is no magician. He is something like a god.

POMPEIA: (*longingly*) His laughter is like a god's. He is strong. I love him.

CALIGULA: (*turning to her—coarsely*) Do not waste your lust. He is faithful to his wife, I warn you.

POMPEIA: (*she points to* MIRIAM) Not that ugly slave?

CALIGULA: Yes. And yet on our journey, whole herds of women—and many as beautiful as you, Pompeia—threw themselves on him and begged for his love.

POMPEIA: (*her voice hardening*) And he?

CALIGULA: He laughed—and passed on. (*She starts.* CALIGULA *goes on wonderingly*) But they seemed as happy as if his laughter had possessed them! You are a woman. Tell me, how could that be?

POMPEIA: (*her voice cruel*) He shall not laugh at me!

CALIGULA: (*tauntingly*) I will bet a string of pearls against your body for a night that he does.

POMPEIA: (*defiantly*) Done! (*Then she laughs—a low, cruel laugh—staring at* MIRIAM) So he loves that woman?

CALIGULA: (*curiously*) What are you planning?

POMPEIA: I shall offer her the fruit Cæsar preserves for those he fears.

CALIGULA: (*with a careless shrug*) You will not win his love by killing her.

POMPEIA: I no longer want his love. I want to see him suffer, to hear his laughter choke in his throat with pain! (*She speaks with more and more voluptuous satisfaction*) Then *I* shall laugh! (*She laughs softly and steps forward*).

CALIGULA: (*concernedly*) Stop. I am his protector. (*Then suddenly*) But what is the Jewess to me? (*With more and more of a spirit of perverse cruelty*) Do it, Pompeia! His laughter is too cruel to us! We must save death from him!

POMPEIA: (*walks to the dais which she ascends slowly until she stands by* CÆSAR'S *couch behind him, confronting* LAZARUS. *But the two men remain unmindful of her presence.* TIBERIUS *continues to stare into* LAZARUS' *eyes. His whole body is now relaxed, at rest, a dreamy smile softens his thin, compressed mouth.* POMPEIA *leans over and takes a peach from the bowl of fruit on* CÆSAR'S *table and, taking* TIBERIUS' *hand in her other, she kisses it and calls insistently*) Cæsar. It is I, Pompeia. (LAZARUS *does not look at her. She stares at him defiantly.* TIBERIUS *blinks his eyes in a daze*).

TIBERIUS: (*dreamily*) Yes! A cloud came from a depth of sky—around me, softly, warmly, and the cloud dissolved into the sky, and the sky into peace! (*Suddenly springing to his feet and staring about him in a confused rage—clutching* POMPEIA *by the shoulder and forcing her to her knees*) What are you doing here?

POMPEIA: Forgive your loving slave! I grew afraid this magician had put you under a spell. (*She stares at* LAZARUS, *her words challenging him*).

TIBERIUS: (*confusedly, sinking back on his couch and releasing her*) A spell? Could it be he laid a dream of death upon me, leading me to death? (*He trembles timorously—appealing to* LAZARUS) Whatever magic thou didst to me, Dæmon, I beseech thee undo it!

LAZARUS: (*smiling*) Do you fear peace?

POMPEIA: (*harshly and insolently*) Mock not at Cæsar, dog! (LAZARUS *continues to smile. His eyes remain on* CÆSAR. *He seems absolutely unaware of* POMPEIA. *This enrages her the more against him. She speaks tauntingly to* TIBERIUS) Surely, Cæsar, this magician must have powerful charms since he dares to mock Tiberius to his face!

TIBERIUS: (*stung*) Be still! (*Then in a low tone to her*) Do you not know this Lazarus died and then by his magic rose from his tomb.

POMPEIA: (*scornfully*) To believe that, I must have seen it, Cæsar!

TIBERIUS: (*impatiently*) Do you think I would believe without good evidence? I have had them take the statements of many witnesses. The miracle was done in conjunction with another Jew acting as this man's tool. This other Jew, the report states, could not possibly have possessed any magic power Himself, for Pilate crucified Him a short time after and He died in pain and weakness within a few hours. But this Lazarus laughs at death!

LAZARUS: (*looks up, smiling with ironical bitterness*) Couldst Thou but hear, Jesus! And men shall keep on in panic nailing Man's soul to the cross of their fear until in the end they do it to avenge Thee, for Thine Honor and Glory! (*He sighs sadly—then after a struggle overcoming himself—with exultance*) Yes! (*His eyes fall again to* TIBERIUS *and he smiles*) Yes! Yes to the stupid as to the wise! To what is understood and to what cannot be understood! Known and unknown! Over and over! Forever and ever! Yes! (*He laughs softly to himself*).

TIBERIUS: (*with superstitious dread*) What dost thou mean, Dæmon?

POMPEIA: (*with indignant scorn*) Let him prove there is no death, Cæsar! (*She appeals to the company who straighten up on their couches with interest*).

CHORUS: (*chant demandingly*)

> Let him prove there is no death!
> We are bored!

CROWD: (*echoing*)

> Prove there is no death!
> We are bored, Cæsar!

TIBERIUS: (*waits to see what* LAZARUS *will say—then as he says nothing, plucking up his courage—his cruelty aroused*) Do you hear, Lazarus?

POMPEIA: Make him perform his miracle again!

CHORUS: (*as before*)

> Let him perform a miracle!
> We are bored, Cæsar!

CROWD: (*they now stand up and coming from behind their tables, move forward toward the dais*).

> A miracle!
> We are bored!

POMPEIA: Let him raise someone from the dead!

CHORUS: (*chanting with a pettish insistence*).

> Raise the dead!
> We are bored!

CROWD: (*echoing—grouping in a big semicircle as of spectators in a theatre, around and to the sides of the dais, one sex on each side.* CALIGULA *moves in from the left in front of them. They form in three ranks, the first squatting on their hams like savages (as* CALIGULA *does), the second rank crouching over them, the third leaning over the second, all with a hectic, morbid interest).*

We are bored!
Raise the dead!

POMPEIA: (*with a cruel smile*) I have thought of a special test for him, Cæsar. (*She whispers in* CÆSAR'S *ear and points to* MIRIAM *and the fruit in her hand*) And he must laugh!

TIBERIUS: (*with a harsh, cruel chuckle*) Yes, I shall command him to laugh! (*Then disgustedly*) But she is sad and old. I will be only doing him a favor.

CALIGULA: (*rocking back and forth on his haunches—looking at* LAZARUS *with taunting cruelty*) No, Cæsar! I know he loves her!

LAZARUS: Yes! (*He steps down from the dais to* MIRIAM'S *side and taking her head in both his hands, he kisses her on the lips*).

TIBERIUS: (*with a malignant grin*) Give her the fruit!

POMPEIA: (*advances and offers the peach to* MIRIAM—*with a hard, cruel little laugh*) Cæsar invites you to eat!

MIRIAM: (*to* LAZARUS—*requesting meekly but longingly*) May I accept, Lazarus? Is it time at last? My love has followed you over long roads among strangers and each league we came from home my heart has grown older. Now it is too old for you, a heart too weary for your loving laughter. Ever your laughter has grown younger, Lazarus! Upward it springs like a lark from a field, and sings! Once I knew your laughter was my child, my son of Lazarus; but then it grew younger and I felt at last it had returned to my womb—and ever younger and younger—until, tonight, when I spoke to you of home, I felt new birth-pains as your laughter, grown too young for me, flew back to the unborn—a birth so like a death! (*She sobs and wipes her eyes with her sleeve—then humbly, reaching out for the fruit*) May I accept it, Lazarus? You should have newborn laughing hearts to love you. My old one labors with memories and its blood is sluggish with the past. Your home on the hills of space is too far away. My heart longs for the warmth of close walls of earth baked in the sun. Our home in Bethany, Lazarus, where you and my children lived and died. Our tomb near our home, Lazarus, in which you and my children wait for me. Is it time at last?

LAZARUS: (*deeply moved*) Poor lonely heart! It has been crueler for you than I remembered. Go in peace—to peace! (*His voice trembles in spite of himself*) I shall be lonely, dear one. (*With a note of pleading*) You have never laughed with my laughter. Will you call back— Yes!— when you know—to tell me you understand and laugh with me at last?

MIRIAM: (*not answering him, to* POMPEIA, *taking the peach and making a humble courtesy before her*) I thank you, pretty lady. (*She raises the peach toward her mouth. Involuntarily one of* LAZARUS' *hands half-reaches out as if to stop her*).

POMPEIA: (*with savage triumph, pointing*) See! He would stop her! He is afraid of death!

CHORUS: (*pointing—jeeringly*) He is afraid of death! Ha-ha-ha-ha!

CROWD: (*jeeringly*) Ha-ha-ha-ha!

MIRIAM: (*bites into the peach and, chewing, begins, as if immediately affected, to talk like a garrulous old woman, her words coming quicker and quicker as her voice becomes fainter and fainter*) Say what you like, it is much better I should go home first, Lazarus. We have been away so long, there will be so much to attend to about the house. And all the children will be waiting. You would be as helpless as a child, Lazarus. Between you and the children, things would soon be in a fine state! (*More and more confused*) No, no! You cannot help me, dearest one. You are only in my way. No, I will make the fire. When you laid it the last time, we all had to run for our lives, choking, the smoke poured from the windows, the neighbors thought the house was burning! (*She laughs—a queer, vague little inward laugh*) You are so impractical. The neighbors all get the best of you. Money slips through your fingers. If it was not for me— (*She sighs—then brightly and lovingly*) But, dearest husband, why do you take it so to heart? Why do you feel guilty because you are not like other men? That is why I love you so much. Is it a sin to be born a dreamer? But God, He must be a dreamer, too, or how would we be on earth? Do not keep saying to yourself so bitterly, you are a failure in life! Do not sit brooding on the hilltop in the evening like a black figure of Job against the sky! (*Her voice trembling*) Even if God has taken our little ones—yes, in spite of sorrow—have you not a good home I make for you, and a wife who loves you? (*She forces a chuckle*) Be grateful, then—for me! Smile, my sad one! Laugh a little once in a while! Come home, bringing me laughter of the wind from the hills! (*Swaying, looking at the peach in her hand*) What a mellow, sweet fruit! Did you bring it home for me? (*She falls back into his arms. Gently he lets her body sink until it rests against the steps of the dais.* TIBERIUS *rises from his couch to bend over with cruel gloating.* POMPEIA *steps nearer to* LAZARUS, *staring at him mockingly.* CALIGULA *hops to her side, looking from* LAZARUS *to* MIRIAM. *The half-circle of masked figures moves closer, straining forward and downward as if to overwhelm the two figures at the foot of the dais with their concentrated death wish*).

TIBERIUS: (*thickly*) She is dead, and I do not hear you laugh!

LAZARUS: (*bending down—supplicatingly*) Miriam! Call back to me! Laugh! (*He pauses. A second of dead silence. Then, with a found that is very like a sob, he kisses her on the lips*) I am lonely!

POMPEIA: (*with savage malice—jeeringly*) See! He weeps, Cæsar! (*She bursts into strident laughter*) Ha-ha-ha-ha!

CHORUS: (*echoing her laughter*)

> Ha-ha-ha-ha!
> There is fear!
> There is death.

CROWD:

> There is death!
> Ha-ha-ha-ha!

CALIGULA: (*in a frenzy of despairing rage, hopping up and down*) Liar! Charlatan! Weakling! How you have cheated Caligula! (*He suddenly slaps* LAZARUS *viciously across the face*) There is death! Laugh, if you dare!

TIBERIUS: (*standing—in a sinister cold rage, the crueler because his dream of a cure for death is baffled, yet feeling his power as* CÆSAR *triumphant nevertheless*) And I thought you might be a dæmon. I thought you might have a magic cure— (*With revengeful fury*) But death is, and death is mine! I shall make you pray for death! And I shall make Death laugh at you! Ha-ha-ha-ha! (*In a frenzy as* LAZARUS *neither makes a sound nor looks up*) Laugh, Lazarus! Laugh at yourself! Laugh with me! (*Then to his soldiers*) Scourge him! Make him laugh!

CALIGULA: (*running to soldiers—fiercely*) Give me a scourge!

POMPEIA: (*running to the soldiers—hysterically*) Ha-ha-ha-ha! Let me beat him, Cæsar! (*They group behind him. The rods and scourges are uplifted over his back to strike, when in the dead expectant silence,* MIRIAM's *body is seen to rise in a writhing tortured last effort*).

MIRIAM: (*in a voice of unearthly sweetness*) Yes! There is only life! Lazarus, be not lonely! (*She laughs and sinks back and is still. A shuddering murmur of superstitious fear comes from them as they shrink back swiftly from* LAZARUS, *remaining huddled one against the other.* POMPEIA *runs to the feet of* TIBERIUS *and crouches down on the steps below him, as if for protection, her terrified eyes on* MIRIAM. CALIGULA *runs to her and crouches beside and beneath her*).

LAZARUS: (*kisses* MIRIAM *again and raises his head. His face is radiant with new faith and joy. He smiles with happiness and speaks to himself with a mocking affection as if to an amusing child*) That much remained hidden in me of the sad old Lazarus who died of self-pity—his loneliness! Lonely no more! Man's loneliness is but his fear of life! Lonely no more! Millions of laughing stars there are around me! And laughing dust, born once of woman on this earth, now freed to dance! New stars are born of dust eternally! The old, grown mellow with God, burst into flaming seed! The fields of infinite space are sown—and grass for sheep springs up on the hills of earth! But there is no death, nor fear, nor loneliness! There is only God's Eternal Laughter! His Laughter flows into the lonely heart! (*He begins to laugh, his laughter clear and ringing—the laughter of a conqueror arrogant with happiness and the pride of a new triumph. He bends and picks up the body of* MIRIAM *in his arms and, his head thrown back, laughing, he ascends the dais and places her on the table as on a bier. He touches one hand on her breast, as if he were taking an oath to life on her heart, looks upward and laughs, his voice ringing more and more with a terrible unbearable power and beauty that beats those in the room into an abject submissive panic.* TIBERIUS *grovels half under the table, his hands covering his ears, his face on the floor; he is laughing with the agony and terror of death.* POMPEIA *lies face down on the first step and beats it with her fist; she is laughing with horror amd self-loathing.* CALIGULA,, *his hands clutching his head, pounds it against the edge of the steps; he is laughing with grief and remorse. The rest, soldiers, slaves and the prostitutes of both sexes, writhe and twist distractedly, seeking to hide their heads against each other, beating each other and the floor with clenched hands. An agonized moan of supplicating laughter comes from them all*).

ALL:

> Ha-ha-ha-ha! Ha-ha-ha-ha!
> Let us die, Lazarus!
> Mercy, Laughing One!
> Mercy of death!
> Ha-ha-ha-ha! Ha-ha-ha-ha!

(*But the laughter of* LAZARUS *is as remote now as the laughter of a god*).

CURTAIN

*S*CENE: *The same as previous Scene—the same night a short while later. All the lamps are out except the one on the table on the dais which, placed beside the head of* MIRIAM, *shines down upon the white mask of her face. In the half-darkness, the walls are lost in shadow, the room seems immense, the dais nearer.*

LAZARUS *sits on the couch at the right on the dais. His face is strong and proud although his eyes are fixed down on the face of* MIRIAM. *He seems more youthful still now, like a young son who keeps watch by the body of his mother, but at the same time retaining the aloof serenity of the statue of a god. His face expresses sorrow and a happiness that transcends sorrow.*

On the other side of the table, at the end of the couch, TIBERIUS *sits facing front, his elbows on his knees, his large hands with bloated veins hanging loosely. He keeps his gaze averted from the corpse. He talks to* LAZARUS *half over his shoulder.*

On the top step, POMPEIA *sits, facing right, her hands clasped about one knee, the other leg stretched down to the lower step. Her head is thrown back and she is gazing up into* LAZARUS' *face.*

On the step below her, CALIGULA *squats on his haunches, his arms on his knees, his fists pressed to his temples. He is staring straight before him.*

Only these four people are in the room now.

TIBERIUS: (*gloomily*) Was she dead, Dæmon, and was it thy power that recalled life to her body for that moment? Or was she still living and her words only the last desire of her love to comfort you, Lazarus? (LAZARUS *does not reply*) If thou dost not tell me, I must always doubt thee, Dæmon.

POMPEIA: (*with a sigh of bewildered happiness, turns to* CALIGULA) I am glad he laughed, Caligula! Did I say I loved him before? Then it was only my body that wanted a slave. Now it is my heart that desires a master! Now I know love for the first time in my life!

437

CALIGULA: (*bitterly*) Fool! What does he care for love? (*Somberly*) He loves everyone—but no one—not even me! (*He broods frowningly*).

POMPEIA: (*following her own thoughts*) And now that hag is dead he will need a woman, young and beautiful, to protect and comfort him, to make him a home and bear his children! (*She dreams, her eyes again fixed on* LAZARUS—*then suddenly turning to* CALIGULA) I am glad I lost our bet. But you must accept some other payment. Now I know love, I may not give myself to any man save him!

CALIGULA: I do not want you! What are you but another animal! Faugh! (*With a grimace of disgust*) Pleasure is dirty and joyless! Or we who seek it are, which comes to the same thing. (*Then grimly*) But our bet can rest. This is not the end. There may still be a chance for you to laugh at him!

POMPEIA: No! Now I could not! I should weep for his defeat!

TIBERIUS: (*gloomily arguing, half to himself*) His laughter triumphed over me, but he has not brought her back to life. I think he knows no cure for another's death, as I had hoped. And I must always doubt that it was not some trick—(*Harshly*) until I have tested him with his own life! He cannot cheat me then! (*A pause—arguing to himself*) But he was dead—that much has been proved— and before he died he was old and sad. What did he find beyond there? (*Suddenly—turning to* LAZARUS *now*) What did you find beyond death, Lazarus?

LAZARUS: (*exaltedly*) Life! God's Eternal Laughter!

TIBERIUS: (*shaking his head*) I want hope—for me, Tiberius Cæsar.

LAZARUS: What is—you? But there is hope for Man! Love is Man's hope—love for his life on earth, a noble love above suspicion and distrust! Hitherto Man has always suspected his life, and in revenge and self-torture his love has been faithless! He has even betrayed Eternity, his mother, with his slave he calls Immortal Soul! (*He laughs softly, gaily, mockingly—then to* TIBERIUS *directly*) Hope for you, Tiberius Cæsar? Then dare to love Eternity without your fear desiring to possess her! Be brave enough to be possessed!

TIBERIUS: (*strangely*) My mother was the wife of Cæsar. (*Then dully*) I do not understand.

LAZARUS: Men are too cowardly to understand! And so the worms of their little fears eat them and grow fat and terrible and become their jealous gods they must appease with lies!

TIBERIUS: (*wearily*) Your words are meaningless, Lazarus. You are a fool. All laughter is malice, all gods are dead, and life is a sickness.

LAZARUS: (*laughs pityingly*) So say the race of men, whose lives are long dyings! They evade their fear of death by becoming so sick of life that by the time death comes they are too lifeless to fear it! Their disease triumphs over death—a noble victory called resignation! "We are sick," they say, "therefore there is no God in us, therefore there is no God!" Oh, if men would but interpret that first cry of man fresh from the womb as the laughter of one who even then says to his heart, "It is my pride as God to become Man. Then let it be my pride as Man to recreate the God in me!" (*He laughs softly but with exultant pride*).

POMPEIA: (*laughing with him—proudly*) He will create a god in me! I shall be proud!

CALIGULA: (*pounding his temples with his fist—tortured*) I am Caligula. I was born in a camp among soldiers. My father was Germanicus, a hero, as all men know. But I do not understand this—and though I burst with pride, I cannot laugh with joy!

TIBERIUS: (*gloomily*) Obscurities! I have found nothing in life that merits pride. I am not proud of being Cæsar—and what is a god but a Cæsar over Cæsars? If fools kneel and worship me because they fear me, should I be proud? But Cæsar is a fact, and Tiberius, a man, is one, and I cling to these certainties—and I do not wish to die! If I were sure of eternal sleep beyond there, deep rest and forgetfulness of all I have ever seen or heard or hated or loved on earth, I would gladly die! But surely, Lazarus, nothing is sure—peace the least sure of all— and I fear there is no rest beyond there, that one remembers there

as here and cannot sleep, that the mind goes on eternally the same—
a long insomnia of memories and regrets and the ghosts of dreams
one has poisoned to death passing with white bodies spotted by the
leprous fingers of one's lusts. (*Bitterly*) I fear the long nights now in
which I lie awake and listen to Death dancing round me in the
darkness, prancing to the drum beat of my heart! (*He shudders*) And
I am afraid, Lazarus—afraid that there is no sleep beyond there,
either!

LAZARUS: There is peace! (*His words are like a benediction he pronounces
upon them. Soothed in a mysterious, childlike way, they repeat the word
after him, wonderingly*).

POMPEIA: Peace?

CALIGULA: Peace?

TIBERIUS: Peace? (*For a long moment there is complete silence. Then* TIBER-
IUS *sighs heavily, shaking his head*) Peace! Another word blurred into
a senseless sigh by men's longing! A bubble of froth blown from the
lips of the dying toward the stars! No! (*He grins bitterly—then looks
at* LAZARUS—*somberly contemptuous and threatening*) You are pleased
to act the mysterious, Jew, but I shall solve you! (*Then with a lawyer-
like incisiveness*) There is one certainty about you and I must know
the cause—for there must be a cause and a rational explanation! You
were fifty when you died—

LAZARUS: (*smiling mockingly*) Yes. When I died.

TIBERIUS: (*unheeding*) And now your appearance is of one younger by
a score. Not alone your appearance! You *are* young. I see the fact,
the effect. And I demand an explanation of the cause without mystic
nonsense or evasion. (*Threateningly*) And I warn you to answer directly in plain words—and not to laugh, you understand!—not to
dare!—or I shall lose patience with you and—(*With a grim smile*) I
can be terrible! (LAZARUS *smiles gently at him. He turns away with
confused annoyance, then back to* LAZARUS, *resuming his lawyer-like manner*) What was it restored your youth? How did you contrive that

your body reversed the natural process and grows younger? Is it a charm by which you invoke a supernatural force? Or is it a powder you dissolve in wine? Or a liquid? Or an unguent you rub into the skin to revitalize the old bones and tissues? Or—what is it, Lazarus?

LAZARUS: (*gently*) I know that age and time are but timidities of thought.

TIBERIUS: (*broodingly—as if he had not heard—persuasively*) Perhaps you ask yourself, what would Tiberius do with youth? Then, because you must have heard rumors of my depravity, you will conclude the old lecher desires youth for his lusts! (*He laughs harshly*) Ha! Why, do not my faithful subjects draw pictures of an old buck goat upon the walls and write above them, Cæsar? And they are just. In self-contempt of Man I have made this man, myself, the most swinish and contemptible of men! Yes! In all this empire there is no man so base a hog as I! (*He grins bitterly and ironically*) My claim to this excellence, at least, is not contested! Everyone admits therein Tiberius is by right their Cæsar! (*He laughs bitterly*) Ha! So who would believe Tiberius if he said, I want youth again because I loathe lust and long for purity!

LAZARUS: (*gently*) I believe you, Cæsar.

TIBERIUS: (*stares at him—deeply moved*) You—believe—? (*Then gruffly*) You lie! You are not mad—and only a madman would believe another man! (*Then confidingly, leaning over toward* LAZARUS) I know it is folly to speak—but—one gets old, one becomes talkative, one wishes to confess, to say the thing one has always kept hidden, to reveal one's unique truth—and there is so little time left—and one is alone! Therefore the old—like children—talk to themselves, for they have reached that hopeless wisdom of experience which knows that though one were to cry it in the streets to multitudes, or whisper it in the kiss to one's beloved, the only ears that can ever hear one's secret are one's own! (*He laughs bitterly*) And so I talk aloud, Lazarus! I talk to my loneliness!

LAZARUS: (*simply*) I hear, Tiberius.

TIBERIUS: (*again moved and confused—forcing a mocking smile*) Liar! Eavesdropper! You merely—listen! (*Then he turns away*) My mother, Livia, that strong woman, giving birth to me, desired not a child, but a Cæsar—just as, married to Augustus, she loved him not but loved herself as Cæsar's wife. She made me feel, in the proud questioning of her scornful eyes, that to win her mother love I must become Cæsar. She poisoned Prince Marcellus and young Gaius and Lucius that the way might be clear for me. I used to see their blood dance in red specks before my eyes when I looked at the sky. Now— (He brushes his hand before his eyes) it is all a red blot! I cannot distinguish. There have been too many. My mother— her blood is in that blot, for I revenged myself on her. I did not kill her, it is true, but I deprived her of her power and she died, as I knew she must, that powerful woman who bore me as a weapon! The murder was subtle and cruel—how cruel only that passionate, deep-breasted woman unslaked by eighty years of devoured desires could know! Too cruel! I did not go to her funeral. I was afraid her closed eyes might open and look at me! (*Then with almost a cry*) I want youth, Lazarus, that I may play again about her feet with the love I felt for her before I learned to read her eyes! (*He half sobs, bowing his head. A pause*).

CALIGULA: (*nudging* POMPEIA—*with a crafty whisper*) Do you hear? The old lecher talks to himself. He is becoming senile. He will soon die. And I shall be Cæsar. Then I shall laugh!

POMPEIA: (*staring up at* LAZARUS' *face, hearing only* CALIGULA'S *words without their meaning*) No. My Lazarus does not laugh now. See. His mouth is silent—and a little sad, I think.

LAZARUS: (*gently and comfortingly*) I hear, Tiberius.

TIBERIUS: (*harshly*) I hated that woman, my mother, and I still hate her! Have you ever loved, Lazarus? (*Then with* a *glance at* MIRIAM'S *body and a shuddering away from it—vaguely*) I was forgetting her. I killed your love, too, did I not? Well, I must! I envy those who are loved. Where I can, I kill love—for retribution's sake—but much of it escapes me. (*Then harshly again*) I loved Agrippina. We were married. A son was born to us. We were happy. Then that proud woman, my mother, saw my happiness. Was she jealous of my love? Or did she know no happy man would wish to be Cæsar? Well, she condemned my happiness to death. She whispered to Augustus and he ordered me to divorce Agrippina. I should have opened her veins and mine, and died with her. But my mother stayed by me, Agrippina was kept away, my mother spoke to me and spoke to me and even wept, that tall woman, strong as a great man, and I consented that my love be murdered. Then my mother married me to a whore. Why? The whore was Cæsar's daughter, true—but I feel that was not all of it, that my mother wished to keep me tortured that I might love her alone and long to be Cæsar! (*He laughs harshly*) Ha! In brief, I married the whore, she tortured me, my mother's scheming prospered—that subtle and crafty woman!—and many years passed in being here and there, in doing this and that, in growing full of hate and revengeful ambition to be Cæsar. At last, Augustus died. I was Cæsar. Then I killed that whore, my wife, and I starved my mother's strength to death until she died, and I began to take pleasure in vengeance upon men, and pleasure in taking vengeance on myself. (*He grins horribly*) It is all very simple, as you see! (*He suddenly starts to his feet—with harsh arrogance and pride, threateningly*) Enough! Why do I tell you these old tales? Must I explain to you why I want youth? It is my whim! I am Cæsar! And now I must lie down and try to sleep! And it is my command that you reveal the secret of your youth to me when I awake, or else— (*With malignant cruelty*) I will have to revenge the death of a hope on you—and a hope at my age demands a terrible expiation on its slayer! (*He walks down and starts to go off, right—then turns and addresses* LAZARUS *with grim irony*) Good night to you, Lazarus. And remember there shall be death while I am Cæsar! (*He turns to go*).

LAZARUS: (*smiling affectionately at him, shakes his head*) Cæsar must believe in death. But does the husband of Agrippina?

TIBERIUS: (*stops short and stares at* LAZARUS, *confused and stuttering*) What—what—do you mean, Lazarus?

LAZARUS: I have heard your loneliness.

TIBERIUS: (*cruelly and grimly again*) So much the more reason why my pride should kill you! Remember that! (*He turns and strides off into the darkness at right*).

CALIGULA: (*peers after him until sure he is gone—then gets up and begins a grotesque, hopping dance, singing a verse of the legionary's song*)

> A bold legionary am I
> March, oh march on!
> A Roman eagle was my daddy
> My mother was a drunken drabby
> Oh march on to the wars!

(*He laughs gratingly, posturing and gesticulating up at* LAZARUS) Ha-ha-ha! He is gone! I can breathe! His breath in the same air suffocates me! The gods grant mine do the same for him! But he is failing! He talks to himself like a man in second childhood. His words are a thick babble I could not hear. They well from his lips like clots of blood from a reopened wound. I kept listening to the beating of his heart. It sounded slow, slower than when I last heard it. Did you detect that, Lazarus? Once or twice I thought it faltered— (*He draws in his breath with an avid gasp—then laughs gratingly*) Ha-ha-ha— (*Grandiloquently*) Tiberius, the old buck goat, will soon be gone, my friends, and in his place you will be blessed with the beautiful young god, Caligula! Hail to Caligula! Hail! Ha-ha-ha— (*His laughter suddenly breaks off into a whimper and he stands staring around him in a panic of fear that he has been overheard. He slinks noiselessly up the steps of the dais and squats coweringly at* LAZARUS' *feet, blinking up at his face in monkeywise, clutching* LAZARUS' *hand in both of his. His teeth can be heard chattering together in nervous fear.* POMPEIA, *whose gaze has remained fixed on* LAZARUS *throughout, has gradually moved closer to him until she, too, is at his feet, half-kneeling beneath the table on which* MIRIAM *lies, side by side with* CALIGULA *but as oblivious of him as he is of her. Having grown calmer now,* CALIGULA *speaks again—mournful and bewildered*).

CALIGULA: Why should I love you, Lazarus? Your laughter taunts me! It insults Cæsar! It denies Rome! But I will warn you again. Escape! Tonight Tiberius' mood is to play sentimental, but tomorrow he will jeer while hyenas gnaw at your skull and lick your brain. And then— there is pain, Lazarus! There is pain!

POMPEIA: (*pressing her hand to her own heart—with a shudder*) Yes, there is pain!

LAZARUS: (*smiling down on them—gently*) If you can answer Yes to pain, there is no pain!

POMPEIA: (*passionately*) Yes! Yes! I love Lazarus!

CALIGULA: (*with a bitter grin*) Do not take pain away from us! It is our one truth. Without pain there is nothing—a nothingness in which even your laughter, Lazarus, is swallowed at one gulp like a whining gnat by the cretin's silence of immensity! Ha-ha! No, we must keep pain! Especially Cæsar must! Pain must twinkle with a mad mirth in a Cæsar's eyes—men's pain—or they would become dissatisfied and disrespectful! Ha-ha! (*He stops his grating laughter abruptly and continues mournfully*) I am sick, Lazarus, sick of cruelty and lust and human flesh and all the imbecilities of pleasure—the unclean antics of half-witted children! (*With a mounting agony of longing*) I would be clean! If I could only laugh your laughter, Lazarus! That would purify my heart. For I could wish to love all men, as you love them—as I love you! If only I did not fear them and despise them! If I could only believe— believe in them—in life—in myself!—believe that one man or woman in the world knew and loved the real Caligula—then I might have faith in Caligula myself—then I might laugh your laughter!

LAZARUS: (*suddenly, in a quiet but compelling voice*) I, who know you, love you, Caligula. (*Gently patting his head*) I love Caligula.

CALIGULA: (*staring up at him in pathetic confusion*) You? You? You, Lazarus? (*He begins to tremble all over as if in a seizure—chokingly*) Beware! It is not good—not just—to make fun of me— to laugh at my misery—saying you love— (*In a frenzy, he jumps to his feet threatening* LAZARUS) Are you trying to fool me, hypocrite? Do you think I have become so abject that you dare—? Because I love you, do you presume—? Do you think I am your slave, dog of a Jew, that you can—insult—to my face—the heir of Cæsar— (*He stutters and stammers with rage, hopping up and down grotesquely, shaking his fist at* LAZARUS, *who smiles at him affectionately as at a child in a tantrum*).

LAZARUS: (*catching his eyes and holding them with his glance—calmly*) Believe, Caligula!

CALIGULA: (*again overcome—stuttering with strange terror*) Believe? But I cannot! I must not! You cannot know me, if— You are a holy man! You are a god in a mortal body—you can laugh with joy to be alive—while I— Oh, no, you cannot love me! There is nothing in me at bottom but a despising and an evil eye! You cannot! You are only being kind! (*Hysterically*) I do not want your kindness! I hate your pity! I am too proud! I am too strong! (*He collapses weepingly, kneeling and clutching* LAZARUS' *hand in both of his*).

LAZARUS: (*smiling*) You are so proud of being evil! What if there is no evil? What if there are only health and sickness? Believe in the healthy god called Man in you! Laugh at Caligula, the funny clown who beats the backside of his shadow with a bladder and thinks thereby he is Evil, the Enemy of God! (*He suddenly lifts the face of* CALIGULA *and stares into his eyes*) Believe! What if you are a man and men are despicable? Men are also unimportant! Men pass! Like rain into the sea! The sea remains! Man remains! Man slowly arises from the past of the race of men that was his tomb of death! For Man death is not! Man, Son of God's Laughter, *is!* (*He begins to laugh triumphantly, staring deep into* CALIGULA'S *eyes*) Is, Caligula! Believe in the laughing god within you!

CALIGULA: (*bursting suddenly into choking, joyful laughter—like a visionary*). I believe! I believe there is love even for Caligula! I can laugh—

now—Lazarus! Free laughter! Clean! No sickness! No lust for death! My corpse no longer rots in my heart! The tomb is full of sunlight! I am alive! I who love Man, I who can love and laugh! Listen, Lazarus! I dream! When I am Cæsar, I will devote my power to your truth. I will decree that there must be kindness and love! I will make the Empire one great Blessed Isle! Rome shall know happiness, it shall believe in life, it shall learn to laugh your laughter, Lazarus, or I— (*He raises his hand in an imperial autocratic gesture*).

LAZARUS: (*gaily mocking*) Or you will cut off its head?

CALIGULA: (*fiercely*) Yes! I will—! (*Then meeting* LAZARUS' *eyes, he beats his head with his fists crazily*) Forgive me! I forget! I forget!

LAZARUS: Go out under the sky! Let your heart climb on laughter to a star! Then make it look down at earth, and watch Caligula commanding Life under pain of death to do his will! (*He laughs*).

CALIGULA: (*laughing*) I will! I do! I laugh at him! Caligula is a trained ape, a humped cripple! Now I take him out under the sky, where I can watch his monkey tricks, where there is space for laughter and where this new joy, your love of me, may dance! (*Laughing clearly and exultantly, he runs out through the arched doorway at rear*).

LAZARUS: (*stops laughing—shaking his head, almost sadly*) They forget! It is too soon for laughter! (*Then grinning at himself*) What, Lazarus? Are you, too, thinking in terms of time, old fool so soon to reënter infinity? (*He laughs with joyous self-mockery*).

POMPEIA: (*who has crept to his feet, kisses his hand passionately*) I love you, Lazarus!

LAZARUS: (*stops laughing, and looks down at her gently*) And I love you, woman.

POMPEIA: (*with a gasp of delight*) You? (*She stares up into his eyes doubtingly, raising her face toward his*) Then—put your arms around me. (*He does so, smiling gently*) And hold me to you. (*He presses her closer to him*) And kiss me. (*He kisses her on the forehead*) No, on the lips! (*He kisses her. She flings her arms about his neck passionately and kisses him again and again—then slowly draws away—remains looking into his eyes a long time, shrinking back from him with bewildered pain which speedily turns to rage and revengeful hatred*) No! No! It is *my* love, not Love! I want you to know *my* love, to give me back love—for me—only for me— Pompeia—my body, my heart—me, a woman— not Woman, women! Do I love Man, men? I hate men! I love you, Lazarus—a man—a lover—a father to children! I want love—as you loved that woman there. (*She points to* MIRIAM) that I poisoned for love of you! But did you love her—or just Woman, wife and mother of men? (*She stares—then as if reading admission in his eyes, she springs to her feet*) Liar! Cheat! Hypocrite! Thief! (*Half hysterical with rage, pain and grief, she bends over* MIRIAM *and smooths the hair back from her forehead*) Poor wife! Poor woman! How he must have tortured you! Now I remember the pity in your eyes when you looked at me! Oh, how his soothing gray words must have pecked at the wound in your heart like doves with bloody beaks! (*Then with sudden harshness*) But perhaps you were too dull to understand, too poor and tired and ugly and old to care, too slavish—! Pah! (*She turns away with contempt and faces* LAZARUS *with revengeful hatred*) Did you think I would take her place—become your slave, wait upon you, give you love and passion and beauty in exchange for phrases about man and gods—you who are neither a man nor a god but a dead thing without desire! You dared to hope I would give my body, my love, to you! (*She spits in his face and laughs harshly*) You insolent fool! I shall punish you! You shall be tortured as you have tortured! (*She laughs wildly—then steps down from the dais and goes off right, crying distractedly*) Cæsar! This man has made you a fool before all the world! Torture him, Cæsar! Now! Let the people witness! Send heralds to wake them! Torture him, Cæsar, the man who laughs at you! Ha-ha-ha-ha! (*Her laughter is caught up by all the* GIRLS *and* YOUTHS *of the palace, who, as she disappears, led by their* CHORUS, *pour in from each side of the room and dance forward to group themselves around the dais as in the previous scene, staring at* LAZARUS, *laughing cruelly, falsely, stridently*).

CHORUS: (*tauntingly*)

> Ha-ha-ha-ha!
> Laugh now, Lazarus!
> Let us see you laugh!
> Ha-ha-ha-ha!

CROWD: (*echoing*)

> Ha-ha-ha-ha!
> Ha-ha-ha-ha!

LAZARUS: (*moves, and immediately there is silence. He bends down and kisses* MIRIAM *and picks her up in his arms. Talking down to her face—with a tender smile*) Farewell! You are home! And now I will take your body home to earth! Space is too far away, you said! Home in the earth! There will be so much for you to do there! Home! Earth (*His voice trembling a bit*) Farewell, body of Miriam. My grief is a lonely cry wailing in the home in my heart that you have left forever! (*Then exultantly*) But what am I? Now your love has become Eternal Love! Now, since your life passed, I feel Eternal Life made nobler by your selflessness! Love has grown purer! The laughter of God is more profoundly tender! (*He looks up in an ecstasy and descends the dais, carrying her*) Yes, that is it! That is it, my Miriam! (*Laughing softly and tenderly, he walks around the dais and carries the body out through the doorway in rear. The* CHORUS *and* YOUTHS *and* GIRLS *make way for him in awed silence—then scurry around to right and left, forming an aisle through which he passes—then after he has gone out through the arch, they close into a semicircular group again, staring after him, and a whisper of strange, bewildered, tender laughter comes from them*).

CHORUS: (*in this whisper*)

> That is it!
> Love is pure!
> Laughter is tender!
> Laugh!

CROWD: (*echoing*)

> Laugh! Laugh!

CURTAIN

SCENE TWO

SCENE: *The arena of an amphitheatre. It is just before dawn of the same night. Cæsar's throne is on the left at the extreme front, facing right, turned a little toward front. It is lighted by four immense lamps. In front of the throne is a marble railing that tops the wall that encloses the arena. In the rear the towering pile of the circular amphitheatre is faintly outlined in deeper black against the dark sky.*

TIBERIUS *sits on the throne, his eyes fixed on the middle of the arena off right, where, bound to a high stake after he had been tortured,* LAZARUS *is now being burnt alive over a huge pile of faggots. The crackling of the flames is heard. Their billowing rise and fall is reflected on the masked faces of the multitude who sit on the banked tiers of marble behind and to the rear of the throne, with their* CHORUS, *seven men masked in Middle Age in the Servile, Hypocritical type, grouped on each side of the throne of* CÆSAR *on a lower tier.*

Half-kneeling before TIBERIUS, *her chin resting on her hands on top of the marble rail,* POMPEIA *also stares at* LAZARUS.

Before the curtain, the crackle of the flames and an uproar of human voices from the multitude, jeering, hooting, laughing at LAZARUS *in cruel mockery of his laughter. This sound has risen to its greatest volume as the curtain rises.*

CHORUS: (*chanting mockingly*)

> Ha-ha-ha-ha!
> Burn and laugh!
> Laugh now, Lazarus!
> Ha-ha-ha-ha!

CROWD: (*chanting with revengeful mockery*) Ha-ha-ha-ha!

TIBERIUS: Who laughs now, Lazarus—thou or Cæsar? Ha-ha—! (*With awe*) His flesh melts in the fire but his eyes shine with peace!

POMPEIA: How he looks at me! (*Averting her eyes with a shudder*) Command them to put out his eyes, Cæsar!

TIBERIUS: (*harshly*) No. I want to read his eyes when they see death! (*Then averting his face—guiltily*) He is looking at me, not you. I should not have listened to your cries for his death.

POMPEIA: (*turning to him again with a shudder of agony—beseechingly*) Have them put out his eyes, Cæsar! They call to me!

TIBERIUS: (*as if not hearing her—to himself*) Why do I feel remorse? His laughter dies and is forgotten, and the hope it raised dies— (*With sudden excitement*) And yet—he must know something—and if he would—even now he could tell— (*Suddenly rising to his feet he calls imploringly*) Lazarus!

CHORUS: (*chanting in a great imploring chorus now*) Lazarus!

CROWD: (*echoing*) Lazarus!

SOLDIER'S VOICE: (*calling from off beside the stake*) You had us gag him, Cæsar, so he might not laugh. Shall we cut away the gag?

POMPEIA: (*in terror*) No, Cæsar! He will laugh! And I will go to him! (*Desperately*) He will laugh at you, Cæsar—and the mob will laugh with him!

TIBERIUS: (*struggles with himself—then calls*) Lazarus! If you hear let your eyes answer, and I will grant the mercy of death to end your agony! Is there hope of love somewhere for men on earth?

CHORUS: (*intoning as before*)

> Is there hope of love
> For us on earth?

CROWD:

> Hope of love
> For us on earth!

SOLDIER'S VOICE: His eyes laugh, Cæsar!

TIBERIUS: (*in a strange frenzy now*) Hear me, thou Dæmon of Laughter! Hear and answer, I beseech thee, who alone hath known joy! (*More and more wildly*) How must we live? Wherein lies happiness?

CHORUS: Wherein lies happiness?

CROWD: Wherein, happiness?

TIBERIUS: Why are we born? To what end must we die?

CHORUS: Why are we born to die?

CROWD: Why are we born?

SOLDIER'S VOICE: His eyes laugh, Cæsar! He is dying! He would speak!

CHORUS AND CROWD: (*in one great cry*) Cæsar! Let Lazarus speak!

POMPEIA: (*terrified*) No, Cæsar! He will laugh—and you will die—and I will go to him!

TIBERIUS: (*torn—arguing with his fear*) But—he may know some hope— (*Then making his decision, with grim fatalism*) Hope—or nothing! (*Calls to the* SOLDIERS) Let him speak!

CHORUS AND CROWD: (*cheering*) Hail, Cæsar!

LAZARUS: (*his voice comes, recognizably the voice of* LAZARUS, *yet with a strange, fresh, clear quality of boyhood, gaily mocking with life*) Hail, Cæsar!

CROWD: (*frantic with hope*) Hail, Lazarus!

TIBERIUS: Pull away the fire from him! I see death in his eyes! (*The flaming reflections in the banked, massed faces dance madly as the* SOLDIERS *rake back the fire from the stake. With a forced, taunting mockery*) What do you say now, Lazarus? You are dying!

CHORUS AND CROWD: (*taking his tone—mockingly*) You are dying, Lazarus!

LAZARUS: (*his voice a triumphant assertion of the victory of life over pain and death*) Yes!

TIBERIUS: (*triumphant yet disappointed—with scorn and rage*) Ha! You admit it, do you, coward! Craven! Knave! Duper of fools! Clown! Liar! Die! I laugh at you! Ha-ha-ha-ha— (*His voice breaks chokingly*).

CROWD: (*led by their* CHORUS—*in the same frenzy of disappointment, with all sorts of grotesque and obscene gestures and noises, thumbing their fingers to their noses, wagging them at their ears, sticking out their tongues, slapping their behinds, barking, crowing like roosters, howling, and hooting in every conceivable manner*) Yah! Yah! Yellow Gut! Bungkisser! Muck-heel! Scumwiper! Liar! Pig! Jackal! Die! We laugh at you! Ha-ha-ha— (*Their voices, too, break*).

POMPEIA: (*rising to her feet like one in a trance, staring toward* LAZARUS) They are tormenting him. I hear him crying to me! (*She moves to the top of the steps leading to the arena*).

LAZARUS: (*his voice thrilling with exultance*) O men, fear not life! You die—but there is no death for Man! (*He begins to laugh, and at the sound of his laughter, a great spell of silence settles upon all his hearers— then as his laughter rises, they begin to laugh with him*).

POMPEIA: (*descending the steps like a sleep-walker*) I hear his laughter calling. I must go to him.

TIBERIUS: (*as if he realized something was happening that was against his will—trying feebly to be imperial*) I command you not to laugh! Cæsar commands— (*Calling feebly to the* SOLDIERS) Put back—the gag! Stop his laughter! (*The laughter of* LAZARUS *gaily and lovingly mocks back at him*).

SOLDIER'S VOICE: (*his voice gently remonstrating*) We may not, Cæsar. We love his laughter! (*They laugh with him*).

CHORUS AND CROWD: (*in a soft, dreamy murmur*)

We love his laughter!
We laugh!

TIBERIUS: (*dreamily*) Then—pile the fire back around him. High and higher! Let him blaze to the stars! I laugh with him!

SOLDIER'S VOICE: (*gently and gravely*) That is just, Cæsar. We love men flaming toward the stars! We laugh with him!

CHORUS AND CROWD: (*as the flames, piled back and fed anew by the* SOL-

DIERS, *flare upward and are reflected on their masks in dancing waves of light*)

> We love men flaming toward the stars!
> We laugh!

POMPEIA: (*in the arena*) The fire calls me. My burning heart calls for the fire! (*She laughs softly and passes swiftly across the arena toward* LAZARUS).

TIBERIUS: (*in a sort of childish complaint*) You must pardon me, Lazarus. This is my Cæsar's duty—to kill you! You have no right to laugh—before all these people—at Cæsar. It is not kind. (*He sobs snuffingly—then begins to laugh at himself. Suddenly the flames waver, die down, then shoot up again and* POMPEIA'S *laughter is heard for a moment, rising clear and passionately with that of* LAZARUS, *then dying quickly out*).

SOLDIER'S VOICE: A woman has thrown herself in the flames, Cæsar! She laughs with Lazarus!

TIBERIUS: (*in a sudden panicky flurry—feverishly*) Quick, Lazarus! You will soon be silent! Speak!—in the name of man's solitude—his agony of farewell—what is beyond there, Lazarus? (*His voice has risen to a passionate entreaty*).

CHORUS: (*in a great pleading echo*) What is beyond there, Lazarus?

CROWD: What is beyond?

LAZARUS: (*his voice speaking lovingly, with a surpassing clearness and exaltation*) Life! Eternity! Stars and dust! God's Eternal Laughter! (*His laughter bursts forth now in its highest pitch of ecstatic summons to the feast and sacrifice of Life, the Eternal. The crowds laugh with him in a frenzied rhythmic chorus. Led by the* CHORUS, *they pour down from the banked walls of the amphitheatre and dance in the flaring reflection of the flames strange wild measures of liberated joy.* TIBERIUS *stands on the raised dais laughing great shouts of clear, fearless laughter*).

CHORUS: (*chanting as they dance*)

Laugh! Laugh!
We are stars!
We are dust!
We are gods!
We are laughter!

CROWD:

We are dust!
We are gods!
Laugh! Laugh!

CALIGULA: (*enters from behind* TIBERIUS. *His aspect is wild, his hair disheveled, his clothes torn, he is panting as if exhausted by running. He stares toward the flames stupidly—then screams despairingly above the chant*) Lazarus! I come to save you! Do you still live, Lazarus?

TIBERIUS: (*has been speaking. His words are now heard as the tumult momentarily dies down*) I have lived long enough! I will die with Lazarus! I no longer fear death! I laugh! I laugh at Cæsar! I advise you, my brothers, fear not Cæsars! Seek Man in the brotherhood of the dust! Cæsar is your fear of Man! I counsel you, laugh away your Cæsars!

CALIGULA: (*with resentful jealousy and rage—in a voice rising to a scream*) What do I hear, Lazarus? You laugh with your murderer? You give him your laughter? You have forgotten me—my love—you make him love you—you make him laugh at Cæsars—at me! (*Suddenly springs on* TIBERIUS *in a fury and grabbing him by the throat chokes him, forcing him back on the throne—screaming*) Die, traitor! Die! (TIBERIUS' *body relaxes in his hands, dead, and slips from the chair.* CALIGULA *rushes madly down the stairs into the midst of the oblivious, laughing, dancing crowd, screaming*) You have betrayed me, dog of a Jew! You have betrayed Cæsar! (*Beginning to be caught by the contagion of the laughter*) Ha-ah— No! I will not laugh! I will kill you! Give me a spear! (*He snatches a spear from a soldier and fights his way drunkenly toward the flames, like a man half overcome by a poisonous gas, shouting, half-laughing in spite of himself, half-weeping with rage*) Ha-ah— The gods be with Cæsar Caligula! O Immortal Gods, give thy brother strength! You shall die, Lazarus—die—Ha-ah—! (*He disappears toward the flames, his spear held ready to stab*).

CHORUS AND CROWD: (*who have been entirely oblivious of him—chanting*)

> Laugh! Laugh!
> We are gods!
> We are dust!

LAZARUS: (*at his first word there is a profound silence in which each dancer remains frozen in the last movement*) Hail, Caligula Cæsar! Men forget! (*He laughs with gay mockery as at a child*).

CHORUS AND CROWD: (*starting to laugh*) Laugh! Laugh! (*Then there is a fierce cry of rage from* CALIGULA *and* LAZARUS' *laughter ceases, and with it the laughter of the crowd turns to a wail of fear and lamentation*).

CALIGULA: (*dashes back among them waving his bloody spear and rushing up to the throne stands on it and strikes a grandiose pose*) I have killed God! I am Death! Death is Cæsar!

CHORUS AND CROWD: (*turning and scurrying away—huddled in fleeing groups, crouching close to the ground like a multitude of terrified rats, their voices squeaky now with fright*) Hail, Cæsar! Hail to Death! (*They are gone*).

CALIGULA: (*keeping his absurd majestic pose, turns and addresses with rhetorical intoning, and flowing gestures, the body of* LAZARUS, *high upon its stake, the flames below it now flickering fitfully*) Hail, Caligula! Hero of heroes, conqueror of the Dæmon, Lazarus, who taught the treason that fear and death were dead! But I am Lord of Fear! I am Cæsar of Death! And you, Lazarus, are carrion! (*Then in a more conversational tone, putting aside his grandiose airs, confidentially*) I had to kill you, Lazarus! Surely your good sense tells you— You heard what the old fool, Tiberius, told the mob. A moment more and there would have been a revolution—no more Cæsar—and my dream—! (*He stops—*

bewilderedly) My dream? Did I kill laughter? I had just learned to
laugh—with love! (*More confusedly*) I must be a little mad, Lazarus.
It was one terror too many, to have been laughing your laughter in
the night, to have been dreaming great yearning dreams of all the
good my love might do for men when I was Cæsar—and then, to
hear the old howling of mob lust, and to run here—and there a high
white flame amidst the fire—you, Lazarus!—dying!—laughing with
him—Tiberius—betraying me—who loved you, Lazarus! Yes, I became mad! I am mad! And I can laugh my own mad laughter, Lazarus—my own! Ha-ha-ha-ha! (*He laughs with a wild triumphant madness and again rhetorically, with sweeping gestures and ferocious capers*)
And all of men are vile and mad, and I shall be their madmen's
Cæsar! (*He turns as if addressing an amphitheatre full of his subjects*) O
my good people, my faithful scum, my brother swine, Lazarus is dead
and we have murdered great laughter, and it befits our madness to
have done so, and it is befitting above all to have Caligula for Cæsar!
(*Then savagely*) Kneel down! Abase yourselves! I am your Cæsar and
your God! Hail! (*He stands saluting himself with a crazy intensity that
is not without grandeur. A pause. Suddenly the silence seems to crush down
upon him; he is aware that he is alone in the vast arena; he whirls about,
looking around him as if he felt an assassin at his back; he lunges with his
spear at imaginary foes, jumping, dodging from side to side, yelping*) Ho,
there! Help! Help! Your Cæsar calls you! Help, my people! To the
rescue! (*Suddenly throwing his spear away and sinking on his knees, his
face toward* LAZARUS, *supplicatingly*) Lazarus! Forgive me! Help me!
Fear kills me! Save me from death! (*He is groveling in a paroxysm of
terror, grinding his face in his fists as if to hide it*).

LAZARUS: (*his voice is heard in a gentle, expiring sigh of compassion, followed
by a faint dying note of laughter that rises and is lost in the sky like the
flight of his soul back into the womb of Infinity*) Fear not, Caligula! There
is no death!

CALIGULA: (*lifts his head at the first sound and rises with the laughter to his
feet, until, as it is finally lost, he is on tip-toes, his arms straining upward*

to the sky, a tender, childish laughter of love on his lips) I laugh, Lazarus! I laugh with you! (*Then grief-stricken*) Lazarus! (*He hides his face in his hands, weeping*) No more! (*Then beats his head with his fists*) I will remember! I will! (*Then suddenly, with a return to grotesqueness— harshly*) All the same, I killed him and I proved there is death! (*Immediately overcome by remorse, groveling and beating himself*) Fool! Madman! Forgive me, Lazarus! Men forget!

CURTAIN

Strange Interlude

✥

CHARACTERS

CHARLES MARSDEN   SAM EVANS

PROFESSOR HENRY LEEDS   MRS. AMOS EVANS, *Sam's mother*

NINA LEEDS, *his daughter*   GORDON EVANS

EDMUND DARRELL   MADELINE ARNOLD

FIRST PART

SECOND PART

Strange Interlude

First Part—Act One

Scene: *The library of* professor leeds' *home in a small university town in New England. This room is at the front part of his house with windows opening on the strip of lawn between the house and the quiet residential street. It is a small room with a low ceiling. The furniture has been selected with a love for old New England pieces. The walls are lined almost to the ceiling with glassed-in bookshelves. These are packed with books, principally editions, many of them old and rare, of the ancient classics in the original Greek and Latin, of the later classics in French and German and Italian, of all the English authors who wrote while s was still like an f and a few since then, the most modern probably being Thackeray. The atmosphere of the room is that of a cosy, cultured retreat, sedulously built as a sanctuary where, secure with the culture of the past at his back, a fugitive from reality can view the present safely from a distance, as a superior with condescending disdain, pity, and even amusement.*

There is a fair-sized table, a heavy armchair, a rocker, and an old bench made comfortable with cushions. The table, with the Professor's armchair at its left, is arranged toward the left of the room, the rocker is at center, the bench at right.

There is one entrance, a door in the right wall, rear.

It is late afternoon of a day in August. Sunshine, cooled and dimmed in the shade of trees, fills the room with a soothing light.

The sound of a maid's voice—*a middle-aged woman—explaining familiarly but respectfully from the right, and* marsden *enters. He is a tall thin man of thirty-five, meticulously well-dressed in tweeds of distinctly English tailoring, his appearance that of an Anglicized New England gentleman. His face is too long for its width, his nose is high and narrow, his forehead broad,*

461

*his mild blue eyes those of a dreamy self-analyst, his thin lips ironical and a
bit sad. There is an indefinable feminine quality about him, but it is nothing
apparent in either appearance or act. His manner is cool and poised. He speaks
with a careful ease as one who listens to his own conversation. He has long
fragile hands, and the stoop to his shoulders of a man weak muscularly, who
has never liked athletics and has always been regarded as of delicate constitution.
The main point about his personality is a quiet charm, a quality of appealing,
inquisitive friendliness, always willing to listen, eager to sympathize, to like
and to be liked.*

MARSDEN: (*standing just inside the door, his tall, stooped figure leaning back
against the books—nodding back at the* MAID *and smiling kindly*) I'll wait
in here, Mary. (*His eyes follow her for a second, then return to gaze
around the room slowly with an appreciative relish for the familiar significance of the books. He smiles affectionately and his amused voice recites the
words with a rhetorical resonance*) Sanctum Sanctorum! (*His voice takes
on a monotonous musing quality, his eyes stare idly at his drifting thoughts*)

How perfectly the Professor's unique haven! . . .

(*He smiles*)

Primly classical . . . when New Englander meets Greek! . . .

(*Looking at the books now*)

He hasn't added one book in years . . . how old was I when I first came
here? . . . six . . . with my father . . . father . . . how dim his face has
grown! . . . he wanted to speak to me just before he died . . . the hospital . . . smell of iodoform in the cool halls . . . hot summer . . . I bent
down . . . his voice had withdrawn so far away . . . I couldn't understand
him . . . what son can ever understand? . . . always too near, too soon, too
distant or too late! . . .

(*His face has become sad with a memory of the bewildered suffering of the
adolescent boy he had been at the time of his father's death. Then he shakes
his head, flinging off his thoughts, and makes himself walk about the room*)

What memories on such a smiling afternoon! . . . this pleasant old town after three months . . . I won't go to Europe again . . . couldn't write a line there . . . how answer the fierce question of all those dead and maimed? . . . too big a job for me! . . .

(*He sighs—then self-mockingly*)

But back here . . . it is the interlude that gently questions . . . in this town dozing . . . decorous bodies moving with circumspection through the afternoons . . . their habits affectionately chronicled . . . an excuse for weaving amusing words . . . my novels . . . not of cosmic importance, hardly . . .

(*Then self-reassuringly*)

but there is a public to cherish them, evidently . . . and I can write! . . . more than one can say of these modern sex-yahoos! . . . I must start work tomorrow . . . I'd like to use the Professor in a novel sometime . . . and his wife . . . seems impossible she's been dead six years . . . so aggressively his wife! . . . poor Professor! now it's Nina who bosses him . . . but that's different . . . she has bossed me, too, ever since she was a baby . . . she's a woman now . . . known love and death . . . Gordon brought down in flames . . . two days before the armistice . . . what fiendish irony! . . . his wonderful athlete's body . . . her lover . . . charred bones in a cage of twisted steel . . . no wonder she broke down . . . Mother said she's become quite queer lately . . . Mother seemed jealous of my concern . . . why have I never fallen in love with Nina? . . . could I? . . . that way . . . used to dance her on my knee . . . sit her on my lap . . . even now she'd never think anything about it . . . but sometimes the scent of her hair and skin . . . like a dreamy drug . . . dreamy! . . . there's the rub! . . . all dreams with me! . . . my sex life among the phantoms! . . .

(*He grins torturedly*)

Why? . . . oh, this digging in gets nowhere . . . to the devil with sex! . . . our impotent pose of today to beat the loud drum on fornication! . . . boasters . . . eunuchs parading with the phallus! . . . giving themselves away . . . whom do they fool? . . . not even themselves! . . .

(*His face suddenly full of an intense pain and disgust*)

Ugh! . . . always that memory! . . . why can't I ever forget? . . . as sickeningly clear as if it were yesterday . . . prep school . . . Easter vacation . . . Fatty Boggs and Jack Frazer . . . that house of cheap vice . . . one dollar! . . . why did I go? . . . Jack, the dead game sport . . . how I admired him!

... afraid of his taunts ... he pointed to the Italian girl ... "Take her!"
... daring me ... I went ... miserably frightened ... what a pig she was!
... pretty vicious face under caked powder and rouge ... surly and contemptuous ... lumpy body ... short legs and thick ankles ... slums of Naples ... "What you gawkin' about? Git a move on, kid" ... kid! ... I *was* only a kid! ... sixteen ... test of manhood ... ashamed to face Jack again unless ... fool! ... I might have lied to him! ... but I honestly thought that wench would feel humiliated if I ... oh, stupid kid! ... back at the hotel I waited till they were asleep ... then sobbed ... thinking of Mother ... feeling I had defiled her ... and myself ... forever! ...

(*Mocking bitterly*)

"Nothing half so sweet in life as love's young dream," what? ...

(*He gets to his feet impatiently*)

Why does my mind always have to dwell on that? ... too silly ... no importance really ... an incident such as any boy of my age ...

(*He hears someone coming quickly from the right and turns expectantly.* PROFESSOR LEEDS *enters, a pleased relieved expression fighting the flurried worry on his face. He is a small, slender man of fifty-five, his hair gray, the top of his head bald. His face, prepossessing in spite of its too-small, over-refined features, is that of a retiring, studious nature. He has intelligent eyes and a smile that can be ironical. Temperamentally timid, his defense is an assumption of his complacent, superior manner of the classroom toward the world at large. This defense is strengthened by a natural tendency toward a prim provincialism where practical present-day considerations are concerned (though he is most liberal—even radical—in his tolerant understanding of the manners and morals of Greece and Imperial Rome!). This classroom poise of his, however, he cannot quite carry off outside the classroom. There is an unconvincing quality about it that leaves his larger audience—and particularly the* PROFESSOR *himself—subtly embarrassed. As* MARSDEN *is one of his old students, whom, in addition, he has known from childhood, he is perfectly at ease with him*).

MARSDEN: (*holding out his hand—with unmistakable liking*) Here I am again, Professor!

PROFESSOR LEEDS: (*shaking his hand and patting him on the back—with genuine affection*) So glad to see you, Charlie! A surprise, too! We didn't expect you back so soon! (*He sits in his chair on the left of the table while* MARSDEN *sits in the rocker*). (*Looking away from* MARSDEN *a moment, his face now full of selfish relief as he thinks*)

Fortunate, his coming back . . . always calming influence on Nina . . .

MARSDEN: And I never dreamed of returning so soon. But Europe, Professor, is the big casualty they were afraid to set down on the list.

PROFESSOR LEEDS: (*his face clouding*) Yes, I suppose you found everything completely changed since before the war. (*He thinks resentfully*)

The war . . . Gordon! . . .

MARSDEN: Europe has "gone west"—(*He smiles whimsically*) to America, let's hope! (*Then frowningly*) I couldn't stand it. There were millions sitting up with the corpse already, who had a family right to be there— (*Then matter-of-factly*) I was wasting my time, too. I couldn't write a line. (*Then gaily*) But where's Nina? I must see Nina!

PROFESSOR LEEDS: She'll be right in. She said she wanted to finish thinking something out— You'll find Nina changed, Charlie, greatly changed! (*He sighs—thinking with a trace of guilty alarm*)

The first thing she said at breakfast . . . "I dreamed of Gordon" . . . as if she wanted to taunt me! . . . how absurd! . . . her eyes positively glared! . . .

(*Suddenly blurting out resentfully*) She dreams about Gordon.

MARSDEN: (*looking at him with amused surprise*) Well, I'd hardly call that a change, would you?

PROFESSOR LEEDS: (*thinking, oblivious to this remark*)

But I must constantly bear in mind that she's not herself . . . that she's a sick girl . . .

MARSDEN: (*thinking*)

> The morning news of Gordon's death came . . . her face like gray putty . . . beauty gone . . . no face can afford intense grief . . . it's only later when sorrow. . .

(*With concern*) Just what do you mean by changed, Professor? Before I left she seemed to be coming out of that horrible numbed calm.

PROFESSOR LEEDS: (*slowly and carefully*) Yes, she has played a lot of golf and tennis this summer, motored around with her friends, and even danced a good deal. And she eats with a ravenous appetite. (*Thinking frightenedly*)

> Breakfast . . . "dreamed of Gordon" . . . what a look of hate for me in her eyes! . . .

MARSDEN: But that sounds splendid! When I left she wouldn't see anyone or go anywhere. (*Thinking pityingly*)

> Wandering from room to room . . . her thin body and pale lost face . . . gutted, love-abandoned eyes! . . .

PROFESSOR LEEDS: Well, now she's gone to the opposite extreme! Sees everyone—bores, fools—as if she'd lost all discrimination or wish to discriminate. And she talks interminably, Charlie—intentional nonsense, one would say! Refuses to be serious! Jeers at everything!

MARSDEN: (*consolingly*) Oh, that's all undoubtedly part of the effort she's making to forget.

PROFESSOR LEEDS: (*absent-mindedly*) Yes. (*Arguing with himself*)

> Shall I tell him? . . . no . . . it might sound silly . . . but it's terrible to be so alone in this . . . if Nina's mother had lived . . . my wife . . . dead! . . . and for a time I actually felt released! . . . wife! . . . help-meet! . . . now I need help! . . . no use! . . . she's gone! . . .

MARSDEN: (*watching him—thinking with a condescending affection*)

> Good little man . . . he looks worried . . . always fussing about something . . . he must get on Nina's nerves. . . .

(*Reassuringly*) No girl could forget Gordon in a hurry, especially after the shock of his tragic death.

PROFESSOR LEEDS: (*irritably*) I realize that. (*Thinking resentfully*)

> Gordon . . . always Gordon with everyone! . . .

MARSDEN: By the way, I located the spot near Sedan where Gordon's machine fell. Nina asked me to, you know.

PROFESSOR LEEDS: (*irritated—expostulatingly*) For heaven's sake, don't remind her! Give her a chance to forget if you want to see her well again. After all, Charlie, life must be lived and Nina can't live with a corpse forever! (*Trying to control his irritation and talk in an objective tone*) You see, I'm trying to see things through clearly and unsentimentally. If you'll remember, I was as broken up as anyone over Gordon's death. I'd become so reconciled to Nina's love for him— although, as you know, I was opposed at first, and for fair reasons, I think, for the boy, for all his good looks and prowess in sport and his courses, really came of common people and had no money of his own except as he made a career for himself.

MARSDEN: (*a trifle defensively*) I'm sure he would have had a brilliant career.

PROFESSOR LEEDS: (*impatiently*) No doubt. Although you must acknowledge, Charlie, that college heroes rarely shine brilliantly in after life. Unfortunately, the tendency to spoil them in the university is a poor training—

MARSDEN: But Gordon was absolutely unspoiled, I should say.

PROFESSOR LEEDS: (*heatedly*) Don't misunderstand me, Charlie! I'd be the first to acknowledge— (*A bit pathetically*) It isn't Gordon, Charlie. It's his memory, his ghost, you might call it, haunting Nina, whose influence I have come to dread because of the terrible change in her attitude toward me. (*His face twitches as if he were on the verge of tears— he thinks desperately*)

> I've got to tell him . . . he will see that I acted for the best . . . that I was justified. . . .

(*He hesitates—then blurts out*) It may sound incredible, but Nina has begun to act as if she hated me!

MARSDEN: (*startled*) Oh, come now!

PROFESSOR LEEDS: (*insistently*) Absolutely! I haven't wanted to admit it. I've refused to believe it, until it's become too appallingly obvious in her whole attitude toward me! (*His voice trembles*).

MARSDEN: (*moved—expostulating*) Oh, now you're becoming morbid! Why, Nina has always idolized you! What possible reason—?

PROFESSOR LEEDS: (*quickly*) I can answer that, I think. She has a reason. But why she should blame me when she must know I acted for the best— You probably don't know, but just before he sailed for the front Gordon wanted their marriage to take place, and Nina consented. In fact, from the insinuations she lets drop now, she must have been most eager, but at the time— However, I felt it was ill-advised and I took Gordon aside and pointed out to him that such a precipitate marriage would be unfair to Nina, and scarcely honorable on his part.

MARSDEN: (*staring at him wonderingly*) You said that to Gordon? (*Thinking cynically*)

A shrewd move! . . . Gordon's proud spot, fairness and honor! . . . but was it honorable of you? . . .

PROFESSOR LEEDS: (*with a touch of asperity*) Yes, I said it, and I gave him my reason. There *was* the possibility he might be killed, in the flying service rather more than a possibility, which needless to say, I did not point out, but which Gordon undoubtedly realized, poor boy! If he were killed, he would be leaving Nina a widow, perhaps with a baby, with no resources, since he was penniless, except what pension she might get from the government; and all this while she was still at an age when a girl, especially one of Nina's charm and beauty, should have all of life before her. Decidedly, I told him, in justice to Nina, they must wait until he had come back and begun to establish his position in the world. That was the square thing. And Gordon was quick to agree with me!

MARSDEN: (*thinking*)

The square thing! . . . but we must all be crooks where happiness is concerned! . . . steal or starve! . . .

(*Then rather ironically*) And so Gordon told Nina he'd suddenly realized it wouldn't be fair to her. But I gather he didn't tell her it was your scruple originally?

PROFESSOR LEEDS: No, I asked him to keep what I said strictly confidential.

MARSDEN: (*thinking ironically*)

Trusted to his honor again! . . . old fox! . . . poor Gordon! . . .

But Nina suspects now that you—?

PROFESSOR LEEDS: (*startled*) Yes. That's exactly it. She knows in some queer way. And she acts toward me exactly as if she thought I had deliberately destroyed her happiness, that I had hoped for Gordon's death and been secretly overjoyed when the news came! (*His voice is shaking with emotion*) And there you have it, Charlie—the whole absurd mess! (*Thinking with a strident accusation*)

And it's true, you contemptible . . . !

(*Then miserably defending himself*)

No! . . . I acted unselfishly . . . for her sake! . . .

MARSDEN: (*wonderingly*) You don't mean to tell me she has accused you of all this?

PROFESSOR LEEDS: Oh, no, Charlie! Only by hints—looks—innuendos. She knows she has no real grounds, but in the present state of her mind the real and the unreal become confused—

MARSDEN: (*thinking cynically*)

As always in all minds . . . or how could men live? . . .

(*Soothingly*) That's just what you ought to bear in your mind—the state of hers—and not get so worked up over what I should say is a combination of imagination on both your parts. (*He gets to his feet as he hears voices from the right*) Buck up! This must be Nina coming. (*The* PROFESSOR *gets to his feet, hastily composing his features into his bland, cultured expression*).

MARSDEN: (*thinking self-mockingly but a bit worried about himself*)

> My heart pounding! . . . seeing Nina again! . . . how sentimental . . . how she'd laugh if she knew! . . . and quite rightly . . . absurd for me to react as if I loved . . . that way . . . her dear old Charlie . . . ha! . . .

(*He smiles with bitter self-mockery*)

PROFESSOR LEEDS: (*thinking worriedly*)

> I hope she won't make a scene . . . she's seemed on the verge all day . . . thank God, Charlie's like one of the family . . . but what a life for me! . . . with the opening of the new term only a few weeks off! . . . I can't do it . . . I'll have to call in a nerve specialist . . . but the last one did her no good . . . his outrageous fee . . . he can take it to court . . . I absolutely refuse . . . but if he should bring suit? . . . what a scandal . . . no, I'll have to pay . . . somehow . . . borrow . . . he has me in a corner, the robber! . . .

NINA: (*enters and stands just inside the doorway looking directly at her father with defiant eyes, her face set in an expression of stubborn resolve. She is twenty, tall with broad square shoulders, slim strong hips and long beautifully developed legs—a fine athletic girl of the swimmer, tennis player, golfer type. Her straw-blond hair, framing her sunburned face, is bobbed. Her face is striking, handsome rather than pretty, the bone structure prominent, the forehead high, the lips of her rather large mouth clearly modelled above the firm jaw. Her eyes are beautiful and bewildering, extraordinarily large and a deep greenish blue. Since* GORDON'S *death they have a quality of continually shuddering before some terrible enigma, of being wounded to their depths and made defiant and resentful by their pain. Her whole manner, the charged atmosphere she gives off, is totally at variance with her healthy outdoor physique. It is strained, nerve-racked, hectic, a terrible tension of will alone maintaining self-possession. She is dressed in smart sport clothes. Too preoccupied with her resolve to remember or see* MARSDEN, *she speaks directly to her father in a voice tensely cold and calm*) I have made up my mind, Father.

PROFESSOR LEEDS: (*thinking distractedly*)

> What does she mean? . . . oh, God help me! . . .

(*Flustered—hastily*) Don't you see Charlie, Nina?

MARSDEN: (*troubled—thinking*)

> She has changed . . . what has happened? . . .

(*He comes forward toward her—a bit embarrassed but affectionately using his pet name for her*) Hello, Nina Cara Nina! Are you trying to cut me dead, young lady?

NINA: (*turning her eyes to* MARSDEN, *holding out her hand for him to shake, in her cool, preoccupied voice*) Hello, Charlie. (*Her eyes immediately return to her father*) Listen, Father!

MARSDEN: (*standing near her, concealing his chagrin*)

> That hurts! . . . I mean nothing! . . . but she's a sick girl . . . I must make allowance . . .

PROFESSOR LEEDS: (*thinking distractedly*)

> That look in her eyes! . . . hate! . . .

(*With a silly giggle*) Really, Nina, you're absolutely rude! What has Charlie done?

NINA: (*in her cool tone*) Why, nothing. Nothing at all. (*She goes to him with a detached, friendly manner*) Did I seem rude, Charlie? I didn't mean to be. (*She kisses him with a cool, friendly smile*) Welcome home. (*Thinking wearily*)

> What has Charlie done? . . . nothing . . . and never will . . . Charlie sits beside the fierce river, immaculately timid, cool and clothed, watching the burning, frozen naked swimmers drown at last. . . .

MARSDEN: (*thinking torturedly*)

> Cold lips . . . the kiss of contempt! . . . for dear old Charlie! . . .

(*Forcing a good-natured laugh*) Rude? Not a bit! (*Banteringly*) As I've often reminded you, what can I expect when the first word you ever

spoke in this world was an insult to me. "Dog" you said, looking
right at me—at the age of one! (*He laughs. The* PROFESSOR *laughs
nervously.* NINA *smiles perfunctorily*).

NINA: (*thinking wearily*)

> The fathers laugh at little daughter Nina ... I must get away! ... nice
> Charlie doggy ... faithful ... fetch and carry ... bark softly in books at
> the deep night. ...

PROFESSOR LEEDS: (*thinking*)

> What is she thinking? ... I can't stand living like this! ...

(*Giggle gone to a twitching grin*) You are a cool one, Nina! You'd
think you'd just seen Charlie yesterday!

NINA: (*slowly—coolly and reflectively*) Well, the war is over. Coming back
safe from Europe isn't such an unusual feat now, is it?

MARSDEN: (*thinking bitterly*)

> A taunt ... I didn't fight ... physically unfit ... not like Gordon ... Gor-
> don in flames ... how she must resent my living! ... thinking of me,
> scribbling in press bureau ... louder and louder lies ... drown the guns
> and the screams ... deafen the world with lies ... hired choir of
> liars! ...

(*Forcing a joking tone*) Little you know the deadly risks I ran, Nina!
If you'd eaten some of the food they gave me on my renovated
transport, you'd shower me with congratulations! (*The* PROFESSOR
forces a snicker).

NINA: (*coolly*) Well, you're here, and that's that. (*Then suddenly expanding in a sweet, genuinely affectionate smile*) And I *am* glad, Charlie,
always glad you're here! You know that.

MARSDEN: (*delighted and embarrassed*) I hope so, Nina!

NINA: (*turning on her father—determinedly*) I must finish what I started
to say, Father. I've thought it all out and decided that I simply must
get away from here at once—or go crazy! And I'm going on the nine-
forty tonight. (*She turns to* MARSDEN *with a quick smile*) You'll have
to help me pack, Charlie! (*Thinking with weary relief*)

Now that's said . . . I'm going . . . never come back . . . oh, how I loathe this room! . . .

MARSDEN: (*thinking with alarm*)

What's this? . . . going? . . . going to whom? . . .

PROFESSOR LEEDS: (*thinking—terrified*)

Going? . . . never come back to me? . . . no! . . .

(*Desperately putting on his prim severe manner toward an unruly pupil*) This is rather a sudden decision, isn't it? You haven't mentioned before that you were considering—in fact, you've led me to believe that you were quite contented here—that is, of course I mean for the time being, and I really think—

MARSDEN: (*looking at* NINA—*thinking with alarm*)

Going away to whom? . . .

(*Then watching the* PROFESSOR *with a pitying shudder*)

He's on the wrong tack with his professor's manner . . . her eyes seeing cruelly through him . . . with what terrible recognition! . . . God, never bless me with children! . . .

NINA: (*thinking with weary scorn*)

The Professor of Dead Languages is talking again . . . a dead man lectures on the past of living . . . since I was born I have been in his class, loving-attentive, pupil-daughter Nina . . . my ears numb with spiritless messages from the dead . . . dead words droning on . . . listening because he is my cultured father . . . a little more inclined to deafness than the rest (let me be just) because he is my father . . . father? . . . what is father? . . .

PROFESSOR LEEDS: (*thinking—terrified*)

I must talk her out of it! . . . find the right words! . . . oh, I know she won't hear me! . . . oh, wife, why did you die, you would have talked to her, she would have listened to you! . . .

(*Continuing in his professor's superior manner*) —and I really think, in justice to yourself above all, you ought to consider this step with great care before you definitely commit yourself. First and foremost, there is your health to be taken into consideration. You've been very ill, Nina, how perilously so perhaps you're not completely aware, but I assure you, and Charlie can corroborate my statement, that six months ago the doctors thought it might be years before—and yet, by staying home and resting and finding healthy outdoor recreation among your old friends, and keeping your mind occupied with the routine of managing the household— (*He forces a prim playful smile*) and managing me, I might add!—you have wonderfully improved and I think it most ill-advised in the hottest part of August, while you're really still a convalescent—

NINA: (*thinking*)

Talking! . . . his voice like a fatiguing dying tune droned on a beggar's organ . . . his words arising from the tomb of a soul in puffs of ashes . . .

(*Torturedly*)

Ashes! . . . oh, Gordon, my dear one! . . . oh, lips on my lips, oh, strong arms around me, oh, spirit so brave and generous and gay! . . . ashes dissolving into mud! . . . mud and ashes! . . . that's all! . . . gone! . . . gone forever from me! . . .

PROFESSOR LEEDS: (*thinking angrily*)

Her eyes . . . I know that look . . . tender, loving . . . not for me . . . damn Gordon! . . . I'm glad he's dead! . . .

(*A touch of asperity in his voice*) And at a couple of hours' notice to leave everything in the air, as it were— (*Then judicially*) No, Nina, frankly, I can't see it. You know I'd gladly consent to anything in the world to benefit you, but—surely, you can't have reflected!

NINA: (*thinking torturedly*)

Gordon darling, I must go away where I can think of you in silence! . . .

(*She turns on her father, her voice trembling with the effort to keep it in control—icily*) It's no use talking, Father. *I have* reflected and I am going!

PROFESSOR LEEDS: (*with asperity*) But I tell you it's quite impossible! I don't like to bring up the money consideration but I couldn't possibly afford— And how will you support yourself, if I may ask? Two years in the University, I am sorry to say, won't be much use to you when applying for a job. And even if you had completely recovered from your nervous breakdown, which it's obvious to anyone you haven't, then I most decidedly think you should finish out your science course and take your degree before you attempt— (*Thinking desperately*)

No use!... she doesn't hear... thinking of Gordon... she'll defy me...

NINA: (*thinking desperately*)

I must keep calm... I mustn't let go or I'll tell him everything... and I mustn't tell him... he's my father...

(*With the same cold calculating finality*) I've already had six months' training for a nurse. I will finish my training. There's a doctor I know at a sanitarium for crippled soldiers—a friend of Gordon's. I wrote to him and he answered that he'll gladly arrange it.

PROFESSOR LEEDS: (*thinking furiously*)

Gordon's friend... Gordon again!...

(*Severely*) You seriously mean to tell me you, in your condition, want to nurse in a soldiers' hospital! Absurd!

MARSDEN: (*thinking with indignant revulsion*)

Quite right, Professor!... her beauty... all those men... in their beds ... it's too revolting!...

(*With a persuasive quizzing tone*) Yes, I must say I can't see you as a peace-time Florence Nightingale, Nina!

NINA: (*coolly, struggling to keep control, ignoring these remarks*) So you see, Father, I've thought of everything and there's not the slightest reason to worry about me. And I've been teaching Mary how to take care of you. So you won't need me at all. You can go along as if nothing had happened—and really, nothing will have happened that hasn't already happened.

PROFESSOR LEEDS: Why, even the manner in which you address me—the tone you take—proves conclusively that you're not yourself!

NINA: (*her voice becoming a bit uncanny, her thoughts breaking through*) No, I'm not myself yet. That's just it. Not all myself. But I've been becoming myself. And I must finish!

PROFESSOR LEEDS: (*with angry significance—to* MARSDEN) You hear her, Charlie? She's a sick girl!

NINA: (*slowly and strangely*) I'm not sick. I'm too well. But they are sick and I must give my health to help them to live on, and to live on myself. (*With a sudden intensity in her tone*) I must pay for my cowardly treachery to Gordon! You should understand this, Father, you who—(*She swallows hard, catching her breath*) (*Thinking desperately*)

I'm beginning to tell him! . . . I mustn't! . . . he's my father! . . .

PROFESSOR LEEDS: (*in a panic of guilty fear, but defiantly*) What do you mean? I am afraid you're not responsible for what you're saying.

NINA: (*again with the strange intensity*) I must pay! It's my plain duty! Gordon is dead! What use is my life to me or anyone? But I must make it of use—by giving it! (*Fiercely*) I must learn to give myself, do you hear—give and give until I can make that gift of myself for a man's happiness without scruple, without fear, without joy except in his joy! When I've accomplished this I'll have found myself, I'll know how to start in living my own life again! (*Appealing to them with a desperate impatience*) Don't you see? In the name of the commonest decency and honor, I owe it to Gordon!

PROFESSOR LEEDS: (*sharply*) No, I can't see—nor anyone else! (*Thinking savagely*)

I hope Gordon is in hell! . . .

MARSDEN: (*thinking*)

Give herself? . . . can she mean her body? . . . beautiful body . . . to crippples? . . . for Gordon's sake? . . . damn Gordon! . . .

(*Coldly*) What do you mean, you owe it to Gordon, Nina?

PROFESSOR LEEDS: (*bitterly*) Yes, how ridiculous! It seems to me when you gave him your love, he got more than he could ever have hoped—

NINA: (*with fierce self-contempt*) I gave him? What did I give him? It's what I didn't give! That last night before he sailed—in his arms until my body ached—kisses until my lips were numb—knowing all that night—something in me knowing he would die, that he would never kiss me again—knowing this so surely yet with my cowardly brain lying, no, he'll come back and marry you, you'll be happy ever after and feel his children at your breast looking up with eyes so much like his, possessing eyes so happy in possessing you! (*Then violently*) But Gordon never possessed me! I'm still Gordon's silly virgin! And Gordon is muddy ashes! And I've lost my happiness forever! All that last night I knew he wanted me. I knew it was only the honorable code-bound Gordon, who kept commanding from his brain, no, you mustn't, you must respect her, you must wait till you have a marriage license! (*She gives a mocking laugh*).

PROFESSOR LEEDS: (*shocked*) Nina! This is really going too far!

MARSDEN: (*repelled—with a superior sneer*) Oh, come now, Nina! You've been reading books. Those don't sound like your thoughts.

NINA: (*without looking at him, her eyes on her father's—intensely*) Gordon wanted me! I wanted Gordon! I should have made him take me! I knew he would die and I would have no children, that there would be no big Gordon or little Gordon left to me, that happiness was calling me, never to call again if I refused! And yet I did refuse! I didn't make him take me! I lost him forever! And now I am lonely and not pregnant with anything at all, but—but loathing! (*She hurls this last at her father—fiercely*) Why did I refuse? What was that cowardly something in me that cried, no, you mustn't, what would your father say?

PROFESSOR LEEDS: (*thinking—furiously*)

> What an animal! . . . and my daughter! . . . she doesn't get it from me!
> . . . was her mother like that? . . .

(*Distractedly*) Nina! I really can't listen!

NINA: (*savagely*) And that's exactly what my father did say! Wait, he
told Gordon! Wait for Nina till the war's over, and you've got a
good job and can afford a marriage license!

PROFESSOR LEEDS: (*crumbling pitifully*) Nina! I—!

MARSDEN: (*flurriedly—going to him*) Don't take her seriously, Professor!
(*Thinking with nervous repulsion*)

> Nina has changed . . . all flesh now . . . lust . . . who would dream she was
> so sensual? . . . I wish I were out of this! . . . I wish I hadn't come here
> today! . . .

NINA: (*coldly and deliberately*) Don't lie any more, Father! Today I've
made up my mind to face things. I know now why Gordon suddenly
dropped all idea of marriage before he left, how unfair to me he
suddenly decided it would be! Unfair to me! Oh, that's humorous!
To think I might have had happiness, Gordon, and now Gordon's
child— (*Then directly accusing him*) You told him it'd be unfair, you
put him on his honor, didn't you?

PROFESSOR LEEDS: (*collecting himself—woodenly*) Yes. I did it for your
sake, Nina.

NINA: (*in the same voice as before*) It's too late for lies!

PROFESSOR LEEDS: (*woodenly*) Let us say then that I *persuaded* myself it
was for your sake. That may be true. You are young. You think one
can live with truth. Very well. It is also true I was jealous of Gordon.
I was alone and I wanted to keep your love. I hated him as one hates
a thief one may not accuse nor punish. I did my best to prevent your
marriage. I was glad when he died. There. Is that what you wish me
to say?

NINA: Yes. Now I begin to forget I've hated you. You were braver than
I, at least.

PROFESSOR LEEDS: I wanted to live comforted by your love until the end. In short, I am a man who happens to be your father. (*He hides his face in his hands and weeps softly*) Forgive that man!

MARSDEN: (*thinking timidly*)

> In short, forgive us our possessing as we forgive those who possessed before us . . . Mother must be wondering what keeps me so long . . . it's time for tea . . . I must go home . . .

NINA: (*sadly*) Oh, I forgive you. But do you understand now that I must somehow find a way to give myself to Gordon still, that I must pay my debt and learn to forgive myself?

PROFESSOR LEEDS: Yes.

NINA: Mary will look after you.

PROFESSOR LEEDS: Mary will do very well, I'm sure.

MARSDEN: (*thinking*)

> Nina has changed . . . this is no place for me . . . Mother is waiting tea. . . .

(*Then venturing on an uncertain tone of pleasantry*) Quite so, you two. But isn't this all nonsense? Nina will be back with us in a month, Professor, what with the depressing heat and humidity, and the more depressing halt and the lame!

PROFESSOR LEEDS: (*sharply*) She must stay away until she gets well. This time I do speak for her sake.

NINA: I'll take the nine-forty. (*Turning to* MARSDEN—*with a sudden girlishness*) Come on upstairs, Charlie, and help me pack! (*She grabs him by the hand and starts to pull him away*).

MARSDEN: (*shrugging his shoulders—confusedly*) Well—I don't understand this!

NINA: (*with a strange smile*) But some day I'll read it all in one of your books, Charlie, and it'll be so simple and easy to understand that I won't be able to recognize it, Charlie, let alone understand it! (*She laughs teasingly*) Dear old Charlie!

MARSDEN: (*thinking in agony*)

> God damn in hell . . . dear old Charlie! . . .

(*Then with a genial grin*) I'll have to propose, Nina, if you continue to be my severest critic! I'm a stickler for these little literary conventions, you know!

NINA: All right. Propose while we pack. (*She leads him off, right*).

PROFESSOR LEEDS: (*blows his nose, wipes his eyes, sighs, clears his throat, squares his shoulders, pulls his coat down in front, sets his tie straight, and starts to take a brisk turn about the room. His face is washed blandly clean of all emotion*)

Three weeks now . . . new term . . . I will have to be looking over my notes. . . .

(*He looks out of window, front*)

Grass parched in the middle . . . Tom forgotten the sprinkler . . . careless . . . ah, there goes Mr. Davis of the bank . . . bank . . . my salary will go farther now . . . books I really need . . . all bosh two can live as cheaply as one . . . there are worse things than being a trained nurse . . . good background of discipline . . . she needs it . . . she may meet rich fellow there . . . mature . . . only students here for her . . . and their fathers never approve if they have anything. . . .

(*He sits down with a forced sigh of peace*)

I am glad we had it out . . . his ghost will be gone now . . . no more Gordon, Gordon, Gordon, love and praise and tears, all for Gordon! . . . Mary will do very well by me . . . I will have more leisure and peace of mind . . . and Nina will come back home . . . when she is well again . . . the old Nina! . . . my little Nina! . . . she knows and she forgave me . . . she said so . . . said! . . . but could she really? . . . don't you imagine? . . . deep in her heart? . . . She still must hate? . . . oh, God! . . . I feel cold! . . . alone! . . . this home is abandoned! . . . the house is empty and full of death! . . . there is a pain about my heart! . . .

(*He calls hoarsely, getting to his feet*) Nina!

NINA'S VOICE: (*her voice, fresh and girlish, calls from upstairs*) Yes, Father. Do you want me?

PROFESSOR LEEDS: (*struggling with himself—goes to door and calls with affectionate blandness*) No. Never mind. Just wanted to remind you to call for a taxi in good time.

NINA'S VOICE: I won't forget.

PROFESSOR LEEDS: (*looks at his watch*)

Five-thirty just . . . nine-forty, the train . . . then . . . Nina no more! . . .
four hours more . . . she'll be packing . . . then good-bye . . . a kiss . . .
nothing more ever to say to each other . . . and I'll die in here some day
. . . alone . . . gasp, cry out for help . . . the president will speak at the
funeral . . . Nina will be here again . . . Nina in black . . . too late! . . .

(*He calls hoarsely*) Nina! (*There is no answer*)

In other room . . . doesn't hear . . . just as well . . .

(*He turns to the bookcase and pulls out the first volume his hands come on
and opens it at random and begins to read aloud sonorously like a child
whistling to keep up his courage in the dark*)

> "Stetit unus in arcem
> Erectus capitis victorque ad sidera mittit
> Sidereos oculos propiusque adspectat Olympum
> Inquiritque Iovem;" . . .

CURTAIN

ACT TWO

SCENE: *The same as Scene One,* PROFESSOR LEEDS' *study. It is about nine o'clock of a night in early fall, over a year later. The appearance of the room is unchanged except that all the shades, of the color of pale flesh, are drawn down, givng the windows a suggestion of lifeless closed eyes and making the room seem more withdrawn from life than before. The reading lamp on the table is lit. Everything on the table, papers, pencils, pens, etc., is arranged in meticulous order.*

MARSDEN *is seated on the chair at center. He is dressed carefully in an English made suit of blue serge so dark as to seem black, and which, combined with the gloomy brooding expression of his face, strongly suggests one in mourning. His tall, thin body sags wearily in the chair, his head is sunk forward, the chin almost touching his chest, his eyes stare sadly at nothing.*

MARSDEN: (*his thoughts at ebb, without emphasis, sluggish and melancholy*)

Prophetic Professor! . . . I remember he once said . . . shortly after Nina went away . . . "some day, in here, . . . you'll find me" . . . did he foresee? . . . no . . . everything in life is so contemptuously accidental! . . . God's sneer at our self-importance! . . .

(*Smiling grimly*)

Poor Professor! he was horribly lonely . . . tried to hide it . . . always telling you how beneficial the training at the hospital would be for her . . . poor old chap! . . .

(*His voice grows husky and uncertain—he controls it—straightens himself*)

What time is it? . . .

(*He takes out his watch mechanically and looks at it*)

Ten after nine. . . . Nina ought to be here. . . .

(*Then with sudden bitterness*)

Will she feel any real grief over his death, I wonder? ... I doubt it! ... but why am I so resentful? ... the two times I've visited the hospital she's been pleasant enough ... pleasantly evasive! ... perhaps she thought her father had sent me to spy on her ... poor Professor! ... at least she answered his letters ... he used to show them to me ... pathetically overjoyed ... newsy, loveless scripts, telling nothing whatever about herself ... well, she won't have to compose them any more ... she never answered mine ... she might at least have acknowledged them. ... Mother thinks she's behaved quite inexcusably ...

(*Then jealously*)

I suppose every single damned inmate has fallen in love with her! ... her eyes seemed cynical ... sick with men ... as though I'd looked into the eyes of a prostitute ... not that I ever have ... except that once ... the dollar house ... hers were like patent leather buttons in a saucer of blue milk! ...

(*Getting up with a movement of impatience*)

The devil! ... what beastly incidents our memories insist on cherishing! ... the ugly and disgusting ... the beautiful things we have to keep diaries to remember! ...

(*He smiles with a wry amusement for a second—then bitterly*)

That last night Nina was here ... she talked so brazenly about giving herself ... I wish I knew the truth of what she's been doing in that house full of men ... particularly that self-important young ass of a doctor! ... Gordon's friend! ...

(*He frowns at himself, determinedly puts an end to his train of thought and comes and sits down again in the chair—in sneering, conversational tones as if he were this time actually addressing another person*)

Really, it's hardly a decent time, is it, for that kind of speculation ... with her father lying dead upstairs? ...

(*A silence as if he had respectably squelched himself—then he pulls out his watch mechanically and stares at it. As he does so a noise of a car is heard approaching, stopping at the curb beyond the garden. He jumps to his feet and starts to go to door—then hesitates confusedly*)

No, let Mary go . . . I wouldn't know what to do . . . take her in my arms? . . . kiss her? . . . right now? . . . or wait until she? . . .

(*A bell rings insistently from the back of the house. From the front voices are heard, first* NINA'S, *then a man's.* MARSDEN *starts, his face suddenly angry and dejected*)

Someone with her! . . . a man! . . . I thought she'd be alone! . . .

(MARY *is heard shuffling to the front door which is opened. Immediately, as* MARY *sees* NINA, *she breaks down and there is the sound of her uncontrolled sobbing and choking, incoherent words drowning out* NINA'S *voice, soothing her*).

NINA: (*as* MARY'S *grief subsides a trifle, her voice is heard, flat and toneless*) Isn't Mr. Marsden here, Mary? (*She calls*) Charlie!

MARSDEN: (*confused—huskily*) In here—I'm in the study, Nina. (*He moves uncertainly toward the door*).

NINA: (*comes in and stands just inside the doorway. She is dressed in a nurse's uniform with cap, a raglan coat over it. She appears older than in the previous scene, her face is pale and much thinner, her cheek bones stand out, her mouth is taut in hard lines of a cynical scorn. Her eyes try to armor her wounded spirit with a defensive stare of disillusionment. Her training has also tended to coarsen her fiber a trifle, to make her insensitive to suffering, to give her the nurse's professionally callous attitude. In her fight to regain control of her nerves she has over-striven after the cool and efficient poise, but she is really in a more highly strung, disorganized state than ever, although she is now more capable of suppressing and concealing it. She remains strikingly handsome and her physical appeal is enhanced by her pallor and the mysterious suggestion about her of hidden experience. She stares at* MARSDEN *blankly and speaks in queer flat tones*) Hello, Charlie. He's dead, Mary says.

MARSDEN: (*nodding his head several times—stupidly*) Yes.

NINA: (*in same tones*) It's too bad. I brought Doctor Darrell. I thought there might be a chance. (*She pauses and looks about the room—thinking confusedly*)

His books . . . his chair . . . he always sat there . . . there's his table . . .
little Nina was never allowed to touch anything . . . she used to sit on his
lap . . . cuddle against him . . . dreaming into the dark beyond the windows . . . warm in his arms before the fireplace . . . dreams like sparks
soaring up to die in the cold dark . . . warm in his love, safe-drifting into
sleep . . . "Daddy's girl, aren't you?" . . .

(*She looks around and then up and down*)

His home . . . my home . . . he was my father . . . he's dead . . .

(*She shakes her head*)

Yes, I hear you, little Nina, but I don't understand one word of it. . . .

(*She smiles with a cynical self-contempt*)

I'm sorry, Father! . . . you see you've been dead for me a long time . . .
when Gordon died, all men died . . . what did you feel for me then? . . .
nothing . . . and now I feel nothing . . . it's too bad . . .

MARSDEN: (*thinking woundedly*)

I hoped she would throw herself in my arms . . . weeping . . . hide her
face on my shoulder . . . "Oh, Charlie, you're all I've got left in the
world . . ."

(*Then angrily*)

Why did she have to bring that Darrell with her?

NINA: (*flatly*) When I said good-bye that night I had a premonition I'd
never see him again.

MARSDEN: (*glad of this opening for moral indignation*) You've never tried
to see him, Nina! (*Then overcome by disgust with himself—contritely*)
Forgive me! It was rotten of me to say that!

NINA: (*shaking her head—flatly*) I didn't want him to see what he would
have thought was me. (*Ironically*) That's the other side of it you
couldn't dissect into words from here, Charlie! (*Then suddenly asking
a necessary question in her nurse's cool, efficient tones*) Is he upstairs?
(*Marsden nods stupidly*) I'll take Ned up. I might as well. (*She turns
and walks out briskly*).

MARSDEN: (*staring after her—dully*)

>That isn't Nina. . . .

(*Indignantly*)

>They've killed her soul down there! . . .

(*Tears come to his eyes suddenly and he pulls out his handkerchief and wipes them, muttering huskily*)

>Poor old Professor! . . .

(*Then suddenly jeering at himself*)

>For God's sake, stop acting! . . . it isn't the Professor! . . . dear old Charlie is crying because she didn't weep on his shoulder . . . as he had hoped! . . .

(*He laughs harshly—then suddenly sees a man outside the doorway and stares—then calls sharply*) Who's that?

EVANS: (*his voice embarrassed and hesitating comes from the hall*) It's all right. (*He appears in the doorway, grinning bashfully*) It's me—I, I mean—Miss Leeds told me to come in here. (*He stretches out his hand awkwardly*) Guess you don't remember me, Mr. Marsden. Miss Leeds introduced us one day at the hospital. You were leaving just as I came in. Evans is my name.

MARSDEN: (*who has been regarding him with waning resentment, forces a cordial smile and shakes hands*) Oh, yes. At first I couldn't place you.

EVANS: (*awkwardly*) I sort of feel I'm butting in.

MARSDEN: (*beginning to be taken by his likable boyish quality*) Not at all. Sit down. (*He sits in the rocker at center as* EVANS *goes to the bench at right.* EVANS *sits uncomfortably hunched forward, twiddling his hat in his hands. He is above the medium height, very blond, with guileless, diffident blue eyes, his figure inclined to immature lumbering outlines. His face is fresh and red-cheeked, handsome in a boyish fashion. His manner is bashful with women or older men, coltishly playful with his friends. There is a lack of self-confidence, a lost and strayed appealing air about him, yet with a hint of some unawakened obstinate force beneath his apparent weakness. Although he is twenty-five and has been out of college three years, he still wears the latest in collegiate clothes and as he looks younger than he is, he is always mistaken for an undergraduate and likes to be. It keeps him placed in life for himself).*

MARSDEN: (*studying him keenly—amused*)

> This is certainly no giant intellect . . . overgrown boy . . . likable quality though . . .

EVANS: (*uneasy under* MARSDEN'S *eyes*)

> Giving me the once-over . . . seems like good egg . . . Nina says he is . . . suppose I ought to say something about his books, but I can't even remember a title of one . . .

(*He suddenly blurts out*) You've known Nina—Miss Leeds—ever since she was a kid, haven't you?

MARSDEN: (*a bit shortly*) Yes. How long have you known her?

EVANS: Well—really only since she's been at the hospital, although I met her once years ago at a Prom with Gordon Shaw.

MARSDEN: (*indifferently*) Oh, you knew Gordon?

EVANS: (*proudly*) Sure thing! I was in his class! (*With admiration amounting to hero-worship*) He sure was a wonder, wasn't he?

MARSDEN: (*cynically*)

> Gordon über alles and forever! . . . I begin to appreciate the Professor's viewpoint . . .

(*Casually*) A fine boy! Did you know him well?

EVANS: No. The crowd he went with were mostly fellows who were good at sports—and I always was a dud. (*Forcing a smile*) I was always one of the first to get bounced off the squad in any sport. (*Then with a flash of humble pride*) But I never quit trying, anyway!

MARSDEN: (*consolingly*) Well, the sport hero usually doesn't star after college.

EVANS: Gordon did! (*Eagerly—with intense admiration*) In the war! He was an ace! And he always fought just as cleanly as he'd played football! Even the Huns respected him!

MARSDEN: (*thinking cynically*)

> This Gordon worshipper must be the apple of Nina's eye!

(*Casually*) Were you in the army?

EVANS: (*shamefacedly*) Yes—infantry—but I never got to the front—never saw anything exciting. (*Thinking glumly*)

> Won't tell him I tried for flying service . . . wanted to get in Gordon's outfit . . . couldn't make the physical exam. . . . never made anything I wanted . . . suppose I'll lose out with Nina, too . . .

(*Then rallying himself*)

> Hey, you! . . . what's the matter with you? . . . don't quit! . . .

MARSDEN: (*who has been staring at him inquisitively*) How did you happen to come out here tonight?

EVANS: I was calling on Nina when your wire came. Ned thought I better come along, too—might be of some use.

MARSDEN: (*frowning*) You mean Doctor Darrell? (EVANS *nods*) Is he a close friend of yours?

EVANS: (*hesitatingly*) Well, sort of. Roomed in the same dorm with me at college. He was a senior when I was a freshman. Used to help me along in lots of ways. Took pity on me, I was so green. Then about a year ago when I went to the hospital to visit a fellow who'd been in my outfit I ran into him again. (*Then with a grin*) But I wouldn't say Ned was close to anyone. He's a dyed-in-the-wool doc. He's only close to whatever's the matter with you! (*He chuckles—then hastily*) But don't get me wrong about him. He's the best egg ever! You know him, don't you?

MARSDEN: (*stiffly*) Barely. Nina introduced us once. (*Thinking bitterly*)

> He's upstairs alone with her . . . I hoped it would be I who . . .

EVANS:

> Don't want him to get the wrong idea of Ned . . . Ned's my best friend . . . doing all he can to help me with Nina . . . he thinks she'll marry me in the end . . . God, if she only would! . . . I wouldn't expect her to love me at first . . . be happy only to take care of her . . . cook her breakfast . . . bring it up to her in bed . . . tuck the pillows behind her . . . comb her hair for her . . . I'd be happy just to kiss her hair! . . .

MARSDEN: (*agitated—thinking suspiciously*)

> What are Darrell's relations with Nina? . . . close to what's the matter with her? . . . damned thoughts! . . . why should I care? . . . I'll ask this Evans . . . pump him while I have a chance . . .

(*With forced indifference*) Is your friend, the Doctor, "close" to Miss Leeds? She's had quite a lot the matter with her since her breakdown, if that's what interests him! (*He smiles casually*).

EVANS: (*gives a start, awakening from his dream*) Oh—er—yes. He's always trying to bully her into taking better care of herself, but she only laughs at him. (*Soberly*) It'd be much better if she'd take his advice.

MARSDEN: (*suspiciously*) No doubt.

EVANS: (*pronounces with boyish solemnity*) She isn't herself, Mr. Marsden. And I think nursing all those poor guys keeps the war before her when she ought to forget it. She ought to give up nursing and be nursed for a change, that's my idea.

MARSDEN: (*struck by this—eagerly*) Exactly my opinion. (*Thinking*)

> If she'd settle down here . . . I could come over every day . . . I'd nurse her . . . Mother home . . . Nina here . . . how I could work then! . . .

EVANS: (*thinking*)

> He certainly seems all for me . . . so far! . . .

(*Then in a sudden flurry*)

> Shall I tell him? . . . he'll be like her guardian now . . . I've got to know how he stands . . .

(*He starts with a solemn earnestness*) Mr. Marsden, I—there's something I ought to tell you, I think. You see, Nina's talked a lot about you. I know how much she thinks of you. And now her old man— (*He hesitates in confusion*) I mean, her father's dead—

MARSDEN: (*in a sort of panic—thinking*)

> What's this? . . . proposal? . . . in form? . . . for her hand? . . . to me? . . . Father Charlie now, eh? . . . ha! . . . God, what a fool! . . . does he imagine she'd ever love him? . . . but she might . . . not bad looking . . . likable, innocent . . . something to mother . . .

EVANS: (*blundering on regardless now*) I know it's hardly the proper time—

MARSDEN: (*interrupting—dryly*) Perhaps I can anticipate. You want to tell me you're in love with Nina?

EVANS: Yes, sir, and I've asked her to marry me.

MARSDEN: What did she say?

EVANS: (*sheepishly*) Nothing. She just smiled.

MARSDEN: (*with relief*) Ah. (*Then harshly*) Well, what could you expect? Surely you must know she still loves Gordon?

EVANS: (*manfully*) Sure I know it—and I admire her for it! Most girls forget too easily. She ought to love Gordon for a long time yet. And I know I'm an awful wash-out compared to him—but I love her as much as he did, or anyone could! And I'll work my way up for her— I know I can!—so I can give her everything she wants. And I wouldn't ask for anything in return except the right to take care of her. (*Blurts out confusedly*) I never think of her—that way—she's too beautiful and wonderful—not that I don't hope she'd come to love me in time—

MARSDEN: (*sharply*) And just what do you expect me to do about all this?

EVANS: (*taken aback*) Why—er—nothing, sir. I just thought you ought to know. (*Sheepishly he glances up at ceiling, then down at floor, twiddling his hat*).

MARSDEN: (*thinking—at first with a grudging appreciation and envy*)

He thinks he means that ... pure love! ... it's easy to talk ... he doesn't know life ... but he might be good for Nina ... if she were married to this simpleton would she be faithful? ... and then I? ... what a vile thought! ... I don't mean that! ...

(*Then forcing a kindly tone*) You see, there's really nothing I can do about it. (*With a smile*) If Nina will, she will—and if she won't, she won't. But I can wish you good luck.

EVANS: (*immediately all boyish gratitude*) Thanks! That's darn fine of you, Mr. Marsden!

MARSDEN: But I think we'd better let the subject drop, don't you? We're forgetting that her father—

EVANS: (*guiltily embarrassed*) Yes—sure—I'm a damn fool! Excuse me! (*There is the noise of steps from the hall and* DOCTOR EDMUND DARRELL *enters. He is twenty-seven, short, dark, wiry, his movements rapid and sure, his manner cool and observant, his dark eyes analytical. His head is handsome and intelligent. There is a quality about him, provoking and disturbing to women, of intense passion which he has rigidly trained himself to control and set free only for the objective satisfaction of studying his own and their reactions; and so he has come to consider himself as immune to love through his scientific understanding of its real sexual nature. He sees* EVANS *and* MARSDEN, *nods at* MARSDEN *silently, who returns it coldly, goes to the table and taking a prescription pad from his pocket, hastily scratches on it*).

MARSDEN: (*thinking sneeringly*)

Amusing, these young doctors! ... perspire with the effort to appear cool! ... writing a prescription ... cough medicine for the corpse, perhaps! ... good-looking? ... more or less ... attractive to women, I dare say. ...

DARRELL: (*tears it off—hands it to* EVANS) Here, Sam. Run along up the street and get this filled.

EVANS: (*with relief*) Sure. Glad of the chance for a walk. (*He goes out, rear*).

DARRELL: (*turning to* MARSDEN) It's for Nina. She's got to get some sleep tonight. (*He sits down abruptly in the chair at center.* MARSDEN *unconsciously takes the* PROFESSOR'S *place behind the table. The two men stare at each other for a moment,* DARRELL *with a frank probing, examining look that ruffles* MARSDEN *and makes him all the more resentful toward him*)

This Marsden doesn't like me . . . that's evident . . . but he interests me . . . read his books . . . wanted to know his bearing on Nina's case . . . his novels just well-written surface . . . no depth, no digging underneath . . . why? . . . has the talent but doesn't dare . . . afraid he'll meet himself somewhere . . . one of those poor devils who spend their lives trying not to discover which sex they belong to! . . .

MARSDEN:

Giving me the fishy, diagnosing eye they practice at medical school . . . like freshmen from Ioway cultivating broad A's at Harvard! . . . what is his specialty? . . . neurologist, I think . . . I hope not psychoanalyst . . . a lot to account for, Herr Freud! . . . punishment to fit his crimes, be forced to listen eternally during breakfast while innumerable plain ones tell him dreams about snakes . . . pah, what an easy cure-all! . . . sex the philosopher's stone . . . "O Oedipus, O my king! The world is adopting you!" . . .

DARRELL:

Must pitch into him about Nina . . . have to have his help . . . damn little time to convince him . . . he's the kind you have to explode a bomb under to get them to move . . . but not too big a bomb . . . they blow to pieces easily . . .

(*Brusquely*) Nina's gone to pot again! Not that her father's death is a shock in the usual sense of grief. I wish to God it were! No, it's a shock because it's finally convinced her she can't feel anything any more. That's what she's doing upstairs now—trying to goad herself into feeling something!

MARSDEN: (*resentfully*) I think you're mistaken. She loved her father—

DARRELL: (*shortly and dryly*) We can't waste time being sentimental, Marsden! She'll be down any minute, and I've got a lot to talk over with you. (*As* MARSDEN *seems again about to protest*) Nina has a real affection for you and I imagine you have for her. Then you'll want as much as I do to get her straightened out. She's a corking girl. She ought to have every chance for a happy life. (*Then sharply driving his words in*) But the way she's conditioned now, there's no chance. She's piled on too many destructive experiences. A few more and she'll dive for the gutter just to get the security that comes from knowing she's touched bottom and there's no farther to go!

MARSDEN: (*revolted and angry, half-springs to his feet*) Look here, Darrell, I'll be damned if I'll listen to such a ridiculous statement!

DARRELL: (*curtly—with authority*) How do you know it's ridiculous? What do you know of Nina since she left home? But she hadn't been nursing with us three days before I saw she really ought to be a patient; and ever since then I've studied her case. So I think it's up to you to listen.

MARSDEN: (*freezingly*) I'm listening. (*With apprehensive terror*)

Gutter . . . has she . . . I wish he wouldn't tell me! . . .

DARRELL: (*thinking*)

How much need I tell him? . . . can't tell him the raw truth about her promiscuity . . . he isn't built to face reality . . . no writer is outside of his books . . . have to tone it down for him . . . but not too much! . . .

Nina has been giving way more and more to a morbid longing for martyrdom. The reason for it is obvious. Gordon went away without—well, let's say marrying her. The war killed him. She was left suspended. Then she began to blame herself and to want to sacrifice herself and at the same time give happiness to various fellow war-victims by pretending to love them. It's a pretty idea but it hasn't worked out. Nina's a bad actress. She hasn't convinced the men of her love—or herself of her good intentions. And each experience of this kind has only left her more a prey to a guilty conscience than before and more determined to punish herself!

MARSDEN: (*thinking*)

What does he mean? . . . how far did she? . . . how many? . . .

(*Coldly and sneeringly*) May I ask on what specific actions of hers this theory of yours is based?

DARRELL: (*coldly in turn*) On her evident craving to make an exhibition of kissing, necking, petting—whatever you call it—spooning in general—with any patient in the institution who got a case on her! (*Ironically—thinking*)

> Spooning! . . . rather a mild word for her affairs . . . but strong enough for this ladylike soul. . . .

MARSDEN: (*bitterly*)

> He's lying! . . . what's he trying to hide? . . . was he one of them? . . . her lover? . . . I must get her away from him . . . get her to marry Evans! . . .

(*With authority*) Then she mustn't go back to your hospital, that's certain!

DARRELL: (*quickly*) You're quite right. And that brings me to what I want you to urge her to do.

MARSDEN: (*thinking suspiciously*)

> He doesn't want her back . . . I must have been wrong . . . but there might be many reasons why he'd wish to get rid of her . . .

(*Coldly*) I think you exaggerate my influence.

DARRELL: (*eagerly*) Not a bit. You're the last link connecting her with the girl she used to be before Gordon's death. You're closely associated in her mind with that period of happy security, of health and peace of mind. I know that from the way she talks about you. You're the only person she still respects—and really loves. (*As* MARSDEN *starts guiltily and glances at him in confusion—with a laugh*) Oh, you needn't look frightened. I mean the sort of love she'd feel for an uncle.

MARSDEN: (*thinking in agony*)

> Frightened? . . . was I? . . . only person she loves . . . and then he said "love she'd feel for an uncle" . . . Uncle Charlie now! . . . God damn him! . . .

DARRELL: (*eyeing him*)

> Looks damnably upset . . . wants to evade all responsibility for her, I suppose . . . he's that kind . . . all the better! . . . he'll be only too anxious to get her safely married. . . .

(*Bluntly*) And that's why I've done all this talking. You've got to help snap her out of this.

MARSDEN: (*bitterly*) And how, if I may ask?

DARRELL: There's only one way I can see. Get her to marry Sam Evans.

MARSDEN: (*astonished*) Evans? (*He makes a silly gesture toward the door— thinking confusedly*)

> Wrong again . . . why does he want her married to . . . it's some trick. . . .

DARRELL: Yes, Evans. He s in love with her. And it's one of those unselfish loves you read about. And she is fond of him. In a maternal way, of course—but that's just what she needs now, someone she cares about to mother and boss and keep her occupied. And still more important, this would give her a chance to have children. She's got to find normal outlets for her craving for sacrifice. She needs normal love objects for the emotional life Gordon's death blocked up in her. Now marrying Sam ought to do the trick. Ought to. Naturally, no one can say for certain. But I think his unselfish love, combined with her real liking for him, will gradually give her back a sense of security and a feeling of being worth something to life again, and once she's got that, she'll be saved! (*He has spoken with persuasive feeling. He asks anxiously*) Doesn't that seem good sense to you?

MARSDEN: (*suspicious—dryly non-commital*) I'm sorry but I'm in no position to say. I don't know anything about Evans, for one thing.

DARRELL: (*emphatically*) Well, I do. He's a fine healthy boy, clean and unspoiled. You can take my word for that. And I'm convinced he's got the right stuff in him to succeed, once he grows up and buckles down to work. He's only a big kid now, but all he needs is a little self-confidence and a sense of responsibility. He's holding down a fair job, too, considering he's just started in the advertising game—enough to keep them living. (*With a slight smile*) I'm prescribing for Sam, too, when I boost this wedding.

MARSDEN: (*his snobbery coming out*) Do you know his family—what sort of people?—

DARRELL: (*bitingly*) I'm not acquainted with their social qualifications, if that's what you mean! They're upstate country folks—fruit growers and farmers, well off, I believe. Simple, healthy people, I'm sure of that although I've never met them.

MARSDEN: (*a bit shamefacedly—changing the subject hastily*) Have you suggested this match to Nina?

DARRELL: Yes, a good many times lately in a half-joking way. If I were serious she wouldn't listen, she'd say I was prescribing. But I think what I've said has planted it in her mind as a possibility.

MARSDEN: (*thinking suspiciously*)

Is this Doctor her lover? . . . trying to pull the wool over my eyes? . . . use me to arrange a convenient triangle for him? . . .

(*Harshly—but trying to force a joking tone*) Do you know what I'm inclined to suspect, Doctor? That you may be in love with Nina yourself!

DARRELL: (*astonished*) The deuce you do! What in the devil makes you think that? Not that any man mightn't fall in love with Nina. Most of them do. But I didn't happen to. And what's more I never could. In my mind she always belongs to Gordon. It's probably a reflection of her own silly fixed idea about him. (*Suddenly, dryly and harshly*) And I couldn't share a woman—even with a ghost! (*Thinking cynically*)

Not to mention the living who have had her! . . . Sam doesn't know about them . . . and I'll bet he couldn't believe it of her even if she confessed! . . .

MARSDEN: (*thinking baffledly*)

Wrong again! . . . he isn't lying . . . but I feel he's hiding something . . .

why does he speak so resentfully of Gordon's memory? . . . why do I sympathize? . . .

(*In a strange mocking ironic tone*) I can quite appreciate your feeling about Gordon. I wouldn't care to share with a ghost-lover myself. That species of dead is so invulnerably alive! Even a doctor couldn't kill one, eh? (*He forces a laugh—then in a friendly confidential tone*) Gordon is too egregious for a ghost. That was the way Nina's father felt about him, too. (*Suddenly reminded of the dead man—in penitently sad tones*) You didn't know her father, did you? A charming old fellow!

DARRELL: (*hearing a noise from the hall—warningly*) Sstt! (NINA *enters slowly. She looks from one to the other with a queer, quick, inquisitive stare, but her face is a pale expressionless mask drained of all emotional response to human contacts. It is as if her eyes were acting on their own account as restless, prying, recording instruments. The two men have risen and stare at her anxiously.* DARRELL *moves back and to one side until he is standing in relatively the same place as* MARSDEN *had occupied in the previous scene while* MARSDEN *is in her father's place and she stops where she had been. There is a pause. Then just as each of the men is about to speak, she answers as if they had asked a question*).

NINA: (*in a queer flat voice*) Yes, he's dead—my father—whose passion created me—who began me—he is ended. There is only his end living—his death. It lives now to draw nearer me, to draw me nearer, to become my end! (*Then with a strange twisted smile*) How we poor monkeys hide from ourselves behind the sounds called words!

MARSDEN: (*thinking frightenedly*)

How terrible she is! . . . who is she? . . . not my Nina! . . .

(*As if to reassure himself—timidly*) Nina! (DARRELL *makes an impatient gesture for him to let her go on. What she is saying interests him and he feels talking it out will do her good. She looks at* MARSDEN *for a moment startledly as if she couldn't recognize him*).

NINA: What? (*Then placing him—with real affection that is like a galling goad to him*) Dear old Charlie!

MARSDEN:

>   Dear damned Charlie! . . . She loves to torture! . . .

(*Then forcing a smile—soothingly*) Yes, Nina Cara Nina! Right here!

NINA: (*forcing a smile*) You look frightened, Charlie. Do I seem queer? It's because I've suddenly seen the lies in the sounds called words. You know—grief, sorrow, love, father—those sounds our lips make and our hands write. You ought to know what I mean. You work with them. Have you written another novel lately? But, stop to think, you're just the one who couldn't know what I mean. With you the lies have become the only truthful things. And I suppose that's the logical conclusion to the whole evasive mess, isn't it? Do you understand me, Charlie? Say lie— (*She says it, drawing it out*) L-i-i-e! Now say life. L-i-i-f-e! You see! Life is just a long drawn out lie with a sniffling sigh at the end! (*She laughs*).

MARSDEN: (*in strange agony*)

>   She's hard! . . . like a whore! . . . tearing your heart with dirty finger nails! . . . my Nina! . . . cruel bitch! . . . some day I won't bear it! . . . I'll scream out the truth about every woman! no kinder at heart than dollar tarts! . . .

(*Then in a passion of remorse*)

>   Forgive me, Mother! . . . I didn't mean all! . . .

DARRELL: (*a bit worried himself now—persuasively*) Why not sit down, Nina, and let us two gentlemen sit down?

NINA: (*smiling at him swiftly and mechanically*) Oh, all right, Ned. (*She sits at center. He comes and sits on the bench.* MARSDEN *sits by the table. She continues sarcastically*) Are you prescribing for me again, Ned? This is my pet doctor, Charlie. He couldn't be happy in heaven unless God called him in because He'd caught something! Did you ever know a young scientist, Charlie? He believes if you pick a lie to pieces, the pieces are the truth! I like him because he's so inhuman. But once he kissed me—in a moment of carnal weakness! I was as startled as if a mummy had done it! And then he looked so disgusted with himself! I had to laugh! (*She smiles at him with a pitying scorn*).

DARRELL: (*good-naturedly smiling*) That's right! Rub it in! (*Ruffled but amused in spite of it*)

> I'd forgotten about that kiss . . . I was sore at myself afterwards . . . she was so damned indifferent! . . .

NINA: (*wanderingly*) Do you know what I was doing upstairs? I was trying to pray. I tried hard to pray to the modern science God. I thought of a million light years to a spiral nebula—one other universe among innumerable others. But how could that God care about our trifling misery of death-born-of-birth? I couldn't believe in Him, and I wouldn't if I could! I'd rather imitate His indifference and prove I had that one trait at least in common!

MARSDEN: (*worriedly*) Nina, why don't you lie down?

NINA: (*jeeringly*) Oh, let me talk, Charlie! They're only words, remember! So many many words have jammed up into thoughts in my poor head! You'd better let them overflow or they'll burst the dam! I wanted to believe in any God at any price—a heap of stones, a mud image, a drawing on a wall, a bird, a fish, a snake, a baboon—or even a good man preaching the simple platitudes of truth, those Gospel words we love the sound of but whose meaning we pass on to spooks to live by!

MARSDEN: (*again—half-rising—frightenedly*) Nina! You ought to stop talking. You'll work yourself into— (*He glances angrily at* DARRELL *as if demanding that, as a doctor, he do something*).

NINA: (*with bitter hopelessness*) Oh, all right!

DARRELL: (*answering his look—thinking*)

> You poor fool! . . . it'll do her good to talk this out of her system . . . and then it'll be up to you to bring her around to Sam . . .

(*Starts toward the door*) Think I'll go out and stretch my legs.

MARSDEN: (*thinking—in a panic*)

I don't want to be alone with her! . . . I don't know her! . . . I'm
afraid! . . .

(*Protestingly*) Well—but—hold on—I'm sure Nina would rather—

NINA: (*dully*) Let him go. I've said everything I can ever say—to him. I
want to talk to you, Charlie. (DARRELL *goes out noiselessly with a meaning look at* MARSDEN—*a pause*).

MARSDEN: (*thinking tremblingly*)

Here . . . now . . . what I hoped . . . she and I alone . . . she will cry . . . I
will comfort her . . . why am I so afraid? . . . whom do I fear? . . . is it she?
. . . or I? . . .

NINA: (*suddenly, with pity yet with scorn*) Why have you always been so
timid, Charlie? Why are you always afraid? What are you afraid of?

MARSDEN: (*thinking in a panic*)

She sneaked into my soul to spy! . . .

(*Then boldly*)

Well then, a little truth for once in a way! . . .

(*Timidly*) I'm afraid of—of life, Nina.

NINA: (*nodding slowly*) I know. (*After a pause—queerly*) The mistake
began when God was created in a male image. Of course, women
would see Him that way, but men should have been gentlemen
enough, remembering their mothers, to make God a woman! But
the God of Gods—the Boss—has always been a man. That makes
life so perverted, and death so unnatural. We should have imagined
life as created in the birth-pain of God the Mother. Then we would
understand why we, Her children, have inherited pain, for we would
know that our life's rhythm beats from Her great heart, torn with
the agony of love and birth. And we would feel that death meant
reunion with Her, a passing back into Her substance, blood of Her
blood again, peace of Her peace! (MARSDEN *has been listening to her
fascinatedly. She gives a strange little laugh*) Now wouldn't that be more
logical and satisfying than having God a male whose chest thunders

with egotism and is too hard for tired heads and thoroughly comfortless? Wouldn't it, Charlie?

MARSDEN: (*with a strange passionate eagerness*) Yes! It would, indeed! It would, Nina!

NINA: (*suddenly jumping to her feet and going to him—with a horrible moaning desolation*) Oh, God, Charlie, I want to believe in something! I want to believe so I can feel! I want to feel that he is dead—my father! And I can't feel anything, Charlie! I can't feel anything at all! (*She throws herself on her knees beside him and hides her face in her hands on his knees and begins to sob—stifled torn sounds*).

MARSDEN: (*bends down, pats her head with trembling hands, soothes her with uncertain trembling words*) There—there—don't—Nina, please—don't cry—you'll make yourself sick—come now—get up—do! (*His hands grasping her arms he half raises her to her feet, but, her face still hidden in her hands, sobbing, she slips on to his lap like a little girl and hides her face on his shoulder. His expression becomes transported with a great happiness—in an ecstatic whisper*)

As I dreamed . . . with a deeper sweetness! . . .

(*He kisses her hair with a great reverence*)

There . . . this is all my desire . . . I am this kind of lover . . . this is my love . . . she is my girl . . . not woman . . . my little girl . . . and I am brave because of her little girl's pure love . . . and I am proud . . . no more afraid . . . no more ashamed of being pure! . . .

(*He kisses her hair again tenderly and smiles at himself—then soothingly with a teasing incongruous gaiety*) This will never do, Nina Cara Nina—never, never do, you know—I can't permit it!

NINA: (*in a muffled voice, her sobbing beginning to ebb away into sighs—in a young girl's voice*) Oh, Charlie, you're so kind and comforting! I've wanted you so!

MARSDEN: (*immediately disturbed*)

Wanted? . . . wanted? . . . not that kind of wanted . . . can she mean? . . .

(*Questioning hesitatingly*) You've wanted me, Nina?

NINA: Yes,—awfully! I've been so homesick. I've wanted to run home and 'fess up, tell how bad I've been, and be punished! Oh, I've got to be punished, Charlie, out of mercy for me, so I can forgive myself! And now Father dead, there's only you. You will, won't you—or tell me how to punish myself? You've simply got to, if you love me!

MARSDEN: (*thinking intensely*)

If I love her! . . . oh, I do love her! . . .

(*Eagerly*) Anything you wish, Nina—anything!

NINA: (*with a comforted smile, closing her eyes and cuddling up against him*) I knew you would. Dear old Charlie! (*As he gives a wincing start*) What is it? (*She looks up into his face*).

MARSDEN: (*forcing a smile—ironically*) Twinge—rheumatics—getting old, Nina. (*Thinking with wild agony*)

Dear old Charlie! . . . descended again into hell! . . .

(*Then in a flat voice*) What do you want to be punished for, Nina?

NINA: (*in a strange, far-away tone, looking up not at him but at the ceiling*) For playing the silly slut, Charlie. For giving my cool clean body to men with hot hands and greedy eyes which they called love! Ugh! (*A shiver runs over her body*).

MARSDEN: (*thinking with sudden agony*)

Then she did! . . . the little filth! . . .

(*In his flat voice*) You mean you— (*Then pleadingly*) But not—Darrell?

NINA: (*with simple surprise*) Ned? No, how could I? The war hadn't maimed him. There would have been no point in that. But I did with others—oh, four or five or six or seven men, Charlie. I forget—and it doesn't matter. They were all the same. Count them all as one, and that one a ghost of nothing. That is, to me. They were important to themselves, if I remember rightly. But I forget.

MARSDEN: (*thinking in agony*)

But why? . . . the dirty little trollop! . . . why? . . .

(*In his flat voice*) Why did you do this, Nina?

NINA: (*with a sad little laugh*) God knows, Charlie! Perhaps I knew at the time but I've forgotten. It's all mixed up. There was a desire to be kind. But it's horribly hard to give anything, and frightful to receive! And to give love—oneself—not in this world! And men are difficult to please, Charlie. I seemed to feel Gordon standing against a wall with eyes bandaged and these men were a firing squad whose eyes were also bandaged—and only I could see! No, I was the blindest! I would not see! I knew it was a stupid, morbid business, that I was more maimed than they were, really, that the war had blown my heart and insides out! And I knew too that I was torturing these tortured men, morbidly super-sensitive already, that they loathed the cruel mockery of my gift! Yet I kept on, from one to one, like a stupid, driven animal until one night not long ago I had a dream of Gordon diving down out of the sky in flames and he looked at me with such sad burning eyes, and all my poor maimed men, too, seemed staring out of his eyes with a burning pain, and I woke up crying, my own eyes burning. Then I saw what a fool I'd been—a guilty fool! So be kind and punish me!

MARSDEN: (*thinking with bitter confusion*)

> I wish she hadn't told me this . . . it has upset me terribly! . . . I positively must run home at once . . . Mother is waiting up . . . oh, how I'd love to hate this little whore! . . . then I could punish! . . . I wish her father were alive . . . "now he's dead there's only you," she said . . . "I've wanted you," . . .

(*With intense bitterness*)

> Dear old Father Charlie now! . . . ha! . . . that's how she wants me! . . .

(*Then suddenly in a matter-of-fact tone that is mockingly like her father's*)
Then, under the circumstances, having weighed the pros and cons, so to speak, I should say that decidedly the most desirable course—

NINA: (*drowsily—her eyes shut*) You sound so like Father, Charlie.

MARSDEN: (*in the tone like her father's*) —is for you to marry that young Evans. He is a splendid chap, clean and boyish, with real stuff in him, too, to make a career for himself if he finds a help-meet who will inspire him to his best efforts and bring his latent ability to the surface.

NINA: (*drowsily*) Sam is a nice boy. Yes, it would be a career for me to bring a career to his surface. I would be busy—surface life—no more depths, please God! But I don't love him, Father.

MARSDEN: (*blandly—in the tone like her father's*) But you like him, Nina. And he loves you devotedly. And it's time you were having children— and when children come, love comes, you know.

NINA: (*drowsily*) I want children. I must become a mother so I can give myself. I am sick of sickness.

MARSDEN: (*briskly*) Then it's all settled?

NINA: (*drowsily*) Yes. (*Very sleepily*) Thank you, Father. You've been so kind. You've let me off too easily. I don't feel as if you'd punished me hardly at all. But I'll never, never do it again, I promise—never, never!— (*She falls asleep and gives a soft little snore*).

MARSDEN: (*still in her father's tones—very paternally—looking down*) She's had a hard day of it, poor child! I'll carry her up to her room. (*He rises to his feet with* NINA *sleeping peacefully in his arms. At this moment* SAM EVANS *enters from the right with the package of medicine in his hand*).

EVANS: (*grinning respectfully*) Here's the— (*As he sees* NINA) Oh! (*Then excitedly*) Did she faint?

MARSDEN: (*smiling kindly at* EVANS—*still in her father's tones*) Sssh! She's asleep. She cried and then she fell asleep—like a little girl. (*Then benignantly*) But first we spoke a word about you, Evans, and I'm sure you have every reason to hope.

EVANS: (*overcome, his eyes on his shuffling feet and twiddling cap*) Thanks— I—I really don't know how to thank—

MARSDEN: (*going to door—in his own voice now*) I've got to go home. My mother is waiting up for me. I'll just carry Nina upstairs and put her on her bed and throw something over her.

EVANS: Can't I help you, Mr. Marsden?

MARSDEN: (*dully*) No. I cannot help myself. (*As* EVANS *looks puzzled and startled he adds with an ironical, self-mocking geniality*) You'd better call me just Charlie after this. (*He smiles bitterly to himself as he goes out*).

EVANS: (*looks after him for a moment—then cannot restrain a joyful, coltish caper—gleefully*) Good egg! Good old Charlie! (*As if he had heard or guessed,* MARSDEN's *bitter laugh comes back from the end of the hallway*).

CURTAIN

ACT THREE

SCENE: *Seven months or so later—the dining room of the* EVANS' *homestead in northern New York state—about nine o'clock in the morning of a day in late spring of the following year.*

The room is one of those big, misproportioned dining rooms that are found in the large, jigsaw country houses scattered around the country as a result of the rural taste for grandeur in the eighties. There is a cumbersome hanging lamp suspended from chains over the exact center of the ugly table with its set of straightbacked chairs set back at spaced intervals against the walls. The wall paper, a repulsive brown, is stained at the ceiling line with damp blotches of mildew, and here and there has started to peel back where the strips join. The floor is carpeted in a smeary brown with a dark red design blurred into it. In the left wall is one window with starched white curtains looking out on a covered side porch, so that no sunlight ever gets to this room and the light from the window, although it is a beautiful warm day in the flower garden beyond the porch, is cheerless and sickly. There is a door in the rear, to left of center, that leads to a hall opening on the same porch. To the right of door a heavy sideboard, a part of the set, displaying some "company" china and glassware. In the right wall, a door leading to the kitchen. NINA *is seated at the foot of the table, her back to the window, writing a letter. Her whole personality seems changed, her face has a contented expression, there is an inner calm about her. And her personal appearance has changed in kind, her face and figure have filled out, she is prettier in a conventional way and less striking and unusual; nothing remains of the strange fascination of her face except her unchangeably mysterious eyes.*

NINA: (*reading what she has just written over to herself*)

It's a queer house, Ned. There is something wrong with its psyche, I'm sure. Therefore you'd simply adore it. It's a hideous old place, a faded gingerbread with orange fixin's and numerous lightning rods. Around it are acres and acres of apple trees in full bloom, all white and pinkish and beautiful, like brides just tripping out of church with the bridegroom, Spring, by the arm.

Which reminds me, Ned, that it's over six months since Sam and I were married and we haven't seen hide nor hair of you since the ceremony. Do you think that is any nice way to act? You might at least drop me a line. But I'm only joking. I know how busy you must be now that you've got the chance you've always wanted to do research work. Did you get our joint letter of congratulation written after we read of your appointment?

But to get back to this house. I feel it has lost its soul and grown resigned to doing without it. It isn't haunted by anything at all—and ghosts of some sort are the only normal life a house has—like our minds, you know. So although last evening when we got here at first I said "obviously haunted" to myself, now that I've spent one night in it I know that whatever spooks there may once have been have packed up their manifestations a long time ago and drifted away over the grass, wisps of mist between the apple trees, without one backward glance of regret or recollection. It's incredible to think Sam was born and spent his childhood here. I'm glad he doesn't show it! We slept last night in the room he was born in. Or rather he slept, I couldn't. I lay awake and found it difficult to breathe, as if all the life in the air had long since been exhausted in keeping the dying living a little longer. It was hard to believe anyone had ever been born alive there. I know you're saying crossly "She's still morbid" but I'm not. I've never been more normal. I feel contented and placid.

(Looking up from the letter, thinking embarrassedly)

Should I have told him? . . . no . . . my own secret . . . tell no one . . . not even Sam . . . why haven't I told Sam? . . . it'd do him so much good . . . he'd feel so proud of himself, poor dear . . . no . . . I want to keep it just my baby . . . only mine . . . as long as I can . . . and it will be time enough to let Ned know when I go to New York . . . he can suggest a good obstetrician . . . how delighted he'll be when he hears! . . . he always said it would be the best thing for me . . . well, I do feel happy when I think . . . and I love Sam now . . . in a way . . . it will be his baby too . . .

(Then with a happy sigh, turns back to letter)

But speaking of Sam's birth, you really must meet his mother sometime. It's amazing how little she is like him, a strange woman from the bit I saw of her last night. She has been writing Sam regularly once a week ever since she's known we were married, the most urgent invitations to visit her. They were really more like commands, or prayers. I suspect she is terribly lonely all by herself in this big house. Sam's feeling toward her puzzles me. I don't believe he ever mentioned her until her letters began coming or that he'd ever have come to see the poor woman if I hadn't insisted. His attitude rather shocked me. It was just as though he'd forgotten he had a mother. And yet as soon as he saw her he was sweet enough. She seemed dreadfully upset to see Charlie with us, until we'd explained it was thanks to his kindess and in his car we were taking this deferred honeymoon. Charlie's like a fussy old woman about his car, he's afraid to let Sam or me drive it—

MARSDEN: (*enters from the rear. He is spruce, dressed immaculately, his face a bit tired and resigned, but smiling kindly. He has a letter in his hand*) Good morning. (*She gives a start and instinctively covers the letter with her hand*).

NINA: Good morning. (*Thinking amusedly*)

If he knew what I'd just written . . . poor old Charlie! . . .

(*Then indicating the letter he carries*) I see you're an early correspondent, too.

MARSDEN: (*with sudden jealous suspicion*)

Why did she cover it up like that? . . . whom is she writing to? . . .

(*Coming toward her*) Just a line to Mother to let her know we've not all been murdered by rum-bandits. You know how she worries.

NINA: (*thinking with a trace of pitying contempt*)

Apron strings . . . still his devotion to her is touching . . . I hope if mine is a boy he will love me as much . . . oh, I hope it is a boy . . . healthy and strong and beautiful . . . like Gordon! . . .

(*Then suddenly sensing* MARSDEN'S *curiosity—perfunctorily*) I'm writing to Ned Darrell. I've owed him one for ages. (*She folds it up and puts it aside*).

MARSDEN: (*thinking glumly*)

I thought she'd forgotten him . . . still I suppose it's just friendly . . . and it's none of my business now she's married. . . .

(*Perfunctorily*) How did you sleep?

NINA: Not a wink. I had the strangest feeling.

MARSDEN: Sleeping in a strange bed, I suppose. (*Jokingly*) Did you see any ghosts?

NINA: (*with a sad smile*) No, I got the feeling the ghosts had all deserted the house and left it without a soul—as the dead so often leave the living— (*She forces a little laugh*) if you get what I mean.

MARSDEN: (*thinking worriedly*)

Slipping back into that morbid tone . . . first time in a long while . . .

(*Teasingly*) Hello! Do I hear graveyards yawning from their sleep— and yet I observe it's a gorgeous morning without, the flowers are flowering, the trees are treeing with one another, and you, if I mistake not, are on your honeymoon!

NINA: (*immediately gaily mocking*) Oh, very well, old thing! "God's in his heaven, all's right with the world!" And Pippa's cured of the pip! (*She dances up to him*).

MARSDEN: (*gallantly*) Pippa is certainly a pippin this morning!

NINA: (*kisses him quickly*) You deserve one for that! All I meant was that ghosts remind me of men's smart crack about women, you can't live with them and can't live without them. (*Stands still and looks at him teasingly*) But there you stand proving me a liar by every breath you draw! You're ghostless and womanless—and as sleek and satisfied as a pet seal! (*She sticks out her tongue at him and makes a face of superior scorn*) Bah! That for you, 'Fraid-cat Charlie, you slacker bachelor! (*She runs to the kitchen door*) I'm going to bum some more coffee! How about you?

MARSDEN: (*with a forced smile*) No, thank you. (*She disappears into the kitchen—thinking with bitter pain*)

Ghostless! . . . if she only knew . . . that joking tone hides her real contempt! . . .

(*Self-mockingly*)

"But when the girls began to play 'Fraid-cat Charlie ran away!"

(*Then rallying himself*)

Bosh! ... I haven't had such thoughts ... not since their marriage ... happy in her happiness ... but is she happy? ... in the first few months she was obviously playing a part ... kissed him too much ... as if she'd determined to make herself a loving wife ... and then all of a sudden she became contented ... her face filled out ... her eyes lazily examined peace ... pregnant ... yes, she must be ... I hope so.... Why? ... for her sake ... my own, too ... when she has a child I know I can entirely accept ... forget I have lost her ... lost her? ... silly ass! ... how can you lose what you never possessed? ... except in dreams! ...

(*Shaking his head exasperatedly*)

Round and round ... thoughts ... damn pests! ... mosquitoes of the soul ... whine, sting, suck one's blood ... why did I invite Nina and Sam on this tour ... it's a business trip with me, really ... I need a new setting for my next novel ... "Mr. Marsden departs a bit from his familiar field" ... well, there they were stuck in the Professor's house ... couldn't afford a vacation ... never had a honeymoon ... I've pretended to be done up every night so they could ... I've gone to bed right after dinner so they could be alone and ... I wonder if she can really like him ... that way? ...

(*The sound of* EVANS' *voice and his mother's is heard from the garden.* MARS-DEN *goes over and carefully peers out*)

Sam with his mother ... peculiar woman ... strong ... good character for a novel ... no, she's too somber ... her eyes are the saddest ... and, at the same time, the grimmest ... they're coming in ... I'll drive around the country a bit ... give them a chance for a family conference ... discuss Nina's pregnancy, I suppose ... does Sam know? ... he gives no indication ... why do wives hide it from their husbands? ... ancient shame ... guilty of continuing life, of bringing fresh pain into the world ...

(*He goes out, rear. The outside door in the hall is heard being opened and* EVANS *and his mother evidently meet* MARSDEN *as he is about to go out. Their voices, his voice explaining, are heard, then the outer door being opened and shut again as* MARSDEN *departs. A moment later* EVANS *and his mother enter the dining room.* SAM *looks timorously happy, as if he could not quite believe in his good fortune and had constantly to reassure himself*)

*about it, yet he is riding the crest of the wave, he radiates love and devotion
and boyish adoration. He is a charming-looking fresh boy now. He wears a
sweater and linen knickers, collegiate to the last degree. His mother is a
tiny woman with a frail figure, her head and face, framed in iron-gray
hair, seeming much too large for her body, so that at first glance she gives
one the impression of a wonderfully made, lifelike doll. She is only about
forty-five but she looks at least sixty. Her face with its delicate features must
have once been of a romantic, tender, clinging-vine beauty, but what has
happened to her has compressed its defenseless curves into planes, its mouth
into the thin line around a locked door, its gentle chin has been forced out
aggressively by a long reliance on clenched teeth. She is very pale. Her big
dark eyes are grim with the prisoner-pain of a walled-in soul. Yet a sweet
loving-kindness, the ghost of an old faith and trust in life's goodness, hovers
girlishly, fleetingly, about the corners of her mouth and softens into deep
sorrow the shadowy grimness of her eyes. Her voice jumps startlingly in
tone from a caressing gentleness to a blunted flat assertiveness, as if what
she said then was merely a voice on its own without human emotion to
inspire it).*

EVANS: (*as they come in—rattling on in the cocksure boastful way of a boy
showing off his prowess before his mother, confident of thrilled adulation*)
In a few years you won't have to worry one way or another about
the darned old apple crop. I'll be able to take care of you then. Wait
and see! Of course, I'm not making so much now. I couldn't expect
to. I've only just started. But I'm making good, all right, all right—
since I got married—and it's only a question of time when— Why,
to show you, Cole—he's the manager and the best egg ever—called
me into his office and told me he'd had his eye on me, that my stuff
was exactly what they wanted, and he thought I had the makings of
a real find. (*Proudly*) How's that? That's certainly fair enough, isn't
it?

MRS. EVANS: (*vaguely—she has evidently not heard much of what he said*)
That's fine, Sammy. (*Thinking apprehensively*)

I do hope I'm wrong! . . . but that old shiver of dread took me the minute she stepped in the door! . . . I don't think she's told Sammy but I got to make sure. . . .

EVANS: (*seeing her preoccupation now—deeply hurt—testily*) I'll bet you didn't hear a word I said! Are you still worrying about how the darn old apples are going to turn out?

MRS. EVANS: (*with a guilty start—protestingly*) Yes, I did hear you, Sammy—every word! That's just what I was thinking about—how proud I am you're doing so wonderful well!

EVANS: (*mollified but still grumbling*) You'd never guess it from the gloomy way you looked! (*But encouraged to go on*) And Cole asked me if I was married—seemed to take a real personal interest—said he was glad to hear it because marriage was what put the right kind of ambition into a fellow—unselfish ambition—working for his wife and not just himself— (*Then embarrassedly*) He even asked me if we were expecting an addition to the family.

MRS. EVANS: (*seeing this is her chance—quickly—forcing a smile*) I've been meaning to ask you that myself, Sammy. (*Blurts out apprehensively*) She—Nina—she isn't going to have a baby, is she?

EVANS: (*with an indefinable guilty air—as if he were reluctant to admit it*) I—why—you mean, is she now? I don't think so, Mother. (*He strolls over to the window whistling with an exaggeratedly casual air, and looks out*).

MRS. EVANS: (*thinking with grim relief*)

He don't know . . . there's that much to be thankful for, anyway. . . .

EVANS: (*thinking with intense longing*)

If that'd only happen! . . . soon! . . . Nina's begun to love me . . . a little . . . I've felt it the last two months . . . God, it's made me happy! . . . before that she didn't . . . only liked me . . . that was all I asked . . . never dared hope she'd come to love me . . . even a little . . . so soon . . . sometimes I feel it's too good to be true . . . don't deserve it . . . and now . . . if that'd happen . . . then I'd feel sure . . . it'd be there . . . half Nina, half me . . . living proof! . . .

(*Then an apprehensive note creeping in*)

And I know she wants a baby so much . . . one reason why she married me . . . and I know she's felt right along that then she'd love me . . . really love me . . .

(*Gloomily*)

I wonder why . . . ought to have happened before this . . . hope it's nothing wrong . . . with me! . . .

(*He starts, flinging off his thought—then suddenly clutching at a straw, turns hopefully to his mother*) Why did you ask me that, Mother? D'you think—?

MRS. EVANS: (*hastily*) No, indeed! I don't think she is! I wouldn't say so at all!

EVANS: (*dejectedly*) Oh—I thought perhaps— (*Then changing the subject*) I suppose I ought to go up and say hello to Aunt Bessie.

MRS. EVANS: (*her face becoming defensive—in blunted tones, a trifle pleadingly*) I wouldn't, Sammy. She hasn't seen you since you were eight. She wouldn't know you. And you're on your honeymoon, and old age is always sad to young folks. Be happy while you can! (*Then pushing him toward door*) Look here! You catch that friend, he's just getting his car out. You drive to town with him, give me a chance to get to know my daughter-in-law, and call her to account for how she's taking care of you! (*She laughs forcedly*).

EVANS: (*bursting out passionately*) Better than I deserve! She's an angel, Mother! I know you'll love her!

MRS. EVANS: (*gently*) I do already, Sammy! She's so pretty and sweet!

EVANS: (*kisses her—joyously*) I'll tell her that. I'm going out this way and kiss her good-bye. (*He runs out through the kitchen door*).

MRS. EVANS: (*looking after him—passionately*)

He loves her! . . . he's happy! . . . that's all that counts! . . . being happy! . . .

(*Thinking apprehensively*)

If only she isn't going to have a baby . . . if only she doesn't care so much about having one . . . I got to have it out with her . . . got to! . . . no other way . . . in mercy . . . in justice . . . this has got to end with my boy . . . and he's got to live happy! . . .

(*At the sound of steps from the kitchen she straightens up in her chair stiffly*).

NINA: (*comes in from the kitchen, a cup of coffee in her hand, smiling happily*) Good morning— (*She hesitates—then shyly*) Mother. (*She comes over and kisses her—slips down and sits on the floor beside her*).

MRS. EVANS: (*flusteredly—hurriedly*) Good morning! It's a real fine day, isn't it? I ought to have been here and got your breakfast, but I was out gallivanting round the place with Sammy. I hope you found everything you wanted.

NINA: Indeed I did! And I ate so much I'm ashamed of myself! (*She nods at the cup of coffee and laughs*) See. I'm still at it.

MRS. EVANS: Good for you!

NINA: I ought to apologize for coming down so late. Sam should have called me. But I wasn't able to get to sleep until after daylight somehow.

MRS. EVANS: (*strangely*) You couldn't sleep? Why? Did you feel anything funny—about this house?

NINA: (*struck by her tone—looks up*) No. Why? (*Thinking*)

How her face changes! . . . what sad eyes! . . .

MRS. EVANS: (*thinking in an agony of apprehension*)

Got to start in to tell her . . . got to . . .

NINA: (*apprehensive herself now*)

That sick dead feeling . . . when something is going to happen . . . I felt it before I got the cable about Gordon . . .

(*Then taking a sip of coffee, and trying to be pleasantly casual*) Sam said you wanted to talk to me.

MRS. EVANS: (*dully*) Yes. You love my boy, don't you?

NINA: (*startled—forcing a smile, quickly*) Why, of course! (*Reassuring herself*)

 No, it isn't a lie . . . I do love him . . . the father of my baby . . .

MRS. EVANS: (*blurts out*) Are you going to have a baby, Nina?

NINA: (*she presses* MRS. EVANS' *hand—simply*) Yes, Mother.

MRS. EVANS: (*in her blunt flat tones—with a mechanical rapidity to her words*) Don't you think it's too soon? Don't you think you better wait until Sammy's making more money? Don't you think it'll be a drag on him and you? Why don't you just go on being happy together, just you two?

NINA: (*thinking frightenedly*)

 What is behind what she's saying? . . . that feeling of death again! . . .

(*Moving away from her—repulsed*) No, I don't think any of those things, Mrs. Evans. I want a baby—beyond everything! We both do!

MRS. EVANS: (*hopelessly*) I know. (*Then grimly*) But you can't! You've got to make up your mind you can't! (*Thinking fiercely—even with satisfaction*)

 Tell her! . . . make her suffer what I was made to suffer! . . . I've been too lonely! . . .

NINA: (*thinking with terrified foreboding*)

 I knew it! . . . Out of a blue sky . . . black! . . .

(*Springing to her feet—bewilderedly*) What do you mean? How can you say a thing like that?

MRS. EVANS: (*reaching out her hand tenderly, trying to touch* NINA) It's because I want Sammy—and you, too, child—to be happy. (*Then as* NINA *shrinks away from her hand—in her blunted tones*) You just can't.

NINA: (*defiantly*) But I can! I have already! I mean—I am, didn't you understand me?

MRS. EVANS: (*gently*) I know it's hard. (*Then inexorably*) But you can't go on!

NINA: (*violently*) I don't believe you know what you're saying! It's too terrible for you—Sam's own mother—how would you have felt if someone—when you were going to have Sam—came to you and said—?

MRS. EVANS: (*thinking fiercely*)

Now's my chance! . . .

(*Tonelessly*) They did say it! Sam's own father did—my husband! And I said it to myself! And I did all I could, all my husband could think of, so's I wouldn't—but we didn't know enough. And right to the time the pains come on, I prayed Sammy'd be born dead, and Sammy's father prayed, but Sammy was born healthy and smiling, and we just had to love him, and live in fear. He doubled the torment of fear we lived in. And that's what you'd be in for. And Sammy, he'd go the way his father went. And your baby, you'd be bringing it into torment. (*A bit violently*) I tell you it'd be a crime—a crime worse than murder! (*Then recovering—commiseratingly*) So you just can't, Nina!

NINA: (*who has been listening distractedly—thinking*)

Don't listen to her! . . . feeling of death! . . . what is it? . . . she's trying to kill my baby! . . . oh, *I* hate her! . . .

(*Hysterically resentful*) What do you mean? Why don't you speak plainly? (*Violently*) I think you're horrible! Praying your baby would be born dead! That's a lie! You couldn't!

MRS. EVANS: (*thinking*)

I know what she's doing now . . . just what I did . . . trying not to believe . . .

(*Fiercely*)

But I'll make her! . . . she's got to suffer, too! . . . I been too lonely! . . . she's got to share and help me save my Sammy! . . .

(*With an even more blunted flat relentless tonelessness*) I thought I was plain, but I'll be plainer. Only remember it's a family secret, and now you're one of the family. It's the curse on the Evanses. My husband's mother—she was an only child—died in an asylum and her father before her. I know that for a fact. And my husband's sister, Sammy's aunt, she's out of her mind. She lives on the top floor of this house, hasn't been out of her room in years, I've taken care of her. She just sits, doesn't say a word, but she's happy, she laughs to herself a lot, she hasn't a care in the world. But I remember when she was all right, she was always unhappy, she never got married, most people around here were afraid of the Evanses in spite of their being rich for hereabouts. They knew about the craziness going back, I guess, for heaven knows how long. I didn't know about the Evanses until after I'd married my husband. He came to the town I lived in, no one there knew about the Evanses. He didn't tell me until after we were married. He asked me to forgive him, he said he loved me so much he'd have gone mad without me, said I was his only hope of salvation. So I forgave him. I loved him an awful lot. I said to myself, I'll be his salvation—and maybe I could have been if we hadn't had Sammy born. My husband kept real well up to then. We'd swore we'd never have children, we never forgot to be careful for two whole years. Then one night we'd both gone to a dance, we'd both had a little punch to drink, just enough—to forget—driving home in the moonlight—that moonlight!—such little things at the back of big things!

NINA: (*in a dull moan*) I don't believe you! I won't believe you!

MRS. EVANS: (*drones on*) My husband, Sammy's father, in spite of all he and I fought against it, he finally gave in to it when Sammy was only eight, he couldn't keep up any more living in fear for Sammy, thinking any minute the curse might get him, every time he was sick, or had a headache, or bumped his head, or started crying, or had a nightmare and screamed, or said something queer like children do naturally. (*A bit stridently*) Living like that with that fear is awful torment! I know that! I went through it by his side! It nearly drove me crazy, too—but I didn't have it in my blood! And that's why I'm telling you! You got to see you can't, Nina!

NINA: (*suddenly breaking out—frenziedly*) I don't believe you! I don't believe Sam would ever have married me if he knew—!

MRS. EVANS: (*sharply*) Who said Sammy knew? He don't know a single thing about it! That's been the work of my life, keeping him from knowing. When his father gave up and went off into it I sent Sammy right off to boarding school. I told him his father was sick, and a little while after I sent word his father was dead, and from then on until his father did really die during Sammy's second year to college, I kept him away at school in winter and camp in summers and I went to see him, I never let him come home. (*With a sigh*) It was hard, giving up Sammy, knowing I was making him forget he had a mother. I was glad taking care of them two kept me so busy I didn't get much chance to think then. But here's what I've come to think since, Nina: I'm certain sure my husband might have kept his mind with the help of my love if I hadn't had Sammy. And if I'd never had Sammy I'd never have loved Sammy—or missed him, would I?—and I'd have kept my husband.

NINA: (*not heeding this last—with wild mockery*) And I thought Sam was so normal—so healthy and sane—not like me! I thought he'd give me such healthy, happy children and I'd forget myself in them and learn to love him!

MRS. EVANS: (*horrified, jumping to her feet*) Learn to? You told me you did love Sammy!

NINA: No! Maybe I almost have—lately—but only when I thought of his baby! Now I hate him! (*She begins to weep hysterically.* MRS. EVANS *goes to her and puts her arms around her.* NINA *sobs out*) Don't touch me! I hate you, too! Why didn't you tell him he must never marry!

MRS. EVANS: What reason could I give, without telling him everything? And I never heard about you till after you were married. Then I wanted to write to you but I was scared he might read it. And I couldn't leave her upstairs to come away to see you. I kept writing Sammy to bring you here right off, although having him come frightened me to death for fear he might get to suspect something. You got to get him right away from here, Nina! I just kept hoping you wouldn't want children right away—young folks don't nowadays—until I'd seen you and told you everything. And I thought you'd love him like I did his father, and be satisfied with him alone.

NINA: (*lifting her head—wildly*) No! I don't! I won't! I'll leave him!

MRS. EVANS: (*shaking her, fiercely*) You can't! He'd go crazy sure then! You'd be a devil! Don't you see how he loves you?

NINA: (*breaking away from her—harshly*) Well, I don't love him! I only married him because he needed me—and I needed children! And now you tell me I've got to kill my—oh, yes, I see I've got to, you needn't argue any more! I love it too much to make it run that chance! And I hate it too, now, because it's sick, it's not my baby, it's his! (*With terrible ironic bitterness*) And still you can dare to tell me I can't even leave Sam!

MRS. EVANS: (*very sadly and bitterly*) You just said you married him because he needed you. Don't he need you now—more'n ever? But I can't tell you not to leave him, not if you don't love him. But you oughtn't to have married him when you didn't love him. And it'll be your fault, what'll happen.

NINA: (*torturedly*) What will happen?—what do you mean?—Sam will be all right—just as he was before—and it's not my fault anyway!—it's not my fault! (*Then thinking conscience-strickenly*)

> Poor Sam . . . she's right . . . it's not his fault . . . it's mine . . . I wanted to use him to save myself . . . I acted the coward again . . . as I did with Gordon . . .

MRS. EVANS: (*grimly*) You know what'll happen to him if you leave him—after all I've told you! (*Then breaking into intense pleading*) Oh, I'd get down on my knees to you, don't make my boy run that risk! You got to give one Evans, the last one, a chance to live in this world! And you'll learn to love him, if you give up enough for him! (*Then with a grim smile*) Why, I even love that idiot upstairs, I've taken care of her so many years, lived her life for her with my life, you might say. You give your life to Sammy, then you'll love him same as you love yourself. You'll have to! That's sure as death! (*She laughs a queer gentle laugh full of amused bitterness*).

NINA: (*with a sort of dull stupid wonderment*) And you've found peace?—

MRS. EVANS: (*sardonically*) There's peace in the green fields of Eden, they say! You got to die to find out! (*Then proudly*) But I can say I feel proud of having lived fair to them that gave me love and trusted in me!

NINA: (*struck—confusedly*) Yes—that's true, isn't it? (*Thinking strangely*)

Lived fair ... pride ... trust ... play the game! ... who is speaking to me... Gordon! ... oh, Gordon, do you mean I must give Sam the life I didn't give you? ... Sam loved you too ... he said, if we have a boy, we'll call him Gordon in Gordon's honor ... Gordon's honor! ... what must I do now in your honor, Gordon? ... yes! ... I know! ...

(*Speaking mechanically in a dull voice*) All right, Mother. I'll stay with Sam. There's nothing else I can do, is there, when it isn't his fault, poor boy! (*Then suddenly snapping and bursting out in a despairing cry*) But I'll be so lonely! I'll have lost my baby! (*She sinks down on her knees at* MRS. EVANS' *feet—piteously*) Oh, Mother, how can I keep on living?

MRS. EVANS: (*thinking miserably*)

Now she knows my suffering ... now I got to help her ... she's got a right to have a baby ... another baby ... sometime ... somehow ... she's giving her life to save my Sammy ... I got to save her! ...

(*Stammeringly*) Maybe, Nina—

NINA: (*dully and resentfully again now*) And how about Sam? You want him to be happy, don't you? It's just as important for him as it is for me that I should have a baby! If you know anything at all about him, you ought to see that!

MRS. EVANS: (*sadly*) I know that. I see that in him, Nina. (*Gropingly*) There must be a way—somehow. I remember when I was carrying

Sam, sometimes I'd forget I was a wife, I'd only remember the child in me. And then I used to wish I'd gone out deliberate in our first year, without my husband knowing, and picked a man, a healthy male to breed by, same's we do with stock, to give the man I loved a healthy child. And if I didn't love that other man nor him me where would be the harm? Then God would whisper: "It'd be a sin, adultery, the worst sin!" But after He'd gone I'd argue back again to myself, then we'd have a healthy child, I needn't be afraid! And maybe my husband would feel without ever knowing how he felt it, that I wasn't afraid and that child wasn't cursed and so he needn't fear and I could save him. (*Then scornfully*) But I was too afraid of God then to have ever done it! (*Then very simply*) He loved children so, my poor husband did, and the way they took to him, you never saw anything like it, he was a natural born father. And Sammy's the same.

NINA: (*as from a distance—strangely*) Yes, Sammy's the same. But I'm not the same as you. (*Defiantly*) I don't believe in God the Father!

MRS. EVANS: (*strangely*) Then it'd be easy for you. (*With a grim smile*) And I don't believe in Him, neither, not any more. I used to be a great one for worrying about what's God and what's devil, but I got richly over it living here with poor folks that was being punished for no sins of their own, and me being punished with them for no sin but loving much. (*With decision*) Being happy, that's the nearest we can ever come to knowing what's good! Being happy, that's good! The rest is just talk! (*She pauses—then with a strange austere sternness*) I love my boy, Sammy. I could see how much he wants you to have a baby. Sammy's got to feel sure you love him—to be happy. Whatever you can do to make him happy is good—is good, Nina! I don't care what! You've got to have a healthy baby—sometime—so's you can both be happy! It's your rightful duty!

NINA: (*confusedly—in a half-whisper*) Yes, Mother. (*Thinking longingly*)

I want to be happy! . . . it's my right . . . and my duty! . . .

(*Then suddenly in guilty agony*)

Oh, my baby . . . my poor baby . . . I'm forgetting you . . . desiring another after you are dead! . . . I feel you beating against my heart for mercy . . . oh! . . .

(*She weeps with bitter anguish*).

MRS. EVANS: (*gently and with deep sympathy*) I know what you're suffering. And I wouldn't say what I just said now only I know us two mustn't see each other ever again. You and Sammy have got to forget me. (*As* NINA *makes a motion of protest—grimly and inexorably*) Oh, yes, you will—easy. People forget everything. They got to, poor people! And I'm saying what I said about a healthy baby so's you will remember it when you need to, after you've forgotten—this one.

NINA: (*sobbing pitifully*) Don't! Please, Mother!

MRS. EVANS: (*with sudden tenderness—gathering* NINA *up in her arms, brokenly*) You poor child! You're like the daughter of my sorrow! You're closer to me now than ever Sammy could be! I want you to be happy! (*She begins to sob, too, kissing* NINA's *bowed head*).

CURTAIN

Act Four

Scene: *An evening early in the following winter about seven months later. The* professor's *study again. The books in the cases have never been touched, their austere array shows no gaps, but the glass separating them from the world is gray with dust, giving them a blurred ghostly quality. The table, although it is the same, is no longer the* professor's *table, just as the other furniture in the room, by its disarrangement, betrays that the* professor's *well-ordered mind no longer trims it to his personality. The table has become neurotic. Volumes of the Encyclopedia Britannica mixed up with popular treatises on Mind Training for Success, etc., looking startlingly modern and disturbing against the background of classics in the original, are slapped helter-skelter on top of each other on it. The titles of these books face in all directions, no one volume is placed with any relation to the one beneath it—the effect is that they have no connected meaning. The rest of the table is littered with an ink bottle, pens, pencils, erasers, a box of typewriting paper, and a typewriter at the center before the chair, which is pushed back, setting the rug askew. On the floor beside the table are an overflowing wastepaper basket, a few sheets of paper and the rubber cover for the typewriter like a collapsed tent. The rocking chair is no longer at center but has been pulled nearer the table, directly faces it with its back to the bench. This bench in turn has been drawn much closer, but is now placed more to the rear and half-faces front, its back squarely to the door in the corner.*

evans *is seated in the* professor's *old chair. He has evidently been typing, or is about to type, for a sheet of paper can be seen in the machine. He smokes a pipe, which he is always relighting whether it needs it or not, and which he bites and shifts about and pulls in and out and puffs at nervously. His expression is dispirited, his eyes shift about, his shoulders are collapsed submissively. He seems much thinner, his face drawn and sallow. The collegiate clothes are no longer natty, they need pressing and look too big for him.*

EVANS: (*turns to his typewriter and pounds out a few words with a sort of aimless desperation—then tears the sheet out of the machine with an exclamation of disgust, crumples it up and throws it violently on the floor, pushing his chair back and jumping to his feet*) Hell! (*He begins pacing up and down the room, puffing at his pipe, thinking tormentedly*)

No use . . . can't think of a darn thing . . . well, who could dope out a novel ad on another powdered milk, anyway? . . . all the stuff been used already . . . Tartars conquering on dried mares' milk . . . Metchnikoff, eminent scientist . . . been done to death . . . but simply got to work out something or . . . Cole said, what's been the matter with you lately? . . . you started off so well . . . I thought you were a real find, but your work's fallen off to nothing . . .

(*He sits down on the edge of the bench nearby, his shoulders hunched—despondently*)

Couldn't deny it . . . been going stale ever since we came back from that trip home . . . no ideas . . . I'll get fired . . . sterile . . .

(*With a guilty terror*)

in more ways than one, I guess! . . .

(*He springs to his feet as if this idea were a pin stuck in him—lighting his already lighted pipe, walks up and down again, forcing his thoughts into other channels*)

Bet the old man turns over in his grave at my writing ads in his study . . . maybe that's why I can't . . . bum influence . . . try tomorrow in my bedroom . . . sleeping alone . . . since Nina got sick . . . some woman's sickness . . . wouldn't tell me . . . too modest . . . still, there are some things a husband has a right to know . . . especially when we haven't . . . in five months . . . doctor told her she mustn't, she said . . . what doctor? . . . she's never said . . . what the hell's the matter with you, do you think Nina's lying? . . . no . . . but . . .

(*Desperately*)

If I was only sure it was because she's really sick . . . not just sick of me! . . .

(*He sinks down in the rocking chair despondently*)

Certainly been a big change in her . . . since that visit home . . . what happened between Mother and her? . . . she says nothing . . . they seemed to like each other . . . both of them cried when we left . . . still, Nina insisted on going that same day and Mother seemed anxious to get rid of us . . . can't make it out . . . next few weeks Nina couldn't be loving enough . . . I never was so happy . . . then she crashed . . . strain of waiting and hoping she'd get pregnant . . . and nothing happening . . . that's what did it . . . my fault! . . . how d'you know? . . . you can't tell that! . . .

(*He jumps to his feet again—walks up and down again distractedly*)

God, if we'd only have a kid! . . . then I'd show them all what I could do! . . . Cole always used to say I had the stuff, and Ned certainly thought so . . . .

(*With sudden relieved excitement*)

By gosh, I was forgetting! . . . Ned's coming out tonight . . . forgot to tell Nina . . . mustn't let her get wise I got him to come to look her over . . . she'd hate me for swallowing my pride after he's never been to see us . . . but I had to . . . this has got my goat . . . I've got to know what's wrong . . . and Ned's the only one I can trust . . .

(*He flings himself on chair in front of desk and, picking up a fresh sheet of paper, jams it into the machine*)

Gosh, I ought to try and get a new start on this before it's time . . .

(*He types a sentence or two, a strained frown of concentration on his face.* NINA *comes silently through the door and stands just inside it looking at him. She has grown thin again, her face is pale and drawn, her movements are those of extreme nervous tension*).

NINA: (*before she can stifle her immediate reaction of contempt and dislike*)

How weak he is! . . . he'll never do anything . . . never give me my desire . . . if he'd only fall in love with someone else . . . go away . . . not be here in my father's room . . . I even have to give him a home . . . if he'd disappear . . . leave me free . . . if he'd die . . .

(*Checking herself—remorsefully*)

I must stop such thoughts . . . I don't mean it . . . poor Sam! . . . trying so hard . . . loving me so much . . . I give so little in return . . . he feels I'm always watching him with scorn . . . I can't tell him it's with pity . . . how can I help watching him? . . . help worrying over his worry because of what it might lead to . . . after what his mother . . . how horrible life is! . . . he's worried now . . . he doesn't sleep . . . I hear him tossing about . . . I must sleep with him again soon . . . he's only home two nights a week . . . it isn't fair of me . . . I must try . . . I must! . . . he suspects my revulsion . . . it's hurting him . . . oh, poor dead baby I dared not bear, how I might have loved your father for your sake! . . .

EVANS: (*suddenly feeling her presence, jerks himself to his feet—with a diffident guilty air which is noticeable about him now whenever he is in her presence*) Hello, dear. I thought you were lying down. (*Guiltily*) Did the noise of my typing bother you? I'm terribly sorry!

NINA: (*irritated in spite of herself*)

Why is he always cringing? . . .

(*She comes forward to the chair at center and sits down—forcing a smile*) But there's nothing to be terribly sorry about! (*As he stands awkward and confused, like a schoolboy who has been called on to recite and cannot and is being "bawled out" before the class, she forces a playful tone*) Goodness, Sam, how tragic you can get about nothing at all!

EVANS: (*still forced to justify himself—contritely*) I know it isn't pleasant for you having me drag my work out here, trying to pound out rotten ads. (*With a short laugh*) Trying to is right! (*Blurts out*) I wouldn't do it except that Cole gave me a warning to buck up—or get out.

NINA: (*stares at him, more annoyed, her eyes hardening, thinking*)

Yes! . . . he'll always be losing one job, getting another, starting with a burst of confidence each time, then . . .

(*Cutting him with a careless sneering tone*) Well, it isn't a job to worry much about losing, is it?

EVANS: (*wincing pitiably*) No, not much money. But I used to think there was a fine chance to rise there—but of course that's my fault, I haven't made good— (*He finishes miserably*) somehow.

NINA: (*her antagonism giving way to remorseful pity*)

What makes me so cruel? . . . he's so defenseless . . . his mother's baby . . . poor sick baby! . . . poor Sam!

(*She jumps to her feet and goes over to him*).

EVANS: (*as she comes—with a defensive, boastful bravery*) Oh, I can get another job just as good, all right—maybe a lot better.

NINA: (*reassuringly*) Certainly, you can! And I'm sure you're not going to lose this one. You're always anticipating trouble. (*She kisses him and sits on the arm of his chair, putting an arm around his neck and pulling his head on to her breast*) And it isn't your fault, you big goose, you! It's mine. I know how hard it makes everything for you, being tied to a wife who's too sick to be a wife. You ought to have married a big strapping, motherly—

EVANS: (*in the seventh heaven now—passionately*) Bunk! All the other women in the world aren't worth your little finger! It's you who ought to have married someone worth while, not a poor fish like me! But no one could love you more than I do, no matter what he was!

NINA: (*presses his head on her breast, avoiding his eyes, kisses him on the forehead*) And I love you, Sam. (*Staring out over his head—with loving pity, thinking*)

I almost do . . . poor unfortunate boy! . . . at these moments . . . as his mother loves him . . . but that isn't enough for him . . . I can hear his mother saying, "Sammy's got to feel sure you love him . . . to be happy." . . . I must try to make him feel sure . . .

(*Speaking gently*) I want you to be happy, Sam.

EVANS: (*his face transformed with happiness*) I am—a hundred times more than I deserve!

NINA: (*presses his head down on her breast so he cannot see her eyes—gently*) Ssshh. (*Thinking sadly*)

I promised her . . . but I couldn't see how hard it would be to let him love me . . . after his baby . . . was gone . . . it was hard even to keep on living . . . after that operation . . . Gordon's spirit followed me from room to room . . . poor reproachful ghost! . . .

(*With bitter mockery*)

Oh, Gordon, I'm afraid this is a deeper point of honor than any that was
ever shot down in flames! . . . what would your honor say now? . . . "Stick
to him! . . . play the game!" . . . oh, yes, I know . . . I'm sticking . . . but he
isn't happy . . . I'm trying to play the game . . . then why do I keep myself
from him? . . . but I was really sick . . . for a time after . . . since then, I
couldn't . . . but . . . oh, I'll try . . . I'll try soon . . .

(*Tenderly—but having to force herself to say it*) Doesn't my boy want
to sleep with me again—sometime soon?

EVANS: (*passionately—hardly able to believe his ears*) Oh, it'd be wonderful,
Nina! But are you sure you really want me to—that you'll feel well
enough?

NINA: (*repeats his words as if she were memorizing a lesson*) Yes, I want
you to. Yes, I'll feel well enough. (*He seizes her hand and kisses it in a
passionately grateful silence—she thinks with resigned finality*)

There, Sammy's mother and Gordon . . . I'll play the game . . . it will
make him happy for a while . . . as he was in those weeks after we'd left
his mother . . . when I gave myself with a mad pleasure in torturing myself
for his pleasure! . . .

(*Then with weary hopelessness*)

He'll be happy until he begins to feel guilty again because I'm not pregnant . . .

(*With a grim bitter smile*)

Poor Sam, if he only knew the precautions . . . as if I wouldn't die rather
than take the slightest chance of that happening! . . . ever again . . . what
a tragic joke it was on both of us! . . . I wanted my baby so! . . . oh, God!
. . . his mother said . . . "You've got to have a healthy baby . . . sometime
. . . it's your rightful duty" . . . that seemed right then . . . but now . . . it
seems cowardly . . . to betray poor Sam . . . and vile to give myself . . .
without love or desire . . . and yet I've given myself to men before without
a thought just to give them a moment's happiness . . . can't I do that
again? . . . when it's a case of Sam's happiness? . . . and my own? . . .

(*She gets up from beside him with a hunted movement*) It must be half
past eight. Charlie's coming to bring his suggestions on my outline
for Gordon's biography.

EVANS: (*his bliss shattered—dejectedly*)

Always happens . . . just as we get close . . . something comes between . . .

(*Then confusedly*) Say, I forgot to tell you Ned's coming out tonight.

NINA: (*astonished*) Ned Darrell?

EVANS: Sure. I happened to run into him the other day and invited him and he said Saturday evening. He couldn't tell what train. Said never mind meeting him.

NINA: (*excitedly*) Why didn't you tell me before, you big booby! (*She kisses him*) There, don't mind. But it's just like you. Now someone'll have to go down to the store. And I'll have to get the spare room ready. (*She hurries to the doorway. He follows her*).

EVANS: I'll help you.

NINA: You'll do nothing of the kind! You'll stay right downstairs and bring them in here and cover up my absence. Thank heavens, Charlie won't stay long if Ned is here. (*The doorbell rings—excitedly*) There's one of them now. I'll run upstairs. Come up and tell me if it's Ned— and get rid of Charlie. (*She kisses him playfully and hurries out*).

EVANS: (*looking after her—thinks*)

She seems better tonight . . . happier . . . she seems to love me . . . if she'll only get all well again, then everything will . . .

(*The bell rings again*)

I must give Ned a good chance to talk to her . . .

(*He goes out to the outer door—returns a moment later with* MARSDEN. *The latter's manner is preoccupied and nervous. His face has an expression of anxiety which he tries to conceal. He seems a prey to some inner fear he is trying to hide even from himself and is resolutely warding off from his consciousness. His tall, thin body stoops as if a part of its sustaining will had been removed*).

EVANS: (*with a rather forced welcoming note*) Come on in, Charlie. Nina's upstairs lying down.

MARSDEN: (*with marked relief*) Then by all means don't disturb her. I just dropped in to bring back her outline with the suggestions I've made. (*He has taken some papers out of his pocket and hands them to* EVANS) I couldn't have stayed but a minute in any event. Mother is a bit under the weather these days.

EVANS: (*perfunctorily*) Too bad. (*Thinking vindictively*)

> Serve her right, the old scandal-monger, after the way she's gossiped about Nina! . . .

MARSDEN: (*with assumed carelessness*) Just a little indigestion. Nothing serious but it annoys her terribly. (*Thinking frightenedly*)

> That dull pain she complains of . . . I don't like it . . . and she won't see anyone but old Doctor Tibbetts . . . she's sixty-eight . . . I can't help fearing . . . no! . . .

EVANS: (*bored—vaguely*) Well, I suppose you've got to be careful of every little thing when you get to her age.

MARSDEN: (*positively bristling*) Her age? Mother isn't so old!

EVANS: (*surprised*) Over sixty-five, isn't she?

MARSDEN: (*indignantly*) You're quite out there! She's still under sixty-five—and in health and spirits she isn't more than fifty! Everyone remarks that! (*Annoyed at himself*)

> Why did I lie to him about her age? . . . I must be on edge . . . Mother is rather difficult to live with these days, getting me worried to death, when it's probably nothing . . .

EVANS: (*annoyed in his turn—thinking*)

> Why all the fuss? . . . as if I gave a damn if the old girl was a million! . . .

(*Indicating the papers*) I'll give these to Nina first thing in the morning.

MARSDEN: (*mechanically*) Righto. Thank *you*. (*He starts to go toward door—then turns—fussily*) But you'd better take a look while I'm here and see if it's clear. I've written on the margins. See if there's anything you can't make out. (EVANS *nods helplessly and begins reading the sheets, going back beneath the lamp*).

MARSDEN: (*looking around him with squeamish disapproval*)

What a mess they've made of this study . . . poor Professor! . . . dead and forgotten . . . and his tomb desecrated . . . does Sam write his ads here of a week-end now? . . . the last touch! . . . and Nina labors with love at Gordon's biography . . . whom the Professor hated! . . . "life is so full of a number of things!" . . . why does everyone in the world think they can write? . . . but I've only myself to blame . . . why in the devil did I ever suggest it to her? . . . because I hoped my helping her while Sam was in the city would bring us alone together? . . . but I made the suggestion before she had that abortion performed! . . . how do you know she did? . . . because I know! . . . there are psychic affinities . . . her body confessed . . . and since then, I've felt an aversion . . . as if she were a criminal . . . she is! . . . how could she? . . . why? . . . I thought she wanted a child . . . but evidently I don't know her . . . I suppose, afraid it would spoil her figure . . . her flesh . . . her power to enslave men's senses . . . mine . . . and I had hoped . . . looked forward to her becoming a mother . . . for my peace of mind. . . .

(*Catching himself—violently*)

Shut up! . . . what a base creature I'm becoming! . . . to have such thoughts when Mother is sick and I ought to be thinking only of her! . . . and it's none of my damn business, anyway! . . .

(*Glaring at* EVANS *resentfully as if he were to blame*)

Look at him! . . . he'll never suspect anything! . . . what a simple-simon! . . . he adored Gordon as a newsboy does a champion pugilist! . . . and Nina writes of Gordon as if he had been a demi-god! . . . when actually he came from the commonest people! . . .

(*He suddenly speaks to* EVANS *with a really savage satisfaction*) Did I tell you I once looked up Gordon's family in Beachampton? A truly deplorable lot! When I remembered Gordon and looked at his father I had either to suspect a lover in the wood pile or to believe in an Immaculate Conception . . . that is, until I saw his mother! Then a stork became the only conceivable explanation!

EVANS: (*who has only half-heard and hasn't understood, says vaguely*) I never saw his folks. (*Indicating the papers*) I can make this all out all right.

MARSDEN: (*sarcastically*) I'm glad it's understandable!

EVANS: (*blunderingly*) I'll give it to Nina—and I hope your mother is feeling better tomorrow.

MARSDEN: (*piqued*) Oh, I'm going. Why didn't you tell me if I was interrupting—your writing!

EVANS: (*immediately guilty*) Oh, come on, Charlie, don't get peevish, you know I didn't mean— (*The bell rings.* EVANS *stammers in confusion, trying at a nonchalant air*) Hello! That must be Ned. You remember Darrell. He's coming out for a little visit. Excuse me. (*He blunders out of the door*).

MARSDEN: (*looking after him with anger mixed with alarmed suspicion and surprise*)

Darrell? . . . what's he doing here? . . . have they been meeting? . . . perhaps he was the one who performed the . . . no, his idea was she ought to have a child . . . but if she came and begged him? . . . but why should Nina beg not to have a baby? . . .

(*Distractedly*)

Oh, I don't know! . . . it's all a sordid mess! . . . I ought to be going home! . . . I don't want to see Darrell! . . .

(*He starts for the door—then struck by a sudden thought, stops*)

Wait . . . I could ask him about Mother . . . yes . . . good idea . . .

(*He comes back to the middle of the room, front, and is standing there when* DARRELL *enters, followed by* EVANS. DARRELL *has not changed in appearance except that his expression is graver and more thoughtful. His manner is more convincingly authoritative, more mature. He takes in* MARSDEN *from head to foot with one comprehensive glance*).

EVANS: (*awkwardly*) Ned, you remember Charlie Marsden?

MARSDEN: (*holding out his hand, urbanely polite*) How are you, Doctor?

DARRELL: (*shaking his hand—briefly*) Hello.

EVANS: I'll go up and tell Nina you're here, Ned. (*He goes, casting a resentful glance at* MARSDEN).

MARSDEN: (*awkwardly, as* DARRELL *sits down in the chair at center, goes over and stands by the table*) I was on the point of leaving when you rang. Then I decided to stop and renew our acquaintance. (*He stoops and picks up one sheet of paper, and puts it back carefully on the table*).

DARRELL: (*watching him—thinking*)

> Neat . . . suspiciously neat . . . he's an old maid who seduces himself in his novels . . . so I suspect . . . I'd like a chance to study him more closely . . . .

MARSDEN: (*thinking resentfully*)

> What a boor! . . . he might say something! . . .

(*Forcing a smile*) And I wanted to ask a favor of you, a word of advice as to the best specialist, the very best, it would be possible to consult—

DARRELL: (*sharply*) On what?

MARSDEN: (*almost naïvely*) My mother has a pain in her stomach.

DARRELL: (*amused—dryly*) Possibly she eats too much.

MARSDEN: (*as he bends and carefully picks another sheet from the floor to place it as carefully on the table*) She doesn't eat enough to keep a canary alive. It's a dull, constant pain, she says. She's terribly worried. She's terrified by the idea of cancer. But, of course, that's perfect rot, she's never been sick a day in her life and—

DARRELL: (*sharply*) She's showing more intelligence about her pain than you are.

MARSDEN: (*bending down for another sheet, his voice trembling with terror*) I don't understand—quite. Do you mean to say you think—?

DARRELL: (*brutally*) It's possible.

(*He has pulled out his pen and a card and is writing. Thinking grimly*)

> Explode a bomb under him, as I did once before . . . only way to get him started doing anything . . . .

MARSDEN: (*angrily*) But—that's nonsense!

DARRELL: (*with satisfaction—unruffledly*) People who are afraid to face unpleasant possibilities until it's too late commit more murders and suicides than— (*Holds out card*) Doctor Schultz is your man. Take her to see him—tomorrow!

MARSDEN: (*bursting out in anger and misery*) Damn it, you're condemning her without—! (*He breaks down chokingly*) You've no damn right!— (*He bends down, trembling all over, to pick up another piece of paper*).

DARRELL: (*genuinely astonished and contrite*)

And I thought he was so ingrown he didn't care a damn about anyone! ... his mother ... now I begin to see him ...

(*He jumps from his chair and going to* MARSDEN *puts a hand on his shoulder—kindly*) I beg your pardon, Marsden. I only wanted to drive it in that all delay is dangerous. Your mother's pain may be due to any number of harmless causes, but you owe it to her to make sure. Here. (*He hands out the card*).

MARSDEN: (*straightens up and takes it, his eyes grateful now—humbly*) Thank you. I'll take her to see him tomorrow. (EVANS *comes in*).

EVANS: (*to* MARSDEN, *blunderingly*) Say, Charlie, I don't want to hurry you but Nina wants some things at the store before it closes, and if you'd give me a lift—

MARSDEN: (*dully*) Of course. Come along. (*He shakes hands with* DARRELL) Good night, Doctor—and thank you.

DARRELL: Good night. (MARSDEN *goes, followed by* EVANS).

EVANS: (*turns in the doorway and says meaningly*) Nina'll be right down. For Pete's sake, have a good heart-to-heart talk with her, Ned!

DARRELL: (*frowning—impatiently*) Oh—all right! Run along. (EVANS *goes.* DARRELL *remains standing near the table looking after them, thinking about* MARSDEN)

Queer fellow, Marsden ... mother's boy still ... if she dies what will he do? ...

(*Then dismissing* MARSDEN *with a shrug of his shoulders*)

Oh, well, he can always escape life in a new book....

(*He moves around the table examining its disorder critically, then sits down in armchair—amused*).

Evidences of authorship . . . Sam's ads? . . . isn't making good, he said . . . was I wrong in thinking he had stuff in him? . . . hope not . . . always liked Sam, don't know why exactly . . . said Nina'd gotten into a bad state again . . . what's happened to their marriage? . . . I felt a bit sorry for myself at their wedding . . . not that I'd ever fallen . . . but I did envy him in a way . . . she always had strong physical attraction for me . . . that time I kissed her . . . one reason I've steered clear since . . . take no chances on emotional didos . . . need all my mind on my work . . . got rid of even that slight suspicion . . . I'd forgotten all about her . . . she's a strange girl . . . interesting case . . . I should have kept in touch on that account . . . hope she'll tell me about herself . . . can't understand her not having child . . . it's so obviously the sensible thing . . .

(*Cynically*)

Probably why . . . to expect common sense of people proves you're lacking in it yourself! . . .

NINA: (*enters silently. She has fixed herself up, put on her best dress, arranged her hair, rouged, etc.—but it is principally her mood that has changed her, making her appear a younger, prettier person for the moment.* DARRELL *immediately senses her presence, and, looking up, gets to his feet with a smile of affectionate admiration. She comes quickly over to him saying with frank pleasure*) Hello, Ned. I'm certainly glad to see you again—after all these years!

DARRELL: (*as they shake hands—smiling*) Not as long as all that, is it? (*Thinking admiringly*)

Wonderful-looking as ever . . . Sam is a lucky devil! . . .

NINA: (*thinking*)

Strong hands like Gordon's . . . take hold of you . . . not like Sam's . . . yielding fingers that let you fall back into yourself . . .

(*Teasingly*) I ought to cut you dead after the shameful way you've ignored us!

DARRELL: (*a bit embarrassedly*) I've really meant to write. (*His eyes examining her keenly*)

> Been through a lot since I saw her . . . face shows it . . . nervous tension pronounced . . . hiding behind her smile . . .

NINA: (*uneasy under his glance*)

> I hate that professional look in his eyes . . . watching symptoms . . . without seeing me . . .

(*With resentful mockery*) Well, what do you suspect is wrong with the patient now, Doctor? (*She laughs nervously*) Sit down, Ned. I suppose you can't help your diagnosing stare. (*She turns from him and sits down in the rocker at center*).

DARRELL: (*quickly averting his eyes—sits down—jokingly*) Same old unjust accusation! You were always reading diagnosis into me, when what I was really thinking was what fine eyes you had, or what a becoming gown, or—

NINA: (*smiling*) Or what a becoming alibi you could cook up! Oh, I know you! (*With a sudden change of mood she laughs gaily and naturally*) But you're forgiven—that is, if you can explain why you've never been to see us.

DARRELL: Honestly, Nina, I've been so rushed with work I haven't had a chance to go anywhere.

NINA: Or an inclination!

DARRELL: (*smiling*) Well—maybe.

NINA: Do you like the Institute so much? (*He nods gravely*) Is it the big opportunity you wanted?

DARRELL: (*simply*) I think it is.

NINA: (*with a smile*) Well, you're the taking kind for whom opportunities are made!

DARRELL: (*smiling*) I hope so.

NINA: (*sighing*) I wish that could be said of more of us— (*Then quickly*) —meaning myself.

DARRELL: (*thinking with a certain satisfaction*)

Meaning Sam . . . that doesn't look hopeful for future wedded bliss! . . .

(*Teasingly*) But I heard you were "taking an opportunity" to go in for literature—collaborating with Marsden.

NINA: No, Charlie is only going to advise. He'd never deign to appear as co-author. And besides, he never appreciated the real Gordon. No one did except me.

DARRELL: (*thinking caustically*)

Gordon myth strong as ever . . . root of her trouble still . . .

(*Keenly inquisitive*) Sam certainly appreciated him, didn't he?

NINA: (*not remembering to hide her contempt*) Sam? Why, he's the exact opposite in every way!

DARRELL: (*caustically thinking*)

These heroes die hard . . . but perhaps she can write him out of her system. . . .

(*Persuasively*) Well, you're going ahead with the biography, aren't you? I think you ought to.

NINA: (*dryly*) For my soul, Doctor? (*Listlessly*) I suppose I will. I don't know. I haven't much time. The duties of a wife— (*Teasingly*) By the way, if it isn't too rude to inquire, aren't you getting yourself engaged to some fair lady or other?

DARRELL: (*smiling—but emphatically*) Not on your life! Not until after I'm thirty-five, at least!

NINA: (*sarcastically*) Then you don't believe in taking your own medicine? Why, Doctor! Think of how much good it would do you!— (*Excitedly with a hectic sarcasm*) —if you had a nice girl to love—or was it learn to love?—and take care of—whose character you could shape and whose life you could guide and make what you pleased, in whose unselfish devotion you could find peace! (*More and more bitterly sarcastic*) And you ought to have a baby, Doctor! You will never know what life is, you'll never be really happy until you've had a baby, Doctor—a fine, healthy baby! (*She laughs a bitter, sneering laugh*).

DARRELL: (*after a quick, keen glance, thinking*)

> Good! . . . she's going to tell . . .

(*Meekly*) I recognize my arguments. Was I really wrong on every point, Nina?

NINA: (*harshly*) On every single point, Doctor!

DARRELL: (*glancing at her keenly*) But how? You haven't given the baby end of it a chance yet, have you?

NINA: (*bitterly*) Oh, haven't I? (*Then bursts out with intense bitterness*) I'll have you know I'm not destined to bear babies, Doctor!

DARRELL: (*startledly*)

> What's that? . . . why not? . . .

(*Again with a certain satisfaction*)

> Can she mean Sam? . . . that he . . .

(*Soothingly—but plainly disturbed*) Why don't you begin at the beginning and tell me all about it? I feel responsible.

NINA: (*fiercely*) You are! (*Then wearily*) And you're not. No one is. You didn't know. No one could know.

DARRELL: (*in same tone*) Know what? (*Thinking with the same eagerness to believe something he hopes*)

> She must mean no one could know that Sam wasn't . . . but I might have guessed it . . . from his general weakness . . . poor unlucky devil . . .

(*Then as she remains silent—urgingly*) Tell me. I want to help you, Nina.

NINA: (*touched*) It's too late, Ned. (*Then suddenly*) I've just thought— Sam said he happened to run into you. That isn't so, is it? He went to see you and told you how worried he was about me and asked you out to see me, didn't he? (*As* DARRELL *nods*) Oh, I don't mind! It's even rather touching. (*Then mockingly*) Well, since you're out here professionally, and my husband wants me to consult you, I might as well give you the whole case history! (*Wearily*) I warn you it isn't pretty, Doctor! But then life doesn't seem to be pretty, does it? And, after all, you aided and abetted God the Father in making this mess. I hope it'll teach you not to be so cocksure in future. (*More and more bitterly*) I must say you proceeded very unscientifically, Doctor! (*Then suddenly starts her story in a dull monotonous tone recalling that of* EVANS' *mother in the previous Act*) When we went to visit Sam's mother I'd known for two months that I was going to have a baby.

DARRELL: (*startled—unable to hide a trace of disappointment*) Oh, then you actually were? (*Thinking disappointedly and ashamed of himself for being disappointed*)

> All wrong, what I thought . . . she was going to . . . then why didn't she? . . .

NINA: (*with a strange happy intensity*) Oh, Ned, I loved it more than I've ever loved anything in my life—even Gordon! I loved it so it seemed at times that Gordon must be its real father, that Gordon must have come to me in a dream while I was lying asleep beside Sam! And I was happy! I almost loved Sam then! I felt he was a good husband!

DARRELL: (*instantly repelled—thinking with scornful jealousy*)

> Ha! . . . the hero again! . . . comes to her bed! . . . puts horns on poor Sam! . . . becomes the father of his child! . . . I'll be damned if hers isn't the most idiotic obsession I ever . . .

NINA: (*her voice suddenly becoming flat and lifeless*) And then Sam's mother told me I couldn't have my baby. You see, Doctor, Sam's great-grandfather was insane, and Sam's grandmother died in an asylum, and Sam's father had lost his mind for years before he died, and an aunt who is still alive is crazy. So of course I had to agree it would be wrong—and I had an operation.

DARRELL: (*who has listened with amazed horror—profoundly shocked and stunned*) Good God! Are you crazy, Nina? I simply can't believe! It would be too hellish! Poor Sam, of all people! (*Bewilderedly*) Nina! Are you absolutely sure?

NINA: (*immediately defensive and mocking*) Absolutely, Doctor! Why? Do you think it's I who am crazy? Sam looks so healthy and sane, doesn't he? He fooled you completely, didn't he? You thought he'd be an ideal husband for me! And poor Sam's fooling himself too because he doesn't know anything about all this—so you can't blame him, Doctor!

DARRELL: (*thinking in a real panic of horror——and a flood of protective affection for her*)

God, this is too awful! ... on top of all the rest! ... how did she ever stand it! ... she'll lose her mind too! ... and it's my fault! ...

(*Getting up, comes to her and puts his hands on her shoulders, standing behind her—tenderly*) Nina! I'm so damn sorry! There's only one possible thing to do now. You'll have to make Sam give you a divorce.

NINA: (*bitterly*) Yes? Then what do you suppose would be his finish? No, I've enough guilt in my memory now, thank you! I've got to stick to Sam! (*Then with a strange monotonous insistence*) I've promised Sam's mother I'd make him happy! He's unhappy now because he thinks he isn't able to give me a child. And I'm unhappy because I've lost my child. So I must have another baby— somehow—don't you think, Doctor?—to make us both happy? (*She looks up at him pleadingly. For a moment they stare into each other's eyes—then both turn away in guilty confusion*).

DARRELL: (*bewilderedly thinking*)

That look in her eyes ... what does she want me to think? ... why does she talk so much about being happy? ... am I happy? ... I don't know ... what is happiness? ...

(*Confusedly*) Nina, I don't know what to think.

NINA: (*thinking strangely*)

That look in his eyes ... what did he mean? ...

(*With the same monotonous insistence*) You must know what to think.

I can't think it out myself any more. I need your advice—your *scientific* advice this time, if you please, Doctor. I've thought and thought about it. I've told myself it's what I ought to do. Sam's own mother urged me to do it. It's sensible and kind and just and good. I've told myself this a thousand times and yet I can't quite convince something in me that's afraid of something. I need the courage of someone who can stand outside and reason it out as if Sam and I were no more than guinea pigs. You've got to help me, Doctor! You've got to show me what's the sane—the truly sane, you understand!—thing I must do for Sam's sake, and my own.

DARRELL: (*thinking confusedly*)

> What do I have to do? . . . this was all my fault . . . I owe her something in return . . . I owe Sam something . . . I owe them happiness! . . .

(*Irritably*)

> Damn it, there's a humming in my ears! . . . I've caught some fever . . . I swore to live coolly . . . let me see. . . .

(*In a cold, emotionless professional voice, his face like a mask of a doctor*) A doctor must be in full possession of the facts, if he is to advise. What is it precisely that Sam's wife has thought so much of doing?

NINA: (*in the same insistent tone*) Of picking out a healthy male about whom she cared nothing and having a child by him that Sam would believe was his child, whose life would give him confidence in his own living, who would be for him a living proof that his wife loved him. (*Confusedly, strangely and purposefully*)

> This doctor is healthy. . . .

DARRELL: (*in his ultra professional manner—like an automaton of a doctor*) I see. But this needs a lot of thinking over. It isn't easy to prescribe—
(*Thinking*)

> I have a friend who has a wife . . . I was envious at his wedding . . . but what has that to do with it? . . . damn it, my mind won't work! . . . it keeps running away to her . . . it wants to mate with her mind . . . in the interest of Science? . . . what damned rot I'm thinking! . . .

NINA: (*thinking as before*)

> This doctor is nothing to me but a healthy male . . . when he was Ned he once kissed me . . . but I cared nothing about him . . . so that's all right, isn't it, Sam's Mother?

DARRELL: (*thinking*)

> Let me see. . . . I am in the laboratory and they are guinea pigs . . . in fact, in the interest of science, I can be for the purpose of this experiment, a healthy guinea pig myself and still remain an observer . . . I observe my pulse is high, for example, and that's obviously because I am stricken with a recurrence of an old desire . . . desire is a natural male reaction to the beauty of the female . . . her husband is my friend . . . . I have always tried to help him . . .

(*Coldly*) I've been considering what Sam's wife told me and her reasoning is quite sound. The child can't be her husband's.

NINA: Then you agree with Sam's mother? She said: "Being happy is the nearest we can ever come to knowing what good is!"

DARRELL: I agree with her decidedly. Sam's wife should find a healthy father for Sam's child at once. It is her sane duty to her husband. (*Worriedly thinking*)

> Have I ever been happy? . . . I have studied to cure the body's unhappiness . . . I have watched happy smiles form on the lips of the dying . . . I have experienced pleasure with a number of women I desired but never loved . . . I have known a bit of honor and a trifle of self-satisfaction . . . this talk of happiness seems to me extraneous . . .

NINA: (*beginning to adopt a timid, diffident, guilty tone*) This will have to be hidden from Sam so he can never know! Oh, Doctor, Sam's wife is afraid!

DARRELL: (*sharply professional*) Nonsense! This is no time for timidity! Happiness hates the timid! So does Science! Certainly Sam's wife must conceal her action! To let Sam know would be insanely cruel of her—and stupid, for then no one could be the happier for her act! (*Anxiously thinking*)

Am I right to advise this? . . . yes, it is clearly the rational thing to do . . . but this advice betrays my friend! . . . no, it saves him! . . . it saves his wife . . . and if a third party should know a little happiness . . . is he any poorer, am I any the less his friend because I saved him? . . . no, my duty to him is plain . . . and my duty as an experimental searcher after truth . . . to observe these three guinea pigs, of which I am one . . .

NINA: (*thinking determinedly*)

I must have my baby! . . .

(*Timidly—gets from her chair and half-turns toward him—pleadingly*) You must give his wife courage, Doctor. You must free her from her feeling of guilt.

DARRELL: There can only be guilt when one deliberately neglects one's manifest duty to life. Anything else is rot! This woman's duty is to save her husband and herself by begetting a healthy child! (*Thinking guiltily and instinctively moving away from her*)

I am healthy . . . but he is my friend . . . there is such a thing as honor! . . .

NINA: (*determinedly*)

I must take my happiness! . . .

(*Frightenedly—comes after him*) But she is ashamed. It's adultery. It's wrong.

DARRELL: (*moving away again—with a cold sneering laugh of impatience*) Wrong! Would she rather see her husband wind up in an asylum? Would she rather face the prospect of going to pot mentally, morally, physically herself through year after year of devilling herself and him? Really, Madame, if you can't throw overboard all such irrelevant moral ideas, I'll have to give up this case here and now! (*Thinking frightenedly*)

Who is talking? . . . is he suggesting me? . . . but you know very well I can't be the one, Doctor! . . . why not, you're healthy and it's a friendly act for all concerned . . .

NINA: (*thinking determinedly*)

> I must have my baby! . . .

(*Going further toward him—she can now touch him with her hand*) Please, Doctor, you must give her strength to do this right thing that seems to her so right and then so wrong! (*She puts out her hand and takes one of his*).

DARRELL: (*thinking frightenedly*)

> Whose hand is this? . . . it burns me . . . I kissed her once . . . her lips were cold . . . now they would burn with happiness for me! . . .

NINA: (*taking his other hand and slowly pulling him around to face her, although he does not look at her—pleadingly*) Now she feels your strength. It gives her the courage to ask you, Doctor, to suggest the father. She has changed, Doctor, since she became Sam's wife. She can't bear the thought now of giving herself to any man she could neither desire nor respect. So each time her thoughts come to the man she must select they are afraid to go on! She needs your courage to choose!

DARRELL: (*as if listening to himself*)

> Sam is my friend . . . well, and isn't she your friend? . . . her two hands are so warm! . . . I must not even hint at my desire! . . .

(*Judicially calm*) Well, the man must be someone who is not unattractive to her physically, of course.

NINA: Ned always attracted her.

DARRELL: (*thinking frightenedly*)

> What's that she said? . . . Ned? . . . attracts? . . .

(*In same tone*) And the man should have a mind that can truly understand—a scientific mind superior to the moral scruples that cause so much human blundering and unhappiness.

NINA: She always thought Ned had a superior mind.

DARRELL: (*thinking frightenedly*)

> Did she say Ned? . . . she thinks Ned . . . ?

(*In same tone*) The man should like and admire her, he should be her good friend and want to help her, but he should not love her—although he might, without harm to anyone, desire her.

NINA: Ned does not love her—but he used to like her and, I think, desire her. Does he now, Doctor?

DARRELL: (*thinking*)

> Does he? . . . who is he? . . . he is Ned! . . . Ned is I! . . . I desire her! . . . I desire happiness! . . .

(*Tremblingly now—gently*) But, Madame, I must confess the Ned you are speaking of is I, and I am Ned.

NINA: (*gently*) And I am Nina, who wants her baby. (*Then she reaches out and turns his head until his face faces hers but he keeps his eyes down—she bends her head meekly and submissively—softly*) I should be so grateful, Ned. (*He starts, looks up at her wildly, makes a motion as though to take her in his arms, then remains fixed for a moment in that attitude, staring at her bowed head as she repeats submissively*) I should be so humbly grateful.

DARRELL: (*suddenly falling on his knees and taking her hand in both of his and kissing it humbly—with a sob*) Yes—yes, Nina—yes—for your happiness—in that spirit! (*Thinking—fiercely triumphant*)

> I shall be happy for a while! . . .

NINA: (*raising her head—thinking—proudly triumphant*)

> I shall be happy! . . . I shall make my husband happy! . . .

CURTAIN

ACT FIVE

SCENE: *The sitting room of a small house* EVANS *has rented in a seashore suburb near New York. It is a bright morning in the following April.*

The room is a typical sitting room of the quantity-production bungalow type. Windows on the left look out on a broad porch. A double doorway in rear leads into the hall. A door on right, to the dining room. NINA *has tried to take the curse of offensive, banal newness off the room with some of her own things from her old home but the attempt has been half-hearted in the face of such overpowering commonness, and the result is a room as disorganized in character as was the* PROFESSOR'S *study in the last Act.*

The arrangement of the furniture follows the same pattern as in preceding scenes. There is a Morris chair and a round golden oak table at left of center, an upholstered chair, covered with bright chintz at center, a sofa covered with the same chintz at right.

NINA *is sitting in the chair at center. She has been trying to read a book but has let this drop listlessly on her lap. A great change is noticeable in her face and bearing. She is again the pregnant woman of Act Three but this time there is a triumphant strength about her expression, a ruthless self-confidence in her eyes. She has grown stouter, her face has filled out. One gets no impression of neurotic strain from her now, she seems nerveless and deeply calm.*

NINA: (*as if listening for something within her—joyfully*)

There! . . . that can't be my imagination . . . I felt it plainly . . . life . . . my baby . . . my only baby . . . the other never really lived . . . this is the child of my love! . . . I love Ned! . . . I've loved him ever since that first afternoon . . . when I went to him . . . so scientifically! . . .

(*She laughs at herself*)

Oh, what a goose I was! . . . then love came to me . . . in his arms . . . happiness! . . . I hid it from him . . . I saw he was frightened . . . his own joy frightened him . . . I could feel him fighting with himself . . . during all those afternoons . . . our wonderful afternoons of happiness! . . . and I said nothing . . . I made myself be calculating . . . so when he finally said . . . dreadfully disturbed . . . "Look here, Nina, we've done all that is necessary, playing with fire is dangerous" . . . I said, "You're quite right, Ned, of all things I don't want to fall in love with you!" . . .

(*She laughs*)

He didn't like that! . . . he looked angry . . . and afraid . . . then for weeks he never even phoned . . . I waited . . . it was prudent to wait . . . but every day I grew more terrified . . . then just as my will was breaking, his broke . . . he suddenly appeared again . . . but I held him to his aloof doctor's pose and sent him away, proud of his will power . . . and sick of himself with desire for me! . . . every week since then he's been coming out here . . . as my doctor . . . we've talked about our child wisely, dispassionately . . . as if it were Sam's child . . . we've never given in to our desire . . . and I've watched love grow in him until I'm sure . . .

(*With sudden alarm*)

But am I? . . . he's never once mentioned love . . . perhaps I've been a fool to play the part I've played . . . it may have turned him against me . . .

(*Suddenly with calm confidence*)

No . . . he does . . . I feel it . . . it's only when I start thinking, I begin to doubt . . .

(*She settles back and stares dreamily before her—a pause*)

There . . . again . . . his child! . . . my child moving in my life . . . my life moving in my child . . . the world is whole and perfect . . . all things are each other's . . . life is . . . and the is is beyond reason . . . questions die in the silence of this peace . . . I am living a dream within the great dream of the tide . . . breathing in the tide I dream and breathe back my dream into the tide . . . suspended in the movement of the tide, I feel life move in me, suspended in me . . . no whys matter . . . there is no why . . . I am a mother . . . God is a Mother . . .

(*She sighs happily, closing her eyes. A pause.* EVANS *enters from the hallway in rear. He is dressed carefully but his clothes are old ones—shabby collegiate gentility—and he has forgotten to shave. His eyes look pitiably harried, his manner has become a distressingly obvious attempt to cover up a chronic state of nervous panic and guilty conscience. He stops inside the doorway and looks at her with a pitiable furtiveness, arguing with himself, trying to get up his courage*)

Tell her! . . . go on! . . . you made up your mind to, didn't you? . . . don't quit now! . . . tell her you've decided . . . for her sake . . . to face the truth . . . that she can't love you . . . she's tried . . . she's acted like a good sport . . . but she's beginning to hate you . . . and you can't blame her . . . she wanted children . . . and you haven't been able . . .

(*Protesting feebly*)

But I don't know for certain . . . that that's my fault . . .

(*Then bitterly*)

Aw, don't kid yourself, if she'd married someone else . . . if Gordon had lived and married her . . . I'll bet in the first month she'd . . . you'd better resign from the whole game . . . with a gun! . . .

(*He swallows hard as if he were choking back a sob—then savagely*)

Stop whining! . . . go on and wake her up! . . . say you're willing to give her a divorce so she can marry some real guy who can give her what she ought to have! . . .

(*Then with sudden terror*)

And if she says yes? . . . I couldn't bear it! . . . I'd die without her! . . .

(*Then with a somber alien forcefulness*)

All right . . . good riddance! . . . I'd have the guts to bump off then, all right! . . . that'd set her free . . . come on now! . . . ask her! . . .

(*But his voice begins to tremble uncertainly again as he calls*) Nina.

NINA: (*opens her eyes and gazes calmly, indifferently at him*) Yes?

EVANS: (*immediately terrified and beaten—thinking*)

I can't! . . . the way she looks at me! . . . she'd say yes! . . .

(*Stammering*) I hate to wake you up but—it's about time for Ned to come, isn't it?

NINA: (*calmly*) I wasn't asleep.

(*Thinking as if she found it hard to concentrate on him, to realize his existence*)

This man is my husband . . . it's hard to remember that . . . people will say he's the father of my child . . ..

(*With revulsion*)

That's shameful! . . . and yet that's exactly what I wanted! . . . wanted! . . . not now! . . . now I love Ned! . . . I won't lose him! . . . Sam must give me a divorce . . . I've sacrificed enough of my life . . . what has he given me? . . . not even a home . . . I had to sell my father's home to get money so we could move near his job . . . and then he lost his job! . . . now he's depending on Ned to help him get another! . . . my love! . . . how shameless! . . .

(*Then contritely*)

Oh, I'm unjust . . . poor Sam doesn't know about Ned . . . and it was I who wanted to sell the place . . . I was lonely there . . . I wanted to be near Ned. . . .

EVANS: (*thinking in agony*)

What's she thinking? . . . probably lucky for me I don't know! . . .

(*Forcing a brisk air as he turns away from her*) I hope Ned brings that letter he promised me to the manager of the Globe company. I'm keen to get on the job again.

NINA: (*with scornful pity*) Oh, I guess Ned will bring the letter. I asked him not to forget.

EVANS: I hope they'll have an opening right off. We can use the money. (*Hanging his head*) I feel rotten, living on you when you've got so little.

NINA: (*indifferently but with authority, like a governess to a small boy*) Now, now!

EVANS: (*relieved*) Well, it's true. (*Then coming to her—humbly ingratiating*) You've felt a lot better lately, haven't you, Nina?

NINA: (*with a start—sharply*) Why?

EVANS: You look ever so much better. You're getting fat. (*He forces a grin*).

NINA: (*curtly*) Don't be absurd, please! As a matter of fact, I don't feel a bit better.

EVANS: (*thinking despondently*)

Lately, she jumps on me every chance she gets . . . as if everything I did disgusted her! . . .

(*He strays over to the window and looks out listlessly*) I thought we'd get some word from Charlie this morning saying if he was coming down or not. But I suppose he's still too broken up over his mother's death to write.

NINA: (*indifferently*) He'll probably come without bothering to write. (*Vaguely—wonderingly*)

Charlie . . . dear old Charlie . . . I've forgotten him, too. . . .

EVANS: I think that's Ned's car now. Yes. It's stopping. I'll go out and meet him. (*He starts for the door in rear*).

NINA: (*sharply, before she can restrain the impulse*) Don't be such a fool!

EVANS: (*stops—stammers confusedly*) What—what's the matter?

NINA: (*controlling herself—but irritably*) Don't mind me. I'm nervous. (*Thinking guiltily*)

One minute I feel ashamed of him for making such a fool of himself over my lover . . . the next minute something hateful urges me to drive him into doing it! . . .

(*The maid has answered the ring and opened the outer door.* NED DARRELL *comes in from the rear. His face looks older. There is an expression of defensive bitterness and self-resentment about his mouth and eyes. This vanishes into one of desire and joy as he sees* NINA. *He starts toward her impulsively*) Nina! (*Then stops short as he sees* EVANS.)

NINA: (*forgetting* EVANS, *gets to her feet as if to receive* DARRELL *in her arms—with love*) Ned!

EVANS: (*affectionately and gratefully*) Hello, Ned! (*He holds out his hand which* DARRELL *takes mechanically*).

DARRELL: (*trying to overcome his guilty embarrassment*) Hello, Sam. Didn't see you. (*Hurriedly reaching in his coat pocket*) Before I forget, here's that letter. I had a talk over the phone with Appleby yesterday. He's pretty sure there's an opening— (*With a condescension he can't help*) —but you'll have to get your nose on the grindstone to make good with him.

EVANS: (*flushing guiltily—forcing a confident tone*) You bet I will! (*Then gratefully and humbly*) Gosh, Ned, I can't tell you how grateful I am!

DARRELL: (*brusquely, to hide his embarrassment*) Oh, shut up! I'm only too glad.

NINA: (*watching* EVANS *with a contempt that is almost gloating—in a tone of curt dismissal*) You'd better go and shave, hadn't you, if you're going to town?

EVANS: (*guiltily, passing his hand over his face—forcing a brisk, purposeful air*) Yes, of course. I forgot I hadn't. Excuse me, will you? (*This to* DARRELL. EVANS *hurries out, rear*).

DARRELL: (*as soon as he is out of earshot—turning on* NINA *accusingly*) How can you treat him that way? It makes me feel—like a swine!

NINA: (*flushing guiltily—protestingly*) What way? (*Then inconsequentially*) He's always forgetting to shave lately.

DARRELL: You know what I mean, Nina! (*Turns away from her—thinking bitterly*)

What a rotten liar I've become! . . . and he trusts me absolutely! . . .

NINA: (*thinking frightenedly*)

Why doesn't he take me in his arms? . . . oh, I feel he doesn't love me now! . . . he's so bitter! . . .

(*Trying to be matter-of-fact*) I'm sorry, Ned. I don't mean to be cross but Sam does get on my nerves.

DARRELL: (*thinking bitterly*)

> Sometimes I almost hate her! . . . if it wasn't for her I'd have kept my peace of mind . . . no good for anything lately, damn it! . . . but it's idiotic to feel guilty . . . if Sam only didn't trust me! . . .

(*Then impatiently*)

> Bosh! . . . sentimental nonsense! . . . end justifies means! . . . this will have a good end for Sam, I swear to that! . . . why doesn't she tell him she's pregnant? . . . what's she waiting for? . . .

NINA: (*thinking passionately, looking at him*)

> Oh, my lover, why don't you kiss me? . . .

(*Imploringly*) Ned! Don't be cross with me, please!

DARRELL: (*fighting to control himself—coldly*) I'm not cross, Nina. Only you must admit these triangular scenes are, to say the least, humiliating. (*Resentfully*) I won't come out here again!

NINA: (*with a cry of pain*) Ned!

DARRELL: (*thinking exultingly at first*)

> She loves me! . . . she's forgotten Gordon! . . . I'm happy! . . . do I love her? . . . no! . . . I won't! . . . I can't! . . . think what it would mean to Sam! . . . to my career! . . . be objective about it! . . . you guinea pig! . . . I'm her doctor . . . and Sam's . . . I prescribed child for them . . . that's all there is to it! . . .

NINA: (*torn between hope and fear*)

> What is he thinking? . . . he's fighting his love . . . oh, my lover! . . .

(*Again with longing*) Ned!

DARRELL: (*putting on his best professional air, going to her*) How do you feel today? You look as if you might have a little fever. (*He takes her hand as if to feel her pulse. Her hand closes over his. She looks up into his face. He keeps his turned away*).

NINA: (*straining up toward him—with intense longing—thinking*)

> I love you! . . . take me! . . . what do I care for anything in the world but you! . . . let Sam die! . . .

DARRELL: (*fighting himself—thinking*)

> Christ! . . . touch of her skin! . . . her nakedness! . . . those afternoons in her arms! happiness! . . . what do I care for anything else? . . . to hell with Sam! . . .

NINA: (*breaking out passionately*) Ned! I love you! I can't hide it any more! I won't! I love you, Ned!

DARRELL: (*suddenly taking her in his arms and kissing her frantically*) Nina! Beautiful!

NINA: (*triumphantly—between kisses*) You love me, don't you? Say you do, Ned!

DARRELL: (*passionately*) Yes! Yes!

NINA: (*with a cry of triumph*) Thank God! At last you've told me! You've confessed it to yourself! Oh, Ned, you've made me so happy! (*There is a ring from the front door bell.* DARRELL *hears it. It acts like an electric shock on him. He tears himself away from her. Instinctively she gets up too and moves to the lounge at right*).

DARRELL: (*stupidly*) Someone—at the door. (*He sinks down in the chair by the table at left. Thinking torturedly*)

> I said I loved her! . . . she won! . . . she used my desire! . . . but I don't love her! . . . I won't! . . . she can't own my life! . . .

(*Violently—almost shouts at her*) I don't, Nina! I tell you I don't!

NINA: (*the maid has just gone to the front door*) Sshh! (*Then in a triumphant whisper*) You do, Ned! You do!

DARRELL: (*with dogged stupidity*) I don't! (*The front door has been opened.* MARSDEN *appears in the rear, walks slowly and woodenly like a man in a trance into the room. He is dressed immaculately in deep mourning. His face is pale, drawn, haggard with loneliness and grief. His eyes have a dazed look as if he were still too stunned to comprehend clearly what has happened to him. He does not seem conscious of* DARRELL'S *presence at first. His shoulders are bowed, his whole figure droops*).

NINA: (*thinking—in a strange superstitious panic*)

Black . . . in the midst of happiness . . . black comes . . . again . . . death . . . my father . . . comes between me and happiness! . . .

(*Then recovering herself, scornfully*)

You silly coward! . . . it's only Charlie! . . .

(*Then with furious resentment*)

The old fool! . . . what does he mean coming in on us without warning? . . .

MARSDEN: (*forcing a pitiful smile to his lips*) Hello, Nina. I know it's an imposition—but—I've been in such a terrible state since Mother—(*He falters, his face becomes distorted into an ugly mask of grief, his eyes water*).

NINA: (*immediately sym pathetic, gets up and goes to him impulsively*) There's no question of imposition, Charlie. We were expecting you. (*She has come to him and put her arms around him. He gives way and sobs, his head against her shoulder*).

MARSDEN: (*brokenly*) You don't know, Nina—how terrible—it's terrible!—

NINA: (*leading him to the chair at center, soothingly*) I know, Charlie.

(*Thinking with helpless annoyance*)

Oh, dear, what can I say? . . . his mother hated me . . . I'm not glad she's dead . . . but neither am I sorry . . .

(*With a trace of contempt*)

Poor Charlie . . . he was so tied to her apron strings . . .

(*Then kindly but condescendingly, comforting him*) Poor old Charlie!

MARSDEN: (*the words and the tone shock his pride to life. He raises his head and half-pushes her away—resentfully, thinking*)

Poor old Charlie! . . . damn it, what am I to her? . . . her old dog who's lost his mother? . . . Mother hated her . . . no, poor dear Mother was so sweet, she never hated anyone . . . she simply disapproved . . .

(*Coldly*) I'm all right, Nina. Quite all right now, thank you. I apologize for making a scene.

DARRELL: (*has gotten up from his chair—with relief—thinking*)

Thank God for Marsden . . . I feel sane again . . .

(*He comes to* MARSDEN—*cordially*) How are you, Marsden? (*Then offering conventional consolation, pats* MARSDEN'S *shoulder*) I'm sorry, Marsden.

MARSDEN: (*startled, looks up at him in amazement*) Darrell! (*Then with instant hostility*) There's nothing to be sorry about that I can discover! (*Then as they both look at him in surprise he realizes what he has said— stammeringly*) I mean—sorry—is hardly the right word—hardly—is it?

NINA: (*worriedly*) Sit down, Charlie. You look so tired. (*He slumps down in the chair at center mechanically.* NINA *and* DARRELL *return to their chairs.* NINA *looks across him at* DARRELL—*triumphantly—thinking*)

You do love me, Ned! . . .

DARRELL: (*thinking—answering her look—defiantly*)

I don't love you! . . .

MARSDEN: (*stares intensely before him. Thinking suspiciously—morbidly agitated*)

Darrell! . . . and Nina! . . . there's something in this room! . . . something disgusting! . . . like a brutal, hairy hand, raw and red, at my throat! . . . stench of human life! . . . heavy and rank! . . . outside it's April . . . green buds on the slim trees . . . the sadness of spring . . . my loss at peace in Nature . . . her sorrow of birth consoling my sorrow of death . . . something human and unnatural in this room! . . . love and hate and passion and possession! . . . cruelly indifferent to my loss! . . . mocking my loneliness! . . . no longer any love for me in any room! . . . lust in this room! . . . lust with a loathsome jeer taunting my sensitive timidities! . . . my purity! . . . purity? . . . ha! yes, if you say prurient purity! . . . lust ogling me for a dollar with oily shoe button Italian eyes! . . .

(*In terror*)

What thoughts! . . . what a low scoundrel you are! . . . and your mother
dead only two weeks! . . . I hate Nina! . . . that Darrell in this room! . . .
I feel their desires! . . . where is Sam? . . . I'll tell him! . . . no, he wouldn't
believe . . . he's such a trusting fool . . . I must punish her some other
way . . .

(*Remorsefully*)

What? . . . punish Nina? . . . my little Nina? . . . why, I want her to be
happy! . . . even with Darrell? . . . it's all so confused! . . . I must stop
thinking! . . . I must talk! . . . forget! . . . say something! . . . forget everything! . . .

(*He suddenly bursts into a flood of garrulity*) Mother asked for you,
Nina—three days before the end. She said, "Where is Nina Leeds
now, Charlie? When is she going to marry Gordon Shaw?" Her
mind was wandering, poor woman! You remember how fond she
always was of Gordon. She used to love to watch the football games
when he was playing. He was so handsome and graceful, she always
thought. She always loved a strong, healthy body. She took such
strict care of her own, she walked miles every day, she loved bathing
and boating in the summer even after she was sixty, she was never
sick a day in her life until— (*He turns on* DARRELL—*coldly*) You were
right, Doctor Darrell. It was cancer. (*Then angrily*) But the doctor
you sent me to, and the others he called in could do nothing for
her—absolutely nothing! I might just as well have imported some
witch doctors from the Solomon Islands! They at least would have
diverted her in her last hours with their singing and dancing, but
your specialists were at total loss! (*Suddenly with an insulting, ugly
sneer, raising his voice*) I think you doctors are a pack of God-damned
ignorant liars and hypocrites!

NINA: (*sharply*) Charlie!

MARSDEN: (*coming to himself—with a groan—shamefacedly*) Don't mind
me. I'm not myself, Nina. I've been through hell! (*He seems about to
sob—then abruptly springs to his feet, wildly*) It's this room! I can't stand
this room! There's something repulsive about it!

NINA: (*soothingly*) I know it's ugly, Charlie. I haven't had a chance to fix it up yet. We've been too broke.

MARSDEN: (*confusedly*) Oh, it s all right. I'm ugly, too! Where's Sam?

NINA: (*eagerly*) Right upstairs. Go on up. He'll be delighted to see you.

MARSDEN: (*vaguely*) Very well. (*He goes to the door, then stops mournfully*) But from what I saw on that visit to his home, he doesn't love his mother much. I don't think he'll understand, Nina. He never writes to her, does he?

NINA: (*uneasily*) No—I don't know.

MARSDEN: She seemed lonely. He'll be sorry for it some day after she— (*He gulps*) Well— (*He goes*).

NINA: (*in a sudden panic—thinking*)

    Sam's mother! ... "Make my boy, Sammy, happy!" ... I promised ... oh, why did Charlie have to remember her? ...

    (*Then resolutely*)

    I can't remember her now! ... I won't! ... I've got to be happy! ...

DARRELL: (*uneasily trying to force a casual conversation*) Poor Marsden is completely knocked off balance, isn't he? (*A pause*) My mother died when I was away at school. I hadn't seen her in some time, so her death was never very real to me; but in Marsden's case—

NINA: (*with a possessive smile of tolerance*) Never mind Charlie, Ned. What do I care about Charlie? I love you! And you love me!

DARRELL: (*apprehensively, forcing a tone of annoyed rebuke*) But I don't! And you don't! You're simply letting your romantic imagination run away with you— (*Showing his jealous resentment in spite of himself*) — as you did once before with Gordon Shaw!

NINA: (*thinking*)

    He is jealous of Gordon! ... how wonderful that is! ...

    (*With provoking calm*) I loved Gordon.

DARRELL: (*irritably ignoring this as if he didn't want to hear it*) Romantic imagination! It has ruined more lives than all the diseases! Other diseases, I should say! It's a form of insanity! (*He gets up forcefully and begins to pace about the room. Thinking uneasily*)

Mustn't look at her . . . find an excuse and get away . . . and this time never come back! . . .

(*Avoiding looking at her, trying to argue reasonably—coldly*) You're acting foolishly, Nina—and very unfairly. The agreement we made has no more to do with love than a contract for building a house. In fact, you know we agreed it was essential that love mustn't enter into it. And it hasn't in spite of what you say. (*A pause. He walks about. She watches him. Thinking*)

She's got to come back to earth! . . . I've got to break with her! . . . bad enough now! . . . but to go on with it! . . . what a mess it'd make of all our lives! . . .

NINA: (*thinking tenderly*)

Let his pride put all the blame on me! . . . I'll accept it gladly!

DARRELL: (*irritably*) Of course, I realize I've been to blame, too. I haven't been able to be as impersonal as I thought I could be. The trouble is there's been a dangerous physical attraction. Since I first met you, I've always desired you physically. I admit that now.

NINA: (*smiling tenderly—thinking*)

Oh, he admits that, does he? . . . poor darling! . . .

(*Enticingly*) And you still do desire me, don't you, Ned?

DARRELL: (*keeping his back turned to her—roughly*) No! That part of it is finished! (NINA *laughs softly, possessively. He whirls around to face her—angrily*) Look here! You're going to have the child you wanted, aren't you?

NINA: (*implacably*) My child wants its father!

DARRELL: (*coming a little toward her—desperately*) But you're crazy! You're forgetting Sam! It may be stupid but I've got a guilty conscience! I'm beginning to think we've wronged the very one we were trying to help!

NINA: You were trying to help me, too, Ned!

DARRELL: (*stammering*) Well—all right—let's say that part of it was all right then. But it's got to stop! It can't go on!

NINA: (*implacably*) Only your love can make me happy now! Sam must give me a divorce so I can marry you.

DARRELL: (*thinking suspiciously*)

Look out! ... there it is! ... marry! ... own me! ... ruin my career! ...

(*Scornfully*) Marry? Do you think I'm a fool? Get that out of your head quick! I wouldn't marry anyone—no matter what! (*As she continues to look at him with unmoved determination—pleadingly*) Be sensible, for God's sake! We're absolutely unsuited to each other! I don't admire your character! I don't respect you! I know too much about your past! (*Then indignantly*) And how about Sam? Divorce him? Have you forgotten all his mother told you? Do you mean to say you'd deliberately—? And you expect me to—? What do you think I am?

NINA: (*inflexibly*) You're my lover! Nothing else matters. Yes, I remember what Sam's mother said. She said, "being happy is the nearest we can come to knowing what good is." And I'm going to be happy! I've lost everything in life so far because I didn't have the courage to take it—and I've hurt everyone around me. There's no use trying to think of others. One human being can't think of another. It's impossible. (*Gently and caressingly*) But this time I'm going to think of my own happiness—and that means you—and our child! That's quite enough for one human being to think of, dear, isn't it? (*She reaches out and takes his hand. A pause. With her other hand she gently pulls him around until he is forced to look into her eyes*).

DARRELL: (*thinking fascinatedly*)

I see my happiness in her eyes ... the touch of her soft skin! ... those afternoons! ... God, I was happy! ...

(*In a strange dazed voice—as if it were forced out of him by an impulse stronger than his will*) Yes, Nina.

NINA: (*in a determined voice*) I've given Sam enough of my life! And it hasn't made him happy, not the least bit! So what's the good? And how can we really know that his thinking our child was his would do him any good? We can't! It's all guesswork. The only thing sure is that we love each other.

DARRELL: (*dazedly*) Yes. (*A noise from the hall and* EVANS *comes in from the rear. He sees their two hands together but mistakes their meaning*).

EVANS: (*genially—with a forced self-confident air*) Well, Doc, how's the patient? I think she's much better, don't you—although she won't admit it.

DARRELL: (*at the first sound of* EVANS' *voice, pulls his hand from* NINA'S *as if it were a hot coal—avoiding* EVANS' *eyes, moving away from her jerkily and self-consciously*) Yes. Much better.

EVANS: Good! (*He pats* NINA *on the back. She shrinks away. His confidence vanishes in a flash. Thinking miserably*)

Why does she shrink away . . . if I even touch her? . . .

NINA: (*matter-of-factly*) I must see how lunch is coming on. You'll stay, of course, Ned?

DARRELL: (*struggling—shakenly*) No, I think I'd better— (*Thinking desperately*)

Got to go! . . . can't go! . . . got to go! . . .

EVANS: Oh, come on, old man!

NINA: (*thinking*)

He must stay . . . and after lunch we'll tell Sam. . . .

(*With certainty*) He'll stay. (*Meaningly*) And we want to have a long talk with you after lunch, Sam—don't we, Ned? (DARRELL *does not answer. She goes out, right*).

EVANS: (*vaguely making talk*) I got Charlie to lie down. He's all in, poor guy. (*Then trying to face* DARRELL *who keeps looking away from him*) What did Nina mean, you want a long talk with me? Or is it a secret, Ned?

DARRELL: (*controlling an impulse toward hysterical laughter*) A secret? Yes, you bet it's a secret! (*He flings himself in the chair at left, keeping his face averted. His thoughts bitter and desperate like a cornered fugitive's*).

> This is horrible! . . . Sam thinks I'm finest fellow in world . . . and I do this to him! . . . as if he hadn't enough! . . . born under a curse! . . . I finish him! . . . a doctor! . . . God damn it! . . . I can see his end! . . . never forgive myself! . . . never forget! . . . break me! . . . ruin my career! . . .

(*More desperately*)

> Got to stop this! . . . while there's time! . . . she said . . . after lunch, talk . . . she meant, tell him . . . that means kill him . . . then she'll marry me! . . .

(*Beginning to be angry*)

> By God, I won't! . . . she'll find out! . . . smiling! . . . got me where she wants me! . . . then be as cruel to me as she is to him! . . . love me? . . . liar! . . . still loves Gordon! . . . her body is a trap! . . . I'm caught in it! . . . she touches my hand, her eyes get in mine, I lose my will! . . .

(*Furiously*)

> By God, she can't make a fool of me that way! . . . I'll go away some place! . . . go to Europe! . . . study! . . . forget her in work! . . . keep hidden until boat sails so she can't reach me! . . .

(*He is in a state of strange elation by this time*)

> Go now! . . . no! . . . got to spike her guns with Sam! . . . by God, I see! . . . tell him about baby! . . . that'll stop her! . . . when she knows I've told him that, she'll see it's hopeless! . . . she'll stick to him! . . . poor Nina! . . . I'm sorry! . . . she does love me! . . . hell! . . . she'll forget! . . . she'll have her child! . . . she'll be happy! . . . and Sam'll be happy! . . .

(*He suddenly turns to* EVANS *who has been staring at him, puzzledly—in a whisper*) Look here, Sam. I can't stay to lunch. I haven't time, I've got a million things to do. I'm sailing for Europe in a few days.

EVANS: (*surprised*) You're sailing?

DARRELL: (*very hurriedly*) Yes—going to study over there for a year or so. I haven't told anyone. I came out today to say good-bye. You won't be able to reach me again. I'll be out of town visiting. (*Then elatedly*) And now for your secret! It ought to make you very happy, Sam. I know how much you've wished for it, so I'm going to tell you although Nina'll be furious with me. She was saving it to surprise you with at her own proper time— (*Still more elatedly*) —but I'm selfish enough to want to see you happy before I go!

EVANS: (*not daring to believe what he hopes—stammering*) What—what is it, Ned?

DARRELL: (*clapping him on the back—with strange joviality*) You're going to be a father, old scout, that's the secret! (*Then as* EVANS *just stares at him dumbly in a blissful satisfaction, he rattles on*) And now I've got to run. See you again in a year or so. I've said good-bye to Nina. Good-bye, Sam. (*He takes his hand and clasps it*) Good luck! Buckle down to work now! You've got the stuff in you! When I get back I'll expect to hear you're on the high-road to success! And tell Nina I'll expect to find you both happy in your child—both of you, tell her!— happy in your child! Tell her that, Sam! (*He turns and goes to the door. Thinking as he goes*)

That does it! . . . honorably! . . . I'm free! . . .

(*He goes out—then out the front door—a moment later his motor is heard starting—dies away*).

EVANS: (*stares after him dumbly in the same state of happy stupefaction— mumbles*) Thank you—Ned. (*Thinking disjointedly*)

Why did I doubt myself? . . . now she loves me . . . she's loved me right along . . . I've been a fool . . .

(*He suddenly falls on his knees*)

Oh, God, I thank you!

(NINA *comes in from the kitchen. She stops in amazement when she sees him on his knees. He jumps to his feet and takes her in his arms with confident happiness and kisses her*) Oh, Nina, I love you so! And now I know you love me! I'll never be afraid of anything again!

NINA: (*bewildered and terror-stricken, trying feebly to push him away—thinking*)

> Has he . . . has he gone crazy? . . .

(*Weakly*) Sam! What's come over you, Sam?

EVANS: (*tenderly*) Ned told me—the secret—and I'm so happy, dear! (*He kisses her again*).

NINA: (*stammering*) Ned told you—what?

EVANS: (*tenderly*) That we're going to have a child, dear. You mustn't be sore at him. Why did you want to keep it a secret from me? Didn't you know how happy it would make me, Nina?

NINA: He told you we—we—you, the father—? (*Then suddenly breaking from him—wildly*) Ned! Where is Ned?

EVANS: He left a moment ago.

NINA: (*stupidly*) Left? Call him back. Lunch is ready.

EVANS: He's gone. He couldn't stay. He's got so much to do getting ready to sail.

NINA: Sail?

EVANS: Didn't he tell you he was sailing for Europe? He's going over for a year or so to study.

NINA: A year or so! (*Wildly*) I've got to call him up! No, I'll go in and see him right now! (*She takes a wavering step toward the door. Thinking in anguish*)

> Go! . . . go to him! . . . find him! . . . my lover! . . .

EVANS: He won't be there, I'm afraid. He said we couldn't reach him, that he'd be visiting friends out of town until he sailed. (*Solicitously*) Why, do you have to see him about something important, Nina? Perhaps I could locate—

NINA: (*stammering and swaying*) No. (*She stifles an hysterical laugh*) No, nothing—nothing important—nothing is important—ha—! (*She stifles another laugh—then on the verge of fainting, weakly*) Sam! Help me—

EVANS: (*rushes to her, supports her to sofa at right*) Poor darling! Lie down
and rest. (*She remains in a sitting position, staring blankly before her. He
chafes her wrists*) Poor darling! (*Thinking jubilantly*)

> Her condition . . . this weakness comes from her condition! . . .

NINA: (*thinking in anguish*)

> Ned doesn't love me! . . . he's gone! . . . gone forever! . . . like Gordon!
> . . . no, not like Gordon! . . . like a sneak, a coward! . . . a liar! . . . oh, I
> hate him! . . . O Mother God, please let me hate him! . . . he must have
> been planning this! . . . he must have known it today when he said he
> loved me! . . .

(*Thinking frenziedly*)

> I won't bear it! . . . he thinks he has palmed me off on Sam forever! . . .
> and his child! . . . he can't! . . . I'll tell Sam he was lying! . . . I'll make Sam
> hate him! . . . I'll make Sam kill him! . . . I'll promise to love Sam if he
> kills him! . . .

(*Suddenly turns to* EVANS—*savagely*) He lied to you!

EVANS: (*letting her wrists drop—appalled—stammers*) You mean—Ned
lied about—?

NINA: (*in same tone*) Ned lied to you!

EVANS: (*stammers*) You're not—going to have a child—

NINA: (*savagely*) Oh, yes! Oh, yes, I am! Nothing can keep me from
that! But you're—you're—I mean, you . . . (*Thinking in anguish*)

> I can't say that to him! . . . I can't tell him without Ned to help me! . . . I
> can't! . . . look at his face! . . . oh, poor Sammy! . . . poor little boy! . . .
> poor little boy! . . .

(*She takes his head and presses it to her breast and begins to weep. Weeping.*) I mean, you weren't to know about it, Sammy.

EVANS: (*immediately on the crest again—tenderly*) Why? Don't you want
me to be happy, Nina?

NINA: Yes—yes, I do, Sammy. (*Thinking strangely*)

> Little boy! . . . little boy! . . . one gives birth to little boys! . . . one doesn't
> drive them mad and kill them! . . .

EVANS: (*thinking*)

> She's never called me Sammy before . . . someone used to . . . oh, yes, Mother. . . .

(*Tenderly and boyishly*) And I'm going to make you happy from now on, Nina. I tell you, the moment Ned told me, something happened to me! I can't explain it, but—I'll make good now, Nina! I know I've said that before but I was only boasting. I was only trying to make myself think so. But now I say it knowing I can do it! (*Softly*) It's because we're going to have a child, Nina. I knew that you'd never come to really love me without that. That's what I was down on my knees for when you came in. I was thanking God—for our baby!

NINA: (*tremblingly*) Sammy! Poor boy!

EVANS: Ned said when he came back he'd expect to find us both happy— in our baby. He said to tell you that. You will be happy now, won't you, Nina?

NINA: (*brokenly and exhaustedly*) I'll try to make you happy, Sammy. (*He kisses her, then hides his head on her breast. She stares out over his head. She seems to grow older. Thinking as if she were repeating the words of some inner voice of life*)

> Not Ned's child! . . . not Sam's child! . . . mine! . . . there! . . . again! . . . I feel my child live . . . moving in my life . . . my life moving in my child . . . breathing in the tide I dream and breathe my dream back into the tide . . . God is a Mother. . . .

(*Then with sudden anguish*)

> Oh, afternoons . . . dear wonderful afternoons of love with you, my lover . . . you are lost . . . gone from me forever! . . .

CURTAIN

SECOND PART—ACT SIX

SCENE: *The same—an evening a little over a year later. The room has undergone a significant change. There is a comfortable, homey atmosphere as though now it definitely belonged to the type of person it was built for. It has a proud air of modest prosperity.*

It is soon after dinner—about eight o'clock. EVANS *is sitting by the table at left, glancing through a newspaper at headlines and reading an article here and there.* NINA *is in the chair at center, knitting a tiny sweater.* MARSDEN *is sitting on the sofa at right, holding a book which he pretends to be looking through, but glancing wonderingly at* EVANS *and* NINA.

There is a startling change in EVANS. *He is stouter, the haggard look of worry and self-conscious inferiority has gone from his face, it is full and healthy and satisfied. There is also, what is more remarkable, a decided look of solidity about him, of a determination moving toward ends it is confident it can achieve. He has matured, found his place in the world.*

The change in NINA *is also perceptible. She looks noticeably older, the traces of former suffering are marked on her face, but there is also an expression of present contentment and calm.*

MARSDEN *has aged greatly. His hair is gray, his expression one of a deep grief that is dying out into a resignation resentful of itself. He is dressed immaculately in dark tweed.*

NINA: (*thinking*)

> I wonder if there's a draft in the baby's room? . . . maybe I'd better close the window? . . . oh, I guess it's all right . . . he needs lots of fresh air . . . little Gordon . . . he does remind me of Gordon . . . something in his eyes . . . my romantic imagination? . . . Ned said that . . . why hasn't Ned ever written? . . . it's better he hasn't . . . how he made me suffer! . . . but I forgive him . . . he gave me my baby . . . the baby certainly doesn't look like him . . . everyone says he looks like Sam . . . how absurd! . . . but Sam makes a wonderful father . . . he's become a new man in the past year . . . and I've helped him . . . he asks me about everything . . . I have a genuine

respect for him now . . . I can give myself without repulsion . . . I am
making him happy . . . I've written his mother I'm making him happy . . .
I was proud to be able to write her that . . . how queerly things work out!
. . . all for the best . . . and I don't feel wicked . . . I feel good . . .

(*She smiles strangely*)

MARSDEN: (*thinking*)

> What a change! . . . the last time I was here the air was poisoned . . .
> Darrell . . . I was sure he was her lover . . . but I was in a morbid state
> . . . why did Darrell run away? . . . Nina could have got Sam to divorce
> her if she really loved Darrell . . . then it's evident she couldn't have loved
> him . . . and she was going to have Sam's baby . . . Darrell's love must
> have seemed like treachery . . . so she sent him away . . . that must be
> it . . .

(*With satisfaction*)

> Yes, I've got it straight now . . . .

(*With contemptuous pity*)

> Poor Darrell . . . I have no use for him but I did pity him when I ran
> across him in Munich . . . he was going the pace . . . looked desperate . . .

(*Then gloomily*)

> My running away was about as successful as his . . . as if one could leave
> one's memory behind! . . . I couldn't forget Mother . . . she haunted me
> through every city of Europe . . .

(*Then irritatedly*)

> I must get back to work! . . . not a line written in over a year! . . . my
> public will be forgetting me! . . . a plot came to me yesterday . . . my mind
> is coming around again . . . I am be ginning to forget, thank God! . . .

(*Then remorsefully*)

> No, I don't want to forget you, Mother! . . . but let me remember . . .
> without pain! . . .

EVANS: (*turning over a page of his paper*) There's going to be the biggest
boom before long this country has ever known, or I miss my guess,
Nina.

NINA: (*with great seriousness*) Do you think so, Sammy?

EVANS: (*decidedly*) I'm dead sure of it.

NINA: (*with a maternal pride and amusement*)

Dear Sam . . . I can't quite believe in this self-confident business man yet . . . but I have to admit he's proved it . . . he asked for more money and they gave it without question . . . they're anxious to keep him . . . they ought to be . . . how he's slaved! . . . for me and my baby! . . .

EVANS: (*has been looking at* MARSDEN *surreptitiously over his paper*)

Charlie's mother must have hoarded up a half million . . . he'll let it rot in government bonds . . . wonder what he'd say if I proposed that he back me? . . . he's always taken a friendly interest . . . well, it's worth a bet, anyway . . . he'd be an easy partner to handle . . .

MARSDEN: (*staring at* EVANS *wonderingly*)

What a changed Sam! . . . I preferred him the old way . . . futile but he had a sensitive quality . . . now he's brash . . . a little success . . . oh, he'll succeed all right . . . his kind are inheriting the earth . . . hogging it, cramming it down their tasteless gullets! . . . and he's happy! . . . actually happy! . . . he has Nina . . . a beautiful baby . . . a comfortable home . . . no sorrow, no tragic memories . . . and I have nothing! . . . but utter loneliness! . . .

(*With grieving self-pity*)

If only Mother had lived! . . . how horribly I miss her! . . . my lonely home . . . who will keep house for me now? . . . it has got to be done sympathetically or I won't be able to work . . . I must write to Jane . . . she'll probably be only too glad . . .

(*Turning to* NINA) I think I'll write to my sister in California and ask her to come on and live with me. She's alone now that her youngest daughter is married, and she has very little money. And my hands are tied as far as sharing the estate with her is concerned. According to Mother's will, I'm cut off too if I give her a penny. Mother never got over her bitter feeling about Jane's marriage. In a way, she was right. Jane's husband wasn't much—no family or position or ability—

and I doubt if she was ever happy with him. (*Sarcastically*) It was one of those love matches!

NINA: (*smiling—teasingly*) There's no danger of your ever making a love match, is there, Charlie?

MARSDEN: (*wincing—thinking*)

She can't believe any woman could possibly love me! . . .

(*Caustically*) I trust I'll never make that kind of a fool of myself, Nina!

NINA: (*teasingly*) Pooh! Aren't you the superior bachelor! I don't see anything to be so proud of! You're simply shirking, Charlie!

MARSDEN: (*wincing but forcing a teasing air*) You were my only true love, Nina. I made a vow of perpetual bachelorhood when you threw me over in Sam's favor!

EVANS: (*has listened to this last—jokingly*) Hello! What's this? I never knew you were my hated rival, Charlie!

MARSDEN: (*dryly*) Oh—didn't you really? (But EVANS *has turned back to his paper. Thinking savagely*)

That fool, too! . . . he jokes about it! . . . as if I were the last one in the world he could imagine . . .

NINA: (*teasingly*) Well, if I'm responsible, Charlie, I feel I ought to do something about it. I'll pick out a wife for you—guaranteed to suit! She must be at least ten years older than you, large and matronly and placid, and a wonderful cook and housekeeper—

MARSDEN: (*sharply*) Don't be stupid! (*Thinking angrily*)

She picks someone beyond the age! . . . she never imagines sex could enter into it! . . .

NINA: (*placatingly—seeing he is really angry*) Why, I was only picking out a type I thought would be good for you, Charlie—and for your work.

MARSDEN: (*sneeringly—with a meaning emphasis*) You didn't mention chaste. I couldn't respect a woman who hadn't respected herself!

NINA: (*thinking—stung*)

He's thinking of those men in the hospital . . . what a fool I was ever to tell him! . . .

(*Cuttingly*) Oh, so you think you deserve an innocent virgin!

MARSDEN: (*coldly—controlling his anger*) Let's drop me, if you please. (*With a look at her that is challenging and malicious*) Did I tell you I ran into Doctor Darrell in Munich?

NINA: (*startled—thinking frightenedly and confusedly*)

Ned! . . . he saw Ned! . . . why hasn't he told me before? . . . why did he look at me like that? . . . does he suspect? . . .

(*Trying to be calm but stammering*) You saw—Ned?

MARSDEN: (*with savage satisfaction*)

That struck home! . . . look at her! . . . guilty! . . . then I was right that day! . . .

(*Casually*) Yes, I chanced to run into him.

NINA: (*more calmly now*) Why on earth didn't you tell us before, Charlie?

MARSDEN: (*coolly*) Why? Is it such important news? You knew he was there, didn't you? I supposed he'd written you.

EVANS: (*looking up from his paper—affectionately*) How was the old scout?

MARSDEN: (*maliciously*) He seemed in fine feather—said he was having a gay time. When I saw him he was with a startling looking female— quite beautiful, if you like that type. I gathered they were living together.

NINA: (*cannot restrain herself—breaks out*) I don't believe it! (*Then immediately controlling herself and forcing a laugh*) I mean, Ned was always so serious-minded it's hard to imagine him messed up in that sort of thing. (*Thinking in a queer state of jealous confusion*)

Hard to imagine! . . . my lover! . . . oh, pain again! . . . why? . . . I don't love him now . . . be careful! . . . Charlie's staring at me. . . .

MARSDEN: (*thinking—jealously*)

Then she did love him! . . . does she still? . . .

(*Hopefully*)

Or is it only pique? . . . no woman likes to lose a man even when she no longer loves him . . . .

(*With malicious insistence*) Why is that hard to imagine, Nina? Darrell never struck me as a Galahad. After all, why shouldn't he have a mistress? (*Meaningly*) He has no tie over here to remain faithful to, has he?

NINA: (*struggling with herself—thinking pitiably*)

He's right . . . why shouldn't Ned? . . . is that why he's never written? . . .

(*Airily*) I don't know what ties he has or hasn't got. It's nothing to me if he has fifty mistresses. I suppose he's no better than the rest of you.

EVANS: (*looking over at her—tenderly reproachful*) That isn't fair, Nina. (*Thinking proudly*)

I'm proud of that . . . never anyone before her . . .

NINA: (*looking at him—with real gratitude*) I didn't mean you, dear. (*Thinking—proudly*)

Thank God for Sammy! . . . I know he's mine . . . no jealousy . . . no fear . . . no pain . . . I've found peace . . .

(*Then distractedly*)

Oh, Ned, why haven't you written? . . . stop it! . . . what a fool I am! . . . Ned's dead for me! . . . oh, I hate Charlie! . . . why did he tell me? . . .

MARSDEN: (*looking at* EVANS—*contemptuously thinking*)

What a poor simpleton Sam is! . . . boasting of his virtue! . . . as if women loved you for that! . . . they despise it! . . . I don't want Nina to think I've had no experiences with women. . . .

(*Mockingly*) So then it's Sam who is the Galahad, eh? Really Nina, you should have him put in the Museum among the prehistoric mammals!

EVANS: (*pleased—comes back kiddingly*) Well, I never had your chances, Charlie! I couldn't run over to Europe and get away with murder the way you have!

MARSDEN: (*foolishly pleased—admitting while denying*) Oh, I wasn't quite as bad as all that, Sam! (*Scornfully ashamed of himself—thinking*)

> Poor sick ass that I am! . . . I want them to think I've been a Don Juan! . . . how pitiful and disgusting! . . . I wouldn't have a mistress if I could! . . . if I could? . . . of course I could! . . . I've simply never cared to degrade myself! . . .

NINA: (*thinking—tormentedly*)

> The thought of that woman! . . . Ned forgetting our afternoons in nights with her! . . . stop these thoughts! . . . I won't give in to them! . . . why did Charlie want to hurt me? . . . is he jealous of Ned? . . . Charlie has always loved me in some queer way of his own . . . how ridiculous!! . . . look at him! . . . he's so proud of being thought a Don Juan! . . . I'm sure he never even dared to kiss a woman except his mother! . . .

(*Mockingly*) Do tell us about all your various mistresses in foreign parts, Charlie!

MARSDEN: (*in confusion now*) I—I really don't remember, Nina!

NINA: Why, you're the most heartless person I've ever heard of, Charlie! Not remember even one! And I suppose there are little Marsdens—and you've forgotten all about them too! (*She laughs maliciously—* EVANS *laughs with her*).

MARSDEN: (*still more confused—with a silly idiotic smirk*) I can't say about that, Nina. It's a wise father who knows his own child, you know!

NINA: (*frightenedly—thinking*)

> What does he mean? . . . does he suspect about the baby too? . . . I must be terribly careful of Charlie! . . .

EVANS: (*looking up from his paper again*) Did Ned say anything about coming back?

NINA: (*thinking—longingly*)

Come back? . . . oh, Ned, how I wish! . . .

MARSDEN: (*looking at her—meaningly*) No, he didn't say. I gathered he was staying over indefinitely.

EVANS: I'd sure like to see him again.

NINA: (*thinking*)

He has forgotten me . . . if he did come, he'd probably avoid me. . . .

MARSDEN: He spoke of you. He asked if I'd heard whether Nina had had her baby yet or not. I told him I hadn't.

EVANS: (*heartily*) Too bad you didn't know. You could have told him what a world-beater we've got! Eh, Nina?

NINA: (*mechanically*) Yes. (*joyfully—thinking*)

Ned asked about my baby! . . . then he hadn't forgotten! . . . if he came back he'd come to see his baby! . . .

EVANS: (*solicitously*) Isn't it time to nurse him again?

NINA: (*starts to her feet automatically*) Yes, I'm going now. (*She glances at* MARSDEN, *thinking calculatingly*)

I must win Charlie over again . . . I don't feel safe . . .

(*She stops by his chair and takes his hand and looks into his eyes gently and reproachfully*).

MARSDEN: (*thinking shamefacedly*)

Why have I been trying to hurt her? . . . my Nina! . . . I am nearer to her than anyone! . . . I'd give my life to make her happy! . . .

NINA: (*triumphantly*)

How his hand trembles! . . . what a fool to be afraid of Charlie! . . . I can always twist him round my finger! . . .

(*She runs her hand through his hair, and speaks as though she were hiding a hurt reproach beneath a joking tone*) I shouldn't like you any more, do you know it, after you've practically admitted you've philandered all over Europe! And I thought you were absolutely true to me, Charlie!

MARSDEN: (*so pleased he can hardly believe his ears*)

Then she did believe me! . . . she's actually hurt! . . . but I can't let her think . . .

(*With passionate earnestness, clasping her hand in both of his, looking into her eyes*) No, Nina! I swear to you!

NINA: (*thinking—cruelly*)

Pah! . . . how limp his hands are! . . . his eyes are so shrinking! . . . is it possible he loves me? . . . like that? . . . what a sickening idea! . . . it seems incestuous somehow! . . . no, it's too absurd! . . .

(*Smiling, gently releases her hand*) All right. I forgive you, Charlie. (*Then matter-of-factly*) Excuse me, please, while I go up and feed my infant, or we're due to hear some lusty howling in a moment. (*She turns away, then impulsively turns back and kisses* MARSDEN *with real affection*) You're an old dear, do you know it, Charlie? I don't know what I'd do without you! (*Thinking*)

It's true, too! . . . he's my only dependable friend . . . I must never lose him . . . never let him suspect about little Gordon . . .

(*She turns to go*).

EVANS: (*jumping up, throwing his paper aside*) Wait a second. I'll come with you. I want to say good night to him. (*He comes, puts his arm about her waist, kisses her and they go out together*).

MARSDEN: (*thinking excitedly*)

I almost confessed I loved her! . . . a queer expression came over her face . . . what was it? . . . was it satisfaction? . . . she didn't mind? . . . was it pleasure? . . . then I can hope? . . .

(*Then miserably*)

Hope for what? . . . what do I want? . . . If Nina were free, what would I do? . . . would I do anything? . . . would I wish to? . . . what would I offer her? . . . money? . . . she could get that from others . . . myself? . . .

(*Bitterly*)

What a prize! . . . my ugly body . . . there's nothing in me to attract her . . . my fame? . . . God, what a shoddy, pitiful! . . . but I might have done something big . . . I might still . . . if I had the courage to write the truth . . . but I was born afraid . . . afraid of myself . . . I've given my talent to making fools feel pleased with themselves in order that they'd feel pleased with me . . . and like me . . . I'm neither hated nor loved . . . I'm liked . . . women like me . . . Nina likes me! . . .

(*Resentfully*)

She can't help letting the truth escape her! . . . "You're an old dear, do you know it, Charlie?" Oh, yes, I know it . . . too damned well! . . . dear old Charlie! . . .

(*In anguish*)

Dear old Rover, nice old doggie, we've had him for years, he's so affectionate and faithful but he's growing old, he's getting cross, we'll have to get rid of him soon! . . .

(*In a strange rage, threateningly*)

But you won't get rid of me so easily, Nina! . . .

(*Then confusedly and shamefacedly*)

Good God, what's the matter with me! . . . since Mother's death I've become a regular idiot! . . .

EVANS: (*comes back from the right, a beaming look of proud parenthood on his face*) He was sleeping so soundly an earthquake wouldn't have made him peep! (*He goes back to his chair—earnestly*) He sure is healthy and husky, Charlie. That tickles me more than anything else. I'm going to start in training him as soon as he's old enough—so he'll be a crack athlete when he goes to college—what I wanted to be and couldn't. I want him to justify the name of Gordon and be a bigger star than Gordon ever was, if that's possible.

MARSDEN: (*with a sort of pity—thinking*)

His is an adolescent mind . . . he'll never grow up . . . well, in this adolescent country, what greater blessing could he wish for? . . .

(*Forcing a smile*) How about training his mind?

EVANS: (*confidently*) Oh, that'll take care of itself. Gordon was always near the top in his studies, wasn't he? And with Nina for a mother, his namesake ought to inherit a full set of brains.

MARSDEN: (*amused*) You're the only genuinely modest person I know, Sam.

EVANS: (*embarrassed*) Oh—me—I'm the boob of the family. (*Then hastily*) except when it comes to business. I'll make the money. (*Confidently*) And you can bet your sweet life I will make it!

MARSDEN: I'm quite sure of that.

EVANS: (*very seriously—in a confidential tone*) I couldn't have said that two years ago—and believed it. I've changed a hell of a lot! Since the baby was born, I've felt as if I had a shot of dynamite in each arm. They can't pile on the work fast enough. (*He grins—then seriously*) It was about time I got hold of myself. I wasn't much for Nina to feel proud about having around the house in those days. Now—well—at least I've improved. I'm not afraid of my own shadow any more.

MARSDEN: (*thinking strangely*)

Not to be afraid of one's shadow! . . . that must be the highest happiness of heaven! . . .

(*Flatteringly*) Yes, you've done wonders in the past year.

EVANS: Oh, I haven't even started yet. Wait till I get my chance! (*Glances at* MARSDEN *sharply, makes up his mind and leans forward toward him confidentially*) And I see my real chance, Charlie—lying right ahead, waiting for me to grab it—an agency that's been allowed to run down and go to seed. Within a year or so they'll be willing to sell out cheap. One of their people who's become a good pal of mine told me that in confidence, put it up to me. He'd take it on himself but he's sick of the game. But I'm not! I love it! It's great sport! (*Then putting a brake on this exuberance—matter-of-factly*) But I'll need a hundred thousand—and where will I get it? (*Looking at* MARSDEN *keenly but putting on a joking tone*) Any suggestion you can make, Charlie, will be gratefully received.

MARSDEN: (*thinking suspiciously*)

Does he actually imagine I...? and a hundred thousand, no less!... over one-fifth of my entire... by Jove, I'll have to throw cold water on that fancy!...

(*Shortly*) No, Sam, I can't think of anyone. Sorry.

EVANS: (*without losing any confidence—with a grin*)

Check!... That's that!... Charlie's out... till the next time!... but I'll keep after him!...

(*Contemplating himself with pride*)

Gee, I have changed all right! I can remember when a refusal like that would have ruined my confidence for six months!

(*Heartily*) Nothing to be sorry about, old man. I only mentioned it on the off chance *you* might know of someone. (*Trying a bold closing stroke—jokingly*) Why don't you be my partner, Charlie? Never mind the hundred thousand. We'll get that elsewhere. I'll bet you might have darn fine original ideas to contribute. (*Thinking—satisfied*)

There!... That'll keep my proposition pinned up in his mind!...

(*Then jumping to his feet—briskly*) What do you say to a little stroll down to the shore and back? Come on—do you good. (*Taking his arm and hustling him genially toward the door*) What you need is exercise. You're soft as putty. Why don't you take up golf?

MARSDEN: (*with sudden resistance pulls away—determinedly*) No, I won't go, Sam. I want to think out a new plot.

EVANS: Oh, all right. If it's a case of work, go to it! See you later. (*He goes out. A moment later the front door is heard closing*).

MARSDEN: (*looks after him with a mixture of annoyance and scornful amusement*)

What a fount of meaningless energy he's tapped!... always on the go ... typical terrible child of the age... universal slogan, keep moving

...moving where?...never mind that...don't think of ends... the means are the end...keep moving!...

(*He laughs scornfully and sits down in* EVANS' *chair, picking up the paper and glancing at it sneeringly*)

It's in every headline of this daily newer testament...going...going ...never mind the gone...we won't live to see it...and we'll be so rich, we can buy off the deluge anyway!...even our new God has His price!...must have!...aren't we made in His image?...or vice-versa?...

(*He laughs again, letting the paper drop disdainfully—then bitterly*)

But why am I so superior?...where am I going?...to the same no-where!...worse!...I'm not even going!...I'm there!...

(*He laughs with bitter self-pity—then begins to think with amused curiosity*)

Become Sam's partner?...there's a grotesque notion!...it might revive my sense of humor about myself, at least...I'm the logical one to help him...I helped him to Nina...logical partner...partner in Nina? ...what inane thoughts!...

(*With a sigh*)

No use trying to think out that plot tonight...I'll try to read....

(*He sees the book he has been reading on the couch and gets up to get it. There is a ring from the front door.* MARSDEN *turns toward it uncertainly. A pause. Then* NINA'S *voice calls down the stairs*).

NINA: The maid's out. Will you go to the door, Charlie?

MARSDEN: Surely. (*He goes out and opens the front door. A pause. Then he can be heard saying resentfully*) Hello, Darrell. (*And someone answering "Hello, Marsden" and coming in and the door closing*).

NINA: (*from upstairs, her voice strange and excited*) Who is it, Charlie?

DARRELL: (*comes into view in the hall, opposite the doorway, at the foot of the stairs—his voice trembling a little with suppressed emotion*) It's I, Nina— Ned Darrell.

NINA: (*with a glad cry*) Ned! (*Then in a voice which shows she is trying to control herself, and is frightened now*) I—make yourself at home. I'll be down—in a minute or two. (DARRELL *remains standing looking up the stairs in a sort of joyous stupor.* MARSDEN *stares at him*).

MARSDEN: (*sharply*) Come on in and sit down. (DARRELL *starts, comes into the room, plainly getting a grip on himself.* MARSDEN *follows him, glaring at his back with enmity and suspicion.* DARRELL *moves as far away from him as possible, sitting down on the sofa at right.* MARSDEN *takes* EVANS' *chair by the table.* DARRELL *is pale, thin, nervous, unhealthy looking. There are lines of desperation in his face, puffy shadows of dissipation and sleeplessness under his restless, harried eyes. He is dressed carelessly, almost shabbily. His eyes wander about the room, greedily taking it in*).

DARRELL: (*thinking disjointedly*)

Here again! . . . dreamed of this house . . . from here, ran away . . . I've come back . . . my turn to be happy! . . .

MARSDEN: (*watching him—savagely*)

Now I know! . . . absolutely! . . . his face! . . . her voice! . . . they did love each other! . . . they do now! . . .

(*Sharply*) When did you get back from Europe?

DARRELL: (*curtly*) This morning on the Olympic. (*Thinking—cautiously*)

Look out for this fellow . . . always had it in for me . . . like a woman . . . smells out love . . . he suspected before . . .

(*Then boldly*)

Well, who gives a damn now? . . . all got to come out! . . . Nina wanted to tell Sam . . . now I'll tell him myself! . . .

MARSDEN: (*righteously indignant*)

What has brought him back? . . . what a devilish, cowardly trick to play on poor unsuspecting Sam! . . .

(*Revengefully*)

But I'm not unsuspecting! . . . I'm not their fool! . . .

(*Coldly*) What brought you back so soon? When I saw you in Munich you weren't intending—

DARRELL: (*shortly*) My father died three weeks ago. I've had to come back about his estate. (*Thinking*)

> Lie . . . Father's death just gave me an excuse to myself . . . wouldn't have come back for that . . . came back because I love her! . . . damn his questions! . . . I want to think . . . before I see her . . . sound of her voice . . . seemed to burn inside my head . . . God, I'm licked! . . . no use fighting it . . . I've done my damnedest . . . work . . . booze . . . other women . . . no use . . . I love her! . . . always! . . . to hell with pride! . . .

MARSDEN: (*thinking*)

> He has two brothers . . . they'll probably all share equally . . . his father noted Philadelphia surgeon . . . rich, I've heard . . .

(*With a bitter grin*)

> Wait till Sam hears that! . . . he'll ask Darrell to back him . . . and Darrell will jump at it . . . chance to avert suspicion . . . conscience money, too! . . . it's my duty to protect Sam . . .

(*As he hears* NINA *coming down the stairs*)

> I must watch them . . . it's my duty to protect Nina from herself . . . Sam is a simpleton . . . I'm all she has . . .

DARRELL: (*hearing her coming—in a panic—thinking*)

> Coming! . . . in a second I'll see her! . . .

(*Terrified*)

> Does she still love me? . . . she may have forgotten . . . no, it's my child . . . she can never forget that! . . .

(NINA *comes in from the rear. She has put on a fresh dress, her hair is arranged, her face newly rouged and powdered, she looks extremely pretty and this is heightened by the feverish state of mind she is in—a mixture of love, of triumphant egotism in knowing her lover has come back to her, and of fear and uncertainty in feeling her new peace, her certainties, her con-*

tented absorption in her child failing her. She hesitates just inside the door, staring into DARRELL'S *eyes, thinking a fierce question*).

NINA.

Does he still love me? . . .

(*Then triumphantly as she reads him*)

Yes! . . . he does! . . . he does! . . .

DARRELL: (*who has jumped to his feet—with a cry of longing*) Nina! (*Thinking with alarm now*)

She's changed! . . . changed! . . . can't tell if she loves! . . .

(*He has started to go to her. Now he hesitates. His voice taking on a pleading uncertain quality*) Nina!

NINA: (*thinking triumphantly—with a certain cruelty*)

He loves me! . . . he's mine . . . now more than ever! . . . he'll never dare leave me again! . . .

(*Certain of herself now, she comes to him and speaks with confident pleasure*) Hello, Ned! This is a wonderful surprise! How are you? (*She takes his hand*).

DARRELL: (*taken aback—confusedly*) Oh—all right, Nina. (*Thinking in a panic*)

That tone! . . . as if she didn't care! . . . can't believe that! . . . she's playing a game to fool Marsden! . . .

MARSDEN: (*who is watching them keenly—thinking*)

She loves his love for her . . . she's cruelly confident . . . much as I hate this man I can't help feeling sorry . . . I know her cruelty . . . it's time I took a hand in this . . . what a plot for a novel! . . .

(*Almost mockingly*) Darrell's father died, Nina. He had to come home to see about the estate.

DARRELL: (*with a glare at* MARSDEN—*protestingly*) I was coming home

anyway. I only intended to stay a year, and it's over that since—
(*Intensely*) I was coming back anyway, Nina!

NINA: (*thinking with triumphant happiness*)

> You dear, you! . . . as if I didn't know that! . . . oh, how I'd love to take
> you in my arms! . . .

(*Happily*) I'm awfully glad you've come, Ned. We've missed you
terribly.

DARRELL: (*thinking—more and more at sea*)

> She looks glad . . . but she's changed . . . I don't understand her . . .
> "we've missed" . . . that means Sam . . . what does that mean? . . .

(*Intensely, pressing her hand*) And I've missed you—terribly!

MARSDEN: (*sardonically*) Yes, indeed, Darrell, I can vouch for their miss-
ing you—Sam in particular. He was asking about you only a short
while ago—how things were going with you when I saw you in
Munich. (*Maliciously*) By the way, who was the lady you were with
that day? She was certainly startling looking.

NINA: (*thinking—triumphantly mocking*)

> A miss, Charlie! . . . he loves me! . . . what do I care about that wo-
> man? . . .

(*Gaily*) Yes, who was the mysterious beauty, Ned? Do tell us! (*She
moves away from him and sits down at center.* DARRELL *remains standing*).

DARRELL: (*glaring at* MARSDEN, *sullenly*) Oh, I don't remember—
(*Thinking apprehensively with a bitter resentment*)

> She doesn't give a damn! . . . if she loved me she'd be jealous! . . . but she
> doesn't give a damn! . . .

(*He blurts out resentfully at* NINA) Well, she was my mistress—for a
time—I was lonely. (*Then with sudden anger turning on* MARSDEN) But
what's all this to you, Marsden?

MARSDEN: (*coolly*) Absolutely nothing. Pardon me. It was a tactless question. (*Then with continued open malice*) But I was starting to say how
Sam had missed you, Darrell. It's really remarkable. One doesn't

encounter such friendship often in these slack days, Why, he'd trust you with anything!

NINA: (*wincing—thinking*)

> That hurts . . . hurts Ned . . . Charlie is being cruel! . . .

DARRELL: (*wincing—in a forced tone*) And I'd trust Sam with anything.

MARSDEN: Of course. He is a person one can trust. They are rare. You're going to be amazed at the change in Sam, Darrell. Isn't he, Nina? He's a new man. I never saw such energy. If ever a man was bound for success Sam is. In fact, I'm so confident he is that as soon as he thinks the time is ripe to start his own firm I'm going to furnish the capital and become his silent partner.

DARRELL: (*puzzled and irritated—thinking confusedly*)

> What's he driving at? . . . why doesn't he get the hell out and leave us alone? . . . but I'm glad Sam is on his feet . . . makes it easier to tell him the truth . . . .

NINA: (*thinking—worriedly*)

> What's Charlie talking about? . . . it's time I talked to Ned . . . Oh, Ned, I do love you! . . . you can be my lover! . . . we won't hurt Sam! . . . he'll never know! . . .

MARSDEN: Yes, ever since the baby was born Sam's been another man—in fact, ever since he knew there was going to be a baby, isn't it, Nina?

NINA: (*agreeing as if she had only half-heard him*) Yes. (*Thinking*)

> Ned's baby! . . . I must talk to him about our baby . . . .

MARSDEN: Sam is the proudest parent I've ever seen!

NINA: (*as before*) Yes, Sam makes a wonderful father, Ned. (*Thinking*)

> Ned doesn't care for children . . . I know what you're hoping, Ned . . . but if you think I'm going to take Sam's baby from him, you're mistaken! . . . or if you think I'll run away with you and leave my baby . . .

MARSDEN: (*with the same strange driving insistence*) If anything happened

to that child I actually believe Sam would lose his reason! Don't you
think so, Nina?

NINA: (*with emphasis*) I know I'd lose mine! Little Gordon has become
my whole life.

DARRELL: (*thinking—with a sad bitter irony*)

Sam . . . wonderful father . . . lose his reason . . . little Gordon! . . . Nina
called my son after Gordon! . . . romantic imagination! . . . Gordon is still
her lover! . . . Gordon, Sam and Nina! . . . and my son! . . . closed cor-
poration! . . . I'm forced out! . . .

(*Then rebelling furiously*)

No! . . . not yet, by God! . . . I'll smash it up! . . . I'll tell Sam the truth no
matter what! . . .

NINA: (*thinking with a strange calculation*)

I couldn't find a better husband than Sam . . . and I couldn't find a better
lover than Ned . . . I need them both to be happy . . .

MARSDEN: (*with sudden despairing suspicion*)

Good God . . . after all, is it Sam's child? . . . mightn't it be Darrell's!
. . . why have I never thought of that? . . . No! . . . Nina couldn't be so
vile! . . . to go on living with Sam, pretending . . . and, after all, why
should she, you fool? . . . there's no sense! . . . she could have gone off
with Darrell, couldn't she? . . . Sam would have given her a divorce . . .
there was no possible reason for her staying with Sam, when she loved
Darrell, unless exactly because this was Sam's baby . . . for its sake . . .

(*Hectically relieved*)

Of course! . . . of course! . . . that's all right! . . . I love that poor baby
now! . . . I'll fight for its sake against these two! . . .

(*Smilingly gets to his feet—thinking*)

I can leave them alone now . . . for they won't be alone, thanks to
me! . . . I leave Sam and his baby in this room with them . . . and their
honor . . .

(*Suddenly raging*)

Their honor! . . . what an obscene joke! . . . the honor of a harlot and a pimp! . . . I hate them! . . . if only God would strike them dead! . . . now! . . . and I could see them die! . . . I would praise His justice! . . . His kindness and mercy to me! . . .

NINA: (*thinking—with horrified confusion*)

Why doesn't Charlie go? . . . What is he thinking? . . . I suddenly feel afraid of him! . . .

(*She gets to her feet with a confused pleading cry*) Charlie!

MARSDEN: (*immediately urbane and smiling*) It's all right. I'm going out to find Sam. When he knows you're here he'll come on the run, Darrell. (*He goes to the door. They watch him suspiciously*) And you two probably have a lot to talk over. (*He chuckles pleasantly and goes into the hall—mockingly warning*) We'll be back before long. (*The front door is heard slamming.* NINA *and* DARRELL *turn and look at each other guiltily and frightenedly. Then he comes to her and takes both of her hands uncertainly*).

DARRELL: (*stammeringly*) Nina—I've come back to you—do you—do you still care—Nina?

NINA: (*giving way to his love passionately, as if to drown her fears*) I love you, Ned!

DARRELL: (*kisses her awkwardly—stammering*) I—I didn't know—you seemed so cold—damn Marsden—he suspects, doesn't he?—but it makes no difference now, does it? (*Then in a flood of words*) Oh, it's been hell, Nina! I couldn't forget you! Other women—they only made me love you more! I hated them and loved you even at the moment when—that's honest! It was always you in my arms—as you used to be—those afternoons—God, how I've thought of them—lying awake—recalling every word you said, each movement, each expression on your face, smelling your hair, feeling your soft body—(*Suddenly taking her in his arms and kissing her again and again—passionately*) Nina! I love you so!

NINA: And I've longed for you so much! Do you think I've forgotten those afternoons? (*Then in anguish*) Oh, Ned, why did you run away? I can never forgive that! I can never trust you again!

DARRELL: (*violently*) I was a fool! I thought of Sam! And that wasn't all! Oh, I wasn't all noble, I'll confess! I thought of myself and my career! Damn my career! A lot of good that did it! I didn't study! I didn't live! I longed for you—and suffered! I paid in full, believe me, Nina! But I know better now! I've come back. The time for lying is past! You've got to come away with me! (*He kisses her*).

NINA: (*letting herself go, kissing him passionately*) Yes! My lover! (*Then suddenly resisting and pushing him away*) No! You're forgetting Sam— and Sam's baby!

DARRELL: (*staring at her wildly*) Sam's baby? Are you joking? Ours, you mean! We'll take him with us, of course!

NINA: (*sadly*) And Sam?

DARRELL: Damn Sam! He's got to give you a divorce! Let him be generous for a change!

NINA: (*sadly but determinedly*) He would be. You must be just to Sam. He'd give his life for my happiness. And this would mean his life. Could we be happy then? You know we couldn't! And I've changed, Ned. You've got to realize that. I'm not your old mad Nina. I still love you. I will always love you. But now I love my baby too. His happiness comes first with me!

DARRELL: But—he's mine, too!

NINA: No! You gave him to Sam to save Sam!

DARRELL: To hell with Sam! It was to make you happy!

NINA: So I could make Sam happy! That was in it too! I was sincere in that, Ned! If I hadn't been, I could never have gone to you that first day—or if I had, I'd never have forgiven myself. But as it is I don't feel guilty or wicked. I have made Sam happy! And I'm proud! I love Sam's happiness! I love the devoted husband and father in him! And I feel it's his baby—that we've made it his baby!

DARRELL: (*distractedly*) Nina! For God's sake! You haven't come to love

Sam, have you? Then—I'll go—I'll go away again—I'll never come back—I tried not to this time—but I had to, Nina!

NINA: (*taking him in her arms—with sudden alarm*) No, don't go away, Ned—ever again. I don't love Sam! I love you!

DARRELL: (*miserably*) But I don't understand! Sam gets everything—and I have nothing!

NINA: You have my love. (*With a strange, self-assured smile at him*) It seems to me you're complaining unreasonably!

DARRELL: You mean—I can be—your lover again?

NINA: (*simply, even matter-of-factly*) Isn't that the nearest we can come to making everyone happy? That's all that counts.

DARRELL: (*with a harsh laugh*) And is that what you call playing fair to Sam?

NINA: (*simply*) Sam will never know. The happiness I have given him has made him too sure of himself ever to suspect me now. And as long as we can love each other without danger to him, I feel he owes that to us for all we've done for him. (*With finality*) That's the only possible solution, Ned, for all our sakes, now you've come back to me.

DARRELL: (*repulsed*) Nina! How can you be so inhuman and calculating!

NINA: (*stung—mockingly*) It was you who taught me the scientific approach, Doctor!

DARRELL: (*shrinking back from her—threateningly*) Then I'll leave again! I'll go back to Europe! I won't endure—! (*Then in a queer, futile rage*) You think I'll stay—to be your lover—watching Sam with my wife and my child—you think that's what I came back to you for? You can go to hell, Nina!

NINA: (*calmly—sure of him*) But what else can I do, Ned? (*Then warningly*) I hear them coming, dear. It's Sam, you know.

DARRELL: (*in a frenzy*) What else can you do? Liar! But I can do something else! I can smash your calculating game for you! I can tell Sam—and I will—right now—by God, I will!

NINA: (*quietly*) No. You won't, Ned. You can't do that to Sam.

DARRELL: (*savagely*) Like hell I can't! (*The front door is opened.* EVANS' *voice is immediately heard, even before he bounds into the room. He rushes up to* NED *hilariously, shakes his hand and pounds his back, oblivious to* DARRELL'S *wild expression*).

EVANS: You old son of a gun! Why didn't you let a guy know you were coming? We'd have met you at the dock, and brought the baby. Let me have a look at you! You look thinner. We'll fatten you up, won't we, Nina? Let us do the prescribing this time! Why didn't you let us know where you were, you old bum? We wanted to write you about the baby. And I wanted to boast about how I was getting on! You're the only person in the world—except Nina and Charlie—I would boast about that to.

NINA: (*affectionately*) Mercy, Sam, give Ned a chance to get a word in! (*Looking at* NED *pityingly but challengingly*) He wants to tell you something, Sam.

DARRELL: (*crushed—stammers*) No—I mean, yes—I want to tell you how damn glad I am . . . (*He turns away, his face is screwed up in his effort to hold back his tears. Thinking miserably*)

I can't tell him! . . . God damn him, I can't! . . .

NINA: (*with a strange triumphant calm*)

There! . . . that's settled for all time! . . . poor Ned! . . . how crushed he looks! . . . I mustn't let Sam look at him! . . .

(*She steps between them protectingly*) Where's Charlie, Sam?

MARSDEN: (*appearing from the hall*) Here, Nina. Always here! (*He comes to her, smiling with assurance*).

NINA: (*suddenly with a strange unnatural elation—looking from one to the other with triumphant possession*) Yes, you're here, Charlie—always! And you, Sam and Ned! (*With a strange gaiety*) Sit down, all of you! Make yourselves at home! You are my three men! This is your home with me! (*Then in a strange half-whisper*) Ssshh! I thought I heard the baby. You must all sit down and be very quiet. You must not wake our baby. (*Mechanically, the three sit down, careful to make no noise—* EVANS *in his old place by the table,* MARSDEN *at center,* DARRELL *on the sofa at right. They sit staring before them in silence.* NINA *remains standing, dominating them, a little behind and to the left of* MARSDEN).

DARRELL: (*thinking abjectly*)

> I couldn't! . . . there are things one may not do and live with oneself afterwards . . . there are things one may not say . . . memory is too full of echoes! . . . there are secrets one must not reveal . . . memory is lined with mirrors! . . . he was too happy! . . . to kill happiness is a worse murder than taking life! . . . I gave him that happiness! . . . Sam deserves my happiness! . . . God bless you, Sam! . . .

(*Then in a strange objective tone—thinking*)

> My experiment with the guinea pigs has been a success . . . the ailing ones, Sam, and the female, Nina, have been restored to health and normal function . . . only the other male, Ned, seems to have suffered deterioration.

(*Then bitterly humble*)

> Nothing left but to accept her terms . . . I love her . . . I can help to make her happy . . . half a loaf is better . . . to a starving man. . . .

(*Glancing over at* EVANS *—bitterly gloating*)

> And your child is mine! . . . your wife is mine! . . . your happiness is mine! . . . may you enjoy my happiness, her husband! . . .

EVANS: (*looking at* DARRELL, *affectionately*)

> Sure good to see Ned again . . . a real friend if there ever was one . . . looks blue about something . . . oh, that's right, Charlie said his old man had kicked in . . . his old man was rich . . . that's an idea . . . I'll bet he'd put up that capital . . .

(*Then ashamed of himself*)

> Aw hell, what's the matter with me? . . . he's no sooner here than I start . . . he's done enough . . . forget it! . . . now anyway . . . he looks pretty dissipated . . . too many women . . . ought to get married and settle down

... tell him that if I didn't think he'd laugh at me giving him advice ...
but he'll soon realize I'm not the old Sam he knew ... I suppose Nina's
been boasting about that already ... she's proud ... she's helped me ...
she's a wonderful wife and mother ...

(*Looking up at her—solicitously*)

She acted a bit nervous just now ... queer ... like she used to ... haven't
noticed her that way in a long time ... suppose it's the excitement of Ned
turning up ... mustn't let her get overexcited ... bad for the baby's
milk. ...

MARSDEN: (*glancing furtively over his shoulder at* NINA *—broodingly thinking*)

She's the old queer Nina now ... the Nina I could never fathom ... her
three men! ... and we are! ... I? ... yes, more deeply than either of the
others since I serve for nothing ... a queer kind of love, maybe ... I am
not ordinary! ... our child ... what could she mean by that? ... child of
us three? ... on the surface, that's insane ... but I felt when she said it
there was something in it ... she has strange devious intuitions that tap
the hidden currents of life ... dark intermingling currents that become
the one stream of desire ... I feel, with regard to Nina, my life queerly
identified with Sam's and Darrell's ... her child is the child of our three
loves for her ... I would like to believe that ... I would like to be her
husband in a sense ... and the father of a child, after my fashion ... I
could forgive her everything ... permit everything ...

(*Determinedly*)

And I do forgive! ... and I will not meddle hereafter more than is necessary to guard her happiness, and Sam's and our baby's ... as for Darrell,
I am no longer jealous of him ... she is only using his love for her own
happiness ... he can never take her away from me! ...

NINA: (*more and more strangely triumphant*)

My three men! ... I feel their desires converge in me! ... to form one
complete beautiful male desire which I absorb ... and am whole ... they
dissolve in me, their life is my life ... I am pregnant with the three! ...
husband! ... lover! ... father! ... and the fourth man! ... little man!
... little Gordon! ... he is mine too! ... that makes it perfect! ...

(*With an extravagant suppressed exultance*)

Why, I should be the proudest woman on earth! . . . I should be the happiest woman in the world! . . .

(*Then suppressing an outbreak of hysterical triumphant laughter only by a tremendous effort*)

Ha-ha . . . only I better knock wood . . .

(*She raps with both knuckles in a fierce tattoo on the table*)

before God the Father hears my happiness! . . .

EVANS: (*as the three turn to her—anxiously*) Nina? What's the matter?

NINA: (*controlling herself with a great effort comes to him—forcing a smile—puts her arms around him affectionately*) Nothing, dear. Nerves, that's all. I've gotten over-tired, I guess.

EVANS: (*bullying her—with loving authority*) Then you go right to bed, young lady! We'll excuse you.

NINA: (*quietly and calmly now*) All right, dear. I guess I do need to rest. (*She kisses him as she might kiss a big brother she loved—affectionately*) Good night, you bossy old thing, you!

EVANS: (*with deep tenderness*) Good night, darling.

NINA: (*she goes and kisses Charlie dutifully on the cheek as she might her father—affectionately*) Good night, Charlie.

MARSDEN: (*with a touch of her father's manner*) That's a good girl! Good night, dear.

NINA: (*she goes and kisses* DARRELL *lovingly on the lips as she would kiss her lover*) Good night, Ned.

DARRELL: (*looks at her with grateful humility*) Thank you. Good night. (*She turns and walks quietly out of the room. The eyes of the three men follow her*).

CURTAIN

Act Seven

SCENE: *Nearly eleven years later. The sitting room of the* EVANS' *apartment on Park Avenue, New York City—a room that is a tribute to* NINA'S *good taste. It is a large, sunny room, the furniture expensive but extremely simple. The arrangement of the furniture shown is as in previous scenes except there are more pieces. Two chairs are by the table at left. There is a smaller table at center, and a chaise longue. A large, magnificently comfortable sofa is at right.*

It is about one in the afternoon of a day in early fall. NINA *and* DARRELL *and their son,* GORDON, *are in the room.* NINA *is reclining on the chaise longue watching* GORDON *who is sitting on the floor near her, turning over the pages of a book.* DARRELL *is sitting by the table at left, watching* NINA.

NINA *is thirty-five, in the full bloom of her womanhood. She is slimmer than in the previous scene. Her skin still retains a trace of summer tan and she appears in the pink of physical condition. But as in the first act of the play, there is beneath this a sense of great mental strain. One notices the many lines in her face at second glance. Her eyes are tragically sad in repose and her expression is set and masklike.*

GORDON *is eleven—a fine boy with, even at this age, the figure of an athlete. He looks older than he is. There is a grave expression to his face. His eyes are full of a quick-tempered sensitiveness. He does not noticeably resemble his mother. He looks nothing at all like his father. He seems to have sprung from a line distinct from any of the people we have seen.*

DARRELL *has aged greatly. His hair is streaked with gray. He has grown stout. His face is a bit jowly and puffy under the eyes. The features have become blurred. He has the look of a man with no definite aim or ambition to which he can relate his living. His eyes are embittered and they hide his inner self-resentment behind a pose of cynical indifference.*

GORDON: (*thinking as he plays—resentfully*)

I wish Darrell'd get out of here! . . . why couldn't Mother let me run my own birthday? . . . I'd never had him here, you bet! . . . what's he always hanging 'round for? . . . why don't he go off on one of his old trips again . . . last time he was gone more'n a year . . . I was hoping he'd died! . . . what makes Mother like him so much? . . . she makes me sick! . . . I'd think she'd get sick of the old fool and tell him to get out and never come back! . . . I'd kick him out if I was big enough! . . . it's good for him he didn't bring me any birthday present or I'd smash it first chance I got! . . .

NINA: (*watching him—brooding with loving tenderness—sadly*)

No longer my baby . . . my little man . . . eleven . . . I can't believe it . . . I'm thirty-five . . . five years more . . . at forty a woman has finished living . . . life passes by her . . . she rots away in peace! . . .

(*Intensely*)

I want to rot away in peace! . . . I'm sick of the fight for happiness! . . .

(*Smiling with a wry amusement at herself*)

What ungrateful thoughts on my son's birthday! . . . my love for him has been happiness . . . how handsome he is! . . . not at all like Ned . . . when I was carrying him I was fighting to forget Ned . . . hoping he might be like Gordon . . . and he is . . . poor Ned, I've made him suffer a great deal . . . !

(*She looks over at* DARRELL—*self-mockingly*)

My lover! . . . so very rarely now, those interludes of passion . . . what has bound us together all these years? . . . love? . . . if he could only have been contented with what I was able to give him! . . . but he has always wanted more . . . yet never had the courage to insist on all or nothing . . . proud without being proud enough! . . . he has shared me for his comfort's sake with a little gratitude and a big bitterness . . . and sharing me has corrupted him! . . .

(*Then bitterly*)

No, I can't blame myself! . . . no woman can make a man happy who has no purpose in life! . . . why did he give up his career? . . . because I had made him weak? . . .

(*With resentful scorn*)

No, it was I who shamed him into taking up biology and starting the station at Antigua . . . if I hadn't he'd simply have hung around me year after year, doing nothing . . .

(*Irritatedly*)

Why does he stay so long? . . . over six months . . . I can't stand having him around me that long any more! . . . why doesn't he go back to the West Indies? . . . I always get a terrible feeling after he's been back a while that he's waiting for Sam to die! . . . or go insane! . . .

DARRELL: (*thinking—with an apathetic bitterness*)

What is she thinking? . . . we sit together in silence, thinking . . . thoughts that never know the other's thoughts . . . our love has become the intimate thinking together of thoughts that are strangers . . . our love! . . . well, whatever it is that has bound us together, it's strong! . . . I've broken with her, run away, tried to forget her . . . running away to come back each time more abject! . . . or, if she saw there was some chance I might break loose, she'd find some way to call me back . . . and I'd forget my longing for freedom, I'd come wagging my tail . . . no, guinea pigs have no tails . . . I hope my experiment has proved something! . . . Sam . . . happy and wealthy . . . and healthy! . . . I used to hope he'd break down . . . I'd watch him and read symptoms of insanity into every move he made . . . despicable? . . . certainly, but love makes one either noble or despicable! . . . he only grew healthier . . . now I've given up watching him . . . almost entirely . . . now I watch him grow fat and I laugh! . . . the huge joke has dawned on me! . . . Sam is the only normal one! . . . we lunatics! . . . Nina and I! . . . have made a sane life for him out of our madness! . . .

(*Watching* NINA—*sadly*)

Always thinking of her son . . . well, I gave him to her . . . Gordon . . . I hate that name . . . why do I continue hanging around here? . . . each time after a few months my love changes to bitterness . . . I blame Nina for the mess I've made of life . . .

NINA: (*suddenly turning on him*) When are you going back to the West Indies, Ned?

DARRELL: (*determinedly*) Soon!

GORDON: (*stops playing to listen—thinking*)

Gosh, I'm glad! . . . How soon, I wonder? . . .

NINA: (*with a trace of a sneer*) I don't see how you can afford to leave your work for such long periods. Don't you grow rusty?

DARRELL: (*looking at her meaningly*) My life work is to rust—nicely and unobtrusively! (*He smiles mockingly*).

NINA: (*sadly—thinking*)

> To rot away in peace . . . that's all he wants now, too! . . . and this is what love has done to us! . . .

DARRELL: (*bitterly*) My work was finished twelve years ago. As I believe you know, I ended it with an experiment which resulted so successfully that any further meddling with human lives would have been superfluous!

NINA: (*pityingly*) Ned!

DARRELL: (*indifferent and cynical*) But you meant my present dabbling about. You know better than to call that work. It's merely my hobby. Our backing Sam has made Marsden and me so wealthy that we're forced to take up hobbies. Marsden goes in for his old one of dashing off genteel novels, while I play at biology. Sam argued that golf would be healthier and less nonsensical for me, but you insisted on biology. And give it its due, it has kept me out in the open air and been conducive to travelling and broadening my mind. (*Then forcing a smile*) But I'm exaggerating. I really am interested, or I'd never keep financing the Station. And when I'm down there I do work hard, helping Preston. He's doing remarkable work already, and he's still in his twenties. He'll be a big man— (*His bitterness cropping up again*) at least if he takes my advice and never carries his experiments as far as human lives!

NINA: (*in a low voice*) How can you be so bitter, Ned—on Gordon's birthday?

DARRELL: (*thinking cynically*)

> She expects me to love the child she deliberately took from me and gave to another man! . . . no, thank you, Nina! . . . I've been hurt enough! . . . I'll not leave myself open there! . . .

(*Regarding his son bitterly*) Every day he gets more like Sam, doesn't he?

GORDON: (*thinking*)

He's talking about me . . . he better look out! . . .

NINA: (*resentfully*) I don't think Gordon resembles Sam at all. He reminds me a great deal of his namesake.

DARRELL: (*touched on a sore spot—with a nasty laugh—cuttingly*) Gordon Shaw? Not the slightest bit in the world! And you ought to thank God he doesn't! It's the last thing I'd want wished on a boy of mine— to be like that rah-rah hero!

GORDON: (*thinking contemptuously*)

Boy of his! . . . He hasn't got a boy! . . .

NINA: (*amused and pleased by his jealousy*)

Poor Ned! . . . isn't he silly? . . . at his age, after all we've been through, to still feel jealous . . .

DARRELL: I'd much rather have him (*Pointing to* GORDON) grow up to be an exact duplicate of the esteemed Samuel!

GORDON: (*thinking resentfully*)

He's always making fun of my father! . . . he better look out! . . .

DARRELL: (*more and more mockingly*) And what could be fairer? The good Samuel is an A one success. He has a charming wife and a darling boy, and a Park Avenue apartment and a membership in an expensive golf club. And, above all, he rests so complacently on the proud assurance that he is self-made!

NINA: (*sharply*) Ned! You ought to be ashamed! You know how grateful Sam has always been to you!

DARRELL: (*bitingly*) Would he be grateful if he knew how much I'd really done for him?

NINA: (*sternly*) Ned!

GORDON: (*suddenly jumps up and confronts* DARRELL, *his fists clenched, trembling with rage, stammers*) You—shut up—making fun of my father!

NINA: (*in dismay*) Gordon!

DARRELL: (*mockingly*) My dear boy, I wouldn't make fun of your father for the world!

GORDON: (*baffledly—his lips trembling*) You—you did, too! (*Then intensely*) I hate you!

NINA: (*shocked and indignant*) Gordon! How dare you talk like that to your Uncle Ned!

GORDON: (*rebelliously*) He's not my uncle! He's not my anything!

NINA: Not another word or you'll be punished, whether it's your birthday or not! If you can't behave better than that, I'll have to phone to all your friends they mustn't come here this afternoon, that you've been so bad you can't have a party! (*Thinking remorsefully*)

> Is this my fault? . . . I've done my best to get him to love Ned! . . . but it only makes him worse! . . . it makes him turn against me! . . . turn from me to Sam!

GORDON: (*sullenly*) I don't care! I'll tell Dad!

NINA: (*peremptorily*) Leave the room! And don't come near me again, do you hear, until you've apologized to Uncle Ned! (*Thinking angrily*)

> Dad! . . . It's always Dad with him now! . . .

DARRELL: (*boredly*) Oh, never mind, Nina!

GORDON: (*going out—mutters*) I won't 'pologize—never! (*Thinking vindictively*)

> I hate her too when she sides with him! . . . I don't care if she is my mother! . . . she has no right! . . .

(*He goes out, rear*).

DARRELL: (*irritably*) What if he does hate me? I don't blame him! He suspects what I know—that I've acted like a coward and a weakling toward him! I should have claimed him no matter what happened to other people! Whose fault is it if he hates me, and I dislike him because he loves another father? Ours! You gave him to Sam and I consented! All right! Then don't blame him for acting like Sam's son!

NINA: But he shouldn't say he hates you. (*Thinking bitterly*)

Sam's! . . . he's becoming all Sam's! . . . I'm getting to mean nothing! . . .

DARRELL: (*sardonically*) Perhaps he realizes subconsciously that I am his father, his rival in your love; but I'm not his father ostensibly, there are no taboos, so he can come right out and hate me to his heart's content! (*Bitterly*) If he realized how little you love me any more, he wouldn't bother!

NINA: (*exasperatedly*) Oh, Ned, do shut up! I can't stand hearing those same old reproaches I've heard a thousand times before! I can't bear to hear myself making the same old bitter counter-accusations. And then there'll be the same old terrible scene of hate and you'll run away—it used to be to drink and women, now it's to the Station. Or I'll send you away, and then after a time I'll call you back, because I'll have gotten so lonely again living this lonely lie of my life, with no one to speak to except Sam's business friends and their deadly wives. (*She laughs helplessly*) Or else you'll get lonely in your lie a little before I do and come back again of your own desire! And then we'll kiss and cry and love each other again!

DARRELL: (*with an ironical grimace*) Or I might cheat myself into believing I'd fallen in love with some nice girl and get myself engaged to be married again as I did once before! And then you'd be jealous again and have to find some way of getting me to break it off!

NINA: (*forlornly amused*) Yes—I suppose the thought of a wife taking you away from me would be too much—again! (*Then helplessly*) Oh, Ned, when are we ever going to learn something about each other? We act like such brainless fools—with our love. It's always so wonderful when you first come back, but you always stay too long—or I always keep you too long! You never leave before we've come to the ugly bitter stage when we blame each other! (*Then suddenly forlornly tender*) Is it possible you can still love me, Ned?

DARRELL: (*mournfully smiling*) I must, or I'd never act this fool way, would I?

NINA: (*smiling back*) And I must love you. (*Then seriously*) After all, I can never forget that Gordon is the child of your love, Ned.

DARRELL: (*sadly*) You'd better forget that, for his sake and your own. Children have sure intuitions. He feels cheated of your love—by me. So he's concentrating his affections on Sam whose love he knows is secure, and withdrawing from you.

NINA: (*frightened—angrily*) Don't be stupid, Ned! That isn't so at all! I hate you when you talk that way!

DARRELL: (*cynically*) Hate me, exactly. As he does! That's what I'm advising you to do if you want to keep his love! (*He smiles grimly*).

NINA: (*sharply*) If Gordon doesn't love you it's because you've never made the slightest attempt to be lovable to him! There's no earthly reason why he should like you, when you come right down to it, Ned! Take today, for instance. It's his birthday but you'd forgotten, or didn't care! You never even brought him a present.

DARRELL: (*with bitter sadness*) I did bring him a present. It's out in the hall. I bought him a costly delicate one so he could get full satisfaction and yet not strain himself when he smashed it, as he's smashed every present of mine in the past! And I left it out in the hall, to be given to him after I've gone because, after all, he is my son and I'd prefer he didn't smash it before my eyes! (*Trying to mock his own emotion back—with savage bitterness*) I'm selfish, you see! I don't want my son to be too happy at my expense, even on his birthday!

NINA: (*tormented by love and pity and remorse*) Ned! For God's sake! How can you torture us like that! Oh, it's too dreadful—what I have done to you! Forgive me, Ned!

DARRELL: (*his expression changing to one of pity for her—goes to her and puts his hand on her head—tenderly*) I'm sorry. (*With remorseful tenderness*)

Dreadful, what you've done, Nina? Why, you've given me the only happiness I've ever known! And no matter what I may say or do in bitterness, I'm proud—and grateful, Nina!

NINA: (*looks up at him with deep tenderness and admiration*) Dearest, it's wonderful of you to say that! (*She gets up and puts her hands on his shoulders and looks into his eyes—tenderly in a sort of pleading*) Can't we be brave enough—for you to go away—now, on this note—sure of our love—with no ugly bitterness for once?

DARRELL: (*joyfully*) Yes! I'll go—this minute if you wish!

NINA: (*playfully*) Oh, you needn't go this minute! Wait and say good-bye to Sam. He'd be terribly hurt if you didn't. (*Then seriously*) And will you promise to stay away two years—even if I call you back before then—and work this time, really work?

DARRELL: I'll try, Nina!

NINA: And then—surely come back to me!

DARRELL: (*smiling*) Surely—again!

NINA: Then good-bye, dear! (*She kisses him*).

DARRELL: Again! (*He smiles and she smiles and they kiss again*. GORDON *appears in the doorway at rear and stands for a moment in a passion of jealousy and rage and grief, watching them*).

GORDON: (*thinking with a strange tortured shame*)

>   I mustn't see her! . . . pretend I didn't see her! . . . mustn't never let her know I saw her! . . .

(*He vanishes as silently as he had come*).

NINA: (*suddenly moving away from* DARRELL, *looking around her uneasily*) Ned, did you see—? I had the queerest feeling just then that some-one—

GORDON: (*his voice sounds from the hall with a strained casualness*) Mother! Uncle Charlie's downstairs. Shall he come right up?

NINA: (*startled, her own voice straining to be casual*) Yes, dear—of course! (*Then worriedly*) His voice sounded funny. Did it to you? Do you suppose he—?

DARRELL: (*with a wry smile*) It's possible. To be on the safe side, you'd better tell him you kissed me good-bye to get rid of me! (*Then angrily*) So Marsden's here again! The damned old woman! I simply can't go him any more, Nina! Why Gordon should take such a fancy to that old sissy is beyond me!

NINA: (*suddenly struck—thinking*)

Why, he's jealous of Gordon liking Charlie! . . .

(*Immediately all affectionate pity*)

Then he must love Gordon a little! . . .

(*Letting her pity escape her*) Poor Ned! (*She makes a movement toward him*).

DARRELL: (*startled and afraid she may have guessed something he doesn't acknowledge to himself*) What? Why do you say that? (*Then rudely defensive*) Don't be silly! (*Resentfully*) You know well enough what I've always held against him! I wanted to put up all the money to back Sam when he started. I wanted to do it for Sam's sake—but especially for my child's sake. Why did Marsden absolutely insist on Sam letting him in equally? It isn't that I begrudge him the money he's made, but I know there was something queer in his mind and that he did it intentionally to spite me! (*From the hallway comes the sound of* MARSDEN'S *voice and* GORDON'S *greeting him vociferously as he lets him into the apartment. As* DARRELL *listens his expression becomes furious again. He bursts out angrily*) You're letting that old ass spoil Gordon, you fool, you! (MARSDEN *comes in from the rear, smiling, immaculately dressed as usual. He looks hardly any older except that his hair is grayer and his tall figure more stooped. His expression and the general atmosphere he gives out are more nearly like those of Act One. If not happy, he is at least living in comparative peace with himself and his environment*).

MARSDEN: (*comes straight to* NINA) Hello, Nina Cara Nina! Congratulations on your son's birthday! (*He kisses her*) He's grown so much bigger and stronger in the two months since I've seen him. (*He turns and shakes hands with* DARRELL *coldly—with a trace of a patronizing air*) Hello, Darrell. Last time I was here you were leaving for the West Indies in a week but I see you're still around.

DARRELL: (*furious—with a mocking air*) And here you are around again yourself! You're looking comfortable these days, Marsden. I hope your sister is well. It must be a great comfort, having her to take your mother's place! (*Then with a harsh laugh*) Yes, we're two bad pennies, eh, Marsden?—counterfeits—fakes—Sam's silent partners!

NINA: (*thinking irritably*)

> Ned's getting hateful again! . . . Poor Charlie! . . . I won't have him insulted! . . . he's become such a comfort . . . he understands so much . . . without my having to tell him . . .

(*Looking rebukingly at* DARRELL) Ned is sailing this week, Charlie.

MARSDEN: (*thinking triumphantly*)

> He's trying to insult me . . . I know all he means . . . but what do I care what he says . . . she's sending him away! . . . intentionally before me! . . . it means he's finished! . . .

DARRELL: (*thinking resentfully*)

> Is she trying to humiliate me before him? . . . I'll teach her! . . .

(*Then struggling with himself—remorsefully*)

> No . . . not this time . . . I promised . . . no quarrel . . . remember . . .

(*Acquiescing—with a pleasant nod to* MARSDEN) Yes, I'm going this week and I expect to be gone at least two years this time—two years of hard work.

MARSDEN: (*thinking with scornful pity*)

> His work! . . . what a pretense! . . . a scientific dilettante! . . . could anything be more pitiable? . . . poor chap! . . .

(*Perfunctorily*) Biology must be an interesting study. I wish I knew more about it.

DARRELL: (*stung yet amused by the other's tone—ironically*) Yes, so do I wish you did, Marsden! Then you might write more about life and less about dear old ladies and devilish bachelors! Why don't you write a novel about life sometime, Marsden? (*He turns his back on* MARSDEN *with a glance of repulsion and walks to the window and stares out*).

MARSDEN: (*confusedly*) Yes—decidedly—but hardly in my line— (*Thinking in anguish—picking up a magazine and turning over the pages aimlessly*)

> That . . . is . . . true! . . . he's full of poison! . . . I've never married the word to life! . . . I've been a timid bachelor of Arts, not an artist! . . . my poor pleasant books! . . . all is well! . . . is this well, the three of us? . . . Darrell has become less and less her lover . . . Nina has turned more and more to me . . . we have built up a secret life of subtle sympathies and confidences . . . she has known I have understood about her mere physical passion for Darrell . . . what woman could be expected to love Sam passionately? . . . some day she'll confide all about Darrell to me . . . now that he's finished . . . she knows that I love her without my telling . . . she even knows the sort of love it is. . . .

(*Passionately—thinking*)

> My love is finer than any she has known! . . . I do not lust for her! . . . I would be content if our marriage should be purely the placing of our ashes in the same tomb . . . our urn side by side and touching one another . . . could the others say as much, could they love so deeply? . . .

(*Then suddenly miserably self-contemptuous*)

> What! . . . platonic heroic at my age! . . . do I believe a word of that? . . . look at her beautiful eyes! . . . wouldn't I give anything in life to see them desire me? . . . and the intimacy I'm boasting about, what more does it mean than that I've been playing the dear old Charlie of her girlhood again? . . .

(*Thinking in anguish*)

> Damned coward and weakling! . . .

NINA: (*looking at him—pityingly—thinking*)

What does he always want of me? . . . me? . . . I am the only one who senses his deep hurt . . . I feel how life has wounded him . . . is that partly my fault, too? . . . I have wounded everyone . . . poor Charlie, what can I do for you? . . . if giving myself to you would bring you a moment's happiness, could I? . . . the idea used to be revolting . . . now, nothing about love seems important enough to be revolting . . . poor Charlie, he only thinks he ought to desire me! . . . dear Charlie, what a perfect lover he would make for one's old age! . . . what a perfect lover when one was past passion! . . .

(*Then with sudden scornful revulsion*)

These men make me sick! . . . I hate all three of them! . . . they disgust me! . . . the wife and mistress in me has been killed by them! . . . thank God, I am only a mother now! . . . Gordon is my little man, my only man! . . .

(*Suddenly*) I've got a job for you, Charlie—make the salad dressing for lunch. You know, the one I'm so crazy about.

MARSDEN: (*springs to his feet*) Righto! (*He puts his arm about her waist and they go out together laughingly, without a glance at* DARRELL).

DARRELL: (*thinking dully*)

I mustn't stay to lunch . . . ghost at my son's feast! . . . I better go now . . . why wait for Sam? . . . what is there to say to him I can say? . . . and there's nothing about him I want to see . . . he's as healthy as a pig . . . and as sane . . . I was afraid once his mother had lied to Nina . . . I went upstate and investigated . . . true, every word of it . . . his great-grand-father, his grandmother, his father, were all insane . . .

(*Moving uneasily*)

Stop it! . . . time to go when those thoughts come . . . sail on Saturday . . . not come here again . . . Nina will soon be fighting Sam for my son's love! . . . I'm better out of that! . . . O Christ, what a mess it all is! . . .

GORDON: (*appears in the doorway in rear. He carries a small, expensive yacht's model of a sloop with the sails set. He is in a terrific state of conflicting emotions, on the verge of tears yet stubbornly determined*)

I got to do it! . . . Gosh, it's awful . . . this boat is so pretty . . . why did it have to come from him? . . . I can get Dad to buy me another boat . . . but now I love this one . . . but he kissed Mother . . . she kissed him . . .

(*He walks up defiantly and confronts* DARRELL *who turns to him in surprise*) Hey—Darrell—did you—? (*He stops chokingly*).

DARRELL: (*immediately realizing what is coming—thinking with somber anguish*)

So this has to happen! . . . what I dreaded! . . . my fate is merciless, it seems! . . .

(*With strained kindliness*) Did what?

GORDON: (*growing hard—stammers angrily*) I found this—out in the hall. It can't be from anybody else. Is this—your present?

DARRELL: (*hard and defiant himself*) Yes.

GORDON: (*in a rage—tremblingly*) Then—here's what—I think of you! (Beginning to cry, he breaks off the mast, bowsprit, breaks the mast in two, tears the rigging off and throws the dismantled hull at DARRELL'S *feet*) There! You can keep it!

DARRELL: (*his anger overcoming him for an instant*) You—you mean little devil, you! You don't get that from me— (*He has taken a threatening step forward.* GORDON *stands white-faced, defying him.* DARRELL *pulls himself up short—then in a trembling voice of deeply wounded affection*) You shouldn't have done that, son. What difference do I make? It was never my boat. But it was your boat. You should consider the boat, not me. Don't you like boats for themselves? It was a beautiful little boat, I thought. That's why I—

GORDON: (*sobbing miserably*) It was awful pretty! I didn't want to do it! (*He kneels down and gathers up the boat into his arms again*) Honest I didn't. I love boats! But I hate you! (*This last with passionate intensity*).

DARRELL: (*dryly*) So I've observed. (*Thinking with angry anguish*)

He hurts, damn him! . . .

GORDON: No, you don't know! More'n ever now! More'n ever! (*The secret escaping him*) I saw you kissing Mother! I saw Mother, too!

DARRELL: (*startled, but immediately forcing a smile*) But I was saying good-bye. We're old friends. You know that.

GORDON: You can't fool me! This was different! (*Explosively*) It would serve you good and right—and Mother, too—if I was to tell Dad on you!

DARRELL: Why, I'm Sam's oldest friend. Don't make a little fool of yourself!

GORDON: You are not his friend. You've always been hanging around cheating him—hanging around Mother!

DARRELL: Keep still! What do you mean cheating him?

GORDON: I don't know. But I know you aren't his friend. And sometime I'm going to tell him I saw you—

DARRELL: (*with great seriousness now—deeply moved*) Listen! There are things a man of honor doesn't tell anyone—not even his mother or father. You want to be a man of honor, don't you? (*Intensely*) There are things we don't tell, you and I! (*He has put his hand around* GORDON's *shoulder impulsively*)

This is my son! ... I love him! ...

GORDON: (*thinking—terribly torn*)

Why do I like him now! ... I like him awful! ...

(*Crying*) We?—who d'you mean?—I've got honor!—more'n you!— you don't have to tell me!—I wasn't going to tell Dad anyway, honest I wasn't!—We?—what d'you mean, we?—I'm not like you! I don't want to be ever like you! (*There is the sound of a door being flung open and shut and* EVANS' *hearty voice*).

EVANS: (*from the entrance hall*) Hello, everybody!

DARRELL: (*slapping* GORDON *on the back*) Buck up, son! Here he is! Hide that boat or he'll ask questions. (GORDON *runs and hides the boat under the sofa. When* EVANS *enters,* GORDON *is entirely composed and runs to him joyfully.* EVANS *has grown stouter, his face is heavy now, he has grown executive and used to command, he automatically takes charge wherever he is. He does not look his age except that his hair has grown scanty and there is a perceptible bald spot on top. He is expensively tailored*).

EVANS: (*hugging* GORDON *to him—lovingly*) How's the old son? How's the birthday coming along?

GORDON: Fine, Dad!

EVANS: Hello, Ned! Isn't this kid of mine a whopper for his age, though!

DARRELL: (*smiling strainedly*) Yes. (*Writhing—thinking*)

> It hurts now! . . . to see my son his son! . . . I've had enough! . . . get out! . . . any excuse! . . . I can phone afterwards! . . . I'll yell out the whole business if I stay! . . .

I was just going, Sam. I've got to step around and see a fellow who lives near—biologist. (*He has gone to the door*).

EVANS: (*disappointedly*) Then you won't be here for lunch?

DARRELL: (*thinking*)

> I'll yell the truth into your ears if I stay a second longer . . . you damned lunatic! . . .

Can't stay. Sorry. This is important. I'm sailing in a few days—lots to do—see you later, Sam. So long—Gordon.

GORDON: (*as he goes out with awkward haste*) Good-bye—Uncle Ned. (*Thinking confusedly*)

> Why did I call him that when I said I never would? . . . I know . . . must be because he said he's sailing and I'm glad . . .

EVANS: So long, Ned. (*Thinking—good-naturedly superior*)

> Ned and his biology! . . . He takes his hobby pretty seriously! . . .

(*With satisfaction*)

> Well, he can afford to have hobbies now! . . . his investment with me has made him a pile. . . .

Where's Mother, son?

GORDON: Out in the kitchen with Uncle Charlie. (*Thinking*)

> I hope he never comes back! . . . why did I like him then? . . . it was only for a second . . . I didn't really . . . I never could! . . . why does he always call me Gordon as if he hated to? . . .

EVANS: (*sitting down at left*) I hope lunch is ready soon. I'm hungry as the devil, aren't you?

GORDON: (*absent-mindedly*) Yes, Dad.

EVANS: Come over here and tell me about your birthday. (GORDON *comes over.* EVANS *pulls him up on his lap*) How'd you like your presents? What'd you get from Uncle Ned?

GORDON: (*evasively*) They were all dandy. (*Suddenly*) Why was I named Gordon?

EVANS: Oh, you know all about that—all about Gordon Shaw. I've told you time and again.

GORDON: You told me once he was Mother's beau—when she was a girl.

EVANS: (*teasingly*) What do you know about beaus? You're growing up!

GORDON: Did Mother love him a lot?

EVANS: (*embarrassedly*) I guess so.

GORDON: (*thinking keenly*)

> That's why Darrell hates me being called Gordon . . . he knows Mother loved Gordon better'n she does him . . . now I know how to get back at him . . . I'll be just like Gordon was and Mother'll love me better'n him! . . .

And then that Gordon was killed, wasn't he? Am I anything like him?

EVANS: I hope you are. If when you go to college you can play football or row like Gordon did, I'll—I'll give you anything you ask for! I mean that!

GORDON: (*dreamily*) Tell me about him again, will you, Dad—about the time he was stroking the crew and the fellow who was Number Seven began to crack, and he couldn't see him but he felt him cracking somehow, and he began talking back to him all the time and sort of gave him his strength so that when the race was over and they'd won Gordon fainted and the other fellow didn't.

EVANS: (*with a fond laugh*) Why, you know it all by heart! What's the use of my telling you?

NINA: (*comes in from the rear while they are talking. She comes forward slowly—thinking resentfully*)

Does he love Sam more than he does me? ... oh, no, he can't! ... but he trusts him more! ... he confides in him more! ...

GORDON: Did you ever used to fight fellows, Dad?

EVANS: (*embarrassedly*) Oh, a little—when I had to.

GORDON: Could you lick Darrell?

NINA: (*thinking frightenedly*)

Why does he ask that? ...

EVANS: (*surprised*) Your Uncle Ned? What for? We've always been friends.

GORDON: I mean, if you weren't friends, could you?

EVANS: (*boastfully*) Oh, yes, I guess so. Ned was never as strong as I was.

NINA: (*thinking contemptuously*)

Ned is weak....

(*Then apprehensively*)

But you're getting too strong, Sam....

GORDON: But Gordon could have licked you, couldn't he?

EVANS: You bet he could!

GORDON: (*thinking*)

She must have loved Gordon better'n Dad even! ...

NINA: (*she comes forward to the chair at center, forcing a smile*) What's all this talk about fighting? That's not nice. For heaven's sake, Sam, don't encourage him—

EVANS: (*grinning*) Never mind the women, Gordon. You've got to know how to fight to get on in this world.

NINA: (*thinking pityingly*)

You poor booby! ... how brave you are now! ...

(*softly*) Perhaps you're right, dear. (*Looking around*) Has Ned gone?

GORDON: (*defiantly*) Yes—and he's not coming back—and he's sailing soon!

NINA: (*with a shudder*)

> Why does he challenge me that way? . . . and cling to Sam? . . . he must have seen Ned and me . . . he doesn't offer to come to my lap . . . he used to . . . Ned was right . . . I've got to lie to him . . . get him back . . . here . . . on my lap! . . .

(*With a sneer—to* EVANS) I'm glad Ned's gone. I was afraid he was going to be on our hands all day.

GORDON: (*eagerly, half-getting down from his father's lap*) You're glad—? (*Then cautiously thinking*)

> She's cheating . . . I saw her kiss him . . . .

NINA: Ned's getting to be an awful bore. He's so weak. He can't get started on anything unless he's pushed.

GORDON: (*moving a little nearer—searching her face—thinking*)

> She doesn't seem to like him so much . . . but I saw her kiss him! . . .

EVANS: (*surprised*) Oh, come now, Nina, aren't you being a little hard on Ned? It's true he's sort of lost his grip in a way but he's our best friend.

GORDON: (*moving away from his father again—resentfully—thinking*)

> What's Dad standing up for him to her for? . . .

NINA: (*thinking triumphantly*)

> That's right, Sam . . . just what I wanted you to say! . . .

(*Boredly*) Oh, I know he is but he gets on my nerves hanging around all the time. Without being too rude, I urged him to get back to his work, and made him promise me he wouldn't return for two years. Finally he promised—and then he became silly and sentimental and asked me to kiss him good-bye for good luck! So I kissed him to get rid of him! The silly fool!

GORDON: (*thinking—over joyed*)

> Then! . . . that's why! . . . that's why! . . . and he'll be gone two years!
> . . . oh, I'm so glad! . . .

(*He goes to her and looks up into her face with shining eyes*) Mother!

NINA: Dear! (*She takes him up on her lap and hugs him in her arms*).

GORDON: (*kisses her*) There! (*Triumphantly thinking*)

> That makes up for his kiss! . . . That takes it off her mouth . . . .

EVANS: (*grinning*) Ned must be falling for you—in his old age! (*Then sentimentally*) Poor guy! He's never married, that's the trouble. He's lonely. I know how he feels. A fellow needs a little feminine encouragement to help him keep his head up.

NINA: (*snuggling* GORDON'S *head against hers—laughing teasingly*) I think your hard-headed Dad is getting mushy and silly! What do you think, Gordon?

GORDON: (*laughing with her*) Yes, he's mushy, Mother! He's silly! (*He kisses her and whispers*) I'm going to be like Gordon Shaw, Mother! (*She hugs him fiercely to her, triumphantly happy*).

EVANS: (*grinning*) You two are getting too hard-boiled for me. (*He laughs. They all laugh happily together*).

NINA: (*suddenly overcome by a wave of conscience-stricken remorse and pity*)

> Oh, I am hard on Ned! . . . poor dear generous Ned! . . . you told me to lie to your son against you . . . for my sake . . . I'm not worthy of your love! . . . I'm low and selfish! . . . but I do love you! . . . this is the son of our love in my arms! . . . oh, Mother God, grant my prayer that some day we may tell our son the truth and he may love his father! . . .

GORDON: (*sensing her thoughts, sits up in her lap and stares into her face, while she guiltily avoids his eyes—in fear and resentment. Thinking*)

> She's thinking about that Darrell now! . . . I know! . . . she likes him too!
> . . . she can't fool me! . . . I saw her kissing! . . . she didn't think he was a silly fool then! . . . she was lying to Dad and me! . . .

(*He pushes off her lap and backs away from her*).

NINA: (*thinking frightenedly*)

He read my thoughts! . . . I mustn't even think of Ned when he's around! . . . poor Ned! . . . no, don't think of him! . . .

(*Leaning forward toward* GORDON *with her arms stretched out entreatingly but adopting a playful tone*) Why, Gordon, what's come over you? You jumped off my lap as though you'd sat on a tack! (*She forces a laugh*).

GORDON: (*his eyes on the floor—evasively*) I'm hungry. I want to see if lunch is nearly ready. (*He turns abruptly and runs out*).

EVANS: (*in a tone of superior manly understanding, kindly but laying down the law to womanly weakness*) He's sick of being babied, Nina. You forget he's getting to be a big boy. And we want him to grow up a real he-man and not an old lady like Charlie. (*Sagaciously*) That's what's made Charlie like he is, I'll bet. His mother never stopped babying him.

NINA: (*submissively—but with a look of bitter scorn at him*) Perhaps you're right, Sam.

EVANS: (*confidently*) I know I am!

NINA: (*thinking with a look of intense hatred*)

Oh, Mother God, grant that I may some day tell this fool the truth! . . .

CURTAIN

ACT EIGHT

SCENE: *Late afternoon in late June, ten years later—the afterdeck of the* EVANS' *motor cruiser anchored in the lane of yachts near the finish line at Poughkeepsie. The bow and amidship of the cruiser are off right, pointed upstream. The portside rail is in the rear, the curve of the stern at left, the rear of the cabin with broad windows and a door is at right. Two wicker chairs are at left and a chaise longue at right. A wicker table with another chair is at center. The afterdeck is in cool shade, contrasted with the soft golden haze of late afternoon sunlight that glows on the river.*

NINA *is sitting by the table at center,* DARRELL *in the chair farthest left,* MARSDEN *in the chaise longue at right.* EVANS *is leaning over the rail directly back of* NINA, *looking up the river through a pair of binoculars.* MADELINE ARNOLD *is standing by his side.*

NINA'S *hair has turned completely white. She is desperately trying to conceal the obvious inroads of time by an over-emphasis on makeup that defeats its end by drawing attention to what it would conceal. Her face is thin, her cheeks taut, her mouth drawn with forced smiling. There is little left of her face's charm except her eyes which now seem larger and more deeply mysterious than ever. But she has kept her beautiful figure. It has the tragic effect of making her face seem older and more worn-out by contrast. Her general manner recalls instantly the* NINA *of Act Four, neurotic, passionately embittered and torn. She is dressed in a white yachting costume.*

DARRELL *seems to have "thrown back" to the young doctor we had seen at the house of* NINA'S *father in Act Two. He has again the air of the cool, detached scientist regarding himself and the people around him as interesting phenomena. In appearance, he is once more sharply defined, his face and body have grown lean and well-conditioned, the puffiness and jowls of the previous Act are gone. His skin is tanned almost black by his years in the tropics. His thick hair is iron-gray. He wears flannel pants, a blue coat, white buckskin shoes. He looks his fifty-one years, perhaps, but not a day more.* MARSDEN *has aged greatly. The stoop of his tall figure is accentuated, his hair has grown whitish. He is an older image of the* MARSDEN *of Act Five, who was so prostrated by his mother's death. Now it is his sister's death two months before that has plunged him into despair. His present grief, however, is more resigned to its fate than the old. He is dressed immaculately in black, as in Act Five.*

EVANS *is simply* EVANS, *his type logically developed by ten years of continued success and accumulating wealth, jovial and simple and good-natured as ever, but increasingly stubborn and self-opinionated. He has grown very stout. His jowly broad face has a heavy, flushed, apoplectic look. His head has grown quite bald on top. He is wearing a yachting cap, blue yachting coat, white flannel pants, buckskin shoes.*

MADELINE ARNOLD *is a pretty girl of nineteen, with dark hair and eyes. Her skin is deeply tanned, her figure tall and athletic, reminding one of* NINA'S *when we first saw her. Her personality is direct and frank. She gives the impression of a person who always knows exactly what she is after and generally gets it, but is also generous and a good loser, a good sport who is popular with her own sex as well as sought after by men. She is dressed in a bright-colored sport costume.*

EVANS: (*nervous and excited—on pins and needles—lowering his binoculars impatiently*) Can't see anything up there! There's a damned haze on the river! (*Handing the binoculars to* MADELINE) Here, Madeline. You've got young eyes.

MADELINE: (*eagerly*) Thank you. (*She looks up the river through the glasses*).

NINA: (*thinking—bitterly*)

> Young eyes! ... they look into Gordon's eyes! ... he sees love in her young eyes! ... mine are old now! ...

EVANS: (*pulling out his watch*) Soon be time for the start. (*Comes forward—exasperatedly*) Of course, the damned radio has to pick out this time to go dead! Brand new one I had installed especially for this race, too! Just my luck! (*Coming to* NINA *and putting his hand on her shoulder*) Gosh, I'll bet Gordon's some keyed-up right at this moment, Nina!

MADELINE: (*without lowering the glasses*) Poor kid! I'll bet he is!

NINA: (*thinking with intense bitterness*)

> That tone in her voice! ... her love already possesses him! ... my son! ...

(*Vindictively*)

> But she won't! ... as long as I live! ...

(*Flatly*) Yes, he must be nervous.

EVANS: (*taking his hand away, sharply*) I didn't mean nervous. He doesn't know what it is to have nerves. Nothing's ever got him rattled yet. (*This last with a resentful look down at her as he moves back to the rail*).

MADELINE: (*with the calm confidence of one who knows*) Yes, you can bank on Gordon never losing his nerve.

NINA: (*coldly*) I'm quite aware my son isn't a weakling— (*Meaningly, with a glance at* MADELINE) even though he does do weak things sometimes.

MADELINE: (*without lowering the glasses from her eyes—thinking good-naturedly*)

> Ouch! ... that was meant for me! ...

(*Then hurt*)

> Why does she dislike me so? ... I've done my best, for Gordon's sake, to be nice to her. ...

EVANS: (*looking back at* NINA *resentfully—thinking*)

> Another nasty crack at Madeline! ... Nina's certainly become the prize bum sport! ... I thought once her change of life was over she'd be ashamed of her crazy jealousy ... instead of that it's got worse ... but I'm not going to let her come between Gordon and Madeline ... he loves her and she loves him ... and her folks have got money and position, too ... and I like her a lot ... and, by God, I'm going to see to it their marriage goes through on schedule, no matter how much Nina kicks up! ...

DARRELL: (*keenly observant—thinking*)

> Nina hates this young lady . . . of course! . . . Gordon's girl . . . she'll
> smash their engagement if she can . . . as she did mine once . . . once!
> . . . thank God my slavery is over! . . . how did she know I was back in
> town? . . . I wasn't going to see her again . . . but her invitation was so
> imploring . . . my duty to Gordon, she wrote . . . what duty? . . . pretty
> late in the day! . . . that's better left dead, too! . . .

EVANS: (*looking at his watch again*) They ought to be lined up at the
start any minute now. (*Pounding his fist on the rail—letting his pent-up
feelings explode*) Come on, Gordon!

NINA: (*startled—with nervous irritation*) Sam! I told you I have a splitting
headache! (*Thinking intensely*)

> You vulgar boor! . . . Gordon's engagement to her is all your fault! . . .

EVANS: (*Resentfully*) I'm sorry. Why don't you take some aspirin?
(*Thinking irritably*)

> Nina in the dumps! . . . Charlie in mourning! . . . what a pair of killjoys!
> . . . I wanted to bring Gordon and his friends on board to celebrate . . .
> no chance! . . . have to take Madeline . . . stage a party in New York . . .
> leave this outfit flat . . . Nina'll be sore as the devil but she'll have to like
> it . . .

DARRELL: (*examining* NINA *critically—thinking*)

> She's gotten into a fine neurotic state . . . reminds me of when I first knew
> her . . .

(*Then exultantly*)

> Thank God, I can watch her objectively again . . . these last three years
> away have finally done it . . . complete cure! . . .

(*Then remorsefully*)

> Poor Nina! . . . we're all deserting her . . .

(*Then glancing at* MARSDEN —*with a trace of a sneer*)

> Even Marsden seems to have left her for the dead! . . .

MARSDEN: (*vaguely irritated—thinking*)

> What am I doing here? . . . what do I care about this stupid race? . . . why did I let Nina bully me into coming? . . . I ought to be alone . . . with my memories of dear Jane . . . it will be two months ago Saturday she died . . .

(*His lips tremble, tears come to his eyes*)

MADELINE: (*with an impatient sigh, lowering the glasses*) It's no use, Mr. Evans, I can't see a thing.

EVANS: (*with angry disgust*) If only that damned radio was working!

NINA: (*exasperatedly*) For heaven's sake, stop swearing so much!

EVANS: (*hurt—indignantly*) What about it if I am excited? Seems to me you could show a little more interest without it hurting you, when it's Gordon's last race, his last appearance on a varsity! (*He turns away from her*).

MADELINE (*thinking*)

> He's right . . . she's acting rotten . . . if I were Gordon's mother, I certainly wouldn't . . .

EVANS: (*turning back to* NINA—*resentfully*) You used to cheer loud enough for Gordon Shaw! And our Gordon's got him beat a mile, as an oarsman, at least! (*Turning to* DARRELL) And that isn't father stuff either, Ned! All the experts say so!

DARRELL: (*cynically*) Oh, come on, Sam! Surely no one could ever touch Shaw in anything! (*He glances at* NINA *with a sneer. Immediately angry at himself*)

> What an idiot! . . . that popped out of me! . . . old habit! . . . I haven't loved her in years! . . .

NINA: (*thinking indifferently*)

> Ned still feels jealous . . . that no longer pleases me . . . I don't feel anything . . . except that I must get him to help me. . . .

(*She turns to* DARRELL *bitterly*) Sam said "our" Gordon. He means his. Gordon's become so like Sam, Ned, you won't recognize him!

MADELINE: (*thinking indignantly*)

> She's crazy! . . . he's nothing like his father! . . . he's so strong and handsome! . . .

EVANS: (*good-naturedly, with a trace of pride*) You flatter me, Nina. I wish I thought that. But he isn't a bit like me, luckily for him. He's a dead ringer for Gordon Shaw at his best.

MADELINE: (*thinking*)

> Shaw . . . I've seen his picture in the gym . . . my Gordon is better looking . . . he once told me Shaw was an old beau of his mother's . . . they say she was beautiful once . . .

NINA: (*shaking her head—scornfully*) Don't be modest, Sam. Gordon *is* you. He may be a fine athlete like Gordon Shaw, because you've held that out to him as your ideal, but there the resemblance ceases. He isn't really like him at all, not the slightest bit!

EVANS: (*restraining his anger with difficulty—thinking*)

> I'm getting sick of this! . . . she's carrying her jealous grouch too far! . . .

(*Suddenly exploding, pounds his fist on the rail*) Damn it, Nina, if you had any feeling you couldn't—right at the moment when he's probably getting into the shell— (*He stops, trying to control himself, panting, his face red*).

NINA: (*staring at him with repulsion—with cool disdain*) I didn't say anything so dire, did I—merely that Gordon resembles you in character. (*With malice*) Don't get so excited. It's bad for your high blood pressure. Ask Ned if it isn't. (*Intensely—thinking*)

> If he'd only die! . . .

(*Thinking—immediately*)

> Oh, I don't mean that . . . I mustn't . . .

DARRELL: (*thinking keenly*)

> There's a death wish . . . things have gone pretty far . . . Sam does look as if he might have a bad pressure . . . what hope that would have given me at one time! . . . no more, thank God! . . .

(*In a joking tone*) Oh, I guess Sam's all right, Nina.

EVANS: (*gruffly*) I never felt better. (*He jerks out his watch again*) Time for the start. Come on in the cabin, Ned, and shoot a drink. We'll see if McCabe's getting the damned radio fixed. (*Passing by* MARSDEN *he claps him on the shoulder exasperatedly*) Come on, Charlie! Snap out of it!

MARSDEN: (*startled out of his trance—bewilderedly*) Eh?—what is it?—are they coming?

EVANS: (*recovering his good nature—with a grin, taking his arm*) You're coming to shoot a drink. You need about ten, I think, to get you in the right spirit to see the finish! (*To* DARRELL *who has gotten up but is still standing by his chair*) Come on, Ned.

NINA: (*quickly*) No, leave Ned with me. I want to talk to him. Take Madeline—and Charlie.

MARSDEN: (*looking at her appealingly*) But I'm perfectly contented sitting— (*Then after a look in her eyes—thinking*)

She wants to be alone with Darrell . . . all right . . . doesn't matter now . . . their love is dead . . . but there's still some secret between them she's never told me . . . never mind . . . she'll tell me sometime . . . I'm all she will have left . . . soon . . . .

(*Then stricken with guilt*)

Poor dear Jane! . . . how can I think of anyone but you! . . . God, I'm contemptible! . . . I'll get drunk with that fool! . . . that's all I'm good for! . . .

MADELINE: (*thinking resentfully*)

She takes a fine do-this-little-girl tone toward me! . . . I'll give in to her now . . . but once I'm married! . . .

EVANS: Come on then, Madeline. We'll give you a small one. (*Impatiently*) Charlie! Head up!

MARSDEN: (*with hectic joviality*) I hope it's strong poison!

EVANS: (*laughing*) That's the spirit! We'll make a sport out of you yet!

MADELINE: (*laughing, goes and takes* MARSDEN'S *arm*) I'll see you get home safe, Mr. Marsden! (*They go into the cabin,* EVANS *following them.* NINA *and* DARRELL *turn and look at each other wonderingly, inquisitively, for a long moment.* DARRELL *remains standing and seems to be a little uneasy*).

DARRELL: (*thinking with melancholy interest*)

And now? . . . what? . . . I can look into her eyes . . . strange eyes that will never grow old . . . without desire or jealousy or bitterness . . . was she ever my mistress? . . . can she be the mother of my child? . . . is there such a person as my son? . . . I can't think of these things as real any more . . . they must have happened in another life . . . .

NINA: (*thinking sadly*)

My old lover . . . how well and young he looks . . . now we no longer love each other at all . . . our account with God the Father is settled . . . afternoons of happiness paid for with years of pain . . . love, passion, ecstasy . . . in what a far-off life were they alive! . . . the only living life is in the past and future . . . the present is an interlude . . . strange interlude in which we call on past and future to bear witness we are living! . . .

(*With a sad smile*) Sit down, Ned. When I heard you were back I wrote you because I need a friend. It has been so long since we loved each other we can now be friends again. Don't you feel that?

DARRELL: (*gratefully*) Yes. I do. (*He sits down in one of the chairs at left, drawing it up closer to her. Thinking cautiously*)

I want to be her friend . . . but I will never . . .

NINA: (*thinking cautiously*)

I must keep very cool and sensible or he won't help me . . . .

(*With a friendly smile*) I haven't seen you look so young and handsome since I first knew you. Tell me your secret. (*Bitterly*) I need it! I'm old! Look at me! And I was actually looking forward to being old! I thought it would mean peace. I've been sadly disillusioned! (*Then forcing a smile*) So tell me what fountain of youth you've found.

DARRELL: (*proudly*) That's easy. Work! I've become as interested in biology as I once was in medicine. And not selfishly interested, that's the difference. There's no chance of my becoming a famous biologist and I know it. I'm very much a worker in the ranks. But our Station is a "huge success," as Sam would say. We've made some damned important discoveries. I say "we." I really mean Preston. You may remember I used to write you about him with enthusiasm. He's justified it. He *is* making his name world-famous. He's what I might have been—I did have the brains, Nina!—if I'd had more guts and less vanity, if I'd hewn to the line! (*Then forcing a smile*) But I'm not lamenting. I've found myself in helping him. In that way I feel I've paid my debt—that his work is partly my work. And he acknowledges it. He possesses the rare virtue of gratitude. (*With proud affection*) He's a fine boy, Nina! I suppose I should say man now he's in his thirties.

NINA: (*thinking with bitter sorrow*)

> So, Ned . . . you remember our love . . . with bitterness! . . . as a stupid mistake! . . . the proof of a gutless vanity that ruined your career! . . . oh! . . .

(*Then controlling herself—thinking cynically*)

> Well, after all, how do I remember our love? . . . with no emotion at all, not even bitterness! . . .

(*Then with sudden alarm*)

> He's forgotten Gordon for this Preston! . . .

(*Thinking desperately*)

> I must make him remember Gordon is his child or I can never persuade him to help me! . . .

(*Reproachfully*) So you have found a son while I was losing mine—who is yours, too!

DARRELL: (*struck by this—impersonally interested*) That's never occurred to me but now I think of it— (*Smiling*) Yes, perhaps unconsciously

Preston is a compensating substitute. Well, it's done both of us good and hasn't harmed anyone.

NINA: (*with bitter emphasis*) Except your real son—and me—but we don't count, I suppose!

DARRELL: (*coolly*) Harmed Gordon? How? He's all right, isn't he? (*With a sneer*) I should say from all I've been hearing that he was your ideal of college hero—like his never-to-be-forgotten namesake!

NINA: (*thinking resentfully*)

He's sneering at his own son! . . .

(*Then trying to be calculating*)

But I mustn't get angry . . . I must make him help me . . . .

(*Speaking with gentle reproach*) And am I the ideal of a happy mother, Ned?

DARRELL: (*immediately moved by pity and ashamed of himself*) Forgive me, Nina. I haven't quite buried all my bitterness, I'm afraid. (*Gently*) I'm sorry you're unhappy, Nina.

NINA: (*thinking with satisfaction*)

He means that . . . he still does care a little . . . if only it's enough to . . . !

(*Speaking sadly*) I've lost my son, Ned! Sam has made him all his. And it was done so gradually that, although I realized what was happening, there was never any way I could interfere. What Sam advised seemed always the best thing for Gordon's future. And it was always what Gordon himself wanted, to escape from me to boarding school and then to college, to become Sam's athletic hero—

DARRELL: (*impatiently*) Oh, come now, Nina, you know you've always longed for him to be like Gordon Shaw!

NINA: (*bursting out in spite of herself—violently*) He's not like Gordon! He's forgotten me for that—! (*Trying to be more reasonable*) What do I care whether he's an athlete or not? It's such nonsense, all this fuss! I'm not the slightest bit interested in this race today, for example! I wouldn't care if he came in last! (*Stopping herself—thinking fright-enedly*)

Oh, if he should ever guess I said that! . . .

DARRELL: (*thinking keenly*)

Hello! . . . she said that as if she'd like to see him come last! . . . why? . . .

(*Then vindictively*)

Well, so would I! . . . it's time these Gordons took a good licking from life! . . .

MADELINE: (*suddenly appears in the door from the cabin, her face flushed with excitement*) They're off! Mr. Evans is getting something—it's terribly faint but—Navy and Washington are leading—Gordon's third! (*She disappears back in the cabin*).

NINA: (*looking after her with hatred*)

Her Gordon! . . . she is so sure! . . . how I've come to detest her pretty face! . . .

DARRELL: (*thinking with a sneer*)

"Gordon's third"! . . . you might think there was no one else pulling the shell! . . . what idiots women make of themselves about these Gordons! . . . she's pretty, that Madeline! . . . she's got a figure like Nina's when I first loved her . . . those afternoons . . . age is beginning to tell on Nina's face . . . but she's kept her wonderful body! . . .

(*With a trace of malice—dryly*) There's a young lady who seems to care a lot whether Gordon comes in last or not!

NINA: (*trying to be sorrowful and appealing*) Yes. Gordon is hers now, Ned. (*But she cannot bear this thought—vindictively*) That is, they're engaged. But, of course, that doesn't necessarily mean— Can you imagine him throwing himself away on a little fool like that? I simply can't believe he really loves her! Why, she's hardly even pretty and she's deadly stupid. I thought he was only flirting with her—or merely indulging in a passing physical affair. (*She winces*) At his age, one has to expect—even a mother must face nature. But for Gordon to take her seriously, and propose marriage—it's too idiotic for words!

DARRELL: (*thinking cynically*)

Oh, so you'll compromise on his sleeping with her . . . if you have to . . . but she must have no real claim to dispute your ownership, eh? . . . you'd like to make her the same sort of convenient slave for him that I was for you! . . .

(*Resentfully*) I can't agree with you. I find her quite charming. It seems to me if I were in Gordon's shoes I'd do exactly what he has done. (*In confusion—thinking bitterly*)

In Gordon's shoes! . . . I always was in Gordon Shaw's shoes! . . . and why am I taking this young Gordon's part? . . . what is he to me, for God's sake? . . .

NINA: (*unheedingly*) If he marries her, it means he'll forget me! He'll forget me as completely as Sam forgot his mother! She'll keep him away from me! Oh, I know what wives can do! She'll use her body until she persuades him to forget me! My son, Ned! And your son, too! (*She suddenly gets up and goes to him and takes one of his hands in both of hers*) The son of our old love, Ned!

DARRELL: (*thinking with a strange shudder of mingled attraction and fear as she touches him*)

Our love . . . old love . . . old touch of her flesh . . . we're old . . . it's silly and indecent . . . does she think she still can own me? . . .

NINA: (*in the tone a mother takes in speaking to her husband about their boy*) You'll have to give Gordon a good talking to, Ned.

DARRELL: (*still more disturbed—thinking*)

Old . . . but she's kept her wonderful body . . . how many years since? . . . she has the same strange influence over me . . . touch of her flesh . . . it's dangerous . . . bosh, I'm only humoring her as a friend . . . as her doctor . . . and why shouldn't I have a talk with Gordon? . . . a father owes something to his son . . . he ought to advise him . . . .

(*Then alarmed*)

But I was never going to meddle again . . .

(*Sternly*) I swore I'd never again meddle with human lives, Nina!

NINA: (*unheedingly*) You must keep him from ruining his life.

DARRELL: (*doggedly—struggling with himself*) I won't touch a life that has more than one cell! (*Harshly*) And I wouldn't help you in this, anyway! You've got to give up owning people, meddling in their lives as if you were God and had created them!

NINA: (*strangely forlorn*) I don't know what you mean, Ned. Gordon is my son, isn't he?

DARRELL: (*with a sudden strange violence*) And mine! Mine, too! (*He stops himself. Thinking*)

Shut up, you fool! . . . is that the way to humor her? . . .

NINA: (*with strange quiet*) I think I still love you a little, Ned.

DARRELL: (*in her tone*) And I still love you a little, Nina. (*Then sternly*) But I will not meddle in your life again! (*With a harsh laugh*) And you've meddled enough with human love, old lady! Your time for that is over! I'll send you a couple of million cells you can torture without harming yourself! (*Regaining control—shamefacedly*) Nina! Please forgive me!

NINA: (*starts as if out of a dream—anxiously*) What were you saying, Ned? (*She lets go of his hand and goes back to her chair*).

DARRELL: (*dully*) Nothing.

NINA: (*strangely*) We were talking about Sam, weren't we? How do you think he looks?

DARRELL: (*confusedly casual*) Fine. A bit too fat, of course. He looks as though his blood pressure might be higher than it ought to be. But that's not unusual in persons of his build and age. It's nothing to hope—I meant, to worry over! (*Then violently*) God damn it, why did you make me say hope?

NINA: (*calmly*) It may have been in your mind, too, mayn't it?

DARRELL: No! I've nothing against Sam. I've always been his best friend. He owes his happiness to me.

NINA: (*strangely*) There are so many curious reasons we dare not think about for thinking things!

DARRELL: (*rudely*) Thinking doesn't matter a damn! Life is something in one cell that doesn't need to think!

NINA: (*strangely*) I know! God the Mother!

DARRELL: (*excitedly*) And all the rest is gutless egotism! But to hell with it! What I started to say was, what possible reason could I have for hoping for Sam's death?

NINA: (*strangely*) We're always desiring death for ourselves or others, aren't we—while we while away our lives with the old surface ritual of coveting our neighbor's ass?

DARRELL: (*frightenedly*) You're talking like the old Nina now—when I first loved you. Please don't! It isn't decent—at our age! (*thinking in terror*)

> The old Nina! . . . am I the old Ned? . . . then that means? . . . but we must not meddle in each other's lives again! . . .

NINA: (*strangely*) I am the old Nina! And this time I will not let my Gordon go from me forever!

EVANS: (*appears in the doorway of the cabin—excited and irritated*) Madeline's listening in now. It went dead on me. (*Raising the binoculars as he goes to the rail, he looks up the river*) Last I got, Gordon third, Navy and Washington leading. They're the ones to fear, he said—Navy especially. (*Putting down the glasses—with a groan*) Damned haze! My eyes are getting old. (*Then suddenly with a grin*) You ought to see Charlie! He started throwing Scotch into him as if he were drinking against time. I had to take the bottle away from him. It's hit him an awful wallop. (*Then looking from one to the other—resentfully*) What's the matter with you two? There's a race going on, don't you know it? And you sit like dead clams!

DARRELL: (*placatingly*) I thought someone'd better stay out here and let you know when they get in sight.

EVANS: (*relieved*) Oh, sure, that's right! Here, take the glasses. You always had good eyes. (DARRELL *gets up and takes the glasses and goes to the rail and begins adjusting them*).

DARRELL: Which crew was it you said Gordon feared the most?

EVANS: (*has gone back to the cabin doorway*) Navy. (*Then proudly*) Oh, he'll beat them! But it'll be damn close. I'll see if Madeline's getting— (*He goes back in the cabin*).

DARRELL: (*looking up the river—with vindictive bitterness—thinking*)

Come on, Navy! . . .

NINA: (*thinking bitterly*)

Madeline's Gordon! . . . Sam's Gordon! . . . the thanks I get for saving Sam at the sacrifice of my own happiness! . . . I won't have it! . . . what do I care what happens to Sam now? . . . I hate him! . . . I'll tell him Gordon isn't his child! . . . and threaten to tell Gordon too, unless! . . . he'll be in deadly fear of that! . . . he'll soon find some excuse to break their engagement! . . . he can! . . . he has the strangest influence over Gordon! . . . but Ned must back me up or Sam won't believe me! . . . Ned must tell him too! . . . but will Ned? . . . he'll be afraid of the insanity! . . . I must make him believe Sam's in no danger . . .

(*Intensely*) Listen, Ned, I'm absolutely sure, from things she wrote me before she died, that Sam's mother must have been deliberately lying to me about the insanity that time. She was jealous because Sam loved me and she simply wanted to be revenged, I'm sure.

DARRELL: (*without lowering glasses—dryly*) No. She told you the truth. I never mentioned it, but I went up there once and made a thorough investigation of his family.

NINA: (*with resentful disappointment*) Oh—I suppose you wanted to make sure so you could hope he'd go insane?

DARRELL: (*simply*) I needed to be able to hope that, then. I loved you horribly at that time, Nina—horribly!

NINA: (*putting her hands on his arm*) And you don't—any more, Ned? (*Thinking intensely*)

Oh, I must make him love me again . . . enough to make him tell Sam! . . .

DARRELL: (*thinking strangely—struggling with himself*)

She'd like to own me again . . . I wish she wouldn't touch me . . . what is this tie of old happiness between our flesh? . . .

(*Harshly—weakly struggling to shake off her hands, without lowering the glasses*) I won't meddle again with human lives, I told you!

NINA: (*unheeding, clinging to him*) And I loved you horribly! I still do love you, Ned! I used to hope he'd go insane myself because I loved you so! But look at Sam! He's sane as a pig! There's absolutely no danger now!

DARRELL: (*thinking—alarmed*)

What is she after now—what does she want me for? . . .

(*Stiffly*) I'm no longer a doctor but I should say he's a healthy miss of Nature's. It's a thousand to one against it at this late day.

NINA: (*with sudden fierce intensity*) Then it's time to tell him the truth, isn't it? We've suffered all our lives for his sake! We've made him rich and happy! It's time he gave us back our son!

DARRELL: (*thinking*)

Aha . . . so that's it! . . . tell Sam the truth? . . . at last! . . . by God, I'd like to tell him, at that! . . .

(*With a sneer*) Our son? You mean yours, my dear! Kindly count me out of any further meddling with—

NINA: (*unruffledly—obsessed*) But Sam won't believe me if I'm the only one to tell him! He'll think I'm lying for spite, that it's only my crazy jealousy! He'll ask you! You've got to tell him too, Ned!

DARRELL: (thinking)

I'd like to see his face when I told him his famous oarsman isn't his son but mine! . . . that might pay me back a little for all he's taken from me! . . .

(*Harshly*) I've stopped meddling in Sam's life, I tell you!

NINA: (*insistently*) Think of what Sam has made us go through, of how he's made us suffer! You've got to tell him! You still love me a little, don't you, Ned? You must when you remember the happiness we've known in each other's arms! You were the only happiness I've ever known in life!

DARRELL: (*struggling weakly—thinking*)

> She lies! ... there was her old lover, Gordon! ... he was always first! ... then her son, Gordon! ...

(*With desperate rancor—thinking*)

> Come on, Navy! ... beat her Gordons for me! ...

NINA: (*intensely*) Oh, if I'd only gone away with you that time when you came back from Europe! How happy we would have been, dear! How our boy would have loved you—if it hadn't been for Sam!

DARRELL: (*thinking—weakly*)

> Yes, if it hadn't been for Sam I would have been happy! ... I would have been the world's greatest neurologist! ... my boy would have loved me and I'd have loved him! ...

NINA: (*with a crowning intensity to break down his last resistance*) You must tell him, Ned! For my sake! Because I love you! Because you remember our afternoons—our mad happiness! Because you love me!

DARRELL: (*beaten—dazedly*) Yes—what must I do?—meddle again? (*The noise of* MADELINE'S *excited voice cheering and clapping her hands, of* MARSDEN'S *voice yelling drunkenly, of* EVANS', *all shouting "Gordon! Gordon! Come on, Gordon!" comes from the cabin.* MARSDEN *appears swaying in the cabin doorway yelling "Gordon!" He is hectically tipsy.* DARRELL *gives a violent shudder as if he were coming out of a nightmare and pushes* NINA *away from him*).

DARRELL: (*thinking—dazedly still, but in a tone of relief*)

> Marsden again! ... thank God! ... he's saved me! ... from her! ... and her Gordons! ...

(*Turning on her triumphantly*) No, Nina—sorry—but I can't help you. I told you I'd never meddle again with human lives! (*More and more confidently*) Besides, I'm quite sure Gordon isn't my son, if the real deep core of the truth were known! I was only a body to you. Your first Gordon used to come back to life. I was never more to you than a substitute for your dead lover! Gordon is really Gordon's son! So you see I'd be telling Sam a lie if I boasted that I— And I'm a man of honor! I've proved that, at least! (*He raises his glasses and looks up the river—thinking exultantly*)

> I'm free! . . . I've beaten her at last! . . . now come on, Navy! . . . you've got to beat her Gordons for me! . . .

NINA: (*after staring at him for a moment—walking away from him—thinking with a dull fatalism*)

> I've lost him . . . he'll never tell Sam now . . . is what he said right? . . . is Gordon Gordon's? . . . oh, I hope so! . . . oh, dear, dead Gordon, help me to get back your son! . . . I must find some way. . . .

(*She sits down again*).

MARSDEN: (*who has been staring at them with a foolish grin*) Hello, you two! Why do you look so guilty? You don't love each other any more! It's all nonsense! I don't feel the slightest twinge of jealousy. That's proof enough, isn't it? (*Then blandly apologetic*) Pardon me if I sound a bit pipped—a good bit! Sam said ten and then took the bottle away when I'd had only five! But it's enough! I've forgotten sorrow! There's nothing in life worth grieving about, I assure you, Nina! And I've gotten interested in this race now. (*He sings raucously*) "Oh, we'll row, row, row, right down the river! And we'll row, row, row—" Remember that old tune—when you were a little girl, Nina? Oh, I'm forgetting Sam said to tell you Gordon was on even terms with the leaders! A gallant spurt did it! Nip and tuck now! I don't care who wins—as long as it isn't Gordon! I don't like him since he's grown up! He thinks I'm an old woman! (*Sings*) "Row, row, row." The field against Gordon!

DARRELL: (*hectically*) Right! (*He looks through the glasses—excitedly*) I see a flashing in the water way up there! Must be their oars! They're coming! I'll tell Sam! (*He hurries into the cabin*).

NINA: (*thinking dully*)

> He'll tell Sam . . . no, he doesn't mean that . . . I must find some other way . . .

MARSDEN: (*walks a bit uncertainly to* NINA's *chair*) Gordon really should get beaten today—for the good of his soul, Nina. That Madeline is pretty, isn't she? These Gordons are too infernally lucky—while we others— (*He almost starts to blubber—angrily*) we others have got to beat him today! (*He slumps clumsily down to a sitting position on the deck by her chair and takes her hand and pats it*) There, there, Nina Cara Nina! Don't worry your pretty head! It will all come out all right! We'll only have a little while longer to wait and then you and I'll be quietly married! (*Thinking frightenedly*)

> The devil! . . . what am I saying? . . . I'm drunk! . . . all right, all the better! . . . I've wanted all my life to tell her! . . .

Of course, I realize you've got a husband at present but, never mind, I can wait. I've waited a lifetime already; but for a long while now I've had a keen psychic intuition that I wasn't born to die before— (EVANS *and* MADELINE *and* DARRELL *come rushing out of the cabin. They all have binoculars. They run to the rail and train their glasses up the river*).

MADELINE: (*excitedly*) I see them! (*Grabbing his arm and pointing*) Look, Mr. Evans—there—don't you see?

EVANS: (*excitedly*) No—not yet— Yes! Now I see them! (*Pounding on the rail*) Come on, Gordon boy!

MADELINE: Come on, Gordon! (*The whistles and sirens from the yachts up the river begin to be heard. This grows momentarily louder as one after another other yachts join in the chorus as the crews approach nearer and nearer until toward the close of the scene there is a perfect pandemonium of sound*).

NINA: (*with bitter hatred—thinking*)

How I hate her! . . .

(*Then suddenly with a deadly calculation—thinking*)

Why not tell her? . . . as Sam's mother told me? . . . of the insanity? . . . she thinks Gordon is Sam's son.

(*With a deadly smile of triumph*)

That will be poetic justice! . . . that will solve everything! . . . she won't marry him! . . . he will turn to me for comfort! . . . but I must plan it out carefully! . . .

MARSDEN: (*driven on—extravagantly*) Listen, Nina! After we're married I'm going to write a novel—my first real novel! All the twenty odd books I've written have been long-winded fairy tales for grown-ups— about dear old ladies and witty, cynical bachelors and quaint characters with dialects, and married folk who always admire and respect each other, and lovers who avoid love in hushed whispers! That's what I've been, Nina—a hush-hush whisperer of lies! Now I'm going to give an honest healthy yell—turn on the sun into the shadows of lies—shout "This is life and this is sex, and here are passion and hatred and regret and joy and pain and ecstasy, and these are men and women and sons and daughters whose hearts are weak and strong, whose blood is blood and not a soothing syrup!" Oh, I can do it, Nina! I can write the truth! I've seen it in you, your father, my mother, sister, Gordon, Sam, Darrell and myself. I'll write the book of us! But here I am talking while my last chapters are in the making—right here and now— (*Hurriedly*) You'll excuse me, won't you, Nina? I must watch—my duty as an artist! (*He scrambles to his feet and peers about him with a hectic eagerness.* NINA *pays no attention to him*).

EVANS: (*exasperatedly, taking down his glasses*) You can't tell a damn thing—which is which or who's ahead—I'm going to listen in again. (*He hurries into the cabin*).

NINA: (*with a smile of cruel triumph—thinking*)

> I can tell her ... confidentially ... I can pretend I'm forced to tell her ... as Sam's mother did with me ... because I feel it's due to her happiness and Gordon's ... it will explain my objection to the engagement ... oh, it can't help succeeding ... my Gordon will come back! ... I'll see he never gets away again!

(*She calls*) Madeline!

MARSDEN: (*thinking*)

> Why is she calling Madeline? ... I must watch all this carefully! ...

EVANS: (*comes rushing out in wild alarm*) Bad news! Navy has drawn ahead—half a length—looks like Navy's race, he said— (*Then violently*) But what does he know, that damn fool announcer—some poor boob—!

MADELINE: (*excitedly*) He doesn't know Gordon! He s always best when he's pushed to the limit!

NINA: (*she calls more sharply*) Madeline!

DARRELL: (*turns around to stare at her—thinking*)

> Why is she calling Madeline? ... she's bound she'll meddle in their lives ... I've got to watch her ... well, let's see ....

(*He touches* MADELINE *on the shoulder*) Mrs. Evans is calling you, Miss Arnold.

MADELINE: (*impatiently*) Yes, Mrs. Evans. But they're getting closer. Why don't you come and watch?

NINA: (*not heeding—impressively*) There's something I must tell you.

MADELINE: (*in hopeless irritation*) But— Oh, all right. (*She hurries over to her, glancing eagerly over her shoulder towards the river*) Yes, Mrs. Evans?

DARRELL: (*moves from the rail toward them—thinking keenly*)

> I must watch this ... she's in a desperate meddling mood! ...

NINA: (*impressively*) First, give me your word of honor that you'll never reveal a word of what I'm going to tell you to a living soul—above all not to Gordon!

MADELINE: (*looking at her in amazement—soothingly*) Couldn't you tell me later, Mrs. Evans—after the race?

NINA: (*sternly—grabbing her by the wrist*) No, now! Do you promise?

MADELINE: (*with helpless annoyance*) Yes, Mrs. Evans.

NINA: (*sternly*) For the sake of your future happiness and my son's I've got to speak! Your engagement forces me to! You've probably wondered why I objected. It's because the marriage is impossible. You can't marry Gordon! I speak as your friend! You must break your engagement with him at once!

MADELINE: (*cannot believe her ears—suddenly panic-stricken*) But why—why?

DARRELL: (*who has come closer—resentfully thinking*)

She wants to ruin my son's life as she ruined mine! . . .

NINA: (*relentlessly*) Why? Because—

DARRELL: (*steps up suddenly beside them—sharply and sternly commanding*) No, Nina! (*He taps* MADELINE *on the shoulder and draws her aside.* NINA *lets go of her wrist and stares after them in a sort of stunned stupor*) Miss Arnold, as a doctor I feel it my duty to tell you that Mrs. Evans isn't herself. Pay no attention to anything she may say to you. She's just passed through a crucial period in a woman's life and she's morbidly jealous of you and subject to queer delusions! (*He smiles kindly at her*) So get back to the race! And God bless you! (*He grips her hand, strangely moved*).

MADELINE: (*gratefully*) Thank you. I understand, I think. Poor Mrs. Evans! (*She hurries back to the rail, raising her glasses*).

NINA: (*springing to her feet and finding her voice—with despairing accusation*) Ned!

DARRELL: (*steps quickly to her side*) I'm sorry, Nina, but I warned you not to meddle. (*Then affectionately*). And Gordon is—well—sort of my stepson, isn't he? I really want him to be happy. (*Then smiling good-naturedly*) All the same, I can't help hoping he'll be beaten in this race. As an oarsman he recalls his father, Gordon Shaw, to me. (*He turns away and raises his glasses, going back to the rail.* NINA *slumps down in her chair again*).

EVANS: Damn! They all look even from here! Can you tell which is which, Madeline?

MADELINE: No—not yet—oh, dear, this is awful! Gordon!

NINA: (*looking about her in the air—with a dazed question*) Gordon?

MARSDEN: (*thinking*)

> Damn that Darrell! . . . if he hadn't interfered Nina would have told . . . something of infinite importance, I know! . . .

(*He comes and again sits on the deck by her chair and takes her hand*) Because what, Nina—my dear little Nina Cara Nina—because what? Let me help you!

NINA: (*staring before her as if she were in a trance—simply, like a young girl*) Yes, Charlie. Yes, Father. Because all of Sam's father's family have been insane. His mother told me that time so I wouldn't have his baby. I was going to tell Madeline that so she wouldn't marry Gordon. But it would have been a lie because Gordon isn't really Sam's child at all, he's Ned's. Ned gave him to me and I gave him to Sam so Sam could have a healthy child and be well and happy. And Sam is well and happy, don't you think? (*Childishly*) So I haven't been such an awfully wicked girl, have I, Father?

MARSDEN: (*horrified and completely sobered by what he has heard —stares at her with stunned eyes*) Nina! Good God! Do you know what you're saying?

MADELINE: (*excitedly*) There! The one on this side! I saw the color on their blades just now!

EVANS: (*anxiously*) Are you sure? Then he's a little behind the other two!

DARRELL: (*excitedly*) The one in the middle seems to be ahead! Is that the Navy? (*But the others pay no attention to him. All three are leaning over the rail, their glasses glued to their eyes, looking up the river. The noise from the whistles is now very loud. The cheering from the observation trains can be heard).*

MARSDEN: (*stares into her face with great pity now*) Merciful God, Nina! Then you've lived all these years—with this horror! And you and Darrell deliberately—?

NINA: (*without looking at him—to the air*) Sam's mother said I had a right to be happy too.

MARSDEN: And you didn't love Darrell then—?

NINA: (*as before*) I did afterwards. I don't now. Ned is dead, too. (*Softly*) Only you are alive now, Father—and Gordon.

MARSDEN: (*gets up and bends over her paternally, stroking her hair with a strange, wild, joyous pity*) Oh, Nina—poor little Nina—my Nina— how you must have suffered! I forgive you! I forgive you everything! I forgive even your trying to tell Madeline—you wanted to keep Gordon—oh, I understand that—and I forgive you!

NINA: (*as before—affectionately and strangely*) And I forgive you, Father. It was all your fault in the beginning, wasn't it? You mustn't ever meddle with human lives again!

EVANS: (*wildly excited*) Gordon's sprinting, isn't he? He's drawing up on that middle one!

MADELINE: Yes! Oh, come on, Gordon!

DARRELL: (*exultantly*) Come on, Navy!

EVANS: (*who is standing next to* NED, *whirls on him in a furious passion*) What's that? What the hell's the matter with you?

DARRELL: (*facing him—with a strange friendliness slaps him on the back*) We've got to beat these Gordons, Sam! We've got to beat—

EVANS: (*raging*) You—! (*He draws back his fist—then suddenly horrified at what he is doing but still angry, grabs* DARRELL *by both shoulders and shakes him*) Wake up! What the hell's got into you? Have you gone crazy?

DARRELL: (*mockingly*) Probably! It runs in my family! All of my father's people were happy lunatics—not healthy, country folk like yours, Sam! Ha!

EVANS: (*staring at him*) Ned, old man, what's the trouble? You said "Navy."

DARRELL: (*ironically—with a bitter hopeless laugh*) Slip of the tongue! I meant Gordon! Meant Gordon, of course! Gordon is always meant—meant to win! Come on, Gordon! It's fate!

MADELINE: Here they come! They're both spurting! I can see Gordon's back!

EVANS: (*forgetting everything else, turns back to the race*) Come on, boy! Come on, son! (*The chorus of noise is now a bedlam as the crews near the finish line. The people have to yell and scream to make themselves heard*).

NINA: (*getting up—thinking with a strange, strident, wild passion*)

I hear the Father laughing! . . . O Mother God, protect my son! . . . let Gordon fly to you in heaven! . . . quick, Gordon! . . . love is the Father's lightning! . . . Madeline will bring you down in flames! . . . I hear His screaming laughter! . . . fly back to me! . . .

(*She is looking desperately up into the sky as if some race of life and death were happening there for her*).

EVANS: (*holding on to a stanchion and leaning far out at the imminent risk of falling in*) One spurt more will do it! Come on, boy, come on! It took death to beat Gordon Shaw! You can't be beaten either, Gordon! Lift her out of the water, son! Stroke! Stroke! He's gaining! Now! Over the line, boy! Over with her! Stroke! That's done it! He's won! He's won!

MADELINE: (*has been shrieking at the same time*) Gordon! Gordon! He's won! Oh, he's fainted! Poor dear darling! (*She remains standing on the rail, leaning out dangerously, holding on with one hand, looking down longingly toward his shell*).

EVANS: (*bounding back to the deck, his face congested and purple with a frenzy of joy, dancing about*) He's won! By God, it was close! Greatest race in the history of rowing! He's the greatest oarsman God ever made! (*Embracing* NINA *and kissing her frantically*) Aren't you happy, Nina? Our Gordon! The greatest ever!

NINA: (*torturedly—trying incoherently to force out a last despairing protest*) No!—not yours!—mine!—and Gordon's!—Gordon is Gordon's!— he was my Gordon!—his Gordon is mine!

EVANS: (*soothingly, humoring her—kissing her again*) Of course he's yours, dear—and a dead ringer for Gordon Shaw, too! Gordon's body! Gordon's spirit! Your body and spirit, too, Nina! He's not like me, lucky for him! I'm a poor boob! I never could row worth a damn! (*He suddenly staggers as if he were very drunk, leaning on* MARSDEN— *then gives a gasp and collapses inertly to the deck, lying on his back*)

MARSDEN: (*stares down at him stupidly—then thinking strangely*)

   I knew it! . . . I saw the end beginning! . . .

   (*He touches* NINA's *arm—in a low voice*) Nina—your husband! (*Touching* DARRELL *who has stood staring straight before him with a bitter ironical smile on his lips*) Ned—your friend! Doctor Darrell—a patient!

NINA: (*stares down at* EVANS—*slowly, as if trying to bring her mind back to him*) My husband? (*Suddenly with a cry of pain, sinks on her knees beside the body*) Sam!

DARRELL: (*looking down at him—thinking yearningly*)

   Is her husband dead . . . at last? . . .

   (*Then with a shudder at his thoughts*)

   No? . . . I don't hope! . . . I don't! . . .

   (*He cries*) Sam! (*He kneels down, feels of his heart, pulse, looks into his face—with a change to a strictly professional manner*) He's not dead. Only a bad stroke.

NINA: (*with a cry of grief*) Oh, Ned, did all our old secret hopes do this at last?

DARRELL: (*professionally, staring at her coldly*) Bosh, Mrs. Evans! We're not in the Congo that we can believe in evil charms! (*Sternly*) In his condition, Mr. Evans must have absolute quiet and peace of mind or— And perfect care! You must tend him night and day! And I will! We've got to keep him happy!

NINA: (*dully*). Again? (*Then sternly in her turn, as if swearing a pledge to herself*) I will never leave his side! I will never tell him anything that might disturb his peace!

MARSDEN: (*standing above them—thinking exultantly*)

> I will not have long to wait now! . . .

(*Then ashamed*)

> How can I think such things . . . poor Sam! . . . he was . . . I mean he is my friend . . .

(*With assertive loyalty*) A rare spirit! A pure and simple soul! A good man—yes, a good man! God bless him! (*He makes a motion over the body like a priest blessing*).

DARRELL: (*his voice suddenly breaking with a sincere human grief*) Sam, old boy! I'm so damned sorry! I will give my life to save you!

NINA: (*in dull anguish*) Save—again? (*Then lovingly, kissing* EVANS' *face*) Dear husband, you have tried to make me happy, I will give you my happiness again! I will give you Gordon to give to Madeline!

MADELINE: (*still standing on the rail, staring after* GORDON'S *shell*)

> Gordon! . . . dear lover . . . how tired . . . but you'll rest in my arms . . . your head will lie on my breast . . . soon! . . .

CURTAIN

ACT NINE

SCENE: *Several months later. A terrace on the* EVANS' *estate on Long Island. In the rear, the terrace overlooks a small harbor with the ocean beyond. On the right is a side entrance of the pretentious villa. On the left is a hedge with an arched gateway leading to a garden. The terrace is paved with rough stone. There is a stone bench at center, a recliner at right, a wicker table and armchair at left.*

It is late afternoon of a day in early fall. GORDON EVANS *is sitting on the stone bench, his chin propped on his hands,* MADELINE *standing behind him, her arm about his shoulders.* GORDON *is over six feet tall with the figure of a trained athlete. His sun-bronzed face is extremely handsome after the fashion of the magazine cover American collegian. It is a strong face but of a strength wholly material in quality. He has been too thoroughly trained to progress along a certain groove to success ever to question it or be dissatisfied with its rewards. At the same time, although entirely an unimaginative code-bound gentleman of his groove, he is boyish and likable, of an even, modest, sporting disposition. His expression is boyishly forlorn, but he is making a manly effort to conceal his grief.*

MADELINE *is much the same as in the previous Act except that there is now a distinct maternal older feeling in her attitude toward* GORDON *as she endeavors to console him.*

MADELINE: (*tenderly, smoothing his hair*) There, dear! I know how horribly hard it is for you. I loved him, too. He was so wonderful and sweet to me.

GORDON: (*his voice trembling*) I didn't really realize he was gone—until out at the cemetery— (*His voice breaks*).

MADELINE: (*kissing his hair*) Darling! Please don't!

GORDON: (*rebelliously*) Damn it, I don't see why he had to die! (*With a groan*) It was that constant grind at the office! I ought to have insisted on his taking better care of himself. But I wasn't home enough, that's the trouble. I couldn't watch him. (*Then bitterly*) But I can't see why Mother didn't!

MADELINE: (*reprovingly but showing she shares his feeling*) Now! You mustn't start feeling bitter toward her.

GORDON: (*contritely*) I know I shouldn't. (*But returning to his bitter tone*) But I can't help remembering how unreasonably she's acted about our engagement.

MADELINE: Not since your father was taken sick, she hasn't, dear. She's been wonderfully nice.

GORDON: (*in the same tone*) Nice? Indifferent, you mean! She doesn't seem to care a damn one way or the other any more!

MADELINE: You could hardly expect her to think of anyone but your father. She's been with him every minute. I never saw such devotion. (*Thinking*)

> Will Gordon ever get old and sick like that? . . . oh, I hope we'll both die before! . . . but I'd nurse him just as she did his father . . . I'll always love him! . . .

GORDON: (*consoled—proudly*) Yes, she sure was wonderful to him, all right! (*Then coming back to his old tone*) But—this may sound rotten of me—I always had a queer feeling she was doing it as a duty. And when he died, I felt her grief was—not from love for him—at least, only the love of a friend, not a wife's love. (*As if under some urgent compulsion from within*) I've never told you, but I've always felt, ever since I was a little kid, that she didn't really love Dad. She liked him and respected him. She was a wonderful wife. But I'm sure she didn't love him. (*Blurting it out as if he couldn't help it*) I'll tell you, Madeline! I've always felt she cared a lot for—Darrell. (*Hastily*) Of course, I might be wrong. (*Then bursting out*) No, I'm not wrong! I've felt it too strongly, ever since I was a kid. And then when I was eleven— something happened. I've been sure of it since then.

MADELINE: (*thinking in amazement, but not without a queer satisfaction*)

Does he mean that she was unfaithful to his father? . . . no, he'd never believe that . . . but what else could he mean? . . .

(*Wonderingly*) Gordon! Do you mean you've been sure that your mother was—

GORDON: (*outraged by something in her tone—jumping to his feet and flinging her hand off—roughly*) Was what? What do you mean, Madeline?

MADELINE: (*frightened—placatingly puts her arms around him*) I didn't mean anything, dear. I simply thought you meant—

GORDON: (*still indignant*) All I meant was that she must have fallen in love with Darrell long after she was married—and then she sent him away for Dad's sake—and mine, too, I suppose. He kept coming back every couple of years. He didn't have guts enough to stay away for good! Oh, I suppose I'm unfair. I suppose it was damned hard on him. He fought it down, too, on account of his friendship for Dad. (*Then with a bitter laugh*) I suppose they'll be getting married now! And I'll have to wish them good luck. Dad would want me to. He was game. (*With a bitter gloomy air*) Life is damn queer, that's all I've got to say!

MADELINE: (*thinking with a sort of tender, loving scorn for his boyish naïveté*)

How little he knows her! . . . Mr. Evans was a fine man but . . . Darrell must have been fascinating once . . . if she loved anyone she isn't the kind who would hesitate . . . any more than I have with Gordon . . . oh, I'll never be unfaithful to Gordon . . . I'll love him always! . . .

(*She runs her fingers through his hair caressingly—comfortingly*) You must never blame them, dear. No one can help love. We couldn't, could we? (*She sits beside him. He takes her in his arms. They kiss each other with rising passion. MARSDEN comes in noiselessly from the garden, a bunch of roses and a pair of shears in his hands. He looks younger, calm and contented. He is dressed in his all black, meticulous, perfectly tailored mourning costume. He stands looking at the two lovers, a queer agitation coming into his face*).

MARSDEN: (*scandalized as an old maid—thinking*)

I must say! . . . his father hardly cold in his grave! . . . it's positively bestial! . . .

(*Then struggling with himself—with a defensive self-mockery*)

Only it wasn't his father . . . what is Sam to Darrell's son? . . . and even if he were Sam's son, what have the living to do with the dead? . . . his duty is to love that life may keep on living . . . and what has their loving to do with me? . . . my life is cool green shade wherein comes no scorching zenith sun of passion and possession to wither the heart with bitter poisons . . . my life gathers roses, coolly crimson, in sheltered gardens, on late afternoons in love with evening . . . roses heavy with after-blooming of the long day, desiring evening . . . my life is an evening . . . Nina is a rose, my rose, exhausted by the long, hot day, leaning wearily toward peace. . . .

(*He kisses one of the roses with a simple sentimental smile—then still smiling, makes a gesture toward the two lovers*)

That is on another planet, called the world . . . Nina and I have moved on to the moon. . . .

MADELINE: (*passionately*) Dear one! Sweetheart!

GORDON: Madeline! I love you!

MARSDEN: (*looking at them—gaily mocking—thinking*)

Once I'd have felt jealous . . . cheated . . . swindled by God out of joy! . . . I would have thought bitterly, "The Gordons have all the luck!" . . . but now I know that dear old Charlie . . . yes, poor dear old Charlie!— passed beyond desire, has all the luck at last! . . .

(*Then matter-of-factly*)

But I'll have to interrupt their biological preparations . . . there are many things still to be done this evening . . . Age's terms of peace, after the long interlude of war with life, have still to be concluded . . . Youth must keep decently away . . . so many old wounds may have to be unbound, and old scars pointed to with pride, to prove to ourselves we have been brave and noble!

(*He lets the shears drop to the ground. They jump startledly and turn around. He smiles quietly*) Sorry to disturb you. I've been picking some roses for your mother, Gordon. Flowers really have the power to soothe grief. I suppose it was that discovery that led to their general use at funerals—and weddings! (*He hands a rose to* MADELINE) Here, Madeline, here's a rose for you. Hail, Love, we who have died, salute you! (*He smiles strangely. She takes the rose automatically, staring at him uncomprehendingly*).

MADELINE: (*thinking suspiciously*)

> What a queer creature! . . . there's something uncanny! . . . oh, don't be silly! . . . it's only poor old Charlie! . . .

(*She makes him a mocking curtsey*) Thank you, Uncle Charlie!

GORDON: (*thinking with sneering pity*)

> Poor old guy! . . . he means well . . . Dad liked him. . . .

(*Pretending an interest in the roses*) They're pretty. (*Then suddenly*) Where's Mother—still in the house?

MARSDEN: She was trying to get rid of the last of the people. I'm going in. Shall I tell her you want to see her? It would give her an excuse to get away.

GORDON: Yes. Will you? (MARSDEN *goes into the house on right*).

MADELINE: You'd better see your mother alone. I'll go down to the plane and wait for you. You want to fly back before dark, don't you?

GORDON: Yes, and we ought to get started soon. (*Moodily*) Maybe it would be better if you weren't here. There are some things I feel I ought to say to her—and Darrell. I've got to do what I know Dad would have wanted. I've got to be fair. He always was to everyone all his life.

MADELINE: You dear, you! You couldn't be unfair to anyone if you tried! (*She kisses him*) Don't be too long.

GORDON: (*moodily*) You bet I won't! It won't be so pleasant I'll want to drag it out!

MADELINE: Good-bye for a while then.

GORDON: So long. (*He looks after her lovingly as she goes out right, rear, around the corner of the house. Thinking*)

Madeline's wonderful! . . . I don't deserve my luck . . . but, God, I sure do love her! . . .

(*He sits down on the bench again, his chin on his hands*)

It seems rotten and selfish to be happy . . . when Dad . . . oh, he understands, he'd want me to be . . . it's funny how I got to care more for Dad than for Mother . . . I suppose it was finding out she loved Darrell . . . I can remember that day seeing her kiss him . . . it did something to me I never got over . . . but she made Dad happy . . . she gave up her own happiness for his sake . . . that was certainly damn fine . . . that was playing the game . . . I'm a hell of a one to criticize . . . my own mother! . . .

(*Changing the subject of his thoughts abruptly*)

Forget it! . . . think of Madeline . . . we'll be married . . . then two months' honeymoon in Europe . . . God, that'll be great! . . . then back and dive into the business . . . Dad relied on me to carry on where he left off . . . I'll have to start at the bottom but I'll get to the top in a hurry, I promise you that, Dad! . . .

(NINA *and* DARRELL *come out of the house on the right. He hears the sound of the door and looks around. Thinking resentfully*)

Funny! . . . I can't stand it even now! . . . when I see him with Mother! . . . I'd like to beat him up! . . .

(*He gets to his feet, his face unconsciously becoming older and cold and severe. He stares accusingly at them as they come slowly toward him in silence.* NINA *looks much older than in the preceding Act. Resignation has come into her face, a resignation that uses no makeup, that has given up the struggle to be sexually attractive and look younger. She is dressed in deep black.* DARRELL'S *deep sunburn of the tropics has faded, leaving his skin a Mongolian yellow. He, too, looks much older. His expression is sad and bitter*).

NINA: (*glancing at* GORDON *searchingly—thinking sadly*)

He sent for me to say good-bye . . . really good-bye forever this time . . .

he's not my son now, nor Gordon's son, nor Sam's, nor Ned's . . . he has become that stranger, another woman's lover. . . .

DARRELL: (*also after a quick keen glance at* GORDON's *face—thinking*)

There's something up . . . some final accounting . . .

(*Thinking resignedly*)

Well, let's get it over . . . then I can get back to work. . . . I've stayed too long up here . . . Preston must be wondering if I've deserted him. . . .

(*Then with a wondering sadness*)

Is that my son? . . . my flesh and blood? . . . staring at me with such cold enmity? . . . how sad and idiotic this all is! . . .

NINA: (*putting on a tone of joking annoyance*) Your message was a godsend, Gordon. Those stupid people with their social condolences were killing me. Perhaps I'm morbid but I always have the feeling that they're secretly glad someone is dead—that it flatters their vanity and makes them feel superior because they're living. (*She sits wearily on the bench.* DARRELL *sits on side of the recliner at right*).

GORDON: (*repelled by this idea—stiffly*) They were all good friends of Dad's. Why shouldn't they be sincerely sorry? His death ought to be a loss to everyone who knew him. (*His voice trembles. He turns away and walks to the table. Thinking bitterly*)

She doesn't care a damn! . . . she's free to marry Darrell now! . . .

NINA: (*thinking sadly, looking at his back*)

He's accusing me because I'm not weeping . . . well, I did weep . . . all I could . . . there aren't many tears left . . . it was too bad Sam had to die . . . living suited him . . . he was so contented with himself . . . but I can't feel guilty . . . I helped him to live . . . I made him believe I loved him . . . his mind was perfectly sane to the end . . . and just before he died, he smiled at me . . . so gratefully and forgivingly, I thought . . . closing our life together with that smile . . . that life is dead . . . its regrets are dead . . . I am sad but there's comfort in the thought that now I am free at last to rot away in peace . . . I'll go and live in Father's old home . . . Sam bought that back . . . I suppose he left it to me . . . Charlie will come in every day to visit . . . he'll comfort and amuse me . . . we can talk together of the old days . . . when I was a girl . . . when I was happy . . . before I fell in love with Gordon Shaw and all this tangled mess of love and hate and pain and birth began! . . .

DARRELL: (*staring at* GORDON'S *back resentfully*)

It gets under my skin to see him act so unfeelingly toward his mother! . . . if he only knew what she's suffered for his sake! . . . the Gordon Shaw ideal passed on through Sam has certainly made my son an insensitive clod! . . .

(*With disgust*)

Bah, what has that young man to do with me? . . . compared to Preston he's only a well-muscled, handsome fool! . . .

(*With a trace of anger*)

But I'd like to jolt his stupid self-complacency! . . . if he knew the facts about himself, he wouldn't be sobbing sentimentally about Sam . . . he'd better change his tune or I'll certainly be tempted to tell him . . . there's no reason for his not knowing now . . .

(*His face is flushed. He has worked himself into a real anger*).

GORDON: (*suddenly, having got back his control, turns to them—coldly*) There are certain things connected with Dad's will I thought I ought to— (*With a tinge of satisfied superiority*) I don't believe Dad told you about his will, did he, Mother?

NINA: (*indifferently*) No.

GORDON: Well, the whole estate goes to you and me, of course. I didn't mean that. (*With a resentful look at* DARRELL) But there is one provision that is peculiar, to say the least. It concerns you, Doctor Darrell—a half-million for your Station to be used in biological research work.

DARRELL: (*his face suddenly flushing with anger*) What's that? That's a joke, isn't it? (*Thinking furiously*)

It's worse! . . . it's a deliberate insult! . . . a last sneer of ownership! . . . of my life! . . .

GORDON: (*coldly sneering*) I thought it must be a joke myself—but Dad insisted.

DARRELL: (*angrily*) Well, I won't accept it—and that's final!

GORDON: (*coldly*) It's not left to you but to the Station. Your supervision is mentioned but I suppose if you won't carry on, whoever is in real charge down there will be only too glad to accept it.

DARRELL: (*stupefied*) That means Preston! But Sam didn't even know Preston—except from hearing me talk about him! What had Sam to do with Preston? Preston is none of his business! I'll advise Preston to refuse it! (*Thinking torturedly*)

> But it's for science! . . . he has no right to refuse! . . . I have no right to ask him to! . . . God damn Sam! . . . wasn't it enough for him to own my wife, my son, in his lifetime? . . . now in death he reaches out to steal Preston! . . . to steal my work! . . .

NINA: (*thinking bitterly*)

> Even in death Sam makes people suffer . . .

(*Sympathetically*) It isn't for you—nor for Preston. It's for science, Ned. You must look at it that way.

GORDON: (*thinking resentfully*)

> What a tender tone she takes toward him! . . . she's forgotten Dad already! . . .

(*With a sneer*) You'd better accept. Half-millions aren't being thrown away for nothing every day.

NINA: (*in anguish—thinking*)

> How can Gordon insult poor Ned like that! . . . his own father! . . . Ned has suffered too much! . . .

(*Sharply*) I think you've said about enough, Gordon!

GORDON: (*bitterly, but trying to control himself—meaningly*) I haven't said all I'm going to say, Mother!

NINA: (*thinking—first frightenedly*)

> What does he mean? . . . does he know about Ned being . . . ?

(*Then with a sort of defiant relief*)

Well, what does it matter what he thinks of me? . . . he's hers now, anyway. . . .

DARRELL: (*thinking vindictively*)

I hope he knows the truth, for if he doesn't, by God, I'll tell him! . . . if
only to get something back from Sam of all he's stolen from me! . . .

(*Authoritatively—as* GORDON *hesitates*) Well, what have you got to
say? Your mother and I are waiting.

GORDON: (*furiously, taking a threatening step toward him*) Shut up, you!
Don't take that tone with me or I'll forget your age— (*Contemptuously*) and give you a spanking!

NINA: (*thinking hysterically*)

Spanking! . . . the son spanks the father! . . .

(*Laughing hysterically*) Oh, Gordon, don't make me laugh! It's all so
funny!

DARRELL: (*jumps from his chair and goes to her—solicitously*) Nina! Don't
mind him! He doesn't realize—

GORDON: (*maddened, comes closer*) I realize a lot! I realize you've acted
like a cur! (*He steps forward and slaps* DARRELL *across the face viciously.*
DARRELL *staggers back from the force of the blow, his hands to his face.*
NINA *screams and flings herself on* GORDON, *holding his arms*).

NINA: (*piteously—hysterically*) For God's sake, Gordon! What would
your father say? You don't know what you're doing! You're hitting
your father!

DARRELL: (*suddenly breaking down—chokingly*) No—it's all right, son—
all right—you didn't know—

GORDON: (*crushed, overcome by remorse for his blow*) I'm sorry—sorry—
you're right, Mother—Dad would feel as if I'd hit him—just as bad
as if I'd hit him!

DARRELL: It's nothing, son—nothing!

GORDON: (*brokenly*) That's damn fine, Darrell—damn fine and sporting
of you! It was a rotten, dirty trick! Accept my apology, Darrell, won't
you?

DARRELL: (*staring at him stupidly—thinking*)

> Darrell? . . . he calls me Darrell! . . . but doesn't he know? . . . I thought she told him. . . .

NINA: (*laughing hysterically—thinking*)

> I told him he hit his father . . . but he can't understand me! . . . why, of course he can't! . . . how could he? . . .

GORDON: (*insistently holding out his hand*) I'm damned sorry! I didn't mean it! Shake hands, won't you?

DARRELL: (*doing so mechanically—stupidly*) Only too glad—pleased to meet you—know you by reputation—the famous oarsman—great race you stroked last June—but I was hoping the Navy would give you a beating.

NINA: (*thinking in desperate hysterical anguish*)

> Oh, I wish Ned would go away and stay away forever! . . . I can't bear to watch him suffer any more! . . . it's too frightful! . . . yes, God the Father, I hear you laughing . . . you see the joke . . . I'm laughing too . . . it's all so crazy, isn't it? . . .

(*Laughing hysterically*) Oh, Ned! Poor Ned! You were born unlucky!

GORDON: (*making her sit down again—soothing her*) Mother! Stop laughing! Please! It's all right—all right between us! I've apologized! (*As she has grown calmer*) And now I want to say what I was going to say. It wasn't anything bad. It was just that I wanted you to know how fine I think you've both acted. I've known ever since I was a kid that you and Darrell were in love with each other. I hated the idea on Father's account—that's only natural, isn't it?—but I knew it was unfair, that people can't help loving each other any more than Madeline and I could have helped ourselves. And I saw how fair you both were to Dad—what a good wife you were, Mother—what a true friend you were, Darrell—and how damn much he loved you both! So all I wanted to say is, now he's dead, I hope you'll get married and I hope you'll be as happy as you both deserve— (*Here he breaks down, kissing her and then breaking away*) I've got to say good-bye—

got to fly back before dark—Madeline's waiting. (*He takes* DARRELL'S *hand and shakes it again. They have both been staring at him stupidly*) Good-bye, Darrell! Good luck!

DARRELL: (*thinking sufferingly*)

Why does he keep on calling me Darrell . . . he's my boy . . . I'm his father . . . I've got to make him realize I'm his father! . . .

(*Holding* GORDON's *hand*) Listen, son. It's my turn. I've got to tell you something—

NINA: (*thinking torturedly*)

Oh, he mustn't! . . . I feel he mustn't! . . .

(*Sharply*) Ned! First, let me ask Gordon a question. (*Then looking her son in the eyes, slowly and impressively*) Do you think I was ever unfaithful to your father, Gordon?

GORDON: (*startled, stares at her—shocked and horrified—then suddenly he blurts out indignantly*) Mother, what do you think I am—as rotten-minded as that! (*Pleadingly*) Please, Mother, I'm not as bad as that! I know you're the best woman that ever lived—the best of all! I don't even except Madeline!

NINA: (*with a sobbing triumphant cry*) My dear Gordon! You do love me, don't you?

GORDON: (*kneeling beside her and kissing her*) Of course!

NINA: (*pushing him away—tenderly*) And now go! Hurry! Madeline is waiting! Give her my love! Come to see me once in a while in the years to come! Good-bye, dear! (*Turning to* DARRELL, *who is standing with a sad resigned expression—imploringly*) Did you still want to tell Gordon something, Ned?

DARRELL: (*forcing a tortured smile*) Not for anything in the world! Good-bye, son.

GORDON: Good-bye, sir. (*He hurries off around the corner of the house at left, rear, thinking troubledly*)

What does she think I am? . . . I've never thought that! . . . I couldn't!

. . . my own mother! I'd kill myself if I ever even caught myself thinking . . . !

(*He is gone*).

NINA: (*turns to* NED, *gratefully taking his hand and pressing it*) Poor dear
Ned, you've always had to give! How can I ever thank you?

DARRELL: (*with an ironical smile—forcing a joking tone*) By refusing me
when I ask you to marry me! For I've got to ask you! Gordon expects
it! And he'll be so pleased when he knows you turned me down.
(MARSDEN *comes out of the house*) Hello, here comes Charlie. I must
hurry. Will you marry me, Nina?

NINA: (*with a sad smile*) No. Certainly not. Our ghosts would torture
us to death! (*Then forlornly*) But I wish I did love you, Ned! Those
were wonderful afternoons long ago! The Nina of those afternoons
will always live in me, will always love her lover, Ned, the father of
her baby!

DARRELL: (*lifting her hand to his lips—tenderly*) Thank you for that! And
that Ned will always adore his beautiful Nina! Remember him! Forget me! I'm going back to work. (*He laughs softly and sadly*) I leave
you to Charlie. You'd better marry him, Nina—if you want peace.
And after all, I think you owe it to him for his life-long devotion.

MARSDEN: (*thinking uneasily*)

> They're talking about me . . . why doesn't he go? . . . she doesn't love him
> any more . . . even now he's all heat and energy and the tormenting drive
> of noon . . . can't he see she is in love with evening? . . .

(*Clearing his throat uneasily*) Do I hear my name taken in vain?

NINA: (*looking at* MARSDEN *with a strange yearning*)

> Peace! . . . yes . . . that is all I desire . . . I can no longer imagine happiness
> . . . Charlie has found peace . . . he will be tender . . . as my father was
> when I was a girl . . . when I could imagine happiness . . .

(*With a girlish coquettishness and embarrassment—making way for him
on the bench beside her—strangely*) Ned's just proposed to me. I refused
him, Charlie. I don't love him any more.

MARSDEN: (*sitting down beside her*) I suspected as much. Then whom do you love, Nina Cara Nina?

NINA: (*sadly smiling*) You, Charlie, I suppose. I have always loved your love for me. (*She kisses him—wistfully*) Will you let me rot away in peace?

MARSDEN: (*strongly*) All my life I've waited to bring you peace.

NINA: (*sadly teasing*) If you've waited that long, Charlie, we'd better get married tomorrow. But I forgot. You haven't asked me yet, have you? Do you want me to marry you, Charlie?

MARSDEN: (*humbly*) Yes, Nina. (*Thinking with a strange ecstasy*)

> I knew the time would come at last when I would hear her ask that! . . . I could never have said it, never! . . . oh, russet-golden afternoon, you are a mellow fruit of happiness ripely falling! . . .

DARRELL: (*amused—with a sad smile*) Bless you, my children! (*He turns to go*).

NINA: I don't suppose we'll ever see you again, Ned.

DARRELL: I hope not, Nina. A scientist shouldn't believe in ghosts. (*With a mocking smile*) But perhaps we'll become part of cosmic positive and negative electric charges and meet again.

NINA: In our afternoons—again?

DARRELL: (*smiling sadly*) Again. In our afternoons.

MARSDEN: (*coming out of his day dream*) We'll be married in the afternoon, decidedly. I've already picked out the church, Nina—a gray ivied chapel, full of restful shadow, symbolical of the peace we have found. The crimsons and purples in the windows will stain our faces with faded passion. It must be in the hour before sunset when the earth dreams in afterthoughts and mystic premonitions of life's beauty. And then we'll go up to your old home to live. Mine wouldn't be suitable for us. Mother and Jane live there in memory. And I'll work in your father's old study. He won't mind me. (*From the bay below comes the roaring hum of an airplane motor.* NINA *and* DARRELL *jump startledly and go to the rear of the terrace to watch the plane ascend from the water, standing side by side.* MARSDEN *remains oblivious*).

NINA: (*with anguish*) Gordon! Good-bye, dear! (*Pointing as the plane climbs higher moving away off to the left—bitterly*) See, Ned! He's leaving me without a backward look!

DARRELL: (*joyfully*) No! He's circling. He's coming back! (*The roar of the engine grows steadily nearer now*) He's going to pass directly over us! (*Their eyes follow the plane as it comes swiftly nearer and passes directly over them*) See! He's waving to us!

NINA: Oh, Gordon! My dear son! (*She waves frantically*).

DARRELL: (*with a last tortured protest*) Nina! Are you forgetting? He's my son, too! (*He shouts up at the sky*) You're my son, Gordon! You're my— (*He controls himself abruptly—with a smile of cynical self-pity*) He can't hear! Well, at least I've done my duty! (*Then with a grim fatalism—with a final wave of his hand at the sky*) Good-bye, Gordon's son!

NINA: (*with tortured exultance*) Fly up to heaven, Gordon! Fly with your love to heaven! Fly always! Never crash to earth like my old Gordon! Be happy, dear! You've got to be happy!

DARRELL: (*sardonically*) I've heard that cry for happiness before, Nina! I remember hearing myself cry it—once—it must have been long ago! I'll get back to my cells—sensible unicellular life that floats in the sea and has never learned the cry for happiness! I'm going, Nina. (*As she remains oblivious, staring after the plane— thinking fatalistically*)

She doesn't hear, either. . . .

(*He laughs up at the sky*)

Oh, God, so deaf and dumb and blind! . . . teach me to be resigned to be an atom! . . .

(*He walks off, right, and enters the house*).

NINA: (*finally lowering her eyes—confusedly*) Gone. My eyes are growing dim. Where is Ned? Gone, too. And Sam is gone. They're all dead. Where are Father and Charlie? (*With a shiver of fear she hurries over and sits on the bench beside* MARSDEN, *huddling against him*) Gordon is dead, Father. I've just had a cable. What I mean is, he flew away to another life—my son, Gordon, Charlie. So we're alone again—just as we used to be.

MARSDEN: (*putting his arm around her—affectionately*) Just as we used to be, dear Nina Cara Nina, before Gordon came.

NINA: (*looking up at the sky—strangely*) My having a son was a failure, wasn't it? He couldn't give me happiness. Sons are always their fathers. They pass through the mother to become their father again. The Sons of the Father have all been failures! Failing they died for us, they flew away to other lives, they could not stay with us, they could not give us happiness!

MARSDEN: (*paternally—in her father's tone*) You had best forget the whole affair of your association with the Gordons. After all, dear Nina, there was something unreal in all that has happened since you first met Gordon Shaw, something extravagant and fantastic, the sort of thing that isn't done, really, in our afternoons. So let's you and me forget the whole distressing episode, regard it as an interlude, of trial and preparation, say, in which our souls have been scraped clean of impure flesh and made worthy to bleach in peace.

NINA: (*with a strange smile*) Strange interlude! Yes, our lives are merely strange dark interludes in the electrical display of God the Father! (*Resting her head on his shoulder*) You're so restful, Charlie. I feel as if I were a girl again and you were my father and the Charlie of those days made into one. I wonder is our old garden the same? We'll pick flowers together in the aging afternoons of spring and summer, won't we? It will be a comfort to get home—to be old and to be home again at last—to be in love with peace together—to love each other's peace—to sleep with peace together—! (*She kisses him—then shuts her eyes with a deep sigh of requited weariness*) —to die in peace! I'm so contentedly weary with life!

MARSDEN: (*with a serene peace*) Rest, dear Nina. (*Then tenderly*) It has been a long day. Why don't you sleep now—as you used to, remember?—for a little while?

NINA: (*murmurs with drowsy gratitude*) Thank you, Father—have I been wicked?—you're so good—dear old Charlie!

MARSDEN: (*reacting automatically and wincing with pain—thinking mechanically*)

God damn dear old . . . !

(*Then with a glance down at* NINA's *face, with a happy smile*)

No, God bless dear old Charlie . . . who, passed beyond desire, has all the luck at last! . . .

(NINA *has fallen asleep. He watches with contented eyes the evening shadows closing in around them*).

CURTAIN

Mourning Becomes Electra

A Trilogy

❦

To Carlotta, my wife

❦

Part One

HOMECOMING

A Play in Four Acts

Part Two

THE HUNTED

A Play in Five acts

Part Three

THE HAUNTED

A Play in Four Acts

General Scene of the Trilogy

THE action of the trilogy, with the exception of an act of the second play, takes place in or immediately outside the Mannon residence, on the outskirts of one of the small New England seaport towns.

A special curtain shows the house as seen from the street. From this, in each play, one comes to the exterior of the house in the opening act and enters it in the following act.

This curtain reveals the extensive grounds—about thirty acres—which surround the house, a heavily wooded ridge in the background, orchards at the right and in the immediate rear, a large flower garden and a greenhouse to the left.

In the foreground, along the street, is a line of locust and elm trees. The property is enclosed by a white picket fence and a tall hedge. A driveway curves up to the house from two entrances with white gates. Between the house and the street is a lawn. By the right corner of the house is a grove of pine trees. Farther forward, along the driveway, maples and locusts. By the left corner of the house is a big clump of lilacs and syringas.

The house is placed back on a slight rise of ground about three hundred feet from the street. It is a large building of the Greek temple type that was the vogue in the first half of the nineteenth century. A white wooden portico with six tall columns contrasts with the wall of the house proper which is of gray cut stone. There are five windows on the upper floor and four on the ground floor, with the main entrance in the middle, a doorway with squared transom and sidelights flanked by intermediate columns. The window shutters are painted a dark green. Before the doorway a flight of four steps leads from the ground to the portico.

The three plays take place in either spring or summer of the years 1865–1866.

Homecoming

CHARACTERS

BRIGADIER-GENERAL EZRA MANNON

CHRISTINE, *his wife*

LAVINIA, *their daughter*

CAPTAIN ADAM BRANT, *of the clipper "Flying Trades"*

CAPTAIN PETER NILES, *U. S. Artillery*

HAZEL NILES, *his sister*

SETH BECKWITH

AMOS AMES

LOUISA, *his wife*

MINNIE, *her cousin*

SCENES

Act One: Exterior of the Mannon house in New England—April, 1865.

Act Two: Ezra Mannon's study in the house—no time has elapsed.

Act Three: The same as Act One—exterior of the house—a night a week later.

Act Four: A bedroom in the house—later the same night.

HOMECOMING

ACT ONE

SCENE—*Exterior of the Mannon house on a late afternoon in April, 1865. At front is the driveway which leads up to the house from the two entrances on the street. Behind the driveway the white Grecian temple portico with its six tall columns extends across the stage. A big pine tree is on the lawn at the edge of the drive before the right corner of the house. Its trunk is a black column in striking contrast to the white columns of the portico. By the edge of the drive, left front, is a thick clump of lilacs and syringas. A bench is placed on the lawn at front of this shrubbery which partly screens anyone sitting on it from the front of the house.*

It is shortly before sunset and the soft light of the declining sun shines directly on the front of the house, shimmering in a luminous mist on the white portico and the gray stone wall behind, intensifying the whiteness of the columns, the somber grayness of the wall, the green of the open shutters, the green of the lawn and shrubbery, the black and green of the pine tree. The white columns cast black bars of shadow on the gray wall behind them. The windows of the lower floor reflect the sun's rays in a resentful glare. The temple portico is like an incongruous white mask fixed on the house to hide its somber gray ugliness.

In the distance, from the town, a band is heard playing "John Brown's Body." Borne on the light puffs of wind this music is at times quite loud, then sinks into faintness as the wind dies.

From the left rear, a man's voice is heard singing the chanty "Shenandoah"—a song that more than any other holds in it the brooding rhythm of the sea. The voice grows quickly nearer. It is thin and aged, the wraith of what must once have been a good baritone.

"Oh, Shenandoah, I long to hear you
A-way, my rolling river
Oh, Shenandoah, I can't get near you
Way-ay, I'm bound away
Across the wide Missouri."

The singer, SETH BECKWITH, *finishes the last line as he enters from around the corner of the house. Closely following him are* AMOS AMES, *his wife* LOUISA, *and her cousin* MINNIE.

SETH BECKWITH, *the Mannons' gardener and man of all work, is an old man of seventy-five with white hair and beard, tall, rawboned and stoop-shouldered, his joints stiffened by rheumatism, but still sound and hale. He has a gaunt face that in repose gives one the strange impression of a life-like mask. It is set in a grim expression, but his small, sharp eyes still peer at life with a shrewd prying avidity and his loose mouth has a strong suggestion of ribald humor. He wears his earth-stained working clothes.*

AMOS AMES, *carpenter by trade but now taking a holiday and dressed in his Sunday best, as are his wife and her cousin, is a fat man in his fifties. In character he is the townsfolk type of garrulous gossip-monger who is at the same time devoid of evil intent, scandal being for him merely the subject most popular with his audience.*

His wife, LOUISA, *is taller and stouter than he and about the same age. Of a similar scandal-bearing type, her tongue is sharpened by malice.*

Her cousin, MINNIE, *is a plump little woman of forty, of the meek, eager-listener type, with a small round face, round stupid eyes, and a round mouth pursed out to drink in gossip.*

These last three are types of townsfolk rather than individuals, a chorus representing the town come to look and listen and spy on the rich and exclusive Mannons.

Led by SETH, *they come forward as far as the lilac clump and stand staring at the house.* SETH, *in a mood of aged playfulness, is trying to make an impression on* MINNIE. *His singing has been for her benefit. He nudges her with his elbow, grinning.*

SETH: How's that fur singin' fur an old feller? I used to be noted fur my chanties. (*Seeing she is paying no attention to him but is staring with open-mouthed awe at the house, he turns to* AMES— *jubilantly*) By jingo, Amos, if that news is true, there won't be a sober man in town tonight! It's our patriotic duty to celebrate!

AMES: (*with a grin*) We'd ought to, that's sartin!

LOUISA: You ain't goin' to git Amos drunk tonight, surrender or no surrender! An old reprobate, that's what you be!

SETH: (*pleased*) Old nothin'! On'y seventy-five! My old man lived to be ninety! Licker can't kill the Beckwiths! (*He and* AMES *laugh.* LOUISA *smiles in spite of herself.* MINNIE *is oblivious, still staring at the house*).

MINNIE: My sakes! What a purty house!

SETH: Wal, I promised Amos I'd help show ye the sights when you came to visit him. 'Taint everyone can git to see the Mannon place close to. They're strict about trespassin'.

MINNIE: My! They must be rich! How'd they make their money?

SETH: Ezra's made a pile, and before him, his father, Abe Mannon, he inherited some and made a pile more in shippin'. Started one of the fust Western Ocean packet lines.

MINNIE: Ezra's the General, ain't he?

SETH: (*proudly*) Ayeh. The best fighter in the hull of Grant's army!

MINNIE: What kind is he?

SETH: (*boastfully expanding*) He's able, Ezra is! Folks think he's cold-blooded and uppish, 'cause he's never got much to say to 'em. But that's only the Mannons' way. They've been top dog around here for near on two hundred years and don't let folks fergit it.

MINNIE: How'd he come to jine the army if he's so rich?

SETH: Oh, he'd been a soldier afore this war. His paw made him go to West P'int. He went to the Mexican war and come out a major. Abe died that same year and Ezra give up the army and took holt of the shippin' business here. But he didn't stop there. He learned law on the side and got made a judge. Went in fur politics and got 'lected mayor. He was mayor when this war broke out but he resigned to once and jined the army again. And now he's riz to be General. Oh, he's able, Ezra is!

AMES: Ayeh. This town's real proud of Ezra.

LOUISA: Which is more'n you kin say fur his wife. Folks all hates her! She ain't the Mannon kind. French and Dutch descended, she is. Furrin lookin' and queer. Her father's a doctor in New York, but he can't be much of a one 'cause she didn't bring no money when Ezra married her.

SETH: (*his face growing grim—sharply*) Never mind her. We ain't talkin' 'bout her. (*Then abruptly changing the subject*) Wal, I've got to see Vinnie. I'm goin' round by the kitchen. You wait here. And if Ezra's wife starts to run you off fur trespassin', you tell her I got permission from Vinnie to show you round. (*He goes off around the corner of the house, left. The three stare about them gawkily, awed and uncomfortable. They talk in low voices*).

LOUISA: Seth is so proud of his durned old Mannons! I couldn't help givin' him a dig about Ezra's wife.

AMES: Wal, don't matter much. He's allus hated her.

LOUISA: Ssshh! Someone's comin' out. Let's get back here! (*They crowd to the rear of the bench by the lilac clump and peer through the leaves as the front door is opened and* CHRISTINE MANNON *comes out to the edge of the portico at the top of the steps.* LOUISA *prods her cousin and whispers excitedly*) That's her! (CHRISTINE MANNON *is a tall striking-looking woman of forty but she appears younger. She has a fine, voluptuous figure and she moves with a flowing animal grace. She wears a green satin dress, smartly cut and expensive, which brings out the peculiar color of her thick curly hair, partly a copper brown, partly a bronze gold, each shade distinct and yet blending with the other. Her face is unusual, handsome rather than beautiful. One is struck at once by the strange impression it gives in repose of being not living flesh but a wonderfully life-like pale mask, in which only the deep-set eyes, of a dark violet blue, are alive. Her black eyebrows meet in a pronounced straight line above her strong nose. Her chin is heavy, her mouth large and sensual, the lower lip full, the upper a thin bow, shadowed by a line of hair. She stands and listens defensively, as if the music held some meaning that threatened her. But at once she shrugs her shoulders with disdain and comes down the steps and walks off toward the flower garden, passing behind the lilac clump without having noticed* AMES *and the women*).

MINNIE: (*in an awed whisper*) My! She's awful handsome, ain't she?

LOUISA: Too furrin lookin' fur my taste.

MINNIE: Ayeh. There's somethin' queer lookin' about her face.

AMES: Secret lookin'—'s if it was a mask she'd put on. That's the Mannon look. They all has it. They grow it on their wives. Seth's growed it on too, didn't you notice—from bein' with 'em all his life. They don't want folks to guess their secrets.

MINNIE: (*breathlessly eager*) Secrets?

LOUISA: The Mannons got skeletons in their closets same as others! Worse ones. (*Lowering her voice almost to a whisper—to her husband*) Tell Minnie about old Abe Mannon's brother David marryin' that French Canuck nurse girl he'd got into trouble.

AMES: Ssshh! Shet up, can't you? Here's Seth comin'. (*But he whispers quickly to* MINNIE) That happened way back when I was a youngster. I'll tell you later. (SETH *has appeared from around the left corner of the house and now joins them*).

SETH: That durned nigger cook is allus askin' me to fetch wood fur her! You'd think I was her slave! That's what we get fur freein' 'em! (*Then briskly*) Wal, come along, folks. I'll show you the peach orchard and then we'll go to my greenhouse. I couldn't find Vinnie. (*They are about to start when the front door of the house is opened and* LAVINIA *comes out to the top of the steps where her mother had stood. She is twenty-three but looks considerably older. Tall like her mother, her body is thin, flat-breasted and angular, and its unattractiveness is accentuated by her plain black dress. Her movements are stiff and she carries herself with a wooden, square-shouldered, military bearing. She has a flat dry voice and a habit of snapping out her words like an officer giving orders. But in spite of these dissimilarities, one is immediately struck by her facial resemblance to her mother. She has the same peculiar shade of copper-gold hair, the same pallor and dark violet-blue eyes, the black eyebrows meeting in a straight line above her nose, the same sensual mouth, the same heavy jaw. Above all, one is struck by the same strange, life-like mask impression her face gives in repose. But it is evident* LAVINIA *does all in her power to emphasize the dissimilarity rather than the resemblance to her parent. She wears her hair pulled tightly back, as if to conceal its natural curliness, and there is not a touch of feminine allurement to her severely plain get-up. Her head is the same size as her mother's, but on her thin body it looks too large and heavy*).

SETH: (*seeing her*) There she be now. (*He starts for the steps—then sees she has not noticed their presence, and stops and stands waiting, struck by something in her manner. She is looking off right, watching her mother as she strolls through the garden to the greenhouse. Her eyes are bleak and hard with an intense, bitter enmity. Then her mother evidently disappears in the greenhouse, for* LAVINIA *turns her head, still oblivious to* SETH *and his friends, and looks off left, her attention caught by the band, the music of which, borne on a freshening breeze, has suddenly become louder. It is still playing "John Brown's Body."* LAVINIA *listens, as her mother had a moment before, but her reaction is the direct opposite to what her mother's had been. Her eyes light up with a grim satisfaction, and an expression of strange vindictive triumph comes into her face*).

LOUSIA: (*in a quick whisper to* MINNIE) That's Lavinia!

MINNIE: She looks like her mother in face—queer lookin'—but she ain't purty like her.

SETH: You git along to the orchard, folks. I'll jine you there. (*They walk back around the left of the house and disappear. He goes to* LAVINIA *eagerly*) Say, I got fine news fur you, Vinnie. The telegraph feller says Lee is a goner sure this time! They're only waitin' now fur the news to be made official. You can count on your paw comin' home!

LAVINIA: (*grimly*) I hope so. It's time.

SETH: (*with a keen glance at her—slowly*) Ayeh.

LAVINIA: (*turning on him sharply*) What do you mean, Seth?

SETH: (*avoiding her eyes—evasively*) Nothin'—'cept what you mean. (LAVINIA *stares at him. He avoids her eyes—then heavily casual*) Where was you gallivantin' night afore last and all yesterday?

LAVINIA: (*starts*) Over to Hazel and Peter's house.

SETH: Ayeh. There's where Hannah said you'd told her you was goin'. That's funny now—'cause I seen Peter upstreet yesterday and he asked me where you was keepin' yourself.

LAVINIA: (*again starts—then slowly as if admitting a secret understanding between them*) I went to New York, Seth.

SETH: Ayeh. That's where I thought you'd gone, mebbe. (*Then with deep sympathy*) It's durned hard on you, Vinnie. It's a durned shame.

LAVINIA: (*stiffening—curtly*) I don't know what you're talking about.

SETH: (*nods comprehendingly*) All right, Vinnie. Just as you say. (*He pauses—then after hesitating frowningly for a moment, blurts out*) There's somethin' been on my mind lately I want to warn you about. It's got to do with what's worryin' you—that is, if there's anythin' in it.

LAVINIA: (*stiffly*) There's nothing worrying me. (*Then sharply*) Warn me? About what?

SETH: Mebbe it's nothin'—and then again mebbe I'm right, and if I'm right, then you'd ought t'be warned. It's to do with that Captain Brant.

LAVINIA: (*starts again but keeps her tone cold and collected*) What about him?

SETH: Somethin' I calc'late no one'd notice 'specially 'ceptin' me, because— (*Then hastily as he sees someone coming up the drive*) Here's Peter and Hazel comin'. I'll tell you later, Vinnie. I ain't got time now anyways. Those folks are waitin' for me.

LAVINIA: I'll be sitting here. You come back afterwards. (*Then her cold disciplined mask breaking for a moment—tensely*) Oh, why do Peter and Hazel have to come now? I don't want to see anyone! (*She starts as if to go into the house*).

SETH: You run in. I'll git rid of 'em fur you.

LAVINIA: (*recovering herself—curtly*) No. I'll see them. (SETH *goes back*

around the corner of the house, left. A moment later HAZEL *and* PETER
NILES *enter along the drive from left, front.* HAZEL *is a pretty, healthy girl
of nineteen, with dark hair and eyes. Her features are small but clearly
modelled. She has a strong chin and a capable, smiling mouth. One gets a
sure impression of her character at a glance—frank, innocent, amiable and
good—not in a negative but in a positive, self-possessed way. Her brother,*
PETER, *is very like her in character—straightforward, guileless and good-
natured. He is a heavily built young fellow of twenty-two, awkward in
movement and hesitating in speech. His face is broad, plain, with a snubby
nose, curly brown hair, fine gray eyes and a big mouth. He wears the
uniform of an artillery captain in the Union Army).*

LAVINIA: (*with forced cordiality*) Good afternoon. How are you? (*She and*
HAZEL *kiss and she shakes hands with* PETER).

HAZEL: Oh, we're all right. But how are you, Vinnie, that's the question?
Seems as if we hadn't seen you in ages! You haven't been sick, I
hope!

LAVINIA: Well—if you call a pesky cold sick.

PETER: Gosh, that's too bad! All over it now?

LAVINIA: Yes—almost. Do sit down, won't you? (HAZEL *sits at left of
bench,* LAVINIA *beside her in the middle.* PETER *sits gingerly on the right
edge so that there is an open space between him and* LAVINIA).

HAZEL: Peter can stay a while if you want him to, but I just dropped in
for a second to find out if you'd had any more news from Orin.

LAVINIA: Not since the letter I showed you.

HAZEL: But that was ages ago! And I haven't had a letter in months. I
guess he must have met another girl some place and given me the
go by. (*She forces a smile but her tone is really hurt*).

PETER: Orin not writing doesn't mean anything. He never was much of
a hand for letters.

HAZEL: I know that, but—you don't think he's been wounded, do you,
Vinnie?

LAVINIA: Of course not. Father would have let us know.

PETER: Sure he would. Don't be foolish, Hazel! (*Then after a little pause*)

Orin ought to be home before long now. You've heard the good news, of course, Vinnie?

HAZEL: Peter won't have to go back. Isn't that fine?

PETER: My wound is healed and I've got orders to leave tomorrow but they'll be cancelled, I guess. (*Grinning*) I won't pretend I'm the sort of hero that wants to go back, either! I've had enough!

HAZEL: (*impulsively*) Oh, it will be so good to see Orin again. (*Then embarrassed, forces a self-conscious laugh and gets up and kisses* LAVINIA) Well, I must run. I've got to meet Emily. Good-bye, Vinnie. Do take care of yourself and come to see us soon (*With a teasing glance at her brother*) And be kind to Peter. He's nice—when he's asleep. And he has something he's just dying to ask you!

PETER: (*horribly embarrassed*) Darn you! (HAZEL *laughs and goes off down the drive, left front.* PETER *fidgets, his eyes on the ground.* LAVINIA *watches him. Since* HAZEL's *teasing statement, she has visibly withdrawn into herself and is on the defensive. Finally* PETER *looks up and blurts out awkwardly*) Hazel feels bad about Orin not writing. Do you think he really—loves her?

LAVINIA: (*stiffening—brusquely*) I don't know anything about love! I don't want to know anything! (*Intensely*) I hate love!

PETER: (*crushed by this but trying bravely to joke*) Gosh, then, if that's the mood you're in, I guess I better not ask—something I'd made up my mind to ask you today.

LAVINIA: It's what you asked me a year ago when you were home on leave, isn't it?

PETER: And you said wait till the war was over. Well, it's over now.

LAVINIA: (*slowly*) I can't marry anyone, Peter. I've got to stay home. Father needs me.

PETER: He's got your mother.

LAVINIA: (*sharply*) He needs me more! (*A pause. Then she turns pityingly and puts her hand on his shoulder*) I'm sorry, Peter.

PETER: (*gruffly*) Oh, that's all right.

LAVINIA: I know it's what girls always say in books, but I do love you as a brother, Peter. I wouldn't lose you as a brother for anything. We've been like that ever since we were little and started playing together—you and Orin and Hazel and I. So please don't let this come between us.

PETER: 'Course it won't. What do you think I am? (*Doggedly*) Besides, I'm not giving up hope but what you'll change your mind in time. That is, unless it's because you love someone else—

LAVINIA: (*snatching her hand back*) Don't be stupid, Peter!

PETER: But how about this mysterious clipper captain that's been calling?

LAVINIA: (*angrily*) Do you think I care anything about that—that—!

PETER: Don't get mad. I only meant, folks say he's courting you.

LAVINIA: Folks say more than their prayers!

PETER: Then you don't—care for him?

LAVINIA: (*intensely*) I hate the sight of him!

PETER: Gosh! I'm glad to hear you say that, Vinnie. I was afraid—I imagined girls all liked him. He's such a darned romantic-looking cuss. Looks more like a gambler or a poet than a ship captain. I got a look as he was coming out of your gate—I guess it was the last time he was here. Funny, too. He reminded me of someone. But I couldn't place who it was.

LAVINIA: (*startled, glances at him uneasily*) No one around here, that's sure. He comes from out West. Grandfather Hamel happened to meet him in New York and took a fancy to him, and Mother met him at Grandfather's house.

PETER: Who is he, anyway, Vinnie?

LAVINIA: I don't know much about him in spite of what you think. Oh, he did tell me the story of his life to make himself out romantic, but I didn't pay much attention. He went to sea when he was young and was in California for the Gold Rush. He's sailed all over the world—he lived on a South Sea island once, so he says.

PETER: (*grumpily*) He seems to have had plenty of romantic experience, if you can believe him!

LAVINIA: (*bitterly*) That's his trade—being romantic! (*Then agitatedly*) But I don't want to talk any more about him. (*She gets up and walks toward right to conceal her agitation, keeping her back turned to* PETER).

PETER: (*with a grin*) Well, I don't either. I can think of more interesting subjects. (CHRISTINE MANNON *appears from left, between the clump of lilacs and the house. She is carrying a big bunch of flowers.* LAVINIA *senses her presence and whirls around. For a moment, mother and daughter stare into each other's eyes. In their whole tense attitudes is clearly revealed the bitter antagonism between them. But* CHRISTINE *quickly recovers herself and her air resumes its disdainful aloofness*).

CHRISTINE: Ah, here you are at last! (*Then she sees* PETER, *who is visibly embarrassed by her presence*) Why, good afternoon, Peter, I didn't see you at first.

PETER: Good afternoon, Mrs. Mannon. I was just passing and dropped in for a second. I guess I better run along now, Vinnie.

LAVINIA: (*with an obvious eagerness to get him off—quickly*) All right. Good-bye, Peter.

PETER: Good-bye. Good-bye, Mrs. Mannon.

CHRISTINE: Good-bye, Peter. (*He disappears from the drive, left.* CHRISTINE *comes forward*) I must say you treat your one devoted swain pretty rudely. (LAVINIA *doesn't reply.* CHRISTINE *goes on coolly*) I was wondering when I was going to see you. When I returned from New York last night you seemed to have gone to bed.

LAVINIA: I had gone to bed.

CHRISTINE: You usually read long after that. I tried your door—but you had locked yourself in. When you kept yourself locked in all day I was sure you were intentionally avoiding me. But Annie said you had a headache. (*While she has been speaking she has come toward* LAVINIA *until she is now within arm's reach of her. The facial resemblance, as they stand there, is extraordinary.* CHRISTINE *stares at her coolly, but one senses an uneasy wariness beneath her pose*) Did you have a headache?

LAVINIA: No. I wanted to be alone—to think over things.

CHRISTINE: What things, if I may ask? (*Then, as if she were afraid of an answer to this question, she abruptly changes the subject*) Who are those people I saw wandering about the grounds?

LAVINIA: Some friends of Seth's.

CHRISTINE: Because they know that lazy old sot, does it give them the privilege of trespassing?

LAVINIA: I gave Seth permission to show them around.

CHRISTINE: And since when have you the right without consulting me?

LAVINIA: I couldn't very well consult you when Seth asked me. You had gone to New York— (*She pauses a second—then adds slowly, staring fixedly at her mother*) to see Grandfather. Is he feeling any better? He seems to have been sick so much this past year.

CHRISTINE: (*casually, avoiding her eyes*) Yes. He's much better now. He'll soon be going the rounds to his patients again, he hopes. (*As if anxious to change the subject, looking at the flowers she carries*) I've been to the greenhouse to pick these. I felt our tomb needed a little brightening. (*She nods scornfully toward the house*) Each time I come back after being away it appears more like a sepulchre! The "whited" one of the Bible—pagan temple front stuck like a mask on Puritan gray ugliness! It was just like old Abe Mannon to build such a monstrosity—as a temple for his hatred. (*Then with a little mocking laugh*) Forgive me, Vinnie. I forgot you liked it. And you ought to. It suits your temperament. (LAVINIA *stares at her but remains silent.* CHRISTINE *glances at her flowers again and turns toward the house*) I must put these in water. (*She moves a few steps toward the house—then turns again— with a studied casualness*) By the way, before I forget, I happened to run into Captain Brant on the street in New York. He said he was coming up here today to take over his ship and asked me if he might drop in to see you. I told him he could—and stay to supper with us. (*Without looking at* LAVINIA, *who is staring at her with a face grown grim and hard*) Doesn't that please you, Vinnie? Or do you remain true to your one and only beau, Peter?

LAVINIA: Is that why you picked the flowers—because he is coming? (*Her mother does not answer. She goes on with a threatening undercurrent in her voice*) You have heard the news, I suppose? It means Father will be home soon!

CHRISTINE: (*without looking at her—coolly*) We've had so many rumors lately. This report hasn't been confirmed yet, has it? I haven't heard the fort firing a salute.

LAVINIA: You will before long!

CHRISTINE: I'm sure I hope so as much as you.

LAVINIA: You can say that!

CHRISTINE: (*concealing her alarm—coldly*) What do you mean? You will kindly not take that tone with me, please! (*Cuttingly*) If you are determined to quarrel, let us go into the house. We might be overheard out here. (*She turns and sees* SETH *who has just come to the corner of the house, left, and is standing there watching them*) See. There is your old crony doing his best to listen now! (*Moving to the steps*) I am going in and rest a while. (*She walks up the steps*).

LAVINIA: (*harshly*) I've got to have a talk with you, Mother—before long!

CHRISTINE: (*turning defiantly*) Whenever you wish. Tonight after the Captain leaves you, if you like. But what is it you want to talk about?

LAVINIA: You'll know soon enough!

CHRISTINE: (*staring at her with a questioning dread—forcing a scornful smile*) You always make such a mystery of things, Vinnie. (*She goes into the house and closes the door behind her.* SETH *comes forward from where he had withdrawn around the corner of the house.* LAVINIA *makes a motion for him to follow her, and goes and sits on the bench at left. A pause. She stares straight ahead, her face frozen, her eyes hard. He regards her understandingly*).

LAVINIA: (*abruptly*) Well? What is it about Captain Brant you want to warn me against? (*Then as if she felt she must defend her question from some suspicion that she knows is in his mind*) I want to know all I can about him because—he seems to be calling to court me.

SETH: (*managing to convey his entire disbelief of this statement in one word*) Ayeh.

LAVINIA: (*sharply*) You say that as if you didn't believe me.

SETH: I believe anything you tell me to believe. I ain't been with the Mannons for sixty years without learning that. (*A pause. Then he asks slowly*) Ain't you noticed this Brant reminds you of someone in looks?

LAVINIA: (*struck by this*) Yes. I have—ever since I first saw him— but I've never been able to place who— Who do you mean?

SETH: Your Paw, ain't it, Vinnie?

LAVINIA: (*startled—agitatedly*) Father? No! It can't be! (*Then as if the conviction were forcing itself on her in spite of herself*) Yes! He does— something about his face—that must be why I've had the strange feeling I've known him before—why I've felt— (*Then tensely as if she were about to break down*) Oh! I won't believe it! You must be mistaken, Seth! That would be too—!

SETH: He ain't only like your Paw. He's like Orin, too—and all the Mannons I've known.

LAVINIA: (*frightenedly*) But why—why should he—?

SETH: More speshully he calls to my mind your Grandpaw's brother, David. How much do you know about David Mannon, Vinnie? I know his name's never been allowed to be spoke among Mannons since the day he left—but you've likely heard gossip, ain't you—even if it all happened before you was born.

LAVINIA: I've heard that he loved the Canuck nurse girl who was taking care of Father's little sister who died, and had to marry her because she was going to have a baby; and that Grandfather put them both out of the house and then afterwards tore it down and built this one because he wouldn't live where his brother had disgraced the family. But what has that old scandal got to do with—

SETH: Wait. Right after they was throwed out they married and went away. There was talk they'd gone out West, but no one knew nothin' about 'em afterwards—'ceptin' your Grandpaw let out to me one time she'd had the baby—a boy. He was cussin' it. (*Then impressively*) It's about her baby I've been thinkin', Vinnie.

LAVINIA: (*a look of appalled comprehension growing on her face*) Oh!

SETH: How old is that Brant, Vinnie?

LAVINIA: Thirty-six, I think.

SETH: Ayeh! That'd make it right. And here's another funny thing—his name. Brant's sort of queer fur a name. I ain't never heard tell of it before. Sounds made up to me—like short fur somethin' else. Remember what that Canuck girl's name was, do you, Vinnie? Marie Brantôme! See what I'm drivin' at?

LAVINIA: (*agitatedly, fighting against a growing conviction*) But—don't be stupid, Seth—his name would be Mannon and he'd be only too proud of it.

SETH: He'd have good reason not to use the name of Mannon when he came callin' here, wouldn't he? If your Paw ever guessed—!

LAVINIA: (*breaking out violently*) No! It can't be! God wouldn't let it! It would be too horrible—on top of—! I won't even think of it, do you hear? Why did you have to tell me?

SETH: (*calmingly*) There now! Don't take on, Vinnie. No need gettin' riled at me. (*He waits—then goes on insistently*) All I'm drivin' at is that it's durned funny—his looks and the name—and you'd ought fur your Paw's sake to make sartin.

LAVINIA: How can I make certain?

SETH: Catch him off guard sometime and put it up to him strong—as if you knowed it—and see if mebbe he don't give himself away. (*He starts to go—looks down the drive at left*) Looks like him comin' up the drive now, Vinnie. There's somethin' about his walk calls back David Mannon, too. If I didn't know it was him I'd think it was David's ghost comin' home. (*He turns away abruptly*) Wal, calc'late I better git back to work. (*He walks around the left corner of the house. A pause. Then* CAPTAIN ADAM BRANT *enters from the drive, left, front. He starts on seeing* LAVINIA *but immediately puts on his most polite, winning air. One is struck at a glance by the peculiar quality his face in repose has of being a life-like mask rather than living flesh. He has a broad, low forehead, framed by coal-black straight hair which he wears noticeably long, pushed back carelessly from his forehead as a poet's might be. He has a big aquiline nose, bushy eyebrows, swarthy complexion, hazel eyes. His wide mouth is sensual and moody—a mouth that can be strong and weak by turns. He wears a mustache, but his heavy cleft chin is clean-shaven. In figure he is tall, broad-shouldered and powerful. He gives the impression of being always on the offensive or defensive, always fighting life. He is dressed with an almost foppish extravagance, with touches of studied carelessness, as if a romantic Byronic appearance were the ideal in mind. There is little of the obvious ship captain about him, except his big, strong hands and his deep voice).*

BRANT: (*bowing with an exaggerated politeness*) Good afternoon. (*Coming and taking her hand which she forces herself to hold out to him*) Hope you don't mind my walking in on you without ceremony. Your mother told me—

LAVINIA: I know. She had to go out for a while and she said I was to keep you company until she returned.

BRANT: (*gallantly*) Well, I'm in good luck, then. I hope she doesn't hurry back to stand watch over us. I haven't had a chance to be alone with you since—that night we went walking in the moonlight, do you remember? (*He has kept her hand and he drops his voice to a low, lover-like tone.* LAVINIA *cannot repress a start, agitatedly snatching her hand from his and turning away from him*).

LAVINIA: (*regaining command of herself—slowly*) What do you think of the news of Lee surrendering, Captain? We expect my father home very soon now. (*At something in her tone he stares at her suspiciously, but she is looking straight before her*) Why don't you sit down?

BRANT: Thank you. (*He sits on the bench at her right. He has become wary now, feeling something strange in her attitude but not able to make her out—casually*) Yes, you must be very happy at the prospect of seeing your father again. Your mother has told me how close you've always been to him.

LAVINIA: Did she? (*Then with intensity*) I love Father better than anyone in the world. There is nothing I wouldn't do—to protect him from hurt!

BRANT: (*watching her carefully—keeping his casual tone*) You care more for him than for your mother?

LAVINIA: Yes.

BRANT: Well, I suppose that's the usual way of it. A daughter feels closer to her father and a son to his mother. But I should think you ought to be a born exception to that rule.

LAVINIA: Why?

BRANT: You're so like your mother in some ways. Your face is the dead image of hers. And look at your hair. You won't meet hair like yours and hers again in a month of Sundays. I only know of one other woman who had it. You'll think it strange when I tell you. It was my mother.

LAVINIA: (*with a start*) Ah!

BRANT: (*dropping his voice to a reverent, hushed tone*) Yes, she had beautiful hair like your mother's, that hung down to her knees, and big, deep, sad eyes that were blue as the Caribbean Sea!

LAVINIA: (*harshly*) What do looks amount to? I'm not a bit like her! Everybody knows I take after Father!

BRANT: (*brought back with a shock, astonished at her tone*) But—you're not angry at me for saying that, are you? (*Then filled with uneasiness and resolving he must establish himself on an intimate footing with her again— with engaging bluntness*) You're puzzling today, Miss Lavinia. You'll excuse me if I come out with it bluntly. I've lived most of my life at sea and in camps and I'm used to straight speaking. What are you holding against me? If I've done anything to offend you, I swear it wasn't meant. (*She is silent, staring before her with hard eyes, rigidly upright. He appraises her with a calculating look, then goes on*) I wouldn't have bad feeling come between us for the world. I may only be flattering myself, but I thought you liked me. Have you forgotten that night walking along the shore?

LAVINIA: (*in a cold, hard voice*) I haven't forgotten. Did Mother tell you you could kiss me?

BRANT: What—what do you mean? (*But he at once attributes the question to her naïveté—laughingly*) Oh! I see! But, come now, Lavinia, you can't mean, can you, I should have asked her permission?

LAVINIA: Shouldn't you?

BRANT: (*again uneasy—trying to joke it off*) Well, I wasn't brought up that strictly and, should or shouldn't, at any rate, I didn't—and it wasn't the less sweet for that! (*Then at something in her face he hurriedly goes off on another tack*) I'm afraid I gabbed to much that night. Maybe I bored you with my talk of clipper ships and my love for them?

LAVINIA: (*dryly*) "Tall, white clippers," you called them. You said they were like beautiful, pale women to you. You said you loved them more than you'd ever loved a woman. Is that true, Captain?

BRANT: (*with forced gallantry*) Aye. But I meant, before I met you. (*Then thinking he has at last hit on the cause of her changed attitude toward him—with a laugh*) So that's what you're holding against me, is it? Well, I might have guessed. Women are jealous of ships. They always suspect the sea. They know they're three of a kind when it comes to a man! (*He laughs again but less certainly this time, as he regards her grim, set expression*) Yes, I might have seen you didn't appear much taken by my sea gamming that night. I suppose clippers are too old a story to the daughter of a ship builder. But unless I'm much mistaken, you were interested when I told you of the islands in the South Seas where I was shipwrecked my first voyage at sea.

LAVINIA: (*in a dry, brittle tone*) I remember your admiration for the naked native women. You said they had found the secret of happiness because they had never heard that love can be a sin.

BRANT: (*surprised—sizing her up puzzledly*) So you remember that, do you? (*Then romantically*) Aye! And they live in as near the Garden of Paradise before sin was discovered as you'll find on this earth! Unless you've seen it, you can't picture the green beauty of their land set in the blue of the sea! The clouds like down on the mountain tops, the sun drowsing in your blood, and always the surf on the barrier reef singing a croon in your ears like a lullaby! The Blessed Isles, I'd call them! You can forget there all men's dirty dreams of greed and power!

LAVINIA: And their dirty dreams—of love?

BRANT: (*startled again—staring at her uneasily*) Why do you say that? What do you mean, Lavinia?

LAVINIA: Nothing. I was only thinking—of your Blessed Isles.

BRANT: (*uncertainly*) Oh! But you said— (*Then with a confused, stupid persistence he comes closer to her, dropping his voice again to his love-making tone*) Whenever I remember those islands now, I will always think of you, as you walked beside me that night with your hair blowing in the sea wind and the moonlight in your eyes! (*He tries to take her hand, but at his touch she pulls away and springs to her feet*).

LAVINIA: (*with cold fury*) Don't you touch me! Don't you dare—! You liar! You—! (*Then as he starts back in confusion, she seizes this opportunity to follow* SETH's *advice—staring at him with deliberately insulting scorn*) But I suppose it would be foolish to expect anything but cheap romantic lies from the son of a low Canuck nurse girl!

BRANT: (*stunned*) What's that? (*Then rage at the insult to his mother overcoming all prudence—springs to his feet threateningly*) Belay, damn you!—or I'll forget you're a woman—no Mannon can insult her while I—

LAVINIA: (*appalled now she knows the truth*) So—it is true— You are her son! Oh!

BRANT: (*fighting to control himself—with harsh defiance*) And what if I am? I'm proud to be! My only shame is my dirty Mannon blood! So that's why you couldn't stand my touching you just now, is it? You're too good for the son of a servant, eh? By God, you were glad enough before—!

LAVINIA: (*fiercely*) It's not true! I was only leading you on to find out things!

BRANT: Oh, no! It's only since you suspected who I was! I suppose your father has stuffed you with his lies about my mother! But, by God, you'll hear the truth of it, now you know who I am— And you'll see if you or any Mannon has the right to look down on her!

LAVINIA: I don't want to hear— (*She starts to go toward the house*).

BRANT: (*grabbing her by the arm—tauntingly*) You're a coward, are you, like all Mannons, when it comes to facing the truth about themselves? (*She turns on him defiantly. He drops her arm and goes on harshly*) I'll bet he never told you your grandfather, Abe Mannon, as well as his brother, loved my mother!

LAVINIA: It's a lie!

BRANT: It's the truth. It was his jealous revenge made him disown my father and cheat him out of his share of the business they'd inherited!

LAVINIA: He didn't cheat him! He bought him out!

BRANT: Forced him to sell for one-tenth its worth, you mean! He knew my father and mother were starving! But the money didn't last my father long! He'd taken to drink. He was a coward—like all Mannons—once he felt the world looked down on him. He skulked and avoided people. He grew ashamed of my mother—and me. He sank down and down and my mother worked and supported him. I can remember when men from the corner saloon would drag him home and he'd fall in the door, a sodden carcass. One night when I was seven he came home crazy drunk and hit my mother in the face. It was the first time he'd ever struck her. It made me blind mad. I hit at him with the poker and cut his head. My mother pulled me back and gave me a hiding. Then she cried over him. She'd never stopped loving him.

LAVINIA: Why do you tell me this? I told you once I don't want to hear—

BRANT: (*grimly*) You'll see the point of it damned soon! (*Unheeding— as if the scene were still before his eyes*) For days after, he sat and stared at nothing. One time when we were alone he asked me to forgive him hitting her. But I hated him and I wouldn't forgive him. Then one night he went out and he didn't come back. The next morning they found him hanging in a barn!

LAVINIA: (*with a shudder*) Oh!

BRANT: (*savagely*) The only decent thing he ever did!

LAVINIA: You're lying! No Mannon would ever—

BRANT: Oh, wouldn't they? They are all fine, honorable gentlemen, you think! Then listen a bit and you'll hear something about another of them! (*Then going on bitterly with his story*) My mother sewed for a living and sent me to school. She was very strict with me. She blamed me for his killing himself. But she was bound she'd make a gentleman of me—like he was!—if it took her last cent and her last strap! (*With a grim smile*) She didn't succeed, as you notice! At seventeen I ran away to sea—and forgot I had a mother, except I took part of her name—Brant was short and easy on ships—and I wouldn't wear the name of Mannon. I forgot her until two years ago when I came back from the East. Oh, I'd written to her now and then and sent her money when I happened to have any. But I'd forgotten her just the same—and when I got to New York I found her dying—of sickness and starvation! And I found out that when she'd been laid up, not able to work, not knowing where to reach me, she'd sunk her last shred of pride and written to your father asking for a loan. He never answered her. And I came too late. She died in my arms. (*With vindictive passion*) He could have saved her—and he deliberately let her die! He's as guilty of murder as anyone he ever sent to the rope when he was a judge!

LAVINIA: (*springing to her feet—furiously*) You dare say that about Father! If he were here—

BRANT: I wish to God he was! I'd tell him what I tell you now—that I swore on my mother's body I'd revenge her death on him.

LAVINIA: (*with cold deadly intensity*) And I suppose you boast that now you've done so, don't you?—in the vilest, most cowardly way—like the son of a servant you are!

BRANT: (*again thrown off guard—furiously*) Belay, I told you, with that kind of talk!

LAVINIA: She is only your means of revenge on Father, is that it?

BRANT: (*stunned—stammers in guilty confusion*) What?—She?—Who?—I don't know what you're talking about!

LAVINIA: Then you soon will know! And so will she! I've found out all I wanted to from you. I'm going in to talk to her now. You wait here until I call you!

BRANT: (*furious at her tone*) No! Be damned if you can order me about as if I was your servant!

LAVINIA: (*icily*) If you have any consideration for her, you'll do as I say and not force me to write my father. (*She turns her back on him and walks to the steps woodenly erect and square-shouldered*).

BRANT: (*desperately now—with a grotesque catching at his lover's manner*) I don't know what you mean, Lavinia. I swear before God it is only you I— (*She turns at the top of the steps at this and stares at him with such a passion of hatred that he is silenced. Her lips move as if she were going to speak, but she fights back the words, turns stiffly and goes into the house and closes the door behind her*).

CURTAIN

Act Two

SCENE—*In the house—*EZRA MANNON'S *study. No time has elapsed.*

The study is a large room with a stiff, austere atmosphere. The furniture is old colonial. The walls are plain plastered surfaces tinted a dull gray with a flat white trim. At rear, right, is a door leading to the hall. On the right wall is a painting of George Washington in a gilt frame, flanked by smaller portraits of Alexander Hamilton and John Marshall. At rear, center, is an open fireplace. At left of fireplace, a bookcase filled with law books. Above the fireplace, in a plain frame, is a large portrait of EZRA MANNON *himself, painted ten years previously. One is at once struck by the startling likeness between him and* ADAM BRANT. *He is a tall man in his early forties, with a spare, wiry frame, seated stiffly in an armchair, his hands on the arms, wearing his black judge's robe. His face is handsome in a stern, aloof fashion. It is cold and emotionless and has the same strange semblance of a life-like mask that we have already seen in the faces of his wife and daughter and* BRANT.

On the left are two windows. Between them a desk. A large table with an armchair on either side, right and left, stands at left center, front. At right center is another chair. There are hooked rugs on the floor.

Outside the sun is beginning to set and its glow fills the room with a golden mist. As the action progresses this becomes brighter, then turns to crimson, which darkens to somberness at the end.

LAVINIA *is discovered standing by the table. She is fighting to control herself, but her face is torn by a look of stricken anguish. She turns slowly to her father's portrait and for a moment stares at it fixedly. Then she goes to it and puts her hand over one of his hands with a loving, protecting gesture.*

LAVINIA: Poor Father! (*She hears a noise in the hall and moves hastily away. The door from the hall is opened and* CHRISTINE *enters. She is uneasy underneath, but affects a scornful indignation*).

CHRISTINE: Really, this unconfirmed report must have turned your head—otherwise I'd find it difficult to understand your sending Annie to disturb me when you knew I was resting.

LAVINIA: I told you I had to talk to you.

CHRISTINE: (*looking around the room with aversion*) But why in this musty room, of all places?

LAVINIA: (*indicating the portrait—quietly*) Because it's Father's room.

CHRISTINE: (*starts, looks at the portrait and quickly drops her eyes.* LAVINIA *goes to the door and closes it.* CHRISTINE *says with forced scorn*) More mystery?

LAVINIA: You better sit down. (CHRISTINE *sits in the chair at rear center.* LAVINIA *goes back to her father's chair at left of table*).

CHRISTINE: Well—if you're quite ready, perhaps you will explain.

LAVINIA: I suppose Annie told you I'd been to visit Hazel and Peter while you were away.

CHRISTINE: Yes. I thought it peculiar. You never visit anyone overnight. Why did you suddenly take that notion?

LAVINIA: I didn't.

CHRISTINE: You didn't visit them?

LAVINIA: No.

CHRISTINE: Then where did you go?

LAVINIA: (*accusingly*) To New York! (CHRISTINE *starts.* LAVINIA *hurries on a bit incoherently*) I've suspected something—lately—the excuse you've made for all your trips there the past year, that Grandfather was sick— (*As* CHRISTINE *is about to protest indignantly*) Oh! I know he has been—and you've stayed at his house—but I've suspected lately that wasn't the real reason—and now I can prove it isn't! Because I waited outside Grandfather's house and followed you. I saw you meet Brant!

CHRISTINE: (*alarmed but concealing it—coolly*) Well, what if you did? I told you myself I ran into him by accident—

LAVINIA: You went to his room!

CHRISTINE: (*shaken*) He asked me to meet a friend of his—a lady. It was her house we went to.

LAVINIA: I asked the woman in the basement. He had hired the room under another name, but she recognized his description. And yours too. She said you had come there often in the past year.

CHRISTINE: (*desperately*) It was the first time I had ever been there. He insisted on my going. He said he had to talk to me about you. He wanted my help to approach your father—

LAVINIA: (*furiously*) How can you lie like that? How can you be so vile as to try to use me to hide your adultery?

CHRISTINE: (*springing up—with weak indignation*) Vinnie!

LAVINIA: Your adultery, I said!

CHRISTINE: No!

LAVINIA: Stop lying, I tell you! I went upstairs! I heard you telling him—"I love you, Adam"—and kissing him! (*with a cold bitter fury*) You vile—! You're shameless and evil! Even if you are my mother, I say it! (CHRISTINE *stares at her, overwhelmed by this onslaught, her poise shattered for the moment. She tries to keep her voice indifferent but it trembles a little*).

CHRISTINE: I—I knew you hated me, Vinnie—but not as bitterly as that! (*Then with a return of her defiant coolness*) Very well! I love Adam Brant. What are you going to do?

LAVINIA: How you say that—without any shame! You don't give one thought to Father—who is so good—who trusts you! Oh, how could you do this to Father? How could you?

CHRISTINE: (*with strident intensity*) You would understand if you were the wife of a man you hated!

LAVINIA: (*horrified—with a glance at the portrait*) Don't! Don't say that—before him! I won't listen!

CHRISTINE: (*grabbing her by the arm*) You will listen! I'm talking to you as a woman now, not as mother to daughter! That relationship has no meaning between us! You've called me vile and shameless! Well, I want you to know that's what I've felt about myself for over twenty years, giving my body to a man I—

LAVINIA: (*trying to break away from her, half putting her hands up to her ears*) Stop telling me such things! Let me go! (*She breaks away, shrinking from her mother with a look of sick repulsion. A pause. She stammers*) You—then you've always hated Father?

CHRISTINE: (*bitterly*) No. I loved him once—before I married him— incredible as that seems now! He was handsome in his lieutenant's uniform! He was silent and mysterious and romantic! But marriage soon turned his romance into—disgust!

LAVINIA: (*wincing again—stammers harshly*) So I was born of your disgust! I've always guessed that, Mother—ever since I was little—when I used to come to you—with love—but you would always push me away! I've felt it ever since I can remember—your disgust! (*Then with a flare-up of bitter hatred*) Oh, I hate you! It's only right I should hate you!

CHRISTINE: (*shaken—defensively*) I tried to love you. I told myself it wasn't human not to love my own child, born of my body. But I never could make myself feel you were born of any body but his! You were always my wedding night to me—and my honeymoon!

LAVINIA: Stop saying that! How can you be so—! (*Then suddenly—with a strange jealous bitterness*) You've loved Orin! Why didn't you hate him, too?

CHRISTINE: Because by then I had forced myself to become resigned in order to live! And most of the time I was carrying him, your father was with the army in Mexico. I had forgotten him. And when Orin was born he seemed my child, only mine, and I loved him for that! (*Bitterly*) I loved him until he let you and your father nag him into the war, in spite of my begging him not to leave me alone. (*Staring at* LAVINIA *with hatred*) I know his leaving me was your doing principally, Vinnie!

LAVINIA: (*sternly*) It was his duty as a Mannon to go! He'd have been sorry the rest of his life if he hadn't! I love him better than you! I was thinking of him!

CHRISTINE: Well, I hope you realize I never would have fallen in love with Adam if I'd had Orin with me. When he had gone there was nothing left—but hate and a desire to be revenged—and a longing for love! And it was then I met Adam. I saw he loved me—

LAVINIA: (*with taunting scorn*) He doesn't love you! You're only his revenge on Father! Do you know who he really is? He's the son of that low nurse girl Grandfather put out of our house!

CHRISTINE: (*concealing a start—coolly*) So you've found that out? Were you hoping it would be a crushing surprise to me? I've known it all along. He told me when he said he loved me.

LAVINIA: Oh! And I suppose knowing who he was gave you all the more satisfaction—to add that disgrace!

CHRISTINE: (*cuttingly*) Will you kindly come to the point and tell me what you intend doing? I suppose you'll hardly let your father get in the door before you tell him!

LAVINIA: (*suddenly becoming rigid and cold again—slowly*) No. Not unless you force me to. (*Then as she sees her mother's astonishment—grimly*) I don't wonder you're surprised! You know you deserve the worst punishment you could get. And Father would disown you publicly, no matter how much the scandal cost him!

CHRISTINE: I realize that. I know him even better than you do!

LAVINIA: And I'd like to see you punished for your wickedness! So please understand this isn't for your sake. It's for Father's. He hasn't been well lately. I'm not going to have him hurt! It's my first duty to protect him from you!

CHRISTINE: I know better than to expect any generosity on my account.

LAVINIA: I won't tell him, provided you give up Brant and never see him again—and promise to be a dutiful wife to Father and make up for the wrong you've done him!

CHRISTINE: (*stares at her daughter—a pause—then she laughs dryly*) What a fraud you are, with your talk of your father and your duty! Oh, I'm not denying you want to save his pride—and I know how anxious you are to keep the family from more scandal! But all the same, that's not your real reason for sparing me!

LAVINIA: (*confused—guiltily*) It is!

CHRISTINE: You wanted Adam Brant yourself!

LAVINIA: That's a lie!

CHRISTINE: And now you know you can't have him, you're determined that at least you'll take him from me!

LAVINIA: No!

CHRISTINE: But if you told your father, I'd have to go away with Adam. He'd be mine still. You can't bear that thought, even at the price of my disgrace, can you?

LAVINIA: It's your evil mind!

CHRISTINE: I know you, Vinnie! I've watched you ever since you were little, trying to do exactly what you're doing now! You've tried to become the wife of your father and the mother of Orin! You've always schemed to steal my place!

LAVINIA: (*wildly*) No! It's you who have stolen all love from me since the time I was born! (*Then her manner becoming threatening*) But I don't want to listen to any more of your lies and excuses! I want to know right now whether you're going to do what I told you or not!

CHRISTINE: Suppose I refuse! Suppose I go off openly with Adam! Where will you and your father and the family name be after that scandal? And what if I were disgraced myself? I'd have the man I love, at least!

LAVINIA: (*grimly*) Not for long! Father would use all his influence and get Brant blacklisted so he'd lose his command and never get another! You know how much the "Flying Trades" means to him. And Father would never divorce you. You could never marry. You'd be an anchor around his neck. Don't forget you're five years older than he is! He'll still be in his prime when you're an old woman with all your looks gone! He'd grow to hate the sight of you!

CHRISTINE: (*stung beyond bearing—makes a threatening move as if to strike her daughter's face*) You devil! You mean little—! (*But* LAVINIA *stares back coldly into her eyes and she controls herself and drops her hand*).

LAVINIA: I wouldn't call names if I were you! There is one you deserve!

CHRISTINE: (*turning away—her voice still trembling*) I'm a fool to let you make me lose my temper—over your jealous spite! (*A pause.* LAVINIA *stares at her.* CHRISTINE *seems considering something. A sinister expression comes to her face. Then she turns back to* LAVINIA—*coldly*) But you wanted my answer, didn't you? Well, I agree to do as you said. I promise you I'll never see Adam again after he calls this evening. Are you satisfied?

LAVINIA: (*stares at her with cold suspicion*) You seem to take giving him up pretty easily!

CHRISTINE: (*hastily*) Do you think I'll ever give you the satisfaction of seeing me grieve? Oh, no, Vinnie! You'll never have a chance to gloat!

LAVINIA: (*still suspiciously—with a touch of scorn*) If I loved anyone—!

CHRISTINE: (*tauntingly*) If? I think you do love him—as much as you can love! (*With a sudden flurry of jealousy*) You little fool! Don't you know I made him flirt with you, so you wouldn't be suspicious?

LAVINIA: (*gives a little shudder—then fiercely*) He didn't fool me! I saw what a liar he was! I just led him on—to find out things! I always hated him! (CHRISTINE *smiles mockingly and turns away, as if to go out of the room.* LAVINIA'S *manner becomes threatening again*) Wait! I don't trust you! I know you're thinking already how you can fool me and break the promise you've just made! But you better not try it! I'll be watching you every minute! And I won't be the only one! I wrote to Father and Orin as soon as I got back from New York!

CHRISTINE: (*startled*) About Adam?

LAVINIA: Only enough so they'd be suspicious and watch you too. I said a Captain Brant had been calling and folks had begun to gossip.

CHRISTINE: Ah! I see what it's going to mean—that you'll always have this to hold over me and I'll be under your thumb for the rest of my life! (*She cannot restrain her rage—threateningly*) Take care, Vinnie! You'll be responsible if—! (*She checks herself abruptly*).

LAVINIA: (*suspiciously*) If what?

CHRISTINE: (*quickly*) Nothing. I only meant if I went off with Adam. But of course you know I won't do that. You know there's nothing I can do now—but obey your orders!

LAVINIA: (*continues to stare at her suspiciously—grimly*) You ought to see it's your duty to Father, not my orders—if you had any honor or decency! (*Then brusquely*) Brant is waiting outside. You can tell him what you've got to do—and tell him if he ever dares come here again—! (*Forcing back her anger*) And see that you get rid of him right now! I'm going upstreet to get the latest news. I won't be gone more than a half-hour and I want him out of the house by the time I get back, do you hear? If he isn't, I'll write Father again. I won't even wait for him to come home! (*She turns her back on her mother and marches out the door, square-shouldered and stiff, without a backward glance.* CHRISTINE *looks after her, waiting until she hears the side door of the house close after her. Then she turns and stands in tense calculating thought. Her face has become like a sinister evil mask. Finally, as if making up her mind irrevocably, she comes to the table, tears off a slip of paper and writes two words on it. She tucks this paper in the sleeve of her dress and goes to the open window and calls*).

CHRISTINE: Adam! (*She moves toward the door to wait for him. Her eyes are caught by the eyes of her husband in the portrait over the fireplace. She stares at him with hatred and addresses him vindictively, half under her breath*) You can thank Vinnie, Ezra! (*She goes to the door and reaches it just as* BRANT *appears from the hall. She takes his hand and draws him into the room, closing the door behind him. One is immediately struck by the resemblance between his face and that of the portrait of* EZRA MANNON).

BRANT: (*glancing uneasily at her, as they come to the center of the room*) She knows—?

CHRISTINE: Yes. She followed me to New York. And she's found out who you are too, Adam.

BRANT: (*with a grim smile*) I know. She got that out of me—the proof of it, at any rate. Before I knew what was up I'd given myself away.

CHRISTINE: She must have noticed your resemblance to Orin. I was afraid that might start her thinking.

BRANT: (*sees the portrait for the first time. Instantly his body shifts to a fighting tenseness. It is as if he were going to spring at the figure in the painting. He says slowly*) That, I take it, is General Mannon?

CHRISTINE: Judge Mannon then. Don't forget he used to be a judge. He won't forget it.

BRANT: (*his eyes still fixed on the portrait—comes and sits in* MANNON's *chair on the left of table. Unconsciously he takes the same attitude as* MANNON, *sitting erect, his hands on the arms of the chair—slowly*) Does Orin by any chance resemble his father?

CHRISTINE: (*stares at him—agitatedly*) No! Of course not! What put such a stupid idea in your head?

BRANT: It would be damned queer if you fell in love with me because I recalled Ezra Mannon to you!

CHRISTINE: (*going to him and putting an arm around his shoulder*) No, no, I tell you! It was Orin you made me think of! It was Orin!

BRANT: I remember that night we were introduced and I heard the name Mrs. Ezra Mannon! By God, how I hated you then for being his! I thought, by God, I'll take her from him and that'll be part of my revenge! And out of that hatred my love came! It's damned queer, isn't it?

CHRISTINE: (*hugging him to her*) Are you going to let him take me from you now, Adam?

BRANT: (*passionately*) You ask that!

CHRISTINE: You swear you won't—no matter what you must do?

BRANT: By God, I swear it!

CHRISTINE: (*kisses him*) Remember that oath! (*She glances at the portrait—then turns back to* BRANT *with a little shiver—nervously*) What made you sit there? It's his chair. I've so often seen him sitting there— (*Forcing a little laugh*) Your silly talk about resemblances— Don't sit there. Come. Bring that chair over here. (*She moves to the chair at right center. He brings the chair at right of table close to hers*).

BRANT: We've got to decide what we must do. The time for skulking and lying is over—and by God I'm glad of it! It's a coward's game I have no stomach for! (*He has placed the chair beside hers. She is staring at the portrait*) Why don't you sit down, Christine?

CHRISTINE: (*slowly*) I was thinking—perhaps we had better go to the sitting-room. (*Then defiantly*) No! I've been afraid of you long enough, Ezra! (*She sits down*).

BRANT: I felt there was something wrong the moment I saw her. I tried my damnedest to put her off the course by giving her some softsoap— as you'd told me to do to blind her. (*Frowning*) That was a mistake, Christine. It made her pay too much attention to me—and opened her eyes!

CHRISTINE: Oh, I know I've made one blunder after another. It's as if love drove me on to do everything I shouldn't. I never should have brought you to this house. Seeing you in New York should have been enough for me. But I loved you too much. I wanted you every possible moment we could steal! And I simply couldn't believe that he ever would come home. I prayed that he should be killed in the war so intensely that I finally believed it would surely happen! (*With savage intensity*) Oh, if he were only dead!

BRANT: That chance is finished now.

CHRISTINE: (*slowly—without looking at him*) Yes—in that way.

BRANT: (*stares at her*) What do you mean? (*She remains silent. He changes the subject uneasily*) There's only one thing to do! When he comes home I'll wait for him and not give Vinnie the satisfaction of telling him. I'll tell him myself. (*Vindictively*) By God! I'd give my soul to see his face when he knows you love Marie Brantôme's son! And then I'll take you away openly and laugh at him! And if he tries to stop me—! (*He stops and glances with savage hatred at the portrait*).

CHRISTINE: What would you do then?

BRANT: If ever I laid hands on him, I'd kill him!

CHRISTINE: And then? You would be hanged for murder! And where would I be? There would be nothing left for me but to kill myself!

BRANT: If I could catch him alone, where no one would interfere, and let the best man come out alive—as I've often seen it done in the West!

CHRISTINE: This isn't the West.

BRANT: I could insult him on the street before everyone and make him fight me! I could let him shoot first and then kill him in self-defense.

CHRISTINE: (*scornfully*) Do you imagine you could force him to fight a duel with you? Don't you know duelling is illegal? Oh, no! He'd simply feel bound to do his duty as a former judge and have you arrested! (*She adds calculatingly, seeing he is boiling inside*) It would be a poor revenge for your mother's death to let him make you a laughing stock!

BRANT: But when I take you off, the laugh will be on him! You can come on the "Flying Trades."

CHRISTINE: (*calculatingly reproachful*) I don't think you'd propose that, Adam, if you stopped thinking of your revenge for a moment and thought of me! Don't you realize he would never divorce me, out of spite? What would I be in the world's eyes? My life would be ruined and I would ruin yours! You'd grow to hate me!

BRANT: (*passionately*) Don't talk like that! It's a lie and you know it!

CHRISTINE: (*with bitter yearning*) If I could only believe that, Adam! But I'll grow old so soon! And I'm afraid of time! (*Then abruptly changing tone*) As for my sailing on your ship, you'll find you won't have a ship! He'll see to it you lose this command and get you blacklisted so you'll have no chance of getting another.

BRANT: (*angrily*) Aye! He can do that if he sets about it. There are twice as many skippers as ships these days.

CHRISTINE: (*calculatingly—without looking at him*) If he had only been killed, we could be married now and I would bring you my share of the Mannon estate. That would only be justice. It's yours by right. It's what his father stole from yours.

BRANT: That's true enough, damn him!

CHRISTINE: You wouldn't have to worry about commands or owners' favors then. You could buy your own ship and be your own master!

BRANT: (*yearningly*) That's always been my dream—some day to own my own clipper! And Clark and Dawson would be willing to sell the "Flying Trades." (*Then forgetting everything in his enthusiasm*) You've seen her, Christine. She's as beautiful a ship as you're a woman. Aye, the two of you are like sisters. If she was mine, I'd take you on a honeymoon then! To China—and on the voyage back, we'd stop at the South Pacific Islands I've told you about. By God, there's the right place for love and a honeymoon!

CHRISTINE: (*slowly*) Yes—but Ezra is alive!

BRANT: (*brought back to earth—gloomily*) I know it's only a dream.

CHRISTINE: (*turning to stare at him—slowly*) You can have your dream—and I can have mine. There is a way. (*Then turning away again*) You remember my telling you he had written complaining of pains about his heart?

BRANT: You're surely not hoping—

CHRISTINE: No. He said it was nothing serious. But I've let it be known that he has heart trouble. I went to see our old family doctor and told him about Ezra's letter. I pretended to be dreadfully worried, until I got him worried too. He's the town's worst old gossip. I'm sure everyone knows about Ezra's weak heart by this time.

BRANT: What are you driving at, Christine?

CHRISTINE: Something I've been thinking of ever since I realized he might soon come home. And now that Vinnie—but even if we didn't have to consider her, it'd be the only way! I couldn't fool him long. He's a strange, hidden man. His silence always creeps into my thoughts. Even if he never spoke, I would feel what was in his mind and some night, lying beside him, it would drive me mad and I'd have to kill his silence by screaming out the truth! (*She has been staring before her—now she suddenly turns on* BRANT—*slowly*) If he died suddenly now, no one would think it was anything but heart failure. I've been reading a book in Father's medical library. I saw it there one day a few weeks ago—it was as if some fate in me forced me to see it! (*She reaches in the sleeve of her dress and takes out the slip of paper she had written on*) I've written something here. I want you to get it for me. (*His fingers close on it mechanically. He stares at it with a strange stupid dread. She hurries on so as not to give him time for reflection*) The work on the "Flying Trades" is all finished, isn't it? You sail to Boston tomorrow, to wait for cargo?

BRANT: (*dully*) Aye.

CHRISTINE: Get this at some druggist's down by the waterfront the minute you reach there. You can make up some story about a sick dog on your ship. As soon as you get it, mail it to me here. I'll be on the lookout, so Vinnie will never know it came. Then you must wait on the "Flying Trades" until you hear from me or I come to you— afterward!

BRANT: (*dully*) But how can you do it—so no one will suspect?

CHRISTINE: He's taking medicine. I'll give him his medicine. Oh, I've planned it carefully.

BRANT: But—if he dies suddenly, won't Vinnie—

CHRISTINE: There'll be no reason for her to suspect. She's worried already about his heart. Besides, she may hate me, but she would never think—

BRANT: Orin will be coming home, too.

CHRISTINE: Orin will believe anything I want him to. As for the people here, they'd never dream of such a thing in the Mannon house! And the sooner I do it, the less suspicion there'll be! They will think the excitement of coming home and the reaction were too much for his weak heart! Doctor Blake will think so. I'll see that's what he thinks.

BRANT: (*harshly*) Poison! It's a coward's trick!

CHRISTINE: (*with fierce scorn now, seeing the necessity of goading him*) Do you think you would be braver to give me up to him and let him take away your ship?

BRANT: No!

CHRISTINE: Didn't you say you wanted to kill him?

BRANT: Aye! But I'd give him his chance!

CHRISTINE: Did he give your mother her chance?

BRANT: (*aroused*) No, damn him!

CHRISTINE: Then what makes you suddenly so scrupulous about his death? (*With a sneer*) It must be the Mannon in you coming out! Are you going to prove, the first time your love is put to a real test, that you're a weak coward like your father?

BRANT: Christine! If it was any man said that to me—!

CHRISTINE: (*passionately*) Have you thought of this side of his homecoming—that he's coming back to my bed? If you love me as much as you claim, I should think that would rid you of any scruples! If it was a question of some woman taking you from me, I wouldn't have qualms about which was or wasn't the way to kill her! (*More tauntingly*) But perhaps your love has been only a lie you told me—to take the sneaking revenge on him of being a backstairs lover! Perhaps—

BRANT: (*stung, grabbing her by the shoulders—fiercely*) Stop it! I'll do anything you want! You know it! (*Then with a change to somber grimness—putting the paper in his pocket*) And you're right. I'm a damn fool to have any feeling about how Ezra Mannon dies!

CHRISTINE: (*a look of exultant satisfaction comes to her face as she sees he is definitely won over now. She throws her arms around him and kisses him passionately*) Ah! Now you're the man I love again, not a hypocritical Mannon! Promise me, no more cowardly romantic scruples! Promise me!

BRANT: I promise. (*The boom of a cannon sounds from the fort that guards the harbor. He and* CHRISTINE *start frightenedly and stand staring at each other. Another boom comes, reverberating, rattling the windows.* CHRISTINE *recovers herself*).

CHRISTINE: You hear? That's the salute to his homecoming! (*She kisses him—with fierce insistence*) Remember your mother's death! Remember your dream of your own ship! Above all, remember you'll have me!—all your own—your wife! (*Then urgently*) And now you must go! She'll be coming back—and you're not good at hiding your thoughts. (*Urging him toward the door*) Hurry! I don't want you to meet her! (*The cannon at the fort keep booming at regular intervals until the end of the scene.* BRANT *goes out in the hall and a moment later the front door is heard closing after him.* CHRISTINE *hurries from the door to the window and watches him from behind the curtains as he goes down the drive. She is in a state of tense, exultant excitement. Then, as if an idea had suddenly come to her, she speaks to his retreating figure with a strange sinister air of elation*) You'll never dare leave me now, Adam—for your ships or your sea or your naked Island girls—when I grow old and ugly! (*She turns back from the window. Her eyes are caught by the eyes of her husband in the portrait and for a moment she stares back into them, as if fascinated. Then she jerks her glance away and, with a little shudder she cannot repress, turns and walks quickly from the room and closes the door behind her*).

CURTAIN

ACT THREE

*S*CENE—*The same as Act One, Scene One—exterior of the Mannon house. It is around nine o'clock of a night a week later. The light of a half moon falls on the house, giving it an unreal, detached, eerie quality. The pure white temple front seems more than ever like an incongruous mask fixed on the somber, stone house. All the shutters are closed. The white columns of the portico cast black bars of shadow on the gray wall behind them. The trunk of the pine at right is an ebony pillar, its branches a mass of shade.*

LAVINIA *is sitting on the top of the steps to the portico. She is dressed, as before, severely in black. Her thin figure, seated stiffly upright, arms against her sides, the legs close together, the shoulders square, the head upright, is like that of an Egyptian statue. She is staring straight before her. The sound of* SETH'S *thin, aged baritone mournfully singing the chanty "Shenandoah" is heard from down the drive, off right front. He is approaching the house and the song draws quickly nearer:*

> *"Oh, Shenandoah, I long to hear you*
> *A-way, my rolling river.*
> *Oh, Shenandoah, I can't get near you*
> *Way-ay, I'm bound away*
> *Across the wide Missouri.*
>
> *"Oh, Shenandoah, I love your daughter*
> *A-way, my rolling river."*

He enters right front. He is a bit drunk but holding his liquor well. He walks up by the lilacs starting the next line "Oh, Shenandoah"—then suddenly sees LAVINIA *on the steps and stops abruptly, a bit sheepish.*

LAVINIA: (*disapprovingly*) This is the second time this week I've caught you coming home like this.

SETH: (*unabashed, approaches the steps—with a grin*) I'm aimin' to do my patriotic duty, Vinnie. The first time was celebratin' Lee's surrender and this time is drownin' my sorrow for the President gittin' shot! And the third'll be when your Paw gits home!

LAVINIA: Father might arrive tonight.

SETH: Gosh, Vinnie, I never calc'lated he could git here so soon!

LAVINIA: Evidently you didn't. He'd give you fits if he caught you drunk. Oh, I don't believe he'll come, but it's possible he might.

SETH: (*is evidently trying to pull himself together. He suddenly leans over toward her and, lowering his voice, asks soberly*) Did you find out anything about that Brant?

LAVINIA: (*sharply*) Yes. There's no connection. It was just a silly idea of yours.

SETH: (*stares at her—then understandingly*) Wal, if you want it left that way, I'll leave it that way. (*A pause. He continues to stand looking at her, while she stares in front of her*).

LAVINIA: (*in a low voice*) What was that Marie Brantôme like, Seth?

SETH: Marie? She was always laughin' and singin'—frisky and full of life—with something free and wild about her like an animile. Purty she was, too! (*Then he adds*) Hair just the color of your Maw's and yourn she had.

LAVINIA: I know.

SETH: Oh, everyone took to Marie—couldn't help it. Even your Paw. He was only a boy then, but he was crazy about her, too, like a youngster would be. His mother was stern with him, while Marie, she made a fuss over him and petted him.

LAVINIA: Father, too!

SETH: Ayeh—but he hated her worse than anyone when it got found out she was his Uncle David's fancy woman.

LAVINIA: (*in a low voice, as if to herself, staring at the house*) It's all so strange! It frightens me! (*She checks herself abruptly— turns to* SETH, *curtly*) I don't believe that about Father. You've had too much whiskey. Go to bed and sleep it off. (*She walks up the steps again*).

SETH: (*gazes at her with understanding*) Ayeh. (*Then warningly, making a surreptitious signal as he sees the front door opening behind her*) Ssstt! (CHRISTINE *appears outlined in the light from the hall. She is dressed in a gown of green velvet that sets off her hair. The light behind her glows along the edges of the dress and in the color of her hair. She closes the door and comes into the moonlight at the edge of the steps, standing above and a little to the right of* LAVINIA. *The moonlight, falling full on them, accentuates strangely the resemblance between their faces and at the same time the hostile dissimilarity in body and dress.* LAVINIA *does not turn or give any sign of knowing her mother is behind her. There is a second's uncomfortable silence.* SETH *moves off left*) Wal, I'll trot along! (*He disappears around the corner of the house. There is a pause. Then* CHRISTINE *speaks in a dry mocking tone*).

CHRISTINE: What are you moongazing at? Puritan maidens shouldn't peer too inquisitively into Spring! Isn't beauty an abomination and love a vile thing? (*She laughs with bitter mockery—then tauntingly*) Why don't you marry Peter? You don't want to be left an old maid, do you?

LAVINIA: (*quietly*) You needn't hope to get rid of me that way. I'm not marrying anyone. I've got my duty to Father.

CHRISTINE: Duty! How often I've heard that word in this house! Well, you can't say I didn't do mine all these years. But there comes an end.

LAVINIA: (*grimly*) And there comes another end—and you must do your duty again!

CHRISTINE: (*starts as if to retort defiantly—then says calmly*) Yes, I realize that.

LAVINIA: (*after a pause—suspiciously*) What's going on at the bottom of your mind? I know you're plotting something!

CHRISTINE: (*controlling a start*) Don't be stupid, please!

LAVINIA: Are you planning how you can see Adam again? You better not!

CHRISTINE: (*calmly*) I'm not so foolish. I said good-bye once. Do you think I want to make it harder for myself?

LAVINIA: Has it been hard for you? I'd never guess it—and I've been watching you.

CHRISTINE: I warned you you would have no chance to gloat! (*After a pause*) When do you expect your father home? You want me to play my part well when he comes, don't you?—for his sake. I'd like to be forewarned.

LAVINIA: His letter said he wouldn't wait until his brigade was disbanded but would try to get leave at once. He might arrive tonight—or tomorrow—or the next day. I don't know.

CHRISTINE: You think he might come tonight? (*Then with a mocking smile*) So he's the beau you're waiting for in the spring moonlight! (*Then after a pause*) But the night train got in long ago.

LAVINIA: (*glances down the drive, left front—then starts to her feet excitedly*) Here's someone! (CHRISTINE *slowly rises. There is the sound of footsteps. A moment later* EZRA MANNON *enters from left, front. He stops short in the shadow for a second and stands, erect and stiff, as if at attention, staring at his house, his wife and daughter. He is a tall, spare, big-boned man of fifty, dressed in the uniform of a Brigadier-General. One is immediately struck by the mask-like look of his face in repose, more pronounced in him than in the others. He is exactly like the portrait in his study, which we have seen in Act Two, except that his face is more lined and lean and the hair and beard are grizzled. His movements are exact and wooden and he has a mannerism of standing and sitting in stiff, posed attitudes that suggest the statues of military heroes. When he speaks, his deep voice has a hollow repressed quality, as if he were continually withholding emotion from it. His air is brusque and authoritative*).

LAVINIA: (*seeing the man's figure stop in the shadow—calls excitedly*) Who's that?

MANNON: (*stepping forward into the moonlight*) It's I.

LAVINIA: (*with a cry of joy*) Father! (*She runs to him and throws her arms around him and kisses him*) Oh, Father! (*She bursts into tears and hides her face against his shoulder*).

MANNON: (*embarrassed—patting her head—gruffly*) Come! I thought I'd taught you never to cry.

LAVINIA: (*obediently forcing back her tears*) I'm sorry, Father—but I'm so happy!

MANNON: (*awkwardly moved*) Tears are queer tokens of happiness! But I appreciate your—your feeling.

CHRISTINE: (*has slowly descended the steps, her eyes fixed on him—tensely*) Is it really you, Ezra? We had just given up hope of your coming tonight.

MANNON: (*going stiffly to meet her*) Train was late. The railroad is jammed up. Everybody has got leave. (*He meets her at the foot of the steps and kisses her with a chill dignity—formally*) I am glad to see you, Christine. You are looking well. (*He steps back and stares at her—then in a voice that betrays a deep undercurrent of suppressed feeling*) You have changed, somehow. You are prettier than ever— But you always were pretty.

CHRISTINE: (*forcing a light tone*) Compliments from one's husband! How gallant you've become, Ezra! (*Then solicitously*) You must be terribly tired. Wouldn't you like to sit here on the steps for a while? The moonlight is so beautiful.

LAVINIA: (*who has been hovering about jealously, now manages to worm herself between them—sharply*) No. It's too damp out here. And Father must be hungry. (*Taking his arm*) Come inside with me and I'll get you something to eat. You poor dear! You must be starved.

MANNON: (*really revelling in his daughter's coddling but embarrassed before his wife—pulling his arm back—brusquely*) No, thanks! I would rather rest here for a spell. Sit down, Vinnie. (*CHRISTINE sits on the top step at center; he sits on the middle step at right; LAVINIA on the lowest step at left. While they are doing this he keeps on talking in his abrupt sentences, as if he were trying to cover up some hidden uneasiness*) I've got leave for a few days. Then I must go back and disband my brigade. Peace ought to be signed soon. The President's assassination is a frightful calamity. But it can't change the course of events.

LAVINIA: Poor man! It's dreadful he should die just at his moment of victory.

MANNON: Yes! (*Then after a pause—somberly*) All victory ends in the defeat of death. That's sure. But does defeat end in the victory of death? That's what I wonder! (*They both stare at him,* LAVINIA *in surprise,* CHRISTINE *in uneasy wonder. A pause*).

CHRISTINE: Where is Orin? Couldn't you get leave for him too?

MANNON: (*hesitates—then brusquely*) I've been keeping it from you. Orin was wounded.

LAVINIA: Wounded! You don't mean—badly hurt?

CHRISTINE: (*half starting to her feet impulsively—with more of angry bitterness than grief*) I knew it! I knew when you forced him into your horrible war—! (*Then sinking back—tensely*) You needn't trouble to break the news gradually, Ezra. Orin is dead, isn't he?

LAVINIA: Don't say that! It isn't true, is it, Father?

MANNON: (*curtly—a trace of jealousy in his tone*) Of course it isn't! If your mother would permit me to finish instead of jumping at conclusions about her baby—! (*With a grim, proud satisfaction*) He's no baby now. I've made a man of him. He did one of the bravest things I've seen in the war. He was wounded in the head— a close shave but it turned out only a scratch. But he got brain fever from the shock. He's all right now. He was in a rundown condition, they say at the hospital. I never guessed it. Nerves. I wouldn't notice nerves. He's always been restless. (*Half turning to* CHRISTINE) He gets that from you.

CHRISTINE: When will he be well enough to come home?

MANNON: Soon. The doctor advised a few more days' rest. He's still weak. He was out of his head for a long time. Acted as if he were a little boy again. Seemed to think you were with him. That is, he kept talking to "Mother."

CHRISTINE: (*with a tense intake of breath*) Ah!

LAVINIA: (*pityingly—with a tinge of scorn in her voice*) Poor Orin!

MANNON: I don't want you to baby him when he comes home, Christine. It would be bad for him to get tied to your apron strings again.

CHRISTINE: You needn't worry. That passed—when he left me. (*Another pause. Then* LAVINIA *speaks*).

LAVINIA: How is the trouble with your heart, Father? I've been so afraid you might be making it out less serious than it really was to keep us from worrying.

MANNON: (*gruffly*) If it was serious, I'd tell you, so you'd be prepared. If you'd seen as much of death as I have in the past four years, you wouldn't be afraid of it. (*Suddenly jumping to his feet— brusquely*) Let's change the subject! I've had my fill of death. What I want now is to forget it. (*He turns and paces up and down to the right of steps.* LAVINIA *watches him worriedly*) All I know is the pain is like a knife. It puts me out of commission while it lasts. The doctor gave me orders to avoid worry or any over-exertion or excitement.

CHRISTINE: (*staring at him*) You don't look well. But probably that's because you're so tired. You must go to bed soon, Ezra.

MANNON: (*comes to a stop in his pacing directly before her and looks into her eyes—a pause—then he says in a voice that he tries to make ordinary*) Yes, I want to—soon.

LAVINIA: (*who has been watching him jealously—suddenly pulling him by the arm—with a childish volubility*) No! Not yet! Please, Father! You've only just come! We've hardly talked at all! (*Defiantly to her mother*) How can you tell him he looks tired? He looks as well as I've ever seen him. (*Then to her father with a vindictive look at* CHRISTINE) We've so much to tell you. All about Captain Brant. (*If she had expected her mother to flinch at this, she is disappointed.* CHRISTINE *is prepared and remains unmoved beneath the searching, suspicious glance Mannon now directs at her*).

MANNON: Vinnie wrote me you'd had company. I never heard of him. What business had he here?

CHRISTINE: (*with an easy smile*) You had better ask Vinnie! He's her latest beau! She even went walking in the moonlight with him!

LAVINIA: (*with a gasp at being defied so brazenly*) Oh!

MANNON: (*now jealous and suspicious of his daughter*) I notice you didn't mention that in your letter, young lady!

LAVINIA: I only went walking once with him—and that was before— (*She checks herself abruptly*).

MANNON: Before what?

LAVINIA: Before I knew he's the kind who chases after every woman he sees.

MANNON: (*angrily to* CHRISTINE) A fine guest to receive in my absence!

LAVINIA: I believe he even thought Mother was flirting with him. That's why I felt it my duty to write you. You know how folks in town gossip, Father. I thought you ought to warn Mother she was foolish to allow him to come here.

MANNON: Foolish! It was downright—!

CHRISTINE: (*coldly*) I would prefer not to discuss this until we are alone, Ezra—if you don't mind! And I think Vinnie is extremely inconsiderate the moment you're home—to annoy you with such ridiculous nonsense! (*She turns to* LAVINIA) I think you've done enough mischief. Will you kindly leave us?

LAVINIA: No.

MANNON: (*sharply*) Stop your squabbling, both of you! I hoped you had grown out of that nonsense! I won't have it in my house!

LAVINIA: (*obediently*) Yes, Father.

MANNON: It must be your bedtime, Vinnie.

LAVINIA: Yes, Father. (*She comes and kisses him—excitedly*) Oh, I'm so happy you're here! Don't let Mother make you believe I— You're the only man I'll ever love! I'm going to stay with you!

MANNON: (*patting her hair—with gruff tenderness*) I hope so. I want you to remain my little girl—for a while longer, at least. (*Then suddenly catching* CHRISTINE's *scornful glance—pushes* LAVINIA *away—brusquely*) March now!

LAVINIA: Yes, Father. (*She goes up the steps past her mother without a look. Behind her mother, in the portico, she stops and turns*) Don't let anything worry you, Father. I'll always take care of you. (*She goes in.* MANNON *looks at his wife who stares before her. He clears his throat as if about to say something—then starts pacing self-consciously up and down at the right of steps*).

CHRISTINE: (*forcing a gentle tone*) Sit down, Ezra. You will only make yourself more tired, keeping on your feet. (*He sits awkwardly two steps below her, on her left, turned sideways to face her. She asks with disarming simplicity*) Now please tell me just what it is you suspect me of?

MANNON: (*taken aback*) What makes you think I suspect you?

CHRISTINE: Everything! I've felt your distrust from the moment you came. Your eyes have been probing me, as if you were a judge again and I were the prisoner.

MANNON: (*guiltily*) I—?

CHRISTINE: And all on account of a stupid letter Vinnie had no business to write. It seems to me a late day, when I am an old woman with grown-up children, to accuse me of flirting with a stupid ship captain!

MANNON: (*impressed and relieved—placatingly*) There's no question of accusing you of that. I only think you've been foolish to give the gossips a chance to be malicious.

CHRISTINE: Are you sure that's all you have in your heart against me?

MANNON: Yes! Of course! What else? (*Patting her hand embarrassedly*) We'll say no more about it. (*Then he adds gruffly*) But I'd like you to explain how this Brant happened—

CHRISTINE: I'm only too glad to! I met him at Father's. Father has taken a fancy to him for some reason. So when he called here I couldn't be rude, could I? I hinted that his visits weren't welcome, but men of his type don't understand hints. But he's only been here four times in all, I think. And as for there having been gossip, that's nonsense! The only talk has been that he came to court Vinnie! You can ask anyone in town.

MANNON: Damn his impudence! It was your duty to tell him flatly he wasn't wanted!

CHRISTINE: (*forcing a contrite air*) Well, I must confess I didn't mind his coming as much as I might have—for one reason. He always brought me news of Father. Father's been sick for the past year, as I wrote you. (*Then with a twitch of the lips, as if she were restraining a derisive smile*) You can't realize what a strain I've been under—worrying about Father and Orin and—you.

MANNON: (*deeply moved, turns to her and takes her hand in both of his— awkwardly*) Christine—I deeply regret—having been unjust. (*He kisses her hand impulsively—then embarrassed by this show of emotion, adds in a gruff, joking tone*) Afraid old Johnny Reb would pick me off, were you?

CHRISTINE: (*controlling a wild impulse to burst into derisive laughter*) Do you need to ask that? (*A pause. He stares at her, fascinated and stirred*).

MANNON: (*finally blurts out*) I've dreamed of coming home to you, Christine! (*Leans toward her, his voice trembling with desire and a feeling of strangeness and awe—touching her hair with an awkward caress*) You're beautiful! You look more beautiful than ever—and strange to me. I don't know you. You're younger. I feel like an old man beside you. Only your hair is the same—your strange beautiful hair I always—

CHRISTINE: (*with a start of repulsion, shrinking from his hand*) Don't! (*Then as he turns away, hurt and resentful at this rebuff—hastily*) I'm sorry, Ezra. I didn't mean—I—I'm nervous tonight. (MANNON *paces to the right and stands looking at the trees.* CHRISTINE *stares at his back with hatred. She sighs with affected weariness and leans back and closes her eyes*).

CHRISTINE: I'm tired, Ezra.

MANNON: (*blurts out*) I shouldn't have bothered you with that foolishness about Brant tonight. (*He forces a strained smile*) But I was jealous a mite, to tell you the truth. (*He forces himself to turn and, seeing her eyes are shut, suddenly comes and leans over her awkwardly, as if to kiss her, then is stopped by some strangeness he feels about her still face*).

CHRISTINE: (*feeling his desire and instinctively shrinking—without opening her eyes*) Why do you look at me like that?

MANNON: (*turns away guiltily*) Like what? (*Uneasily*) How do you know? Your eyes are shut. (*Then, as if some burden of depression were on him that he had to throw off, he blurts out heavily*) I can't get used to home yet. It's so lonely. I've got used to the feel of camps with thousands of men around me at night—a sense of protection, maybe! (*Suddenly uneasy again*) Don't keep your eyes shut like that! Don't be so still! (*Then, as she opens her eyes—with an explosive appeal*) God, I want to talk to you, Christine! I've got to explain some things—inside me—to my wife—try to, anyway! (*He sits down beside her*) Shut your eyes again! I can talk better. It has always been hard for me to talk—about feelings. I never could when you looked at me. Your eyes were always so—so full of silence! That is, since we've been married. Not before, when I was courting you. They used to speak then. They made me talk—because they answered.

CHRISTINE: (*her eyes closed—tensely*) Don't talk, Ezra.

MANNON: (*as if he had determined, once started, to go on doggedly without heeding any interruption*) It was seeing death all the time in this war got me to thinking these things. Death was so common, it didn't mean anything. That freed me to think of life. Queer, isn't it? Death made me think of life. Before that life had only made me think of death!

CHRISTINE: (*without opening her eyes*) Why are you talking of death?

MANNON: That's always been the Mannons' way of thinking. They went to the white meeting-house on Sabbaths and meditated on death. Life was a dying. Being born was starting to die. Death was being born. (*Shaking his head with a dogged bewilderment*) How in hell people ever got such notions! That white meeting-house. It stuck in my mind—clean-scrubbed and whitewashed—a temple of death! But in this war I've seen too many white walls splattered with blood that counted no more than dirty water. I've seen dead men scattered about, no more important than rubbish to be got rid of. That made the white meeting-house seem meaningless—making so much solemn fuss over death!

CHRISTINE: (*opens her eyes and stares at him with a strange terror*) What has this talk of death to do with me?

MANNON: (*avoiding her glance—insistently*) Shut your eyes again. Listen and you'll know. (*She shuts her eyes. He plods on with a note of desperation in his voice*) I thought about my life—lying awake nights—and about your life. In the middle of battle I'd think maybe in a minute I'll be dead. But my life as just me ending, that didn't appear worth a thought one way or another. But listen, me as your husband being killed that seemed queer and wrong—like something dying that had never lived. Then all the years we've been man and wife would rise up in my mind and I would try to look at them. But nothing was clear except that there'd always been some barrier between us—a wall hiding us from each other! I would try to make up my mind exactly what that wall was but I never could discover. (*With a clumsy appealing gesture*) Do you know?

CHRISTINE: (*tensely*) I don't know what you're talking about.

MANNON: But you've known it was there! Don't lie, Christine! (*He looks at her still face and closed eyes, imploring her to reassure him—then blunders on doggedly*) Maybe you've always known you didn't love me. I call to mind the Mexican War. I could see you wanted me to go. I had a feeling you'd grown to hate me. Did you? (*She doesn't answer*) That was why I went. I was hoping I might get killed. Maybe you were hoping that too. Were you?

CHRISTINE: (*stammers*) No, no, I— What makes you say such things?

MANNON: When I came back you had turned to your new baby, Orin. I was hardly alive for you any more. I saw that. I tried not to hate Orin. I turned to Vinnie, but a daughter's not a wife. Then I made up my mind I'd do my work in the world and leave you alone in your life and not care. That's why the shipping wasn't enough—why I became a judge and a mayor and such vain truck, and why folks in town look on me as so able! Ha! Able for what? Not for what I wanted most in life! Not for your love! No! Able only to keep my mind from thinking of what I'd lost! (*He stares at her—then asks pleadingly*) For you did love me before we were married. You won't deny that, will you?

CHRISTINE: (*desperately*) I don't deny anything!

MANNON: (*drawing himself up with a stern pride and dignity and surrendering himself like a commander against hopeless odds*) All right, then. I came home to surrender to you—what's inside me. I love you. I loved you then, and all the years between, and I love you now.

CHRISTINE: (*distractedly*) Ezra! Please!

MANNON: I want that said! Maybe you have forgotten it. I wouldn't blame you. I guess I haven't said it or showed it much—ever. Something queer in me keeps me mum about the things I'd like most to say—keeps me hiding the things I'd like to show. Something keeps me sitting numb in my own heart—like a statue of a dead man in a town square. (*Suddenly he reaches over and takes her hand*) I want to find what that wall is marriage put between us! You've got to help me smash it down! We have twenty good years still before us! I've been thinking of what we could do to get back to each other. I've a notion if we'd leave the children and go off on a voyage together— to the other side of the world—find some island where we could be alone a while. You'll find I have changed, Christine. I'm sick of death! I want life! Maybe you could love me now! (*In a note of final desperate pleading*) I've got to make you love me!

CHRISTINE: (*pulls her hand away from him and springs to her feet wildly*) For God's sake, stop talking. I don't know what you're saying. Leave me alone! What must be, must be! You make me weak! (*Then abruptly*) It's getting late.

MANNON: (*terribly wounded, withdrawn into his stiff soldier armor—takes out his watch mechanically*) Yes—six past eleven. Time to turn in. (*He ascends two steps, his face toward the door. He says bitterly*) You tell me to stop talking! By God, that's funny!

CHRISTINE: (*collected now and calculating—takes hold of his arm, seductively*) I meant—what is the good of words? There is no wall between us. I love you.

MANNON: (*grabs her by the shoulders and stares into her face*) Christine! I'd give my soul to believe that—but—I'm afraid! (*She kisses him. He presses her fiercely in his arms—passionately*) Christine! (*The door behind him is opened and* LAVINIA *appears at the edge of the portico behind and above him. She wears slippers over her bare feet and has a dark dressing-gown over her night dress. She shrinks back from their embrace with aversion. They separate, startled*).

MANNON: (*embarrassed—irritably*) Thought you'd gone to bed, young lady!

LAVINIA: (*woodenly*) I didn't feel sleepy. I thought I'd walk a little. It's such a fine night.

CHRISTINE: We are just going to bed. Your father is tired. (*She moves up, past her daughter, taking* MANNON's *hand, leading him after her to the door*).

MANNON: No time for a walk, if you ask me. See you turn in soon.

LAVINIA: Yes, Father.

MANNON: Good night. (*The door closes behind them.* LAVINIA *stands staring before her—then walks stiffly down the steps and stands again. Light appears between the chinks of the shutters in the bedroom on the second floor to the left. She looks up*).

LAVINIA: (*in an anguish of jealous hatred*) I hate you! You steal even Father's love from me again! You stole all love from me when I was born! (*Then almost with a sob, hiding her face in her hands*) Oh, Mother! Why have you done this to me? What harm had I done you? (*Then looking up at the window again—with passionate disgust*) Father, how can you love that shameless harlot? (*Then frenziedly*) I can't bear it! I won't! It's my duty to tell him about her! I will! (*She calls desperately*)

Father! Father! (*The shutter of the bedroom is pushed open and* MANNON *leans out*).

MANNON: (*sharply*) What is it? Don't shout like that!

LAVINIA: (*stammers lamely*) I—I remembered I forgot to say good night, Father.

MANNON: (*exasperated*) Good heavens! What— (*Then gently*) Oh—all right—good night, Vinnie. Get to bed soon, like a good girl.

LAVINIA: Yes, Father. Good night. (*He goes back in the bedroom and pulls the shutter closed. She stands staring fascinatedly up at the window, wringing her hands in a pitiful desperation*).

CURTAIN

ACT FOUR

*S*CENE—EZRA MANNON'S *bedroom. A big four-poster bed is at rear, center, the foot front, the head against the rear wall. A small stand, with a candle on it, is by the head of the bed on the left. To the left of the stand is a door leading into* CHRISTINE'S *room. The door is open. In the left wall are two windows. At left, front, is a table with a lamp on it and a chair beside it. In the right wall, front, is a door leading to the hall. Further back, against the wall, is a bureau.*

None of these details can be discerned at first because the room is in darkness, except for what moonlight filters feebly through the shutters. It is around dawn of the following morning.

CHRISTINE'S *form can be made out, a pale ghost in the darkness, as she slips slowly and stealthily from the bed. She tiptoes to the table, left front, and picks up a light-colored dressing-gown that is flung over the chair and puts it on. She stands listening for some sound from the bed. A pause. Then* MANNON'S *voice comes suddenly from the bed, dull and lifeless.*

MANNON: Christine.

CHRISTINE: (*starts violently—in a strained voice*) Yes.

MANNON: Must be near daybreak, isn't it?

CHRISTINE: Yes. It is beginning to get gray.

MANNON: What made you jump when I spoke? Is my voice so strange to you?

CHRISTINE: I thought you were asleep.

MANNON: I haven't been able to sleep. I've been lying here thinking. What makes you so uneasy?

CHRISTINE: I haven't been able to sleep either.

MANNON: You slunk out of bed so quietly.

CHRISTINE: I didn't want to wake you.

MANNON: (*bitterly*) Couldn't you bear it—lying close to me?

CHRISTINE: I didn't want to disturb you by tossing around.

MANNON: We'd better light the light and talk a while.

CHRISTINE: (*with dread*) I don't want to talk! I prefer the dark.

MANNON: I want to see you. (*He takes matches from the stand by the bed and lights the candle on it.* CHRISTINE *hastily sits down in the chair by the table, pushing it so she sits facing left, front, with her face turned three-quarters away from him. He pushes his back up against the head of the bed in a half-sitting position. His face, with the flickering candle light on its side, has a grim, bitter expression*) You like the dark where you can't see your old man of a husband, is that it?

CHRISTINE: I wish you wouldn't talk like that, Ezra. If you are going to say stupid things, I'll go in my own room. (*She gets to her feet but keeps her face turned away from him*).

MANNON: Wait! (*Then a note of pleading in his voice*) Don't go. I don't want to be alone. (*She sits again in the same position as before. He goes on humbly*) I didn't mean to say those things. I guess there's bitterness inside me—my own cussedness, maybe—and sometimes it gets out before I can stop it.

CHRISTINE: You have always been bitter.

MANNON: Before we married?

CHRISTINE: I don't remember.

MANNON: You don't want to remember you ever loved me!

CHRISTINE: (*tensely*) I don't want to talk of the past! (*Abruptly changing the subject*) Did you hear Vinnie the first part of the night? She was pacing up and down before the house like a sentry guarding you. She didn't go to bed until two. I heard the clock strike.

MANNON: There is one who loves me, at least! (*Then after a pause*) I feel strange, Christine.

CHRISTINE: You mean—your heart? You don't think you are going to be—taken ill, do you?

MANNON: (*harshly*) No! (*A pause—then accusingly*) Is that what you're waiting for? Is that why you were so willing to give yourself tonight? Were you hoping—?

CHRISTINE: (*springing up*) Ezra! Stop talking like that! I can't stand it! (*She moves as if to go into her own room*).

MANNON: Wait! I'm sorry I said that. (*Then, as she sits down again, he goes on gloomily*) It isn't my heart. It's something uneasy troubling my mind—as if something in me was listening, watching, waiting for something to happen.

CHRISTINE: Waiting for what to happen?

MANNON: I don't know. (*A pause—then he goes on somberly*) This house is not my house. This is not my room nor my bed. They are empty— waiting for someone to move in! And you are not my wife! You are waiting for something!

CHRISTINE: (*beginning to snap under the strain—jumps to her feet again*) What would I be waiting for?

MANNON: For death—to set you free!

CHRISTINE: Leave me alone! Stop nagging at me with your crazy suspicions! (*Then anger and hatred come into her voice*) Not your wife! You acted as if I were your wife—your property—not so long ago!

MANNON: (*with bitter scorn*) Your body? What are bodies to me? I've seen too many rotting in the sun to make grass greener! Ashes to ashes, dirt to dirt! Is that your notion of love? Do you think I married a body? (*Then, as if all the bitterness and hurt in him had suddenly burst its dam*) You were lying to me tonight as you've always lied! You were only pretending love! You let me take you as if you were a nigger slave I'd bought at auction! You made me appear a lustful beast in my own eyes!—as you've always done since our first marriage night! I would feel cleaner now if I had gone to a brothel! I would feel more honor between myself and life!

CHRISTINE: (*in a stifled voice*) Look out, Ezra! I won't stand—

MANNON: (*with a harsh laugh*) And I had hoped my homecoming would mark a new beginning—new love between us! I told you my secret feelings. I tore my insides out for you—thinking you'd understand! By God, I'm an old fool!

CHRISTINE: (*her voice grown strident*) Did you think you could make me weak—make me forget all the years? Oh, no, Ezra! It's too late! (*Then her voice changes, as if she had suddenly resolved on a course of action, and becomes deliberately taunting*) You want the truth? You've guessed it! You've used me, you've given me children, but I've never once been yours! I never could be! And whose fault is it? I loved you when I married you! I wanted to give myself! But you made me so I couldn't give! You filled me with disgust!

MANNON: (*furiously*) You say that to me! (*Then trying to calm himself—stammers*) No! Be quiet! We mustn't fight! I mustn't lose my temper! It will bring on—!

CHRISTINE: (*goading him with calculating cruelty*) Oh, no! You needn't adopt that pitiful tone! You wanted the truth and you're going to hear it now!

MANNON: (*frightened—almost pleading*) Be quiet, Christine!

CHRISTINE: I've lied about everything! I lied about Captain Brant! He is Marie Brantôme's son! And it was I he came to see, not Vinnie! I made him come!

MANNON: (*seized with fury*) You dared—! You—! The son of that—!

CHRISTINE: Yes, I dared! And all my trips to New York weren't to visit Father but to be with Adam! He's gentle and tender, he's everything you've never been. He's what I've longed for all these years with you—a lover! I love him! So now you know the truth!

MANNON: (*in a frenzy—struggling to get out of bed*) You—you whore—I'll kill you! (*Suddenly he falls back, groaning, doubled up on his left side, with intense pain*).

CHRISTINE: (*with savage satisfaction*) Ah! (*She hurries through the doorway into her room and immediately returns with a small box in her hand. He is facing away from her door, and, even if the intense pain left him any perception, he could not notice her departure and return, she moves so silently*).

MANNON: (*gaspingly*) Quick—medicine!

CHRISTINE: (*turned away from him, takes a pellet from the box, asking tensely as she does so*) Where is your medicine?

MANNON: On the stand! Hurry!

CHRISTINE: Wait. I have it now. (*She pretends to take something from the stand by the head of the bed—then holds out the pellet and a glass of water which is on the stand*) Here. (*He turns to her, groaning and opens his mouth. She puts the pellet on his tongue and presses the glass of water to his lips*) Now drink.

MANNON: (*takes a swallow of water—then suddenly a wild look of terror comes over his face. He gasps*) That's not—my medicine! (*She shrinks back to the table, the hand with the box held out behind her, as if seeking a hiding place. Her fingers release the box on the table top and she brings her hand in front of her as if instinctively impelled to prove to him she has nothing. His eyes are fixed on her in a terrible accusing glare. He tries to call for help but his voice fades to a wheezy whisper*) Help! Vinnie! (*He falls back in a coma, breathing stertorously.* CHRISTINE *stares at him fascinatedly—then starts with terror as she hears a noise from the hall and frantically snatches up the box from the table and holds it behind her back, turning to face the door as it opens and* LAVINIA *appears in the doorway. She is dressed as at the end of Act Three, in nightgown, wrapper and slippers. She stands, dazed and frightened and hesitating, as if she had just awakened*).

LAVINIA: I had a horrible dream—I thought I heard Father calling me—it woke me up—

CHRISTINE: (*trembling with guilty terror—stammers*) He just had—an attack.

LAVINIA: (*hurries to the bed*) Father! (*She puts her arms around him*) He's fainted!

CHRISTINE: No. He's all right now. Let him sleep. (*At this moment* MANNON, *with a last dying effort, straightens up in a sitting position in* LAVINIA'S *arms, his eyes glaring at his wife, and manages to raise his arm and point an accusing finger at her*).

MANNON: (*gasps*) She's guilty—not medicine! (*He falls back limply*).

LAVINIA: Father! (*Frightenedly she feels for his pulse, puts her ear against his chest to listen for a heartbeat*).

CHRISTINE: Let him alone. He's asleep.

LAVINIA: He's dead!

CHRISTINE: (*repeats mechanically*) Dead? (*Then in a strange flat tone*) I hope—he rests in peace.

LAVINIA: (*turning on her with hatred*) Don't you dare pretend—! You wanted him to die! You— (*She stops and stares at her mother with a horrified suspicion—then harshly accusing*) Why did he point at you like that? Why did he say you were guilty? Answer me!

CHRISTINE: (*stammers*) I told him—Adam was my lover.

LAVINIA: (*aghast*) You told him that—when you knew his heart—! Oh! You did it on purpose! You murdered him!

CHRISTINE: No—it was your fault—you made him suspicious—he kept talking of love and death—he forced me to tell him! (*Her voice becomes thick, as if she were drowsy and fighting off sleep. Her eyes half close*).

LAVINIA: (*grabbing her by the shoulders—fiercely*) Listen! Look at me! He said "not medicine"! What did he mean?

CHRISTINE: (*keeping the hand with the poison pressed against her back*) I— I don't know.

LAVINIA: You do know! What was it? Tell me!

CHRISTINE: (*with a last effort of will manages to draw herself up and speak with a simulation of outraged feeling*) Are you accusing your mother of—

LAVINIA: Yes! I—! (*Then distractedly*) No—you can't be that evil!

CHRISTINE: (*her strength gone—swaying weakly*) I don't know what— you're talking about. (*She edges away from* LAVINIA *toward her bedroom door, the hand with the poison stretched out behind her—weakly*) I—feel faint. I must go—and lie down. I—(*She turns as if to run into the room, takes a tottering step—then her knees suddenly buckle under her and she falls in a dead faint at the foot of the bed. As her hand strikes the floor the fingers relax and the box slips out onto one of the hooked rugs*).

LAVINIA: (*does not notice this. Startled by* CHRISTINE'S *collapse, she automatically bends on one knee beside her and hastily feels for her pulse. Then satisfied she has only fainted, her anguished hatred immediately returns and she speaks with strident denunciation*) You murdered him just the same—by telling him! I suppose you think you'll be free to marry Adam now! But you won't! Not while I'm alive! I'll make you pay for your crime! I'll find a way to punish you! (*She is starting to her feet when her eyes fall on the little box on the rug. Immediately she snatches it up and stares at it, the look of suspicion changing to a dreadful, horrified certainty. Then with a shuddering cry she shrinks back along the side of the bed, the box clutched in her hand, and sinks on her knees by the head of the bed, and flings her arms around the dead man. With anguished beseeching*) Father! Don't leave me alone! Come back to me! Tell me what to do!

CURTAIN

The Hunted

❧

CHARACTERS

CHRISTINE, *Ezra Mannon's widow*

LAVINIA (VINNIE), *her daughter*

ORIN, *her son, First Lieutenant of Infantry*

CAPTAIN ADAM BRANT

HAZEL NILES

PETER, *her brother, Captain of Artillery*

JOSIAH BORDEN, *manager of the shipping company*

EMMA, *his wife*

EVERETT HILLS, D.D., *of the First Congregational Church*

HIS WIFE

DOCTOR JOSEPH BLAKE

THE CHANTYMAN

SCENES

Act One: Exterior of the Mannon house—a moonlight night two days after the murder of EZRA MANNON.

Act Two: Sitting-room in the house—immediately follows Act One.

Act Three: EZRA MANNON's study—Immediately follows Act Two.

Act Four: The stern of the clipper ship "Flying Trades," at a wharf in East Boston—a night two days later.

Act Five: Same as Act One—Exterior of the Mannon house the night of the following day.

722

THE HUNTED

ACT ONE

*S*CENE—*The same as Acts One and Three of "Homecoming"— Exterior of the Mannon House.*

It is a moonlight night two days after the murder of EZRA MANNON. *The house has the same strange eerie appearance, its white portico like a mask in the moonlight, as it had on that night. All the shutters are closed. A funeral wreath is fixed to the column at the right of steps. Another wreath is on the door.*

There is a sound of voices from inside the house, the front door is opened and JOSIAH BORDEN *and his wife,* EVERETT HILLS, *the Congregational minister, and his wife, and* DOCTOR JOSEPH BLAKE, *the Mannons' family physician, come out.* CHRISTINE *can be seen in the hall just inside the door. There is a chorus of "Good night, Mrs. Mannon," and then turn to the steps and the door is closed.*

These people—the BORDENS, *HILLS and his wife and* DOCTOR BLAKE—*are, as were the Ames of Act one of "Homecoming," types of townsfolk, a chorus representing as those others had, but in a different stratum of society, the town as a human background for the drama of the Mannons.*

JOSIAH BORDEN, the manager of the Mannon shipping company, is shrewd and competent He is around sixty, small and wizened, white hair and beard, rasping nasal voice, and little sharp eyes. His wife, about ten years his junior, is a typical New England woman of pure English ancestry, with a horse face, buck teeth and big feet, her manner defensively sharp and assertive. HILLS *is the type of well-fed minister of a prosperous small-town congregation—stout and unctuous, snobbish and ingratiating, conscious of godliness, but timid and always feeling his way. He is in the fifties, as is his wife, a sallow, flabby, self-*

effacing minister's wife. DOCTOR BLAKE *is the old kindly best-family physician—a stout, self-important old man with a stubborn opinionated expression.*

They come down the steps to the drive. MRS. BORDEN *and* MRS. HILLS *walk together toward left front until they are by the bench. There they stop to wait for the men who stand at the foot of the steps while* BORDEN *and* BLAKE *light cigars.*

MRS. BORDEN: (*tartly*) I can't abide that woman!

MRS. HILLS: No. There's something queer about her.

MRS. BORDEN: (*grudgingly honest*) Still and all, I come nearer to liking her now than I ever did before when I see how broken down she is over her husband's death.

MRS. HILLS: Yes. She looks terrible, doesn't she? Doctor Blake says she will have herself in bed sick if she doesn't look out.

MRS. BORDEN: I'd never have suspected she had that much feeling in her. Not but what she hasn't always been a dutiful wife, as far as anyone knows.

MRS. HILLS: Yes. She's seemed to be.

MRS. BORDEN: Well, it only goes to show how you can misjudge a person without meaning to—especially when that person is a Mannon. They're not easy to make head or tail of. Queer, the difference in her and Lavinia—the way they take his death. Lavinia is cold and calm as an icicle.

MRS. HILLS: Yes. She doesn't seem to feel as much sorrow as she ought.

MRS. BORDEN: That's where you're wrong. She feels it as much as her mother. Only she's too Mannon to let anyone see what she feels. But did you notice the look in her eyes?

MRS. HILLS: I noticed she never said a word to anyone. Where did she disappear to all of a sudden?

MRS. BORDEN: Went to the train with Peter Niles to meet Orin. I overheard her mother talking to Lavinia in the hall. She was insisting Peter should escort her to meet the train. Lavinia must have been starting to go alone. Her mother seemed real angry about it. (*Then glancing toward the men who have moved a little away from the steps and are standing talking in low tones*) Whatever are those men gossiping about? (*She calls*) Josiah! It's time we were getting home.

BORDEN: I'm coming, Emma. (*The three men join the women by the bench, BORDEN talking as they come*) It isn't for me to question the arrangements she's made, Joe, but it does seem as if Ezra should have been laid out in the town hall where the whole town could have paid their respects to him, and had a big public funeral tomorrow.

HILLS: That's my opinion. He was mayor of the town and a national war hero—

BLAKE: She says it was Ezra's wish he'd often expressed that everything should be private and quiet. That's just like Ezra. He never was one for show. He did the work and let others do the showing-off.

HILLS: (*unctuously*) He was a great man. His death is a real loss to everyone in this community. He was a power for good.

BORDEN: Yes. He got things done.

HILLS: What a tragedy to be taken his first night home after passing unharmed through the whole war!

BORDEN: I couldn't believe the news. Who'd ever suspect— It's queer. It's like fate.

MRS. HILLS: (*breaks in tactlessly*) Maybe it is fate. You remember, Everett, you've always said about the Mannons that pride goeth before a fall and that some day God would humble them in their sinful pride. (*Everyone stares at her, shocked and irritated*).

HILLS: (*flusteredly*) I don't remember ever saying—

BLAKE: (*huffily*) If you'll excuse me, that's darn nonsense! I've known Ezra Mannon all my life, and to those he wanted to know he was as plain and simple—

HILLS: (*hastily*) Of course, Doctor. My wife entirely misunderstood me. I was, perhaps wrongly, referring to Mrs. Mannon.

BLAKE: She's all right too—when you get to know her.

HILLS: (*dryly*) I have no doubt.

BLAKE: And it's a poor time, when this household is afflicted by sudden death, to be—

HILLS: You are quite right, Doctor. My wife should have remembered—

MRS. HILLS: (*crushed*) I didn't mean anything wrong, Doctor.

BLAKE: (*mollifiedly*) Let's forget it then. (*Turning to* BORDEN—*with a self-satisfied, knowing air*) As for your saying who'd ever expect it—well, you and Emma know I expected Ezra wouldn't last long.

BORDEN: Yes. I remember you said you were afraid his heart was bad.

MRS. BORDEN: I remember you did too.

BLAKE: From the symptoms Mrs. Mannon described from his letter to her, I was as certain as if I'd examined him he had angina. And I wasn't surprised neither. I'd often told Ezra he was attempting more than one man could handle and if he didn't rest he'd break down. The minute they sent for me I knew what'd happened. And what she told me about waking up to find him groaning and doubled with pain confirmed it. She'd given him his medicine—it was what I would have prescribed myself—but it was too late. And as for dying, his first night home—well, the war was over, he was worn out, he'd had a long, hard trip home—and angina is no respecter of time and place. It strikes when it has a mind to.

BORDEN: (*shaking his head*) Too bad. Too durned bad. The town won't find another as able as Ezra in a hurry. (*They all shake their heads and look sad. A pause*).

MRS. BORDEN: Well, we aren't doing anyone any good standing here. We ought to get home, Josiah.

MRS. HILLS: Yes. We must, too, Everett. (*They begin moving slowly off left,* HILLS *going with the two women.* DOCTOR BLAKE *nudges* BORDEN *and motions him to stay behind. After the others disappear, he whispers with a meaning grin*).

BLAKE: I'll tell you a secret, Josiah—strictly between you and me.

BORDEN: (*sensing something from his manner—eagerly*) Of course. What is it, Joe?

BLAKE: I haven't asked Christine Mannon any embarrassing questions, but I have a strong suspicion it was love killed Ezra!

BORDEN: Love?

BLAKE: That's what! Leastways, love made angina kill him, if you take my meaning. She's a damned handsome woman and he'd been away a long time. Only natural between man and wife—but not the treatment I'd recommend for angina. He should have known better, but—well—he was human.

BORDEN: (*with a salacious smirk*) Can't say as I blame him! She's a looker! I don't like her and never did but I can imagine worse ways of dying! (*They both chuckle*) Well, let's catch up with the folks. (*They go off, left. They have hardly disappeared before the door of the house is opened and* CHRISTINE MANNON *comes out and stands at the head of the steps a moment, then descends to the drive. She is obviously in a terrible state of strained nerves. Beneath the mask-like veneer of her face there are deep lines about her mouth, and her eyes burn with a feverish light. Feeling herself free from observation for a moment she lets go, her mouth twitches, her eyes look desperately on all sides, as if she longed to fly from something.* HAZEL NILES *comes out of the house to the head of the steps. She is the same as in "Homecoming."* CHRISTINE *at once senses her presence behind her and regains her tense control of herself*).

HAZEL: (*with a cheering, sympathetic air*) So here you are. I looked everywhere around the house and couldn't find you.

CHRISTINE: (*tensely*) I couldn't stay in. I'm so nervous. It's been a little harrowing—all these people coming to stand around and stare at the dead—and at me.

HAZEL: I know. But there won't be any more now. (*Then a tone of eagerness breaking through in spite of herself*) Peter and Vinnie ought to be back soon, if the train isn't late. Oh, I hope Orin will surely come!

CHRISTINE: (*strangely*) The same train! It was late that night he came! Only two days ago! It seems a lifetime! I've grown old.

HAZEL: (*gently*) Try not to think of it.

CHRISTINE: (*tensely*) As if I hadn't tried! But my brain keeps on—over and over and over!

HAZEL: I'm so afraid you will make yourself sick.

CHRISTINE: (*rallying herself and forcing a smile*) There, I'm all right. I mustn't appear too old and haggard when Orin comes, must I? He always liked me to be pretty.

HAZEL: It will be so good to see him again! (*Then quickly*) He ought to be such a comfort to you in your grief.

CHRISTINE: Yes. (*Then strangely*) He used to be my baby, you know—before he left me. (*Suddenly staring at* HAZEL, *as if struck by an idea*) You love Orin, don't you?

HAZEL: (*embarrassed—stammers shyly*) I—I—

CHRISTINE: I am glad. I want you to. I want him to marry you. (*Putting an arm around her—in a strained tone*) We'll be secret conspirators, shall we, and I'll help you and you'll help me?

HAZEL: I don't understand.

CHRISTINE: You know how possessive Vinnie is with Orin. She's always been jealous of you. I warn you she'll do everything she can to keep him from marrying you.

HAZEL: (*shocked*) Oh, Mrs. Mannon, I can't believe Vinnie—!

CHRISTINE: (*unheeding*) So you must help me. We mustn't let Orin come under her influence again. Especially now in the morbid, crazy state of grief she's in! Haven't you noticed how queer she's become? She hasn't spoken a single word since her father's death! When I talk to her she won't answer me. And yet she follows me around everywhere—she hardly leaves me alone a minute. (*Forcing a nervous laugh*) It gets on my nerves until I could scream!

HAZEL: Poor Vinnie! She was so fond of her father. I don't wonder she—

CHRISTINE: (*staring at her—strangely*) You are genuinely good and pure of heart, aren't you?

HAZEL: (*embarrassed*) Oh, no! I'm not at all—

CHRISTINE: I was like you once—long ago—before— (*Then with bitter longing*) If I could only have stayed as I was then! Why can't all of us remain innocent and loving and trusting? But God won't leave us alone. He twists and wrings and tortures our lives with others' lives until—we poison each other to death! (*Seeing* HAZEL's *look, catches herself—quickly*) Don't mind what I said! Let's go in, shall we? I would rather wait for Orin inside. I couldn't bear to wait and watch him coming up the drive—just like—he looks so much like his father at times—and like—but what nonsense I'm talking! Let's go in. I hate moonlight. It makes everything so haunted. (*She turns abruptly and goes into the house.* HAZEL *follows her and shuts the door. There is a pause. Then footsteps and voices are heard from off right front and a moment later* ORIN MANNON *enters with* PETER *and* LAVINIA. *One is at once struck by his startling family resemblance to* EZRA MANNON *and* ADAM BRANT (*whose likeness to each other we have seen in "Homecoming"*). *There is the same lifelike mask quality of his face in repose, the same aquiline nose, heavy eyebrows, swarthy complexion, thick straight black hair, light hazel eyes. His mouth and chin have the same general characteristics as his father's had, but the expression of his mouth gives an impression of tense oversensitiveness quite foreign to the General's, and his chin is a refined, weakened version of the dead man's. He is about the same height as* MANNON *and* BRANT, *but his body is thin and his swarthy complexion sallow. He wears a bandage around his head high up on his forehead. He carries himself by turns with a marked slouchiness or with a self-conscious square-shouldered stiffness that indicates a soldierly bearing is unnatural to him. When he speaks it is jerkily, with a strange, vague, preoccupied air. But when he smiles naturally his face has a gentle boyish charm which makes women immediately want to mother him. He wears a mustache similar to* BRANT's *which serves to increase their resemblance to each other. Although he is only twenty, he looks thirty. He is dressed in a baggy, ill-fitting uniform—that of a first lieutenant of infantry in the Union Army*).

ORIN: (*as they enter looks eagerly toward the house—then with bitter, hurt disappointment in his tone*) Where's Mother? I thought she'd surely be waiting for me. (*He stands staring at the house*) God, how I've dreamed of coming home! I thought it would never end, that we'd go on murdering and being murdered until no one was left alive! Home at last! No, by God, I must be dreaming again! (*Then in an awed tone*) But the house looks strange. Or is it something in me? I was out of my head so long, everything has seemed queer since I came back to earth. Did the house always look so ghostly and dead?

PETER: That's only the moonlight, you chump.

ORIN: Like a tomb. That's what mother used to say it reminded her of, I remember.

LAVINIA: (*reproachfully*) It is a tomb—just now, Orin.

ORIN: (*hurriedly—shamefacedly*) I—I'd forgotten. I simply can't realize he's dead yet. I suppose I'd come to expect he would live forever. (*A trace of resentment has crept into his tone*) Or, at least outlive me. I never thought his heart was weak. He told me the trouble he had wasn't serious.

LAVINIA: (*quickly*) Father told you that, too? I was hoping he had. (*Then turning to* PETER) You go ahead in, Peter. Say we're coming a little behind. I want to speak to Orin a moment.

PETER: Sure thing, Vinnie. (*He goes in the front door, closing it behind him*).

ORIN: I'm glad you got rid of him. Peter is all right but—I want to talk to you alone. (*With a boyish brotherly air—putting an arm around her*) You certainly are a sight for sore eyes, Vinnie! How are you, anyway, you old bossy fuss-buzzer! Gosh, it seems natural to hear myself calling you that old nickname again. Aren't you glad to see me?

LAVINIA: (*affectionately*) Of course I am!

ORIN: I'd never guess it! You've hardly spoken a word since you met me. What's happened to you? (*Then, as she looks at him reproachfully, he takes away his arm—a bit impatiently*) I told you I can't get used to the idea of his being dead. Forgive me, Vinnie. I know what a shock it must be to you.

LAVINIA: Isn't it a shock to you, Orin?

ORIN: Certainly! What do you think I am? But—oh, I can't explain!

You wouldn't understand, unless you'd been at the front. I hardened myself to expect my own death and everyone else's, and think nothing of it. I had to—to keep alive! It was part of my training as a soldier under him. He taught it to me, you might say! So when it's his turn he can hardly expect— (*He has talked with increasing bitterness.* LAVINIA *interrupts him sharply*).

LAVINIA: Orin! How can you be so unfeeling?

ORIN: (*again shamefaced*) I didn't mean that. My mind is still full of ghosts. I can't grasp anything but war, in which he was so alive. He was the war to me—the war that would never end until I died. I can't understand peace—his end! (*Then with exasperation*) God damn it, Vinnie, give me a chance to get used to things!

LAVINIA: Orin!

ORIN: (*resentfully*) I'm sorry! Oh, I know what you're thinking! I used to be such a nice gentlemanly cuss, didn't I?—and now—Well, you wanted me to be a hero in blue, so you better be resigned! Murdering doesn't improve one's manners! (*Abruptly changing the subject*) But what the devil are we talking about me for? Listen, Vinnie. There's something I want to ask you before I see Mother.

LAVINIA: Hurry, then! She'll be coming right out! I've got to tell you something too!

ORIN: What was that stuff you wrote about some Captain Brant coming to see Mother? Do you mean to tell me there's actually been gossip started about her? (*Then without waiting for a reply, bursting into jealous rage*) By God, if he dares come here again, I'll make him damned sorry he did!

LAVINIA: (*grimly*) I'm glad you feel that way about him. But there's no time to talk now. All I want to do is warn you to be on your guard. Don't let her baby you the way she used to and get you under her thumb again. Don't believe the lies she'll tell you! Wait until you've talked to me! Will you promise me?

ORIN: (*staring at her bewilderedly*) You mean—Mother? (*Then angrily*) What the hell are you talking about, anyway? Are you loony? Honestly, Vinnie, I call that carrying your everlasting squabble with Mother a bit too far! You ought to be ashamed of yourself! (*Then suspiciously*) What are you being so mysterious about? Is it Brant—?

LAVINIA: (*at a sound from inside the house*) Ssshh! (*The front door of the house is opened and* CHRISTINE *hurries out*).

CHRISTINE: (*angrily to* PETER *who is in the hall*) Why didn't you call me, Peter? You shouldn't have left him alone! (*She calls uncertainly*) Orin.

ORIN: Mother! (*She runs down the steps and flings her arms around him*).

CHRISTINE: My boy! My baby! (*She kisses him*).

ORIN: (*melting, all his suspicion forgotten*) Mother! God, it's good to see you! (*Then almost roughly, pushing her back and staring at her*) But you're different! What's happened to you?

CHRISTINE: (*forcing a smile*) I? Different? I don't think so, dear. Certainly I hope not—to you! (*Touching the bandage on his head—tenderly*) Your head! Does it pain dreadfully? You poor darling, how you must have suffered! (*She kisses him*) But it's all over now, thank God. I've got you back again! (*Keeping her arm around him, she leads him up the steps*) Let's go in. There's someone else waiting who will be so glad to see you.

LAVINIA: (*who has come to the foot of the steps—harshly*) Remember, Orin! (CHRISTINE *turns around to look down at her. A look of hate flashes between mother and daughter.* ORIN *glances at his mother suspiciously and draws away from her*).

CHRISTINE: (*immediately recovers her poise—to* ORIN, *as if* LAVINIA *hadn't spoken*) Come on in, dear. It's chilly. Your poor head— (*She takes his hand and leads him through the door and closes it behind them.* LAVINIA *remains by the foot of the steps, staring after them. Then the door is suddenly opened again and* CHRISTINE *comes out, closing it behind her, and walks to the head of the steps. For a moment mother and daughter stare into each other's eyes. Then* CHRISTINE *begins haltingly in a tone she vainly tries to make kindly and persuasive*) Vinnie, I—I must speak with you a moment—now Orin is here. I appreciate your grief has made you—not quite normal—and I make allowances. But I cannot understand your

attitude toward me. Why do you keep following me everywhere—
and stare at me like that? I had been a good wife to him for twenty-
three years—until I met Adam. I was guilty then, I admit. But I
repented and put him out of my life. I would have been a good wife
again as long as your father had lived. After all, Vinnie, I am your
mother. I brought you into the world. You ought to have some
feeling for me. (*She pauses, waiting for some response, but* LAVINIA *simply
stares at her, frozen and silent. Fear creeps into* CHRISTINE'S *tone*) Don't
stare like that! What are you thinking? Surely you can't still have
that insane suspicion—that I— (*Then guiltily*) What did you do that
night after I fainted? I—I've missed something—some medicine I
take to put me to sleep— (*Something like a grim smile of satisfaction
forms on* LAVINIA'S *lips.* CHRISTINE *exclaims frightenedly*) Oh, you did—
you found—and I suppose you connect that—but don't you see how
insane—to suspect—when Doctor Blake knows he died of—! (*Then
angrily*) I know what you've been waiting for—to tell Orin your lies
and get him to go to the police! You don't dare do that on your own
responsibility—but if you can make Orin— Isn't that it? Isn't that
what you've been planning the last two days? Tell me! (*Then, as*
LAVINIA *remains silent,* CHRISTINE *gives way to fury and rushes down the
steps and grabs her by the arm and shakes her*) Answer me when I speak
to you! What are you plotting? What are you going to do? Tell me!
(LAVINIA *keeps her body rigid, her eyes staring into her mother's.* CHRIS-
TINE *lets go and steps away from her. Then* LAVINIA, *turning her back,
walks slowly and woodenly off left between the lilac clump and the house.*
CHRISTINE *stares after her, her strength seems to leave her, she trembles
with dread. From inside the house comes the sound of* ORIN'S *voice calling
sharply "Mother! Where are you?"* CHRISTINE *starts and immediately by
an effort of will regains control over herself. She hurries up the steps and
opens the door. She speaks to* ORIN *and her voice is tensely quiet and normal*)
Here I am, dear! (*She shuts the door behind her*).

CURTAIN

ACT TWO

SCENE—*The sitting-room of the Mannon house. Like the study, but much larger, it is an interior composed of straight severe lines with heavy detail. The walls are plain plastered surfaces, light gray with a white trim. It is a bleak room without intimacy, with an atmosphere of uncomfortable, stilted stateliness. The furniture is stationed about with exact precision. On the left, front, is a doorway leading to the dining-room. Further back, on the left, are a wall table and chair and a writing desk and chair. In the rear wall, center, is the doorway giving on the main hall and the stairs. At right is a fireplace with a chimneypiece of black marble, flanked by two windows. Portraits of ancestors hang on the walls. At the rear of the fireplace, on the right, is one of a grim-visaged minister of the witch-burning era. Between fireplace and front is another of* EZRA MANNON'S *grandfather, in the uniform of an officer in Washington's army. Directly over the fireplace is the portrait of* EZRA'S *father,* ABE MANNON, *done when he was sixty. Except for the difference in ages, his face looks exactly like* EZRA'S *in the painting in the study.*

*Of the three portraits on the other walls, two are of women—*ABE MANNON'S *wife and the wife of Washington's officer. The third has the appearance of a prosperous shipowner of Colonial days. All the faces in the portraits have the same mask quality of those of the living characters in the play.*

At the left center of the room, front, is a table with two chairs. There is another chair at center, front, and a sofa at right, front, facing left.

The opening of this scene follows immediately the close of the preceding one. HAZEL *is discovered sitting on the chair at center, front.* PETER *is sitting on the sofa at right. From the hall* ORIN *is heard calling "Mother! Where are you?" as at the close of the preceding act.*

HAZEL: Where can she have gone? She's worked herself into such a state of grief I don't think she knows what she's doing.

PETER: Vinnie's completely knocked out, too.

HAZEL: And poor Orin! What a terrible homecoming this is for him! How sick and changed he looks, doesn't he, Peter?

PETER: Head wounds are no joke. He's darned lucky to have come out alive. (*They stop talking self-consciously as* ORIN *and* CHRISTINE *enter from the rear.* ORIN *is questioning her suspiciously*).

ORIN: Why did you sneak away like that? What were you doing?

CHRISTINE: (*forcing a wan smile*) The happiness of seeing you again was a little too much for me, I'm afraid, dear. I suddenly felt as if I were going to faint, so I rushed out in the fresh air.

ORIN: (*immediately ashamed of himself—tenderly, putting his arm around her*) Poor Mother! I'm sorry— Look here, then. You sit down and rest. Or maybe you better go right to bed.

HAZEL: That's right, Orin, you make her. I've been trying to get her to but she won't listen to me.

CHRISTINE: Go to bed the minute he comes home! I should say not!

ORIN: (*worried and pleased at the same time*) But you mustn't do anything to—

CHRISTINE: (*patting his cheek*) Fiddlesticks! Having you again is just the medicine I need to give me strength—to bear things. (*She turns to* HAZEL) Listen to him, Hazel! You'd think I was the invalid and not he.

HAZEL: Yes. You've got to take care of yourself, too, Orin.

ORIN: Oh, forget me. I'm all right.

CHRISTINE: We'll play nurses, Hazel and I, and have you your old self again before you know it. Won't we, Hazel?

HAZEL: (*smiling happily*) Of course we will.

CHRISTINE: Don't stand, dear. You must be worn out. Wait. We'll make you comfortable. Hazel, will you bring me a cushion? (HAZEL *gets a cushion and helps to place it behind his back in the chair at right of table.* ORIN's *eyes light up and he grins boyishly, obviously revelling in being coddled*).

ORIN: How's this for the comforts of home, Peter? The front was never like this, eh?

PETER: Not so you'd notice it!

ORIN: (*with a wink at* HAZEL) Peter will be getting jealous! You better call Vinnie in to put a pillow behind him!

HAZEL: (*with a smile*) I can't picture Vinnie being that soft.

ORIN: (*a jealous resentment creeping into his voice*) She can be soft—on occasion. She's always coddling Father and he likes it, although he pretends—

CHRISTINE: (*turning away and restraining a shudder*) Orin! You're talking as if he were—alive! (*There is an uncomfortable silence.* HAZEL *goes quietly back to her chair at center.* CHRISTINE *goes around the table to the chair opposite* ORIN *and sits down*).

ORIN: (*with a wry smile*) We'd all forgotten he's dead, hadn't we? Well, I can't believe it even yet. I feel him in this house—alive!

CHRISTINE: Orin!

ORIN: (*strangely*) Everything is changed—in some queer way—this house, Vinnie, you, I—everything but Father. He's the same and always will be—here—the same! Don't you feel that, Mother? (*She shivers, looking before her but doesn't answer*).

HAZEL: (*gently*) You mustn't make your mother think of it, Orin.

ORIN: (*staring at her—in a queer tone of gratitude*) You're the same, Hazel—sweet and good. (*He turns to his mother accusingly*) At least Hazel hasn't changed, thank God!

CHRISTINE: (*rousing herself—turns to force a smile at him*) Hazel will never change, I hope. I am glad you appreciate her. (HAZEL *looks embarrassed.* CHRISTINE *goes on—with motherly solicitude*) Wasn't the long train trip terribly hard on you, dear?

ORIN: Well, it wasn't a pleasure trip exactly. My head got aching till I thought it would explode.

CHRISTINE: (*leans over and puts her hand on his forehead*) Poor boy! Does it pain now?

ORIN: Not much. Not at all when your hand is there. (*Impulsively he takes her hand and kisses it—boyishly*) Gosh, Mother, it feels so darned good to be home with you! (*Then staring at her suspiciously again*) Let me have a good look at you. You're so different. I noticed it even outside. What is it?

CHRISTINE: (*avoiding his eyes—forcing a smile*) It's just that I'm getting old, I'm afraid, dear.

ORIN: No. You're more beautiful than ever! You're younger, too, some-how. But it isn't that. (*Almost pushing her hand away—bitterly*) Maybe I can guess!

CHRISTINE: (*forces a laugh*) Younger and more beautiful! Do you hear him going on, Hazel? He has learned to be very gallant, I must say! (LAVINIA *appears in the doorway at rear. She enters but remains standing just inside the doorway and keeps her eyes fixed on her mother and* ORIN).

ORIN: (*who is again looking at* HAZEL, *breaks out harshly*) Do you remem-ber how you waved your handkerchief, Hazel, the day I set off to become a hero? I thought you would sprain your wrist! And all the mothers and wives and sisters and girls did the same! Sometime in some war they ought to make the women take the men's place for a month or so. Give them a taste of murder!

CHRISTINE: Orin!

ORIN: Let them batter each other's brains out with rifle butts and rip each other's guts with bayonets! After that, maybe they'd stop waving handkerchiefs and gabbing about heroes! (HAZEL *gives a shocked excla-mation*).

CHRISTINE: Please!

PETER: (*gruffly*) Give it a rest, Orin! It's over. Give yourself a chance to forget it. None of us liked it any more than you did.

ORIN: (*immediately shamefaced*) You're right, Peter. I'm a damned whin-ing fool! I'm sorry, Hazel. That was rotten of me.

HAZEL: It was nothing, Orin. I understand how you feel. Really I do.

ORIN: I—I let off steam when I shouldn't. (*Then suddenly*) Do you still sing, Hazel? I used to hear you singing—down there. It made me feel life might still be alive somewhere—that, and my dreams of

Mother, and the memory of Vinnie bossing me around like a drill sergeant. I used to hear you singing at the queerest times—so sweet and clear and pure! It would rise above the screams of the dying—

CHRISTINE: (*tensely*) I wish you wouldn't talk of death!

LAVINIA: (*from the doorway—in a brusque commanding tone like her father's*) Orin! Come and see Father.

ORIN: (*starts up from his chair and makes an automatic motion as if to salute—mechanically*) Yes, sir. (*Then confusedly*) What the devil—? You sounded just like him. Don't do that again, for heaven's sake! (*He tries to force a laugh—then shamefacedly*) I meant to look at him the first thing—but I got talking—I'll go in right now.

CHRISTINE: (*her voice tense and strained*) No! Wait! (*Angrily to* LAVINIA) Can't you let your brother have a minute to rest? You can see how worn out he is! (*Then to* ORIN) I've hardly had a chance to say a word to you yet—and it has been so long! Stay with me a little while, won't you?

ORIN: (*touched, coming back to her*) Of course, Mother! You come before everything!

LAVINIA: (*starts to make a bitter retort, glances at* PETER *and* HAZEL, *then remarks evenly*) Very well. Only remember what I said, Orin. (*She turns her back and starts to go into the hall*).

CHRISTINE: (*frightenedly*) Vinnie! Where are you going?

LAVINIA: (*does not answer her but calls back to her brother over her shoulder*) You'll come in a little while, won't you? (*She disappears across the hall.* ORIN *gives his mother a sidelong glance of uneasy suspicion.* CHRISTINE *is desperately trying to appear calm.* PETER *and* HAZEL *stand up, feeling uncomfortable*).

HAZEL: Peter, we really must be getting home.

PETER: Yes.

CHRISTINE: It was so kind of you to come.

HAZEL: (*giving her hand to* ORIN) You must rest all you can now, Orin—and try not to think about things.

ORIN: You're darned kind, Hazel. It's fine to see you again—the same as ever!

HAZEL: (*delighted but pulling her hand away shyly*) I'm glad, too. Good night, Orin.

PETER: (*shakes his hand*) Good night. Rest up and take it easy.

ORIN: Good night, Peter. Thanks for meeting me.

CHRISTINE: (*goes with them to the hall*) I'm afraid this isn't a very cheerful house to visit just now—but please come soon again. You will do Orin more good than anyone, Hazel. (*The look of suspicion again comes to* ORIN'S *eyes. He sits down in the chair at left of table and stares before him bitterly.* CHRISTINE *returns from the hall, closing the sliding doors behind her silently. She stands for a moment looking at* ORIN, *visibly bracing herself for the ordeal of the coming interview, her eyes full of tense calculating fear*).

ORIN: (*without looking at her*) What's made you take such a fancy to Hazel all of a sudden? You never used to think much of her. You didn't want me going around with her.

CHRISTINE: (*coming forward and sitting across the table from him—in her gentle motherly tone*) I was selfish then. I was jealous, too, I'll confess. But all I want now is your happiness, dear. I know how much you used to like Hazel—

ORIN: (*blurts out*) That was only to make you jealous! (*Then bitterly*) But now you're a widow, I'm not home an hour before you're trying to marry me off! You must be damned anxious to get rid of me again! Why?

CHRISTINE: You mustn't say that! If you knew how horribly lonely I've been without you—

ORIN: So lonely you've written me exactly two letters in the last six months!

CHRISTINE: But I wrote you much more! They must have been lost—

ORIN: I received all of Hazel's letters—and Vinnie's. It's darned funny yours should be the only ones to get lost! (*Unable to hold back any longer, he bursts forth*) Who is this Captain Brant who's been calling on you?

CHRISTINE: (*prepared for this—with well-feigned astonishment*) On me? You mean on Vinnie, don't you? (*Then as* ORIN *looks taken aback*) Wherever did you get that silly idea? Oh, of course, I know! Vinnie must have written you the same nonsense she did your father.

ORIN: She wrote him? What did he do?

CHRISTINE: Why, he laughed at it, naturally! Your father was very fond of Vinnie but he knew how jealous she's always been of me and he realized she'd tell any lie she could to—

ORIN: Oh, come on now, Mother! Just because you're always getting on each other's nerves it doesn't mean Vinnie would ever deliberately—

CHRISTINE: Oh, doesn't it, though? I think you'll discover before you're much older that there isn't anything your sister will stop at—that she will even accuse me of the vilest, most horrible things!

ORIN: Mother! Honestly now! You oughtn't to say that!

CHRISTINE: (*reaching out and taking his hand*) I mean it, Orin. I wouldn't say it to anyone but you. You know that. But we've always been so close, you and I. I feel you are really—my flesh and blood! She isn't! She is your father's! You're a part of me!

ORIN: (*with strange eagerness*) Yes! I feel that, too, Mother!

CHRISTINE: I know I can trust you to understand now as you always used to. (*With a tender smile*) We had a secret little world of our own in the old days, didn't we?—which no one but us knew about.

ORIN: (*happily*) You bet we did! No Mannons allowed was our password, remember!

CHRISTINE: And that's what your father and Vinnie could never forgive us! But we'll make that little world of our own again, won't we?

ORIN: Yes!

CHRISTINE: I want to make up to you for all the injustice you suffered at your father's hands. It may seem a hard thing to say about the dead, but he was jealous of you. He hated you because he knew I loved you better than anything in the world!

ORIN: (*pressing her hand in both of his—intensely*) Do you, Mother? Do you honestly? (*Then he is struck by what she said about his father—woundedly*) I knew he had it in for me. But I never thought he went as far as to—hate me.

CHRISTINE: He did, just the same!

ORIN: (*with resentful bitterness*) All right, then! I'll tell you the truth, Mother! I won't pretend to you I'm sorry he's dead!

CHRISTINE: (*lowering her voice to a whisper*) Yes. I am glad, too!—that he has left us alone! Oh, how happy we'll be together, you and I, if you only won't let Vinnie poison your mind against me with her disgusting lies!

ORIN: (*immediately uneasy again*) What lies? (*He releases her hand and stares at her, morbidly suspicious*) You haven't told me about that Brant yet.

CHRISTINE: There's nothing to tell—except in Vinnie's morbid revengeful mind! I tell you, Orin, you can't realize how she's changed while you've been away! She's always been a moody and strange girl, you know that, but since you've gone she has worried and brooded until I really believe she went a little out of her head. She got so she'd say the most terrible things about everyone. You simply wouldn't believe it, if I told you some of the things. And now, with the shock of your father's death on top of everything, I'm convinced she's actually insane. Haven't you noticed how queerly she acts? You must have!

ORIN: I saw she'd changed a lot. She seemed strange. But—

CHRISTINE: And her craziness all works out in hatred for me! Take this Captain Brant affair, for example—

ORIN: Ah!

CHRISTINE: A stupid ship captain I happened to meet at your grandfather's who took it into his silly head to call here a few times without being asked. Vinnie thought he was coming to court her. I honestly believe she fell in love with him, Orin. But she soon discovered that he wasn't after her at all!

ORIN: Who was he after—you?

CHRISTINE: (*sharply*) Orin! I'd be very angry with you if it weren't so ridiculous! (*She forces a laugh*) You don't seem to realize I'm an old married woman with two grown-up children! No, all he was after was to insinuate himself as a family friend and use your father when he came home to get him a better ship! I soon saw through his little scheme and he'll never call here again, I promise you that! (*She laughs—then with a teasing air*) And that's the whole of the great Captain Brant scandal! Are you satisfied now, you jealous goose, you?

ORIN: (*penitent and happy*) I'm a fool! The war has got me silly, I guess! If you knew all the hell I've been through!

CHRISTINE: It was Vinnie's fault you ever went to war! I'll never forgive her for that! It broke my heart, Orin! (*Then quickly*) But I was going to give you an example of her insane suspicions from the Captain Brant incident. Would you believe it that she has worked it all out that because his name is Brant, he must be the son of that nurse girl Marie Brantôme? Isn't that crazy? And to imagine for a moment, if he were, he'd ever come here to visit!

ORIN: (*his face hardening*) By God, I'd like to see him! His mother brought disgrace enough on our family without—

CHRISTINE: (*frightened, shrinking from him*) Orin! Don't look like that! You're so like your father! (*Then hurrying on*) But I haven't told you the worst yet. Vinnie actually accuses me—your mother—of being in love with that fool and of having met him in New York and gone to his room! I am no better than a prostitute in your sister's eyes!

ORIN: (*stunned*) I don't believe it! Vinnie couldn't!

CHRISTINE: I told you she'd gone crazy! She even followed me to New York, when I went to see your sick grandfather, to spy on me. She saw me meet a man—and immediately to her crazy brain the man was Brant. Oh, it's too revolting, Orin! You don't know what I've had to put up with from Vinnie, or you'd pity me!

ORIN: Good God! Did she tell Father that? No wonder he's dead! (*Then harshly*) Who was this man you met in New York?

CHRISTINE: It was Mr. Lamar, your grandfather's old friend who has known me ever since I was a baby! I happened to meet him and he asked me to go with him to call on his daughter. (*Then, seeing* ORIN *wavering, pitifully*) Oh, Orin! You pretend to love me! And yet you question me as if you suspected me, too! And you haven't Vinnie's excuse! You aren't out of your mind! (*She weeps hysterically*).

ORIN: (*overcome at once by remorse and love*) No! I swear to you! (*He throws himself on his knees beside her and puts his arm around her*) Mother! Please! Don't cry! I do love you! I do!

CHRISTINE: I haven't told you the most horrible thing of all! Vinnie suspects me of having poisoned your father!

ORIN: (*horrified*) What! No, by God, that's too much! If that's true, she ought to be put in an asylum!

CHRISTINE: She found some medicine I take to make me sleep, but she is so crazy I know she thinks— (*Then, with real terror, clinging to him*) Oh, Orin, I'm so afraid of her! God knows what she might do, in her state! She might even go to the police and— Don't let her turn you against me! Remember you're all I have to protect me! You are all I have in the world, dear!

ORIN: (*tenderly soothing her*) Turn me against you? She can't be so crazy as to try that! But listen. I honestly think you— You're a little hysterical, you know. That—about Father—is all such damned nonsense! And as for her going to the police—do you suppose I wouldn't prevent that—for a hundred reasons—the family's sake—my own sake and Vinnie's, too, as well as yours—even if I knew—

CHRISTINE: (*staring at him—in a whisper*) Knew? Orin, you don't believe—?

ORIN: No! For God's sake! I only meant that no matter what you ever did, I love you better than anything in the world and—

CHRISTINE: (*in an outburst of grateful joy—pressing him to her and kissing him*) Oh, Orin, you are my boy, my baby! I love you!

ORIN: Mother! (*Then seizing her by the shoulders and staring into her eyes—with somber intensity*) I could forgive anything— anything!—in my mother—except that other—that about Brant!

CHRISTINE: I swear to you—!

ORIN: If I thought that damned—! (*With savage vengefulness*) By God, I'd show you then I hadn't been taught to kill for nothing!

CHRISTINE: (*full of new terror now—for* BRANT's *life—distractedly*) For God's sake, don't talk like that! You're not like my Orin! You're cruel and horrible! You frighten me!

ORIN: (*immediately contrite and soothing, petting her*) There, there, Mother! We won't ever think about it again! We'll talk of something else. I want to tell you something. (*He sits on the floor at her feet and looks up into her face. A pause. Then he asks tenderly, taking her hand*) Did you really want me to come back, Mother?

CHRISTINE: (*has calmed herself, but her eyes are still terrified and her voice trembles*) What a foolish question, dear.

ORIN: But your letters got farther and farther between—and they seemed so cold! It drove me crazy! I wanted to desert and run home—or else get killed! If you only knew how I longed to be here with you—like this! (*He leans his head against her knee. His voice becomes dreamy and low and caressing*) I used to have the most wonderful dreams about you. Have you ever read a book called "Typee"—about the South Sea Islands?

CHRISTINE: (*with a start—strangely*) Islands! Where there is peace?

ORIN: Then you did read it?

CHRISTINE: No.

ORIN: Someone loaned me the book. I read it and reread it until finally those Islands came to mean everything that wasn't war, everything that was peace and warmth and security. I used to dream I was there. And later on all the time I was out of my head I seemed really to be there. There was no one there but you and me. And yet I never saw you, that's the funny part. I only felt you all around me. The breaking of the waves was your voice. The sky was the same color as your eyes. The warm sand was like your skin. The whole island was you. (*He smiles with a dreamy tenderness*) A strange notion, wasn't it? But you needn't be provoked at being an island because this was the most beautiful island in the world—as beautiful as you, Mother!

CHRISTINE: (*has been staring over his head, listening fascinatedly, more and more deeply moved. As he stops, an agonizing tenderness for him wells up in her—with tortured longing*) Oh, if only you had never gone away! If you only hadn't let them take you from me!

ORIN: (*uneasily*) But I've come back. Everything is all right now, isn't it?

CHRISTINE: (*hastily*) Yes! I didn't mean that. It had to be.

ORIN: And I'll never leave you again now. I don't want Hazel or anyone. (*With a tender grin*) You're my only girl!

CHRISTINE: (*again with tenderness, stroking his hair—smiling*) You're a big man now, aren't you? I can't believe it. It seems only yesterday when I used to find you in your nightshirt hiding in the hall upstairs on the chance that I'd come up and you'd get one more good-night kiss! Do you remember?

ORIN: (*with a boyish grin*) You bet I remember! And what a row there was when Father caught me! And do you remember how you used to let me brush your hair and how I loved to? He hated me doing that, too. You've still got the same beautiful hair, Mother. That hasn't changed. (*He reaches up and touches her hair caressingly. She gives a little shudder of repulsion and draws away from him but he is too happy to notice*) Oh, Mother, it's going to be wonderful from now on! We'll get Vinnie to marry Peter and there will be just you and I! (*The sliding doors in rear are opened a little and* LAVINIA *slips silently in and stands looking at them*).

CHRISTINE: (*immediately senses her presence—controlling a start, harshly*) What do you want? (ORIN *turns to look at his sister resentfully*).

LAVINIA: (*in a flat, emotionless voice*) Aren't you coming in to see Father, Orin?

ORIN: (*scrambling to his feet—irritably*) Oh, all right, I'll come now. (*He hurries out past* LAVINIA *with the air of one with a disagreeable duty he wants to get over quickly and closes the door with a bang behind him.* LAVINIA *stares at her mother a moment—then about-faces stiffly to follow him).*

CHRISTINE: (*springs to her feet*) Vinnie! (*As* LAVINIA *turns to face her— sharply*) Come here—please. I don't want to shout across the room. (LAVINIA *comes slowly forward until she is at arm's length. Her eyes grow bleak and her mouth tightens to a thin line. The resemblance between mother and daughter as they stand confronting each other is strikingly brought out.* CHRISTINE *begins to speak in a low voice, coolly defiant, almost triumphant*) Well, you can go ahead now and tell Orin anything you wish! I've already told him—so you might as well save yourself the trouble. He said you must be insane! I told him how you lied about my trips to New York—for revenge!—because you loved Adam your-self! (LAVINIA *makes a movement like a faint shudder but is immediately stiff and frozen again.* CHRISTINE *smiles tauntingly*) So hadn't you better leave Orin out of it? You can't get him to go to the police for you. Even if you convinced him I poisoned your father, you couldn't! He doesn't want—any more than you do, or your father, or any of the Mannon dead—such a public disgrace as a murder trial would be! For it would all come out! Everything! Who Adam is and my adultery and your knowledge of it—and your love for Adam! Oh, believe me, I'll see to it that comes out if anything ever gets to a trial! I'll show you to the world as a daughter who desired her mother's lover and then tried to get her mother hanged out of hatred and jealousy! (*She laughs tauntingly.* LAVINIA *is trembling but her face remains hard and emotionless. Her lips open as if to speak but she closes them again.* CHRISTINE *seems drunk with her own defiant recklessness*) Go on! Try and convince Orin of my wickedness! He loves me! He hated his father! He's glad he's dead! Even if he knew I had killed him, he'd protect me! (*Then all her defiant attitude collapses and she pleads, seized by an hysterical terror, by some fear she has kept hidden*) For God's sake, keep Orin out of this! He's still sick! He's changed! He's grown hard and cruel! All he thinks of is death! Don't tell him about Adam! He would kill him! I couldn't live then! I would kill myself! (LAVINIA *starts and her eyes light up with a cruel hatred. Again her pale lips part as if she were about to say something but she controls the impulse and about-faces abruptly and walks with jerky steps from the room like some tragic mechanical doll.* CHRISTINE *stares after her—then as she disappears, collapses, catching at the table for support—terrifiedly*) I've got to see Adam! I've got to warn him! (*She sinks in the chair at right of table*).

CURTAIN

ACT THREE

SCENE—*The same as Act Two of "Homecoming"* —EZRA MANNON'S *study. His body, dressed in full uniform, is laid out on a bier draped in black which is placed lengthwise directly before the portrait of him over the fireplace. His head is at right. His mask-like face is a startling reproduction of the face in the portrait above him, but grimly remote and austere in death, like the carven face of a statue.*

The table and chairs which had been at center have been moved to the left. There is a lamp on this table. Two stands of three lighted candles are at each end of the black marble chimneypiece, throwing their light above on the portrait and below on the dead man. There is a chair by the dead man's head, at front of bier.

ORIN *is standing by the head of the bier, at the rear of it, stiffly-erect like a sentinel at attention. He is not looking down at his father but is staring straight before him, deep in suspicious brooding. His face in the candlelight bears a striking resemblance to that of the portrait above him and the dead man's.*

The time of the opening of this act precedes by a few moments that of the end of the previous act.

ORIN: (*ashamed and guilty—bursts out angrily at himself*) Christ, I won't have such thoughts! I am a rotten swine to— Damn Vinnie! She must be crazy! (*Then, as if to distract his mind from these reflections, he turns to gaze down at his father. At the same moment* LAVINIA *appears silently in the doorway from the hall and stands looking at him. He does not notice her entrance. He stares at his father's mask-like face and addresses it with a strange friendly mockery*) Who are you? Another corpse! You and I have seen fields and hillsides sown with them—and they meant nothing!—nothing but a dirty joke life plays on life! (*Then with a dry smile*) Death sits so naturally on you! Death becomes the Mannons!

You were always like a statue of an eminent dead man—sitting on a
chair in a park or straddling a horse in a town square—looking over
the head of life without a sign of recognition—cutting it dead for the
impropriety of living! (*He chuckles to himself with a queer affectionate
amusement*) You never cared to know me in life—but I really think
we might be friends now you are dead!

LAVINIA: (*sternly*) Orin!

ORIN: (*turns to her startledly*) Damn it, don't sneak around like that!
What are you trying to do, anyway? I'm jumpy enough without—
(*Then as she turns and locks the door behind her—suspiciously*) What are
you locking the door for?

LAVINIA: I've got to talk to you—and I don't want to be interrupted.
(*Then sternly*) What made you say such things just then? I wouldn't
believe you could have grown so callous to all feeling of respect—

ORIN: (*guilty and resentful*) You folks at home take death so solemnly!
You would have soon learned at the front that it's only a joke! You
don't understand, Vinnie. You have to learn to mock or go crazy,
can't you see? I didn't mean it in an unkind way. It simply struck me
he looks so strangely familiar—the same familiar stranger I've never
known. (*Then glancing at the dead man with a kindly amused smile*) Do
you know his nickname in the army? Old Stick—short for Stick-in-
the-Mud. Grant himself started it—said Father was no good on an
offensive but he'd trust him to stick in the mud and hold a position
until hell froze over!

LAVINIA: Orin! Don't you realize he was your father and he is dead?

ORIN: (*irritably*) What Grant said was a big compliment in a way.

LAVINIA: When I think of how proud of you he was when he came
home! He boasted that you had done one of the bravest things he'd
seen in the war!

ORIN: (*astonished—then grins with bitter mockery*) One of the bravest
things he'd seen! Oh, that's too rich! I'll tell you the joke about that
heroic deed. It really began the night before when I sneaked through
their lines. I was always volunteering for extra danger. I was so scared

anyone would guess I was afraid! There was a thick mist and it was so still you could hear the fog seeping into the ground. I met a Reb crawling toward our lines. His face drifted out of the mist toward mine. I shortened my sword and let him have the point under the ear. He stared at me with an idiotic look as if he'd sat on a tack—and his eyes dimmed and went out— (*His voice has sunk lower and lower, as if he were talking to himself. He pauses and stares over his father's body fascinatedly at nothing*).

LAVINIA: (*with a shudder*) Don't think of that now!

ORIN: (*goes on with the same air*) Before I'd gotten back I had to kill another in the same way. It was like murdering the same man twice. I had a queer feeling that war meant murdering the same man over and over, and that in the end I would discover the man was myself! Their faces keep coming back in dreams—and they change to Father's face—or to mine— What does that mean, Vinnie?

LAVINIA: I don't know! I've got to talk to you! For heaven's sake, forget the war! It's over now!

ORIN: Not inside us who killed! (*Then quickly—with a bitter, joking tone*) The rest is all a joke! The next morning I was in the trenches. This was at Petersburg. I hadn't slept. My head was queer. I thought what a joke it would be on the stupid Generals like Father if everyone on both sides suddenly saw the joke war was on them and laughed and shook hands! So I began to laugh and walked toward their lines with my hand out. Of course, the joke was on me and I got this wound in the head for my pains. I went mad, wanted to kill, and ran on, yelling. Then a lot of our fools went crazy, too, and followed me and we captured a part of their line we hadn't dared tackle before. I had acted without orders, of course—but Father decided it was better policy to overlook that and let me be a hero! So do you wonder I laugh!

LAVINIA: (*soothingly, coming to him and taking his arm*) You were brave and you know it. I'm proud of you, too.

ORIN: (*helplessly*) Oh, all right! Be proud, then! (*He leaves her and sprawls in the chair at left of table. She stands by the head of the bier and faces him. He says resentfully*) Well? Fire away and let's get this over! But you're wasting your breath. I know what you're going to say. Mother warned me. (*The whole memory of what his mother had said rushes over him*) My God, how can you think such things of Mother? What the hell's got into you? (*Then humoringly*) But I realize you're not yourself. I know how hard his death has hit you. Don't you think it would be better to postpone our talk until—

LAVINIA: No! (*Bitterly*) Has she succeeded in convincing you I'm out of my mind? Oh, Orin, how can you be so stupid? (*She goes to him and, grasping him by his shoulders, brings her face close to him—compellingly*) Look at me! You know in your heart I'm the same as I always was— your sister—who loves you, Orin!

ORIN: (*moved*) I didn't mean—I only think the shock of his death—

LAVINIA: I've never lied to you, have I? Even when we were little you always knew I told you the truth, didn't you?

ORIN: Yes—but—

LAVINIA: Then you must believe I wouldn't lie to you now!

ORIN: No one is saying you'd deliberately lie. It's a question of—

LAVINIA: And even if she's got you so under her thumb again that you doubt my word, you can't doubt the absolute proof!

ORIN: (*roughly*) Never mind what you call proofs! I know all about them already! (*Then excitedly*) Now, listen here, if you think you're going to tell me a lot of crazy stuff about Mother, I warn you I won't listen! So shut up before you start!

LAVINIA: (*threateningly now*) If you don't, I'll go to the police!

ORIN: Don't be a damn fool!

LAVINIA: As a last resort I will—if you force me to!

ORIN: By God, you must be crazy even to talk of—!

LAVINIA: They won't think so!

ORIN: Vinnie! Do you realize what it would mean—?

LAVINIA: I realize only too well! You and I, who are innocent, would suffer a worse punishment than the guilty—for we'd have to live on! It would mean that Father's memory and that of all the honorable

Mannon dead would be dragged through the horror of a murder trial! But I'd rather suffer that than let the murder of our father go unpunished!

ORIN: Good God, do you actually believe—?

LAVINIA: Yes! I accuse her of murder! (*She takes the little box she has found in* CHRISTINE'S *room right after the murder [Act Four "Homecoming"] from the bosom of her dress and holds it out to him*) You see this? I found it right after Father died!

ORIN: Don't be a damned lunatic! She told me all about that! It's only some stuff she takes to make her sleep!

LAVINIA: (*goes on implacably, ignoring his interruptions*) And Father knew she'd poisoned him! He said to me, "She's guilty!"

ORIN: That's all your crazy imagination! God, how can you think—? Do you realize you're deliberately accusing your own mother— It's too horrible and mad! I'll have you declared insane by Doctor Blake and put away in an asylum!

LAVINIA: I swear by our dead father I am telling you the truth! (*She puts her hand on the dead man and addresses him*) Make Orin believe me, Father!

ORIN: (*harshly*) Don't drag him in! He always sided with you against Mother and me! (*He grabs her arm and forces the box from her hand*) Here! Give me that! (*He slips it into his coat pocket*).

LAVINIA: Ah! So you are afraid it's true!

ORIN: No! But I'm going to stop your damned— But I'm a fool to pay any attention to you! The whole thing is too insane! I won't talk to a crazy woman! But, by God, you look out, Vinnie! You leave Mother alone or—!

LAVINIA: (*regarding him bitterly*) Poor Father! He thought the war had made a man of you! But you're not! You're still the spoiled crybaby that she can make a fool of whenever she pleases!

ORIN: (*stung*) That's enough from you!

LAVINIA: Oh, she warned me just now what to expect! She boasted that you wouldn't believe me, and that even if you knew she'd murdered Father you would be glad because you hated him! (*Then a note of entreaty in her voice*) Orin! For God's sake—here, before him!—tell me that isn't true, at least!

ORIN: (*overcome by a sense of guilt—violently defensive*) Of course, I never said that—and I don't believe she did. But Mother means a thousand times more to me than he ever did! I say that before him now as I would if he could hear me!

LAVINIA: (*with a calculated scornful contempt now*) Then if I can't make you see your duty one way, I will another! If you won't help me punish her, I hope you're not such a coward that you're willing to let her lover escape!

ORIN: (*in a tone of awakening suspicion*) Lover? Who do you mean?

LAVINIA: I mean the man who plotted Father's murder with her, who must have got the poison for her! I mean the Captain Brant I wrote you about!

ORIN: (*thickly, trying to fight back his jealous suspicion*) You lie! She told me your rotten lies—about him—about following her to New York. That was Mr. Lamar she met.

LAVINIA: So that's what she told you! As if I could mistake Lamar for Adam Brant! What a fool you are, Orin! She kisses you and pretends she loves you—when she'd forgotten you were ever alive, when all she's thought of is this low lover of hers—!

ORIN: (*wildly*) Stop! I won't stand—!

LAVINIA: When all she is thinking of right now is how she can use you to keep me from doing anything, so she'll get a chance to run off and marry him!

ORIN: You lie!

LAVINIA: She pets you and plays the loving mother and you're so blind you can't see through her! I tell you she went to his room! I followed them upstairs. I heard her telling him, "I love you, Adam." She was kissing him!

ORIN: (*grabs her by the shoulder and shakes her, forcing her to her knees—frenziedly*) Damn you! Tell me you're lying or—!

LAVINIA: (*unafraid—looking up into his eyes—coldly*) You know I'm not lying! She's been going to New York on the excuse of visiting Grandfather Hamel, but really to give herself to—!

ORIN: (*in anguish*) You lie, damn you! (*Threateningly*) You dare say that about Mother! Now you've got to prove it or else—! You're not insane! You know what you're saying! So you prove it—or by God, I'll—!

LAVINIA: (*taking his hands off her shoulders and rising*) All I ask is a chance to prove it! (*Then intensely*) But when I do, will you help me punish Father's murderers?

ORIN: (*in a burst of murderous rage*) I'll kill that bastard! (*In anguished uncertainty again*) But you haven't proved anything yet! It's only your word against hers! I don't believe you! You say Brant is her lover! If that's true, I'll hate her! I'll know she murdered Father then! I'll help you punish her! But you've got to prove it!

LAVINIA: (*coldly*) I can do that very soon. She's frightened out of her wits! She'll go to see Brant the first chance she gets. We must give her that chance. Will you believe me when you find them together?

ORIN: (*torturedly*) Yes. (*Then in a burst of rage*) God damn him, I'll—!

LAVINIA: (*sharply*) Ssshh! Be quiet. There's someone in the hall! (*They wait, staring at the door. Then someone knocks loudly*).

CHRISTINE: (*her voice comes through the door, frightened and strained*) Orin!

ORIN: (*stammers*) God! I can't face her now!

LAVINIA: (*in a quick whisper*) Don't let her know you suspect her. Pretend you think I'm out of my mind, as she wanted you to.

CHRISTINE: Orin! Why don't you answer me? (*She tries the doorknob, and finding the door locked, her voice becomes terrified*) Why have you locked me out? Let me in! (*She pounds on the door violently*).

LAVINIA: (*in a whisper*) Answer her. Let her in.

ORIN: (*obeying mechanically—calls in a choked voice*) All right. I'm coming. (*He moves reluctantly toward the door*).

LAVINIA: (*struck by a sudden idea—grasps his arm*) Wait! (*Before he can prevent it, she reaches in his pocket and gets possession of the box and puts it conspicuously on the body over the dead man's heart*) Watch her when she sees that—if you want proof!

CHRISTINE: Open the door! (*He forces himself to open the door and steps aside.* CHRISTINE *almost falls in. She is in a state bordering on collapse. She throws her arms around* ORIN *as if seeking protection from him*) Orin! I got so afraid—when I found the door locked!

ORIN: (*controls a furious jealous impulse to push her violently away from him—harshly*) What made you afraid, Mother?

CHRISTINE: (*stammers*) Why do you look at me—like that? You look—so like—your father!

ORIN: I am his son, too, remember that!

LAVINIA: (*warningly*) Orin!

CHRISTINE: (*turning on* LAVINIA *who stands by the head of the bier*) I suppose you've been telling him your vile lies, you—

ORIN: (*remembering his instructions, forces himself to blurt out*) She—she's out of her head, Mother.

CHRISTINE: Didn't I tell you! I knew you'd see that! (*Then anxiously, keeping her eyes on* LAVINIA) Did she tell you what she's going to do, Orin? I know she's plotting something—crazy! Did she threaten to go to the police? They might not believe she's crazy— (*Pleading desperately, her eyes still on* LAVINIA) You won't let her do anything dreadful like that, will you?

ORIN: (*feeling her guilt, stammers*) No, Mother.

CHRISTINE: (*her eyes, which have been avoiding the corpse, now fasten on the dead man's face with fascinated horror*) No—remember your father wouldn't want—any scandal—he mustn't be worried, he said—he needs rest and peace— (*She addresses the dead man directly in a strange tone of defiant scorn*) You seem the same to me in death, Ezra! You were always dead to me! I hate the sight of death! I hate the thought of it! (*Her eyes shift from his face and she sees the box of poison. She starts back with a stifled scream and stares at it with guilty fear*).

ORIN: Mother! For God's sake, be quiet! (*The strain snaps for him and he laughs with savage irony*) God! To think I hoped home would be an escape from death! I should never have come back to life—from my island of peace! (*Then staring at his mother strangely*) But that's lost now! You're my lost island, aren't you, Mother? (*He turns and stumbles blindly from the room.* LAVINIA *reaches out stealthily and snatches up the box. This breaks the spell for* CHRISTINE *whose eyes have been fixed on it hypnotically. She looks wildly at* LAVINIA's *frozen accusing face*).

LAVINIA: (*in a cold, grim voice*) It was Brant who got you this—medicine to make you sleep—wasn't it?

CHRISTINE: (*distractedly*) No! No! No!

LAVINIA: You're telling me it was. I knew it—but I wanted to make sure. (*She puts the box back in the bosom of her dress—turns, rigid and square-shouldered, and walks woodenly from the room*).

CHRISTINE: (*stares after her wildly, then her eyes fasten again on the dead man's face. Suddenly she appeals to him distractedly*) Ezra! Don't let her harm Adam! I am the only guilty one! Don't let Orin—! (*Then, as if she read some answer in the dead man's face, she stops in terror and, her eyes still fixed on his face, backs to the door and rushes out*).

CURTAIN

Act Four

*T*HE *stern section of a clipper ship moored alongside a wharf in East Boston, with the floor of the wharf in the foreground. The vessel lies with her bow and amidships off left and only the part aft of the mizzenmast is visible with the curve of the stern at right. The ship is unloaded and her black side rises nine or ten feet above the level of the wharf. On the poop deck above, at right, is the wheel. At left is the chart room and the entrance to the companionway stairs leading below to the cabin. At extreme left is the mizzenmast, the lowest yard just visible above, the boom of the spanker extending out above the deck to the right. Below the deck the portholes show a faint light from the interior of the cabin. On the wharf the end of a warehouse is at left front.*

It is a night two days after Act Two—the day following EZRA MANNON'S *funeral. The moon is rising above the horizon off left rear, its light accentuating the black outlines of the ship.*

Borne on the wind the melancholy refrain of the capstan chanty "Shenandoah," sung by a chantyman with the crew coming in on the chorus, drifts over the water from a ship that is weighing anchor in the harbor. Half in and half out of the shadow of the warehouse, the CHANTYMAN *lies sprawled on his back, snoring in a drunken slumber. The sound of the singing seems to strike a responsive chord in his brain, for he stirs, grunts, and with difficulty raises himself to a sitting position in the moonlight beyond the shadow.*

He is a thin, wiry man of sixty-five or so, with a tousled mop of black hair, unkempt black beard and mustache. His weather-beaten face is dissipated, he has a weak mouth, his big round blue eyes are bloodshot, dreamy and drunken. But there is something romantic, a queer troubadour-of-the-sea quality about him.

CHANTYMAN: (*listens to the singing with critical disapproval*) A hell of a chantyman that feller be! Screech owls is op'ry singers compared to him! I'll give him a taste of how "Shenandoah" ought t' be sung!

(*He begins to sing in a surprisingly good tenor voice, a bit blurry with booze now and sentimentally mournful to a degree, but still managing to get full value out of the chanty*)

"Oh, Shenandoah, I long to hear you—
A-way, my rolling river!
Oh, Shenandoah, I can't get near you—
Way—ay, I'm bound away
Across the wide Missouri!

"Oh, Shenandoah, I love your daughter
A-way, my rolling river!"

(*He stops abruptly, shaking his head—mournfully*) No good! Too drunk to do myself jestice! Pipe down, my John! Sleep it off! (*He sprawls back on his elbows—confusedly*) Where am I? What the hell difference is it? There's plenty o' fresh air and the moon fur a glim. Don't be so damn pertic'lar! What ye want anyways? Featherbed an' a grand piany? (*He sings with a maudlin zest*).

"A bottle o' wine and a bottle o' beer
And a bottle of Irish whiskey oh!
So early in the morning
The sailor likes his bottle oh!"

(*He stops and mutters*) Who'll buy a drink fur the slickest chantyman on the Western or any other damn ocean? Go to hell then! I kin buy it myself! (*He fumbles in his pants pocket*) I had it in this pocket—I remember I put it there pertic'lar—ten dollars in this pocket— (*He pulls the pocket inside out—with bewildered drunken anger*) By Christ, it's gone! I'm plucked clean! (*He struggles to a sitting position*) Where was I last? Aye, I remember! That yaller haired pig with the pink dress on! Put her arm around me so lovin'! Told me how fine I could sing! (*He scrambles unsteadily to his feet*) By Christ, I'll go back an' give her a seaboot in her fat tail that'll learn her—! (*He takes a step but lurches into the shadow and leans against the warehouse*) Hard down!

Heavy gales around Cape Stiff! All is sunk but honor, as the feller says, an' there's damn little o' that afloat! (*He stands against the warehouse, waiting for the swaying world to subside. The companionway door on the poop deck of the vessel is opened and* ADAM BRANT *comes cautiously out. He looks around him quickly with an uneasy suspicious air. He is dressed in a merchant captain's blue uniform. Satisfied that there is no one on the deck, he comes to the rail and stares expectantly up the wharf, off left. His attitude is tense and nervous and he keeps one hand in his coat pocket. The* CHANTYMAN *loses his balance, lurches forward, then back against the warehouse with a thump.* BRANT *leaps back from the rail startledly, jerking a revolver from his coat pocket—then leans over the rail again and calls threateningly*).

BRANT: Who's there? Come out and let me have a look at you or by God I'll shoot!

CHANTYMAN: (*stares up, startled in his turn and momentarily sobered— hastily*) Easy goes, shipmate! Stow that pistol! I'm doin' you no harm. (*He lurches out into the moonlight—suddenly pugnacious*) Not that I'm skeered o' you or your shooter! Who the hell are you to be threatenin' the life of an honest chantyman? Tryin' to hold me up, air ye? I been robbed once tonight! I'll go to the police station and tell 'em there's a robber here—

BRANT: (*hastily, with a placating air*) No harm meant. I'm skipper of this vessel and there have been a lot of waterfront thieves around here lately. I'm lacking a watchman and I've got to keep my weather eye open.

CHANTYMAN: (*again momentarily sobered—touching his forehead*) Aye— aye, sir. Mind your eye. I heer'd tell robbers broke in the "Annie Lodge's" cabin two nights back. Smashed everything and stole two hundred dollars off her skipper. Murderous, too, they be! Near beat the watchman's brains out! (*Then drunken pugnaciousness comes over him again*) Think I'm one o' that gang, do ye? Come down out o' that and I'll show ye who's a thief! I don't give a damn if ye air a skipper! Ye could be Bully Watermann himself an' I'd not let you insult me! I ain't signed on your old hooker! You've got no rights over me! I'm on dry land, by Christ, and this is a free country and— (*His voice has risen to a shout.* BRANT *is alarmed that this uproar will attract someone. He puts the pistol back in his pocket hastily and peers anxiously down the wharf. Then he interrupts the* CHANTYMAN's *tirade by a sharp command*).

BRANT: Stow your damned jaw! Or, by the Eternal, I'll come down and pound some sense in your head!

CHANTYMAN: (*automatically reacts to the voice of authority— quietly*) Aye— aye, sir. (*Then inconsequentially*) You ain't needin' a chantyman fur your next vi'ge, are ye, sir?

BRANT: I'm not sailing for a month yet. If you're still out of a job then—

CHANTYMAN: (*proudly*) You don't know me, that's plain! I'm the finest damn chantyman that ever put a tune to his lip! I ain't lookin' fur berths—they're lookin' fur me! Aye! Skippers are on'y too glad to git me! Many's a time I've seed a skipper an' mates sweatin' blood to beat work out of a crew but nary a lick could they git into 'em till I raised a tune—and then there'd be full sail on her afore ye knowed it!

BRANT: (*impatiently*) I'm not doubting your ability. But I'd advise you to turn in and sleep it off.

CHANTYMAN: (*not heeding this—sadly*) Aye, but it ain't fur long, steam is comin' in, the sea is full o' smoky tea-kettles, the old days is dyin', an' where'll you an' me be then? (*Lugubriously drunken again*) Everything is dyin'! Abe Lincoln is dead. I used to ship on the Mannon packets an' I seed in the paper where Ezra Mannon was dead! (BRANT *starts guiltily. The* CHANTYMAN *goes on maudlinly*) Heart failure killed him, it said, but I know better! I've sailed on Mannon hookers an' been worked t' death and gotten swill fur grub, an' I know he didn't have no heart in him! Open him up an' you'd find a dried turnip! The old skinflint must have left a pile o' money. Who gits it, I wonder? Leave a widder, did he?

BRANT: (*harshly*) How would I know? (*Changing the subject calculatingly*) What are you doing here, Chantyman? I'd expect a man with your voice would be in a saloon, singing and making merry!

CHANTYMAN: So I would! So I would! But I was robbed, sir—aye —an' I know who done it—a yaller-haired wench had her arm around me. Steer clear o' gals or they'll skin your hide off an' use it fur a carpet! I warn ye, skipper! They're not fur sailormen like you an' me, 'less we're lookin' fur sorrow! (*Then insinuatingly*) I ain't got the price of a drink, that's why I'm here, sir.

BRANT: (*reaches in his pocket and tosses him down a silver dollar*) Here!

CHANTYMAN: (*fumbles around and finds the dollar*) Thank ye, sir. (*Then flatteringly*) It's a fine ship you've got there, sir. Crack sail on her and she'll beat most of 'em—an' you're the kind to crack sail on, I kin tell by your cut.

BRANT: (*pleased, glancing up at his ship's lofty rig*) Aye! I'll make her go right enough!

CHANTYMAN: All you need is a good chantyman to help ye. Here's "Hanging Johnny" fur ye! (BRANT *starts at this. The* CHANTYMAN *suddenly begins to sing the chanty "Hanging Johnny" with sentimental mournfulness*)

> "Oh, they call me Hanging Johnny
> Away—ay—i—oh!
> They says I hangs for money
> Oh, hang, boys, hang!"

BRANT: (*harshly*) Stop that damned dirge! And get out of here! Look lively now!

CHANTYMAN: (*starting to go*) Aye—aye, sir. (*Then resentfully*) I see ye ain't got much ear fur music. Good night.

BRANT: (*with exasperated relief*) Good night. (*The* CHANTYMAN *goes un-steadily off left, between the warehouse and the ship. He bursts again into his mournful dirge, his voice receding*)

"*They say I hanged my mother
Away—ay—i—oh!
They say I hanged my mother
Oh, hang, boys, hang!*"

(BRANT, *standing by the rail looking after him, mutters a curse and starts pacing up and down the deck*) Damn that chanty! It's sad as death! I've a foreboding I'll never take this ship to sea. She doesn't want me now—a coward hiding behind a woman's skirts! The sea hates a coward! (*A woman's figure dressed in black, heavily veiled, moves stealthily out from the darkness between the ship and the warehouse, left. She sees the figure on the deck above her and shrinks back with a stifled gasp of fear. BRANT hears the noise. Immediately his revolver is in his hand and he peers down into the shadows of the warehouse*) Who's there?

CHRISTINE: (*with a cry of relief*) Adam!

BRANT: Christine! (*Then quickly*) Go back to the gangplank. I'll meet you there. (*She goes back. He hurries along the deck and disappears off left to meet her. Their voices are heard and a moment later they enter on the poop deck, from left. She leans against him weakly and he supports her with his arm around her*) I have to bring you this way. I bolted the door to the main deck.

CHRISTINE: I was so frightened! I wasn't sure which ship! Some drunken man came along singing—

BRANT: Aye. I just got rid of him. I fired the watchman this morning so I'd be alone at night. I was hoping you'd come soon. Did that drunk see you?

CHRISTINE: No. I hid behind some boxes. (*Then frightenedly*) Why have you got that pistol?

BRANT: (*grimly*) I was going to give them a fight for it—if things went wrong.

CHRISTINE: Adam!

BRANT: By God, you don't think I'll ever let them take me alive, do you?

CHRISTINE: Please, please! Don't talk of that for a moment! Only hold me close to you! Tell me you love me!

BRANT: (*harshly*) It's no time! I want to know what's happened! (*Then immediately repentant he kisses her—with rough tenderness*) Don't mind me! My nerves are gone from waiting alone here not knowing anything but what I read in the papers—that he was dead. These last days have been hell!

CHRISTINE: If you knew what they have been for me!

BRANT: There's something gone wrong! I can read that in your face! What is it, Christine?

CHRISTINE: (*falteringly*) Vinnie knows—! She came into the room when he was dying! He told her—

BRANT: (*harshly*) God! What is she going to do? (*Then, without giving her time to answer his question, he suddenly looks around uneasily*) Christine! How did you get away? She'd suspect you weren't going to your father's now. She followed you once before—

CHRISTINE: No. It's all right. This morning Orin said his cousins, the Bradfords, had invited him and Vinnie to visit them overnight at Blackridge and he was taking Vinnie with him because he thought a change would bring her back to her senses. I've made him think she's out of her head with grief—so he wouldn't listen to her—

BRANT: (*eagerly*) And he believes that?

CHRISTINE: (*weakly*) Yes—he does—now—but I don't know how long—

BRANT: Ah!

CHRISTINE: So I told him by all means to go. It gave me the chance I wanted to come to you. They went this morning. They don't know I've gone and even after they've found out they can't prove where I went. I can only stay a little while, Adam—we've got to plan—so many things have happened I couldn't foresee—I came to warn you—

BRANT: Ssshh! Come below in the cabin! We're fools to be talking out here. (*He guides her with his arm around her through the door to the companionway stairs and closes it quietly behind them. A pause in which the singing of the crew on the ship in the harbor comes mournfully over the water. Then* ORIN *and* LAVINIA *come in stealthily along the deck from the left. She is dressed in black as before. He wears a long cloak over his uniform and has a slouch hat pulled down over his eyes. Her manner is cold and grim.* ORIN *is holding in a savage, revengeful rage. They approach the cabin skylight silently.* ORIN *bends down by it to listen. His face, in the light from the skylight, becomes distorted with jealous fury.* LAVINIA *puts a restraining hand on his arm.*

The scene fades out into darkness. Several minutes are supposed to elapse. When the light comes on again, a section of the ship has been removed to reveal the interior of the cabin, a small compartment, the walls newly painted a light brown. The skylight giving on the deck above is in the middle of the ceiling. Suspended in the skylight is a ship's compass. Beneath it is a pine table with three chairs, one at rear, the other two at the table ends, left and right. On the table is a bottle of whiskey, half full, with a glass and a pitcher of water.

Built against the right wall of the cabin is a long narrow couch, like a bunk, with leather cushions. In the rear wall, at right, is a door leading into the captain's stateroom. A big sideboard stands against the left wall, center. Above it, a ship's clock. Farther back is a door opening on the alleyway leading to the main deck. The companionway stairs lead down to this alleyway.

There is a lighted lamp on the sideboard and a ship's lantern, also lighted, at the right end of the table.

In the cabin, BRANT *is seated at the right of table,* CHRISTINE *to the rear of it. Her face looks haggard and ageing, the mouth pinched and drawn down at the corners, and her general appearance, the arrangement of her hair and clothes, has the dishevelled touch of the fugitive. She is just finishing her story of the murder and the events following it. He is listening tensely. On the deck above,* ORIN *and* LAVINIA *are discovered as before, with* ORIN *bending down by the transom, listening*).

CHRISTINE: When he was dying he pointed at me and told her I was guilty! And afterwards she found the poison—

BRANT: (*springing to his feet*) For God's sake, why didn't you—

CHRISTINE: (*pitifully*) I fainted before I could hide it! And I had planned it all so carefully. But how could I foresee that she would come in just at that moment? And how could I know he would talk to me the way he did? He drove me crazy! He kept talking of death! He was torturing me! I only wanted him to die and leave me alone!

BRANT: (*his eyes lighting up with savage satisfaction*) He knew before he died whose son I was, you said? By God, I'll bet that maddened him!

CHRISTINE: (*repeats pitifully*) I'd planned it so carefully—but something made things happen!

BRANT: (*overcome by gloomy dejection, sinks down on his chair again*) I knew it! I've had a feeling in my bones! It serves me right, what has happened and is to happen! It wasn't that kind of revenge I had sworn on my mother's body! I should have done as I wanted—fought with Ezra Mannon as two men fight for love of a woman! (*With bitter self-contempt*) I have my father's rotten coward blood in me, I think! Aye!

CHRISTINE: Adam! You make me feel so guilty!

BRANT: (*rousing himself—shamefacedly*) I didn't mean to blame you, Christine. (*Then harshly*) It's too late for regrets now, anyway. We've got to think what to do.

CHRISTINE: Yes! I'm so terrified of Vinnie! Oh, Adam, you must promise me to be on your guard every minute! If she convinces Orin you are my lover— Oh, why can't we go away, Adam? Once we're out of her reach, she can't do anything.

BRANT: The "Flying Trades" won't be sailing for a month or more. We can't get cargo as soon as the owners thought.

CHRISTINE: Can't we go on another ship—as passengers—to the East— we could be married out there—

BRANT: (*gloomily*) But everyone in the town would know you were gone. It would start suspicion—

CHRISTINE: No. Orin and Vinnie would lie to people. They'd have to for their own sakes. They'd say I was in New York with my father. Oh, Adam, it's the only thing we can do! If we don't get out of Vinnie's reach right away I know something horrible will happen!

BRANT: (*dejectedly*) Aye. I suppose it's the only way out for us now. The "Atlantis" is sailing on Friday for China. I'll arrange with her skipper to give us passage—and keep his mouth shut. She sails at daybreak Friday. You'd better meet me here Thursday night. (*Then with an effort*) I'll write Clark and Dawson tonight they'll have to find another skipper for the "Flying Trades."

CHRISTINE: (*noticing the hurt in his tone—miserably*) Poor Adam! I know how it hurts you to give up your ship.

BRANT: (*rousing himself guiltily—pats her hand—with gruff tenderness*) There are plenty of ships—but there is only one you, Christine!

CHRISTINE: I feel so guilty! I've brought you nothing but misfortune!

BRANT: You've brought love—and the rest is only the price. It's worth it a million times! You're all mine now, anyway! (*He hugs her to him, staring over her head with sad blank eyes*).

CHRISTINE: (*her voice trembling*) But I'm afraid I'm not much to boast about having—now. I've grown old in the past few days. I'm ugly. But I'll make myself beautiful again—for you—! I'll make up to you for everything! Try not to regret your ship too much, Adam!

BRANT: (*gruffly*) Let's not talk of her any more. (*Then forcing a wry smile*) I'll give up the sea. I think it's through with me now, anyway! The sea hates a coward.

CHRISTINE: (*trying pitifully to cheer him*) Don't talk like that! You have me, Adam! You have me! And we will be happy—once we're safe on your Blessed Islands! (*Then suddenly, with a little shudder*) It's strange. Orin was telling me of an island— (*On the deck above, ORIN, who has bent closer to the transom, straightens up with a threatening movement. LAVINIA grips his arm, restraining him*).

BRANT: (*with a bitter, hopeless yearning*) Aye—the Blessed Isles—Maybe we can still find happiness and forget! (*Then strangely, as if to himself*) I can see them now—so close—and a million miles away! The warm earth in the moonlight, the trade winds rustling the coco palms, the surf on the barrier reef singing a croon in your ears like a lullaby! Aye! There's peace, and forgetfulness for us there—if we can ever find those islands now!

CHRISTINE: (*desperately*) We will find them! We will! (*She kisses him. A pause. Suddenly she glances frightenedly at the clock*) Look at the time! I've got to go, Adam!

BRANT: For the love of God, watch out for Vinnie. If anything happened to you now—!

CHRISTINE: Nothing will happen to me. But you must be on your guard in case Orin— Good-bye, my lover! I must go! I must! (*She tears herself from his arms but immediately throws herself in them again— terrifiedly*) Oh! I feel so strange—so sad—as if I'd never see you again! (*She begins to sob hysterically*) Oh, Adam, tell me you don't regret! Tell me we're going to be happy! I can't bear this horrible feeling of despair!

BRANT: Of course we'll be happy! Come now! It's only a couple of days. (*They start for the door*) We'll go by the main deck. It's shorter. I'll walk to the end of the wharf with you. I won't go further. We might be seen.

CHRISTINE: Then we don't have to say good-bye for a few minutes yet! Oh, thank God! (*They go out to the alleyway,* BRANT *closing the door behind him. A pause. On the deck above* ORIN *pulls a revolver from under his cloak and makes a move, as if to rush off left down to the main deck after them.* LAVINIA *has been dreading this and throws herself in his way, grasping his arm*).

ORIN: (*in a furious whisper*) Let me go!

LAVINIA: (*struggling with him*) No! Be quiet! Ssshh! I hear them on the main deck! Quick! Come to his cabin! (*She urges him to the companionway door, gets him inside and shuts the door behind them. A moment later the door on the left of the cabin below is opened and they enter*).

LAVINIA: He's going to the end of the wharf. That gives us a few minutes. (*Grimly*) You wanted proof! Well, are you satisfied now?

ORIN: Yes! God damn him! Death is too good for him! He ought to be—

LAVINIA: (*sharply commanding*) Orin! Remember you promised not to lose your head. You've got to do everything exactly as we planned it, so there'll be no suspicion about us. There would be no justice if we let ourselves—

ORIN: (*impatiently*) You've said all that before! Do you think I'm a fool? I'm not anxious to be hanged—for that skunk! (*Then with bitter anguish*) I heard her asking him to kiss her! I heard her warn him against me! (*He gives a horrible chuckle*) And my island I told her about—which was she and I—she wants to go there—with him! (*Then furiously*) Damn you! Why did you stop me? I'd have shot his guts out in front of her!

LAVINIA: (*scornfully*) Outside on deck where the shot would be sure to be heard? We'd have been arrested—and then I'd have to tell the truth to save us. She'd be hanged, and even if we managed to get off, our lives would be ruined! The only person to come off lucky would be Brant! He could die happy, knowing he'd revenged himself on us more than he ever dared hope! Is that what you want?

ORIN: (*sullenly*) No.

LAVINIA: Then don't act like a fool again. (*Looks around the cabin calculatingly—then in a tone of command*) Go and hide outside. He won't see you when he passes along the alleyway in the dark. He'll come straight in here. That's the time for you—

ORIN: (*grimly*) You needn't tell me what to do. I've had a thorough training at this game—thanks to you and Father.

LAVINIA: Quick! Go out now! He won't be long!

ORIN: (*goes to the door—then quickly*) I hear him coming. (*He slips out silently. She hurriedly hides herself by the sideboard at left, front. A moment later* BRANT *appears in the doorway and stands just inside it blinking in the light. He looks around the cabin sadly*).

BRANT: (*huskily*) So it's good-bye to you, "Flying Trades"! And you're right! I wasn't man enough for you! (ORIN *steps through the door and with the pistol almost against* BRANT's *body fires twice.* BRANT *pitches forward to the floor by the table, rolls over, twitches a moment on his back and lies still.* ORIN *springs forward and stands over the body, his pistol aimed down at it, ready to fire again*).

LAVINIA: (*stares fascinatedly at* BRANT's *still face*) Is he—dead?

ORIN: Yes.

LAVINIA: (*sharply*) Don't stand there! Where's the chisel you brought? Smash open everything in his stateroom. We must make it look as if thieves killed him, remember! Take anything valuable! We can sink it overboard afterwards! Hurry! (ORIN *puts his revolver on the table and takes a chisel that is stuck in his belt under his cloak and goes into the stateroom. A moment later there is the sound of splintering wood as he pries open a drawer*).

LAVINIA: (*goes slowly to the body and stands looking down into* BRANT's *face. Her own is frozen and expressionless. A pause.* ORIN *can be heard in the stateroom prying open* BRANT's *desk and scattering the contents of drawers around. Finally* LAVINIA *speaks to the corpse in a grim bitter tone*) How could you love that vile old woman so? (*She throws off this thought— harshly*) But you're dead! It's ended! (*She turns away from him reso- lutely—then suddenly turns back and stands stiffly upright and grim beside the body and prays coldly, as if carrying out a duty*) May God find forgiveness for your sins! May the soul of our cousin, Adam Mannon, rest in peace! (ORIN *comes in from the stateroom and overhears the last of her prayer*).

ORIN: (*harshly*) Rest in hell, you mean! (*He comes to her*) I've pried open everything I could find.

LAVINIA: Then come along. Quick. There's your pistol. Don't forget that. (*She goes to the door*).

ORIN: (*putting it in his pocket*) We've got to go through his pockets to make everything look like a burglary. (*He quickly turns* BRANT's *pockets inside out and puts the revolver he finds, along with bills and coins, watch and chain, knife, etc., into his own*) I'll sink these overboard from the dock, along with what was in his stateroom. (*Having finished this, he still remains stooping over the body and stares into* BRANT'S *face, a queer fascinated expression in his eyes*).

LAVINIA: (*uneasily*) Orin!

ORIN: By God, he does look like Father!

LAVINIA: No! Come along!

ORIN: (*as if talking to himself*) This is like my dream. I've killed him before—over and over.

LAVINIA: Orin!

ORIN: Do you remember me telling you how the faces of the men I killed came back and changed to Father's face and finally became my own? (*He smiles grimly*) He looks like me, too! Maybe I've committed suicide!

LAVINIA: (*frightenedly—grabbing his arm*) Hurry! Someone may come!

ORIN: (*not heeding her, still staring at* BRANT—*strangely*) If I had been he I would have done what he did! I would have loved her as he loved her—and killed Father too—for her sake!

LAVINIA: (*tensely—shaking him by the arm*) Orin, for God's sake, will you stop talking crazy and come along? Do you want us to be found here? (*She pulls him away forcibly*).

ORIN: (*with a last look at the dead man*) It's queer! It's a rotten dirty joke on someone! (*He lets her hustle him out to the alleyway*).

CURTAIN

ACT FIVE

SCENE—*The same as Act Three of "Homecoming"—exterior of the Mannon house. It is the following night. The moon has just risen. The right half of the house is in the black shadow cast by the pine trees but the moonlight falls full on the part to the left of the doorway. The door at center is open and there is a light in the hall behind. All the shutters of the windows are closed.*

CHRISTINE is discovered walking back and forth on the drive before the portico, passing from moonlight into the shadow of the pines and back again. She is in a frightful state of tension, unable to keep still.

She sees someone she is evidently expecting approaching the house from up the drive, off left, and she hurries down as far as the bench to meet her.

HAZEL: (*enters from left—with a kindly smile*) Here I am! Seth brought your note and I hurried right over.

CHRISTINE: (*kissing her—with unnatural effusiveness*) I'm so glad you've come! I know I shouldn't have bothered you.

HAZEL: It's no bother at all, Mrs. Mannon. I'm only too happy to keep you company.

CHRISTINE: I was feeling so terribly sad—and nervous here. I had let Hannah and Annie have the night off. I'm all alone. (*She sits on the bench*) Let's sit out here. I can't bear it in the house. (HAZEL *sits beside her*).

HAZEL: (*pityingly*) I know. It must be terribly lonely for you. You must miss him so much.

CHRISTINE: (*with a shudder*) Please don't talk about— He is buried! He is gone!

HAZEL: (*gently*) He is at peace, Mrs. Mannon.

CHRISTINE: (*with bitter mockery*) I was like you once! I believed in heaven! Now I know there is only hell!

HAZEL: Ssshh! You mustn't say that.

CHRISTINE: (*rousing herself—forcing a smile*) I'm not fit company for a young girl, I'm afraid. You should have youth and beauty and freedom around you. I'm old and ugly and haunted by death! (*Then, as if to herself—in a low desperate tone*) I can't let myself get ugly! I can't!

HAZEL: You're only terribly worn out. You ought to try and sleep.

CHRISTINE: I don't believe there's such a thing on this earth as sleep! It's only in the earth one sleeps! One must feel so at peace—at last—with all one's fears ended! (*Then forcing a laugh*) Good heavens, what a bore it must be for you, listening to my gloomy thoughts! I honestly didn't send for you to— I wanted to ask if you or Peter had heard anything from Orin and Vinnie.

HAZEL: (*surprised*) Why, no. We haven't seen them since the funeral.

CHRISTINE: (*forcing a smile*) They seem to have deserted me. (*Then quickly*) I mean they should have been home before this. I can't imagine what's keeping them. They went to Blackridge to stay overnight at the Bradfords'.

HAZEL: Then there's nothing to worry about. But I don't see how they could leave you alone—just now.

CHRISTINE: Oh, that part is all right. I urged them to go. They left soon after the funeral, and afterwards I thought it would be a good opportunity for me to go to New York and see my father. He's sick, you know, but I found him so much better I decided to come home again last night. I expected Vinnie and Orin back this noon, but here it's night and no sign of them. I—I must confess I'm worried—and frightened. You can't know the horror of being all night—alone in that house! (*She glances at the house behind her with a shudder*).

HAZEL: Would it help you if I stayed with you tonight—I mean if they don't come?

CHRISTINE: (*eagerly*) Oh, would you? (*Hysterical tears come to her eyes. She kisses* HAZEL *with impulsive gratitude*) I can't tell you how grateful I'd be! You're so good! (*Then forcing a laugh*) But it's an imposition to ask you to face such an ordeal. I can't stay still. I'm terrified at every sound. You would have to sit up.

HAZEL: Losing a little sleep won't hurt me any.

CHRISTINE: I mustn't sleep! If you see me falling asleep you must promise to wake me!

HAZEL: But it's just what you need.

CHRISTINE: Yes—afterwards—but not now. I must keep awake. (*In tense desperation*) I wish Orin and Vinnie would come!

HAZEL: (*worriedly*) Perhaps Orin got so sick he wasn't able to. Oh, I hope that isn't it! (*Then getting up*) If I'm going to stay all night I'll have to run home and tell Mother, so she won't worry.

CHRISTINE: Yes—do. (*Then frightenedly*) You won't be long, will you? I'm afraid—to be alone.

HAZEL: (*kisses her—pityingly*) I'll be as quick as I possibly can. (*She walks down the drive, off left, waving her hand as she disappears.* CHRISTINE *stands by the bench—then begins to pace back and forth again*).

CHRISTINE: (*her eyes caught by something down the drive—in a tense whisper*) She's met someone by the gate! Oh, why am I so afraid! (*She turns, seized by panic, and runs to the house—then stops at the top of the steps and faces around, leaning against a column for support*) Oh, God, I'm afraid to know! (*A moment later* ORIN *and* LAVINIA *come up the drive from the left.* LAVINIA *is stiffly square-shouldered, her eyes hard, her mouth grim and set.* ORIN *is in a state of morbid excitement. He carries a newspaper in his hand*).

ORIN: (*speaking to* VINNIE *as they enter—harshly*) You let me do the talking! I want to be the one— (*He sees his mother—startledly*) Mother! (*Then with vindictive mockery*) Ah! So this time at least you are waiting to meet me when I come home!

CHRISTINE: (*stammers*) Orin! What kept you—?

ORIN: We just met Hazel. She said you were terribly frightened at being alone here. That is strange—when you have the memory of Father for company!

CHRISTINE: You—you stayed all this time—at the Bradfords'?

ORIN: We didn't go to the Bradfords'!

CHRISTINE: (*stupidly*) You didn't go—to Blackridge?

ORIN: We took the train there but we decided to stay right on and go to Boston instead.

CHRISTINE: (*terrifiedly*) To—Boston—?

ORIN: And in Boston we waited until the evening train got in. We met that train.

CHRISTINE: Ah!

ORIN: We had an idea you would take advantage of our being in Blackridge to be on it—and you were! And we followed you when you called on your lover in his cabin!

CHRISTINE: (*with a pitiful effort at indignation*) Orin! How dare you talk—! (*Then brokenly*) Orin! Don't look at me like that! Tell me—

ORIN: Your lover! Don't lie! You've lied enough, Mother! I was on deck, listening! What would you have done if you had discovered me? Would you have gotten your lover to murder me, Mother? I heard you warning him against me! But your warning was no use!

CHRISTINE: (*chokingly*) What—? Tell me—!

ORIN: I killed him!

CHRISTINE: (*with a cry of terror*) Oh—oh! I knew! (*Then clutching at* ORIN) No—Orin! You—you're just telling me that—to punish me, aren't you? You said you loved me—you'd protect me—protect your mother—you couldn't murder—!

ORIN: (*harshly, pushing her away*) You could murder Father, couldn't you? (*He thrusts the newspaper into her hands, pointing to the story*) Here! Read that, if you don't believe me! We got it in Boston to see whom the police would suspect. It's only a few lines. Brant wasn't important—except to you! (*She looks at the paper with fascinated horror. Then she lets it slip through her fingers, sinks down on the lowest step and begins to moan to herself, wringing her hands together in stricken anguish.* ORIN *turns from her and starts to pace up and down by the steps.* LAVINIA *stands at the left of the steps, rigid and erect, her face mask-like*).

ORIN: (*harshly*) They think exactly what we planned they should think— that he was killed by waterfront thieves. There's nothing to connect us with his death! (*He stops by her. She stares before her, wringing her hands and moaning. He blurts out*) Mother! Don't moan like that! (*She gives no sign of having heard him. He starts to pace up and down again— with savage resentment*) Why do you grieve for that servant's bastard? I know he was the one who planned Father's murder! You couldn't have done that! He got you under his influence to revenge himself! He hypnotized you! I saw you weren't yourself the minute I got home, remember? How else could you ever have imagined you loved that low swine! How else could you ever have said the things— (*He stops before her*) I heard you planning to go with him to the island I had told you about—our island—that was you and I! (*He starts to pace up and down again distractedly. She remains as before except that her moaning has begun to exhaust itself.* ORIN *stops before her again and grasps her by the shoulders, kneeling on the steps beside her—desperately pleading now*) Mother! Don't moan like that! You're still under his influence! But you'll forget him! I'll make you forget him! I'll make you happy! We'll leave Vinnie here and go away on a long voyage—to the South Seas—

LAVINIA: (*sharply*) Orin!

ORIN: (*not heeding her, stares into his mother's face. She has stopped moaning, the horror in her eyes is dying into blankness, the expression of her mouth congealing to one of numbed grief. She gives no sign of having heard him.* ORIN *shakes her—desperately*) Mother! Don't you hear me? Why won't you speak to me? Will you always love him? Do you hate me now? (*He sinks on his knees before her*) Mother! Answer me! Say you forgive me!

LAVINIA: (*with bitter scorn*) Orin! After all that's happened, are you becoming her crybaby again? (ORIN *starts and gets to his feet, staring at her confusedly, as if he had forgotten her existence.* LAVINIA *speaks again in curt commanding tone that recalls her father*) Leave her alone! Go in the house! (*As he hesitates—more sharply*) Do you hear me? March!

ORIN: (*automatically makes a confused motion of military salute—vaguely*) Yes, sir. (*He walks mechanically up the steps—gazing up at the house— strangely*) Why are the shutters still closed? Father has gone. We ought to let in the moonlight. (*He goes into the house.* LAVINIA *comes and stands beside her mother.* CHRISTINE *continues to stare blankly in front of her. Her face has become a tragic death mask. She gives no sign of being aware of her daughter's presence.* LAVINIA *regards her with bleak, condemning eyes*).

LAVINIA: (*finally speaks sternly*) He paid the just penalty for his crime. You know it was justice. It was the only way true justice could be done. (*Her mother starts. The words shatter her merciful numbness and awaken her to agony again. She springs to her feet and stands glaring at her daughter with a terrible look in which a savage hatred fights with horror and fear. In spite of her frozen self-control,* LAVINIA *recoils before this. Keeping her eyes on her,* CHRISTINE *shrinks backward up the steps until she stands at the top between the two columns of the portico before the front door.* LAVINIA *suddenly makes a motion, as if to hold her back. She calls shakenly as if the words were wrung out of her against her will*) Mother! What are you going to do? You can live!

CHRISTINE: (*glares at her as if this were the last insult—with strident mockery*) Live! (*She bursts into shrill laughter, stops it abruptly, raises her hands between her face and her daughter and pushes them out in a gesture of blotting* LAVINIA *forever from her sight. Then she turns and rushes into the house.* LAVINIA *again makes a movement to follow her. But she immediately fights down this impulse and turns her back on the house determinedly, standing square-shouldered and stiff like a grim sentinel in black*).

LAVINIA: (*implacably to herself*) It is justice! (*From the street, away off right front,* SETH'S *thin wraith of a baritone is raised in his favorite mournful* "Shenandoah," *as he nears the gateway to the drive, returning from his nightly visit to the saloon*).

> "*Oh, Shenandoah, I long to hear you*
> *A-way, my rolling river!*
> *Oh, Shenandoah, I can't get near you*
> *Way—ay, I'm bound away*
> *Across the wide—*"

(*There is the sharp report of a pistol from the left ground floor of the house where* EZRA MANNON'S *study is.* LAVINIA *gives a shuddering gasp, turns back to the steps, starts to go up them, stops again and stammers shakenly*) It is justice! It is your justice, Father! (ORIN'S *voice is heard calling from the sitting-room at right* "What's that!" *A door slams. Then* ORIN'S *horrified cry comes from the study as he finds his mother's body, and a moment later he rushes out frantically to* LAVINIA).

ORIN: Vinnie! (*He grabs her arm and stammers distractedly*) Mother— shot herself—Father's pistol—get a doctor—(*Then with hopeless anguish*) No—it's too late—she's dead! (*Then wildly*) Why—why did she, Vinnie? (*With tortured self-accusation*) I drove her to it! I wanted to torture her! She couldn't forgive me! Why did I have to boast about killing him? Why—?

LAVINIA: (*frightenedly, puts her hand over his mouth*) Be quiet!

ORIN: (*tears her hand away—violently*) Why didn't I let her believe burglars killed him? She wouldn't have hated me then! She would have forgotten him! She would have turned to me! (*In a final frenzy of self-denunciation*) I murdered her!

LAVINIA: (*grabbing him by the shoulders*) For God's sake, will you be quiet?

ORIN: (*frantically—trying to break away from her*) Let me go! I've got to find her! I've got to make her forgive me! I—! (*He suddenly breaks down and weeps in hysterical anguish.* LAVINIA *puts her arm around him soothingly. He sobs despairingly*) But she's dead— She's gone—how can I ever get her to forgive me now?

LAVINIA: (*soothingly*) Ssshh! Ssshh! You have me, haven't you? I love you. I'll help you to forget. (*He turns to go back into the house, still sobbing helplessly.* SETH'S *voice comes from the drive, right, close at hand:*

"She's far across the stormy water
Way-ay, I'm bound away—"

(*He enters right, front.* LAVINIA *turns to face him*).

SETH: (*approaching*) Say, Vinnie, did you hear a shot—?

LAVINIA: (*sharply*) I want you to go for Doctor Blake. Tell him Mother has killed herself in a fit of insane grief over Father's death. (*Then as he stares, dumbfounded and wondering, but keeping his face expressionless—more sharply*) Will you remember to tell him that?

SETH: (*slowly*) Ayeh. I'll tell him, Vinnie—anything you say. (*His face set grimly, he goes off, right front.* LAVINIA *turns and, stiffly erect, her face stern and mask-like, follows* ORIN *into the house*).

CURTAIN

The Haunted

CHARACTERS

LAVINIA MANNON

ORIN, *her brother*

PETER NILES

HAZEL, *his sister*

SETH

AMOS AMES

IRA MACKEL

JOE SILVA

ABNER SMALL

SCENES

Act One—Scene I: Exterior of the Mannon house—an evening in the summer of 1866.

Act One—Scene II: Sitting-room in the house (immediately follows Scene One).

Act Two: The study—an evening a month later.

Act Three: The sitting-room (immediately follows Act Two).

Act Four: Same as Act One, Scene One—Exterior of the Mannon house—a late afternoon three days later.

The Haunted

Act One—Scene One

Exterior of the Mannon house (as in the two preceding plays) on an evening of a clear day in summer a year later. It is shortly after sunset but the afterglow in the sky still bathes the white temple portico in a crimson light. The columns cast black bars of shadow on the wall behind them. All the shutters are closed and the front door is boarded up, showing that the house is unoccupied.

A group of five men is standing on the drive by the bench at left, front. SETH BECKWITH *is there and* AMOS AMES, *who appeared in the first Act of "Homecoming." The others are* ABNER SMALL, JOE SILVA *and* IRA MACKEL.

*These four—*AMES, SMALL, SILVA *and* MACKEL*—are, as were the townsfolk of the first acts of "Homecoming" and "The Hunted," a chorus of types representing the town as a human background for the drama of the Mannons.*

SMALL *is a wiry little old man of sixty-five, a clerk in a hardware store. He has white hair and a wispy goat's beard, bright inquisitive eyes, ruddy complexion, and a shrill rasping voice.* SILVA *is a Portuguese fishing captain— a fat, boisterous man, with a hoarse bass voice. He has matted gray hair and a big grizzled mustache. He is sixty.* MACKEL, *who is a farmer, hobbles along with the aid of a cane. His shiny wrinkled face is oblong with a square white chin whisker. He is bald. His yellowish brown eyes are sly. He talks in a drawling wheezy cackle.*

All five are drunk. SETH *has a stone jug in his hand. There is a grotesque atmosphere of boys out on a forbidden lark about these old men.*

SMALL: God A'mighty, Seth, be you glued to that jug?
MACKEL: Gol durn him, he's gittin' stingy in his old age!

SILVA: (*bursts into song*)

> "*A bottle of beer and a bottle of gin*
> *And a bottle of Irish whiskey oh!*
> *So early in the morning*
> *A sailor likes his bottle oh!*"

AMES: (*derisively*) You like your bottle 'ceptin' when your old woman's got her eye on ye!

SILVA: She's visitin' her folks to New Bedford. What the hell I care! (*Bursts into song again*)

> "*Hurrah! Hurrah! I sing the jublilee*
> *Hurrah! Hurrah! Her folks has set me free!*"

AMES: (*slapping him on the back*) God damn you, Joe, you're gittin' to be a poet! (*They all laugh*).

SMALL: God A'mighty, Seth, ain't ye got no heart in ye? Watch me perishin' fur lack o' whiskey and ye keep froze to that jug! (*He reaches out for it*).

SETH: No, ye don't! I'm onto your game! (*With a wink at the others*) He's aimin' to git so full of Injun courage he wouldn't mind if a ghost sot on his lap! Purty slick you be, Abner! Swill my licker so's you kin skin me out o' my bet!

MACKEL: That's it, Seth! Don't let him play no skin games!

JOE: By God, if ghosts look like the livin', I'd let Ezra's woman's ghost set on my lap! M'm! (*He smacks his lips lasciviously*).

AMES: Me, too! She was a looker!

SMALL: (*with an uneasy glance at the house*) It's her ghost folks is sayin' haunts the place, ain't it?

SETH: (*with a wink at the others*) Oh, hers and a hull passel of others. The graveyard's full of Mannons and they all spend their nights to hum here. You needn't worry but you'll have plenty o' company, Abner! (*The others laugh, their mirth a bit forced, but* SMALL *looks rather sick*).

SMALL: It ain't in our bet for you to put sech notions in my head afore I go in, be it? (*Then forcing a perky bravado*) Think you kin scare me? There ain't no sech thing as ghosts!

SETH: An' I'm sayin' you're scared to prove there ain't! Let's git our bet set out plain afore witnesses. I'm lettin' you in the Mannon house and I'm bettin' you ten dollars and a gallon of licker you dassn't stay there till moonrise at ten o'clock. If you come out afore then, you lose. An' you're to stay in the dark and not even strike a match! Is that agreed?

SMALL: (*trying to put a brave face on it*) That's agreed—an' it's like stealin' ten dollars off you!

SETH: We'll see! (*Then with a grin*) An' you're supposed to go in sober! But I won't make it too dead sober! I ain't that hardhearted. I wouldn't face what you'll face with a gallon under my belt! (*Handing him the jug*) Here! Take a good swig! You're lookin' a mite pale about the gills a'ready!

SMALL: No sech thing! (*But he puts the jug to his lips and takes an enormous swallow*).

MACKEL: Whoa thar! Ye ain't drinkin fur all on us! (SMALL *hands the jug to him and he drinks and passes it around until it finally reaches* SETH *again. In the meantime* SMALL *talks to* SETH).

SMALL: Be it all right fur me to go in afore dark? I'd like to know where I'm at while I kin see.

SETH: Wal, I calc'late you kin. Don't want you runnin' into furniture an' breakin' things when them ghosts git chasin' you! Vinnie an' Orin's liable to be back from Chiny afore long an' she'd give me hell if anythin' was broke. (*The jug reaches him. He takes a drink—then sets it down on the drive*) Come along! I've took the screws out o' that door. I kin let you right in. (*He goes toward the portico,* SMALL *following him, whistling with elaborate nonchalance*).

SMALL: (*to the others who remain where they are*) So long, fellers. We'll have a good spree on that ten dollars.

MACKEL: (*with a malicious cackle*) Mebbe! Would you like me fur one o' your pallbearers, Abner?

AMES: I'll comfort your old woman—providin' she'll want comfortin', which ain't likely!

SILVA: And I'll water your grave every Sunday after church! That's the kind of man I be, by God. I don't forget my friends when they're gone!

SETH: (*from the portico*) We'll all jine in, Joe! If he ain't dead, by God, we'll drown him! (*They all roar with laughter.* SMALL *looks bitter. The jest strikes him as being unfeeling—All glow has faded from the sky and it is getting dark*).

SMALL: To hell with ye! (SETH *pries off the board door and unlocks the inner door*).

SETH: Come on. I'll show you the handiest place to say your prayers. (*They go in. The group outside becomes serious*).

AMES: (*voicing the opinion of all of them*) Wal, all the same, I wouldn't be in Abner's boots. It don't do to monkey with them thin's.

MACKEL: You believe in ghosts, Amos?

AMES: Mebbe. Who knows there ain't?

MACKEL: Wal, I believe in 'em. Take the Nims' place out my way. Asa Nims killed his wife with a hatchet—she'd nagged him—then hung himself in the attic. I knew Ben Willett that bought the place. He couldn't live thar—had to move away. It's fallen to ruins now. Ben used to hear things clawin' at the walls an' winders and see the chairs move about. He wasn't a liar nor chicken-hearted neither.

SILVA: There is ghosts, by God! My cousin, Manuel, he seen one! Off on a whaler in the Injun Ocean, that was. A man got knifed and pushed overboard. After that, on moonlight nights, they'd see him a-settin' on the yards and hear him moanin' to himself. Yes, sir, my cousin Manuel, he ain't no liar neither—'ceptin' when he's drunk—and he seen him with his own eyes!

AMES: (*with an uneasy glance around, reaching for the jug*) Wal, let's have a drink. (*He takes a swig just as* SETH *comes out of the house, shutting the door behind him*).

MACKEL: That's Seth. He ain't anxious to stay in thar long, I notice! (SETH *hurries down to them, trying to appear to saunter*).

SETH: (*with a forced note to his joking*) God A'mighty, ye'd ought to see Abner! He's shyin' at the furniture covers an' his teeth are clickin' a'ready. He'll come runnin' out hell fur leather afore long. All I'm wonderin' is, has he got ten dollars.

MACKEL: (*slyly*) You seem a mite shaky.

SETH: (*with a scowl*) You're a liar. What're ye all lookin' glum as owls about?

MACKEL: Been talkin' of ghosts. Do you really believe that there house is haunted, Seth, or are ye only jokin' Abner?

SETH: (*sharply*) Don't be a durned fool! I'm on'y jokin' him, of course!

MACKEL: (*insistently*) Still, it'd be only natural if it was haunted. She shot herself there. Do you think she done it fur grief over Ezra's death, like the daughter let on to folks?

SETH: 'Course she did!

MACKEL: Ezra dyin' sudden his first night to hum—that was durned queer!

SETH: (*angrily*) It's durned queer old fools like you with one foot in the grave can't mind their own business in the little time left to 'em. That's what's queer!

MACKEL: (*angry in his turn*) Wal, all I say is if they hadn't been Mannons with the town lickin' their boots, there'd have been queer doin's come out! And as fur me bein' an old fool, you're older an' a worse fool! An' your foot's deeper in the grave than mine be!

SETH: (*shaking his fist in* MACKEL's *face*) It ain't so deep but what I kin whale the stuffin' out o' you any day in the week!

SILVA: (*comes between them*) Here, you old roosters! No fightin' allowed!

MACKEL: (*subsiding grumpily*) This is a free country, ain't it? I got a right to my opinions!

AMES: (*suddenly looking off down left*) Ssshh! Look, Seth! There's some-one comin' up the drive.

SETH: (*peering*) Ayeh! Who the hell—? It's Peter'n Hazel. Hide that jug, durn ye! (*The jug is hidden under the lilacs. A moment later, HAZEL and PETER enter. They stop in surprise on seeing SETH and his friends. SETH greets them self-consciously*) Good evenin'. I was just showin' some friends around—

PETER: Hello, Seth. Just the man we're looking for. We've just had a telegram. Vinnie and Orin have landed in New York and— (*He is interrupted by a muffled yell of terror from the house. As they all turn to look, the front door is flung open and SMALL comes tearing out and down the portico steps, his face chalky white and his eyes popping*).

SMALL: (*as he reaches them—terrifiedly*) God A'mighty! I heard 'em comin' after me, and I run in the room opposite, an' I seed Ezra's ghost dressed like a judge comin' through the wall—and, by God, I run! (*He jerks a bill out of his pocket and thrusts it on SETH*) Here's your money, durn ye! I wouldn't stay in there fur a million! (*This breaks the tension, and the old men give way to an hysterical, boisterous, drunken mirth, roaring with laughter, pounding each other on the back*).

PETER: (*sharply*) What's this all about? What was he doing in there?

SETH: (*controlling his laughter—embarrassedly*) Only a joke, Peter. (*Then turning on SMALL—scornfully*) That was Ezra's picture hangin' on the wall, not a ghost, ye durned idjut!

SMALL: (*indignantly*) I know pictures when I see 'em an' I knowed him. This was him! Let's get out o' here. I've had enough of this durned place!

SETH: You fellers trot along. I'll jine you later. (*They all mutter good evenings to PETER and HAZEL and go off, left front. SMALL's excited voice can be heard receding as he begins to embroider on the horrors of his adventure. SETH turns to PETER apologetically*) Abner Small's always braggin' how brave he is—so I bet him he dasn't stay in there—

HAZEL: (*indignantly*) Seth! What would Vinnie say if she knew you did such things?

SETH: There ain't no harm done. I calc'late Abner didn't break nothin'. And Vinnie wouldn't mind when she knew why I done it. I was aimin' to stop the durned gabbin' that's been goin' round town about this house bein' haunted. You've heard it, ain't ye?

PETER: I heard some silly talk but didn't pay any attention—

SETH: That durned idjut female I got in to clean a month after Vinnie and Orin sailed started it. Said she'd felt ghosts around. You know how them things grow. Seemed to me Abner's braggin' gave me a good chance to stop it by turnin' it all into a joke on him folks'd laugh at. An' when I git through tellin' my story of it round town tomorrow you'll find folks'll shet up and not take it serious no more.

PETER: (*appreciatively*) You're right, Seth. That was a darned slick notion! Nothing like a joke to lay a ghost!

SETH: Ayeh. But— (*He hesitates—then decides to say it*) Between you 'n' me 'n' the lamp-post, it ain't all sech a joke as it sounds—that about the hauntin', I mean.

PETER: (*incredulously*) You aren't going to tell me you think the house is haunted too!

SETH: (*grimly*) Mebbe, and mebbe not. All I know is I wouldn't stay in there all night if you was to give me the town!

HAZEL: (*impressed but forcing a teasing tone*) Seth! I'm ashamed of you!

PETER: First time I ever heard you say you were afraid of anything!

SETH: There's times when a man's a darn fool not to be scared! Oh, don't git it in your heads I take stock in spirits trespassin' round in windin' sheets or no sech lunatic doin's. But there is sech a thing as evil spirit. An' I've felt it, goin' in there daytimes to see to things— like somethin' rottin' in the walls!

PETER: Bosh!

SETH: (*quietly*) 'Tain't bosh, Peter. There's been evil in that house since it was first built in hate—and it's kept growin' there ever since, as what's happened there has proved. You understand I ain't sayin' this to no one but you two. An' I'm only tellin' you fur one reason— because you're closer to Vinnie and Orin than anyone and you'd ought to persuade them, now they're back, not to live in it. (*He adds impressively*) Fur their own good! (*Then with a change of tone*) An' now I've got that off my chest, tell me about 'em. When are they comin'?

PETER: Tomorrow. Vinnie asked us to open the house. So let's start right in.

SETH: (*with evident reluctance*) You want to do it tonight?

HAZEL: We must, Seth. We've got so little time. We can at least tidy up the rooms a little and get the furniture covers off.

SETH: Wal, I'll go to the barn and git lanterns. There's candles in the house. (*He turns abruptly and goes off left between the lilacs and the house*).

HAZEL: (*looking after him—uneasily*) I can't get over Seth acting so strangely.

PETER: Don't mind him. It's rum and old age.

HAZEL: (*shaking her head—slowly*) No. There is something queer about this house. I've always felt it, even before the General's death and her suicide. (*She shudders*) I can still see her sitting on that bench as she was that last night. She was so frightened of being alone. But I thought when Vinnie and Orin came back she would be all right. (*Then sadly*) Poor Orin! I'll never forget to my dying day the way he looked when we saw him at the funeral. I hardly recognized him, did you?

PETER: No. He certainly was broken up.

HAZEL: And the way he acted—like someone in a trance! I don't believe when Vinnie rushed him off on this trip to the East he knew what he was doing or where he was going or anything.

PETER: A long voyage like that was the best thing to help them both forget.

HAZEL: (*without conviction*) Yes. I suppose it was—but— (*She stops and sighs—then worriedly*) I wonder how Orin is. Vinnie's letters haven't said much about him, or herself, for that matter—only about the trip. (*She sees* SETH *approaching, whistling loudly, from left, rear, with two lighted lanterns*) Here's Seth. (*She walks up the steps to the portico.* PETER *follows her. She hesitates and stands looking at the house—in a low tone, almost of dread*) Seth was right. You feel something cold grip you the moment you set foot—

PETER: Oh, nonsense! He's got you going, too! (*Then with a chuckle*) Listen to him whistling to keep his courage up! (SETH *comes in from the left. He hands one of the lanterns to* PETER).

SETH: Here you be, Peter.

HAZEL: Well, let's go in. You better come out to the kitchen and help me first, Peter. We ought to start a fire. (*They go in. There is a pause in which* PETER *can be heard opening windows behind the shutters in the downstairs rooms. Then silence. Then* LAVINIA *enters, coming up the drive from left, front, and stands regarding the house. One is at once aware of an extraordinary change in her. Her body, formerly so thin and undeveloped, has filled out. Her movements have lost their square-shouldered stiffness. She now bears a striking resemblance to her mother in every respect, even to being dressed in the green her mother had affected. She walks to the clump of lilacs and stands there staring at the house*).

LAVINIA: (*turns back and calls coaxingly in the tone one would use to a child*) Don't stop there, Orin! What are you afraid of? Come on! (*He comes slowly and hesitatingly in from left, front. He carries himself woodenly erect now like a soldier. His movements and attitudes have the statue-like quality that was so marked in his father. He now wears a close-cropped beard in addition to his mustache, and this accentuates his resemblance to his father. The Mannon semblance of his face in repose to a mask is more pronounced than ever. He has grown dreadfully thin and his black suit hangs loosely on his body. His haggard swarthy face is set in a blank lifeless expression*).

LAVINIA: (*glances at him uneasily—concealing her apprehension under a coaxing motherly tone*) You must be brave! This is the test! You have got to face it! (*Then anxiously as he makes no reply*) Do you feel you can—now we're here?

ORIN: (*dully*) I'll be all right—with you.

LAVINIA: (*takes his hand and pats it encouragingly*) That's all I wanted—

to hear you say that. (*Turning to the house*) Look, I see a light through the shutters of the sitting-room. That must be Peter and Hazel. (*Then as she sees he still keeps his eyes averted from the house*) Why don't you look at the house? Are you afraid? (*Then sharply commanding*) Orin! I want you to look now! Do you hear me?

ORIN: (*dully obedient*) Yes, Vinnie. (*He jerks his head around and stares at the house and draws a deep shuddering breath*).

LAVINIA: (*her eyes on his face—as if she were willing her strength into him*) Well? You don't see any ghosts, do you? Tell me!

ORIN: (*obediently*) No.

LAVINIA: Because there are none! Tell me you know there are none, Orin!

ORIN: (*as before*) Yes.

LAVINIA: (*searches his face uneasily—then is apparently satisfied*) Come. Let's go in. We'll find Hazel and Peter and surprise them— (*She takes his arm and leads him to the steps. He walks like an automaton. When they reach the spot where his mother had sat moaning, the last time he had seen her alive (Act Five of "The Hunted") he stops with a shudder*).

ORIN: (*stammers—pointing*) It was here—she—the last time I saw her alive—

LAVINIA: (*quickly, urging him on commandingly*) That is all past and finished! The dead have forgotten us! We've forgotten them! Come! (*He obeys woodenly. She gets him up the steps and they pass into the house*).

CURTAIN

SCENE TWO

*S*AME *as Act Two of "The Hunted"—The sitting-room in the Mannon house.* PETER *has lighted two candles on the mantel and put the lantern on the table at front. In this dim, spotty light the room is full of shadows. It has the dead* *appearance of a room long shut up, and the covered furniture has a ghostly look. In the flickering candlelight the eyes of the Mannon portraits stare with a grim forbiddingness.*

LAVINIA *appears in the doorway at rear. In the lighted room, the change in her is strikingly apparent. At a first glance, one would mistake her for her mother as she appeared in the First Act of "Homecoming." She seems a mature woman, sure of her feminine attractiveness. Her brown-gold hair is arranged as her mother's had been. Her green dress is like a copy of her mother's in Act One of "Homecoming." She comes forward slowly. The movements of her body now have the feminine grace her mother's had possessed. Her eyes are caught by the eyes of the Mannons in the portraits and she approaches as if compelled in spite of herself until she stands directly under them in front of the fireplace. She suddenly addresses them in a harsh resentful voice.*

LAVINIA: Why do you look at me like that? I've done my duty by you! That's finished and forgotten! (*She tears her eyes from theirs and, turning away, becomes aware that* ORIN *has not followed her into the room, and is immediately frightened and uneasy and hurries toward the door, calling*) Orin!

ORIN: (*his voice comes from the dark hall*) I'm here.

LAVINIA: What are you doing out there? Come here! (ORIN *appears in the doorway. His face wears a dazed expression and his eyes have a wild, stricken look. He hurries to her as if seeking protection. She exclaims frightenedly*) Orin! What is it?

ORIN: (*strangely*) I've just been in the study. I was sure she'd be waiting for me in there, where— (*Torturedly*) But she wasn't! She isn't any-where. It's only they— (*He points to the portraits*) They're everywhere! But she's gone forever. She'll never forgive me now!

LAVINIA: (*harshly*) Orin! Will you be quiet!

ORIN: (*unheeding—with a sudden turn to bitter resentful defiance*) Well, let her go! What is she to me? I'm not her son any more! I'm Father's! I'm a Mannon! And they'll welcome me home!

LAVINIA: (*angrily commanding*) Stop it, do you hear me!

ORIN: (*shocked back to awareness by her tone—pitifully confused*) I—I didn't—don't be angry, Vinnie!

LAVINIA: (*soothing him now*) I'm not angry, dear—only do get hold of yourself and be brave. (*Leading him to the sofa*) Here. Come. Let's sit down for a moment, shall we, and get used to being home? (*They sit down. She puts an arm around him reproachfully*) Don't you know how terribly you frighten me when you act so strangely? You don't mean to hurt me, do you?

ORIN: (*deeply moved*) God knows I don't, Vinnie! You're all I have in the world! (*He takes her hand and kisses it humbly*).

LAVINIA: (*soothingly*) That's a good boy. (*Then with a cheerful matter-of-fact note*) Hazel and Peter must be back in the kitchen Won't you be glad to see Hazel again?

ORIN: (*dully now*) You've kept talking about them all the voyage home. Why? What can they have to do with us—now?

LAVINIA: A lot. What we need most is to get back to simple normal things and begin a new life. And their friendship and love will help us more than anything to forget.

ORIN: (*with sudden harshness*) Forget? I thought you'd forgotten long ago—if you ever remembered, which you never seemed to! (*Then with somber bitterness*) Love! What right have I—or you— to love?

LAVINIA: (*defiantly*) Every right!

ORIN: (*grimly*) Mother felt the same about— (*Then with a strange, searching glance at her*) You don't know how like Mother you've become, Vinnie. I don't mean only how pretty you've gotten—

LAVINIA: (*with a strange shy eagerness*) Do you really think I'm as pretty now as she was, Orin?

ORIN: (*as if she hadn't interrupted*) I mean the change in your soul, too. I've watched it ever since we sailed for the East. Little by little it grew like Mother's soul—as if you were stealing hers— as if her death had set you free—to become her!

LAVINIA: (*uneasily*) Now don't begin talking nonsense again, please!

ORIN: (*grimly*) Don't you believe in souls any more? I think you will after we've lived in this house awhile! The Mannon dead will convert you. (*He turns to the portraits mockingly*) Ask them if I'm not right!

LAVINIA: (*sharply*) Orin! What's come over you? You haven't had one of these morbid spells since we left the Islands. You swore to me you were all over them, or I'd never have agreed to come home.

ORIN: (*with a strange malicious air*) I had to get you away from the Islands. My brotherly duty! If you'd stayed there much longer— (*He chuckles disagreeably*).

LAVINIA: (*with a trace of confusion*) I don't know what you're talking about. I only went there for your sake.

ORIN: (*with another chuckle*) Yes—but afterwards—

LAVINIA: (*sharply*) You promised you weren't going to talk any more morbid nonsense. (*He subsides meekly. She goes on reproachfully*) Remember all I've gone through on your account. For months after we sailed you didn't know what you were doing. I had to live in constant fear of what you might say. I wouldn't live through those horrible days again for anything on earth. And remember this homecoming is what you wanted. You told me that if you could come home and face your ghosts, you knew you could rid yourself forever of your silly guilt about the past.

ORIN: (*dully*) I know, Vinnie.

LAVINIA: And I believed you, you seemed so certain of yourself. But now you've suddenly become strange again. You frighten me. So much depends on how you start in, now we're home. (*Then sharply commanding*) Listen, Orin! I want you to start again—by facing all your ghosts right now! (*He turns and his eyes remain fixed on hers from now on. She asks sternly*) Who murdered Father?

ORIN: (*falteringly*) Brant did—for revenge because—

LAVINIA: (*more sternly*) Who murdered Father? Answer me!

ORIN: (*with a shudder*) Mother was under his influence—

LAVINIA: That's a lie! It was he who was under hers. You know the truth!

ORIN: Yes.

LAVINIA: She was an adulteress and a murderess, wasn't she?

ORIN: Yes.

LAVINIA: If we'd done our duty under the law, she would have been hanged, wouldn't she?

ORIN: Yes.

LAVINIA: But we protected her. She could have lived, couldn't she? But she chose to kill herself as a punishment for her crime—of her own free will! It was an act of justice! You had nothing to do with it! You see that now, don't you? (*As he hesitates, trembling violently, she grabs his arm fiercely*) Tell me!

ORIN: (*hardly above a whisper*) Yes.

LAVINIA: And your feeling of being responsible for her death was only your morbid imagination! You don't feel it now! You'll never feel it again!

ORIN: No.

LAVINIA: (*gratefully—and weakly because the strength she has willed into him has left her exhausted*) There! You see! You can do it when you will to! (*She kisses him. He breaks down, sobbing weakly against her breast. She soothes him*) There! Don't cry! You ought to feel proud. You've proven you can laugh at your ghosts from now on. (*Then briskly, to distract his mind*) Come now. Help me to take off these furniture covers. We might as well start making ourselves useful. (*She starts to work. For a moment he helps. Then he goes to one of the windows and pushes back a shutter and stands staring out.* PETER *comes in the door from rear. At the sight of* LAVINIA *he stops startledly, thinks for a second it is her mother's ghost and gives an exclamation of dread. At the same moment she sees him. She stares at him with a strange eager possessiveness. She calls softly*).

LAVINIA: Peter! (*She goes toward him, smiling as her mother might have smiled*) Don't you know me any more, Peter?

PETER: (*stammers*) Vinnie! I—I thought you were—! I can't realize it's you! You've grown so like your— (*Checking himself awkwardly*) I mean you've changed so—and we weren't looking for you until— (*He takes her hand automatically, staring at her stupidly*).

LAVINIA: I know. We had intended to stay in New York tonight but we decided later we'd better come right home. (*Then taking him in with a smiling appreciative possessiveness*) Let me look at you, Peter. You haven't gone and changed, have you? No, you're the same, thank goodness! I've been thinking of you all the way home and wondering—I was so afraid you might have.

PETER: (*plucking up his courage—blurts out*) You—you ought to know I'd never change—with you! (*Then, alarmed by his own boldness, he hastily looks away from her*).

LAVINIA: (*teasingly*) But you haven't said yet you're glad to see me!

PETER: (*has turned back and is staring fascinatedly at her. A surge of love and desire overcomes his timidity and he bursts out*) I—you know how much I—! (*Then he turns away again in confusion and takes refuge in a burst of talk*) Gosh, Vinnie, you ought to have given us more warning. We've only just started to open the place up. I was with Hazel, in the kitchen, starting a fire—

LAVINIA: (*laughing softly*) Yes. You're the same old Peter! You're still afraid of me. But you mustn't be now. I know I used to be an awful old stick, but—

PETER: Who said so? You were not! (*Then with enthusiasm*) Gosh, you look so darned pretty—and healthy. Your trip certainly did you good! (*Staring at her again, drinking her in*) I can't get over seeing you dressed in color. You always used to wear black.

LAVINIA: (*with a strange smile*) I was dead then.

PETER: You ought always to wear color.

LAVINIA: (*immensely pleased*) Do you think so?

PETER: Yes. It certainly is becoming. I— (*Then embarrassedly changing the subject*) But where's Orin?

LAVINIA: (*turning to look around*) Why, he was right here. (*She sees him at the window*) Orin, what are you doing there? Here's Peter. (ORIN *closes the shutter he has pushed open and turns back from the window. He comes forward, his eyes fixed in a strange preoccupation, as if he were unaware of their presence.* LAVINIA *watches him uneasily and speaks sharply*) Don't you see Peter? Why don't you speak to him? You mustn't be so rude.

PETER: (*good-naturedly*) Give him a chance. Hello, Orin. Darned glad to see you back. (*They shake hands.* PETER *has difficulty in hiding his pained surprise at* ORIN'S *sickly appearance*).

ORIN: (*rousing himself, forces a smile and makes an effort at his old friendly manner with* PETER) Hello, Peter. You know I'm glad to see you without any polite palaver. Vinnie is the same old bossy fuss-buzzer—you remember—always trying to teach me manners!

PETER: You bet I remember! But say, hasn't she changed, though? I didn't know her, she's grown so fat! And I was just telling her how well she looked in color. Don't you agree?

ORIN: (*in a sudden strange tone of jeering malice*) Did you ask her why she stole Mother's colors? I can't see why—yet—and I don't think she knows herself. But it will prove a strange reason, I'm certain of that, when I do discover it!

LAVINIA: (*making a warning sign to* PETER *not to take this seriously—forcing a smile*) Don't mind him, Peter.

ORIN: (*his tone becoming sly, insinuating and mocking*) And she's become romantic! Imagine that! Influence of the "dark and deep blue ocean"—and of the Islands, eh, Vinnie?

PETER: (*surprised*) You stopped at the Islands?

ORIN: Yes. We took advantage of our being on a Mannon ship to make the captain touch there on the way back. We stopped a month. (*With resentful bitterness*) But they turned out to be Vinnie's islands, not mine. They only made me sick—and the naked women disgusted me. I guess I'm too much of a Mannon, after all, to turn into a pagan. But you should have seen Vinnie with the men—!

LAVINIA: (*indignantly but with a certain guiltiness*) How can you—!

ORIN: (*jeeringly*) Handsome and romantic-looking, weren't they, Vinnie?—with colored rags around their middles and flowers stuck over their ears! Oh, she was a bit shocked at first by their dances, but afterwards she fell in love with the Islanders. If we'd stayed another month, I know I'd have found her some moonlight night dancing under the palm trees—as naked as the rest!

LAVINIA: Orin! Don't be disgusting!

ORIN: (*points to the portraits mockingly*) Picture, if you can, the feelings of the God-fearing Mannon dead at that spectacle!

LAVINIA: (*with an anxious glance at* PETER) How can you make up such disgusting fibs?

ORIN: (*with a malicious chuckle*) Oh, I wasn't as blind as I pretended to be! Do you remember Avahanni?

LAVINIA: (*angrily*) Stop talking like a fool! (*He subsides meekly again. She forces a smile and a motherly tone*) You're a naughty boy, do you know it? What will Peter think? Of course, he knows you're only teasing me—but you shouldn't go on like that. It isn't nice. (*Then changing the subject abruptly*) Why don't you go and find Hazel? Here. Let me look at you. I want you to look your best when she sees you. (*She arranges him as a mother would a boy, pulling down his coat, giving a touch to his shirt and tie.* ORIN *straightens woodenly to a soldierly attention. She is vexed by this*) Don't stand like a ramrod! You'd be so handsome if you'd only shave off that silly beard and not carry yourself like a tin soldier!

ORIN: (*with a sly cunning air*) Not look so much like Father, eh? More like a romantic clipper captain, is that it? (*As she starts and stares at him frightenedly, he smiles an ugly taunting smile*) Don't look so frightened, Vinnie!

LAVINIA: (*with an apprehensive glance at* PETER—*pleading and at the same time warning*) Ssshh! You weren't to talk nonsense, remember! (*Giving him a final pat*) There! Now run along to Hazel.

ORIN: (*looks from her to* PETER *suspiciously*) You seem damned anxious to get rid of me. (*He turns and stalks stiffly with hurt dignity from the room.* LAVINIA *turns to* PETER *The strain of* ORIN'S *conduct has told on her. She seems suddenly weak and frightened*).

PETER: (*in shocked amazement*) What's come over him?

LAVINIA: (*in a strained voice*) It's the same thing—what the war did to him—and on top of that Father's death—and the shock of Mother's suicide.

PETER: (*puts his arm around her impulsively—comfortingly*) It'll be all right! Don't worry, Vinnie!

LAVINIA: (*nestling against him gratefully*) Thank you, Peter. You're so good. (*Then looking into his eyes*) Do you still love me, Peter?

PETER: Don't have to ask that, do you? (*He squeezes her awkwardly—then stammers*) But do you—think now—you maybe—can love me?

LAVINIA: Yes!

PETER: You really mean that!

LAVINIA: Yes! I do! I've thought of you so much! Things were always reminding me of you—the ship and the sea—everything that was honest and clean! And the natives on the Islands reminded me of you too. They were so simple and fine— (*Then hastily*) You mustn't mind what Orin was saying about the Islands. He's become a regular bigoted Mannon.

PETER: (*amazed*) But, Vinnie—!

LAVINIA: Oh, I know it must sound funny hearing me talk like that. But remember I'm only half Mannon, (*She looks at the portraits defiantly*) And I've done my duty by them! They can't say I haven't!

PETER: (*mystified but happy*) Gosh, you certainly have changed! But I'm darned glad!

LAVINIA: Orin keeps teasing that I was flirting with that native he spoke about, simply because he used to smile at me and I smiled back.

PETER: (*teasingly*) Now, I'm beginning to get jealous, too.

LAVINIA: You mustn't. He made me think of you. He made me dream of marrying you—and everything.

PETER: Oh, well then, I take it all back! I owe him a vote of thanks! (*He hugs her*).

LAVINIA: (*dreamily*) I loved those Islands. They finished setting me free. There was something there mysterious and beautiful—a good spirit—of love—coming out of the land and sea. It made me forget death. There was no hereafter. There was only this world— the warm earth in the moonlight—the trade wind in the coco palms —the surf on the reef—the fires at night and the drum throbbing in my heart— the natives dancing naked and innocent—without knowledge of sin! (*She checks herself abruptly and frightenedly*) But what in the world! I'm gabbing on like a regular chatterbox. You must think I've become awfully scatter-brained!

PETER: (*with a chuckle*) Gosh no! I'm glad you've grown that way! You never used to say a word unless you had to!

LAVINIA: (*suddenly filled with grateful love for him, lets herself go and throws her arms around him*) Oh, Peter, hold me close to you! I want to feel love! Love is all beautiful! I never used to know that! I was a fool! (*She kisses him passionately. He returns it, aroused and at the same time a little shocked by her boldness. She goes on longingly*) We'll be married soon, won't we, and settle out in the country away from folks and their evil talk. We'll make an island for ourselves on land, and we'll have children and love then and teach them to love life so that they can never be possessed by hate and death! (*She gives a start—in a whisper as if to herself*) But I'm forgetting Orin!

PETER: What's Orin got to do with us marrying?

LAVINIA: I can't leave him—until he's all well again. I'd be afraid—

PETER: Let him live with us.

LAVINIA: (*with sudden intensity*) No! I want to be rid of the past. (*Then after a quick look at him—in a confiding tone*) I want to tell you what's wrong with Orin—so you and Hazel can help me. He feels guilty about Mother killing herself. You see, he'd had a quarrel with her that last night. He was jealous and mad and said things he was sorry for after and it preyed on his mind until he blames himself for her death.

PETER: But that's crazy!

LAVINIA: I know it is, Peter, but you can't do anything with him when he gets his morbid spells. Oh, I don't mean he's the way he is tonight most of the time. Usually he's like himself, only quiet and sad—so sad it breaks my heart to see him—like a little boy who's been punished for something he didn't do. Please tell Hazel what I've told you, so she'll make allowances for any crazy thing he might say.

PETER: I'll warn her. And now don't you worry any more about him. We'll get him all right again one way or another.

LAVINIA: (*again grateful for his simple goodness—lovingly*) Bless you, Peter! (*She kisses him. As she does so,* HAZEL *and* ORIN *appear in the doorway at rear.* HAZEL *is a bit shocked, then smiles happily.* ORIN *starts as if he'd been struck. He glares at them with jealous rage and clenches his fists as if he were going to attack them*).

HAZEL: (*with a teasing laugh*) I'm afraid we're interrupting, Orin. (PETER *and* VINNIE *jump apart in confusion*).

ORIN: (*threateningly*) So that's it! By God—!

LAVINIA: (*frightened but managing to be stern*) Orin!

ORIN: (*pulls himself up sharply—confusedly, forcing a sickly smile*) Don't be so solemn—Fuss Buzzer! I was only trying to scare you—for a joke! (*Turning to* PETER *and holding out his hand, his smile becoming ghastly*) I suppose congratulations are in order. I—I'm glad. (PETER *takes his hand awkwardly.* HAZEL *moves toward* LAVINIA *to greet her, her face full of an uneasy bewilderment.* LAVINIA *stares at* ORIN *with eyes full of dread*).

CURTAIN

ACT TWO

*S*CENE—*Same as Act Three of "The Hunted"—*EZRA MANNON'S *study—on an evening a month later. The shutters of the windows are closed. Candles on the mantel above the fireplace light up the portrait of* EZRA MANNON *in his judge's robes.* ORIN *is sitting in his father's chair at left of table, writing by the light of a lamp. A small pile of manuscript is stacked by his right hand. He is intent on his work. He has aged in the intervening month. He looks almost as old now as his father in the portrait. He is dressed in black and the resemblance between the two is uncanny. A grim smile of satisfaction twitches his lips as he stops writing and reads over the paragraph he has just finished. Then he puts the sheet down and stares up at the portrait, sitting back in his chair.*

ORIN: (*sardonically, addressing the portrait*) The truth, the whole truth and nothing but the truth! Is that what you're demanding, Father? Are you sure you want the whole truth? What will the neighbors say if this whole truth is ever known? (*He chuckles grimly*) A ticklish decision for you, Your Honor! (*There is a knock on the door. He hastily grabs the script and puts it in the drawer of the desk*) Who's there?

LAVINIA: It's I.

ORIN: (*hastily locking the drawer and putting the key in his pocket*) What do you want?

LAVINIA: (*sharply*) Please open the door!

ORIN: All right. In a minute. (*He hurriedly straightens up the table and grabs a book at random from the bookcase and lays it open on the table as if he had been reading. Then he unlocks the door and comes back to his chair as* LAVINIA *enters. She wears a green velvet gown similar to that worn by* CHRISTINE *in Act Three of "Homecoming." It sets off her hair and eyes. She is obviously concealing beneath a surface calm a sense of dread and desperation*).

LAVINIA: (*glances at him suspiciously, but forces a casual air*) Why did you lock yourself in? (*She comes over to the table*) What are you doing?

ORIN: Reading.

LAVINIA: (*picks up the book*) Father's law books?

ORIN: (*mockingly*) Why not? I'm considering studying law. He wanted me to, if you remember.

LAVINIA: Do you expect me to believe that, Orin? What is it you're really doing?

ORIN: Curious, aren't you?

LAVINIA: (*forcing a smile*) Good gracious, why wouldn't I be? You've acted so funny lately, locking yourself in here with the blinds closed and the lamp burning even in the daytime. It isn't good for you staying in this stuffy room in this weather. You ought to get out in the fresh air.

ORIN: (*harshly*) I hate the daylight. It's like an accusing eye! No, we've renounced the day, in which normal people live—or rather it has renounced us. Perpetual night—darkness of death in life—that's the fitting habitat for guilt! You believe you can escape that, but I'm not so foolish!

LAVINIA: Now you're being stupid again!

ORIN: And I find artificial light more appropriate for my work—man's light, not God's—man's feeble striving to understand himself, to exist for himself in the darkness! It's a symbol of his life—a lamp burning out in a room of waiting shadows!

LAVINIA: (*sharply*) Your work? What work?

ORIN: (*mockingly*) Studying the law of crime and punishment, as you saw.

LAVINIA: (*forcing a smile again and turning away from him*) All right, if you won't tell me. Go on being mysterious, if you like. (*In a tense voice*) It's so close in here! It's suffocating! It's bad for you! (*She goes to the window and throws the shutters open and looks out*) It's black as pitch tonight. There isn't a star.

ORIN: (*somberly*) Darkness without a star to guide us! Where are we going, Vinnie? (*Then with a mocking chuckle*) Oh, I know you think you know where you're going, but there's many a slip, remember!

LAVINIA: (*her voice strident, as if her will were snapping*) Be quiet! Can't you think of anything but— (*Then controlling herself, comes to him— gently*) I'm sorry. I'm terribly nervous tonight. It's the heat, I guess. And you get me so worried with your incessant brooding over the past. It's the worst thing for your health. (*She pats him on the arm— soothingly*) That's all I'm thinking about, dear.

ORIN: Thank you for your anxiety about my health! But I'm afraid there isn't much hope for you there! I happen to feel quite well!

LAVINIA: (*whirling on him—distractedly*) How can you insinuate such horrible—! (*Again controlling herself with a great effort, forcing a smile*) But you're only trying to rile me—and I'm not going to let you. I'm so glad you're feeling better. You ate a good supper tonight—for you. The long walk we took with Hazel did you good.

ORIN: (*dully*) Yes. (*He slumps down in his chair at left of table*) Why is it you never leave me alone with her more than a minute? You approved of my asking her to marry me—and now we're engaged you never leave us alone! (*Then with a bitter smile*) But I know the reason well enough. You're afraid I'll let something slip.

LAVINIA: (*sits in the chair opposite him—wearily*) Can you blame me, the way you've been acting?

ORIN: (*somberly*) No. I'm afraid myself of being too long alone with her—afraid of myself. I have no right in the same world with her. And yet I feel so drawn to her purity! Her love for me makes me appear less vile to myself! (*Then with a harsh laugh*) And, at the same time, a million times more vile, that's the hell of it! So I'm afraid you can't hope to get rid of me through Hazel. She's another lost island! It's wiser for you to keep Hazel away from me, I warn you. Because when I see love for a murderer in her eyes my guilt crowds up in my throat like poisonous vomit and I long to spit it out—and confess!

LAVINIA: (*in a low voice*) Yes, that is what I live in terror of—that in one of your fits you'll say something before someone—now after it's all past and forgotten—when there isn't the slightest suspicion—

ORIN: (*harshly*) Were you hoping you could escape retribution? You can't! Confess and atone to the full extent of the law! That's the only way to wash the guilt of our mother's blood from our souls!

LAVINIA: (*distractedly*) Ssshh! Will you stop!

ORIN: Ask our father, the Judge, if it isn't! He knows! He keeps telling me!

LAVINIA: Oh, God! Over and over and over! Will you never lose your stupid guilty conscience! Don't you see how you torture me? You're becoming my guilty conscience, too! (*With an instinctive flare-up of her old jealousy*) How can you still love that vile woman so—when you know all she wanted was to leave you without a thought and marry that—

ORIN: (*with fierce accusation*) Yes! Exactly as you're scheming now to leave me and marry Peter! But, by God, you won't! You'll damn soon stop your tricks when you know what I've been writing!

LAVINIA: (*tensely*) What have you written?

ORIN: (*his anger turned to gloating satisfaction*) Ah! That frightens you, does it? Well, you better be frightened!

LAVINIA: Tell me what you've written!

ORIN: None of your damned business.

LAVINIA: I've got to know!

ORIN: Well, as I've practically finished it—I suppose I might as well tell you. At his earnest solicitation— (*He waves a hand to the portrait mockingly*) as the last male Mannon—thank God for that, eh!—I've been writing the history of our family! (*He adds with a glance at the portrait and a malicious chuckle*) But I don't wish to convey that he approves of all I've set down—not by a damned sight!

LAVINIA: (*trying to keep calm—tensely*) What kind of history do you mean?

ORIN: A true history of all the family crimes, beginning with Grand-

father Abe's—all of the crimes, including ours, do you understand?

LAVINIA: (*aghast*) Do you mean to tell me you've actually written—

ORIN: Yes! I've tried to trace to its secret hiding place in the Mannon
past the evil destiny behind our lives! I thought if I could see it clearly
in the past I might be able to foretell what fate is in store for us,
Vinnie—but I haven't dared predict that—not yet— although I can
guess— (*He gives a sinister chuckle*).

LAVINIA: Orin!

ORIN: Most of what I've written is about you! I found you the most
interesting criminal of us all!

LAVINIA: (*breaking*) How can you say such dreadful things to me, after
all I—

ORIN: (*as if he hadn't heard—inexorably*) So many strange hidden things
out of the Mannon past combine in you! For one example, do you
remember the first mate, Wilkins, on the voyage to Frisco? Oh, I
know you thought I was in a stupor of grief—but I wasn't blind! I
saw how you wanted him!

LAVINIA: (*angrily, but with a trace of guilty confusion*) I never gave him a
thought! He was an officer of the ship to me, and nothing more!

ORIN: (*mockingly*) Adam Brant was a ship's officer, too, wasn't he? Wilkins reminded you of Brant—

LAVINIA: No!

ORIN: And that's why you suddenly discarded mourning in Frisco and
bought new clothes—in Mother's colors!

LAVINIA: (*furiously*) Stop talking about her! You'd think, to hear you, I
had no life of my own!

ORIN: You wanted Wilkins just as you'd wanted Brant!

LAVINIA: That s a lie!

ORIN: You're doing the lying! You know damned well that behind all
your pretense about Mother's murder being an act of justice was your
jealous hatred! She warned me of that and I see it clearly now! You
wanted Brant for yourself!

LAVINIA: (*fiercely*) It's a lie! I hated him!

ORIN: Yes, after you knew he was her lover! (*He chuckles with a sinister mockery*) But we'll let that pass for the present—I know it's the last thing you could ever admit to yourself!—and come to what I've written about your adventures on my lost islands. Or should I say, Adam Brant's islands! He had been there too, if you'll remember! Probably he'd lived with one of the native women! He was that kind! Were you thinking of that when we were there?

LAVINIA: (*chokingly*) Stop it! I—I warn you—I won't bear it much longer!

ORIN: (*as if he hadn't heard—in the same sinister mocking tone*) What a paradise the Islands were for you, eh? All those handsome men staring at you and your strange beautiful hair! It was then you finally became pretty—like Mother! You knew they all desired you, didn't you? It filled you with pride! Especially Avahanni! You watched him stare at your body through your clothes, stripping you naked! And you wanted him!

LAVINIA: No!

ORIN: Don't lie! (*He accuses her with fierce jealousy*) What did you do with him the night I was sick and you went to watch their shameless dance? Something happened between you! I saw your face when you came back and stood with him in front of our hut!

LAVINIA: (*quietly—with simple dignity now*) I had kissed him good night, that was all—in gratitude! He was innocent and good. He had made me feel for the first time in my life that everything about love could be sweet and natural.

ORIN: So you kissed him, did you? And that was all?

LAVINIA: (*with a sudden flare of deliberately evil taunting that recalls her mother in the last act of "Homecoming," when she was goading Ezra Mannon to fury just before his murder*) And what if it wasn't? I'm not your property! I have a right to love!

ORIN: (*reacting as his father had—his face grown livid—with a hoarse cry of fury grabs her by the throat*) You—you whore! I'll kill you! (*Then suddenly he breaks down and becomes weak and pitiful*) No! You're lying about him, aren't you? For God's sake, tell me you're lying, Vinnie!

LAVINIA: (*strangely shaken and trembling—stammers*) Yes—it was a lie— how could you believe I—Oh, Orin, something made me say that to you—against my will—something rose up in me—like an evil spirit!

ORIN: (*laughs wildly*) Ghosts! You never seemed so much like Mother as you did just then!

LAVINIA: (*pleading distractedly*) Don't talk about it! Let's forget it ever happened! Forgive me! Please forget it!

ORIN: All right—if the ghosts will let us forget! (*He stares at her fixedly for a moment—then satisfied*) I believe you about Avahanni. I never really suspected, or I'd have killed him—and you, too! I hope you know that! (*Then with his old obsessed insistence*) But you were guilty in your mind just the same!

LAVINIA: (*in a flash of distracted anger*) Stop harping on that! Stop torturing me or I—! I've warned you! I warn you again! I can't bear any more! I won't!

ORIN: (*with a mocking diabolical sneer—quietly*) Then why don't you murder me? I'll help you plan it, as we planned Brant's, so there will be no suspicion on you! And I'll be grateful! I loathe my life!

LAVINIA: (*speechless with horror—can only gasp*) Oh!

ORIN: (*with a quiet mad insistence*) Can't you see I'm now in Father's place and you're Mother? That's the evil destiny out of the past I haven't dared predict! I'm the Mannon you're chained to! So isn't it plain—

LAVINIA: (*putting her hands over her ears*) For God's sake, won't you be quiet! (*Then suddenly her horror turning into a violent rage—unconsciously repeating the exact threat she had goaded her mother to make to her in Act Two of "Homecoming"*) Take care, Orin! You'll be responsible if—! (*She stops abruptly, terrified by her own words*).

ORIN: (*with a diabolical mockery*) If what? If I should die mysteriously of heart failure?

LAVINIA: Leave me alone! Leave me alone! Don't keep saying that! How can you be so horrible? Don't you know I'm your sister, who loves you, who would give her life to bring you peace?

ORIN: (*with a change to a harsh threatening tone*) I don't believe you! I know you're plotting something! But you look out! I'll be watching you! And I warn you I won't stand your leaving me for Peter! I'm going to put this confession I've written in safe hands—to be read in case you try to marry him—or if I should die—

LAVINIA: (*frantically grabbing his arm and shaking him fiercely*) Stop having such thoughts! Stop making me have them! You're like a devil torturing me! I won't listen! (*She breaks down and sobs brokenly.* ORIN *stares at her dazedly—seems half to come back to his natural self and the wild look fades from his eyes leaving them glazed and lifeless*).

ORIN: (*strangely*) Don't cry. The damned don't cry. (*He slumps down heavily in his father's chair and stares at the floor. Suddenly he says harshly again*) Go away, will you? I want to be alone—to finish my work. (*Still sobbing, her hand over her eyes,* LAVINIA *feels blindly for the door and goes out closing it after her.* ORIN *unlocks the table drawer, pulls out his manuscript, and takes up his pen*).

CURTAIN

ACT THREE

SCENE—*Same as Act One, Scene Two—the sitting-room. The lamp on the table is lighted but turned low. Two candles are burning on the mantel over the fireplace at right, shedding their flickering light on the portrait of* ABE MANNON *above, and of the other Mannons on the walls on each side of him. The eyes of the portraits seem to possess an intense bitter life, with their frozen stare "looking over the head of life, cutting it dead for the impropriety of living," as* ORIN *had said of his father in Act Two of "The Hunted."*

No time has elapsed since the preceding act. LAVINIA *enters from the hall in the rear, having just come from the study. She comes to the table and turns up the lamp. She is in a terrific state of tension. The corners of her mouth twitch, she twines and untwines the fingers of her clasped hands with a slow wringing movement which recalls her mother in the last Act of "The Hunted."*

LAVINIA: (*torturedly—begins to pace up and down, muttering her thoughts aloud*) I can't bear it! Why does he keep putting his death in my head? He would be better off if— Why hasn't he the courage—? (*Then in a frenzy of remorseful anguish, her eyes unconsciously seeking the Mannon portraits on the right wall, as if they were the visible symbol of her God*) Oh, God, don't let me have such thoughts! You know I love Orin! Show me the way to save him! Don't let me think of death! I couldn't bear another death! Please! Please! (*At a noise from the hall she controls herself and pretends to be glancing through a book on the table.* SETH *appears in the doorway*).

SETH: Vinnie!

LAVINIA: What is it, Seth?

SETH: That durned idjut, Hannah, is throwin' fits agin. Went down cellar and says she felt ha'nts crawlin' behind her. You'd better come and git her calmed down—or she'll be leavin'. (*Then he adds disgustedly*) That's what we git fur freein' 'em!

LAVINIA: (*wearily*) All right. I'll talk to her. (*She goes out with* SETH. *A pause. Then a ring from the front door bell. A moment later* SETH *can be seen coming back along the hall. He opens the front door and is heard greeting* HAZEL *and* PETER *and follows them in as they enter the room*).

SETH: Vinnie's back seein' to somethin'. You set down and she'll be here soon as she kin.

PETER: All right, Seth. (SETH *goes out again. They come forward and sit down.* PETER *looks hearty and good-natured, the same as ever, but* HAZEL'S *face wears a nervous, uneasy look although her air is determined*).

PETER: I'll have to run along soon and drop in at the Council meeting. I can't get out of it. I'll be back in half an hour—maybe sooner.

HAZEL: (*suddenly with a little shiver*) I hate this house now. I hate coming here. If it wasn't for Orin—He's getting worse. Keeping him shut up here is the worst thing Vinnie could do.

PETER: He won't go out. You know very well she has to force him to walk with you.

HAZEL: And comes along herself! Never leaves him alone hardly a second!

PETER: (*with a grin*) Oh, that's what you've got against her, eh?

HAZEL: (*sharply*) Don't be silly, Peter! I simply think, and I'd say it to her face, that she's a bad influence for Orin! I feel there's something awfully wrong—somehow. He scares me at times—and Vinnie—I've watched her looking at you. She's changed so. There's something bold about her.

PETER: (*getting up*) If you're going to talk like that—! You ought to be ashamed, Hazel!

HAZEL: Well, I'm not! I've got some right to say something about how he's cared for! And I'm going to from now on! I'm going to make her let him visit us for a spell. I've asked Mother and she'll be glad to have him.

PETER: Say, I think that's a darned good notion for both of them. She needs a rest from him, too.

HAZEL: Vinnie doesn't think it's a good notion! I mentioned it yesterday and she gave me such a look! (*Determinedly*) But I'm going to make him promise to come over tomorrow, no matter what she says!

PETER: (*soothingly, patting her shoulder*) Don't get angry now—about nothing. I'll help you persuade her to let him come. (*Then with a grin*) I'll help you do anything to help Orin get well—if only for selfish reasons. As long as Vinnie's tied down to him we can't get married.

HAZEL: (*stares at him—slowly*) Do you really want to marry her—now?

PETER: Why do you ask such a fool question? What do you mean, do I want to now?

HAZEL: (*her voice trembles and she seems about to burst into tears*) Oh, I don't know, Peter! I don't know!

PETER: (*sympathetic and at the same time exasperated*) What in the dickens is the matter with you?

HAZEL: (*hears a noise from the hall and collects herself—warningly*) Ssshh! (ORIN *appears in the doorway at rear. He glances at them, then quickly around the room to see if* LAVINIA *is there. They both greet him with "Hello, Orin"*).

ORIN: Hello! (*Then in an excited whisper, coming to them*) Where's Vinnie?

HAZEL: She's gone to see to something, Seth said.

PETER: (*glancing at his watch*) Gosh, I've got to hurry to that darned Council meeting.

ORIN: (*eagerly*) You're going?

PETER: (*jokingly*) You needn't look so darned tickled about it! It isn't polite!

ORIN: I've got to see Hazel alone!

PETER: All right! You don't have to put me out! (*He grins, slapping* ORIN *on the back and goes out.* ORIN *follows him with his eyes until he hears the front door close behind him*).

ORIN: (*turning to* HAZEL—*with queer furtive excitement*) Listen, Hazel! I want you to do something! But wait! I've got to get— (*He rushes out and can be heard going across the hall to the study.* HAZEL *looks after him worriedly. A moment later he hurries back with a big sealed envelope in his hand which he gives to* HAZEL, *talking breathlessly, with nervous jerks of his head, as he glances apprehensively at the door*) Here! Take this! Quick! Don't let her see it! I want you to keep it in a safe place and never let anyone know you have it! It will be stolen if I keep it here! I know her! Will you promise?

HAZEL: But—what is it, Orin?

ORIN: I can't tell you. You mustn't ask me. And you must promise never to open it—unless something happens to me.

HAZEL: (*frightened by his tone*) What do you mean?

ORIN: I mean if I should die—or—but this is the most important, if she tries to marry Peter—the day before the wedding—I want you to make Peter read what's inside.

HAZEL: You don't want her to marry Peter?

ORIN: No! She can't have happiness! She's got to be punished! (*Suddenly taking her hand—excitedly*) And listen, Hazel! You mustn't love me any more. The only love I can know now is the love of guilt for guilt which breeds more guilt—until you get so deep at the bottom of hell there is no lower you can sink and you rest there in peace! (*He laughs harshly and turns away from her*).

HAZEL: Orin! Don't talk like that! (*Then conquering her horror—resolutely tender and soothing*) Ssshh! Poor boy! Come here to me. (*He comes to her. She puts an arm around him*) Listen. I know something is worrying you—and I don't want to seem prying—but I've had such a strong feeling at times that it would relieve your mind if you could tell me what it is. Haven't you thought that, Orin?

ORIN: (*longingly*) Yes! Yes! I want to confess to your purity! I want to be forgiven! (*Then checking himself abruptly as he is about to speak—dully*) No. I can't. Don't ask me. I love her.

HAZEL: But, you silly boy, Vinnie told Peter herself what it is and told him to tell me.

ORIN: (*staring at her wildly*) What did she tell?

HAZEL: About your having a quarrel with your poor mother that night before she—and how you've brooded over it until you blame yourself for her death.

ORIN: (*harshly*) I see! So in case I did tell you—oh, she's cunning! But not cunning enough this time! (*Vindictively*) You remember what I've given you, Hazel, and you do exactly what I said with it. (*Then with desperate pleading*) For God's sake, Hazel, if you love me help me to get away from here—or something terrible will happen!

HAZEL: That's just what I want to do! You come over tomorrow and stay with us.

ORIN: (*bitterly*) Do you suppose for a moment she'll ever let me go?

HAZEL: But haven't you a right to do as you want to?

ORIN: (*furtively*) I could sneak out when she wasn't looking and then you could hide me and when she came for me tell her I wasn't there.

HAZEL: (*indignantly*) I won't do any such thing! I don't tell lies, Orin! (*Then scornfully*) How can you be so scared of Vinnie?

ORIN: (*hearing a noise from the hall—hastily*) Ssshh! She's coming! Don't let her see what I gave you. And go home right away and lock it up! (*He tiptoes away as if he were afraid of being found close to her and sits on the sofa at right, adopting a suspiciously careless attitude.* HAZEL *looks self-conscious and stiff.* LAVINIA *appears in the doorway and gives a start as she sees* HAZEL *and* ORIN *are alone. She quickly senses something in the atmosphere and glances sharply from one to the other as she comes into the room*).

LAVINIA: (*to* HAZEL, *forcing a casual air*) I'm sorry being so long.

HAZEL: I didn't mind waiting.

LAVINIA: (*sitting down on the chair at center*) Where's Peter?

HAZEL: He had to go to a Council meeting. He's coming back.

LAVINIA: (*uneasiness creeping into her tone*) Has he been gone long?

HAZEL: Not very long.

LAVINIA: (*turning to* ORIN—*sharply*) I thought you were in the study.

ORIN: (*sensing her uneasiness—mockingly*) I finished what I was working on.

LAVINIA: You finished—? (*She glances sharply at* HAZEL—*forcing a joking tone*) My, but you two look mysterious! What have you been up to?

HAZEL: (*trying to force a laugh*) Why, Vinnie? What makes you think—?

LAVINIA: You're hiding something. (HAZEL *gives a start and instinctively moves the hand with the envelope farther behind her back.* LAVINIA *notices this. So does* ORIN *who uneasily comes to* HAZEL'S *rescue*).

ORIN: We're not hiding anything. Hazel has invited me over to their house to stay for a while—and I'm going.

HAZEL: (*backing him up resolutely*) Yes. Orin is coming tomorrow.

LAVINIA: (*alarmed and resentful—coldly*) It's kind of you. I know you mean it for the best. But he can't go.

HAZEL: (*sharply*) Why not?

LAVINIA: I don't care to discuss it, Hazel. You ought to know—

HAZEL: (*angrily*) I don't know! Orin is of age and can go where he pleases!

ORIN: Let her talk all she likes, Hazel. I'll have the upper hand for a change, from now on! (LAVINIA *looks at him, frightened by the triumphant satisfaction in his voice*).

HAZEL: (*anxious to score her point and keep* ORIN'S *mind on it*) I should think you'd be glad. It will be the best thing in the world for him.

LAVINIA: (*turns on her—angrily*) I'll ask you to please mind your own business, Hazel!

HAZEL: (*springs to her feet, in her anger forgetting to hide the envelope which she now holds openly in her hand*) It is my business! I love Orin better than you! I don't think you love him at all, the way you've been acting!

ORIN: (*sees the envelope in plain sight and calls to her warningly*) Hazel! (*She catches his eye and hastily puts her hand behind her.* LAVINIA *sees the movement but doesn't for a moment realize the meaning of it.* ORIN *goes on warningly*) You said you had to go home early. I don't want to remind you but—

HAZEL: (*hastily*) Yes, I really must. (*Starting to go, trying to keep the envelope hidden, aware that* LAVINIA *is watching her suspiciously—defiantly to* ORIN) We'll expect you tomorrow, and have your room ready. (*Then to* LAVINIA—*coldly*) After the way you've insulted me, Vinnie, I hope you realize there's no more question of any friendship between us. (*She tries awkwardly to sidle toward the door*).

LAVINIA: (*suddenly gets between her and the door—with angry accusation*) What are you hiding behind your back? (HAZEL *flushes guiltily, but refusing to lie, says nothing.* LAVINIA *turns on* ORIN) Have you given her what you've written? (*As he hesitates—violently*) Answer me!

ORIN: That's my business! What if I have?

LAVINIA: You—you traitor! You coward! (*Fiercely to* HAZEL) Give it to me! Do you hear?

HAZEL: Vinnie! How dare you talk that way to me! (*She tries to go but* LAVINIA *keeps directly between her and the door*).

LAVINIA: You shan't leave here until—! (*Then breaking down and pleading*) Orin! Think what you're doing! Tell her to give it to me!

ORIN: No!

LAVINIA: (*goes and puts her arms around him—beseechingly as he avoids her eyes*) Think sanely for a moment! You can't do this! You're a Mannon!

ORIN: (*harshly*) It's because I'm one!

LAVINIA: For Mother's sake, you can't! You loved her!

ORIN: A lot she cared! Don't call on her!

LAVINIA: (*desperately*) For my sake, then! You know I love you! Make Hazel give that up and I'll do anything—anything you want me to!

ORIN: (*stares into her eyes, bending his head until his face is close to hers—with morbid intensity*) You mean that?

LAVINIA: (*shrinking back from him—falteringly*) Yes.

ORIN: (*laughs with a crazy triumph—checks this abruptly—and goes to* HAZEL *who has been standing bewilderedly, not understanding what is behind their talk but sensing something sinister, and terribly frightened.* ORIN *speaks curtly, his eyes fixed on* LAVINIA) Let me have it, Hazel.

HAZEL: (*hands him the envelope—in a trembling voice*) I'll go home. I suppose—we can't expect you tomorrow—now.

ORIN: No. Forget me. The Orin you loved was killed in the war. (*With a twisted smile*) Remember only that dead hero and not his rotting ghost! Good-bye! (*Then harshly*) Please go! (HAZEL *begins to sob and hurries blindly from the room.* ORIN *comes back to* LAVINIA *who remains kneeling by the chair. He puts the envelope in her hand—harshly*) Here! You realize the promise you made means giving up Peter? And never seeing him again?

LAVINIA: (*tensely*) Yes.

ORIN: And I suppose you think that's all it means, that I'll be content with a promise I've forced out of you, which you'll always be plotting to break? Oh, no! I'm not such a fool! I've got to be sure— (*She doesn't reply or look at him. He stares at her and slowly a distorted look of desire comes over his face*) You said you would do anything for me. That's a large promise, Vinnie—anything!

LAVINIA: (*shrinking from him*) What do you mean? What terrible thing have you been thinking lately—behind all your crazy talk? No, I don't want to know! Orin! Why do you look at me like that?

ORIN: You don't seem to feel all you mean to me now—all you have made yourself mean—since we murdered Mother!

LAVINIA: Orin!

ORIN: I love you now with all the guilt in me—the guilt we share! Perhaps I love you too much, Vinnie!

LAVINIA: You don't know what you're saying!

ORIN: There are times now when you don't seem to be my sister, nor Mother, but some stranger with the same beautiful hair— (*He touches her hair caressingly. She pulls violently away. He laughs wildly*) Perhaps you're Marie Brantôme, eh? And you say there are no ghosts in this house?

LAVINIA: (*staring at him with fascinated horror*) For God's sake—! No! You're insane! You can't mean—!

ORIN: How else can I be sure you won't leave me? You would never dare leave me—then! You would feel as guilty then as I do! You would be as damned as I am! (*Then with sudden anger as he sees the growing horrified repulsion on her face*) Damn you, don't you see I must find some certainty some way or go mad? You don't want me to go mad, do you? I would talk too much! I would confess! (*Then as if the word stirred something within him his tone instantly changes to one of passionate pleading*) Vinnie! For the love of God, let's go now and confess and pay the penalty for Mother's murder, and find peace together!

LAVINIA: (*tempted and tortured, in a longing whisper*) Peace! (*Then summoning her will, springs to her feet wildly*) No! You coward! There is nothing to confess! There was only justice!

ORIN: (*turns and addresses the portraits on the wall with a crazy mockery*) You hear her? You'll find Lavinia Mannon harder to break than me! You'll have to haunt and hound her for a lifetime!

LAVINIA: (*her control snapping—turning on him now in a burst of frantic hatred and rage*) I hate you! I wish you were dead! You're too vile to live! You'd kill yourself if you weren't a coward!

ORIN: (*starts back as if he'd been struck, the tortured mad look on his face changing to a stricken terrified expression*) Vinnie!

LAVINIA: I mean it! I mean it! (*She breaks down and sobs hysterically*).

ORIN: (*in a pitiful pleading whisper*) Vinnie! (*He stares at her with the lost stricken expression for a moment more—then the obsessed wild look returns to his eyes—with harsh mockery*) Another act of justice, eh? You want to drive me to suicide as I drove Mother! An eye for an eye, is that it? But— (*He stops abruptly and stares before him, as if this idea were suddenly taking hold of his tortured imagination and speaks fascinatedly to himself*) Yes! That would be justice—now you are Mother! She is speaking now through you! (*More and more hypnotized by this train of thought*) Yes! It's the way to peace—to find her again—my lost island—Death is an Island of Peace, too—Mother will be waiting for me there— (*With excited eagerness now, speaking to the dead*) Mother! Do you know what I'll do then? I'll get on my knees and ask your forgiveness—and say— (*His mouth grows convulsed, as if he were retching up poison*) I'll say, I'm glad you found love, Mother! I'll wish you happiness—you and Adam! (*He laughs exultantly*) You've heard me! You're here in the house now! You're calling me! You're waiting to take me home! (*He turns and strides toward the door*).

LAVINIA: (*who has raised her head and has been staring at him with dread during the latter part of his talk—torn by remorse, runs after him and throws her arms around him*) No, Orin! No!

ORIN: (*pushes her away—with a rough brotherly irritation*) Get out of my way, can't you? Mother's waiting! (*He gets to the door. Then he turns back and says sharply*) Ssshh! Here's Peter! Shut up, now! (*He steps back in the room as* PETER *appears in the doorway*).

PETER: Excuse my coming right in. The door was open. Where's Hazel?

ORIN: (*with unnatural casualness*) Gone home. (*Then with a quick, meaning, mocking glance at* LAVINIA) I'm just going in the study to clean my pistol. Darn thing's gotten so rusty. Glad you came now, Peter. You can keep Vinnie company. (*He turns and goes out the door.* PETER *stares after him puzzledly*).

LAVINIA: (*with a stifled cry*) Orin! (*There is no answer but the sound of the study door being shut. She starts to run after him, stops herself, then throws herself into* PETER'S *arms, as if for protection against herself and begins to talk volubly to drown out thought*) Hold me close, Peter! Nothing matters but love, does it? That must come first! No price is too great, is it? Or for peace! One must have peace—one is too weak to forget—no one has the right to keep anyone from peace! (*She makes a motion to cover her ears with her hands*).

PETER: (*alarmed by her hectic excitement*) He's a darned fool to monkey with a pistol—in his state. Shall I get it away from him?

LAVINIA: (*holding him tighter—volubly*) Oh, won't it be wonderful, Peter—once we're married and have a home with a garden and trees! We'll be so happy! I love everything that grows simply—up toward the sun—everything that's straight and strong! I hate what's warped and twists and eats into itself and dies for a lifetime in shadow. (*Then her voice rising as if it were about to break hysterically—again with the instinctive movement to cover her ears*) I can't bear waiting—waiting and waiting and waiting—! (*There is a muffled shot from the study across the hall*).

PETER: (*breaking from her and running for the door*) Good God! What's that? (*He rushes into the hall*).

LAVINIA: (*sags weakly and supports herself against the table—in a faint, trembling voice*) Orin! Forgive me! (*She controls herself with a terrible effort of will. Her mouth congeals into a frozen line. Mechanically she hides the sealed envelope in a drawer of the table and locks the drawer*) I've got to go in— (*She turns to go and her eyes catch the eyes of the* MANNONS *in the portraits fixed accusingly on her—defiantly*) Why do you look at me like that? Wasn't it the only way to keep your secret, too? But I'm through with you forever now, do you hear? I'm Mother's daughter—not one of you! I'll live in spite of you! (*She squares her shoulders, with a return of the abrupt military movement copied from her father which she had of old—as if by the very act of disowning the* MANNONS *she had returned to the fold—and marches stiffly from the room*).

CURTAIN

ACT FOUR

SCENE—*Same as Act One, Scene One—exterior of the house. It is in the late afternoon of a day three days later. The Mannon house has much the same appearance as it had in the first act of "Homecoming." Soft golden sunlight shimmers in a luminous mist on the Greek temple portico, intensifying the whiteness of the columns, the deep green of the shutters, the green of the shrubbery, the black and green of the pines. The columns cast black bars of shadow on the gray stone wall behind them. The shutters are all fastened back, the windows open. On the ground floor, the upper part of the windows, raised from the bottom, reflect the sun in a smouldering stare, as of brooding revengeful eyes.*

SETH *appears walking slowly up the drive from right, front. He has a pair of grass clippers and potters along pretending to trim the edge of the lawn along the drive. But in reality he is merely killing time, chewing tobacco, and singing mournfully to himself, in his aged, plaintive wraith of a once good baritone, the chanty "Shenandoah":*

SETH: "*Oh, Shenandoah, I long to hear you*
         A-way, my rolling river,
         Oh, Shenandoah, I can't get near you
         Way-ay, I'm bound away
         Across the wide Missouri.

         "*Oh, Shenandoah, I love your daughter*
         A-way, you rolling river."

SETH: (*stops singing and stands peering off left toward the flower garden— shakes his head and mutters to himself*) There she be pickin' my flowers agin. Like her Maw used to—on'y wuss. She's got every room in the house full of 'em a'ready. Durn it, I hoped she'd stop that once the funeral was over. There won't be a one left in my garden! (*He looks away and begins pottering about again, and mutters grimly*) A durn queer thin' fur a sodger to kill himself cleanin' his gun, folks is sayin'. They'll fight purty shy of her now. A Mannon has come to mean sudden death to 'em. (*Then with a grim pride*) But Vinnie's able fur 'em. They'll never git her to show nothin'. Clean Mannon strain!

(LAVINIA *enters from the left. The three days that have intervened have effected a remarkable change in her. Her body, dressed in deep mourning, again appears flat-chested and thin. The* MANNON *mask-semblance of her face appears intensified now. It is deeply lined, haggard with sleeplessness and strain, congealed into a stony emotionless expression. Her lips are bloodless, drawn taut in a grim line. She is carrying a large bunch of flowers. She holds them out to* SETH *and speaks in a strange, empty voice*).

LAVINIA: Take these, Seth, and give them to Hannah. Tell her to set them around inside. I want the house to be full of flowers. Peter is coming, and I want everything to be pretty and cheerful. (*She goes and sits at the top of the steps, bolt upright, her arms held stiffly to her sides, her legs and feet pressed together, and stares back into the sun-glare with unblinking, frozen, defiant eyes*).

SETH: (*stands holding the flowers and regarding her worriedly*). I seed you settin' out here on the steps when I got up at five this mornin'—and every mornin' since Orin— Ain't you been gittin' no sleep? (*She stares before her as if she had not heard him. He goes on coaxingly*) How'd you like if I hauled one of them sofas out fur you to lie on, Vinnie? Mebbe you could take a couple o' winks an' it'd do you good.

LAVINIA: No, thank you, Seth. I'm waiting for Peter. (*Then after a pause, curiously*) Why didn't you tell me to go in the house and lie down? (SETH *pretends not to hear the question, avoiding her eyes*) You understand, don't you? You've been with us Mannons so long! You know there's no rest in this house which Grandfather built as a temple of Hate and Death!

SETH: (*blurts out*) Don't you try to live here, Vinnie! You marry Peter and git clear!

LAVINIA: I'm going to marry him! And I'm going away with him and forget this house and all that ever happened in it!

SETH: That's talkin', Vinnie!

LAVINIA: I'll close it up and leave it in the sun and rain to die. The portraits of the Mannons will rot on the walls and the ghosts will fade back into death. And the Mannons will be forgotten. I'm the last and I won't be one long. I'll be Mrs. Peter Niles. Then they're finished! Thank God! (*She leans back in the sunlight and closes her eyes.* SETH *stares at her worriedly, shakes his head and spits. Then he hears something and peers down the drive, off left*).

SETH: Vinnie. Here's Hazel comin'.

LAVINIA: (*jerks up stiffly with a look of alarm*) Hazel? What does she want? (*She springs up as if she were going to run in the house, then stands her ground on the top of the steps, her voice hardening*) Seth, you go work in back, please!

SETH: Ayeh. (*He moves slowly off behind the lilacs as* HAZEL *enters from left, front—calling back*) Evenin', Hazel.

HAZEL: Good evening, Seth. (*She stops short and stares at* LAVINIA. LAVINIA'S *eyes are hard and defiant as she stares back.* HAZEL *is dressed in mourning. Her face is sad and pale, her eyes show evidence of much weeping, but there is an air of stubborn resolution about her as she makes up her mind and walks to the foot of the steps*).

LAVINIA: What do you want? I've got a lot to attend to.

HAZEL: (*quietly*) It won't take me long to say what I've come to say, Vinnie. (*Suddenly she bursts out*) It's a lie about Orin killing himself by accident! I know it is! He meant to!

LAVINIA: You better be careful what you say. I can prove what happened. Peter was here—

HAZEL: I don't care what anyone says!

LAVINIA: I should think you'd be the last one to accuse Orin—

HAZEL: I'm not accusing him! Don't you dare say that! I'm accusing you! You drove him to it! Oh, I know I can't prove it—any more than I can prove a lot of things Orin hinted at! But I know terrible things must have happened—and that you're to blame for them, somehow!

LAVINIA: (*concealing a start of fear—changing to a forced reproachful tone*) What would Orin think of you coming here the day of his funeral to accuse me of the sorrow that's afflicted our family?

HAZEL: (*feeling guilty and at the same time defiant and sure she is right*) All right, Vinnie. I won't say anything more. But I know there's something—and so do you—something that was driving Orin crazy—(*She breaks down and sobs*) Poor Orin!

LAVINIA: (*stares straight before her. Her lips twitch. In a stifled voice between her clenched teeth*) Don't—do that!

HAZEL: (*controlling herself—after a pause*) I'm sorry. I didn't come to talk about Orin.

LAVINIA: (*uneasily*) What did you come for?

HAZEL: About Peter.

LAVINIA: (*as if this were something she had been dreading—harshly*) You leave Peter and me alone!

HAZEL: I won't! You're not going to marry Peter and ruin his life! (*Pleading now*) You can't! Don't you see he could never be happy with you, that you'll only drag him into this terrible thing—whatever it is—and make him share it?

LAVINIA: There is no terrible thing!

HAZEL: I know Peter can't believe evil of anyone, but living alone with you, married, you couldn't hide it, he'd get to feel what I feel. You could never be happy because it would come between you! (*Pleading again*) Oh, Vinnie, you've got to be fair to Peter! You've got to consider his happiness—if you really love him!

LAVINIA: (*hoarsely*) I do love him!

HAZEL: It has started already—his being made unhappy through you!

LAVINIA: You're lying!

HAZEL: He fought with Mother last night when she tried to talk to him—the first time he ever did such a thing! It isn't like Peter. You've changed him. He left home and went to the hotel to stay. He said he'd never speak to Mother or me again. He's always been such a wonderful son before—and brother. We three have been so happy. It's broken Mother's heart. All she does is sit and cry. (*Desperately*) Oh, Vinnie, you can't do it! You will be punished if you do! Peter would get to hate you in the end!

LAVINIA: No!

HAZEL: Do you want to take the risk of driving Peter to do what Orin did? He might—if he ever discovered the truth!

LAVINIA: (*violently*) What truth, you little fool! Discover what?

HAZEL: (*accusingly*) I don't know—but you know! Look in your heart and ask your conscience before God if you ought to marry Peter!

LAVINIA: (*desperately—at the end of her tether*) Yes! Before God! Before anything! (*Then glaring at her—with a burst of rage*) You leave me alone—go away—or I'll get Orin's pistol and kill you! (*Her rage passes, leaving her weak and shaken. She goes to her chair and sinks on it*).

HAZEL: (*recoiling*) Oh! You are wicked! I believe you would—! Vinnie! What's made you like this?

LAVINIA: Go away!

HAZEL: Vinnie! (LAVINIA *closes her eyes.* HAZEL *stands staring at her. After a pause—in a trembling voice*) All right. I'll go. All I can do is trust you. I know in your heart you can't be dead to all honor and justice— you, a Mannon! (LAVINIA *gives a little bitter laugh without opening her eyes*) At least you owe it to Peter to let him read what Orin had in that envelope. Orin asked me to make him read it before he married you. I've told Peter about that, Vinnie.

LAVINIA: (*without opening her eyes—strangely, as if to herself*) The dead! Why can't the dead die!

HAZEL: (*stares at her frightenedly, not knowing what to do—looks around her uncertainly and sees someone coming from off left, front—quickly*) Here he comes now. I'll go by the back. I don't want him to meet me. (*She starts to go but stops by the clump of lilacs—pityingly*) I know you're suffering, Vinnie—and I know your conscience will make you do what's right—and God will forgive you. (*She goes quickly behind the lilacs and around the house to the rear*).

LAVINIA: (*looks after her and calls defiantly*) I'm not asking God or anybody for forgiveness. I forgive myself! (*She leans back and closes her eyes again—bitterly*) I hope there is a hell for the good somewhere! (PETER *enters from the left, front. He looks haggard and tormented. He walks slowly, his eyes on the ground—then sees* LAVINIA *and immediately makes an effort to pull himself together and appear cheerful*).

PETER: Hello, Vinnie. (*He sits on the edge of the portico beside her. She still keeps her eyes closed, as if afraid to open them. He looks at her worriedly*) You look terribly worn out. Haven't you slept? (*He pats her hand with awkward tenderness. Her mouth twitches and draws down at the corners as she stifles a sob. He goes on comfortingly*) You've had an awfully hard time of it, but never mind, we'll be married soon.

LAVINIA: (*without opening her eyes—longingly*) You'll love me and keep me from remembering?

PETER: You bet I will! And the first thing is to get you away from this darned house! I may be a fool but I'm beginning to feel superstitious about it myself.

LAVINIA: (*without opening her eyes—strangely*) Yes. Love can't live in it. We'll go away and leave it alone to die—and we'll forget the dead.

PETER: (*a bitter resentful note coming into his voice*) We can't move too far away to suit me! I hate this damned town now and everyone in it!

LAVINIA: (*opens her eyes and looks at him startledly*) I never heard you talk that way before, Peter—bitter!

PETER: (*avoiding her eyes*) Some things would make anyone bitter!

LAVINIA: You've quarreled with your mother and Hazel—on account of me—is that it?

PETER: How did you know?

LAVINIA: Hazel was just here.

PETER: She told you? The darned fool! What did she do that for?

LAVINIA: She doesn't want me to marry you.

PETER: (*angrily*) The little sneak! What right has she—? (*Then a bit uneasily—forcing a smile*) Well, you won't pay any attention to her, I hope.

LAVINIA: (*more as if she were answering some voice in herself than him— stiffening in her chair—defiantly*) No!

PETER: She and Mother suddenly got a lot of crazy notions in their heads. But they'll get over them.

LAVINIA: (*staring at him searchingly—uneasily*) Supposing they don't?

PETER: They will after we are married—or I'm through with them!

LAVINIA: (*a pause. Then she takes his face in her hands and turns it to hers*) Peter! Let me look at you! You're suffering! Your eyes have a hurt look! They've always been so trustful! They look suspicious and afraid of life now! Have I done this to you already, Peter? Are you beginning to suspect me? Are you wondering what it was Orin wrote?

PETER: (*protesting violently*) No! Of course I'm not! Don't I know Orin was out of his mind? Why would I pay any attention—?

LAVINIA: You swear you'll never suspect me—of anything?

PETER: What do you think I am?

LAVINIA: And you'll never let anyone come between us? Nothing can keep us from being happy, can it? You won't let anything, will you?

PETER: Of course I won't!

LAVINIA: (*more and more desperately*) I want to get married right away, Peter! I'm afraid! Would you marry me now—this evening? We can find a minister to do it. I can change my clothes in a second and put on the color you like! Marry me today, Peter! I'm afraid to wait!

PETER: (*bewildered and a bit shocked*) But—you don't mean that, do you? We couldn't. It wouldn't look right the day Orin—out of respect for him. (*Then suspicious in spite of himself*) I can't see why you're so afraid of waiting. Nothing can happen, can it? Was there anything in what Orin wrote that would stop us from—?

LAVINIA: (*with a wild beaten laugh*) The dead coming between! They always would, Peter! You trust me with your happiness! But that means trusting the Mannon dead—and they're not to be trusted with love! I know them too well! And I couldn't bear to watch your eyes grow bitter and hidden from me and wounded in their trust of life! I love you too much!

PETER: (*made more uneasy and suspicious by this*) What are you talking about, Vinnie? You make me think there was something—

LAVINIA: (*desperately*) No—nothing! (*Then suddenly throwing her arms around him*) No! Don't think of that—not yet! I want a little while of happiness—in spite of all the dead! I've earned it! I've done enough—! (*Growing more desperate—pleading wildly*) Listen, Peter! Why must we wait for marriage? I want a moment of joy—of love— to make up for what's coming! I want it now! Can't you be strong, Peter? Can't you be simple and pure? Can't you forget sin and see that all love is beautiful? (*She kisses him with desperate passion*) Kiss me! Hold me close! Want me! Want me so much you'd murder anyone to have me! I did that—for you! Take me in this house of the dead and love me! Our love will drive the dead away! It will shame them back into death! (*At the topmost pitch of desperate, frantic abandonment*) Want me! Take me, Adam! (*She is brought back to herself with a start by this name escaping her—bewilderedly, laughing idiotically*) Adam? Why did I call you Adam? I never even heard that name before—outside of the Bible! (*Then suddenly with a hopeless, dead finality*) Always the dead between! It's no good trying any more!

PETER: (*convinced she is hysterical and yet shocked and repelled by her display of passion*) Vinnie! You're talking crazy! You don't know what you're saying! You're not—like that!

LAVINIA: (*in a dead voice*) I can't marry you, Peter. You mustn't ever see me again. (*He stares at her, stunned and stupid*) Go home. Make it up with your mother and Hazel. Marry someone else. Love isn't permitted to me. The dead are too strong!

PETER: (*his mind in a turmoil*) Vinnie! You can't—! You've gone crazy—! What's changed you like this? (*Then suspiciously*) Is it— what Orin wrote? What was it? I've got a right to know, haven't I? (*Then as she doesn't answer—more suspiciously*) He acted so queer about— what happened to you on the Islands. Was it something there— something to do with that native—?

LAVINIA: (*her first instinctive reaction one of hurt insult*) Peter! Don't you dare—! (*Then suddenly seizing on this as a way out—with calculated coarseness*) All right! Yes, if you must know! I won't lie any more! Orin suspected I'd lusted with him! And I had!

PETER: (*shrinking from her aghast—brokenly*) Vinnie! You've gone crazy! I don't believe— You—you couldn't!

LAVINIA: (*stridently*) Why shouldn't I? I wanted him! I wanted to learn love from him—love that wasn't a sin! And I did, I tell you! He had me! I was his fancy woman!

PETER: (*wincing as if she had struck him in the face, stares at her with a stricken look of horrified repulsion—with bitter, broken anger*) Then— Mother and Hazel were right about you—you are bad at heart—no wonder Orin killed himself—God, I—I hope you'll be punished— I—! (*He hurries blindly off down the drive to the left*).

LAVINIA: (*watches him go—then with a little desperate cry starts after him*) Peter! It's a lie! I didn't—! (*She stops abruptly and stiffens into her old, square-shouldered attitude. She looks down the drive after him—then turns away, saying in a lost, empty tone*) Good-bye, Peter. (SETH *enters from the left rear, coming around the corner of the house. He stands for a moment watching her, grimly wondering. Then to call her attention to his presence, he begins singing half under his breath his melancholy "Shenandoah" chanty, at the same time looking at the ground around him as if searching for something*).

SETH: *"Oh, Shenandoah, I can't get near you*
          Way-ay, I'm bound away—"

LAVINIA: (*without looking at him, picking up the words of the chanty—with a grim writhen smile*) I'm not bound away—not now, Seth. I'm bound here—to the Mannon dead! (*She gives a dry little cackle of laughter and turns as if to enter the house*).

SETH: (*frightened by the look on her face, grabs her by the arm*) Don't go in there, Vinnie!

LAVINIA: (*grimly*) Don't be afraid. I'm not going the way Mother and Orin went. That's escaping punishment. And there's no one left to punish me. I'm the last Mannon. I've got to punish myself! Living alone here with the dead is a worse act of justice than death or prison! I'll never go out or see anyone! I'll have the shutters nailed closed so no sunlight can ever get in. I'll live alone with the dead, and keep their secrets, and let them hound me, until the curse is paid out and the last Mannon is let die! (*With a strange cruel smile of gloating over the years of self-torture*) I know they will see to it I live for a long time! It takes the Mannons to punish themselves for being born!

SETH: (*with grim understanding*) Ayeh. And I ain't heard a word you've been sayin', Vinnie. (*Pretending to search the ground again*) Left my clippers around somewheres.

LAVINIA: (*turns to him sharply*) You go now and close the shutters and nail them tight.

SETH: Ayeh.

LAVINIA: And tell Hannah to throw out all the flowers.

SETH: Ayeh. (*He goes past her up the steps and into the house. She ascends to the portico—and then turns and stands for a while, stiff and square-shouldered, staring into the sunlight with frozen eyes.* SETH *leans out of the window at the right of the door and pulls the shutters closed with a decisive bang. As if this were a word of command,* LAVINIA *pivots sharply on her heel and marches woodenly into the house, closing the door behind her*).

CURTAIN

A NOTE ON THE TYPE

The principal text of this Modern Library edition
was set in a digitized version of Janson,
a typeface that dates from about 1690 and was cut by Nicholas Kis,
a Hungarian working in Amsterdam. The original matrices have
survived and are held by the Stempel foundry in Germany.
Hermann Zapf redesigned some of the weights and sizes for Stempel,
basing his revisions on the original design.